Identification	Education and The Preschool Child	Education and the Schoolchild	Tips for Teachers
Classification and labeling	PL 99-457	PL 101-476	Making LRE decisions
Traditional assessments (Portfolio Assessment)	Individualized Family Service Plan (IFSP): PL 99-457	Individualized Education Program (IEP)	Guidelines for implementing multidisciplinary teams
Overrepresentation, court cases and discrimination	Head Start, cultural awareness	Cultural diversity, language and instruction, building self-esteem	Teacher checklist—getting to know students and families
Discrepancy scores, discrepancy formulas, standard scores	Early intervention preschool programs, screening	Reading learning strategies	Learning how to learn
Articulation errors, formal and informal assessments	Strategies that promote preschoolers' communication	Teacher's language, language instruction	Creating a language-sensitive environment
IQ, mental age, adaptive behavior, supports	The power of early intervention	Functional curriculum, community based instruction, making choices	Improving generalization
Gardner's seven intelligences	Enriched experiences	Enrichment approach, acceleration approach, eclectic approaches	Considerations for twice exceptional children
Ecological assessments, criteria for determining degree of disturbance	Early identification and intervention	Curriculum based assessment, effective discipline, corporal punishment, self-determination	Cardinal rules for conducting social skills training
Multidisciplinary teams, assessment and collaboration	Motor development, positioning, developing communication skills	Instructional and physical accommodations	Treatment guidelines for epileptic seizure
Hertz, decibels, audiometry: Air conduction and bone conduction	Language development, modes of communication	Instructional considerations, instructional methods, teaming with educational interpreters	Towards early identification of Deaf and hard of hearing students
Acuity versus functional approaches	Play, learning independence, quality indicators of preschool programs	Classroom organization and instructional management, literacy orientation & mobility	Helping sighted students feel more comfortable with blind peers
Checklists, acuity measures, medical examinations	Autism: Delayed language, early signs of autism Deaf-blindness: inhibited mobility, problems with incidental learning	Deaf-blindness: Strategies for teachers TBI: Accommodations in the classroom	Video technology and communication with families

INTRODUCTION TO
Special Education

Teaching in an Age of Challenge

THIRD EDITION

Deborah Deutsch Smith
University of New Mexico

Allyn and Bacon

Boston   London   Toronto   Sydney   Tokyo   Singapore

Series Editor: Ray Short
Developmental Editor: Alicia Reilly
Series Editorial Assistant: Karen Huang
Marketing Manager: Kris Farnsworth
Production Manager: Elaine M. Ober
Composition and Prepress Buyer: Linda Cox
Manufacturing Buyer: Megan Cochran
Cover Administrator: Linda Knowles
Photo Researcher: Susan Duane
Editorial-Production Service: Barbara Gracia, Woodstock Publishers' Services
Interior Designer: Deborah Schneck
Electronic Composition: Schneck-DePippo Graphics

Library of Congress Cataloging-in-Publication Data

Smith, Deborah Deutsch.
    Introduction to special education : teaching in an age of challenge / Deborah Deutsch Smith. — 3rd ed.
      p.   cm.
    Includes bibliographical references and indexes.
    ISBN 0–205–26594-4 (hardcover)
    1. Special education—United States. I. Title.
LC3981.S56 1998
371.9'0973—dc21

97–13816
CIP

Printed in the United States of America
10 9 8 7 6 5 4 3 2 1 —VHP— 01 00 99 98 97

Photo Credits:

Cover photo: Stephen Wiltshire's *Grand Canyon.* Reprinted from *Stephen Wiltshire's American Dream* (Michael Joseph, 1993), p. 104, by permission of Penquin Books, Ltd.; p. 2: Henri de Toulouse-Lautrec, *La Goulue,* 1891, poster, Musée Toulouse-Lautrec, Albi, photograph by Giraudon/Art Resource, New York; p. 16: Lyrl Ahern (left) , Evans Picture Library (right); p. 17: AP/Wide World; p. 21: Courtesy of the National Easter Seal Society; p. 31: Will Faller; p. 32: José Luis Villegas/*The Sacramento Bee;* p. 40: Edouard Manet, *The Piper,* oil on canvas, Musée d'Orsay, Paris, photograph by, Erich Lessing/Art Resource, New York; p. 46: Will Hart; p. 53: Stephen Marks; p. 55: Jim Pickerell; p. 58: Jim Pickerell; p. 65: Will Faller; p. 69: Brian Smith; p. 78: Michael A. Naranjo, *The Eagle's Song,* 1992, bronze, edition of 12, 12" tall, courtesy of the artist; p. 82: Luc Novovitch/Gamma Liaison; p. 85: Will Hart; p. 91: Will Faller; p. 98: Will Faller; p. 105: Brian Smith; p. 122: P. Buckley Moss. *Sunday Afternoon.* © P. Buckley Moss, 1987. No reproduction, lamination, mounting, trimming, matting, framing may be made using the Moss image contained herein. The image may not be used, in whole or in part, for any other product. To do so violates P. Buckley Moss's copyright, trademark and trade dress rights. p. 129: Stephen Marks; p. 134: Courtesy of the Council for Exceptional Children; p. 138: Will Faller; p. 142: Brian Smith; p. 146: Will Faller; p. 154: Brian Smith; p. 168: Will Hart; p. 178: Lewis Carroll, *Alice Liddell as a Beggar Child.* Christ Church Governing Body, Oxford. By permission of Mrs. M. St. Clair. Photograph by Michael R. Dudley; p. 182: Will Hart; p. 186: Will Faller; p. 195: Courtesy of the American Speech, Language & Hearing Association; p. 211: Will Faller; p. 221: Will Faller; p. 228: William Britt, *Winter Cityscape,* 1990, acrylic on canvas, Very Special Arts Gallery, Washington, DC; p. 234: Stephen Marks; p. 246: Paul Kennedy/Liaison International; p. 252: Lester Sloan/Woodfin Camp & Associates; p. 255: Will Faller; p. 260: AP/Wide World Photos; p. 272: Michelangelo Buonarroti, *Pieta* (detail), St. Peter's Basilica, Vatican, Scala/Art Resource, New York; p. 277: Will Hart; p. 287: Special Collections, Milbank Memorial Library, Teachers College, Columbia University;

Photo credits are continued on page iv and are considered an extension of the copyright page.

*To the best newspaper clipping service
in the nation, my mom,*

Marion Deutsch Meyer

CONTENTS

To the Student

The creation of the third edition of *Introduction to Special Education: Teaching in an Age of Challenge* has a major purpose: that you will find the information presented so interesting, and possibly so intriguing, that it will entice you to devote your career to students with disabilities and their families. First, I have tried to create a personal experience where the stories of real people—their challenges and achievements—come to life. Through their stories, it is hoped that you will come to a better understanding and acceptance of differences. Second, every attempt was made to bring you the most current knowledge about disabilities, best educational practices, and individualized education. This information comes to you through discussions of research findings, but, more importantly, through practical examples translating research to practice.

It is also hoped that my vision of schools will influence your vision of educational environments and what they can be. What I see is every school, not just isolated examples, being places where all children—those with and without disabilities—are engaged and excited by learning. I see schools as places where students learn with and from each other, helped by excellent teachers and other professionals. In these schools families are integral to the educational process, and their family traditions, culture, and language are respected and reflected in educational programs. I know that this vision is just that: a vision of what schools should and can be. Maybe, those of you who learn from this text will help make this vision a reality.

My career in special education is long, beginning in my teen years. What has sustained me over the years is the excitement in watching a child with dis- abilities achieve an important goal, perform a task that seemed impossible to accomplish only a few weeks before, and share a funny happening with everyone in class. In no way does this text attempt to minimize disabilities, but it also does not mean to describe them as so complex and difficult that most cannot be compensated for or even overcome. One important message conveyed in this book is that people with disabilities can assume their places, alongside people without significant disabilities, in modern society when special education is truly special. May the child's laughter and joy over an accomplishment entice you to devote your career to the field of disabilities as it did me.

Organization of This Text

Facts, figures, research findings, and the special education and disability knowledge base are important to all professionals and to the public so that the needs of people with disabilities can be met at school and in the community. Such information is important, but it is not the only essence of this field. To approach what is really important about special education, we must listen to individuals with disabilities and their family members. We must "hear their voices" and "see their accomplishments" and become caring, sensitive, and respectful in our interactions with them. For these reasons, this text has included some very special features. Each chapter begins with a piece of art, created by a master who had or has a disability. Those of you who are taking an art history course or have visited museums may be surprised to see some of the same works of beauty in a text about disabilities. All of the artists included here were exceptional in ways beyond their creative and artistic abilities. The inclusion of this artwork is intended to make an important point that you should consider: People, despite their abilities or disabilities, are capable of creating great beauty. Every chapter also includes an opening vignette written by a person with the disability discussed therein, a family member, or a professional. These personal perspectives reflect the real lives of people and how a disability has affected them.

The first two chapters explain the foundation of special education. Chapter 1 describes the context of special education: its definition, the services it provides, its origins, and landmark legislation and court cases that outline the rights of children with disabilities and their families. Chapter 2 is devoted to the individualized special education process and the three plans—Individualized Family Service Plan, Individual Education Program, and Individualized Transition Plan—that guarantee each child with disabilities a free appropriate education in the least restrictive environment possible.

Chapter 3 provides a comprehensive look at multicultural and bilingual special education. The number of culturally and linguistically diverse youngsters attending our nation's schools is growing, and educators must be increasingly sensitive to these students' very complex learning needs. For these reasons, throughout the text information is integrated about diverse children and their families and a special box, Focus on Diversity, is included in each chapter to draw your attention to important issues. The remaining chapters in this book are devoted to specific disabilities recognized by federal law. Those disabilities found with the highest prevalence in schools are presented first. Therefore, the chapter about learning disabilities, the largest special education category, comes first, followed by the chapter about speech or language impairments.

Because prevalence determined the order of chapters, the low-incidence disabilities are discussed in later chapters. Chapter 6 presents the latest information about mental retardation. It is followed by chapters about gifted and talented children (including those with disabilities), behavior disorders and emotional disturbance, physical impairments and special health care needs, deafness and hard of hearing, and low vision and blindness. The final chapter deals with three very low-incidence disabilities: autism, traumatic brain injury, and deaf-blindness.

Tools for Students

In this book, you will find many features to facilitate your study during this semester or academic quarter. At the beginning of every chapter you will find a set of Advance Organizers. The chapter overview, the five self-test questions, and one challenge question should help focus your attention on some important concepts presented in that chapter. Please notice that these questions are repeated in the Summary found at the end of every chapter, and this time concise answers are provided. This feature should allow you to check your understanding of some of the most important concepts presented in the text.

The advance organizer/summary feature is only one of many elements of this text that should help you master the content. Chapters 3 through 12 are written using a standardized organizational format, so you will know where to find topical information on a specific disability. These chapters have the following structure:

- Definition, identification, and significance
- History of the field
- Prevalence
- Causes and prevention
- Students with this disability
- Educational considerations, such as early intervention, placement and inclusion, interventions and accommodations, transition through adulthood
- Technology
- Concepts and controversy
- Supplementary resources, including scholarly texts, popular books and videos, consumer and professional organizations and agencies

Key terms and brief definitions are found in the margin at the bottom of each page where an important concept is first introduced and discussed. The glossary at the end of the text provides you with an alphabetically organized, comprehensive set of these terms and their definitions. Reviewing the glossary at the end of the semester should give you a good overview and review of the content presented over the semester or academic quarter. Another feature should help you bridge information across chapters. The Making Connections statements found in the margins are intended to help you find supporting and complementary information across the text.

Throughout the text, you will find a number of boxes that contain practical information that can be applied to the education of students with disabilities and work with their families. Mentioned earlier, the Focus on Diversity boxes address the unique needs of culturally and linguistically diverse students with disabilities. Each box addresses a different issue that educators must consider when planning appropriate education programs for these students. The Tips for Teachers boxes are designed to give you practical information about identifying and working with students with disabilities. The Making Accommodations boxes include many suggestions about ways to more effectively include students with disabilities in classroom settings and also to meet their individual educational needs. In the Teaching Tactics boxes, you will find examples of instructional techniques that have been verified through research and proven effective with many students with special needs. The references cited in each chapter are organized at the back of the text by chapter and in headings that correspond to the standardized outline. If you want to learn more about a topic or write a paper for class, the arrangement of these references should be helpful. At the end of the book, you will also find two indices: a list of all of the authors cited in the text and selected people who have contributed significantly to the field, and a subject list that allows you to find quickly topics discussed in the text.

The *Students' Resource Manual* accompanying this text offers many tips on how to study more efficiently and effectively for this and other courses. It also includes many practice activities to help you learn the content of the course and practically apply your knowledge to classroom settings. In addition, the resource book includes practice test items to help you self-test and assess your mastery of the content presented in each chapter.

Acknowledgments

The greatest thanks goes to the one person who lost his playmate and travel companion, saw the manuscript and all its various pieces fill my office at home (which is supposed to be "a room of my own") and then consume the dining room, had his life totally interrupted, learned what patience really means, and kept asking "when will you be done": Jim Smith. The debt of gratitude to the book team, who became

known as Charlie's Angels—Claudia C'de Baca, Zina Yzquierdo McLean, and Naomi Chowdhuri Tyler—can never be fully repaid. Without this tireless team, the marginal annotations would be in all the wrong places, the Test Bank would be asking stupid questions, the references would not be double-checked or perfect, the agency and organization information at the end of the chapters might not be accurate, the indexes could not have been done on time, and all of the odds and ends would have driven me crazier than my baseline. Thanks also goes to Chris Curren for helping to conceptualize the advance organizer component and for the case study handouts; to Valerie Appert for handling the permissions and who after two editions could provide technical assistance on this arduous task; to Paula Lucero for help with word processing and manuscript preparation for all three editions; to Cindy Cantou-Clarke for taking those phone calls and making those arrangements for the Alliance 2000 Project, which gave the Angels and me the extra time to devote to this project; and to Arthur Kaufman who made sure the book actually got finished.

For sharing their lives and their stories in such a special way, I thank the exceptional people, parents, family members, and professionals: Lilly Rong-Cheng, Omar Chavez, Betty Dominguez, Gloria Enlow, Leslie Palanker, Robert Pasternak, Ian and Ann Park, Samantha Reed, Karen Canellas-U'Ren, Rebecca Viers, and Judy Zanotti.

Thanks also must go to the Allyn and Bacon team. Ray Short, the editor for all three editions, helped facilitate the project in every way possible and advocated for elements that I wanted included but made his job more difficult. It has been such an honor to be able to work with Elaine Ober, Allyn and Bacon's production manager who decided to take this book on as hers. She immediately caught my vision and added her creativity and sense of aesthetics to the project; the outcome is wonderful and apparent. To my chief problem-solver, question-answerer, go-between, bridge from Albuquerque to Needham Heights, for all of those e-mails and calls, thanks to my developmental editor, Alicia Reilly. Toward the end of a big book project like this one, there is nothing more important to an author than to find a production packager who is professional and efficient, attends to details from the beginning, is available and pleasant, and sets the highest quality standard for those in her business. Barbara Gracia and I have worked together twice, and I hope that we will be able to do so again. The creative graphic design and layouts provided by Deborah Schneck have made this edition interesting to look at and easier for you, the student, to use.

A number of people helped me create a third edition that contains current information and accurately reflects each field's trends, issues, and directions, and all of their efforts are greatly appreciated. These folks took extra time to find what appeared to be unavailable data, or shared their personal materials, or carefully and painstakingly explained the nuances of their area of expertise; and all of them patiently kept answering question after question. Special thanks to these generous professionals: Len Baca, University of Colorado–Boulder; Vic Baldwin, Teaching Research, Monmouth; Jim Banks, University of Washington; Dale Brown, President's Committee on Employment and the Handicapped; Teresa Castalano, University of New Mexico Hospital; Phil Chinn, California State University–Los Angeles; Jane Clarke, University of New Mexico Hospital; Lani Florian, University of Birmingham; Jim Green, Rural America Initiative; Andy Hsi, University of New Mexico Hospital; Elizabeth Nielsen, University of New Mexico; Doug Palmer, University of Texas–A&M; Mike Rosenberg, Johns Hopkins University; Martyn Rouse, University of Cambridge Institute of Education; Loretta Serna, University of New Mexico; Steve Smith, Trinity University; Judy Smith-Davis, Alliance 2000 Project; Ann Taylor, University of New Mexico; Janeen Taylor, Johns Hopkins University; Jo Thomason, Council for Administrators of Special Education (CASE); Jane West, Consultant; and Lindsay L. Whitcomb, March of Dimes Resource Center. And, I also thank the folks at the National Information Center on Deafness and the Research Institute at Gallaudet University, Center for Disease Control, who time and time again answered even the most trivial question and called back with answers when I was uncertain.

A number of professionals helped by reviewing drafts of the third edition. Their reviews of draft manuscript were invaluable and helped toward the creation of an accurate and current text, but also a most useful and usable one. To these professionals who gave of their time and expertise goes my gratitude: Rhoda Cummings, University of Nevada–Reno; Gary Davis, University of Wisconsin–Madison; Mary Kay Dykes, University of Florida–Gainesville; Jane N. Erin, Ph.D., The University of Arizona; Laura Latta Gaudet, Panhandle Mental Health Center, Scotts Bluff, Nevada; Patricia Maurer, National Federation of the Blind; Donald F. Moores, Ph.D., Gallaudet University; Festus E. Obiakor, Ph.D., Emporia State University; Douglas J. Palmer, Texas A&M University; Thomas B. Pierce, Ph.D., University of Nevada–Las Vegas; Michael S. Rosenberg, Johns Hopkins University; Brenda Sheuerman, Southwest Texas State University; Steven F. Warren, Peabody College, Vanderbilt University.

I also wish to acknowledge the following professionals for providing content input, reviews, and assistance on earlier editions of this text: James M. Alarid, New Mexico Highlands University; Leonard Baca, University of Colorado at Denver; Isaura Barrera, University of New Mexico; Barbara Baskin, SUNY at Stony Brook; Diane Bassett, University of Northern Colorado; John Beattie, University of North Carolina at Charlotte; Ann Beckwith, Albuquerque Public Schools; Gary Best, California State University–Los Angeles; Daniel R. Boone, University of Arizona; Sharon Borthwick-Duffy, University of California, Riverside; Virginia Cavaluzzo, Children's Psychiatric Hospital at the University of New Mexico; Bertram Chiang, University of Wisconsin–Oshkosh; Philip C. Chinn, California State University, Los Angeles; Barbara Clark, California State University, Los Angeles; Linda Clark, Department of Human Services, Spokane; Patricia A. Connard, The Ohio State University; Jozi De Leon, New Mexico State University; Floyd Dennis, Peabody College, Vanderbilt University; Amy Dietrich, Memphis State University; Linda Duncan Malone, Ball State University; Mary Kay Dykes, SpEdCon, Inc.; June H. Eliot, Lydon State College; Rebecca R. Fewell, University of Miami; Marie Fritz, Indiana State University; Cheryl Hanley-Maxwell, University of Wisconin–Madison; Suki Harada, Albuquerque Public Schools; Kathryn Haring, University of Oklahoma; Randall Harley, Peabody College, Vanderbilt University; Ben Harper, East Central University; Bill Healey, University of Nevada–Las Vegas; Kyle Higgins, University of Nevada–Las Vegas; Dick Hood, University of New Mexico; Marcia Horne, University of Oklahoma; Betty Greenwood Houbion, Cooperative Extension Service Education Center; Andy Hsi, University of New Mexico Hospital; Selma Hughes, East Texas State University; Roger Kroth, University of New Mexico; Jeanette W. Lee, West Virginia State College; Elliot Lessen, Northern Illinois University; David Lovett, University of Oklahoma; Tom Lovitt, University of Washington; Jean Lowe, University of New Mexico Hospital; Sheila Lowenbraun, University of Washington; Barbara MacDonald and the staff of the New Mexico School for the Visually Handicapped; Donald MacMillan, University of California at Riverside; Donald F. Maietta, Boston University; June Maker, University of Arizona; Horace Mann, State University College at Buffalo; Sheldon Maron, Portland State University; Ed Martin, National Center on Employment and Disability; Christine Marvin, University of Nebraska–Lincoln; C. Julius Meisel, University of Delaware; Cecil Mercer, University of Florida; Linda Metzke, Lyndon State College; Jeanice Midgett, University of Central Florida; Donald F. Moores, Gallaudet University; Sharon R. Morgan, University of Texas; Elizabeth Neilsen, University of New Mexico; John T. Neisworth, The Pennsylvania State University; Daniel H. Nelson, Walla Walla College; Bengt Nirje, Swedish Organization of Sports for the Handicapped; A. Harry Passow, Columbia University; Peter V. Paul, The Ohio State University; Tom Pierce, University of Nevada–Las Vegas; Fran Reed, Olivet Nazarene University; Suzanne Robinson, Kansas University; Raymond Rodriguez, Colorado State University; Robert B. Rutherford, Jr., Arizona State University; Jerome J. Schultz, Lesley College; Jack Scott, Florida Atlantic University; Kathlene S. Shank, Eastern Illinois University; Art Shildroth, Gallaudet Center for Assessment and Demographic Studies; Corinne R. Smith, Syracuse University; Stephen W. Smith, University of Florida; Cathe Snyder, Albuquerque Public Schools; Mårten Söder, University of Uppsala; Scott Sparks, Ohio University, Zanesville Branch; Janet Spector, University of Maine–Orono; Keith Stearns; Nonda Stone, University of Oregon; Qaisar Sultana, Eastern Kentucky University; Krista Swensson, Ball State University; Janis Tabeck-Keene, Albuquerque Public Schools; Jo Thomason, Council for Administrators of Special Education; James Van Tassel, Ball State University; Kevin Vieze, Information Center of Deafness at Gallaudet University; Donna F. Wadsworth, The University of Southwestern Louisiana; Steven F. Warren, Peabody College, Vanderbilt University; Phyllis Wilcox, University of New Mexico; Sherman Wilcox, University of New Mexico; Mary Kay Zabel, Kansas State University.

D.D.S.

Henri Toulouse-Lautrec. *La Goulue,* 1891.

Henri Toulouse-Lautrec was born into a noble French family that was closely related to the royal families of France, England, and Aragon. The countess and count, his parents, were first cousins. Their son's childhood, in the middle of the nineteenth century, was privileged, but also tragic. Probably due to a hereditary condition, he was not a strong child and early on showed signs that he was not developing normally physically. He had a speech impairment and was frail, although he was highly intelligent. Fragile health caused him to miss months of school, and it was clear his bones were weak. He used a wheelchair for many long periods during his childhood. During his teen years and within a fifteen-month period, he fell and broke first the left then the right legs. Lautrec never developed normally, being abnormally short, and he retreated to painting. He became a talented and highly productive painter. However, because of his disabilities, his adult life was often in turmoil and plagued by alcoholism. (Denvir, 1991; Perruchot, 1962)

The Context of Special Education

1

ADVANCE ORGANIZERS

OVERVIEW

Special education provides students with disabilities and their families individually determined educational programs. Special education comprises a free appropriate education provided in the least restrictive environment possible and includes all of the related and support services the student needs. Special education employs teams of professionals from many disciplines. The services included in special education are mandated by law (legislation), called the Individuals with Disabilities Education Act (IDEA), and are interpreted by the courts (litigation).

FOCUS QUESTIONS

SELF-TEST QUESTIONS

▶ How is special education defined, and what are its categories of special needs?

▶ What are the roots of the special education movement in the United States?

▶ What are the eight major provisions Congress addressed when it first passed PL 94–142, the Individuals with Disabilities Act, in 1975?

▶ How might the principle of least restrictive environment be described?

▶ What major roles do legislation and litigation play in special education?

CHALLENGE QUESTION

▶ How do the perspectives of diverse societies and cultures influence the concepts of "disability" and "handicapped"?

A *Personal Perspective*: Lilly Cheng and the Starfish Story

*L*illy Rong Cheng, a professional in special education with particular expertise in multicultural issues, brings to us a perspective we can all ponder and learn. She often tells a story about a wise little girl and her individualized approach to solving a problem.

An old man was walking on a beach one morning and saw some movements from a distance. He was very curious about the movements and as he walked closer, he saw a young girl picking something from the beach and throwing it into the ocean. When he got very near, he saw that the girl was throwing starfish that had washed up on the beach into the ocean. The old man said to the girl, "The sun is out and there are hundreds of starfish on the beach. You can't save them all. They'll all perish." The young girl picked up one more starfish, and while she was throwing the starfish into the ocean, she said, "This one won't." (Cheng, 1996)

1. What is the lesson for special educators found in the Starfish Story?

2. Change this story to be about real people and their experiences.

*T*he right to an education is one of the most widely held values for all young people in the United States. Americans widely recognize that the success of our democracy depends on citizens who are educated, who actively participate in the political process, live independently, and are economically productive. In the early days of the United States (and in many other countries even today), education was a right of a select and privileged few: generally, white males. Not until the mid-nineteenth century did universal education become a reality for most children and youth in this country. Today, all children in the United States have the right to attend school. In most states, in fact, it is their legal obligation to attend school until they reach age 16. Side by side, girls and boys, rich and poor, all races and ethnic groups, children of all skill levels and abilities arrive at schools every morning. Such student diversity demands skilled teachers and other professionals who are adept at meeting challenges and who eagerly meet students and pledge to help and guide the process of education.

Special education teachers and other professionals who work with children with disabilities and their families are committed to such special challenges. All children with disabilities in the United States now have access to public schools and a right to education. Special education children include those with learning disabilities, speech or language impairments, mental retardation, gifted abilities, behavior disorders and emotional disturbance, physical impairments and special health care needs, hearing loss, visual impairments, and other low-incidence disabilities (autism, deaf-blindness, and traumatic brain injury). Because of the very special challenges that culturally and linguistically diverse children face, many of them are at greater risk of being identified as having a disability, and those who do have disabilities often have very unique educational needs. Gifted children have historically been included in discussions of special education but have not been

"Forget it, pal. I thought I recognized you, but, as it turns out, it was just your type that I recognized."

Source: Drawing by Ziegler, © 1983. The New Yorker Magazine, Inc.

protected by the federal laws that guarantee educational opportunities to children with disabilities. Although programs for gifted children exist in many schools, they are not as universal as programs for students with disabilities because gifted education is not protected by federal laws.

Of course, all children are unique individuals, and stereotypes or suggestions that certain children are a "type" must be avoided. However, children—especially those with exceptionalities—frequently share certain characteristics. In this book, we describe some of those shared characteristics and show how you can address the special needs of these students. Special education—along with positive attitudes, high expectations, and well-prepared teachers and related service professionals—can make the difference between a child's success or failure in school and later in life.

Disabilities Defined

Many different paths can lead to an understanding of disabilities and their effect on individuals, their loved ones, and their communities. Definitions often put into place a language system that describes individuals and their generalized characteristics. Definitions can also explain how individuals are treated. Definitions, in their existence, might even contribute to how people react to others who are different in appearance, learning style, or behavior.

Often, different disciplines offer different definitions of disabilities; in other words, nothing is absolute when studying the human condition. For example, some definitions include analyses of a group of individuals' common characteristics (e.g., cognitive abilities, stereotypic behaviors). Other definitions take a more sociological view and discuss how differences are socially constructed and are as much a part of the social system as is the individual (Turner & Louis, 1996). A good example of such differences in definitional orientations might be Jane Mercer's sociological view of mental retardation as compared to a definition that describes mental retardation by an individual's score on a test of intelligence. For decades, definitions approved and adopted by the American Association of Mental Retardation (AAMR) determined the existence and severity of mental retardation in individuals on the basis of the score an individual obtained on a test of intelligence (IQ score). For example, a person with mild mental retardation would have received an IQ score between 50 and 75, a person with moderate mental retardation would have an IQ between 35 and 50, someone with severe mental retardation would score between 25 and 35, and those with scores below 25 would be considered to have profound mental retardation. In 1973, Mercer proposed a different concept about mental retardation through the following definition:

> From a social system perspective, "mental retardate" is an achieved social status and mental retardation is the role associated with that status. A mental retardate is one who occupies the status of mental retardate and plays the role of mental retardate in one or more of the social systems in which he participates. (p. 27)

Through her definition, Mercer suggested that, irrespective of a person's IQ score, what is important is whether the individual is assigned the role of being mentally retarded in the particular social system. Under the sociological definition, *normal* means that the individual is achieving role expectations in a satisfactory manner. Such an evaluation requires a comparison of how the individual performs in

MAKING CONNECTIONS

In every chapter about an exceptionality, you will find a section devoted to definitions.

MAKING CONNECTIONS

In Chapter 6, you will find sections about the evolution of definitions for mental retardation in these sections:
• Defined
• History of the Field

Cultural Basis for the Concept of Disabilities

The relationship between the individual and the group varies across cultures. What also varies are comparisons made from individual to individual: How does this individual's behavior compare with other members of the group? In mainstream U.S. culture, concern about an individual often focuses on how that individual's behavior varies from the "norm." If it differs too much, the behavior is considered deviant. What would happen in cultures that did not compare individuals to a standard? Might the concept of "handicapped" not even exist? Would there be any meaning to the term *disability*? Many Native American cultures block and disvalue any attempt to compare an individual child to another child or to a group norm, and for them there appears to be little operative meaning for terms like *handicapped* or *disabilities* (Green, 1996).

relation to the group. Possibly, whether and how such comparisons are made across different cultures, in part, defines the concept of "being handicapped." The Focus on Diversity box continues with this point.

Whether "disabilities" is an internal condition or a condition imposed on some individuals as a result of how others perceive them and their abilities is a complex concept. In the following sections, we discuss and provide some examples about how, in some cases, having a disability and being handicapped because of that disability is a provocative issue to consider. We also discuss some benefits and disadvantages of labeling and classifying people into disability categories; and, finally, we help you understand how to best talk about people with disabilities. As you read this part of the text and continue your studies throughout the academic term, consider how a person's disability is influenced by the actions of others. On the other side, always be careful not to minimize the effects of a disability on the individual.

Is Having a Disability Necessarily a Handicap?

Not only is the relationship between disabilities and being handicapped an important concept, it is also an interesting topic for discussion. The main questions here may be: To what degree does the way people are treated limit their independence and opportunities? Does discrimination and bias handicap groups of individuals, particularly those with disabilities? What is the difference between being handicapped and having a disability? The answers to these seemingly simple, yet truly complex, questions may lead us to understand that the concept of "being handicapped" is more societally determined than we often acknowledge.

Typically, disability is viewed as a difference, a characteristic that sets an individual apart from everyone else, something that makes the individual less able or inferior. Many professions (medicine, psychology) view disabilities in terms of deviance, a model whereby the majority of the population is considered normal and a disability sets the individual apart. Often, the way society views the disability restricts that individual's ability to reach his or her potential. In other words, the individual is handicapped by society's attitudes.

MAKING CONNECTIONS

For more about deafness, see Chapter 10.

Some evidence exists that supports the idea that people can be handicapped and not be stigmatized by society. Without such bias, people with disabilities might have rates of success and failure similar to everyone else's. The case of the English settlers of Martha's Vineyard serves as a fine example of how the way people are treated can affect their lives. Apparently, the island's seventeenth-century settlers came from Kent, England, and carried with them both a recessive gene for deafness and the ability to use sign language. The hearing people living on the island were bilingual, developing their oral and sign language skills simultaneously early in life. Generation after generation, the prevalence of deafness on the island was exceptionally high, being 1:4 in one small community and 1:25 in several others. Probably because deafness occurred at such a high rate and in almost everyone's family, people who were deaf were not treated like deaf people who lived on the mainland. They were integrated into society and were included in all of the community's work and play situations.

MAKING CONNECTIONS

• For more information about previous restrictions on Deaf people marrying each other, see the History section (Chapter 10).
• For more about employment outcomes of people with disabilities, see the Transition sections in each chapter of this text.

So, what was the result of such integration and adaptation to the needs of people with the disability rather than requiring them to adapt to the ways of those without disabilities? These individuals were free to marry whomever they wished. Of those born before 1817, 73 percent of the Vineyard Deaf* married, whereas only 45 percent of deaf Americans married. Only 35 percent of the Vineyard Deaf married other deaf people, as compared to 79 percent of deaf mainlanders. According to tax records, they generally earned average or above average incomes, with some Deaf people actually being quite wealthy. Also, these individuals were active in all aspects of church affairs. Deaf individuals did have some advantages over their hearing neighbors and family members. They were better educated than the general population because they received tuition assistance to attend the school for the deaf in Connecticut. According to the reports of their descendants, these people were able to read and write, and there are numerous accounts about hearing people asking their Deaf neighbors to read something to them or write a letter for them.

The amazing story about the English settlers on Martha's Vineyard shows how deafness, a disability historically considered to be extremely serious, did not affect the way of life or achievement of those who lived on the island. For more than two hundred years, life on this relatively restricted and confined environment was much the same for those who had this disability and those who did not. Groce (1985) provides an explanation for this situation:

> The most striking fact about these deaf men and women is that they were *not* handicapped, because no one perceived their deafness as a handicap. As one woman said to me, "You know we didn't think anything special about them. They were just like anyone else. When you think about it, the Island was an awfully nice place to live." Indeed it was. (p. 110)

---

* Capital D is used here because the Deaf people on Martha's Vineyard represent an important historical group in Deaf Culture.

Classification and Labeling

When the Individuals with Disabilities Education Act (IDEA), the national law protecting students with disabilities and mandating their educational rights, was being considered for reauthorization in 1995 and in 1996 during the 104th Session of Congress*, the U.S. Department of Education's Office of Special Education Programs recommended that children with disabilities not be labeled or identified with a disability category. Such has been the common practice with preschoolers, who can qualify for special education services without being identified as having a specific disability such as mental retardation or a behavioral disorder. Presently thirteen disability categories (a listing of these categories is found in Figure 1.1) are used to determine which schoolchildren are eligible for service under IDEA (Harrison, 1995). New categories are proposed every so often, however, such as the proposal in 1996 for a category for neurobiological brain disorders. Why would professionals from this government agency make such a proposal? It was their belief that

> many of the 13 categories in the law are based on medical models and stereotypical patterns of performance for groups and persons (Atkins & Pelham, 1992; Reschly, 1988), and do not convey accurate information about an *individual* student's educational needs or how the disability affects an *individual* student's ability to succeed educationally. (U.S. Department of Education, 1995a, p. 22)

This position, however, did not meet with full support. For example, the Learning Disabilities Association of America maintained that the legal and educational needs of students with learning disabilities make the category/label absolutely necessary (1995). The label assists parents in understanding what is "wrong" with their child. It also has other benefits, such as assisting in identifying appropriate services, synthesizing research, providing an effective means for communication, clarifying funding support, and preparing specialists to meet the specific needs of these students.

Students with special needs are individuals who require special education and related special services in order to achieve their fullest potential. Figure 1.1 shows the number and percentage of students identified in each category compared with all children in special education. This text also includes chapters about multicultural and bilingual special education and the delivery of special education services and individualized education programs and plans.

Keep in mind, however, that no individual can be categorized precisely. For example, a particular student may have the special education needs of more than one category. Some may have multiple disabilities—for example, one child may have a visual impairment, a hearing loss, a behavior disorder, *and* a learning disability. The needs of and intensities of support required by students are as individual as are the children themselves. Mere recognition of a disability cannot dictate either a particular **educational placement** or a label into which the student's individuality is forced to fit.

As we all know, and as the U.S. Department of Education (1995a) has officially acknowledged, the names we use to describe persons with special needs can influence the way people think about these individuals and their abilities. These

 MAKING CONNECTIONS

- Multicultural and bilingual education topics are found in every chapter of this text and also in a chapter devoted to these topics (Chapter 3).
- IEPs are discussed in detail in Chapter 2.
- Service delivery options are discussed in Chapter 2 and in every chapter in the Inclusion section (Educational Interventions).

educational placement. The location or type of classroom program (e.g., resource room) arranged for a child's education; the setting in which a student receives educational services.

---

* That attempt at reauthorizing the special education law was unsuccessful, and it is now up to this current session of Congress for a renewal of the law.

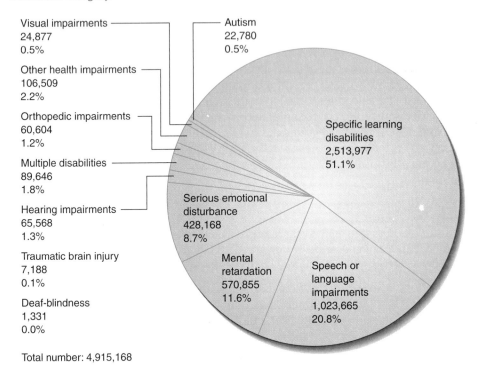

~~~

FIGURE 1.1

Percentage of students with disabilities identified as belonging to each special education category.

Visual impairments
24,877
0.5%

Autism
22,780
0.5%

Other health impairments
106,509
2.2%

Orthopedic impairments
60,604
1.2%

Multiple disabilities
89,646
1.8%

Hearing impairments
65,568
1.3%

Traumatic brain injury
7,188
0.1%

Deaf-blindness
1,331
0.0%

Specific learning
disabilities
2,513,977
51.1%

Serious emotional
disturbance
428,168
8.7%

Mental
retardation
570,855
11.6%

Speech or
language
impairments
1,023,665
20.8%

Total number: 4,915,168

Source: U.S. Department of Education (1996). *Eighteenth Annual Report to Congress on the Implementation of the Individuals with Disabilities Education Act.*

labels can also affect how individuals with special needs regard themselves. Early in the history of mental retardation, for example, people with this disability were labeled "morons," "imbeciles," and "idiots." When first used, these labels may not have had strong negative connotations; but today, we all recognize the devaluation in those labels. We realize that to continue using these terms to describe students with mental retardation would negatively influence the way they perceive themselves, the way others regard them, and probably the attitudes of educators toward them.

Many special educators differentiate *classification* from *labeling*. **Classification** typically refers to a structured system that identifies and organizes characteristics to establish order. Biology, chemistry, geology, and many other disciplines use classification systems for that purpose. To be useful, a classification system must meet four criteria: It must be reliable, cover all relevant aspects, be logically consistent, and have clinical utility (Cromwell, Blashfield, & Strauss, 1975). The classification system we use in this text is **categorical,** organizing special education into the categories learning disabilities, speech or language impairments, mental retardation, giftedness, behavior disorders and emotional disturbance, physical impairments and special health care needs, low vision and

classification. A structured system that identifies and organizes characteristics to establish order.

categorical. A system of classification using specific categories such as learning disabilities or mental retardation.

blindness, hard of hearing and deafness, and **low-incidence disabilities** (autism, deaf-blindness, and traumatic brain injury). Each category has its own internal classification system, or subcategorization. For example, the category mental retardation is now subcategorized into four intensities of supports: intermittent, limited, extensive, and pervasive.

What are the advantages of a classification system for special education? First, a classification system enables us to name disabilities, to differentiate one from another, and to communicate in a meaningful and efficient way about a specific disability. Second, a classification system categorizing a disability and the needs of those who have it is essential for research so that a coherent body of knowledge about the condition can be developed. Third, the system helps citizens form special interest groups to lobby for improved services and promote enlightened attitudes. Finally, categories facilitate relating a certain treatment to a certain diagnosis or category.

What are the disadvantages of using a system of classification? Many professionals support a **noncategorical approach** to educating children with disabilities. They argue that when categories are used, children with special needs are not treated as individuals, that classification places too much emphasis on the group and not enough emphasis on matching the services to individual needs. However, even when a noncategorical approach is used, educators must sometimes classify according to level of disability, for example, mild, moderate, and severe.

Labeling identifies individuals or groups according to a category assigned to them. For example, a child who has been diagnosed as having a behavioral disorders might subsequently be labeled "behaviorally disordered." Labeling can be formal—imposed by an authority such as a psychologist or **diagnostician**—or it can be informal—imposed by nonexperts, such as other children on the playground. Many have criticized labeling as limiting and stigmatizing; some argue that when you impose a label, the person is seen as a stereotype rather than as an individual. Certainly, labeling is harmful when, as a result of a label, individuals are degraded, discriminated against, excluded from society, or placed in classrooms without regard for their individuality. Yet, by providing a common language to describe a disability, labeling can be advantageous. Labeling may also be inevitable and necessary.

The Language of Disabilities

Language evolves to reflect changing concepts and beliefs. What is socially acceptable at one point in history can be viewed as funny or offensive at another. For example, after reading this section, read again Mercer's sociological definition of mental retardation. Think about how, some thirty years ago, she referred to the disability and to those affected by the condition.

People First. Over the past two decades, people with disabilities have become very effective advocates for themselves. In particular, individuals who face physical challenges have joined together to form citizen-action committees, seeking to change laws, policies, and practices that affect their lives. In many respects, the development and passage of the *Americans with Disabilities Act (ADA)* in 1990 was due to the advocacy and vigilance of adults who believe they have been handicapped by society's treatment of them. Today, parents and people

low-incidence disability. A disability that occurs infrequently; the prevalence and incidence are very low.

noncategorical approach. In special education, not classifying or differentiating among disabilities in providing services.

labeling. Assigning a special education category to an individual.

diagnostician. A professional trained to test and analyze a student's areas of strength and weakness to determine whether an individual is eligible for special services and to help in setting educational goals and planning for instruction.

MAKING CONNECTIONS

For more on the ADA law, see the Legislation section found later in this chapter.

with disabilities are the two most powerful lobbying groups at work on behalf of people with disabilities. They have created powerful political action organizations that work to improve opportunities available to *all* individuals with disabilities.

The language we use to talk about these people is very important. It is important to them and it should also be important to us: The words we select send a message to others about our respect for them. Although most of us try to "get it right" all of the time, we occasionally use language offensive to others. The language preferred by people with disabilities can be confusing because different groups and individuals have very different preferences. Although there are many exceptions (especially for the Deaf), there are two basic rules to follow:

1. Put people first.

2. Do not make the person equal the disability.

TABLE 1.1

Getting It Right: Do Say

Adjective	People	Qualifier
Culturally and linguistically diverse	students with ...	• disabilities
	students who have ...	• mental retardation
	individuals with ...	• learning disabilities
	individuals who have ...	• speech impairments
	children with ...	• language impairments
	youth with ...	• severe emotional disturbance
	toddlers with ...	• behavior disorders
	adults with ...	• cerebral palsy • physical disabilities • hearing impairments • visual impairments
Exceptions		
	people	• who face physical challenges
	toddlers	• who use a wheelchair
Blind	students	• who are blind
	youth	• who have low vision
Deaf	individuals	• who are deaf • who are hard of hearing
	the deaf	
	the blind	

The Right Phrases. In light of these rules, therefore, it is proper to use phrases such as the following: students with mental retardation, individuals who have learning disabilities. Two groups of individuals with disabilities prefer a different language system. Specifically, the Deaf (who prefer this term as a reflection of their heritage and culture) and those who are blind provide for most of the exceptions found in disability language systems. You might find the "Do Say" and "Don't Say" tables (see Tables 1.1 and 1.2) helpful as you explain the language of disabilities and its exceptions. Remember, however, that not all members of any group agree unanimously on every issue; some people with disabilities might not agree with the rules of language described here.

Special Education Defined

Special education can be described, defined, and explained in many ways. These different perceptions about what special education is result from people's diverse orientations and experiences. For example, professionals who primarily consult with teachers might be more likely to view special education as a service, whereas those professionals who provide a considerable amount of direct instruction and collaborate with others who also teach and work with students with disabilities might describe it as an educational system. In other words, special education is different things to different people. To us, the most obvious way to define the field of special education is to describe the services it provides and the people who have dedicated themselves to it and to children with special needs and their families.

Special Education Services

First and foremost, **special education** is individualized and tailor-made education for each child with a special need. According to federal regulations, special education means "specially designed instruction, at no cost to the parent, to meet the unique needs of a child with a disability, including instruction conducted in the classroom, in the home, in hospitals and institutions, and in other settings; and instruction in physical education" (34 Code of Federal 17 [a], [1]). Special education includes direct instruction in the classroom, consultation to the general education teacher, coordination of the student's educational program, orchestration of those learning opportunities necessary for each youngster to profit from instruction, and all the related services (speech therapy, physical therapy, occupational therapy, assistive technology) required to meet the unique learning needs of the youngster. In addition, special education monitors progress so that no student with special needs is overlooked or neglected.

So that students with special needs can achieve their maximum potential and continue to grow and learn throughout their lives, special education provides them with the opportunity to learn to read, write, and compute. Although learning academic skills is appropriate for most youngsters with disabilities, it may not be appropriate for some who need more basic life skills instruction. All students with special needs should develop social, leisure time, and community skills, as well; for many, intensive direct instruction on those targets is necessary in order to master these functional life skills. In fact, sometime during their school careers, they

TABLE 1.2

Getting It Right: Don't Say

Article	Adjective or Noun
The	crippled
	disabled
	disturbed
	handicapped
	hearing impairments
	learning disabled
	mentally retarded
	wheelchair bound

special education. Individualized education for children and youth with special needs.

should begin the kind of job preparation necessary to become economically independent. Special education has provided opportunities to students with disabilities, opportunities for an education and a chance to gain the skills necessary for independence in later life. Until relatively recently, not all children with disabilities were afforded this chance. Our future must be one in which no youngster faces a verdict of "noneducable." *Remember, all children can learn.*

Special education is a dynamic, changing, exciting, and controversial field. Although great strides have been made in the past fifty years, further work remains to be done as we strive to "get it right" and provide wonderful educational programs that truly meet the needs of each student with a disability.

Special Education and Related Service Professionals

Special education can also be defined by the wide array of disciplines and professionals that comprise the very special educational effort put forth on behalf of individual students with exceptionalities. Figure 1.2 illustrates, in addition to special education teachers, the variety of professionals providing **related services** to students with disabilities.

One barrier to the provision of an appropriate education to all students with special needs is the shortage of teachers and other professionals: The field needs more trained teachers and support personnel. According to the *Eighteenth Annual Report to Congress on the Implementation of the IDEA,* during the 1994–1995 school year, the nation needed an additional 24,697 certified special education teachers and 23,867 certified related services professionals (U.S. Department of Education, 1996). Special education also needs a work force with improved abilities to collaborate, team teach, modify curricular materials, adapt instructional procedures, design exciting learning environments where all children can learn and grow, and create new educational systems. Special education needs more professionals who will take risks and apply their creative talents to solve the problems faced by many individuals with disabilities and their families. Special education also needs more people from diverse backgrounds (NASDSE, 1994). Culturally and linguistically diverse students will soon comprise 33 percent of the U.S. student body, yet only 5 percent of their teachers will be diverse. Also, additional special education research is needed to develop improved teaching techniques, expand the capabilities of advanced technology, decrease the incidence of disabilities, and create more sensitive communities and school environments.

History of Special Education

related services. A part of special education that includes services from professionals from a wide range of disciplines typically outside of education all designed to meet the learning needs of individual children with disabilities.

People with disabilities and special education (even if it didn't go by that name) have probably existed since the human condition began. Unfortunately, during some periods of history people with disabilities were the victims of discrimination and cruelty. It is also true that at some times, many were cared for and treated well. In the United States, long before 1975 and the passage of the national law that guarantees a free appropriate education to each and every child with a disability, educational services were available to many, but not all, students with exceptional learning needs. We feel strongly that it is important to know the his-

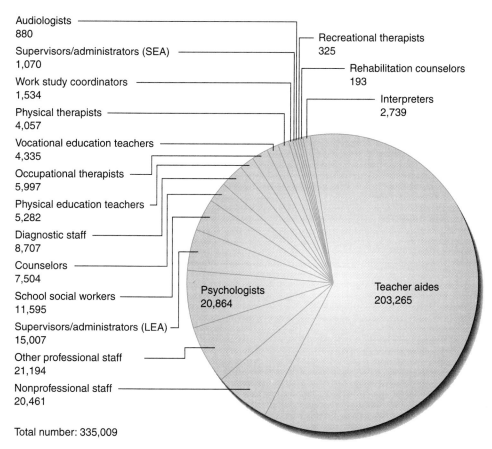

FIGURE 1.2

Types of Related Services Personnel

Audiologists
880

Supervisors/administrators (SEA)
1,070

Work study coordinators
1,534

Physical therapists
4,057

Vocational education teachers
4,335

Occupational therapists
5,997

Physical education teachers
5,282

Diagnostic staff
8,707

Counselors
7,504

School social workers
11,595

Supervisors/administrators (LEA)
15,007

Other professional staff
21,194

Nonprofessional staff
20,461

Recreational therapists
325

Rehabilitation counselors
193

Interpreters
2,739

Psychologists
20,864

Teacher aides
203,265

Total number: 335,009

Source: U.S. Department of Education (1996). *Eighteenth Annual Report to Congress on the Implementation of the Individuals with Disabilities Education Act.*

 MAKING CONNECTIONS

For these reasons, Chapters 3 to 12 include sections about the history of that field.

tory of people with disabilities and of special education. We think that the mistakes of the past are less likely to be repeated if they are known and recognized.

Origins of Special Education

Special education grew from an initial awareness that some children, in order to achieve their potential, require a type or intensity of education different from typical education. This awareness evolved over many years and can be traced to Europe in the 1700s, when certain innovators began to make isolated attempts to provide education to children with disabilities.

One innovator was Jean-Marc-Gaspard Itard, a French physician considered to be the father of special education. Itard worked with deaf children, but his most important work came out of his efforts to help the so-called wild boy of Aveyron.

 MAKING CONNECTIONS

For more on the importance of Itard and Victor, see the History section of Chapter 6.

Jean-Marc-Gaspard Itard, considered to be the father of special education, kept a detailed diary on his teaching of Victor.

Victor, the wild boy of Aveyron, contributed to the development of special education theory and techniques as a student of Itard.

In 1799, a young boy, later named Victor, was discovered in the woods of France. The boy was thought to be a "wild child," untouched by civilization. It is likely that he had mental retardation as well as environmental deprivation. Most people thought the case was hopeless. But Itard, believing in the power of education, took on the task of teaching Victor all the things that typical children learn from their families and in school. He used carefully designed techniques to teach Victor to speak a few words, to walk upright, to eat with dishes and utensils, and to interact with other people.

Fortunately, Itard wrote detailed reports of his techniques and his philosophy, as well as of Victor's progress. Many of these techniques are still used in modern special education. Here are Itard's five aims for Victor's "mental and moral education."

> First aim: To interest him in social life . . . .
>
> Second aim: To awaken his nervous sensibility . . . .
>
> Third aim: To extend the range of his ideas . . . .
>
> Fourth aim: To lead him to the use of speech . . . .
>
> Fifth aim: To make him exercise the simplest mental operations . . . . (Itard, 1806/1962, pp. 10–11).

Another major early figure in the field of special education is Edouard Seguin, a student of Itard. In 1846, he published *The Moral Treatment, Hygiene, and Education of Idiots and Other Backward Children*, the first special education treatise addressing the needs of children with disabilities. After he moved to the United States, he helped found the Association of Medical Officers of American Institutions for Idiots and Feebleminded Persons in 1876. This organization later

Maria Montessori, a pioneer in creating concrete experiences and environments that enhanced learning. She first studied children with mental disabilities and then extended her work to the study of young children.

became the American Association on Mental Deficiency (AAMD) and later yet the American Association on Mental Retardation (AAMR), the oldest and largest interdisciplinary professional association in the field of mental retardation. Seguin believed that sensorimotor exercises could help stimulate learning for children with disabilities. His ideas were integrated into many schools in the United States in the 1800s. The legacy of Seguin's work can be found today in many aspects of special education. For example, the use of motor exercises as an aid to learning was reintroduced in the 1960s in the United States and is often part of the curriculum in special education (Barsh, 1965; Frostig & Horne, 1964; Kephart, 1960).

Seguin, in turn, influenced Maria Montessori, the first female physician in Italy. Before she began the study of young children, Montessori (1912) worked first with children with mental disabilities. She showed that children could learn at young ages and that concrete experiences and an environment rich in manipulative materials facilitated their learning. Her educational methods were published in 1912, helping to spread special education strategies. Today, Montessori is probably most familiar as a leader in early childhood education and the founder of the Montessori preschool movement.

By the early 1800s, residential schools and institutions were established in the United States for teaching children with most disabilities. For example, the American Asylum for the Education of the Deaf and Dumb (now the American School for the Deaf) was started in 1817 by Thomas Hopkins Gallaudet. Samuel Gridley Howe, the famous American reformer and abolitionist, founded the New England Asylum for the Blind (later the Perkins Institute) in 1832. He was the first

For more on Samuel Gridley Howe, also see History sections in
• Chapter 6,
• Chapter 10.

to successfully teach a person who was both blind and deaf. Later, in 1848, Howe created the Massachusetts School for Idiotic and Feeble-Minded Children. Howe successfully persuaded the Massachusetts legislature to appropriate $2,500 to educate children with cognitive disabilities for an experimental three-year program (Barr, 1913). In 1825, the House of Refuge, the first American institution for juvenile delinquents, was founded in New York (Kauffman, 1997). The first hospital devoted to children with physical disabilities, the Home of the Merciful Savior, was founded in 1884 in Philadelphia (Eberle, 1922). By 1917, most states had at least one residential institution housing children and adults with disabilities, often for their entire lives (Scheerenberger, 1983).

Special education classes in neighborhood schools appeared in the late nineteenth century. In 1878, two special education classes opened in Cleveland (Kanner, 1964), apparently for children with behavior problems. Sarason and Doris (1979) describe the early efforts of Elizabeth Farrell, beginning in 1898, to create "ungraded" classes in New York. Farrell's work teaching "backward" students was tied to the settlement house movement, a social service movement to assist the poor and to help immigrants become Americanized. Farrell later founded the Council for Exceptional Children (CEC). Although by the early twentieth century most states had residential institutions, special classes in neighborhood schools existed in only a few cities: Providence, Rhode Island; Springfield, Massachusetts; Chicago; Boston; New York; Philadelphia; Los Angeles; Detroit; Elgin, Illinois; Trenton, New Jersey; Bridgeport, Connecticut; Newton, Massachusetts; Rochester, New York; and Washington, D.C.

As they do today, professionals in the late nineteenth century believed in the individual worth of each student, regardless of that student's special learning needs, and were prepared to work hard to make achievement a reality for all students. In 1891, one institution superintendent described the perfect special education teacher. He urged the teachers to be "sweet-tempered":

> The ideal teacher is well educated, refined, intensely interested in her pupils, and has a professional zeal to grow in her work: she is original, striving to introduce new and bright methods, but not passing hastily from subject to subject before the child has grasped the first. She is patient but energetic, sweet-tempered but persistent, and to the influences of her education and character she adds the charms of personal neatness and attractive manners. She possesses naturally a well grounded religious sense, which finds its best expression in self-sacrifice, conscientious duty, and instinctive kindness. (Isaac N. Kerlin, Manual of Elwyn, 1891, quoted in Nazzaro, 1977, p. 11)

The first training opportunity for teachers of special classes was offered in 1905 at the New Jersey Training School for Feebleminded Boys and Girls (Kanner, 1964). In 1907, the tuition for a six-week summer course in special education was $25. (See Figure 1.3.)

While the idea of special education was taking root in the early 1900s, special education classes remained rare. Only a small number of all students with special needs were able to attend these classes. As late as 1948, for example, only 12 percent of all children and youth *with disabilities* received a special education (Ballard, Ramirez, & Weintraub, 1982). What happened to the others? Many were probably able to function to some degree in their home communities. Others were forced to enter isolated, segregated institutions. Certainly, some died from lack of care, and others were hidden by families fearing discrimination and prejudice.

FIGURE 1.3

Newsletter from the Training School in Vineland, New Jersey.

The Training School

Entered March 14, 1904, at Vineland, N.J., as second-class matter,
under act of Congress of July 16, 1894.

No. 36.   FEBRUARY 1907.   25c. per Annum.

"I gave a beggar from my little store
Of well-earned gold. He spent the
  shining ore
And came again, and yet again, still
  cold
  And hungry as before.

I gave a thought and through that
  thought of mine
He found himself a man, supreme,
  divine,
Bold, clothed, and crowned with bless-
  ings manifold,
  And now he begs no more."

THE SUMMER SCHOOL FOR TEACHERS.

The announcements of our Summer School for 1907 are now ready for distribution. The purpose of the School is to give professional training to those who desire to teach in the special classes in the public schools and to fit teachers and others to better understand peculiar, backward and "special" children. We have unusual facilities for this work, a splendid general equipment and quite a complete laboratory. The plan of work includes observation and teaching, laboratory work, lectures and reading. The tuition fee is $25 and those students who first apply may be boarded at the School at an additional cost of $25. The course extends from July 15th to August 24th.

Information concerning the Summer School may be obtained by addressing E. R. Johnstone, Vineland, N. J.

AS IT APPEARS TO THE PSYCHOLOGIST.

You remember the fable of the lion looking at the picture of a man conquering a lion and saying: "if a lion had painted the picture the man would have gotten the worst of it." It makes a difference who paints the picture.

Men strong of intellect have for long had a monopoly of painting the picture of the feeble-minded. While at times the feeble-minded child has been regarded as a supernatural being possessed of a spirit either good or bad, he has been among the more intellectual races more often treated much as the Spartans treated him—regarded as an outcast and either exposed to die or, where some reverence for human life as such has developed, been preserved from death indeed, but preserved for a life that is possibly worse than death. He has been not only useless, but a drag on society, an incurable disease, a horrible nightmare, one of God's blunders.

But how would the picture look if the lion and not the man painted it?

The feeble-minded child is a human being. He differs from those who call themselves normal, in degree, not in kind. No one of us but might have been of his grade had any one of a score of very possible contingencies taken place. Not one of us but might tomorrow become as "defective" as any of these by the slightest change in our organism. (It is true we should call it insanity, but that is only a matter of terminology.)

What then are we and who is this child? He is somewhere near the

Concept of Normalization

When the field of special education began, the few services that were available were offered primarily in segregated settings, sometimes in special schools within a school district, but more often in residential schools, which in many cases became terrible institutions. These schools usually were geographically isolated in the rural parts of a state. Students often continued living in these facilities even after school age, frequently living their entire lives there. The students spent their time with other students of similar disabilities, rarely interacting with noninstitutionalized peers or participating in the normal patterns of life. Even many children and adults with mild disabilities found themselves in these facilities. Until the 1970s, much of the day-to-day work in institutions—such as caring for individuals with severe disabilities or performing farm or laundry work—was provided by residents with mild and moderate disabilities. Because of the widely held belief that individuals with disabilities would contaminate the "normal" population, many people spent their entire lives in these institutions, isolated from mainstream society.

Normalization is an essential dimension of special education. Although the concept was suggested in 1959 by Bank-Mikkelsen of Denmark (Biklen, 1985), the word itself was coined by Bengt Nirje of Sweden (1969; 1976), who encouraged the United States to incorporate this principle in services to people with disabilities. According to Nirje (1985), normalization means "making available to all persons with disabilities or other handicaps, patterns of life and conditions of everyday living which are as close as possible to or indeed *the same as* the regular circumstances and ways of life of society" (p. 67; emphasis in original). The principle of normalization applies to every aspect of a student's life. Nirje referred to a set of normal life patterns: the normal rhythm of the day, the normal rhythm of the week, the normal rhythm of the year, and the normal development of the life cycle (see also Wolfensberger, 1972; 1995).

Advocacy Movements

The recognition that special education required a particular expertise spurred the development of this new profession. The National Education Association (NEA), a professional educators' organization, approved a Department of Special Education in 1897, although it was disbanded by 1918. In 1922, the International Council for the Education of Exceptional Children (CEC) was founded (Aiello, 1976) when members of a summer special education class conducted at Teachers' College, Columbia University, decided to meet annually to continue sharing exciting ideas about special education. Their professor, Elizabeth Farrell, became the group's first president. Membership grew, and in later years "International" was dropped from the title and the organization became known as the Council for Exceptional Children, or CEC. CEC became affiliated with the National Education Association in 1924 and with the World Federation of Education Associations in 1929. Independent for over thirty years, CEC remains the largest special education professional organization in the United States, with about 61,000 members. CEC was not the only professional organization concerned about people with disabilities that was active during the 1920s. The American Speech and Hearing Association (ASHA) was established in 1935 and has a current membership of 85,000 professionals. The American Occupational Therapy Association (AOTA), the National Association of Social

MAKING CONNECTIONS

Normalization and its evolution is also discussed in Chapter 6.

normalization. Making available ordinary patterns of life and conditions of everyday living.

Workers (NASW), and the American Physical Therapy Association (APTA) have all been instrumental in advocating for the availability of special education-related services for all students with disabilities who need them.

Many volunteer and parent organizations began to organize after World War II to fight for the initiation of educational services in the public schools for students with disabilities. The Arc (formerly the Association for Retarded Citizens of the United States), founded in 1950 as the National Association of Parents and Friends of Mentally Retarded Children, worked to have special education services provided to all students with disabilities through the public education system. Other influential groups were United Cerebral Palsy Associations, Inc. (UCP), which began in 1949; the National Society for Autistic Children, formed in 1961; the Learning Disability Association of America (LDA), founded in 1963 as the Association for Children with Learning Disabilities; and the Epilepsy Foundation of America, which grew out of several earlier epilepsy groups in 1968. The power and importance of the parent advocacy groups must be recognized and applauded. It was and continues to be the strength of the parent movement and its organization that improves federal laws, argues successfully for funding at the state and national levels, and serves as a "watchdog" over local education programs to guard that each student with a disability has access to a free appropriate public education.

People with disabilities formed their own advocacy groups, becoming effectively organized during the late 1980s and 1990s. The first phase was a quest for civil rights, and the second phase is focusing on the development of a disability culture (Longmore, 1995; Treanor, 1993). In Chapter 9, you will learn about Ed Roberts, a catalyst in the organization of people with disabilities in the demand for access to mainstream U.S. society and the fulfillment of basic civil rights. The Council for Citizens with Disabilities (a coalition of many advocacy groups) was instrumental in shaping the Americans with Disabilities Act and provided considerable input during the last attempt to reauthorized IDEA. It continues to be active in shaping national laws and policies. Today, there are many adult advocacy organizations and many other less formal support groups formed by and for adults with disabilities (read your local Sunday newspaper to see a range of these groups in your city).

For *some* kids
school segregation
DIDN'T END IN THE SIXTIES.

Students with disabilities should be evaluated individually to decide their best situations for learning. Because when students are kept apart just for being different, it teaches all the wrong things.

G I V E   A B I L I T Y   A   C H A N C E

 MAKING CONNECTIONS

The self-advocacy movement is discussed in the History sections of Chapters 6 and 9.

Reasons for a National Special Education Law: Pattern of School Exclusion

In 1975, the stage was clearly set for a national special education law. Years of exclusion, segregation, and denial of basic educational opportunities to students with disabilities and their families set an imperative for civil rights law guaranteeing these students access to the education system. Why was this so? In 1948, only 12 percent of all children with disabilities received special education (Ballard et al., 1982). Even as late as 1962, only sixteen states had laws including "educable" mentally retarded children under mandatory school attendance requirements (Roos, 1970). In most states, even those children with the mildest levels of dis-

TABLE 1.3

Landmark Court Cases Setting the Stage for Special Education

Case	Date	Ruling	Importance
Brown v. Board of Education	1954	Ended white "separate but equal" schools	Basis for future rulings that children with disabilities cannot be excluded from school
Pennsylvania Association for Retarded Children (PARC) v. Commonwealth of Pennsylvania	1972	Guaranteed special education to children with mental retardation	Court case that signaled a new period for special education
Mills v. Board of Education of the District of Columbia	1972	Extended the right for special education to children with all disabilities	Reinforced the right to a free public education to all children with disabilities

abilities were not allowed to attend school. Children with more severe disabilities were routinely excluded even until the 1970s. While children without disabilities were required to attend school under compulsory school attendance laws, children *with* disabilities were *prevented* from attending school. The excuses presented for excluding these children from school are shocking by today's standards. One state supreme court justified excluding a young boy with cerebral palsy because he "produces a depressing and nauseating effect upon the teachers and school children" (*State ex rel. Beattie v. Board of Education*, 1919).

Finally, the rights of children with special needs gradually gained momentum. In the 1970s, the courts and Congress addressed the issue of education for children with disabilities. Table 1.3 summarizes early landmark court cases setting the stage for special education.

Legislation

Modern special education reflects the thinking of many practicing educators as well as the contributions of people with disabilities and their families. But special education also reflects legal and political realities in the United States. Federal and state laws govern many aspects of special education. Let's consider some of this disability **legislation**.

PL 94–142: Individuals with Disabilities Education Act (IDEA)

legislation. Laws passed by a legislature or congress and signed by a governor or president.

The face of special education has changed steadily in the United States over the past one hundred years. The progress achieved in the nineteenth and early twentieth centuries can be attributed to the efforts of individuals. The progress of recent years can be attributed in large part to court cases and the passage of a national special education law. The landmark law protecting children with special needs—the **Education for All Handicapped Children Act (EHA)**, **Public Law (PL) 94–142**—was passed in 1975; this law is now called **Individuals with Disabilities Education Act (IDEA)**. With this law, Congress designed federal legislation that guarantees education to every child with disabilities in the country.

The Need for National Legislation. Why did Congress pass this revolutionary law? Let us look at Congress's own words.[*]

The Congress found that

1. There are more than 8 million children with disabilities in the United States today;
2. The special educational needs of such children are not being fully met;
3. More than half of the children with disabilities in the United States do not receive appropriate educational services which would enable them to have full equality of opportunity;
4. 1 million of the children with disabilities in the United States are excluded entirely from the public school system and will not go through the educational process with their peers;
5. There are many children with disabilities throughout the United States participating in regular school programs whose handicaps prevent them from having a successful educational experience because their disabilities are undetected;
6. Because of the lack of adequate services within the public school system, families are often forced to find services outside the public school system, often at great distance from their residence and at their own expense;
7. Developments in the training of teachers and in diagnostic and instructional procedures and methods have advanced to the point that, given appropriate funding, State and local educational agencies can and will provide effective special education and related services to meet the needs of children with disabilities;
8. State and local educational agencies have a responsibility to provide education for all children with disabilities, present financial resources are inadequate to meet the special educational needs of children with disabilities; and
9. It is in the national interest that the Federal Government assist State and local efforts to provide programs to meet the educational needs of children with disabilities in order to assure equal protection of the law. (20 U.S.C. section 1400 [b])

Clearly, Congress recognized the importance of special education for children with disabilities and was concerned about widespread discrimination. Congress pointed out that many students with disabilities were excluded from education; and those who entered school frequently failed to benefit from the school experience because their disabilities went undetected or ignored. Congress realized that special education could make a positive difference in the lives of these children and their families with proper financial assistance and educational support. Congress found these facts so compelling that it declared that it was "in the national interest" to stop discrimination against children with disabilities.

---

[*] Notice how language referring to people with disabilities has changed quickly. The federal law quoted here used language appropriate at that time.

Education for All Handicapped Children Act (EHA). A federal law, PL 94-142, passed in 1975 with many provisions for assuring free appropriate public education for all students with disabilities; later renamed the Individuals with Disabilities Education Act (IDEA).

Public Law (PL) 94-142. Education for All Handicapped Children Act (now IDEA).

Individuals with Disabilities Education Act (IDEA). New name given in 1990 to the Education for All Handicapped Children Act (EHA).

What did Congress intend to accomplish with this law? Again, Congress was specific:

> It is the purpose of this chapter to assure that all handicapped children have available to them . . . a free appropriate public education which emphasizes special education and related services designed to meet their unique needs, to assure that the rights of handicapped children and their parents or guardians are protected, to assist States and localities to provide for the education of all handicapped children, and to assess and assure the effectiveness of efforts to educate handicapped children. (20 U.S.C. section 1400[c])

The Purposes of IDEA. In 1995, the U.S. Department of Education (1995a) rearticulated the purposes of the national law as follows:

1. To ensure that all children with disabilities have available to them a **free appropriate public education (FAPE)** that emphasizes special education and related services designed to meet their particular needs;
2. To ensure that the rights of children with disabilities and of their parents or guardians are protected;
3. To assist states and localities to provide for the education of all children with disabilities; and
4. To assess and ensure the effectiveness of efforts to educate children with disabilities. (p. 1)

Fundamental Provisions. A most ambitious law, IDEA not only guarantees students with disabilities access to education but also describes the process that must be followed as the law is implemented in every school district across this country. Congress outlined seven major provisions when it first passed the law in 1975. Later in this chapter, you will learn how IDEA has been changed through its reauthorizations and amendments over its twenty-five-year existence.

1. *Free appropriate public education (FAPE):* Any special education received by a student with disabilities is to be provided at no cost to the student and family. Special education must be free (at no cost) to the parents *and* must also be appropriate—that is, the education must be suitable to the individual needs of the child. During the course of your study in special education, you will learn about techniques, methods, materials, and approaches designed to provide students with appropriate special education programs.

2. *Parental notification and procedural rights:* Many parents do not know their rights about permitting their children to be tested or evaluated or to participate in the special education planning process. Parents have the right to examine the records, and to obtain an independent educational evaluation, of their child. They have the right to receive a clearly written notice that states the school's **evaluation** of the child's performance. If the school believes the student has special needs, it will recommend further evaluation, placement, and other special services. If the team of experts evaluating the student does not believe the child has a disability, the notice will state that as the reason for denying special services. The parents have the right to consent or object to this notice, to make formal complaints, and to pursue a **due process hearing** and, ultimately, a **judicial hearing** if they disagree with the services provided by the school to the child. These rights include the right to legal counsel and other rights concerning witnesses, written evidence, verbatim documentation of the hearing, and an appeal.

 MAKING CONNECTIONS

For more information on IDEA, see the Legislation section found later in this chapter.

free appropriate public education (FAPE). One of the provisions of IDEA that ensures that children with disabilities receive necessary education and services without cost to the child and family.

evaluation. Assessment or judgment of special characteristics such as intelligence, physical abilities, sensory abilities, learning preferences, and achievement.

due process hearing. A noncourt proceeding before an impartial hearing officer that can be used if parents and school personnel disagree on a special education issue.

judicial hearing. A hearing before a judge in court.

3. *Individualized education and services to all children identified as having disabilities:* IDEA requires that states and schools specifically seek out and identify *all* children with disabilities. States are required to make considerable efforts—through public information campaigns, direct contact with social service agencies, and other types of outreach efforts—to locate and provide services to every child with a disability.

4. *Necessary related services:* For some children with disabilities, special education alone is not enough to comprise an appropriate education. IDEA therefore includes a right to related services such as developmental, corrective, and other support services that may be needed to enable a child to benefit from special education. Typical related services might include transportation, speech therapy, audiology, psychological services, physical therapy, occupational therapy, adaptive physical education, assistive technology, and certain medical and counseling services.

5. *Individualized assessments:* Special education that is truly individualized is the result of individualized and nondiscriminatory assessments. Assessments include evaluations and tests by trained professionals to determine what disabilities a child might have and the most appropriate ways for dealing with the disabilities. This **identification** process qualifies youngsters whose disabilities require special education and related services in order to receive an appropriate education.

6. *Individualized education program (IEP) plans:* The road map for a student's special education is the **individualized educational program (IEP)** plan. The law requires that, for each child or youth with a disability, a written statement be developed in a meeting attended by the following persons: a qualified representative of the local education agency, generally, the child's proposed special education teacher; the child's current teacher; the parents of the child; and the child.

7. *Least restrictive environment (LRE):* IDEA not only provides every child with a disability the right to an appropriate education, but also requires **integration** with students without disabilities. The law requires that these youngsters be included in the **least restrictive environment (LRE)** to the fullest extent possible. This seems to be the case, for over 95 percent of students with disabilities receive at least some portion of their education in **general education** classes (U.S. Department of Education, 1996). For many years, this practice was universally referred to as **mainstreaming.** But what, according to IDEA, does this extension of the normalization principle mean for children? It means that

> to the maximum extent appropriate, children with disabilities, including children in public or private institutions or other care facilities, are educated with children who do not have disabilities, and that special classes, separate schooling, or other removal of children with disabilities from the regular educational environment occurs only when the nature or severity of the disability is such that education in regular classes with the use of supplementary aids and services cannot be achieved satisfactorily.... (20 U.S.C., section 1412 [5][B])

Great controversy exists today over the interpretation of LRE. Almost everyone agrees with the principle that segregation harms *all* students—students without and with disabilities. But not everyone agrees on what the principle of LRE means in the case of a particular child. In 1995, almost all (95 percent) students with disabilities received some of their education in general education settings (U.S. Department of Education, 1996). For some, the criticism is that 100 percent of

 MAKING CONNECTIONS

- The inclusion section, included in every chapter, relates to the interpretation of LRE; review those sections for a better understanding of the issues.
- For more on normalization see the History section of this chapter and sections throughout Chapter 6.

identification. The process of seeking out and designating children with disabilities who require special education and related services.

individualized education program (IEP). A requirement of IDEA that guarantees a specifically tailored program to meet the individualized needs of each student with disabilities.

integration. Being included and having full access to mainstream society.

least restrictive environment (LRE). One of the principles outlined in IDEA that must be balanced when considering the best educational placement for an individual student with disabilities.

general education. A typical classroom and curriculum designed to serve students without disabilities.

mainstreaming. Including students with special needs in general education classrooms for some or all of their school day.

these students did not participate in general education 100 percent of their school day. It does not mean simply the choice of one type of classroom over another, although that choice is tremendously important. At one level, it must mean that the students' environment should give them maximum freedom. However, maximum freedom has to be appropriate to the student's age and educational goals. The courts have recently ruled, and most professio nals tend to agree, that the balance between FAPE and LRE must be individually and carefully determined (Bateman, 1996; LaRue, 1996). For example, in one case the courts decided that LRE was a special education classroom with partial mainstreaming rather than a general education classroom because it was thought that the gains that could be made with a smaller teacher–pupil ratio far outweighed other placement options and because the child's presence in general education settings had proven to be a disruptive force in the past. In another case, the courts even ruled that LRE was only attainable in a comprehensive development class at an elementary school away from the student's neighborhood school. In both cases, the courts ruled against the preferences of the parents. What else does *least restrictive* mean? The Tips for Teachers box should help you better understand the meaning of LRE and serve as a guide to making better decisions about this concept.

8. *Federal assistance to states and school districts:* Even though most students with disabilities are served in general education classrooms, extra funds are needed to provide special education services. This extra cost, referred to as **excess cost**, is to be shared by the individual states and the federal government. In 1975, Congress authorized the federal government to pay up to 40 percent of the average general education expenditure to help support the educational costs of students with disabilities. Although the amount of federal assistance has increased considerably ($2.5 million in 1977 to $2.15 billion in 1994 and from $71 per child to $413 per child in 1994), the federal allocations have never approached 40 percent (NASDSE, 1996). In fact, in most states the federal government is paying less than 10 percent of the special education costs. Although many people believe that special education is becoming increasingly expensive, the average per child expenditure for special students in relation to average per child expenditure for general students is about where it was in 1977, consistently at about twice the cost of students without disabilities (Parrish, 1996). However, it is important to remember that the number of children being served has increased by about 45 percent, so actual costs have risen substantially.

We believe that spending money during the schoolyears is a good investment, one that saves money ultimately because the individuals are more likely to become independent, taxpaying adults. However, in the past several years growing criticism of special education and its costs have been voiced (Whitmire, 1996). One reason for these concerns stems from the fact that budgets for general education have not increased much during recent years, and a growing notion that "if we didn't have to spend this money on these kids, we would have more money to spend for supplies, materials, athletics, art, music, and other activities." Another reason is based in the rising numbers of students identified as having disabilities. For example, while the national average is under 10 percent, in some school districts—Dayton, for example—the special education population has risen from 11 to 14.5 percent in the past five years. Clearly, these issues must be addressed before animosity becomes directed toward specific students with disabilities.

excess cost. Expenses for the education of a child with disabilities that exceed the average expenses of education for a child without disabilities.

Making LRE Decisions

Feature	Application
Maximum freedom	Do not restrict the student's ability to physically and intellectually explore environments.
Similar to age-peers	Ensure that activities are age appropriate.
Not harmful	Some restrictions may be necessary to protect the individual or may be extended until specific skills are mastered.
Similar to peers with similar ability	Activities and freedom should be based on the individual's ability and age; the individual should not be put in a dangerous situation.
Not controlling	Rather than having others control the many aspects of their lives, individuals with disabilities need to develop those skills necessary to control their world.
Not dangerous	Care must be taken to balance the "dignity of risk" principle and safety.
Not intrusive	Although teaching others is an intrusive activity, always respect the privacy and dignity of each student.
Most respectful	Be sensitive, considerate, and respectful of the needs and wishes of students and their families.
Most appropriate	The essence of individualization is to develop students' educational programs, taking into account their unique needs, abilities, learning styles, family circumstances, age, and all other relevant factors.
Most integrated	Full acceptance by peers and others, the ability to be one's self in group situations, and spontaneous inclusion are measures of integration.
Most normalized	Make available to the student with disabilities opportunities for lives similar to those of others in their society.

Fundamental Principles. Special education is framed and has developed with some guiding principles. For example, the principle of normalization is an essential dimension of LRE. It demands that professionals and parents make choices that provide services that are as close to normal as possible. For one child, normalization may mean riding the same bus to school as other children, using ordinary books and materials that have been adapted to his or her disability, receiving all special education services in the general classroom, and having an after-school job delivering newspapers. For a student with severe disabilities, it may mean that designer jeans have Velcro closings to fit over leg braces, that wheelchair wheels are wide enough to enable the student to play on the sandy playground during recess, and that a specially equipped bus does not have reference to special education painted on the side. Normalization also requires allowing the individual the **dignity of risk** (Perske, 1972). Frequently, students with disabilities are overprotected, deprived of the ordinary risks and challenges necessary for human development and essential to growing up. Students with disabilities should be allowed the dignity of risk to succeed or fail like others.

Most special educators cherish a vision of *all* children working and playing together whether at school or in their neighborhoods. Although in some cases this is a challenging goal, the concept of integration is central to special education and the development of appropriate educational programs. Unfortunately, many people with disabilities are still isolated and segregated today, although this practice is disappearing. New principles focusing on inclusion and the community guide the design of services for individuals with disabilities.

Another fundamental principle of special education is that the learning environment is central to considerations about normalization, educational placement, and the creation of an appropriate education program. Special educators tend to focus on the environment as an important variable in the creation of learning programs for children. What does *environment* mean? There is no simple answer. A student's educational environment is multifaceted; it includes the physical environment in which the student works, the human environment or the individuals with whom the student has the opportunity to interact, the affective environment or the feelings and emotional tone surrounding the student, and the geographical environment or the location of the school. Table 1.4 provides some examples of these four aspects of educational environments.

With all these possible interpretations and combinations, you can see why there might be disagreement over what *the* least restrictive environment is for a particular student. Some educators suggest that a general education classroom is the most restrictive educational placement for some students with special needs; others maintain that a special education classroom is always the most restrictive

MAKING CONNECTIONS

For more information about inclusion and educational placements used by students with different disabilities, see each chapter's Inclusion section (Educational Interventions).

dignity of risk. The principle that taking ordinary risks and chances is part of growing up and is essentially human.

TABLE 1.4

Environmental Features

Physical	Human	Affective	Geographical
Student work area	Family members	Feelings and attitudes of students	Community's culture
Books and materials	Friends	Feelings and attitudes of others	Rural or urban setting
Communication devices	Other students without disabilities	Quality of personal interactions	Proximity to family and friends
Braces, glasses, and clothing	Other students with disabilities		Proximity to services
Sights, sounds, and smells	Teachers		Availability of transportation
The classroom	Related services personnel		Availability of work opportunities
The school			
Transportation			

placement. Professionals and parents must weigh all the considerations, constantly balancing students' needs for freedom with their needs to learn certain skills and their needs for opportunities to live lives as normal as possible. The important point to remember is that special education choices must be individualized and based on the particular needs of each individual.

During the 1990s, a great debate about education programs for students with disabilities centered on the interpretation of LRE and the concept of **full inclusion**. Almost every major organization concerned with all or a particular group of students with disabilities responded to the debate. In each chapter in this text, we summarize the position of those groups particularly concerned with the education of students with that specific disability. In 1993, CEC developed a position statement about inclusive schools and communities for all children with disabilities. CEC's position was that educational decisions be based on the individual needs and desired outcomes of each student with a disability and that a full continuum of educational options be available to support this individually determined education.

Reauthorizations and Amendments to PL 94–142

Since the initial passage of PL 94–142 in 1975 (and implementation in 1977), Congress has had to reauthorize the law twice and, during those activities, tried to improve the IDEA through several amendments. The **reauthorization** process is required by law. The first passage, PL 99–457, occurred eleven years after its initial passage in 1975. The next reauthorization occurred about four years later, in 1990. These amendments expanded the age range of children entitled to special education. From 1994 to 1996, the 104th session of Congress attempted to renew the IDEA law, but the Senate and the House were unsuccessful. A new IDEA law did not pass Congress. The reasons for this roadblock are also discussed in this section.

PL 99–457. The first reauthorization of what was originally called the Education for All Handicapped Children's Act (PL 94–142) added infants and toddlers, provided individualized family services plans (IFSPs), and suggested individualized transition plans (ITPs) for adolescents with disabilities.

PL 101–476. The Education of the Handicapped Act (EHA) Amendments of 1990 was signed into law by President George Bush on October 30, 1990. This document made a number of revisions to PL 94–142.

- ■ It changed the title of the special education law to Individuals with Disabilities Education Act (IDEA).
- ■ It changed the language in the law from "handicapped children" to "children with disabilities."
- ■ It specified two additional categories: autism and traumatic brain injury.
- ■ It required transition services no later than age 16.
- ■ It required further public comments on defining "attention deficit disorder" in the law.
- ■ It clarified that states may be sued in federal courts for violating the law.

 MAKING CONNECTIONS

For more on IFSPs and ITPs, see those sections in Chapter 2.

 MAKING CONNECTIONS

- • For specific information about autism and TBI, see Chapter 12.
- • For more about transition programs for youth with disabilities, see the Transition section found in every chapter (Educational Interventions).

full inclusion. The practice of assuring that all students with disabilities participate with other students in all aspects of school.
reauthorization. The act of amending and renewing a law.

PL 105-17: The 1997 Reauthorization of IDEA. The IDEA law was scheduled for reauthorization during the 104th session of Congress (1994 to 1996). Those efforts were unsuccessful in part because for the first time this national law became controversial (West, 1996), but through a remarkable process, IDEA was reauthorized by the 105th Congress in 1997. Three major, contentious issues about special education were difficult to resolve: (1) escalating costs (lawyers' fees and private school placements), (2) discipline, and (3) inclusion (Maroldo, 1995).

To reduce rising costs of special education and to correct the increasingly litigious process involved in due process hearings, Congress strengthened the *mediation* process. Participation of attorneys in educational meetings has been limited. School districts may now share costs of related services and alternative placements with other agencies. Also, parents must work with school districts before making *private school placements* if they expect reimbursement.

IDEA has always protected students with disabilities from expulsion and not allowed *cessation of services* when inappropriate behavior is related to the disability. The **Stay-Put Provision** (Council for Exceptional Children, 1994), however, is often considered a "double standard" (Briand, 1995a): children without disabilities who carry guns to school or who are violent can be suspended or expelled but somechildren with disabilities exhibiting similar behavior are protected. The 1997 version of IDEA encourages districts to seek *alternative placements* and does not allow for cessation of services. Among some educators, a concern remains: ensuring that a positive learning environment for all general education students is retained despite the inclusion of disruptive students (Garnett, 1996).

Lastly, considerable debate focused on LRE and participation in the general education curriculum. While some argued that specialized instruction in separate instructional topics (life skills) constitutes segregation, others argued that FAPE consists of individualized instruction tailored to the specific needs and outcomes expected for each child regardless of placement. IDEA has retained support for a *continuum of services* while encouraging as much participation in general education assessments and curriculum as possible.

Section 504 of the Rehabilitation Act of 1973

Section 504 of the Rehabilitation Act of 1973, passed by Congress prior to IDEA, set the stage for this important special education law. The 504 provision includes some protection of the rights of students with disabilities to a free appropriate public education, but it is neither an education law specifically nor a law that provides federal funding to support its implementation. Section 504 guarantees basic civil rights to people with disabilities in many important aspects of American society and was extended through the Americans with Disabilities Act, passed in 1990.

Over its history, Section 504 has provided many benefits to students with disabilities, despite the fact that it covers all Americans with disabilities. Probably, its greatest benefit to children who do not qualify for IDEA services, but still have very special needs, is its requirement to make accommodations and have a plan for those modifications (Conderman & Katsiyannis, 1995). Section 504 requires classroom teachers and other school staff to detail the adjustments and modifications they make so these students can benefit from their educational programs (Reid & Katsiyannis, 1995). So, who is protected by Section 504 but not by IDEA? Many children with health impairments (AIDS, asthma, other chronic illnesses) need special accommodations such as alternate physical education classes, more breaks during the school day, and special tutors when they are ill and cannot

MAKING CONNECTIONS

For details about FAPE, review these sections:
• The Fundamental Provisions section, found earlier in this chapter
• The Service Delivery section found in Chapter 2

MAKING CONNECTIONS

For more about ADD, see that section in Chapter 4.

Stay-Put Provision. The legal mandate prohibiting students with disabilities from being expelled because of behavior associated with their disabilities.

The excitement of achievement is shared by everyone when there is team spirit.

attend school. Many children with attention deficit disorder (ADD) do not qualify for special education but do require more structure in their school day and even some adjustments in the standard curriculum. Section 504 also guarantees that all aspects of the learning environment (review again Table 1.4) are accessible. Over the years educators have learned time and time again that even the simplest of accommodations can be the difference between school success and failure.

Americans with Disabilities Act (ADA)

On July 26, 1990, President Bush signed the **Americans with Disabilities Act (ADA),** which bars discrimination in employment, transportation, public accommodations, and telecommunications. He said, "Let the shameful walls of exclusion finally come tumbling down." Senator Tom Harkin (D–IA), the chief sponsor of the act, spoke of this law as the "emancipation proclamation" for people with disabilities (West, 1994). ADA guarantees access to all aspects of life—not just those that are federally funded—to people with disabilities and implements the concept of normalization across all of American life.

Both Section 504 of the Rehabilitation Act of 1973 and the Americans with Disabilities Act are considered civil rights and antidiscrimination laws (Roberts & Mather, 1995). ADA supports and extends Section 504, which is almost twenty years older. What does ADA do? The answer is many things, particularly for adults with disabilities in the workplace and in the community. It provides them with greater access to employment and participation in everyday activities that adults without disabilities enjoy. The ADA requires that employers not discriminate against qualified applicants or employees with disabilities; that new buses, trains, and subways be accessible to persons with disabilities; that new or remodeled public accommodations, such as hotels, stores, restaurants, banks, and theaters, be accessible;

Americans with Disabilities Act (ADA). Federal disability antidiscrimination legislation passed in 1990.

Michela Alioto waves to the audience at the 1996 Democratic National Convention in Chicago where she introduced Vice President Al Gore.

and that telephone companies provide relay services so that deaf individuals and people with speech impairments can use ordinary telephones. For students who are making the transition from school to adult life, these improvements in access and non-discrimination will help them achieve genuine participation in their communities.

Many secondary benefits have resulted from the passage of the ADA law. For example, books, like the guidebook to Washington, D.C. for people with disabilities, contain helpful information on accommodations and accessibility of places of interest (American Society of Interior Designers, 1994). The benefits to the tourist industry are great as well. The Census Bureau reports that the 49 million people with disabilities have combined disposable income of $188 billion, and these individuals do travel, spending 3.5 times more nights in hotels a year than most other Americans (Vukelich, 1995). People with disabilities are profiting in other ways from the ADA law. Architects are now using a concept called "universal design" to remodel and build homes that are accessible to everyone (Werne, 1995). Lever handles on doors are easier to handle for those whose arms are laden with shopping bags, those who have arthritis, and those with restricted mobility. Wheelchairs can roll under sinks. Driveways gradually slope to the level of the front door, which eliminates the need for steps and is also aesthetically pleasing. The principles of universal design can have great benefits to almost everyone, not just those with disabilities.

ADA has brought many personal benefits to people with disabilities. DuPont, among many other businesses, has made accommodations in the workplace that allow all of its employees, including the over 3,000 with disabilities, to perform at levels they might not otherwise be able (DuPont, 1993). Despite her worsening condition, Meg Masterson is able to continue her work with the voice-activated computer. Tom Tufano, a director of laboratory research in photographic science, is able to continue his important work because of the closed circuit TV equipment that magnifies printed material he could not otherwise see. Such stories are repeated over and over again across America. People with disabilities are also making their mark on American politics. A new contender, Michela Alioto, showed the strength, fortitude, and commitment to run a strong race (Klein, 1996). Although this young woman, who uses a wheelchair, was unsuccessful in her bid to unseat the incumbent in her northern California district, she certainly gave him a tough race. Unfortunately these stories do not yet represent all people with disabilities.

Section 504 and ADA do affect the education system, but there are some important differences between them and IDEA that you should understand. Section 504 and ADA have a broader definition of disabilities than does IDEA, for they guarantee the right to accommodations even for those who do not need special education services. For example, it is under the authority of ADA that students are entitled to special testing situations (untimed tests, a person reading the test to the person, a special Braille version), even for those who do not qualify for IDEA services.

The ADA law holds many promises for people with disabilities, and it has made a real difference in many people's lives. With the average cost of an accommodation being $36, the burden to the employer creates an incredible relief for the individuals involved (Levoy, 1995). The ADA law, however, has not fulfilled many promises and hopes. The unemployment rate for individuals with disabilities is still at an unacceptable 66 percent (Levoy, 1995). Even those with outstanding skills, like data processor Samar Saalo, who is deaf, have had to wait over five years for a job.

ADA does not come without controversy, however. On the first level, many individuals with disabilities do not believe that the law is being implemented or enforced. Although there is no research about the implementation or impact of ADA (West, 1994), the number of complaints (about 50,000 between 1992 and

1995) is an indication that many people with disabilities do not believe that the law or its intent is being followed. One of those people is Burns Taylor, who has won a Texas lawsuit that will allow him to vote in secret through either Braille or tape recorded ballots (Montes, 1995). On the second level are the many small business-people who claim that ADA requires them to make expensive accommodations to their businesses that are never used. Take the case of Blair Taylor, owner of the Barolo Grill in Denver, who bore the expenses for building a ramp (which took ten months to obtain the necessary variances from the city) and sacrificed four of his twenty-eight dining tables (all twenty-four are now accessible). The ramp has never been used, and Taylor is certain that seventeen wheelchairs will never be in his business at the same time (Mills, 1995). Despite the controversy, and in some cases even hard feelings, the overwhelming opinion of most Americans is that the ADA law guarantees people with disabilities the rights to which they are entitled: participation in and access to the mainstream of American society. In particular, people with disabilities overwhelmingly support continuation of the ADA law despite their continued frustration with specifics about its implementation (Pfeiffer, 1996).

MAKING CONNECTIONS

For more on the ADA law and the reauthorizations of IDEA, see the Legislation section later in this chapter.

Litigation to Interpret and Define IDEA

Since 1975, when PL 94–142 became law, a very small percentage of all children served have been involved in formal disputes. Those disputes concern the identification of children with disabilities, evaluations, educational placements, and the provision of a free appropriate public education. Many of these disputes are resolved in noncourt proceedings (due process hearings).

Some disputes, however, must be settled in courts of law—a few even in the U.S. Supreme Court. From this **litigation**, many different questions about special education have been addressed and clarified. A few of the more important cases that the Supreme Court has decided are listed in Table 1.5.

Prevalence of Children with Special Needs

MAKING CONNECTIONS

For specific prevalence figures for each exceptionality, see the Prevalence sections in Chapters 3 through 12.

How many students in this country need special education services? Professionals use two methods to describe the number of children with disabilities. **Prevalence** refers to the *total* number of cases at a given time. A slightly different calculation is made by **incidence**, which is the number of *new* cases that occur within a certain time period.

What is the prevalence of students requiring special education in the United States? The *Eighteenth Annual Report to Congress on the Implementation of the Individuals with Disabilities Act* indicates that in the 1994–1995 schoolyear, 4,665,279 children and youth from ages 6 through 17 were served in special education programs under the IDEA (U.S. Department of Education, 1996). This total represents 10.43 percent of all children and youth in this age group. Because many students are not identified as having a disability until they are of school age, the percentage of children and youth receiving special education services is highest between ages 6 and 17. Remember also that in this group most of these students have mild disabilities; thus, their special education needs are often mild. Only 4.37 percent of children between the ages of 3 and 5 are identified as having disabilities, but their needs are often more severe, and their special education needs are likely to be more intense and long-standing.

litigation. A lawsuit or legal proceeding.
prevalence. The total number of cases at a given time.
incidence. The number of new cases that occur within a certain time period.

TABLE 1.5

U.S. Supreme Court Cases Interpreting IDEA

Case	Date	Issue	Finding
Rowley v. Hendrick Hudson School District	1984	Free appropriate public education (FAPE)	School districts must provide those services that permit a student with disabilities to benefit from instruction.
Irving Independence School District v. Tatro	1984	Defining *related services*	Clean intermittent catheterization (CIC) is a related service when necessary to allow a student to stay in school.
Smith v. Robinson	1984	Attorneys' fees	IDEA does not provide for attorneys' fees for special education litigation. Congress objected to this interpretation and passed a law authorizing fees to parents who win the case.
Burlington School Committee v. Department of Education	1984	Private school placement	In some cases, public schools may be required to pay for private school placements when an appropriate education is not provided by the district.
Honig v. Doe	1988	Exclusion from school	Students whose misbehavior is related to their disability cannot be denied education.
Timothy W. v. Rochester New Hampshire School District	1989	FAPE	Regardless of the existence or severity of a student's disability, a public education is the right of every child.
Zobrest v. Catalina Foothills School District	1993	Paid interpreter at parochial high school	Paying a sign language interpreter does not violate the constitutional separation of church and state.
Florence County School District 4 v. Carter	1993	Reimbursement for private school	A court may order reimbursement for parents who unilaterally withdraw their children from a public school that provides inappropriate education and place their child in a private school that is proper under IDEA but does not meet all requirements.
Doe v. Withers	1993	FAPE	Teachers are responsible for the implementation of accommodations specified in individual students' IEPs.

Educators and policymakers are concerned about the rising prevalence rate of students with disabilities (Briand, 1995b). A record increase of 4.2 percent was noted between the 1992–1993 and 1993–1994 schoolyears, and another 3.2 percent increase occurred between 1994–1995 (U.S. Department of Education, 1996). Although general education enrollment has increased as well, it has been surpassed by the increase in special education enrollment.

Outcomes and Results of People with Disabilities

Another way to help evaluate services for people with disabilities is to consider **outcomes,** the results of decisions. Thinking about outcomes forces us to focus on the future effects of decisions made today and on what is ultimately important to the individual with the disability (Accreditation Council, 1993). O'Brien and Lyle-O'Brien (1992) suggest a framework of five essential accomplishments useful for determining desirable environments:

MAKING CONNECTIONS

For more about outcomes of people with disabilities, see the Transition sections in every chapter in this text.

1. *Community presence,* the sharing of the ordinary places that define community lives.

2. *Choice, the experience of autonomy,* decision making, and control.

3. *Competence,* the opportunity to learn and perform functional and meaningful activities and to have the opportunity to express one's gifts and capacities.

4. *Respect,* the reality of having a valued place in one's community.

5. *Community participation,* being part of a network of personal relationships.

These values are also important for analyzing special education, supports, and related services. Also, for many, these goals include integrated employment, community living, citizenship, and personal autonomy and life satisfaction. Figure 1.4 illustrates one way of thinking about outcomes for students with disabilities.

FIGURE 1.4

Reaching Adult Outcomes

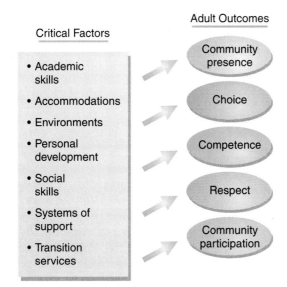

outcomes. The results of decisions and actions.

Others have conceptualized "outcomes" or "results" for people with disabilities somewhat differently. For example, the National Center on Educational Outcomes identified six outcome domains: physical health, responsibility and independence, contribution and citizenship, academic and functional literacy, personal and social adjustment, and satisfaction (U.S. Department of Education, 1995b). Yet, another way to consider the outcomes of people with disabilities is to think about those components that comprise quality of life indicators. This is a complicated assessment task, for research has just begun to determine the dimensions of quality of life. One set of researchers (Hughes, Hwang, Kim, Eisenman, & Killian, 1995) has identified and rank ordered fifteen such dimensions: "psychological well-being and personal satisfaction; social relationships and interaction; employment; physical and material well-being; self-determination, autonomy, and personal choice; personal competence, community adjustment, and independent living skills; community integration; social acceptance, social status, and ecological fit; personal development and fulfillment; residential environment; recreation and leisure; normalization; individual and social demographic indicators; civic responsibility; and support services received" (p. 625). They are seeking to identify "fundamental dimensions (outcomes) of a model that does not vary for individuals with or without disabilities" (p. 633), although they acknowledge that the way of achieving these outcomes will vary by individual.

Since the passage of IDEA in 1975, individuals with disabilities have made great gains (Hehir, 1996). Although more progress can be achieved, on every outcome indicator substantial improvement has been seen. As you have just learned, different outcome indicators can be monitored to evaluate progress. The National Longitudinal Transition Studies (conducted by the Stanford Research Institute) uses these three important indicators: employment, postsecondary education, and residential independence (Blackorby & Wagner, 1996). At the present time, individuals with disabilities do not fare as well as their peers without disabilities on any of these measures. However, people with disabilities can achieve excellent outcomes if they have access to a rich diversity of life and school experiences. These experiences might include not only academic instruction but also social skills training, career education, extracurricular activities, self-advocacy training, leisure and recreation assistance, and family living skills. Outside school, these experiences include club activities, church activities, citizenship involvement such as voting, employment, and any opportunities to practice personal autonomy.

Concepts and Controversy: Should the Stay-Put Provision Be a Right of Children with Disabilities?

MAKING CONNECTIONS

A Concepts and Controversy section is found in each chapter of this text.

IDEA, the original law and its amendments through 1991, clearly specified that children with disabilities cannot be expelled from school because of their disabilities or behaviors relating to them. This component of the law was put into place in 1975 to ensure that children would no longer be denied a free appropriate education for any reason relating to their disability. However, in the 1990s this part of the law came under great criticism, particularly for students with behavior disorders and emotional disturbance who are also violent at school. Under those versions of IDEA, if a parent objected, a student would have to stay in his or her current placement until the dispute was resolved. Specifically, Congress was concerned about such students who brought guns to school and yet could not be expelled as could their nondisabled, violent peers (Briand, 1995a; Garnett, 1996).

The U.S. Department of Education (1995a) proposed the following procedures to ensure safe and disciplined classrooms: Allow for a child to be removed from the classroom and be placed in an alternative setting for up to forty-five calendar days when a child brings a gun or other dangerous weapon to school. Also, the department proposed that regardless of the parents' objections, the school district could request an immediate due process hearing and the child may be removed from the classroom, possibly be assigned to an alternative placement, for forty-five days pending final decision about whether the child is dangerous.

1. Should students with disabilities be afforded the rights to an education that exceed the rights of children without disabilities?

2. What solutions to this dilemma might you offer to Congress and to educators who work directly with disruptive and violent schoolchildren?

~~~ SUMMARY ~~~

After many years of neglect and exclusion, children and youth with disabilities today have the right to receive a free appropriate public school education.

Thus many children receive special education services for at least part of their school career.

FOCUS QUESTIONS

Self-Test Questions

▶ *How is special education defined, and what are its categories of special needs?*

Special education is, first and foremost, individualized education. It is designed to address the unique needs of children with disabilities and to help them achieve their maximum potential. The primary vehicle for designing the program is the individualized education program. All children with disabilities also have rights to appropriate identification and educational services, necessary related services, and least restrictive environments. Parents have notification and procedural rights on behalf of their children. The special education categories are learning disabilities, speech or language impairments, mental retardation, behavior disorders and emotional disturbance, physical impairments and special health care needs, low vision and blindness, hard of hearing and deafness, autism, deaf-blindness, traumatic brain injury. Special education also includes multicultural and bilingual special education for culturally and

linguistically diverse students with disabilities and, in many states, gifted education. Neither multicultural nor bilingual special education nor gifted education programs are mandated or protected by federal law.

▶ *What are the roots of the special education movement in America?*

The history of special education is relatively short. Special education roots in the United States trace back to France, where less than two hundred years ago, Itard worked with Victor, the wild boy of Aveyron. Special education history has included periods of optimism, periods of neglect, periods of fear, and, finally, acceptance of exceptionalities in children. We must learn from history and not let the cruelties of the past (some not so long ago) be repeated. Also from France, Edouard Seguin brought special education to this country. Seguin founded a professional organization to advocate for services and communicate new treatments for mental retardation, and in 1846 he published the first book on special education in this country. A period of hope, positive care and treatment, and education flourished during the late 1800s and early 1900s, but it was later clouded by a period of fear and inhumane treatment of people with disabilities.

▶ *What are the eight major provisions Congress addressed when it first passed PL 94–142, the Individuals with Disabilities Act in 1975?*

The federal law guaranteeing special education and related services to all children with disabilities, the Individuals with Disabilities Education Act (IDEA) (originally called the Education for All Handicapped Children Act, EHA) was passed in 1995. Although the law has been amended and reauthorized, the basic eight provisions remain: free appropriate public education (FAPE), parental notification and procedural rights, individualized services to all students identified as having disabilities, necessary related services, individualized assessments, individualized education program plans, education provided in the least restrictive environment (LRE) possible, and federal assistance to states and school districts.

▶ *How might the principle of least restrictive environment be described?*

The principles of least restrictive environment, normalization, mainstreaming, and inclusion mean more than mere physical classroom placement. They describe a philosophical commitment to ensure that children with disabilities have opportunities for living normal lives and are integrated into the flow and pattern of our society. Schools must ensure an array of services so that the individual needs of children can be accommodated. A variety of professional opportunities are available for special educators to help educate and provide related services to all children with disabilities, and the balance between LRE and FAPE must be individually determined for each child with exceptionalities.

▶ *What are the major roles that legislation and litigation play in special education?*

Congress passes laws, such as IDEA and ADA, to protect the rights and provide greater access to American society to people with disabilities. The courts uphold the rights of children and their families to free appropriate public education for all children with disabilities. The process of legislation causes the courts to further refine and interpret what Congress meant when it drafted and passed laws through the legislative process. Other legal issues (such as payment of legal fees, payment for unauthorized educational placements, exclusion of students with behavioral disorders and emotional disturbance) have also been addressed by the courts, clarifying and defining the federal law.

Challenge Question

▶ *How do different societies and cultures influence the concepts of "disability" and "handicapped"?*

Culture influences the way groups and individuals are perceived. In some cultures, the individual is never compared to some norm or expected standard. In other cultures, the range of tolerance to differences from conceptions of "typical behavior" includes a great range of behaviors. In the United States, the tolerance for deviance is usually not great and comparisons against perceived standards are frequent. For these reasons, judgments about people and their behavioral patterns often vary from cultural group to cultural group, in some cases, ascribing the assessment of "disability" to individuals who would not universally be considered as having a disability.

~~~ **SUPPLEMENTARY RESOURCES** ~~~

Scholarly Books

Osborne, Jr., A. G. (1996). Legal issues in special education. Boston: Allyn and Bacon.

Rosenberg, M. S., & Edmond-Rosenberg, I. (1994). The special education sourcebook: A teacher's guide to programs, materials, and information sources. Rockville, MD: Woodbine House.

Safford, P. L., & Safford, E. J. (1996). A history of childhood and disability. New York: Teachers College Press.

Treanor, R. B. (1993). We overcame: The story of civil rights for disabled people. Falls Church, VA: Regal Direct Publishing.

Gallagher, H. G. (1994). FDR's splendid deception (Rev. Ed.) Arlington, VA: Vandamere Press.

Parent, Professional, and Consumer Organizations and Agencies

Council for Exceptional Children (CEC)
1920 Association Drive
Reston, VA 22091
Phone: (703) 620-3660
Web site: http://www.cec.spec.org

ERIC
Clearinghouse on Disabilities and Gifted Education (CEC)
1920 Association Drive
Reston, VA 22091
Phone: (703) 264-9476
TTY: (703) 724-9480
Web site: http://www.cec.sped.org/ericec.htm

NICHCY
National Information Center for Children and Youth with Disabilities
PO Box 1492
Washington, D.C. 20013
Voice/TTY: (800) 695-0285
Voice/TTY: (202) 884-8200
E-mail: nichy@aed.org

Office of Special Education Programs
U.S. Office of Special Education and Rehabilitative Services
U.S. Department of Education
Washington, D.C. 20202-2641
Phone: (202) 205-9675
Web site: www.ed.gov/offices/osers

National Clearinghouse for Professions in Special Education (CEC)
1920 Association Drive
Reston, VA 22091-1589
Phone: (703) 274-9476
E-mail: ncpse@cec.sped.org

President's Committee on Employment of People with Disabilities
1331 F. St. N. W.
Washington, D.C. 2000
Phone: (202) 376-6200
Web site: http://www.pcepd.gov

Edouard Manet. *The Piper*. 1866.

Edouard Manet was born in Paris in 1832. His father had ambitions for him to carry on the family tradition and become a lawyer, but despite outraged protests about becoming an artist, Manet became one of the most famous Impressionist painters of his day. It is quite possible he turned to art because of his difficulties in school. One headmaster considered him to be "feeble"; another referred to him as "distracted," not "very studious," and "mediocre" (Schneider, 1968, p. 15). Had Manet's father not been a highly respected community leader and a friend of one school's director, he would have been dismissed. At age 16, after taking an art course at school, Manet announced that he wanted to become an artist. His father, exceptionally displeased, channeled his son to become a naval officer. Fortunately for the art world, Manet failed the naval examination (Bolton, 1989). In the 1800s the special education category of learning disabilities had not yet been identified. So, whether Manet actually had a learning disability is unknown. What does seem clear from the accounts, however, is that academic learning was a considerable challenge.

IFSP, IEP, ITP: Planning and Delivering Services

2

ADVANCE ORGANIZERS

OVERVIEW

IDEA mandates that students with disabilities receive a free appropriate education in the least restrictive environment possible. Designing an appropriate education requires the combined efforts of educators, related service providers, and the child's family. Three individualized education program plans, required by IDEA—the Individualized Family Service Plan (IFSP), the Individualized Education Program (IEP), the Individualized Transition Plan (ITP)—are the blueprints for the special education every student with disabilities receives.

FOCUS QUESTIONS

SELF-TEST QUESTIONS

▶ What are the seven steps to developing an individualized program for each student with disabilities?

▶ What roles do special services committees fill?

▶ What factors must be considered when determining the least restrictive environment for individual students?

▶ What are the different educational placement options that comprise the continuum of services for special education?

▶ How would you compare and contrast the three different program plans: Individualized Family Service Plan, Individualized Education Program, Individualized Transition Plan?

CHALLENGE QUESTION

▶ How should the array of educational services and supports available to students with disabilities be implemented?

A *Personal Perspective*: Multidisciplinary Team Members Share Their Thoughts About the IEP Process

We asked professionals who have served on many special services committees a set of questions that reveal their perspectives on the individualized planning process required by IDEA for every student receiving special education.

Chris Arbus	Physical therapist
Dora Garcia	Teacher of students with severe disabilities
Carol Hearon	Adaptive physical education teacher
Maggie Brest	Regular education teacher
Peter Sops	Special education teacher
Jill Wallitsch	Special education teacher
Zina McLean	Speech/language pathologist
Myla Pitts	Occupational therapist
Lea Getts	Resource room teacher

From your perspective, what are the benefits of the IEP process?

PETER SOPS: The IEP aids the teacher in setting realistic and achievable goals for special education students and provides a plan for reaching these goals.

JILL WALLITSCH: Parents have an opportunity to participate in their child's educational program.

ZINA McLEAN: One great benefit is the team approach where one team member may observe a behavior no one else on the team has observed.

From your perspective, what are the disadvantages of the IEP process?

MAGGIE BREST: Finding out that the services a child should have are not available.

MYLA PITTS: Sometimes, these meetings seem to be merely a process of getting the blanks filled in. Sometimes not enough care is taken to draw parents out or they are simply ignored. Sometimes, even simple courtesies are not extended to them.

LEA GETTS: Often, there is no follow-through or checkup.

How do people representing so many different perspectives work together at these meetings?

CAROL HEARON: We all have one common goal, the *child*. With that in mind, we can help each other since areas of instruction overlap.

ZINA McLEAN: By respecting each others' different approaches, we learn from each other and integrate our joint disciplines.

LEA GETTS: One person needs to assume leadership.

Is the IEP meeting typically the first time you have met the child's parents? If so, how does this affect your interaction with them?

CHRIS ARBUS: Yes, and I want to listen to them more and be sure they understand me.

JILL WALLITSCH: No, usually I have done some home visits before this meeting.

ZINA McLEAN: Ideally not. I find it helpful to be in contact with parents before the meeting through home visits. I regard parents as members of the IEP team, and this affects the way I interact with them.

If you ever changed your mind about the needs of a child after participating in an IEP meeting, what caused you to change?

DORA GARCIA: I remember one time in particular. After working with a little girl, I realized that she was able to do a lot more than we expected or anticipated based on the information we had at the time of the IEP meeting.

CHRIS ARBUS: It has been not so much a change of mind, as an occasional feeling of "unease" that I have not done my homework sufficiently before the IEP meeting and haven't presented goals or ways to meet them clearly. Generally, all team members are familiar enough with common goals that there are no "surprises" from my colleagues.

1. Why might people coming from different professions have different perspectives?

2. What are some of the common beliefs shared by members of individualized education teams?

*I*n this chapter, you will learn about the various educational placements and services available to students with disabilities. You will also learn about the wide range of professionals from a variety of disciplines who offer highly specialized expertise to students with disabilities. Individualized educational programs set goals and objectives for youngsters with disabilities and bring professionals together to offer an appropriate education. To help you understand the process of planning an individualized educational program, we discuss and interpret three major plans: one designed for infants, one designed for students, and one that aids in the transition to adulthood. You will learn about the planning process that leads to the development of the individualized program plan. Let's begin with a discussion of what services special education provides.

Special Education Services

As discussed in Chapter 1, the law that provides the framework for special education is the Individuals with Disabilities Education Act (IDEA). Originally passed as Public Law (PL) 94-142 in 1975, IDEA is reauthorized and amended periodically. It is a civil rights law, guaranteeing a free appropriate public education (FAPE) for all youngsters with disabilities from birth through age 21. This law mandates that states provide infants and toddlers with disabilities, and their families, educational services. It also requires an individualized education in the least restrictive environment (LRE) possible for all schoolchildren with disabilities, and it assists high school students with disabilities to make the transition from school to adult life.

MAKING CONNECTIONS

To review the special education law, IDEA see
- all of Chapter 1,
- and, in particular, see the Legislative section in Chapter 1.

Education Environments

Special education should *always* be based on the individual needs of the student and his or her family. This individualized instruction is delivered in a wide range of settings, from **itinerant teachers**, who travel from school to school, to **center schools**, separate schools that only students with disabilities attend. Although the law requires placement in the least restrictive environment, where the educational services are delivered and who delivers those services do not always indicate whether an environment is least restrictive or appropriate. This delineation of educational environments, however, does serve as quick and easy measures when research data are collected or program offerings are evaluated. Educational placements (also called **service delivery options**), used as the location of special education, can be described in different ways. Table 2.1 lists and explains the terms schools commonly use to denote service delivery options and matches those terms with the educational categories used by the federal government. It appears that a new service delivery option is developing that is not yet part of the government's educational placement list. This new model, called by some as **pull-in programming**, provides to children with disabilities all of their education in the general education classroom (Welch, Richards, Okada, Richards, & Prescott, 1995). This means that special education and related service therapies (e.g., speech, physical therapy) are brought to the child.

Look at the data presented on Figure 2.1. It shows the percentage of students with disabilities who receive their education in each of the government's official

itinerant teachers. Teachers who teach students or consult with others in more than one setting.

center schools. Separate schools (some residential), typically dedicated to serving students with a particular disability.

service delivery options. Different special education services and placements, sometimes described as a continuum and other times as an array.

pull-in programming. Rather than having students with disabilities leave the general education classes for special education or for related services, delivering those services to them in the general education classroom.

TABLE 2.1

Service Delivery Options

Type	Description	Government Category	Government Criterion
Itinerant or consultative	Student remains in the general class. The teacher and/or student receives assistance from a specialist.	Regular (general education) class	Students receive special education and related services outside the general education class for less than 21 percent of the school day.
Resource room	Student attends a regular class most of the day but goes to a special education class several hours per day or for blocks of time each week.	Resource room	Includes students who receive special education and related services for at least 21 percent and not more than 60 percent of their school day.
Special education class (partially self-contained)	Student attends a special class but is integrated in general education classes for a considerable amount of time each day.	Separate class	Students receive special education, outside of the general education classroom, for more than 60 percent of their day.
Special education class (self-contained)	Student attends a special class most of the school day and is included in general education activities minimally.	Separate class	Students receive special education, outside of the general education classroom, for more than 60 percent of their day.
Special education schools (center schools)	Center schools—some private, others supported by the state—serve only students with a specific category of disability. Some offer residential services; others do not.	Public separate school facility; private separate school facility; public residential facility; private residential facility.	Includes students who receive their education for more than 50 percent of the day in (a) a separate day school, (b) a public or private residential facility at public expense, (c) a hospital setting, or (d) at home.

MAKING CONNECTIONS

See the Prevalence sections included in each chapter for more information about geographical differences in identification rates.

educational categories. These data are clear: Most students with disabilities receive their education primarily in general education settings, with some support. If you consider that students who attend resource rooms and even special education classes also receive a good portion of their education in the general education setting as well, you will realize that relatively few students with disabilities today are totally segregated from the peers without disabilities. In fact, as a group, students with disabilities spend 70 percent of their time in general education settings, ranging from 87 percent for students with visual impairments and 32 percent for those with multiple disabilities (U.S. Department of Education, 1996). And, approximately 95 percent of students with disabilities receive their education and related services in typical school buildings. However, placement rates are not consistent from state to state. One might assume that, because each state has about the same proportion of youngsters with disabilities, and because students with disabilities have similar needs for education no matter where they live, we would see in each state roughly the same percentages of students in each type of

FIGURE 2.1

American Special Education Placement Rates

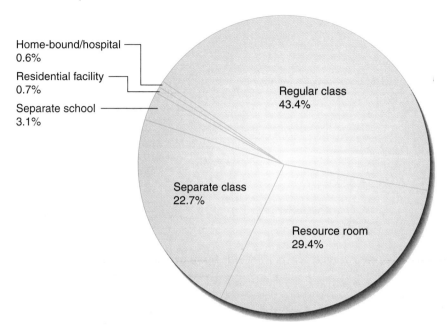

Source: From *Eighteenth Annual Report to Congress on the Implementation of the Individuals with Disabilities Education Act* (p. 71) by the U.S. Department of Education, 1996, Washington, DC: U.S. Government Printing Office.

educational environment. However, the types of placements states use for teaching children with disabilities vary tremendously. For example, New York's rate of segregated day and residential placements is more than four times Oregon's rate. Clearly, it is not only students' characteristics that determine their LRE. What do you think are some of the reasons for the differences between states?

Special education services should be flexible and responsive to the needs of each student. Children and youth with special needs should have access to a variety of services, according to the support needed to achieve their potential. This support will vary by type, intensity, location, personnel, and duration of special education. The types and combinations of placement and curricular options in many school districts are great. For example, one research project working in the Seattle area identified a wide variety of different educational situations available to secondary-level students with disabilities (Lovitt, 1995). These options ranged from general education classes, to resource rooms, self-contained classes, vocational classes, community placements, alternative high schools, and a separate special school.

An *array,* or wide selection, of services should be readily available. The term **array of services** means that students do not have to travel step by step up and down a ladder of services but have available many selections. For example, in some cases, the general education classroom can meet the needs of the student with some support from a consulting teacher or specialist (for instance, a

 MAKING CONNECTIONS

As you study this book, the answer to this question will become clearer; see the Prevalence sections included in each chapter.

array of services. A constellation of services, personnel, and educational placements.

General and special education teachers work side by side in the pull-in service delivery model.

speech/language pathologist). Other cases require more intensive services from many different specialists. As long as an array of services is available, students should not be forced to prove themselves at every step of the ladder before finally entering a general classroom program. The critical point is that the system must respond to the needs of these students rather than forcing them into a rigid or unidimensional system.

Although we believe that visualizing the range of educational services as an array is preferable, the word *continuum* is often used to describe the educational placements (or service delivery options) available. A **continuum of services** implies a full range of services reflecting the most to the least restrictive. For example, a continuum of living arrangements for people with disabilities would probably include a large congregate institution, smaller congregate facilities, foster care, structured group homes, independent group homes, apartments with roommates, and independent apartments and homes. The continuum model is often referred to as a **cascade of services** (Deno, 1970). This model is criticized because it is lockstepped, although it can also be very useful when describing the range of options that should be available to all students with disabilities. The main criticism of the cascade approach is that students often find it difficult, almost impossible, to move to each successively more integrated placement. As a result, many students who were placed in a self-contained classroom for special education remained in that type of placement throughout their school careers, even though their educational needs changed and an appropriate educational experience for them would have been a resource room or a general education class.

Another risk in the cascade model is that professionals may assume that a classroom placement necessarily corresponds to a determination of the severity of the student's disability. They might assume, for instance, that youngsters with

continuum of services. A graduated range of educational services, each level of service leading directly to the next one.

cascade of services. A linear and sequential model used to describe educational environments from the most to the least restrictive.

the most severe disabilities belong automatically in a full-time, self-contained classroom. But that assumption is often erroneous. It may be that one student with a severe disability is most appropriately served in the general education classroom and another with a moderate disability requires temporary placement in a full-day special education classroom. For example, one child with a severe physical disability may require accommodations to the physical organization of a classroom environment but no modification to the instructional program. Another child with a learning disability may not be able to profit from the type of initial reading instruction offered in the general education classroom and until his basic reading skills are mastered would be better served in an intensive special education program.

One way to evaluate the effectiveness of the types of educational services provided under the continuum of special education services is to ask the consumers about their satisfaction with the programs offered. Lovitt (1995) found that most youth with moderate disabilities who have experienced both general and special education situations prefer special education, while students with mild disabilities tend to prefer general education settings. The first group believes that they receive more help and that the classes are easier, and the second group thinks that classes in general education are more challenging and that they learn more. About 75 percent of the parents were pleased with special education programs. Another study supports Lovitt's findings (Padeliadu & Zigmond, 1996). In this study, special education students were asked how they felt about their educational experiences. Of these elementary students, 90 percent said that they received extra help in their special education classes and about 60 percent felt that they did not miss anything important while away from their general education classes. These students were also asked if they liked going to special education, and 76 percent answered yes, 9 percent answered no, and 14 percent said that it was just "okay." If consumer satisfaction is a consideration, we believe that these findings support the retention of an array or continuum of options for students with disabilities in order to best meet their individual needs and abilities.

A Model for LRE Considerations

We believe a fluid approach is necessary when professionals determine services, supports, and placements for students with disabilities. A key factor in this process is the analysis of the outcomes or goals for each student. For example, careful consideration of the goals of integrated employment, community living, citizenship and involvement, and personal autonomy and life satisfaction should all factor into the decisions about the topics of instruction each individual should receive. Figure 2.2 diagrams some of the factors that must be considered when identifying what services an individual requires and where they should be delivered. This diagram shows the student with disabilities at the center of factors related to both an appropriate education and the least restrictive environment (factors such as the intensity of the required services, the professionals who have the expertise to deliver the services, the estimated length of time the services will be needed, where services are available). Keep in mind that the arrangement of any specialized service impacts the student's entire educational program. For this reason, all the factors shown in Figure 2.2 must be considered when professionals balance an appropriate education with the concept of least restrictive environment.

 MAKING CONNECTIONS

See Chapter 1 for a full discussion of the desired outcomes for all individuals with disabilities.

FIGURE 2.2

Considerations for Individualized Determination of LRE

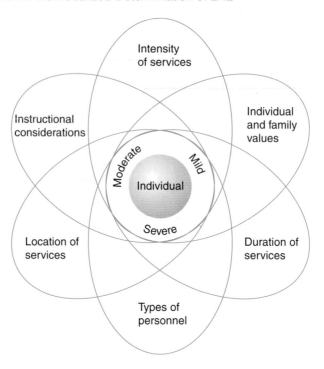

Let us take Becky's case as an example. Eight-year-old Becky is blind, lives on a ranch in a sparsely populated rural community, and has been attending a general education class at an elementary school in the town nearest to her home. No teachers with special training in visual impairment live within 250 miles. Becky needs to learn how to use some special equipment and technology that will assist her with reading and writing, and she needs to begin specialized mobility training. After considerable consultation among Becky's state residential school for students with visual impairments, her teacher, principal, and family members, her parents and the professionals decided that Becky would attend the residential school for at least one month. There, the teachers at the school for students with visual impairments will continue with the curriculum used at Becky's home school. She will be trained to use a computerized print enlarger and a microcomputer for word processing. In addition, a mobility specialist will initiate an orientation and mobility program. Also, the experts from the center school agreed that Becky's third grade teacher, Mrs. Marcus, would visit the center school twice, spending several days on each visit. Mrs. Marcus will be certain that Becky is making progress on her class assignments, but more importantly, Mrs. Marcus will be learning how to use the special equipment so that she can help if Becky has difficulties when she returns home. Mrs. Marcus will also learn how to reinforce and continue the mobility program. Throughout her school years, Becky, her family, and her general education teachers will make many visits to her state's center school for students with visual impairments. As this example indicates, flexible services that are

MAKING CONNECTIONS
• For information about orientation and mobility, see that section in Chapter 11.

Guidelines for Implementing Multidisciplinary Teams

1. *Create working relationships with the student's entire support team.* Partnerships must be developed between the school and the family, between the school and the medical providers, and among school personnel to coordinate services and share information.

2. *Develop systems for collaboration and communication at the beginning of every schoolyear* (or as the child is being identified for special education services). At a meeting with all parties present, be sure to create understandings for as many "what-if" situations as possible, conduct a needs assessment (if necessary), develop an evaluation plan, create formal and informal channels for communication, and set dates for contacts and meetings.

3. *Establish a school-based team that will coordinate services.* Particularly for students who receive services from related services personnel who are not from the school district, key contact persons must be identified to coordinate services, approaches, and information.

4. *Achieve mutual understandings of long-term goals for the child.* Specific goals for transition, adult independence, and employment—held by each stakeholder—should be shared among and understood by all members of the child's support team.

5. *Implement ongoing evaluation procedures.* The student's progress must be monitored directly, consistently, and frequently, and the results must be shared with all members of the child's support team.

6. *Adjust the student's program as needed.* The student's performance should determine any needed modifications in the educational program and must reflect any changes in the psychological, educational, and behavioral needs of the child.

individually applied can be the best answer for a student. It also shows the importance of professionals working together so the educational needs of individual students with special needs can be fully met.

Special Education and Related Service Professionals

Many types of professionals are needed to provide the multidisciplinary services required by individuals with disabilities. A special educator might be a paraprofessional (teacher's aide), a resource teacher, a consultant, an itinerant teacher, a special education classroom teacher, a job coach, an **assistive technology** specialist, a **home or hospital teacher**, a diagnostician, or an administrator. Furthermore, a teacher may assume several of these professional roles during his or her career. In addition, a special education professional might work in a related service as a school psychologist, a speech/language pathologist, an audiologist, an occupational therapist, a physical therapist, a counselor, a nurse or physician, a transportation specialist, a recreational therapist, a supported living worker, a personal care attendant, a vocational rehabilitation worker, or a lawyer.

assistive technology. Devices that help students with disabilities in their daily lives; they include hearing aids, wheelchairs, computers that offer augmentative communication, and a wide array of equipment that helps compensate for an individual's disabilities.

home or hospital teacher. A special teacher who teaches in the child's home or hospital when the child must be absent from school due to health problems.

MAKING CONNECTIONS

To review all of the professionals who comprise special education and related services, see Special Education (defined) in Chapter 1.

Special education teachers and others who work with individuals with disabilities must be able to collaborate—work cooperatively—with professionals from a variety of disciplines. They work together in multidisciplinary teams comprised of those professionals each individual student needs. The Tips for Teachers box (p. 49) should help you understand how these teams are established and how they work together. One method they use is collaboration. It is through this method and working together as a team that is ultimately the key to successful integration for individual students, given that students with disabilities require various combinations of services over their school careers.

Special education teachers collaborate in many areas that touch a child's life. They use collaboration skills when working with parents and families, performing multidisciplinary assessments, working with a team to develop individualized program plans, coordinating the components of students' individualized plans, and helping them make the transitions through the school years and from school to work.

Individualized Special Education Programs

To safeguard the principles contained in the concept of a free appropriate public education, IDEA requires that an individual program plan be developed and implemented for every child identified as having a disability and in need of special education. Individualized plans are required by other laws as well. For example, federal regulations, such as those for Medicaid and Social Security, require that individualized plans also be developed and implemented for individuals residing in institutions or community-based living arrangements, such as group homes. For example, individual written rehabilitation plans (IWRPs) provide vocational rehabilitation. People living in intermediate care facilities for the mentally retarded (ICF/MR) and persons with related conditions must have individualized habilitation plans (IHPs) developed. Individualized plans thus cover a range of educational, social, and vocational goals of people with disabilities. Although the various types of plans respond to different goals, all share some basic principles. For example, such plans typically include a description of the individual's current abilities and disabilities, goals and related objectives, a summary of services to be provided, and the ways these services are to be evaluated.

For those concerned with schools and educational systems, it is only IDEA that requires an individual plan for children. So, only students with disabilities have individual programs that detail the services they require for an appropriate education that has been agreed upon by their parents. Later in the chapter, we discuss the three kinds of individualized program plans. The **Individualized Family Service Plan (IFSP)** serves children under age 3; the IFSP addresses both the infant's or toddler's needs and the needs of the family. For preschoolers age 3 and above and for schoolchildren, an **Individualized Education Program (IEP)** ensures that educational and related services required to meet their individual special needs in academic, social, speech and language, motoric, and vocational areas are met. For adolescents making the transition from school to job placement under the guidance of special education personnel, an **Individualized Transition Plan (ITP)** lists needed transition services. ITPs help students prepare

collaboration. Professionals working cooperatively to provide educational services.

Individualized Family Service Plan (IFSP). A written plan that identifies and organizes services and resources for infants and toddlers with special needs who are under age 3 and for their families.

Individualized Education Program (IEP). A management tool used to identify and organize individualized education and related services for preschoolers and schoolchildren.

Individualized Transition Plan (ITP). A statement of the transition services required for coordination and delivery of services as the student moves to adulthood.

for the transition from school to work and adult life and help agencies coordinate services that will be provided after the student leaves school. Before presenting the individualized programs, however, we will discuss the process or steps that lead from concern over a child's performance, to identification of a disability, to development of a plan to provide special services for that child.

Seven Steps to an Individualized Program Plan: The Planning Process

Individualized program plans are the means by which the educational concepts outlined in IDEA are guaranteed to each student and that student's family. The formation of an individualized program involves seven steps in a comprehensive process, beginning with a referral and ending with a formal plan for a youngster's program. Figure 2.3 highlights the phases of identification and decision making. As you read this section, refer to the figure to see how each step fits into the entire process.

Step 1: Referral. In this first step, a child is referred for special education services. For preschoolers, the referral can come from a variety of sources—the parents, a social service agency, a public health nurse, a day care or preschool teacher, or a doctor. For example, parents might be concerned about a child who is not walking by age 2 or not talking by age 3. Preschool teachers may be troubled by children who have frequent and excessive bursts of violent behavior or inappropriate displays of temper. Pediatricians may be concerned about children whose physical or motor development is slow. Delayed language, difficulties in eating, inability to locate the source of sounds, or excessive crying are other signals that normal child development may be delayed.

Typically, children with severe disabilities begin the referral process sooner than do other children with disabilities. For example, some infants with severe disabilities may be identified at birth or early in infancy. Children who are at risk because of improper prenatal care, low birth weight, accident, or trauma during infancy are also often referred for special services. Infants in need of **neonatal intensive care (NIC)** as a result of prematurity or other health reasons are typically referred to an infant social services agency for assessment and follow-up. In ideal situations, a transition plan is developed in the hospital for medically fragile infants to ensure a smooth transfer from hospital to home. This plan also addresses consistent early intervention services and communication between various agencies and the family.

Individual states use a special office or function called "child find" to help in the referral process. The professionals who work in this capacity can provide information for parents of very young children. The staff of your state's Department of Education's Special Education Division, located in your state capitol, can provide information on child find offices and the procedures for individual states.

For schoolchildren, referral usually begins when the general education teacher becomes concerned about a particular student's behavior or academic achievement. Candidates for referral are students whose academic performance is significantly behind their classmates' or who continually misbehave and disrupt the learning environment. Students who are thought to be gifted and talented because of their accelerated academic performance or high levels of creativity may

 MAKING CONNECTIONS

For a more thorough discussion of preschool children at risk for disabilities and the educational services for which they might be eligible, see the section Education and the Preschool Child in Chapter 5.

neonatal intensive care (NIC). A specialized hospital unit for infants who are in need of intensive medical attention.

FIGURE 2.3

Steps of the Individualized Education Program Process

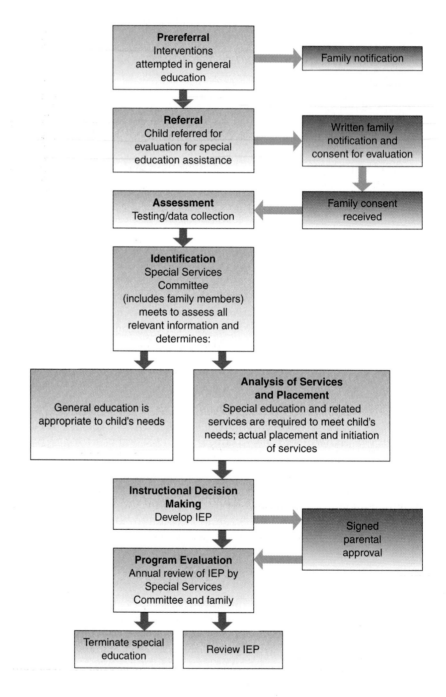

Source: From *Teaching Students with Learning and Behavioral Problems* (3rd ed.) (p. 52) by D. P. Rivera and D. D. Smith, 1997, Boston: Allyn and Bacon. Reprinted with permission.

Members of special services committees represent the many different viewpoints of professionals from a variety of disciplines and the child's parents. By working together, members prepare plans for the balance between FAPE and LRE.

also be referred for evaluation. Although gifted education is not included in IDEA, many states follow the guidelines outlined in these laws and develop IEPs for gifted students. Teachers are careful in their recommendations for referrals, but not all students they refer will qualify for special education services. Estimates indicate that 75 to 81 percent of children referred actually qualify for special education services (Algozzine, Ysseldyke, & Christenson, 1983; Kroth, 1990).

The actual referral process for schoolchildren starts when the general classroom teacher notifies the school's principal, counselor, or the **special services committee,** which can also be called the *appraisal and review team* or the *child study team*. This committee then decides whether a child should be evaluated more thoroughly. The person who refers a student for special education services must provide clear and specific reasons for the referral. He or she must present data, such as behavioral observations, samples of academic work, or anecdotal notes. For example, a teacher might include the results from an achievement test, scores from weekly quizzes, and samples from a student's writing. If social behavior is of concern, the teacher provides a written description of the child's atypical behavior in the classroom and on the playground.

Special services committees review the material presented. The permanent members of the committee normally include the school's principal, the counselor, the school psychologist, and a special education teacher. Rotating members, who change for each referral, are the student's classroom teacher and the parents. If a social service agency is working with a child and family, a representative from that agency would also be included. In each case of referral, the special services committee decides whether a formal evaluation is needed. If the committee decides to proceed, a written notice of the referral and a request for permission to evaluate is sent to the parents. The parents must consent in writing before formal assessment (diagnosis) can begin.

special services committee. The multidisciplinary team of professionals that determines whether a student qualifies for special education and, if so, develops the individualized plan.

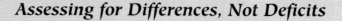

Assessing for Differences, Not Deficits

The assessment process is viewed as flawed and biased by many, particularly for culturally and linguistically diverse children and youth. The assessment process is biased when it either includes or excludes individuals from services because of their minority status (Midgette, 1995). Unfairness and discrimination can occur because of many factors: inappropriate referrals, uninformed or ill-prepared test administrators, inadequacies in the testing instruments, poor interpretation of the results, and insensitivity to cultural differences. Many of our nation's diverse children and their families face challenges that are incomprehensible to those from mainstream society (Figueroa & Garcia, 1994). Although potentially enriching and providing considerable opportunities for strength, the bicultural and bilingual experience places many families in conflict, having to negotiate competed values and practices. Many of these families also find themselves in dangerous living situations. These differences must be understood, as well as influence and be reflected, in the assessment process.

Step 2: Assessment. The assessment (diagnosis) stage is initiated to determine whether a youngster has a disability, whether special education is required, and what types of special or related services are needed. This stage should contribute to the development of an appropriate education for those students identified as having disabilities. The information gathered about the child during this stage is used throughout the rest of the process. Assessment is the foundation for the planning process. And, the result should be a baseline of performance that guides the development of the individualized education program and will later be used to judge the effectiveness of the educational program that was implemented. As you will note from the information included in the Focus on Diversity box, the assessment process can easily be confounded by bias, discrimination, and lack of information. All educators must be particularly sensitive to the different backgrounds of all children.

Because of the potentially negative effect on the individual and the family of incorrectly identifying an individual as having a disability, assessments should be conducted by a team of experts who can judge the abilities and disabilities of the youngster. This team must gather the most accurate and current information available so that the individual's strengths and needs—and, ultimately, the services and supports required—can be determined. The information collected should relate to the individual's major life activities: how the person performs at home, at school, in interpersonal relationships, and during leisure time. These data should be gathered in the person's natural environment through interviews with people who know the person best. The team's planning should focus on life goals and outcomes, so instruction is relevant to the individual's long-term needs (living independently, holding a job, participating in the community). For some students,

MAKING CONNECTIONS

For a review of adult outcomes for individuals with disabilities, see the Outcomes and Results of People with Disabilities in Chapter 1.

This child is responding to questions in one of the subtests of a frequently administered test of intelligence. During the assessment process, she may be tested by several different professionals.

 MAKING CONNECTIONS

For more information about adaptive behavior, see these sections in Chapter 6:
• Mental Retardation Defined
• Identification

 MAKING CONNECTIONS

Every chapter about a disability category includes a section called Identification (in the Defined section); see those sections for specific information about each disability area.

 MAKING CONNECTIONS

For more information about the very special needs of culturally and linguistically diverse students, please see
• All of Chapter 3,
• All Focus on Diversity boxes, found in every chapter of this text.

these assessments will target academic skills, as well as adaptive behavior. For students suspected of having mental retardation, for example, assessment in specific **adaptive skill areas** is typically required (Luckasson et al., 1992). Adaptive skill areas include communication, self-care, home living, social skills, community use, self-direction, health and safety, functional academics, leisure, and work. As you would expect, the persons best qualified to evaluate an individual's adaptive skill areas are those with expertise in these skill areas and who are familiar with the person's daily demands in community-based and age-appropriate living, school, and work situations.

The assessment team includes an array of professionals and an array of assessment instruments and procedures. In many states, the team leader is a **school psychologist**, an educational diagnostician, or a psychometrician. Usually, formal tests—tests of intelligence, academic achievement, **acuity** (vision and hearing), and learning style—comprise the assessment battery for determining whether the student has a disability. Many states also request that less formal assessments—such as classroom observations of both social and academic behavior—be used as well. Today, many professionals are advocating the use of **authentic assessments**, which use the work students generate in classroom settings as the assessment measurements (Fuchs & Deno, 1994). In other words, the testing material comes directly from the curriculum and the students' work. Authentic assessments include curriculum based assessments, test results on students' class assignments (spelling tests, math tests), anecdotal records, writing samples, and observational data. They can even be on abstract cognitive skills such as solving complex problems (Maker, 1994).

adaptive skill areas. Targets of instruction that focus on the ability of an individual to function in a typical environment and on successful adult outcomes (independent living, employment, and community participation).

school psychologist. Psychologist trained to test and evaluate individual students' abilities.

acuity. Sharpness of response to visual, auditory, or tactile stimuli.

authentic assessments. Performance measures that use work generated by the student or observational data on social behaviors for assessment and evaluation purposes.

Assessment must be nondiscriminatory: Tests and procedures must be validated for the purposes for which they are used. Tests must be given in a child's primary language or other mode of communication (for example, sign language) by a school psychologist or diagnostician. The formal and informal tests must not be culturally, linguistically, or ethnically discriminatory. As a safeguard against unfair identification of children as having disabilities—identification based, for example, on cultural or ethnic differences—multidisciplinary teams should assess the child's abilities. The team must give considerable weight to samples of students' classroom work and teachers' descriptions of social behavior. The details of the identification procedure are established by each state. Because the state determines the process used to identify children with disabilities, teams of professionals must be involved to ensure that the procedures adopted represent the points of view of all ethnic groups.

In many cases, various experts participate in the assessment stage. Children suspected of having hearing losses, for example, are assessed by at least three different specialists. In addition to a school psychologist or educational diagnostician, who assesses intelligence, academic achievement, and learning style, an **audiologist** will determine whether the child has a hearing loss and, if so, the extent of the hearing loss. A **speech/language pathologist (SLP)** will assess the impact of the hearing loss upon speech and language abilities.

Because of the importance of the assessment process and its potentially detrimental impact on the individual and the family, new and innovative approaches are gaining in popularity. Some states and school districts are experimenting with an approach referred to as **portfolio assessments**. Advocates of this process claim that the result is a more nearly accurate and fair judgment of students' overall abilities and performance (Bloom & Bacon, 1995; Curran & Harris, 1996). A portfolio assessment for a specific child might include a variety of samples from the student's work taken across a period of time to show growth and development. Portfolios are a type of authentic assessment because they include direct observations of children's performance in the classroom setting or actual samples of their schoolwork for the purpose of evaluation (Pike & Salend, 1995). Students help to select the work included in the portfolio, so the process involves them in the analysis and evaluation of their own work and may give them a more realistic view of their own strengths and weaknesses. The portfolio may also include prizes, certificates of award, pictures, dictated work, photographs, lists of books read, and selections from work done with others. Finally, the portfolio might include narratives written by the teacher or others who work with the child about challenging situations or patterns of behavior that should be a target of concern.

Portfolio assessment is intended to focus on students' abilities rather than on their deficits and involves students in the assessment process (Carpenter, Ray, & Bloom, 1995). Because much of the information required for the portfolio is taken from the students' work in the classroom, the assessment procedure requires little additional teacher time. In fact, the process is so closely related to instruction that it offers teachers immediately useful information for modifying students' instructional programs. Certainly, this assessment procedure is more subjective than the traditional, standardized diagnostic testing format. It could, however, provide a more complete and useful picture of children and the instructional programs they require.

MAKING CONNECTIONS

For more information about hearing impairments and deafness, see Chapter 10.

audiologist. Professional trained to diagnose hearing losses and auditory problems.

speech/language pathologist (SLP). A professional who diagnoses and treats problems in the area of speech and language development.

portfolio assessment. An alternative form of individualized assessment that includes many samples of the student's work across all curriculum targets and reports of teachers and parents about that individual's social skills.

Step 3: Identification. The assessment stage is the foundation for identifying a child as having one or more disabilities. Assessment tests, first, identify whether a student has a disability and, second, classify the disability (mental retardation, learning disabilities, behavior disorders, low vision or blind, deafness or hard of hearing, speech or language impairment). The test results, observations, and the child's educational and medical history (if available) are then summarized. The results and summary become part of the student's confidential school record.

Confidential school records are private; sometimes they are not even kept at the child's school. They contain all the student's test scores; professional observations about the child's social, academic, and other skills, such as motor and language development; and the family's history. The file should also contain a report from the special services committee regarding service and placement recommendations. Although it is sometimes difficult to gain access to this material, special education teachers may find this information useful as they plan specific remediation programs for the child.

Step 4: Analysis of Services. What happens next? Slightly less than 25 percent of children tested are ineligible for special services because they do not meet the criteria set by individual states (Algozzine et al., 1983; Kroth, 1990). These youngsters continue to be served by general education. Special education is intended only for those students with disabilities. IDEA permits the federal government to reimburse states for excess costs for no more than 12 percent of all children (ages 6–17). Most states serve somewhat fewer children, the national average being less than 10 percent (U.S. Department of Education, 1996). For those identified with a disability, the next step requires decisions about appropriate placement and services. The assessment results are used to help make these decisions.

What happens to the 75 percent of children who are identified as having a disability and who require special education services? For each of them, the process requires a determination of the specific services needed. Many schools, school districts, and all states offer a variety of options to deliver special services. In many instances, professionals work with students with special needs in areas beyond the expertise of most special education teachers. For example, many students with learning disabilities also have a language impairment. These students need the services of an SLP. Many with mental retardation have motor coordination difficulties requiring the assistance of a **physical therapist (PT)** and an **occupational therapist (OT)**. Deaf individuals might need the services of an audiologist, an SLP, and possibly an interpreter. Many students with disabilities also require and profit from the services of an assistive technology expert, who can help the individuals learn compensatory skills through the use of technological aids such as communication devices. In some cases, assistive technology is included in a child's special education program, but in other cases (for example, when a special device needs to be created or adapted specially for the student by an expert) it is a related service (Menlove, 1996). Also contributing to the appropriate education of many students with disabilities are **school nurses**. Although not listed in IDEA as a related service, these professionals are vital to the educational programs for many students with disabilities, particularly those with special health care needs.

 MAKING CONNECTIONS

Specific criteria for each disabling condition are discussed in each chapter of this text.

 MAKING CONNECTIONS

For information about each disability, see the Prevalence sections in each chapter.

 MAKING CONNECTIONS

Chapter 5 includes information about augmentative communication devices in the Technology section.

confidential school records. Private files of a student.

physical therapist (PT). A professional who treats physical disabilities through many nonmedical means.

occupational therapist (OT). A professional who directs activities that help improve muscular control and develop self-help skills.

school nurses. Professionals who participate in delivering FAPE to students with disabilities; those not listed by IDEA as an actual related service.

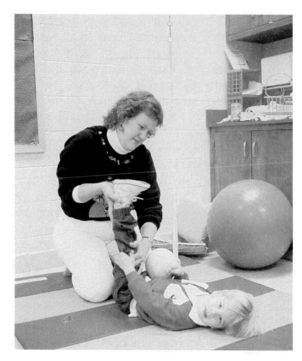

Some children require the services of professionals from different disciplines, such as physical therapy.

The analysis of services is the basis for the student's IEP, which must indicate what the student needs in order to receive a free appropriate education with regard to both special education and related services. Thus a child's IEP should specify particular therapeutic services, such as speech and language therapy, occupational therapy, or physical therapy; services related to transition to the world of work, such as job coaches or programs for supported employment; and, certainly, instructional needs in academic subject areas, such as reading, writing, and arithmetic. Remember, meeting the individual needs of a child with disabilities often requires education in areas that are not usually considered "academic." Each student with disabilities needs such a tailor-made educational program complete with supportive services and individually designed to meet the needs of the child, not the convenience of the school district. The cost of the services cannot be a factor in whether they are provided to a child who requires them (Parette, Murdick, & Gartin, 1996). For example, if Jane requires a special communications device to benefit from special education and to participate in a general education placement for part of the day, that device and the training in how to use it must be part of her IEP. The school district must provide the equipment for Jane. Because of districts' limited resources, many are looking to community leaders to help find private funding to help provide the equipment students need. Teachers must understand that when the school district purchases equipment, the district, not Jane, owns the device. Depending on the district's policy, Jane may or may not be able to take the equipment home with her or practice using the equipment in a variety of settings. If Jane's insurance company purchases the assistive technology equipment, however, then it belongs to Jane.

~~~
**FIGURE 2.4**

*Achieving a Balance Between FAPE and LRE Can Be a Difficult Goal*

The special services committee uses the data gathered during the assessment stage to determine which abilities need strengthening and which disabilities need remediating. Once those needs are determined and noted on the IEP, the services of experts in specialized areas are to be made available regardless of placement.

**Step 5: Placement.** The fifth step in planning the individual program involves possible placement for the student. Placement encompasses two critical and controversial concepts introduced in Chapter 1: (1) least restrictive environment (LRE) and (2) free appropriate public education (FAPE). As the illustration in Figure 2.4 shows, the special services committee must balance these two concepts as it reaches decisions on the programs for a child.

The concept of LRE requires that the student be integrated with nondisabled peers as much as possible and included in the mainstream of society. Debate among parents, special educators, general educators, politicians, and the media focuses on the concept of LRE and how it should be interpreted. On one side of the issue are those who believe that a full array of options should be available to youngsters with disabilities (Hallahan & Kauffman, 1995; Vaughn & Schumm, 1995). They believe in integration in general classrooms and general education activities whenever possible, but they also believe that other services, even separate schooling, may be necessary. On the other side of the issue is the

 MAKING CONNECTIONS
To better understand the range of beliefs about inclusion for students with different disabilities, see the Inclusion section found in each chapter.

interpretation that LRE is a legal mandate that ensures the right of those with disabilities to be fully included in general education settings (Turnbull, Turnbull, Shank, & Leal, 1995; Sailor, 1991; Stainback & Stainback, 1989). No side is arguing for complete segregation, but how to make decisions about LRE and integration has not been resolved. Those who support an array or continuum approach believe that LRE focuses on integration but also allows for separation when it is in the best educational interests of the child involved. As some professionals (Keogh, 1988; Smith, 1988) have pointed out, the general education classroom teacher referred the child in the first place, indicating that at least this professional believes that the general education classroom, as it is currently structured, is not the most appropriate placement for the child. In that teacher's view, the child needs additional support in the general education classroom, supplemental services, or possibly a separate curriculum in order to have a successful educational experience. Finally, many parents and professionals, particularly those concerned with students who are blind or deaf, also feel that the array of placement options must include residential center schools. Clearly, the debate about **full inclusion** and where students with disabilities should receive their education is one of the hottest and most contentious issues in education today.

LRE is an important concept. Special educators must be constantly aware of how placement decisions can segregate students by removing them from normal role models, social interactions, and curriculum—and can fragment their daily lives. Placement decisions further identify a student as being different. Finally, removing a child from the general education classroom has serious implications for today and the future. If, however, the student's needs cannot be met in the general classroom or if that environment impedes learning, then placement there is not appropriate. Tom Lovitt's research indicates that, at least in many schools today, full inclusion and the general education setting might not be meeting students' educational needs or their families' expectations (Pautier, 1995). He concluded that most high schools were not doing a satisfactory job of educating students with learning disabilities, students many would assume might be the easiest group of students to include in the general education setting. He found that these students and their parents did not know what goals and objectives they were expected to meet, they rarely received help from the general education teacher, and they were not graduating with the skills they need to become independent adults. Clearly, general assumptions about any single placement option providing the "best" education for groups of students with disabilities should be held with caution. We believe, along with others, that for students with disabilities there should be no single answer to what comprises either LRE or FAPE (Bateman, 1996).

The second concept in placement is that each child with a disability should be provided with a free appropriate public education. The word *education* is broadly defined. It includes all types of supportive services, a curriculum that may differ from that presented in general education (Levine & Edgar, 1994), and a highly individualized educational program. Because few special education graduates, particularly those with cognitive disabilities, successfully complete postsecondary education programs, the education community should consider more curriculum options designed specifically to prepare youngsters to assume the responsibilities of adulthood immediately after high school. The concept of an array of curricular options fits with the concept of FAPE. For some students with disabilities, it may

MAKING CONNECTIONS

As a reminder about how contentious issues surrounding inclusion is, see these sections in Chapter 1:
• Concepts and Controversy
• Legislation, the 104th Congress.

**full inclusion.** An interpretation that states that the least restrictive environment for all children with disabilities is the general education classroom.

include a functional curriculum where the traditional emphasis on academics is less important than focusing on adult outcomes, such as living and working in the community satisfactorily (Edgar & Polloway, 1994). And, for some youngsters it may mean the need for community based instruction that allows students to learn important job and life skills in the natural environment—that is, in the community, not in a general education class.

After reviewing and analyzing all the available information, the special services committee must make important suggestions about placement and related services. After summarizing their findings and suggestions, they invite the child's parents to a meeting and inform them, in their native language, of their child's abilities and disabilities and discuss their recommendations for the child's education. Adolescents and young adults with disabilities should be invited to participate in this meeting. A major goal of this meeting is to form a partnership between the parents and the agency or professional who will provide the needed services. In most cases, parents and professionals are in agreement about the types of services and the educational placement a child requires. If the parents do not agree with the special services committee, they have a right to challenge any of the team's decisions. If agreement between the two parties cannot be reached, a due process hearing may be called, in which an impartial third party settles the dispute. If either party does not agree to the decision made at the due process hearing, they can appeal to the state education agency. If they still do not agree, they may take the matter to the courts.

***Step 6: Instructional Decision Making.*** At this stage, decisions must be made about the educational program the child will receive. At this time the teacher writes the actual program plan, which includes a statement of the present abilities of the child as well as a summary of the annual goals and objectives that the teacher and the school hope to attain.

Goals and objectives should focus on the child, indicating what is expected of the student after the instructional program is completed. Goals and objectives must be conceptualized to specify the task or concept to be taught and to reflect the level of performance the student should be able to achieve. Each area of instruction could include many overall goals, each comprising many behavioral objectives. As an example, Table 2.2 shows part of one teacher's detailed lesson plan for one goal and some related objectives for telling time, a skill that needs to be taught to many students with disabilities. Although not all students require direct instruction on telling time, the table gives you a useful example about how goals and objectives can guide instruction.

Creating behavioral goal and objective statements for each child can be a daunting task for a teacher. Fortunately, help is readily available. For example, the teachers' manuals accompanying many basal reading and mathematics textbooks provide detailed targets of instruction. Also, many school districts have standard goal and objective statements for various curriculum areas, including computer-generated statements. Although prepared goals and objectives can be a convenient tool for a teacher writing a plan for a student, teachers who use them need to remember to individualize the program. Materials must match a child's needs, so the wise teacher uses the prepared materials as a foundation and tailors them to the individual student. The teacher may often need to prepare supplemental materials to complement commercially available instructional packages. When the

MAKING CONNECTIONS
• Community based instruction is discussed in the Educational Interventions section of Chapter 6.
• For debates about what comprises most restrictive environments, also see the Concepts and Controversy section of this chapter.

**TABLE 2.2**

Behavioral Goals and Objectives for Telling Time

| Abbreviated Objective | Behavioral Statement | Criterion |
|---|---|---|
| Clock hand discrimination | 2.01 The student is able to point to and name both the hour and minute hands. | 2.01 with 100 percent accuracy within 15 seconds |
| Hour hand | 2.02 The student is able to identify all hour hand placements.<br><br>2.02.01 The student is able to identify the hour for exact hour hand placements.<br><br>2.02.02 The student is able to identify the hour for any hour hand placement. | 2.02 (.01–.02) with 100 percent accuracy within 10 seconds |
| Minute hand | 2.03 The student is able to identify all minute hand placements.<br><br>2.03.01 The student is able to identify the minute for minute placements on any interval of five.<br><br>2.03.02 The student is able to identify the minute for exact minute hand placements.<br><br>2.03.03 The student is able to identify fractions of hours using the minute hand (e.g., quarter after). | 2.03 (.01–.03) with 100 percent accuracy within 10 seconds |
| Combination of hour and minute hands | 2.04 The student is able to identify the correct time using both the hour and the minute hands.<br><br>2.04.01 The student is able to identify the time for the "o'clock" times.<br><br>2.04.02 The student is able to identify the time for all intervals of five.<br><br>2.04.03 The student is able to identify the exact time.<br><br>2.04.04 The student is able to identify the time for fractions of the hour. | 2.04 (.01–.04) with 100 percent accuracy within 10 seconds |

individualized program plan is truly individualized—written specifically for one student—it is a useful and reliable management tool that assists the teacher by guiding the instructional program.

**Step 7: Program Evaluation.** The individualized program—whether an IFSP, an IEP, or an ITP—must contain frequent evaluations of student performance. A student's individualized program is evaluated in three ways.

First, the student's program is evaluated while he or she is actively participating in the plan during the school year. One method that many special educators use is a data collection system. In this system, often referred to as **curriculum based assessment (CBA)**, teachers collect data about a child's

**curriculum based assessment (CBA).** A method of evaluating children's performance by collecting data on their daily progress.

daily progress on each instructional task. For example, a teacher instructing a youngster in math would keep a daily record of the number or percentage of problems the child correctly solved. This record helps the teacher judge whether the instructional methods selected are both efficient and effective. With CBA, teachers know how well their students are learning and whether the chosen instructional methods help the child meet the goals and objectives of the individualized plan.

Second, every student's individualized program plan must be reevaluated every year. As the student grows and learns, the educational decisions made one year may not be the best for the ensuing years. At the time of the annual review, a new program is developed. Decisions about placement, supportive services, and the goals and objectives for the upcoming year are made. In some cases, a child's progress may have been so great that special services are no longer required. In other cases, the degree of special services may change. For example, a child's progress may indicate that only periodic attendance in a special education class or resource room is necessary to maintain growth and continued progress. In other cases, more intensive special services may be needed. For example, a student with a behavior disorder may have been placed in a resource room under a behavior management program. If the student showed insufficient progress over the year, this student may need to spend at least part of the upcoming year in a self-contained special education class taught by a teacher trained to work with children with behavior disorders.

Third, the law requires that a full evaluation of every child with special needs over age 3 be conducted every three years. In other words, three years after a child's initial identification, steps 2 through 6 in the process are repeated. This comprehensive evaluation may be conducted earlier if the child's parents or teachers request it. At this point, students who are no longer in need of special services are returned to the general education system.

## Roles and Responsibilities in Planning the Individualized Program

The IFSP, IEP, and ITP guide educators in providing an appropriate education in the least restrictive environment for each child. Developing these plans is a tremendous responsibility: Educators must guarantee that students without disabilities are not mistakenly identified as having disabilities, that students with disabilities are identified and receive the educational and related services they require, and that parents and families are properly involved in decision making. In addition, educators must safeguard students' rights to an education in the least restrictive environment. This chapter has reviewed the steps involved in the planning process, showing you the various people who participate. Table 2.3 summarizes the process and the roles and responsibilities of the participants.

## The Three Different Individualized Education Plans

As mentioned earlier, IDEA specifies that three different individualized plans be developed for children with disabilities. The Individualized Family Service Plan (IFSP), added to IDEA in 1990, serves young children with disabilities (birth to age 3) and their families. The second plan, the Individualized Education Program (IEP), serves preschoolers through high school students. It is available for use with

~~~
TABLE 2.3

Roles and Responsibilities in the Individual Program/Plan Process

Steps	Responsibility	Action	Process Stopped If
1. Referral	Parents, teachers, doctors, or social services	Request assessment to determine eligibility	Child's behavior or performance does not indicate a possible disability. Parents do not give approval in writing. Negotiation. Due process/arbitration.
Parents given written notice of referral			
Parental consent obtained			
2. Assessment	Special services committee	Collect performance data	
3. Identification	Special services committee	Analysis of performance data	Child does not have a disability.
4. Service analysis	Special services committee	Listing of special education and related services needed by student	No special services are required.
5. Planning and instructional decision making	Special services committee	Plan/programs developed, including placement recommendations and goals and objectives	
Signed parental approval			Negotiation. Parent and district disagreement.
6. Implementation	Teacher and/or related services	Placement and initiation of services	
7. Program evaluation	Teachers/related service providers, special services committee	Annual review with recommendation for new program/plan	

students from ages 3 to 21. The third plan, the Individualized Transition Plan (ITP), is used to help those students make the transition from school to work. Although many suggest that ITPs be developed when a student is in middle school, the law mandates only that such coordinating plans must exist for those who need them from the time they are age 16. Keep in mind that these plans must show that the school is providing an appropriate education in a setting that is least restrictive. Let's first look at the IFSP in a little more detail.

Children need opportunities to learn and play together.

Individualized Family Service Plans (IFSPs). Infants or toddlers (birth through age 2) who have a disability or who are at risk for a disability are guaranteed the right to early intervention programs by PL 99-457, passed in 1986. The 1991–1992 schoolyear was the first year that preschool special education services were mandated in every state for youngsters from age 3 to age 5, and most states offer programs for infants (from birth to age 3). The process starts with referral and assessment and, for those who qualify for services, results in the development of an IFSP drawn up by the special services team. Johnson, McGonigel, & Kaufmann (1989) state the purposes and intent of IFSPs:

> The purpose of the IFSP is to identify and organize formal and informal resources to facilitate families' goals for their children and themselves. The IFSP is a promise to children and families—a promise that their strengths will be recognized and built on, that their needs will be met in a way that is respectful of their beliefs and values, and that their hopes and aspirations will be encouraged and enabled. (p. 1)

The required contents of the IFSP differ from those of plans for older children. One key difference is that, like all individualized programs, the plan is evaluated once a year but the IFSP must also be reviewed with the family every six months. The key components of the IFSP include the following descriptions:

- The child's current functioning levels in all relevant areas (physical development, cognitive development, language and speech development, psychosocial development, and self-help skills)

 MAKING CONNECTIONS

Refer to each chapter's section about the Preschool Child (Educational Interventions sections) for more information about what comprises good early education practices.

- The family's strengths and needs, to assist them in enhancing the development of their child
- The major outcomes expected including criteria, procedures, and a timeline, so progress can be evaluated
- The services necessary and a schedule for their delivery
- Projected dates for initiation of services
- The name of the service manager
- A biannual review with the child's family of progress made and the need for modifications in the IFSP
- Indication of methods for transitioning the child to services available for children ages 3 to 5

To many **service managers** and early childhood specialists, the IFSP is a working document for an ongoing process in which parents and specialists work together, continually modifying, expanding, and developing a child's educational program. For this reason, many early childhood specialists use pencil to write up the contents of an individual child's IFSP; parents can then easily modify the goals and objectives suggested by the early childhood specialist.

Children and families who participate in early intervention programs often find these years to be an intense period, with many professionals offering advice, guidance, personalized services, and care and concern. The transition to kindergarten and elementary school is particularly difficult and frightening, and so early childhood experts now recommend special transition efforts for these youngsters and their families (Fowler, Schwartz, & Atwater, 1991). The IFSP should also include special goals and objectives that address the issue of transition to public school.

IFSPs should include a summary of the child's current performance abilities. This information is often gathered from a developmental checklist, a criterion-referenced test, or a traditional standardized test. For young children, it often includes information about cognitive, gross and fine motor, and language abilities. To ensure high-quality IFSPs and IEPs for young children, teachers should remember that they must be relevant and meaningful and have practical application to the child's daily environment. The instructional targets included must be easily incorporated into the student's and family's daily routines. The behaviors taught should lead to the development of other meaningful skills, and progress in mastery of these skills should be easily measurable (Notari-Syverson & Shuster, 1995). The National Center on Educational Outcomes also suggests that the topics of instruction for very young children should focus on these general outcomes: participation in group activities, family involvement, physical health, responsibility and independence, compliance with rules and expectations, academic and functional literacy, and social adjustment (Ysseldyke, Thurlow, & Erickson, 1994). Putting these concerns together should lead to the development of fine early intervention programs for young children with disabilities.

Individualized Education Program (IEP). The IEP is a management tool designed to ensure that schoolchildren with special needs receive the special education and related services appropriate to their needs. First required in 1975 by PL 94-142, the IEP remains a cornerstone of every educational program planned for

MAKING CONNECTIONS

Refer to each chapter's section about the Schoolchild (Educational Interventions sections) for more information about what comprises good early education practices.

service manager. The case manager who oversees the implementation and evaluation of an Individualized Family Service Plan.

each student with a disability. Congress delineated the minimal contents of the IEP, and it is important that every educator knows these key components:

- The child's present levels of educational performance
- Annual goals and short-term instructional objectives
- Specific educational services to be provided
- The extent to which the child will participate in general education
- Projected date for initiation of services
- Expected duration of those services
- Objective criteria and evaluation procedures
- Annual evaluation of progress made on the IEP

Bateman (1996) reminds us of five important principles that should be followed when developing and implementing IEPs. These principles are included in the law and have been verified and supported through hundreds of rulings from a variety of agencies and the courts. First, all of the student's needs must be met, not just a selected few. Academic areas may be reflected, but they might also represent areas not typically part of educational programs of students without disabilities (e.g., fine and gross motor skills, functional life skills). Second, whether services are available does not determine whether they are included on the IEP. If a student needs the services of an assistive technologist, they shall be made available. Third, the IEP indicates services that must be provided. Through this process, they become legally binding. They cannot be denied without another IEP meeting and mutual approval by the family and the school district. Fourth, the IEP should be individually determined. All students who need services of an SLP, for example, should not have identical IEPs. And, lastly, the IEP itself must contain all of the components required and identified in IDEA (see the foregoing list).

Another important principle should be followed when implementing IEPs: Communicate their contents to everyone who should have the information. Too often, teachers do not know what the student's IEP comprises, and at the secondary level, many general education teachers of specific students with disabilities do not even know that they have an IEP that spells out accommodations and modifications that should be met (Bateman, 1996; Lovitt, Cushing, & Stump, 1994; Pautier, 1995). This situation leaves one to ask: How can an appropriate education be delivered when the educators who interact with students with disabilities do not even know what services, goals, and objectives their education should include? The answer is obvious. An appropriate education cannot be delivered under these circumstances. At least some modifications in instruction and accommodations to the learning environment are required for even those with the mildest disabilities. Although IEPs are part of the students' school records, they are not private for those educators who have legitimate educational reasons for having access to them (Bateman, 1996). For those who believe that they are part of the student's confidential record—which was certainly not the intention of the creators of IDEA, the law that mandated IEPs—certainly parents can give permission to share their child's IEP with the educators with whom their child will interact.

The IEP is intended to guarantee an individualized education to every student with disabilities. This program needs to reflect the individual needs of the student

TABLE 2.4

Setting Meaningful IEP Goals

Criterion	Explanation
1. Is the goal educationally useful?	IEP goals should relate and lead to the outcomes expected for that individual student. Without this relationship, it is questionable whether the goals have value to either the student or the family.
2. Is the goal worth achieving?	Any goal must be valued, be within the belief system of the student and the family. For culturally and linguistically diverse students, goals must be set that fit within the individual's cultural belief system, or they will not be considered important.
3. Can it be met?	Goals must be challenging but also attainable and realistic. The individual must believe that through personal effort goals can be accomplished.
4. Is the goal stated, and will it be taught so it can be evaluated?	Progress on achieving the goal must be monitored, so the student's performance must be measurable. This requires determining whether mastery of the objectives leading to the overall goal and contributing to improved outcomes for the individual occurred.
5. Is the goal desirable?	Does achieving this goal make a difference to the individual with disabilities or the family? Does it improve relevant performance of the individual?

and those goals and objectives that will ensure the best adult outcomes possible. This means that the goals and objectives must be relevant and meaningful. Table 2.4, developed with some of the ideas of Edelen-Smith (1995) and Bateman (1996), helps us better understand how to develop useful goals that will become the framework for each child's IEP.

 MAKING CONNECTIONS

Refer to each chapter's section about Transition (Educational Interventions sections) for more information about what comprises good early education practices.

Individualized Transition Plan (ITP). IDEA, through PL 101-476, the Education of Handicapped Children Act Amendments of 1990, provides details about expectations of programs that serve adolescents and young adults with disabilities through age 21 who are in school or have recently left school. It stresses the importance of vocational and life skills for these individuals, and it ensures that transitional services are provided throughout the school years (Patton & Blalock, 1996). This law states that for students who need transitional services, the IEP must include at least a statement of interagency responsibilities and linkages before the student leaves school. By no later than age 16, an ITP should be a facet of the IEP. The ITP adds an important component to adolescents' educational programs. In the past, there was little dialogue between special educators and the vocational rehabilitation counselors who assume some responsibility for many of these youngsters after their school years. As a result, many young adults with disabilities were ill-prepared for community living or the world of work. This recent effort toward collaboration of special and vocational education promises to bene-

Learning job skills at actual work sites are components of many students' IEPs.

fit many individuals and prepare them for independent living and employment. Because young adults can interact with so many different social service agencies, postsecondary job training opportunities, and potential employers, Blalock (1996) suggested that permanently functioning community transition teams be appointed to facilitate the process involved in becoming an independent adult.

In most cases, the ITP supplements and complements the school-based IEP process. While the IEP describes the educational goals and objectives that a student should achieve during a schoolyear, the ITP addresses the skills and the supportive services required in the future (being able to shop, make leisure time choices, and cooperate with co-workers). An ITP should reflect the goals and objectives that ensure that the individual can function on the job, at home, and in the community. Although the ITP for students with disabilities matches their unique needs, some overall goals apply to everyone, to people with or without disabilities. In Chapter 1, we discussed outcomes—integrated employment, community living, citizenship and involvement, and personal autonomy and life satisfaction—that should be included in the educational goals for all students. These outcomes are what educators must consider carefully when designing a student's ITP. For many students with disabilities, the ITP is their last educational opportunity before assuming the responsibilities of adulthood. Consequently, ITPs should cover a variety of topics, such as money management, independent travel from home to work, and social interaction (Clark, 1996).

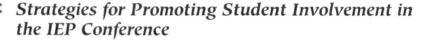
Strategies for Promoting Student Involvement in the IEP Conference

Effective self-advocacy and personal decision-making skills are qualities of more successful, self-determined individuals. Yet, many students with disabilities are unprepared to plan and advocate actively for current and future personal needs and desires. The IEP and transition planning conferences provide ideal opportunities for students to use such skills. IDEA specifies that students may participate in their IEP conference, as appropriate. Far too few students, however, are truly involved. Based on the student's age, disability, ability, and interest to participate, teachers must provide appropriate opportunities for involvement and must teach the needed skills and strategies (Strickland & Turnbull, 1993).

Students may participate for part or all of the meeting. Before the IEP meeting, students should have knowledge of the meeting's purpose, agenda and participants, and their rights. Students should also be prepared to use effective communication skills and to set and share personal goals. Here is an example of how one teacher prepares a student for active participation in her annual IEP conference:

Because Nora will soon be attending high school, it will be important for her to participate and plan for this transition. Nora is a seventh grade student with a learning disability. Her annual IEP is in December.

Initially, Ms. Begay decided to interview Nora (see the interview form). She wanted to find out her level of skill development in personal awareness and goal setting and her knowledge of the IEP conference by using the self-advocacy strategy (Van Reusen, Bos, Schumaker, & Deshler, 1994), which can systematically teach students how to be involved actively at the IEP meetings. She recorded Nora's responses. She soon realized that Nora indeed needed specific instruction facilitating personal awareness and goal setting and the purpose of an IEP meeting.

Next Ms. Begay utilized curriculum materials to instruct Nora on utilizing the following skills:

1. Assess and articulate personal strengths, limitations, preferences, and learning styles.
2. Use this awareness to create personal goals for the present and for the future.
3. Share these personal goals, learning strengths, needs, and desirable learning modifications with others, including adults.
4. State and show knowledge of the content of an IEP, procedures followed during an IEP conference, and personal rights.
5. Practice and use effective communication and listening skills, such as active listening in role-playing activities.

Ms. Begay used direct instruction to teach each of these skills. She provided adequate practice and gave frequent, specific feedback to Nora on her performance.

It was now time for Nora to bring together the skills she had learned in a simulated IEP conference. It was important that Nora coalesce the separate skills she had learned into a more realistic situation. Nora rehearsed during several sessions. She first practiced with a script, verbalizing what specific behaviors and language she would use. She then practiced these skills during a

Personal Awareness and Goal-Setting Interview

Student: _____ Date _____

Interviewer: _____

1. What are your personal strengths? _____

2. What strengths do you have in school? _____

3. How do you learn best? _____

4. In what areas/subjects do you have difficulties? _____

5. What are your specific difficulties? _____

6. What goal(s) do you have for school this year? _____

   What would you like to do in high school? _____

7. Are there specific careers you have thought about for the future? _____

   What are they? _____

8. How do you feel about your friendships with peers? _____

   About your interactions with adults? _____

9. Name any social goals you might have. _____

10. What is an IEP? _____

11. Have you ever attended an IEP conference before? _____

    What was it like? _____

12. Would you like to attend and participate in a meeting in which goals and plans are made about your schoolyear? These plans influence what happens this year during school and can assist in planning for your future.

    _____

mock IEP meeting. Other classmates and adults played roles of potential IEP committee members. Ms. Begay observed and provided Nora feedback on the skills she had exhibited. If needed, she suggested improvements. Additional simulations occurred as needed. When Nora displayed all the necessary skills, she was ready.

On the day of the IEP meeting, Ms. Begay ensured that the physical environment was appropriate and fostered student participation. She made sure that Nora was seated comfortably; to provide support, she seated herself next to the student. Prior to the meeting, she informed all meeting participants that Nora would be in attendance. She stated that Nora would actively participate by asking questions and sharing information such as goals and interests.

Throughout the IEP conference Ms. Begay also used active listening, asking Nora open-ended questions (avoiding yes/no questions), and provided Nora with adequate response time. She made sure that Nora also signed the IEP. Finally, at an appropriate time following the IEP conference, Ms. Begay reinforced Nora for her attendance at the IEP meeting. She also gave her feedback and solicited her reactions.

By the time some youngsters reach high school, their attitudes and their involvement with school and the educational process have lessened. These last years of school, however, can be critical to their achievement of special education outcomes and to their smooth and successful transition to adulthood. Unfortunately, many adolescents with disabilities find the process used to develop IEPs and ITPs frustrating and meaningless (Lovitt, Cushing, & Stump, 1994). Although the law encourages the active involvement of adolescents in the development of their ITPs, many feel that they are not really included in the process of making decisions about their future and their educational programs, that they do not understand the language used at the meeting or in the document, that the evaluation process is unclear, and that the goals and objectives do not reflect their interests. Many parents of high school students have similar feelings, which they demonstrate by not coming to their youngster's IEP/ITP meeting (Haring, Lovett, & Saren, 1991). Successful school-to-work transitions are crucial to positive adult outcomes for students with disabilities; the ITP process is intended to facilitate this growth and development. ITP goals differ from those included in typical IEPs. For example, ITP goals include interagency collaborative arrangements along with skills needed for employment, community integration, independent residential living, and recreation and leisure activities; IEPs do not.

ITPs are important for many reasons. First, they ensure that school-based personnel set appropriate goals and objectives for their students. The goals and objectives should address training in the skills that will help the student as an adult. Second, they can assist individuals with disabilities to make the sometimes difficult transition from the structure of school to the freedom of adulthood. Third, they can help the student to get a job in competitive work. Fourth, they offer a mechanism for the coordination of services available from different agencies and adult service providers (schools, vocational rehabilitation, agencies for community-based living). Finally, they can help students and parents participate more actively in the next phase of their lives. Let's review the major elements of the ITP:

- Is developed by age 16 for those who need transition planning
- Is based on present level of performance
- Plans for transitional services
- Focuses on adult outcomes (independent living, personal social adjustment, and occupational adjustment)
- Coordinates services with agencies that serve adults
- Includes the student as a full participating member of the IEP/ITP team
- Reviews performance annually

 MAKING CONNECTIONS

Also see the Inclusion sections in every chapter (Educational Interventions).

Concepts and Controversy: Least Restrictive Environment (LRE) and Full Inclusion, or Where Should Children with Disabilities Be Served?

Since the concept of LRE was introduced in 1975 (in PL 94-142, the original version of IDEA), this issue has been hotly discussed and debated. Full inclusion, a concept added to the discussion in recent years, continues the dialogue about where students with disabilities should receive their education. The push toward more integration was begun in 1986 by Madeline Will, then director of the federal Office of Special Education and Rehabilitation Services and called the Regular (general) Education Initiative (REI). At the heart of the REI and full inclusion debates are a number of questions and issues:

- What constitutes a least restrictive environment?
- What constitutes an appropriate education?
- Where are students with disabilities best educated?
- Is the general education classroom truly the least restrictive setting for all students?
- Can classroom teachers adjust their instructional programs to meet the needs of youngsters diverse on many dimensions?
- Who should deliver special education? and
- Which sets of peers should be classmates of students with disabilities?

Opinions of professionals, parents, and students with disabilities fall along a continuum. At one end of this debate are professionals who maintain that all children with disabilities should be placed and educated exclusively in general education classrooms (NASBE, 1992; Roach, Ascroft, Stamp, & Kysilko, 1995; Sailor, 1991; Snell, 1988; Stainback & Stainback, 1989). At the other are professionals (Commission on the Education of the Deaf, 1988; Hallahan & Kauffman, 1995) who maintain that the special needs of some of these students are so great that they can be met only in residential programs exclusively designed to meet the needs of that particular group. Most special educators find themselves somewhere between these two extremes, believing that a continuum of services should be maintained (Vaughn & Schumm, 1995).

This complex debate—which has serious ramifications for all of education—encompasses many issues. One teachers' union, the American Federation of Teachers (AFT), has become active in the debate and is calling for a moratorium on full inclusion (Huestis, 1993). Its belief is that the general education learning environment is damaged, educational achievement for typical learners is harmed, and discipline is more difficult to achieve when students with disabilities are fully included into these classrooms. Until class size is reduced, until general education teachers are better prepared to handle greater cognitive and learning diversity, and until extensive support is available on a consistent basis, these educators maintain, full inclusion should not be implemented (Briand, 1994). Now, another interesting issue is being added to the debate: Can students with disabilities make friends who have similar problems and concerns when there is no critical mass and they can never meet others with disabilities like their own (Stainback, Stainback, East, & Sapon-Shevin, 1994)? Of course, such acquaintances can be made through clubs, but they could also be made at school. Certainly, this issue provides yet another dimension to the inclusion debate.

The courts are beginning to hear cases where parents and school officials are in disagreement about the placement of a child with disabilities (LaRue, 1996). And, it appears that the courts are ruling in support of those who argue for a continuum of services and the position that there is no single answer to the interpretation of LRE. For example, in one case (*Poolaw v. Bishop*), the courts ruled that a state residential school, not the general education placement wanted by the parents, was the appropriate placement for a 13-year-old deaf student with severe communication needs. In another case (*Kari v. Franklin S.S.D*), the courts determined that the appropriate educational placement was a separate school for a 14-year-old with severe mental retardation. In both cases, general education placements had been provided in the past; and in both cases, the judges believed that FAPE could not be met in the general education setting and that these youngsters were disruptive forces in their inclusive placements. In a complementary case (*Urban v. Jefferson County School District R-1*), the court decided that students with disabilities did not have a guaranteed right to attend their neighborhood school when it determined that a school closer to a student with cerebral palsy did not have to make accommodations for the youngster when another school had the accessibility the student needed (Briand, 1995).

Regardless of recent court findings, some special education professionals still advocate that all children, despite the severity of their disabilities, receive their education in the general education setting, where special education and related services personnel work alongside the general education teacher (Stainback & Stainback, 1989). These professionals have called for massive education reform that could dismantle special education in the future and has already seen reductions in the number of resource rooms available (Hyman, 1993; U.S. Department of Education, 1996). Some educators worry that once support services are unavailable, students with disabilities will be encouraged to drop out of school, resulting in exclusion rather than inclusion (Silber, 1991). Recent history provides an example of what could happen: In the deinstitutionalization movement of the 1960s and 1970s, people with mental illness were moved out of institutions, but the array of community-based programs promised them were never delivered. The result is the significant number of homeless people who have mental illness and live on the streets today (estimated to be over 51 percent).

Special educators, general educators, those who work with individuals with disabilities in a variety of capacities, and the public need to develop their own positions in this debate. Many special educators adopt a moderate position: They suggest that an array of services be maintained; and at the same time, they encourage more integration of students with disabilities into integrated settings (general education, parks and recreation programs, social clubs). Even if you adopt a middle-of-the-road point of view, what should guide your decisions about how, when, and to what degree individuals with disabilities should be included?

～～ *SUMMARY* ～～

A cornerstone of the federal laws assuring a free appropriate education to all children and youth with disabilities is a mandated process of individualized educational programs. They are the Individualized Family Service Plan, the Individualized Education Program, and the supplemental Individualized Transition Plan. Each of these management tools guides the education system as it plans for and delivers an appropriate education to these individuals.

Self-Test Questions

▶ *What are the seven steps to developing an individualized program for each student with disabilities?*

The seven steps to every individualized special education program are referral, assessment, identification, analysis of services, placement, instructional decision making, and program evaluation. All of these programs (IFSPs, IEPs, and ITPs) follow a general process in the development of individualized program plans. For youngsters first being considered for placement into special education, three steps are completed before the program plan is written: referral, assessment, and identification. Not all children referred for special education services qualify. Some referred do not have a disability and do not require special assistance; others with disabilities do not require special services to meet their educational needs. A wide range of services are available to children with disabilities, from short-term assistance of a specialist to intensive full-time services. Also, many different professionals are available to children with disabilities: special education teachers, speech/language pathologists, occupational therapists, physical therapists, vocational educators, audiologists, counselors, social workers. Special education placement decisions must be made by balancing an appropriate education with the concept of least restrictive environment. Every student receiving special services must have a program individually tailored to meet his or her needs, and this program must be specified in terms of annual goals and objectives, complete with measurable ways to evaluate their attainment. Evaluation and review of these goals and objectives must occur at least once a year. At the time of the annual evaluation, a determination about next year's program must be made. For children requiring continuing special services, a new program plan is developed. For those who no longer require special services, transition to the general education system is made.

▶ *What roles do special services committees fill?*

In many school districts, the special education referral process begins with the special services committee, sometimes called the child study team or the appraisal and review team. When, for example, a general education teacher suspects that a student might have a disability (or a prereview or screening committee holds this belief about a child), it is this committee that receives the referral. This group first must determine whether sufficient information about the child's academic and social performance is available or presented. The special services committee actually makes the decision about whether formal testing and evaluation should commence. If that decision is positive, then the committee seeks permission from the child's parents to conduct the assessments. In some school districts, some members of the special services committee actively participate in the assessment process; in other districts, these professionals do not actually conduct any of the evaluations. Regardless, it is usually this committee that collects the information from the assessment stage and determines which of the child's abilities need strengthening and which problem areas require direct attention. The special services committee is instrumental in writing the student's IEP.

▶ *What factors must be considered when determining the least restrictive environment for individual students?*

All children and youth with disabilities, ages birth to 21, are entitled to a free appropriate education in the least restrictive environment possible. These rights are guaranteed by the Individuals with Disabilities Education Act. When balancing FAPE with LRE, parents and professionals should consider the goals and objectives developed for the student. These goals, of course, should reflect the adult outcomes that will need direct intervention to achieve. These outcomes should include integrated employment, community living, citizenship, and life satisfaction. Attaining these outcomes requires substantial effort by many including the students with disabilities themselves, their families, and the array of educators and related service professionals who have dedicated their careers to these goals. Most importantly, LRE must be individually determined with no single service delivery option being able to meet the needs of all students with any single disability or all students with disabilities. It requires an array of educational placements and services to meet the needs of these students and to define LRE for each of them.

▶ *What are the different educational placement options that comprise the continuum of services for special education?*

New and innovative placement options and service delivery systems are being developed by the creative professionals who work to see special education evolve and improve. For example, pull-in programs have not yet become part of the federal accountability system but are being implemented in many schools today. Under this fully inclusive system, special education and related services are brought to the individual in the general education setting, instead of having the student go to the services. The more traditional options that tend to comprise the continuum of services include itinerant or consultative general education placements, resource rooms, special education classes or self-contained special education classes, special schools or center schools, and home-bound services.

▶ *How would you compare and contrast the three different program plans: the Individualized Family Service Plan, the Individualized Education Program, and the Individualized Transition Plan?*

For infants and toddlers, PL 99-457 mandates that an Individualized Family Service Plan be developed and implemented. The IFSP must contain information about the child's current functioning levels, the strengths and needs of the family, measurable goals and objectives, the services required and the time of their delivery, and the name of the person responsible for coordination of these services. Developing IFSPs is the responsibility of a multidisciplinary team of professionals who must address the needs of the child and the family. Usually, services are provided by many different professionals, with some or all of these services provided in the child's home. As a culminating activity, the multidisciplinary team assists the child and the family in making a transition to preschool.

Children with disabilities from ages 3 to 21 are served by the public schools. PL 94-142 mandates that Individualized Education Programs be prepared for them. The IEP is the management tool that guides their educational program, including related services. It includes an assessment of the child's present level of educational performance, annual goals and objectives, the extent to which the student will participate in general education, the specific services to be provided, and the date for initiation of those services.

The Individualized Transition Plan must be developed and implemented no later than four years before graduation. The ITP coordinates services from different agencies (the schools, vocational rehabilitation, community services) and helps the student prepare for employment and community-based independent living. ITPs supplement and complement IEPs; its goals and objectives center on skills needed for independent living and work, such as learning how to use public transportation, maintain an apartment, or shop for food and clothing.

Challenge Question

▶ *How should the array of educational services and supports available to students with disabilities be implemented?*

The array of educational services should be, first, individually determined, and second, delivered to support the child with disabilities and his or her family at the intensity the services are required and only for the duration needed for the problem to be met. Participation by the student and the family must be integral components of the educational decision-making process. The development of a partnership among school officials, the student's teachers, the student, and the family should be a most important element that is active when determining and implementing educational services. One criticism of the continuum of special education services model, one that has been widely voiced nationwide for over thirty years, is that it is too lock-stepped. In other words, students become identified with a level of classroom placement and seem unable to move to a less restrictive placement despite the academic and social progress they make. "Once a self-contained special education classroom student, always a special education classroom student" seems to be the common trap of this model. Therefore the array of services model is being used to describe supports and placements because it tends to be a more fluid and flexible approach. The array provides many options of programs, placements, intensities of services, and duration of support. It is neither rigid nor unidimensional.

Scholarly Books

Bateman, B. (1996). Better IEPs: How to develop legally correct and educationally useful programs. Longmont, CO: Sopris West.

Hallahan, D. P., & Kauffman, J. M. (1995). The illusion of inclusion. Austin, TX: Pro-Ed.

Patton, J. R., & Blalock, G. (1996). Transition and students with learning disabilities: Facilitating the movement from school to adult life. Austin, TX: Pro-Ed.

Parent, Professional, and Consumer Organizations and Agencies

American Bar Association: Commission on Mental and Physical Disability Law
1800 M Street, NW
Suite 200 South
Washington, DC 20036-5886
Phone: (202) 662-1570
Web site: http://www.abanet.lrd/disability

National Association of State Directors of Special Education (NASDSE)
1800 Diagonal Road, Suite 320
Alexandria, VA 22314
Phone: (703) 519-3800
Web site: http://www.lrp.com

National Council on Disability
1331 F Street, NW
Washington, DC 20004
Phone: (202) 272-2004
E-mail: mquigley@ncd.gov

National Association of School Psychologists
1929 K Street, Suite 250
Washington, DC 20006
Phone: (301) 657-0270
E-mail: nasp8455@aol.com

Michael A. Naranjo. *The Eagle's Song,* 1992.

Michael Naranjo realized that he wanted to make a career of sculpting during the Vietnam War while recovering from wounds from a grenade explosion that left him blind (Smith & Plimpton, 1993). In the hospital, he was given clay and grew determined to succeed as an artist. Since that time, he has become a leading sculptor. Originally from Santa Clara Pueblo, Naranjo has gained considerable national attention, and many of his works are shown in museums and other important collections, including the White House and the Vatican. He has gained an international reputation as "the artist who sees with his hands." His work reflects his American Indian Pueblo culture and his disability. Observers often note that few of his artwork, whether of animals or people, have eyes.

Multicultural and Bilingual Special Education

3

▼

OVERVIEW

Only about 3 percent of Americans can consider themselves true natives; the rest of us are immigrants or the descendants of immigrants. The diversity of America's schools is changing more rapidly than ever before. Schoolchildren today come from hundreds of different cultures and speak almost as many languages. These children are at great risk for being overidentified as having disabilities and underidentified as being gifted. Culturally and linguistically diverse students with exceptionalities require special education programs that accommodate both their diversity and their disabilities.

▼

FOCUS QUESTIONS

SELF-TEST QUESTIONS

▶ What is meant by multicultural special education, and who is served by these programs?

▶ What is meant by bilingual special education, and who is served by these programs?

▶ Why are educators so concerned about culturally and linguistically diverse children?

▶ In what ways can biases occur in the identification and assessment process?

▶ How can school personnel integrate children's home cultures and languages into the educational environment and curriculum?

CHALLENGE QUESTION

▶ Why is there such a national debate about the issue of overrepresentation of culturally and linguistically diverse students in disability categories and their underrepresentation in gifted education?

A *Personal Perspective*: A Bilingual Education Experience Gone Right

Omar Chavez is a 17-year-old college student who recently completed high school. A very intelligent and talented young man, he began school in the United States with no command of the English language. His dream today is to study astrophysics.

School is a little more challenging in Mexico. They teach you harder stuff at a younger age. It was easy up to the eighth grade. During high school I learned new stuff. The teachers are more strict in Mexico. One teacher takes the second grade class all the way to sixth grade. It's just one teacher.

To this day I don't know why they put me into the sixth grade. It might be because of the language. I was in the seventh grade in Mexico, but when I came to the United States they put me in sixth grade. I think it was because of the language. I was a year or two younger than the rest of the students. We came here on vacation and all of a sudden I found myself in school. I didn't bring my transcript.

I've been successful mostly because of my parents' support and understanding and teachers' support and encouragement. When I was 3, my mom taught me to read and write before I went to school. From the beginning they treated me as if I was really smart. Not like, "You're a kid and you don't need to know this or that!" At first my mom taught me the alphabet. She taught me how to write it despite the fact my mother didn't have the opportunity to complete middle school. That was the first thing I learned. I skipped through first and second grade. I only went to kindergarten for a month. Actually, I didn't mind. It was fun. When I got to second grade, it was fun learning new things. The students were already learning mathematics. I was almost 6. A lot of parents don't take the time; I'm glad mine did. My parents were very involved in my education. They always kept an eye on me and how I was doing. They kept close to me even when I came to school here in Albuquerque. Up to high school in the tenth grade they told me, 'This is your responsibility now. If you fail, it is going to be your fault. We can't keep an eye on you every single day.'

My teachers tried not to treat me differently because I didn't speak English. They tried to encourage me to learn it. They saw that I was getting the stuff okay, but still they tried to encourage me to learn more in spite of my language problem at the time. They realized that I was understanding the stuff pretty well. They didn't do anything to give me more work.

When I first came to the United States, the teacher introduced me to another student. He was the first person I met, and he helped me a lot. The teacher knew he spoke Spanish and English. We were friends throughout middle school and part of high school. One day he dropped out of school. He had to uh, I don't know. Some economical problems or something. I lost track of him.

Since the beginning, when I went from the sixth grade to the eighth grade, I took ESL. I had the same teacher for my ESL classes. This teacher was very supportive of the students in the class. When she taught, she was very calm, and very, very patient with her students. There were a couple of Vietnamese students. I got to meet a lot of interesting people from diverse cultures in the high school. Especially in my communications class. There were some students from Vietnam, China, and India. The teacher was very patient with the students who couldn't understand the lessons well. Sometimes we had tutors going in and working with one special group, like the Vietnamese people or the Hispanics. It was pretty fun.

Up to the eighth grade I had all my classes bilingual. In middle school they have lots of tutors and student teachers. They helped us a lot. Almost 80 percent of the teachers weren't bilingual, so they offered us a bilingual class which used the tutors. The teachers who didn't speak Spanish gave a format to the tutor which described what we were going to do and what we were going to talk about. But that was in the eighth grade and I was speaking and understanding English a little better then. I didn't need it too much. By the time I was in high school I didn't have bilingual classes anymore.

In high school, none of my teachers knew I was in ESL. I was in regular English throughout ninth grade and tenth grade, and my tenth grade teacher recommended me for enriched English. So I took enriched English in my junior year, and during my junior year my teacher recommended me for honors English. My junior and senior year I took honors English. They asked, 'Do you want to do this,' and I said, 'I'll give it a try.' Honors English was a real challenge for me. I did learn, but it was really a challenge."

1. Does Omar fit your stereotype of students who begin school without knowing how to speak English?

2. What challenges do you think you would face if you had to move to a foreign country and begin school without speaking the host language?

3. What do you think contributed to Omar's successes in school?

As it has since its founding, the face of the United States continues to change. At this point in the nation's history, its schools are rapidly becoming different as well. Some experts predict that by the year 2010, white students will be in a minority (Smith-Davis & Billingsley, 1993). They are in many school districts today. It is a fact that the United States is a multicultural country. In and of itself, this is neither bad nor good. It is what we do about and with our diversity, how we treat each other, how we understand each others' similarities and differences, and how we learn from one another that require value judgments. We believe that schools will be better places for all children and their parents if educators both understand and capitalize on their students' diversity of race, ethnicity, culture, language, socioeconomic class, religion, regional differences, and gender. By using this diversity to our advantage, the educational environment can be richer, and all children can flourish.

 MAKING CONNECTIONS

Every chapter includes a Focus on Diversity box that is intended to broaden general understanding and sensitivity to differences in culture.

Multicultural and Bilingual Special Education Defined

Multicultural and bilingual special education is a combination of the fields of multicultural education, bilingual education, and special education. Table 3.1 was designed to help you understand each of these three educational systems. As you study this table, think about how teachers might, using these approaches, stress the acquisition of academic and social skills in culturally and linguistically diverse

TABLE 3.1

Multicultural Education, Bilingual Education, and Bilingual Special Education Definitions

Concept	Definition	Source
Multicultural education	Multicultural education is at least three things: an idea or concept, an educational reform movement, and a process. Multicultural education incorporates the idea that all students—regardless of their gender and social class and their ethnic, racial, or cultural characteristics—should have an equal opportunity to learn in school.	Banks and Banks (1993, p. 3)
Bilingual education	The purpose of this educational methodology is to develop greater competence in English, more proficiency in the dominant language, and increased educational opportunity. While affirming the importance of English, bilingual education uses and develops the child's native language for primary instruction until sufficient command of English is attained.	U.S. Office of Education, Office of Bilingual Education (1980)
Bilingual special education	Bilingual special education begins with an individually designed educational program that uses the home language and home culture, along with English, as the foundations for and the means of delivering special instruction that emphasizes the academic and social needs of the child.	Baca and Cervantes (1989)

 MAKING CONNECTIONS

For more information about the relationships among disabilities and poverty, see
• Causes and Prevention in this chapter,
• Information about access to health care in Chapter 6 (Prevention section).

children with exceptionalities. For these children, their special education needs are important, but it is through language and culture that appropriate special education intervention is enhanced.

Culturally and linguistically diverse students are at greater risk for being identified as having a disability, particularly because of factors associated with poverty (e.g., access to health care). We discuss these issues later in this chapter, but for now it is important that you recognize that many culturally and linguistically diverse students and their families face special circumstances as they seek to benefit from educational opportunities available to them.

Types of Culturally and Linguistically Diverse Students

Sometimes it is helpful to understand how the federal government classifies its citizenry and how people describe themselves. In national census reports and other official documents, citizens are divided into five general ethnic groups: Native

Valuing every student's culture provides a wealth of rich experiences that can enhance instruction about traditional topics.

American, Asian/Pacific Islander, White (non-Hispanic), Hispanic, and Black (African American). The diversity within each of these groups is enormous along a multitude of dimensions: language, home country, years and generations in the United States, ethnicity, and social and economic status (SES).

In addition to classifying students by ethnic groups, educators often base their research and clinical findings on two dimensions of diversity: linguistic and cultural. Remember, these issues are not mutually exclusive. Many students who do not come from the dominant U.S. culture (Western European) also are not native English speakers. Some families have retained their cultural heritage even though they have been in this country for several generations, and many have not. Clearly, it is important not to make any assumptions.

Linguistically Diverse Students. One of the fastest growing segments of the U.S. student population is **limited English proficient (LEP)**, sometimes called English Language Learners (ELL) (U.S. Department of Education, 1993). These students' native languages are not English. In classrooms where English is the language of instruction, their reading, writing, speaking, and understanding skills usually hinder their ability to learn successfully. Their exact number is unknown, but the federal government has made some estimates. It is thought that LEP students represent over 18 percent of the student population in California and possibly over 5 percent of the overall student population in the nation. Nationally, the vast majority (78 percent) of these students are Spanish-speaking, but great variance exists by locale, and changes in regional demographics are occurring rapidly. For example, Asian Americans now constitute over 10 percent of the California school population and are one-fourth of the LEP population in that state (Cheng, 1995).

The challenges these students present school district personnel are great. Some of these students come to school speaking no English. Many others are able to communicate in English but are not proficient enough to profit from academic instruction without supports. And, being able to determine when they have truly mastered the language can be difficult. The challenges these students present are compounded by the number of languages they speak. In four school districts—New York City; Chicago; Los Angeles; and Fairfax County, Virginia—children speak over 100 languages. Not enough teachers who speak these children's native languages are available. For example, in 1993, California had only 87 certified bilingual education teachers for 159,380 Southeast Asian LEP students. Only one could speak Lao, another could speak Cambodian, two spoke Hmong, and 83 spoke Vietnamese (Cheng, 1995). Those children who did not have a teacher who could speak their language had to rely on assistance from a paraprofessional for language support, when someone was available.

As you will learn in this chapter, many of these students are at great risk of being incorrectly identified as having a disability. Their language differences do impair their educational opportunities and can mask their potential. Clearly, they do need special programs. For those students without disabilities, however, the answer should *not* be special education.

Culturally Diverse Students. Only about 3 percent of us can claim native status (American Indians, Eskimos, Aleutian Islanders, and Hawaiians), and such diversity demands changes in the way teachers teach (Siccone, 1995). As there are hundreds of languages spoken at schools across the nation, there must be thou-

 MAKING CONNECTIONS

See the Prevalence section found later in this chapter.

 MAKING CONNECTIONS

More about literacy, see
• Reading section (Educational Interventions) in Chapter 4,
• Cognitive and Academic Performance (Children with Speech or Language Impairments) in Chapter 5.

 MAKING CONNECTIONS

More information about language development is located in this chapter in these sections:
• Language and Communication Differences (Culturally and Linguistically Diverse Children with Exceptionalities)
• Language and Instruction (Educational Interventions)
Additional information is also located in other chapters:
• Language instruction (Educational Interventions) in Chapter 5
• Focus on Diversity box in Chapter 4

limited English proficient (LEP). Limited ability to read, write, or speak English.

sands of different cultures represented by its schoolchildren. Many demographers believe that by the year 2000, over one-third of our nation's children will come from historically underrepresented groups (Gottlieb, Alter, Gottlieb, & Wishner, 1994). Today, they are the majority in states such as California, Texas, and New Mexico. Being from a culture different from the dominant American culture does not directly cause disabilities or poor academic performance. However, culturally diverse students are more likely to live in poverty, a definite risk factor for having a disability. And, culture does influence an individual's learning style and experiences, influences which must be reflected in the assessment process and in the delivery of instruction (U.S. Department of Education, 1993).

Why should educators be aware of and sensitive to cultural differences? Let's start with the basics. What is culture? Banks and Banks (1993) help us better understand the term and the concept *culture*, which to them

> consists of knowledge, concepts, and values shared by group members through systems of communication. Culture also consists of shared beliefs, symbols, and interpretation within a human group... .The essence of a culture is not its artifacts, tools, or other tangible cultural elements but how the members of the group interpret, use and perceive them. It is the values, symbols, interpretations, and perspectives that distinguish one people from another. . . .(p. 8)

Why is culture important to children and their schooling? The values, traditions, and beliefs that children bring to school provide the experiences on which new knowledge is learned and understood. Children from different backgrounds often approach learning in different ways, and if the instructional methods used at school conflict with their home culture, their educational performance can ultimately be affected. For example, some cultures value cooperation and do not value competitiveness. For children from these cultures, cooperative learning activities rather than competitive games might be better instructional strategies to implement.

Certainly, educators must be sensitive to children's cultural and learning styles when they select their instructional methods, but that is not enough. They must also respect these students and the cultures they come from (Ogbu, 1992). What teachers do and say sends important messages to children about their abilities and their worth. So, too, do the curriculum adopted and the instructional materials used. Children learn best when they can associate new concepts with those they have already learned and understand. Banks (1994a) suggests that the curriculum should be modified to reflect "the experiences, cultures, and perspectives of a range of cultural and ethnic groups as well as both genders" (p. 11). The benefits of broadening the curriculum can be many. The motivational levels of students are peaked when they learn information they can associate with and build on. They will learn that there are many different approaches to solving problems and understanding perspectives about daily situations.

A Very Special Population: Native Americans. According to the 1990 census, 1.9 million Americans (0.8 percent of the population) claimed Native American[1] status. Of those, about 637,000 lived on reservations or trust lands. Half of the Native American population is concentrated in five states (Oklahoma,

MAKING CONNECTIONS

See Cultural Differences (Culturally and Linguistically Diverse Children with Exceptionalities) in this chapter.

---

[1] The term *Native American* includes Alaskan Natives, Aleuts, and American Indians.

California, Arizona, New Mexico, and Utah). Navajo Nation claims the largest resident population (143,000 people). The Native American population increased by 54 percent between 1980 and 1990 because of a high birthrate and a reduced infant mortality rate. As a group, they are disadvantaged in many ways. They have high rates of unemployment and poverty, low educational attainment, a 36 percent dropout rate (25 percent higher than the national average), and increased health problems (U.S. Department of Education, 1994). These students are more likely to attend isolated, rural schools that offer few resources. Native Americans speak as many as 187 languages, and many of these children, particularly those living in rural areas and on reservations, come to school without previous exposure to the English language (Krause, 1992). Unfortunately, many of the teachers do not speak these children's native languages or understand the student's cultures, which are often in conflict with their own. Many questions have been raised about these children and their education. Should individual tribes take over educational responsibilities for their children? Should the Bureau of Indian Affairs retain some role in the education of Indian children? Should states insist that the curriculum offered on reservations match the curriculum taught in that state's local public schools? Clearly, how to better meet the needs of these children will be a continuing debate well into the next century.

MAKING CONNECTIONS

The Concept and Controversies section in Chapter 7 reinforces these concepts.

Identification

In recent years, we have come to understand that standardized tests used in our schools frequently discriminate against culturally and linguistically diverse students. In the early 1970s, it became apparent that standard methods of testing and

Sometimes, assessment and testing situations discriminate against culturally and linguistically diverse students. Every attempt must be made to help all children reach their potential.

MAKING CONNECTIONS

This chapter's History section provides more information about these and other court cases.

evaluation were identifying too many of them as having disabilities and too few as being gifted. The question, "Are intelligence (IQ) tests discriminating against culturally and linguistically diverse students?" was asked and reasked over and over during the 1970s by educators, policymakers, court judges, and parents. Two California cases, *Larry P. v. Riles* and *Diana v. State Board of Education*, dramatically illustrated the problem. These cases brought national attention to the overrepresentation of African American children in classes for students with mental retardation, the misidentification of bilingual children as having disabilities, and the possibility of discrimination in intelligence testing.

How can discrimination in the testing process occur? There are many reasons for bias, but some of the major ones are worthy of attention and thought. The content level of the test's items might give preference toward specific groups' experiences and interests. For example, asking a child who has never been fishing to explain how to bait a fishing line might negatively affect the impression others have of that child's expressive language and cognitive abilities. When minority groups are not represented in the standardization population, or when an individual untrained in multicultural and bilingual techniques conducts the evaluation, opportunities for unfair evaluations are created. To stress the importance of nonbiased evaluations, IDEA requires that **nondiscriminatory testing** be established in each state:

> procedures to assure that testing and evaluation materials and procedures utilized for the purpose of evaluation and placement of children with disabilities will be selected and administered so as not to be racially or culturally discriminatory. Such materials or procedures shall be provided and administered in the child's native language or mode of communication, unless it is clearly not feasible to do so, and no single procedure shall be the sole criterion for determining an appropriate educational program for a child. (20 U.S.C. section 1412 [5] [C])

Courts have challenged schools' use of standardized tests of intelligence, saying that they place many students from various ethnic and racial groups at a disadvantage because many of the test items are unfair to students from different cultures. The use of such tests has contributed to some students being misidentified as having a disability; for others, test results present an incorrect and depressed picture of their abilities. Remember, the underrepresentation of these students in gifted education is just as unfortunate as their overrepresentation in disability categories. Despite all of the negative attention given to IQ and other standardized tests and despite decisions in the courts indicating that bias exists in these testing procedures, standardized tests of intelligence are still the most common, single source of information used to identify youngsters for gifted education (Maker, 1994). One way to minimize bias is for educators to use their professional judgment when making important decisions about children and their education. Many factors not revealed with standardized tests should be considered: family history, students' length of stay in the United States, socioeconomic status, prior educational experience, and cultural background (Cuccaro, 1996).

Partially because identification of students with disabilities is not always an easy task, educators rely on what appears to be the simplest and most clear-cut form of student evaluation: the standardized test. Unfortunately, these tests do not guarantee fair or accurate results. Some exceptionalities are especially difficult to diagnose when the child has difficulty with English. For example, the diagnosis of a learning disability usually depends on a significant discrepancy between the IQ

nondiscriminatory testing. Assessment that properly takes into account a child's cultural and linguistic diversity.

and academic achievement scores. The first problem is that children with genuine learning disabilities may not be identified because they do not show the necessary discrepancy between potential and achievement to qualify for services. These children may get an artificially low IQ score because they do not have proficient language skills in English (Palmer, Olivarez, Willson, & Fordyce, 1989). The second problem is that some children may be wrongly identified as having a learning disability when, in fact, it is their difficulty with English—their underachievement in a second language—that is the problem (Ruiz, 1995a). Underachievement, language differences, or differences in cultural experiences can cause children to score so low on an achievement test that it artificially creates an IQ/achievement discrepancy that is then misinterpreted as a learning disability. Third, to find a speech or language impairment in a bilingual child, the impairment must occur in the dominant language. For example, a Spanish-speaking child who converses perfectly in Spanish with his brothers on the playground but who has limited ability to discuss academic subjects in English in the classroom certainly has a problem; however, it is due to a communication difference, not a language impairment. Caution is advised, though, when the child is tested using native language instruments. When the child's school instruction has not been in the native language, the child can appear to have a problem because diagnostic instruments primarily assess school language.

Even with the great attention educators pay to potential problems of discrimination in the testing process, bias is often present in the assessment procedures used in the educational system today. In fact, some believe that bias can never be eliminated from the identification process, only reduced (Salas, 1994). It has been suggested that the concept of nonbiased assessment should be changed to "least biased assessment." Because of the continuing problems with traditional assessment procedures, diagnosticians should change the nation's identification and assessment processes. Progress is being made, and we have selected a few innovations to share here.

One problem with standardized tests is that they take a very narrow view of intelligence. Students from culturally and linguistically diverse groups will continue to be unidentified, misidentified, and underrepresented until such time that alternative culturally relevant indicators of giftedness are used in the assessment process (Callahan & McIntire, 1994). For over a decade, educators have had a growing interest in Gardner's (1983) theory of **multiple intelligences**. To Gardner, intelligence centers on problem solving abilities. He identified seven different intelligences: linguistic, logical-mathematical, spatial, musical, bodily-kinesthetic, interpersonal, and intrapersonal. Maker and her colleagues (Maker, Nielson, & Rogers, 1994) applied Gardner's theory to children from diverse backgrounds. They make the point that one's culture may influence how giftedness is expressed. They give the example that oral storytelling may be a common form of linguistic giftedness in one culture, where writing a novel may be another form in another culture. Maker and her colleagues developed a matrix of problem solving skills requiring a range of divergent and convergent thinking across Gardner's seven intelligences. They claim that students identified as gifted through this process, many of whom are not so recognized through traditional methods, do exceptionally well in special enrichment programs. In fact, culturally and linguistically diverse students identified in this way often make gains equal to or greater than those of students identified through the standard IQ testing process.

MAKING CONNECTIONS

The Defined section in Chapter 4 includes information about the identification of students with learning disabilities.

MAKING CONNECTIONS

The theory of multiple intelligences is discussed in the Defined section of Chapter 7.

multiple intelligences. A multidimensional approach to intelligence, providing an alternative view for the concept of IQ, allowing those exceptional in any one of seven areas to be identified as being gifted.

Some other innovative and performance-based diagnostic procedures, such as authentic and portfolio assessments, have particular merit for students at risk for over- or underrepresentation in special education (Figueroa & Garcia, 1994). Ruiz (1995a; 1995b) suggests that small-group activities in the classroom—oral language story building, combination reading and written language lesson, story writing—can be used for both instruction and assessment. The result is a better understanding of individual bilingual children's communicative competence and intellectual abilities than what often results from traditional diagnostic procedures. Remember, language differences are not the only source of concern when identifying diverse youngsters for special education services. Differences in culture, style, and values also demand flexible ways to identify students as having exceptional learning needs. Patton (1992) argues that a new schema incorporating African American world views must guide the development of tests and procedures for that group of students. The methods used to identify children need to change depending on the individual's situation, family, culture, and region. Particularly for gifted education programs, the referral process should change and include input from multiple sources such as parents, extended family members, church and community leaders, and service clubs (Patton & Baytops, 1995). The argument for innovative and flexible identification procedures can be made for all children, but particularly for those who are culturally and linguistically diverse.

MAKING CONNECTIONS

Concerns about the low percentage of students from diverse backgrounds served in gifted education are also examined in
• Gifted Students Who Are Culturally and Linguistically Diverse (Gifted Children) in Chapter 7,
• Focus on Diversity box in Chapter 7,
• Prevalence section of this chapter.

Significance

Unfortunately, many educators lack positive attitudes about students who do not come from the dominant culture or from a middle-class background (Banks, 1994a). When teachers believe students from a language-different background, students of color, and low-income students are unable to achieve at high levels of academic achievement, their expectations for these students are lower. Without high expectations for students, many teachers tend to slow the pace of instruction, select instructional materials that are not challenging, and teach "down" to their students. The result of such negative attitudes and low expectations often is low achievement. Banks (1994a) also maintains that students tend to internalize negative expectations and perceptions. In some cases, such negative attitudes may come from parents' cynicism from their own experiences with American society (Erickson, 1993). Internalizing negative attitudes can lead to reduced motivation to learn difficult skills and concepts. Educators must create positive learning climates in which children are stimulated to do their best, supported to take risks, and encouraged to have fun learning.

To be more effective when working with all of their students' families, educators must become more aware of the cultures their students come from and be sensitive to differing cultural values and beliefs. Differences in cultural perceptions about disabilities are interesting, but sensitivity to these perceptions can be critical when working with different families. Educators should be aware of how each of their student's culture views disabilities, what that culture believes causes disabilities, and what can be done about them. They also need to know whether blame, guilt, shame, or rejection is associated with a disability. This knowledge can influence how educators communicate, interact, and involve families in their child's educational program.

Perceptions About Disabilities

Attitudes about disabilities vary from culture to culture. Different religions hold very different rationales about why disabilities occur and how they reflect on the family. These beliefs are most likely based in folk beliefs, superstitions, and tradition, and understanding the cultural perceptions about disability held by individual families can greatly improve home–school interactions (Cheng, Nakasato, & Wallace, 1995). For example, educators who understand the differences among cultures will reflect that understanding when working with the families of their students with disabilities. Buddhists believe that nothing can be done about a disability and that it is established by karma, or fate. Most Pacific Islanders believe that disabilities are the result of an ancestor's wrongdoing, with the result being guilt and shame. Many from the Philippines view disabilities as a curse and often reject the individual with the disability. The Chamorro culture holds that a birth defect or a disability is a gift from God and the individual with the disability is protected and sheltered by everyone in the community. Knowledge about a family's cultural beliefs and orientation can help educators work with them during the development of the individualized education plan through the implementation of the student's educational program.

History of the Field

Education in the United States has been faced with issues of bilingualism and multiculturalism throughout its history. In the late nineteenth and early twentieth centuries, total exclusion (or separate language schools) began to give way to a new era of "Americanization." Antiforeign feelings and sentiments were on the rise. The guiding principle during the new period was the **melting pot** model, in which individuals were expected to assimilate and abandon their home languages and cultures as soon as possible for a new, homogenized American experience. But the melting pot model appears to have failed. Instead of creating a harmonious new culture, it led to racism, segregation, poverty, and aggression toward individuals in each new immigrant group. It also led to a loss of the richness that can result when a country welcomes many cultures and languages.

Cultural pluralism, a model that was reproposed in the 1960s, actually emerged in the early years of the twentieth century (between 1915 and 1925) as an alternative to the assimilation argument (Banks, 1994a). Cultural pluralism does not require abandoning one's home culture, as did the melting pot model. Rather, it allows people to maintain their various ethnic languages, cultures, and institutions while encouraging their participation in society as a whole. Both early in the century and later, the belief was that diversity would enrich the nation and guide the development of policies for educational and social systems.

melting pot. The concept of an homogenized United States where cultural traditions and home languages are abandoned for the new American culture.

cultural pluralism. All cultural groups are valued components of the society, and the language and traditions of each group are maintained.

MAKING CONNECTIONS

See the sections on
Overrepresentation and
Underrepresentation (Prevalence) in
this chapter.

The concern about overrepresentation of culturally and linguistically diverse students in disability categories is not new. This issue was brought to national attention in several ways. First, in 1968, Lloyd Dunn published an article in which he estimated that

> about 60 percent to 80 percent of the pupils in special education classes [for mental retardation] are children from low status backgrounds—including Afro-Americans, American Indians, Mexicans, and Puerto Rican Americans, those from nonstandard English-speaking, broken, disorganized, and inadequate homes; and children from other non middle class environments (p. 6).

In 1970, the President's Committee on Mental Retardation (PCMR) published *The Six Hour Retarded Child*, which dramatically exposed the ways in which cultural differences were causing some children to be inappropriately labeled as having mental retardation. In California, also in 1970, the case of *Diana v. State Board of Education* began to bring issues about bias in the assessment process into focus. This case was a class action suit on behalf of Hispanic children placed in classrooms for students with mental retardation on the basis of IQ tests that were argued to be discriminatory. Additionally in California, the case of *Larry P. v. Riles* (1971) brought to the attention of the courts and schools the overrepresentation of African American children in classes for students with mental retardation and the possibility of discrimination in intelligence testing. In 1974, the U.S. Supreme Court ruled in a case brought in San Francisco on behalf of students with limited English proficiency (LEP) who were Chinese speaking (*Lau v. Nichols*, 1974). Following the favorable decision in Lau, Congress enacted legislation that incorporated the Court's rationale:

> Public education is not a "right" granted to individuals by the Constitution. But neither is it merely some governmental "benefit" indistinguishable from other forms of social welfare legislation. Both the importance of education in maintaining our basic institutions, and the lasting impact of its deprivation on the life of the child, mark the distinction. The American people have always regarded education and the acquisition of knowledge as matters of supreme importance. We have recognized the public school as a most vital civic institution for the preservation of a democratic system of government, and as the primary vehicle for transmitting the values on which our society rests. As noted early in our history, some degree of education is necessary to prepare citizens to participate effectively and intelligently in our open political system if we are to preserve freedom and independence . . . .
> In sum, education has a fundamental role in maintaining the fabric of our society. We cannot ignore the significant social costs borne by our Nation when select groups are denied the means to absorb the values and skills upon which our social order rests. (Citations omitted; p. 2397)

Nationally normed, standardized tests continue to be at the center of concern about accurate identification of diverse students. Jane Mercer (1973) viewed mental retardation from a sociological perspective (rather than a psychological construct). She extended her work from theory to practice with the development of a test aimed at reducing bias in the identification process. The test, called *The System of Multicultural Pluralistic Assessment (SOMPA)*, significantly decreased the number of African American and Hispanic children placed in special education classes (Gonzales, 1989).

Attention to the very special learning needs of this unique and heterogeneous group of learners was brought to the professional community in the professional literature. The journal of the Council for Exceptional Children, *Exceptional Children*, published a special issue on cultural diversity in 1974 (Bransford, Baca, & Lane, 1974) that brought together many authors to discuss multicultural and bilingual special education issues. Several landmark books called professionals' attention to the unique learning needs of these students. For example, Donna Gollnick and Phil Chinn in their 1983 landmark book, *Multicultural Education in a Pluralistic Society,* helped educators better understand the influence of culture on children's educational performance. Len Baca and Hermes Cervantes's textbook, *The Bilingual Special Education Interface*, first published in 1984, brought the question of language-different youngsters with disabilities to the attention of people in the fields of multicultural education, bilingual education, and special education.

Children's right to an education even gained the attention of the courts. Some states attempted to limit the right to education and to exclude culturally and linguistically diverse children who are not citizens (children who are undocumented and do not have immigration papers). In 1982, the Supreme Court decided a Texas case that questioned whether undocumented children of Mexican nationals residing in Texas without proper documentation had a right to free public school education (*Phyler v. Doe,* 1982). The Supreme Court ruled that children do have this right. Interestingly, history seems to be repeating itself. In 1994, California voters passed Proposition 187 prohibiting undocumented immigrants from receiving public benefits, including education. This component of Proposition 187 was put on the state ballot despite the *Phyler v. Doe* decision but was later ruled illegal by the federal government.

All children living in America have a right to an education and the opportunity to profit from the educational system. Without this right, they will be excluded from mainstream society.

Prevalence

The number of children and youth from different ethnic groups served in special education should reflect the prevalence of those groups in the general population. So, are the nation's demographics changing? The following data come from a variety of sources. Put together, they describe a very different present and future for our nation's schools.

- Between 1980 and 1990, the total U.S. population grew by 9.8 percent with whites experiencing the smallest proportional increase (Bureau of the Census, 1991).

- Approximately 32 percent of today's public school students are from historically underrepresented groups (Office of Civil Rights, 1992).

- In 1990, white students made up 70 percent of the U.S. student population, but by 2026, they may well comprise only 30 percent (Figueroa & Garcia, 1994).

- In twenty-five of the nation's largest public school systems, over half of the student population today is from minority groups (Zawaiza, 1995).

- By the turn of the century, Hispanics may well comprise more than 25 percent of the school population (Center for Research on Elementary and Middle Schools, 1990).

- The number of students from many ethnic and racial groups identified as having a disability is disproportionately high, with some groups having twice the percentage identified as the white group (Harry, 1992a; 1994).

- Placement rates of Hispanic and Native American students in special education tend not to indicate overrepresentation when aggregated nationally, but when analyzed by state, a different picture is apparent (Harry, 1992a).

- African American students, even when national data are presented, are overrepresented in classes for students with mental retardation, at almost twice the expected rate (Harry, 1992a).

- Only 10 percent of today's teachers are from historically underrepresented groups, and that percentage will drop to 5 percent by the year 2000 (Smith-Davis & Billingsley, 1993).

- California, Texas, New York, and Florida have the largest number of documented LEP students and also the largest concentration of illegal immigrants, which in 1993 was estimated to be over 3.3 million nationally (Booth, 1993).

- Six states (California, Texas, New York, Illinois, New Jersey, and Florida) have 72 percent of all LEP students in the nation (Cheng & Chang, 1995).

What are the implications of these demographic statistics? While the U.S. population grew by almost 10 percent, the Bureau of the Census (1991) reports that this growth was not evenly distributed across racial and ethnic groups (whites increased by 6 percent, African Americans by 13 percent, Native Americans by 38 percent, Hispanics by 53 percent, and Asians/Pacific Islanders by 108 percent). The Office of Civil Rights and the U.S. Department of Education (Harry, 1994) reported the following make-up of America's school population in 1990: 68 percent white, 16 percent African American, 12 percent

Hispanic, 3 percent Asian American, and 1 percent Native American. If growth continues at these rates, whites will be a minority group during the life-time of children born today.

The demographics of American inner cities are quite different from the national picture. Let's look at New York City as an example. In this city school district, 93 percent of the entire school population are members of minority groups and 80 percent live in poverty. Most of the city's students in special education are culturally and linguistically diverse and poor: 95 percent are from a minority group, 70 percent are male, the vast majority are poor, 75–90 percent are from single families, 44 percent come from households where English is not the primary language spoken, and 19 percent are foreign born (Gottlieb et al., 1994).

The fact that these children are from diverse backgrounds should not be disturbing. What should be disconcerting is the fact that youngsters from underrepresented groups have a much higher probability of being born of mothers who did not receive early prenatal care, living in poverty, having limited access to health care, and being raised in a single-parent household (*CDF Reports,* 1995). All of these factors put these children at great risk of having a disability. In addition, for many of them their cultural and language differences increase their chances for failure in the educational system and being referred to special education. As we discuss in the next section of this chapter, many of these youngsters are misidentified.

 MAKING CONNECTIONS

For more information about the importance of access to health care, see the Causes and Prevention section in Chapter 6.

Overrepresentation

From the early days of special education, professionals called the nation's attention to the disproportionate participation of various racial and ethnic groups in special education programs (Deno, 1970; Dunn, 1968). Over twenty-five years ago, higher percentages of African American students than should be expected were identified as having mental retardation. Despite the attention that overrepresentation of some of these groups of students in some disability categories received in the press, in the courts (e.g., *Diana v. State Board of Education, Larry P. v. Riles, Lau v. Nichols*), in Congress (e.g., Individuals with Disabilities Act, 1990), and by the federal government (e.g., U.S. Department of Education, 1993), the situation persists. Although some of the national data should cause concern, the data from some locales are truly alarming.

First, consider the national data. While African American students make up 12 percent of the public education student body, they comprise 24 percent of the special education population (Artiles & Trent, 1994). While Hispanics are somewhat underrepresented in most special education categories, they are almost twice as likely to be identified as having moderate mental retardation (Harry, 1994). Students from an Asian background are less than half as likely to be identified as having a disability (U.S. Department of Education, 1993).

At the local level, more disconcerting data are available. Harry (1994) reports that in areas in which certain ethnic groups are more prevalent, more alarming identification patterns prevail. For example, in Alaska Native American students account for 25 percent of the total population, but comprise 44 percent of the placements in classes for students with mild mental retardation, 35 percent in classes for students with moderate mental retardation, 26 percent in classes for students with serious emotional disturbance, and 36 percent in classes for stu-

 MAKING CONNECTIONS

For more information about mental retardation, see Chapter 6.

 MAKING CONNECTIONS

Entire chapter coverage is devoted to these specific disabilities; for more about
• learning disabilities, see Chapter 4;
• giftedness, see Chapter 7;
• emotional disturbance and behavioral disorders, see Chapter 8.

Prevalence ⟿ **93**

dents with learning disabilities. She reports similar patterns in North and South Dakota and in Montana. In Arizona, where Hispanics comprise 26 percent of the school population, these students are clearly overrepresented in almost all disability categories and substantially underrepresented in the gifted education. Table 3.2 provides us with some "red flags" that might indicate that diverse students are improperly being identified for special education services.

Is overrepresentation in disability categories a problem? This is a complex question. Possibly, the simplest answer is no if special education is truly and universally special. Unfortunately, in many cases it is not very special and does not lead to positive outcomes for children (Gottlieb et al., 1994). For many it leads to lower educational expectations and stigmatization. The problem is compounded because special education is plagued by an excessive number of untrained teachers (those teaching before they are licensed) and a high attrition rate (Smith-Davis & Billingsley, 1993). Reschly (1991) and his colleagues (Reschly, Kicklighter, & McKee, 1988) take the position that the overall identification of students with disabilities is small (7.7 percent for African Americans, 5.33 percent for Hispanics, and 5.73 percent for whites). Also, Reschly maintains that the high correlation of poverty to disabilities and the high probability of members of minority groups being in the lower-income categories explains the higher rate of special education identification for these groups of students. It is also more likely that poor children are less ready for school and that children who are not from the dominant culture and language system are more vulnerable to school failure.

Underrepresentation

Although Asian Americans are underrepresented in disabilities categories, they are twice as likely to be identified as gifted (U.S. Department of Education, 1993). Remember the statistics about Native American students in Alaska, Montana, South Dakota, and Arizona; these students are overwhelmingly identified as having disabilities. In Alaska, for example, where Native Americans comprise 25 percent of the population, only 15 percent of them are receiving educational services in gifted programs (Harry, 1994).

Causes and Prevention of Disabilities in Diverse Students

Diversity does not cause disabilities, of course, although poverty and related life circumstances can result in a variety of disabilities. Also remember Reschly's premise about the correlation between poverty and disabilities. This is important, but the impact of multiculturalism must be separated from the effects of poverty. Terrible mistakes are made when people assume that all diverse students are poor or all poor students have disabilities. In fact, the economic conditions for many families from historically underrepresented groups have improved greatly over the last decades. Many culturally and linguistically diverse students do not live in poverty. For those who do, the effects of poverty are sometimes confused with the effects of their diversity. The issues of multiculturalism, bilingualism, cultural and linguistic diversity, and poverty are complex and intertwined. It is important not to oversimplify the causes of disabilities in students from diverse backgrounds or how they can be prevented.

TABLE 3.2

Danger Signs of Overrepresentation of Minorities in Special Education

The following "red flags" may indicate that a school or district has a disproportionate number of students from diverse cultures in special education programs:

- High proportions of special education students that are ethnically diverse

- High proportions of culturally diverse students within certain special education programs, such as programs for behavior impairment or mental retardation

- Students of all races and ethnic groups not having equal access to a district's prereferral intervention program or the same quality of program

- High number of students from one race or ethnic group being referred for evaluation

- Reasons given for special education referrals being disproportionate by race or ethnicity

- Patterns of placement differing by race or ethnicity

Source: Developed by J. Peenan, September 1995, *CEC Today, 2,* p. 7. Reprinted by permission.

Causes

Social and economic inequities have a significant impact on our nation's children (Children's Defense Fund, 1995; Kozol, 1991, 1995; Reed & Sautter, 1990). Childhood poverty is a major problem in the United States, and one that is rising. According to the Children's Defense Fund (1995), almost 23 percent (15.7 million) of our nation's children live in poverty, and 27 percent of them are under age 3. Minority children are more likely to live in poverty: 46 percent of African American children, 41 percent of Hispanic children, compared to 14 percent of white children. Because they have reduced access to health care, poor children are more than two times more likely to have physical and cognitive impairments. Why might this be so? One reason is access to health insurance and health care. For example, in 1993, one in seven (9.4 million) children and 500,000 pregnant women were uninsured (Children's Defense Fund, 1995). As you will learn throughout this text, prenatal care is a very important factor in the prevention of disabilities. In 1992, 4.2 percent of white women and 9.9 percent of African American women received late or no prenatal care, clearly putting their babies at risk for disabilities (Black Community Crusade for Children and the Children's Defense Fund, 1995).

Causation of disabilities should also be viewed within its cultural context. Different cultures sometimes think about the causes of disabilities in children differently. In general, people from the dominant American culture believe in a direct scientific cause-and-effect relationship between a biological problem and the developing baby. Those from other cultures may, in contrast, consider fate, bad luck, sins of a parent, food the mother ate, or evil spirits potential causes of disabilities (Cheng, 1995; Hanson, Lynch, & Wayman, 1990). These alternative views affect the way a child with a disability is considered within the culture and the types of intervention services a family might be willing to pursue to address the child's disabilities and needs.

 MAKING CONNECTIONS

The importance of expectant mother's prenatal care is stressed throughout the text, particularly in the causes and prevention sections. Specifically see those sections in
- Chapter 5,
- Chapter 6.

~~~

TABLE 3.3

Comparison of Cost of Prevention to Cost of Supports

A Healthy Start

All children need basic health care. The following costs and savings apply to every child.

$1 on childhood immunizations	saves	$10.00 in later medical costs
$1 on comprehensive maternity care for pregnant women	saves	$3.38 in later medical costs
$1 on food and nutrition counseling for pregnant women in the Special Supplemental Food Program for Women, Infants, and Children (WIC)	saves	$3.13 in Medicaid costs due to low–birth weight babies

A Head Start

Good preschool and comprehensive child care help children get ready for school, keep up in school, and prepare for future work.

$1 for quality preschool education like comprehensive Headstart	saves	at least $3.00 in later special education, crime, welfare, and other costs

A Fair Start

All parents need adequate income. All parents should support their children to the best of their ability. Children's parents need jobs at decent wages, income supports, fair tax policies, and paid parental leave so that parents have an option to remain at home to meet children's needs. Parents also need quality child care if they choose to work outside the home. Preserving families through family preservation services rather than breaking them up through foster care, and decent, stable housing rather than homeless shelters must be incorporated in social policy for all children and families.

$1 for comprehensive job training, education, and support services through the Job Corps	saves	$1.46 in later crime, welfare, and other costs and lost tax revenues
$765 a month for homelessness prevention and support services (in one model program)	saves	$3,000 a month to shelter a homeless family in a hotel
$4,500 per family for family preservation services that help keep families together	saves	$10,000 for one year of foster family care for one child

Source: The State of America's Children (p. xv) by Children's Defense Fund, 1992, (Washington, DC: Author). Reprinted by permission.

Inappropriately referring culturally and linguistically diverse children to educational diagnosticians can increase the likelihood of misidentifying children. Inappropriate referrals of these students to special education has led to the incorrect labeling of some students as having disabilities as in the situation we described for *Larry P. v. Riles*. On the other hand, the denial of services to children whose exceptionalities are overlooked can cause their disabilities to intensify over time or their giftedness to be ignored and potential inhibited.

Prevention

Prevention should be considered an investment, both in human and in financial terms. Compare the cost of prevention to the cost of supports in Table 3.3.

Prevention can be directly tied to immunization for preventable diseases. For example, the shock of the measles epidemic of 1989, when nearly 60,000 Americans (40 percent of whom were preschoolers) were struck by this terrible disease, caused health officials to renew efforts to protect all Americans from this and other diseases. As seen in Figure 3.1, the situation has improved, but rates are still unacceptable with only 67 percent of 2-year-olds fully immunized (Children's Defense Fund, 1995). This situation left more than one million 2-year-olds vulnerable to preventable diseases like measles, tetanus, polio, and hepatitis B. One federal program has made a difference. Called "Vaccines for Children," this program was passed in 1993 and implemented in the last months of 1994. In eighteen months, this program was clearly the reason more American toddlers are protected from disease. In that short time, the percentage of those fully immunized rose from

 MAKING CONNECTIONS

Immunizations and the prevention of disabilities is discussed in Chapter 5 in these sections:
• Prevention
• Concepts and Controversy

FIGURE 3.1

Immunization Shortfall: Percentage of Children Ages 19–35 Months Not Adequately Immunized

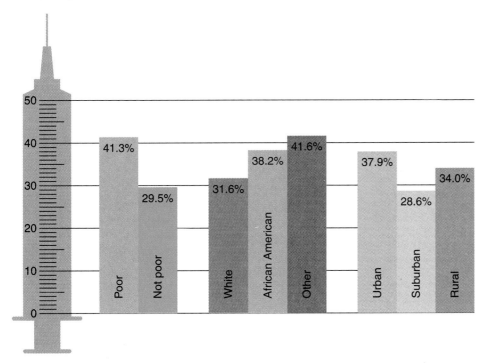

Source: From The *State of America's Children: Yearbook* (p.32) by Children's Defense Fund, 1995, Washington, DC: Author. Reprinted by permission.

30 percent to 55 percent (*CDF Reports,* August 1995). Although there is still great room for improvement, this program is a great start to correcting one factor (prevention of disease through access to vaccines) that contributes to the prevalence of disabilities.

Exceptional Culturally and Linguistically Diverse Children

Culturally and linguistically diverse children with special education needs often have problems in several unique areas. First, language and communication differences can cause challenges for these children and for special education personnel. Second, cultural differences may raise questions about the behavior of these children and their families and about the appropriateness of interventions. In addition, mobility (homelessness, migrant worker transience, or refugee circumstances) can add stress and logistical difficulties to educating some children.

Language and Communication Differences

By definition, culturally and linguistically diverse children exhibit language and communication differences that sometimes raise educational issues (Langdon with Cheng, 1992). Some children may speak forms of a language that vary from its literate or standard form. For example, the spoken Spanish used in South Texas usually varies from the spoken Spanish used in New Mexico, both of which may vary from the standard form of Spanish. These variations are dialects and should not

Communication skills are important components of many students' IEPs and result in improved abilities for meaningful human interactions throughout their lives.

automatically be considered language deficiencies. Some languages do not have certain sounds or grammatical structures found in English. For example, the *f*, *r*, *th*, *v*, and *z* sounds do not exist in Korean. Many English consonant sounds do not exist in Chinese, so a Chinese-speaking child's difficulty with some English sounds may be a result of the child's inexperience with the sounds rather than a speech or language impairment. Although many of these children are referred for speech therapy for an articulation problem, the distinctive speech is simply an accent and therapy is unnecessary.

Language is a major issue for many students, even those who speak English at home. Many African American children, for example, come to school speaking a **dialect** of English. While many Hispanic children come to school speaking Spanish, some come to school speaking combinations of two languages (Sileo, Sileo, & Prather, 1996). Native Americans speak over 187 different languages (Krause, 1992), and people from Southeast Asia and the Pacific speak hundreds of different languages and dialects (Cheng & Chang, 1995). Regardless of the language or dialect a child speaks, Banks (1994a) reminds us that it should be respected while the youngster learns to use the standard English skills required in school. It is estimated that over 14 percent of the current school population does not speak English at home (Waggoner, 1993). When there is a critical mass of these youngsters (enough speaking the same language), many professionals recommend that a bilingual education approach be implemented (Cheng, 1995). Under this system, children are taught in both their primary language and in English until such time that their English proficiency is good enough to benefit from academic instruction in this language.

Some educators are facing new and troubling challenges with a small but growing group of youngsters (Pyle, 1996). More than 6,800 preschool, kindergarten, and first graders in the Los Angeles Unified School district have been identified as being nonverbal in both English and their home language. Called "non-nons," these youngsters (who do not have mental retardation) have increased in number by over 7 percent in just a two-year period. These students need intensive early intervention to develop the speech and language skills necessary to succeed in school. For them, special preschool programs are crucial.

As you have learned, language and communication differences influence students' oral language skills and their overall academic performance. Recognize that these differences also affect the acquisition of reading, a skill imperative to academic success. The overall low achievement of diverse children is very troubling for, at least in American society, it is a predictor of future success. The interrelationships between reading and academics in general is obvious. What should then be quite disconcerting to everyone is when a large group of students experience difficulty mastering such a fundamental skill. The Children's Defense Fund (1995) draws our attention to the poor reading abilities of twelfth graders (see Figure 3.2), which should sound the alarms of teachers of young children to concentrate their efforts on reading instruction.

Cultural Differences

Cultural conflicts may well contribute to some diverse children being identified as having disabilities (Cummins, 1984; Sileo et al., 1996). For some, behaviors perceived as problems in the school setting might be related to differences between the standards of behavior in the home and standards of behavior in school.

 MAKING CONNECTIONS

See Chapter 5,
- Language Impairments section (Causes) for more about language differences;
- Speech Impairments sections (Defined, Causes, Children with Speech or Language Impairments) for more about articulation.

 MAKING CONNECTIONS

- For more about Native Americans, review the Very Special Population section (Defined) found earlier in this chapter.
- For more about developing proficiency in English, see Language and Instruction (Educational Interventions) in this chapter.

 MAKING CONNECTIONS

For more about literacy and reading, see
- Reading section (Educational Interventions) in Chapter 4,
- Significance section (Defined) of Chapter 5,
- Educational Interventions in Chapter 5.

dialect. Words and pronunciation from a particular area, different from the form of the language used by the normative group.

FIGURE 3.2

Percentage of Twelfth Grade Students Reading Below Grade Level

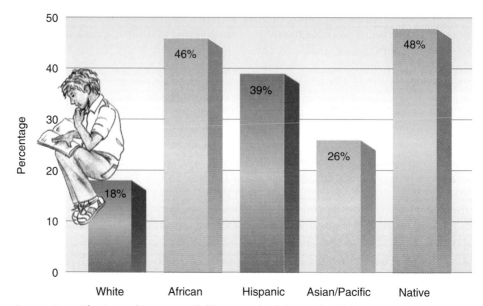

Source: From *The State of America's Children: Yearbook* (p. 93) by Children's Defense Fund, 1995, Washington, DC: Author. Reprinted by permission.

Table 3.4 compares the Hawaiian and dominant white values and clearly illustrates how cultures can differ and how those differences can affect children's learning.

Other issues can arise when behavior appropriate in one environment, such as the home, is inappropriate in another environment, such as the school. A silent child might behave in a desirable way according to standards of his home culture, for example, but be characterized as "withdrawn" or "anxious." Look at Table 3.4 again. Contrast the white focus on individual competitiveness and the standard of cooperation and cooperative learning in the Hawaiian culture. A similar case can be made for Native Americans and other diverse learners. For these children, intense competitiveness at home might be interpreted as a behavior disorder, and the lack of it at school could be interpreted as lack of motivation. When home and school cultures clash, children can become terribly confused and poorly educated (Obiakor, 1994).

Mobility

Some culturally and linguistically diverse children experience great mobility in their lives. Homeless children and those of migrant workers often experience disruption and dislocation, circumstances that can adversely affect their physical, mental, and academic abilities. Because many homeless, refugee, or migrant children have little formal experience with school, special education teachers may need to address years of missed educational opportunities in addition to language and cultural issues.

TABLE 3.4

Hawaiian American Compared with White American Values

Hawaiian	White
Overall Values	
Affiliation/maintenance of interpersonal harmony	Personal achievement
Group goals	Individual goals
Affirmation of relationships as status	Accumulation of material capital as status
Deference to rank and authority	Personal autonomy
Interdependency	Independency
Care and affection	Development of competencies
Learning Styles	
Na'au (sharing of personal information, establishing lineage, relationships)	Separation of public and private life
Ho'olohe (listen)	Questions encouraged
'Ike pono (look)	Adult-child interchanges and feedback
Ho'opili (watch and mimic)	Originality encouraged
Peers as source of information	Adults as source of information
Risk minimization ("ain't no big thing")	Creativity and spontaneity rewarded
Educational Process	
Hawaii Education Process	*Special Education Process*
Group	Individual
Social-interpersonal skills	Individual achievement in math and reading
Ho'oponopono as conflict resolution	Due process
Verbal word important	Written paper trails
Deference to experts	Equal partnerships
Holistic view of child	Fragmented

Source: From G. Kishi and M. Hanohano (November 1992), Hawaiian children. Presentation at Council for Exceptional Children, Multicultural Conference, Minneapolis, MN. Reprinted with permission.

Over 80 percent of migrant and seasonal farm workers are U.S. citizens or legal immigrants (Henning-Stout, 1996). These workers earn less than $7,500 a year, clearly below the federal poverty level. Most migrant families live in

Florida, Texas, or California between November and April and move to find agricultural work the rest of the year. Approximately one-half million migrant students live in the United States (Black Community Crusade for Children and the Children's Defense Fund, 1995). Seventy-five percent are Hispanic, and about a third of them live in California (U.S. Department of Education, 1992). Most have limited English abilities. These culturally and linguistically diverse children who are migrant are very likely to be affected by disabilities because of the poverty and health problems that accompany migrant working. This group experiences high rates of tuberculosis, cervical cancer, and hypertension (Henning-Stout, 1996). Although 64 percent of these students are reported as having learning disabilities, they tend to be underidentified and underserved in special education. These children face other hardships. Their parents must make a difficult choice: keeping their families together but being highly mobile or separating the family by leaving their children with relatives for a more stable school experience. Many middle and high school students also work long hours in the fields before and after school. Their high mobility only aggravates their educational problems, a few of which are listed here:

- Identification is difficult because of the short time they are in any given district.

- Delays in providing appropriate educational services often occur because of the time it takes to transfer special education records from one school district to another.

- Educational time is wasted by creating duplicate educational records.

- Gaps in services occur due to differences in services provided in each school district.

- Inappropriate placements often are made due to language barriers and to the delay in processing special education referrals.

- The efficient identification of and service delivery to migrant students with disabilities are impeded by lack of coordination between migrant education and special education agencies.

- Little data about best educational practices for this group of students are available.

- Migrant workers typically complete 7.7 years of school, compared to 12.5 for the rest of U.S. students.

Homelessness raises severe problems. Families with children account for 39 percent of the homeless in the United States (Children's Defense Fund, 1995). More than 500,000 children experience homelessness in the United States each year, and more than 100,000 children (at least 272,000 of them are school-age) are homeless on any given night (Smith-Davis & Smith, 1993). Although the Education for Homeless Children's Act of 1994 guarantees children a right to an education and allows them to attend any school the parent requests, many of these youngsters experience a fractured education. Homeless children with special needs can experience exceptional hardships because they may have to move from the school where these needs were being met (or in the process of being assessed) to possibly a series of schools, depending on the shelters to which the child is sent. The stress, hunger, disease, and feelings of hopelessness that often accompany homelessness and mobility can create new special education needs in a child or exacerbate existing ones. The ability of the family to implement aspects of an IEP at home are impaired when the family is separated in large dormitories, for example, or when living conditions are so crowded or dangerous that physical survival requires all the family's energy (Kozol, 1988).

Educational Interventions

Clearly, teachers are working in an age of challenge. The demands on them and their students, though great, can be met with innovative, individually sensitive, and culturally responsive approaches. Throughout the remainder of this century and beyond, teachers across the nation will have to deal with a variety of learning styles, values, customs, and behavioral patterns in the classroom. Our hope is that they will do so with an awareness of some important differences among students. We trust that such an awareness will help in celebrating the unique diversity every child brings to school.

Meeting the special education needs of exceptional culturally and linguistically diverse children can be especially challenging, because their multicultural and bilingual needs must be considered (Obiakor, Patton, & Ford, 1992). The professional must assist students in their mastery of English, address their academic needs, help them develop self-confidence, and heighten their awareness of and sensitivity to other linguistic and cultural backgrounds.

In each of the following chapters, we describe specific special education categories and provide suggestions for teaching children with those exceptionalities. Throughout this chapter, we offer tips on incorporating multicultural and bilingual considerations into the general and special education classroom. But most special educators who serve culturally and linguistically diverse students with disabilities speak only English (Ortiz, Yates, & Garcia, 1990). In 1990, U.S. Secretary of Education Lauro Cavazos called on colleges of education to make proficiency in a second language mandatory for all teachers (*New York Times*, 1990). How times can change quickly. Think about Cavazos' request and compare it to the political platform of an "English only America."

Education and the Preschool Child

Young children benefit from early educational experiences in many ways. Headstart programs were initiated in 1964, as part of the federal initiative called "War on Poverty." Today, about 28 percent (622,000) of eligible 3- to 5-year-olds attend Headstart programs (Currie & Thomas, 1995); some of these children have disabilities and many could be considered **at risk** for being identified as having disabilities during their school careers. One of the great benefits to children attending Headstart is access to a variety of health care services: a physical examination and full health assessments (immunization status, growth, vision, hearing, speech, anemia, sickle cell anemia, lead poisoning, tuberculosis, and infections). Access to health care is an important factor in preventing disabilities. Remember, Headstart was designed primarily for children from low-income families. It is IDEA—the Individuals with Disabilities Education Act

 MAKING CONNECTIONS

For more about developing cultural understanding, see
- The Focus on Diversity boxes throughout the text,
- The boxes in this chapter.

 MAKING CONNECTIONS

The issue of "English Only" is debated in the Concepts and Controversy section of this chapter.

 MAKING CONNECTIONS

More information about the concept of "at risk" is found in Education and the Preschool Child (Educational Interventions) in Chapter 5.

at risk. Children whose condition or situation makes it probable for them to develop disabilities.

1. Reflect the various cultural groups at school by providing in the different languages of the community

    - signs in public areas that welcome people,

    - sections in the school newsletters and other official school communications.

2. Provide opportunities for students from the same ethnic group to

    - communicate with one another in their home language,

    - work together in extracurricular activities,

    - study elective subjects in their primary language,

    - read literature written in their native language and work in small groups to discuss what they have read,

    - share information about special holidays and events with their classmates.

3. Recruit volunteers and/or parents who can

    - tutor students in their primary language,

    - serve as translators in meetings with non–English speaking parents,

    - help in the classroom, library, playground, and in clubs,

    - act as resources,

    - present at awards ceremonies,

    - be active partners in classroom instruction,

    - connect the curriculum with the students' personal experiences.

4. Decorate the school and classrooms with

    - pictures and objects of the various cultures represented at the school,

    - pictures of culturally diverse individuals in the professions and high-status occupations,

    - calendars that show special holidays from different countries.

MAKING CONNECTIONS

For a review of special education laws, see Chapter 1.

(PL 94-142) in 1975 and its amendments of 1986 and 1990 (PLs 99-457 and 101-476)—that provides infants and toddlers with disabilities access to early education programs. Usually, public school preschool programs serve children between ages 3 and 5.

Children have an awareness of cultural differences very early. Some believe that by age 3, the first year children typically attend preschool, they already recognize physical differences between groups of people (King, Chipman, & Cruz-Janzen, 1994). It also appears that they are being taught to be more aware of their own cultural identities early in life. Preschool teachers often report their children introducing themselves on the first day of school: "My name is Diana, and I am a Chicana." "My name is Tega. I am beautiful, and I am black." What should teachers do about this early cultural awareness? King and her colleagues (King et al., 1994) believe that cultural knowledge and experiences should be infused into the curriculum. They argue that having a "unit" on each cultural group is insufficient. Rather, the history, customs, art, literature, music, and famous people from all cultures should be woven into every curriculum topic presented across the schoolyear (not just during a designated week). Because children come to school with a

The cultural reality of children's lives is an important component of their experiences. Creative teachers incorporate this reality into school learning experiences.

forming cluster of cultural awareness and knowledge, teachers should increase their students' information, to reduce stereotypes and fear of people who may seem different or strange.

Education and the Schoolchild

Several crucial issues for culturally and linguistically diverse schoolchildren with exceptionalities must be considered when planning educational programs. We selected three to discuss here: cultural diversity, language and instruction, and self-esteem.

Cultural Diversity. Siccone (1995) points out a very important fact, one that we all should think about: Only about 3 percent of Americans can truly claim to be native. The rest of us are immigrants or descendants of immigrants. Many of our families retained at least a part of their cultural heritage; some replaced the old with newer American traditions. The United States is ever evolving, with one guarantee: Its diversity is increasing. U.S. classrooms are, and will be, comprised of students from different ethnic groups and different cultures. Teachers must "anchor" their instruction with examples from many American experiences. How can a teacher incorporate multicultural and bilingual aspects in a classroom? Instructional materials should reflect the cultural diversity of students (Cloud, 1993; Crawford, 1993; Obiakor, 1994). Some teachers have their students celebrate Mexican holidays, and they incorporate culturally relevant examples in their

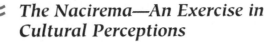

The Nacirema—An Exercise in Cultural Perceptions

Learning about different cultures and how others perceive them is a very important lesson for children and for adults. The result should be enhanced cultural sensitivity and an increased awareness of how individuals and their cultures can be misunderstood.

Mr. Justiz told his class about an article written by Miner and published in the *American Anthropologist* in 1956. The article was entitled, "Body Ritual Among the Nacirema," a tribe that Miner had observed. Mr. Justiz explained to his students that the article described the "magical beliefs and practices" of this tribe in great detail, and the author expressed concern about several slightly masochistic tendencies of this group of people. Mr. Justiz told the class that other researchers have also studied the tribe and support Miner's findings. He then listed some of the Nacirema customs: scraping and lacerating the face or legs with a sharp instrument; piercing the skin with sharp instruments and then taking great care to keep the holes from closing again; ceremonial painting of the body; and insertion and ritualistic movement of a bundle of hog hairs in the mouth several times a day. The people of this tribe seek out the assistance of medicine men many times during the course of a year to treat physical ailments, release them from the power of devils that have lodged in their heads, and gouge holes in their teeth. (This last is done in the hopes of avoiding oral decay and offending one's friends.) The Nacirema gather in large numbers to watch clans within the tribe enact small battles, often with many physical injuries, and to observe individual tribal members fight to unconsciousness.

Mr. Justiz led class discussion by asking the following questions:

1. Where do you think the Nacirema live?

2. List at least ten adjectives to describe this tribe's customs. How many were positive? negative?

3. If you were a teacher, how would you deal with Nacirema children in your classroom who insisted on maintaining their tribal customs?

4. What does Nacirema spell backward?

Mr. Justiz then encouraged his class to think about how it might be possible for all cultures to sound crude, bizarre, and ritualistic when viewed through the eyes of outsiders. He asked the class to describe such everyday events as shaving, ear piercing, and brushing of teeth so they could not sound like primitive customs. The class talked about how doctors, dentists, and psychologists can be made to sound unusual, and football games and boxing matches to sound sadistic. His concluding point was how easy it is to place negative interpretations on customs that seem foreign.

instruction. Schools can also recognize and value different cultures by supporting their clubs and groups (e.g., ESL clubs, Movimiento Estudiantil Chicano de Aztlan [MEChA] clubs, chapters of African American sororities and fraternities, arts, music, dance, and crafts clubs).

Teachers can help students become more sensitive to other cultures by helping them understand that there are many different ways to accomplish the same tasks and that not all cultures value the same experiences in the same ways. Students need to understand that each of them enters the classroom with a set of values and beliefs unique to their life situations. These beliefs can be influenced not only by the cultural background of students, but also by such factors as the length of time their families have been in the United States; the geographic region of the country in which they live; the age, gender, and birthplace of each child; the language spoken at home; the religion practiced by the family; the proximity to other extended family members; and the socioeconomic level of the family (Gollnick & Chinn, 1994). Teachers must become aware of and respect the cultural differences among their students, and their students must gain such acceptance as well. The activity described in the Teaching Tactics box is one activity that should expand students' cultural awareness and possibly help you think of other ways students can come to understand each other better.

In attempting to incorporate cultural diversity into the day-to-day activities of a school, teachers must be careful not to use stereotypical images of students' cultures, yet they should select content that reflects central aspects of a culture (Lynch & Hanson, 1992). For example, the assumption that a second-generation, American-born child of Japanese heritage maintains the same cultural belief system as a recent Japanese immigrant is just as erroneous as the assumption that a child of Cherokee heritage who lives in Denver is completely assimilated into the dominant U.S. culture. In other words, children must not be stereotyped. Teachers must not think, "If Sergio is from Mexico, I can turn to this book to see what he's like." Instead, they should utilize as much information as possible from a variety of sources: written materials, the student's family, the student, multicultural experts, and individuals from that child's culture. Multicultural classrooms and contexts should be considered for their complexity, not their simplicity.

Language and Instruction. What language does the teacher use to *teach* culturally and linguistically diverse students? As you learned in the history section, this question was easily answered for most of our nation's history—English. Until recently, educators believed that bilingualism caused academic problems and that bilingual children would suffer unless they were transformed into monolingual children. Educators believed that children's learning problems would be aggravated if they were required to deal with two languages of instruction. Some argued that this situation would lead to confusion, language interference, or further academic problems. As a result, many schools established rules that only English could be spoken, and many children were punished (for example, having their mouths washed out with soap or being kept after school) for speaking their home language at school; even recently, seven states prohibited bilingual education (Langdon with Cheng, 1992). Professional educators now know that the questions about whether to allow bilingual education programs and how they should be delivered are very complex.

Contrary to common belief, the original intent of bilingual education was not to promote bilingualism. Rather, it was to develop proficiency in English (Langdon with Cheng, 1992). Although there still are many vocal critics of bilingual education (Henry, 1994), research continues to indicate that this method is effective and contributes to the development of language skills and improved academic

MAKING CONNECTIONS

Review the definition of bilingual education found in Table 3.1.

achievement (Banks, 1994b; Corson, 1993). Experts in this field do debate among themselves about many issues, for example, when exactly to discontinue instruction in the student's primary language, but they do not disagree about the power of this instructional system. One positive outcome from good bilingual education programs can be a high level of proficiency in two languages, which can be an advantage to children across the curriculum. Another is the ability to profit from instruction delivered entirely in English.

Research indicates a few key elements included in effective programs, and one of those important keys is sensitivity to the background of the individual child (Pyle, 1996). For example, immigrant children who have already received two to three years of schooling in their native language and come from homes in which their parents are highly educated seem to cope in immersion classes with some supports and achieve equally to their English-speaking peers in about five years (Collier, 1995). Children who do not possess the prerequisites for academic learning, however, are better served in programs that stress the development of language proficiency in both languages (Collier, 1995). Greater academic gains are achieved when they are instructed in their native language until English is completely mastered. In such bilingual programs, students outachieve many other groups. They typically score at or above grade level in all subjects when tested in their first language and surpass their native English-speaking peers after four to seven years. Language acquisition and the development of enough proficiency to profit from academic instruction in English is a slow and complex process—and, as Gersten and his colleagues point out, is not an automatic or natural process for many children (Gersten, Brengilman, and Jiménez, 1994). It often requires that teachers help students make explicit connections between what they read and write in one language and their activities in the other language. Teachers also need to understand that the mere ability to translate from one language to another is not sufficient (Cheng, 1996). Complete understanding also requires understanding of feelings, anecdotes, and culturally based nonverbal messages.

The fields of special education and bilingual education began to come together in the 1970s, in part because of two important pieces of legislation: the Bilingual Education Act of 1968 (PL 90-247) and IDEA (formerly called Education for All Handicapped Children Act of 1975, PL 94-142). These laws helped educators begin to understand the connection between bilingualism and special education (Baca & Cervantes, 1989). Today, professionals understand the importance of bilingual special education services for culturally and linguistically diverse students with disabilities (Arreaga-Mayer, Carta, & Tapia, 1994; Garcia & Yates, 1994); however, many challenges to providing such services exist. Bilingual special education for linguistically diverse students with disabilities does not always occur, even for those in most need (U.S. Department of Education, 1993). According to this federal agency, few states have either established programs or have trained teachers available. Only five states have defined a category or specified student eligibility criterion. Only 2 percent of IEPs written for LEP Hispanic students address language proficiency.

MAKING CONNECTIONS

For more about IEPs, review Chapter 2.

Dual language instruction, bilingual education, is particularly effective for LEP students with disabilities. Unfortunately, it is not always possible to provide bilingual education (or bilingual special education), because teachers are not trained in this methodology or because teachers who themselves are bilingual are not available. Table 3.5 shows the four basic instructional approaches often used with bilingual children.

TABLE 3.5

Approaches Used with Bilingual Students

Approach	Explanation
English as a second language (ESL)	Children are taught English in their classrooms or in special classes until English proficiency is achieved. This method is used when teachers fluent in the child's native language are not available.
Bilingual transitional approach	Students are taught academic subjects in their native language and English is emphasized with the purpose of being able to participate in an English-only curriculum as soon as possible. Although three years of exposure to English is not always sufficient, that is usually how long students are taught in their native language.
Bilingual maintenance approach	Students are taught partly in English and partly in their home language so that they maintain proficiency in the home language but also gain proficiency in English. This method is not used very much today.
Total immersion*	Frequently used in Canada or with very young children, the student is taught entirely in English, and no English instruction or home language instruction is provided. Usually, the other students are also non–native English speakers, and the teacher speaks the students' home language.

*This approach should not be confused with *submersion*, placement in an all-English classroom with no assistance.

Experts in the field of bilingual education now tend to agree that the appropriate time to move a child from the bilingual class to the all-English class is when the dominant language is fully developed, which is at about age 12. The proper timing for such a move is crucial. Research conducted by Cummins (1984) highlights the issues. The first stages of language proficiency include conversational fluency, the mastery of pronunciation, vocabulary, and grammar. Only later does the individual develop the more complex, conceptual linguistic ability, the deeper functions of language necessary for competent participation in academic settings. (See Figure 3.3, which shows the surface and the deeper levels of language proficiency.) Cummins cautions that children first develop face-to-face conversational skills and are transferred to all-English instruction, because they then *appear* to have English proficiency. But they then fall further and further behind academically because they do not have the more complex linguistic abilities required for academic success. Their **basic interpersonal communicative skills (BICS)** are more developed than their **cognitive/academic linguistic proficiency (CALP)**. Conversational skills in a second language can be acquired within two to three years, but the more complex language abilities required for academic work require about five to seven years of meaningful exposure and practice.

English as a second language (ESL). Children are given English instruction in their classrooms or in special classes until English proficiency is achieved.

bilingual transitional approach. Students are taught primarily in English and partly in their home language until they learn enough English to learn academic subjects.

bilingual maintenance approach. Students are taught partly in English using ESL strategies partly in their home language so that they maintain proficiency.

total immersion. The student is taught entirely in English; all the other students are also non–native English speakers, and the teacher can speak the students' home language.

basic interpersonal communicative skills (BICS). Face-to-face conversational language.

cognitive/academic linguistic proficiency (CALP). The abstract language abilities required for academic work.

FIGURE 3.3

Surface and Deeper Levels of Language Proficiency

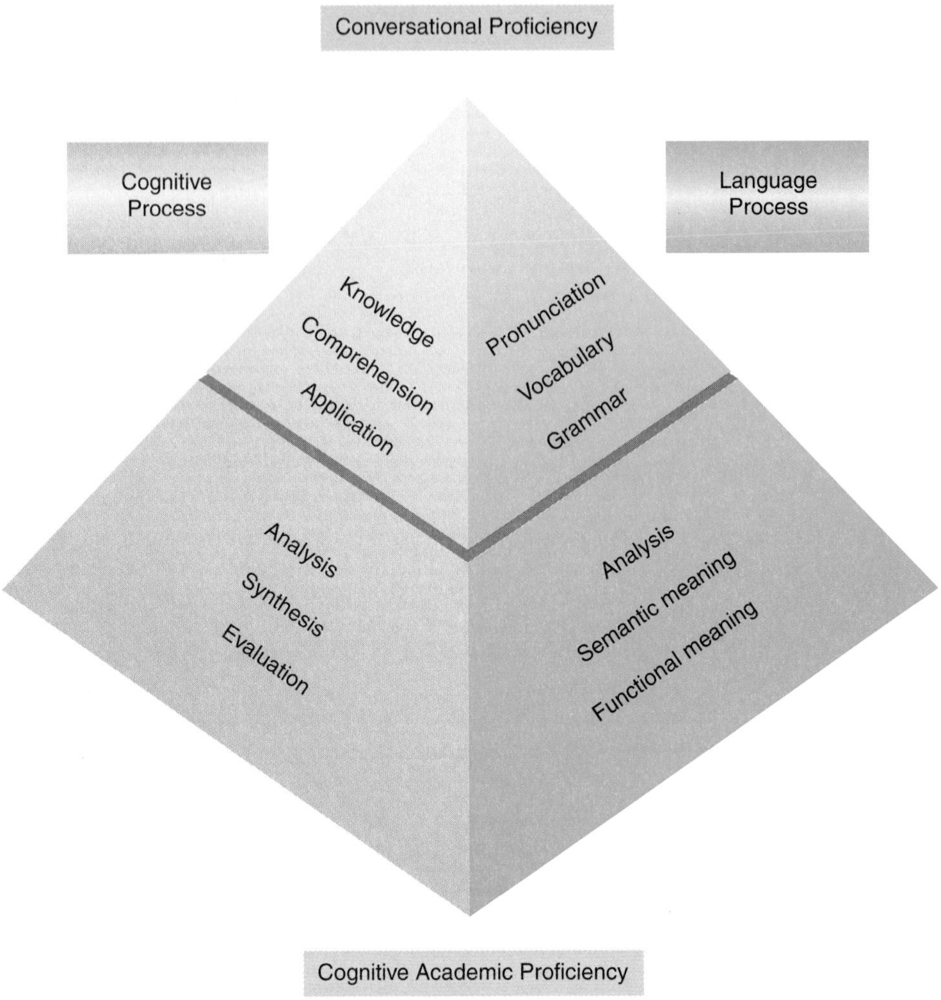

Conversational Proficiency

Cognitive Process

Language Process

Knowledge
Comprehension
Application

Pronunciation
Vocabulary
Grammar

Analysis
Synthesis
Evaluation

Analysis
Semantic meaning
Functional meaning

Cognitive Academic Proficiency

Source: Bilingualism and Special Education: Issues in Assessment and Pedagogy (p. 138)
by J. I. Cummins, 1984, Austin: Pro-Ed. Reprinted by permission.

The student's understanding is affected by how many contextual clues accompany the language, such as explanatory pictures, specific people speaking, or particular tone of voice. In addition, understanding is affected by how demanding the activity is; if the task is concrete, it is easier to understand than if it is quite complex. Second language ability must be greater when fewer contextual clues suggest meaning, or when the communication requires more cognitive ability. Therefore in Figure 3.3 the bottom half of the pyramid requires the highest level of language and cognitive skills.

Controversy over bilingual education has spread beyond the field of education and into local and national politics. The choice of instructional method often becomes a political issue, with communities objecting to non-English instruction. In fact, some politicians, communities, and states have even attempted to declare English the "official" language. How does the discussion of multicultural and bilingual education affect special education? Certainly, the approaches suggested for general education classes can be equally effective in special education classes. The models for multicultural and bilingual education work in concert with the methods developed to teach children with specific exceptionalities.

Building Self-Esteem. Culture is not just customs, heritage, traditions, and beliefs; it incorporates values and a way of interpreting the world (Siccone, 1995). Children who do not come from the dominant culture often are not sure about where they fit. When their culture is not valued, they question whether they, as individuals, have value. For these students, their self-esteem is in question and they need to become empowered (Webb-Johnson, Obiaker, & Algozzine, 1995). Research has shown that culturally and linguistically diverse students gain benefits from or can be disabled by their experiences with teachers. Cummins (1989) notes that schools that empower minority students tend to do the following:

- Incorporate minority students' language and culture into the school program.

- Encourage minority community participation as an integral component of children's education.

- Establish a curriculum that promotes intrinsic motivation for students to use language actively to generate their own knowledge.

- Understand, with help from assessment professionals, the ways in which minority students' academic difficulty is a function of interactions within the school context rather than legitimizing the location of the problem as being within students.

Inclusion

As you will learn throughout this text, the word *inclusion* means many different things to different people. You will also learn that issues related to inclusion are extremely complex and vary from individual to individual and group to group. It is imperative that the special education environment for culturally and linguistically diverse students be responsive to their cultural and language needs. At the same time, for those with disabilities the environment needs to be directed toward their special educational needs, including integration. Depending on students' specific requirements, schedules, classrooms, staff, and appropriate supports should vary.

It might surprise you, but LEP students are more likely to receive their education in segregated settings, even those with mild disabilities. For example, New York state was cited in federal court for not taking into account children's language needs, assessing Spanish-speaking Puerto Rican students in English only, and for not providing the possibility of educational opportunities in least restrictive settings (Hoff, 1995). Clearly, culturally and linguistically diverse students with disabilities are just as entitled to the LRE mandates specified in IDEA as other students with disabilities. However, while they are instructed in either their native language or in a special bilingual setting, it may not be possible or appropriate for them to receive much of their instruction in the general education program.

MAKING CONNECTIONS

For more about English Only, see the Concepts and Controversy section in this chapter.

MAKING CONNECTIONS

For more on educational placements, service delivery models, and inclusion,
- See the Inclusion sections (Educational Interventions) of each chapter about a disability area in this text,
- Review Chapter 2.

Many opportunities for inclusion exist; we just need to be creative and seize them. "Spirit weaving" proved to be such an opportunity for white and Native American children with and without disabilities to explore and learn about cultural heritage, traditions, and have fun (Very Special Arts, 1995). Over 800 school-children gathered in Shawnee, Oklahoma, for the "1995 National Native American Very Special Arts Festival." During the three-day event (which happened to be held shortly after the bombing in Oklahoma City), children learned tribal dances and songs, held an authentic powwow, carved wood, made pots and baskets, learned more about each other as people, and, most importantly, united spirits in time of need.

Transition Through Adulthood

The relationship between education and wages is clear: High school graduates are less likely to be unemployed. Every year of high school completed increases life-time wages by 8 percent and improves job satisfaction (Currie & Thomas, 1995). Statistics show that low-income and culturally and linguistically diverse students tend to drop out of school at a higher rate than do others. Although there has been improvement in the past twenty years, the dropout rate remains troubling, particularly for Hispanic students (National Center for Educational Statistics, 1994). High school dropouts suffer more unemployment than all other groups. More low-income students across ethnic and racial groups drop out of high school (see Figure 3.4), which contributes to the low employment of multicultural and bilingual adults and the continuing cycle of poverty.

High school graduation is one criterion for entrance into college and, as you have just learned, is important to future employment opportunities and the potential for economic success. Unfortunately, data indicate that African American and Hispanic students are underrepresented in colleges and universities. In many cases, minority students are advised not to take the core required courses for college entrance (e.g., enough science, math, and foreign language courses). Often, they attend high schools with fewer financial resources, which translates to outdated textbooks, old instructional materials, and lower-paid teachers. The outcome is usually unfortunate. In twelve southern states, 25 percent of college-age students are African American, but only 16 percent of full-time freshmen are African American. The pattern worsens in their graduation rate: They receive only 10 percent of the total bachelor degrees awarded each year. The degree attainment for Hispanic students in the southern states is comparable to that of African Americans (Panel on Educational Opportunity and Postsecondary Desegregation, 1995).

For most Americans, employment is one important goal of education, but for some the possibilities of economic independence appear bleak. Those living on the White Mountain Apache Indian Reservation are a good example (Ramasamy, 1996). Of those students from both general and special education who graduated from high school across a five-year period, only 33 percent were employed (27 percent of special education graduates and 35 percent of general education graduates). This situation is partly due to the paucity of jobs on the reservation, but other factors need to be considered as well. Only two individuals had requested assistance from rehabilitation services. The vast majority of the entire group were satisfied with their employment situation. Possibly, transition goals for individuals who live on reservations where employment opportunities are limited should be

MAKING CONNECTIONS

Also see the transition sections in
• Chapter 4,
• Chapter 7,
• Chapter 10,
• Chapter 11.

FIGURE 3.4

High School Dropout Rates

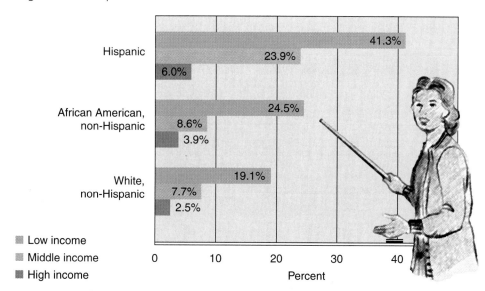

Source: From *The State of America's Children: Yearbook* (p. 94) by Children's Defense Fund, 1995, Washington, DC: Author. Reprinted by permission.

developed with traditional values (participation in cultural and religious activities) considered.

The life situation for many African Americans appears desperate and sad. Consider some of these statistics assembled by the Black Community Crusade for Children of the Children's Defense Fund (1995). Homicide is the leading cause of death for African American males between the ages of 15 and 24, which is eight times higher than the American white rate and over 102 times higher than the homicide rate of males in the same age group from any European country. These children represented about 26 percent of the reported child abuse cases. They are two times more likely to be unemployed as teens and as adults than their white counterparts. While only 86,000 African American young men under age 25 are living in college dorms, more than 150,000 African American men in that age group are in prison. In other words, African American males comprise 14 percent of all 18- to 24-year-old males but over 40 percent of that age group in prison. Clearly, these data demonstrate the waste of human resources, a tragedy for all of us. To avoid this tragedy, Ford, Obiakor, and Patton (1995) suggest a home–community–school pyramid connection to help African Americans and other students from diverse backgrounds transition to adulthood, maximize their potential, and become fully participating members in American life.

Families

Families of culturally and linguistically diverse children often have very special needs when interacting with social service agencies, particularly the schools.

Teacher Checklist—Getting to Know My Students and Their Families

▸ Have I taken the time to get to know my students as individuals–their likes and dislikes, fears and dreams?

▸ Have I identified each student's strengths and given each of them opportunities to experience being successful?

▸ Am I helping my students to develop healthy relationships with their classmates, supporting them in solving their own problems, and encouraging them to appreciate cultural diversity?

▸ How well do I know my students' families, and have my efforts to reach out to them been effective?

▸ Have I found ways of facilitating communication with families whose native language is different from mine?

▸ Have I informed my students' parents and guardians about our educational objectives and how they can help at home?

▸ How many families and community members representing all cultures have been in my classroom to interact with the students?

▸ Have I discovered that prejudice among students often reflects biases that they learn from their parents, and have I formulated a plan for educating parents on the value of diversity?

▸ Have I recognized approaches to parenting that do not enhance children's self-esteem, and have I formulated a plan for educating parents on the importance of self-esteem and how it is developed?

Source: From *Celebrating diversity: Building self-esteem in today's multicultural classrooms* (p. 108) by F. Siccone, 1995. Boston: Allyn and Bacon. Reprinted by permission.

Many come to the school situation with feelings of distrust and alienation (Voltz, 1994). For some, their children are the first generation in their family to enter an education system where English is spoken. These families may speak little, if any, English at home. Even those who speak English may not have enough comfort or proficiency in this second language to truly understand and communicate with educators using technical language or jargon (Wilson & Hughes, 1994). Also, the culture of their homes may differ from the culture represented by the teacher and the school. A significant risk under these circumstances is that the family may feel excluded, rejected, or even offended by their child's school and the educators who provide the education program to their child. Thus, teachers must be aware of these potential challenges and barriers and the risk of alienating families even more. They must know about the cultural background of their students' families (see the checklist in the Tips for Teachers box), dissolve barriers, and develop partnerships with all of the family members who wish to be included. Most importantly, educators must develop trust and respect between home and school (Prater & Tanner, 1995).

Cross-Cultural Dissonance

Teachers may inadvertently set up barriers by excluding parents from more meaningful special education roles. Urging that African American parents be accepted full partners in the special education of their sons and daughters, Harry (1992b) criticizes the practice of limiting parents to the roles of "consent-giver" and "educational planner." Educators do need to change their expectations, particularly of parents from diverse backgrounds. Instead of assuming that parents will assume the roles of loyal supporter and passive recipient of information, educators should seek parents' input about how they would like to be involved in their child's educational program (Prater & Tanner, 1995; Voltz, 1994). Educators also need to communicate more completely to parents about their educational philosophies and methods (Harry, Allen, and McLaughlin, 1996). To be full partners, parents need to understand what educational options are available—like phonics vs. whole language approaches—and why one method was selected over another or how they are being used in combination. Such openness in communication can foster active dialogues about children's instructional programs.

In many school–home relationships, **cross-cultural dissonance**—a situation of extreme misunderstanding of fundamental issues and values about education, disability, and home–school interaction—may undermine special education for students with disabilities (Harry, 1992b). Teachers must understand the risks of dissonance between culturally and linguistically diverse students and their families and the special education system. They must develop educational programs that incorporate the values of diversity.

Children from diverse backgrounds may have a family constellation that differs from that of children from the dominant culture. Often, these **extended family** members play a crucial role in the life of the individual with disabilities. The families of culturally and linguistically diverse children may include many extended family members as well as individuals outside the family (Rogers-Dulan & Blacher, 1995). For example, for some African American families church and community leaders often lend support and resources to the student with disabilities. For that child, the concept of extended family may well include key members from the community. For Native American children, it may be tribal elders whose exclusion would be considered an offense. Before making any decisions about treatments or educational strategies, it may be necessary to consult with these tribal elders and allow time for such consultations. Without understanding the cultural demands and expectations of the child's family, educators can inadvertently create unfortunate and unnecessary barriers.

Family–Teacher Partnerships

Teachers must help the child and family have a positive school experience by developing meaningful partnerships (Voltz, 1994). This requires the development of an atmosphere of trust and respect. Here are a few ways such a climate can be fostered:

- Use titles (Mr., Mrs., Ms., Dr.) when addressing family members; being too familiar by using first names is interpreted as being disrespectful in some cultures.

cross-cultural dissonance. When the home and school cultures are in conflict.

extended family. Includes immediate family members—mother, father, and siblings—and other relatives—aunts, uncles, grandparents.

- Use a polite, courteous, and respectful tone of voice, being careful not to demean or condescend.

- Use language that family members can understand, language that is free from jargon and is nontechnical.

- Listen actively to family members and gain all the information possible about the child from their input.

- Respond to every question and concern with clear and straight responses.

- Treat families with individual respect and avoid stereotyping on any characteristic (race, ethnicity, language, or socioeconomic class).

In some families, the child's parents are not the direct caregivers. Drug abuse, financial hardship, and divorce have caused grandparents to assume the parental role for many children. For instance, in 1989, about 1.2 million African American children lived with their grandparents (Bell & Smith, 1996). In about half of these multigenerational households, the children's mothers live with them. Unfortunately for 38 percent of these children, neither parent was present. In many African American communities, where the church is a central focus of the community, formal and informal adoption and foster care placements re-create the family unit when the natural family cannot function (Rogers-Dulan & Blacher, 1995). Once again, it is important to stress that all direct caregivers be included in home–school partnerships. Educators must not assume their students come from traditional family structures. As indicated in the Tips for Teachers box, they must know their families and be certain to involve the direct caregivers as well as the extended family group when appropriate.

In part, a child's success in school depends on respect between the school and the family. Children must feel confident that their cultural heritage and language are valued by the teacher and school. To encourage confidence and cooperation, a teacher can bring the strengths, contributions, culture, and language of the family directly into the school experience. For example, a grandfather might teach the class a special skill like making silver jewelry. A grandmother who creates pottery following the ancient techniques might demonstrate her art. A mother who programs computers might teach the class how to make drawings or large signs using the computer. A parent who is a migrant agricultural worker might sing folk songs in the home language or tell traditional stories. An aunt who has recently immigrated might have photos, musical instruments, examples of clothing, or other items from her home country to help students dramatize a myth and better understand the customs of the country. Finally, a tribal leader might be asked to officiate at a school awards ceremony. Any such family participation in school events helps foster home–school partnerships and promote children's success at school.

MAKING CONNECTIONS

Review the Tips for Teachers box.

Technology

Technology has changed all of our lives. There is no question that it will continue to impact the lives of those with disabilities and their families. In each section on technology you will come to wonder about the future possibilities. Our hope is to have you dream with us about how even the greatest challenges can be facilitated by advances in technology.

As **computerized language translators** are developed, they may have a significant impact for special education students with a primary language other than

computerized language translators. Microcomputers that provide translations of written text from one language to another.

English. For instance, the student may be able to use a computer to write an assignment in his or her primary language, check the spelling and punctuation, and then press a button to translate the work into English and give it to the teacher. Students could write their assignments in a dialect, and then have the computer translate it into the standard English. Computers can save time for the bilingual teacher or volunteer by being used for immediate translations of specific words or explanations of phrases and idioms.

Language translators can also combine fun and instruction. George Earl (1984) created a Spanish-to-English and an English-to-Spanish computerized version of the word game hangman. Hangman is one of the many instructional games used by special education teachers to help improve language skills. Although the program had some difficulty with dialects (it translates standard Spanish), it demonstrates how technology can be applied to the learning needs of children who are multicultural and bilingual.

Concepts and Controversy: Laws That Mandate Speaking English

Twenty-three states have now passed English-only laws; although unsuccessful so far, legislation has been introduced in the U.S. Congress, and the Supreme Court is considering the issue (Biskupic, 1996). Formal organizations have been created (e.g., U.S. English) to promote official language policies. Most likely, these actions are in response to the recent influx of immigrants from non-European countries and to the increase in the number of foreign languages spoken in this country (14 percent of the 230 million people in the United States over the age of 5 speak a

language other than English, a jump of 38 percent since 1980). Proponents of English-only laws argue that for the social fabric of the United States to stay intact, for economic stability, and to guarantee the American lifestyle, this nation must use one language: English. Defenders of this position maintain that English is a unifying force in the United States, and they fear that the country is being divided along language lines (Piatt, 1990; Tatalovich, 1995). Many look to the recent problems in Canada with conflict over the use of French and English and strengthen their stance that we should adopt a single-language policy.

What motivates the development of single-language policies? What would be so wrong with an English-only America? What might be the outcomes of such laws? It is possible that English-only laws could cause discrimination against bilingual individuals. They could create an atmosphere of hostility, repression, and divisiveness in cities and towns with large communities of non-English speakers. Funding for bilingual education would be threatened. Should speaking more than one language be regarded as a valued skill? Supporters of the alternative position, English Plus, contend that pluralism is an American strength, and that there are great benefits to proficiency of English Plus mastery of at least a second language. Four states (New Mexico, Oregon, Washington, and Rhode Island) along with some major cities (Atlanta, Cleveland, Dallas, San Antonio, Tucson, and Washington, DC) have laws or resolutions supporting the concept of English Plus. How will this national debate conclude? What issues should be considered in this national conversation? What will the impact be on bilingual education and bilingual special education?

~~~ SUMMARY ~~~

Education should reflect the rich diversity of culture and language found in communities across this country, and special education should capitalize on each student's background as an appropriate individualized education program is created. Many exceptional children are bilingual, and many more come from diverse cultural backgrounds. The combinations of disability, giftedness, cultural diversity, and LEP present many challenges to these children, their families, and educators as schools attempt to ensure that special education services are delivered to children who need and are entitled to them.

FOCUS QUESTIONS

Self-Test Questions

▶ *What is meant by multicultural special education, and who is served by these programs?*

The demographics of the United States and its school population is changing rapidly, creating complex challenges for educators and the educational system. The number of multicultural and bilingual students in the United States is increasing rapidly. Almost one-third of today's public schoolchildren come from diverse backgrounds, and it is predicted that by 2026 white children will represent only one-third of the school population. Today, in twenty-five of the country's largest cities and metropolitan areas, at least half the students are from culturally and linguistically diverse groups. The largest and fastest-growing group is Hispanic, which includes 75 percent of all LEP students.

▶ *What is meant by bilingual special education, and who is served by these programs?*

Bilingual special education stresses the development of academic and social skills through an individually designed program that capitalizes on the child's home language and culture, along with English, as a foundation for delivering instruction to culturally and linguistically diverse children with exceptionalities. These programs typically serve children who have limited English proficiency, have not mastered English well enough to receive academic instruction in their non-dominant language, and have been identified as having a disability. A central issue in the instruction of LEP students is the type of instructional approach to use. Four basic instructional approaches are often used in bilingual special education classes: English as a second language (ESL), the bilingual transitional approach, the bilingual maintenance approach (not used much today), and total immersion approach. It is difficult to implement bilingual special education, using any of the four available approaches, because of the unavailability of trained teachers who are also proficient in the child's native language. In such cases, teachers must seek help from family and community volunteers and bilingual paraprofessionals to help children to become proficient in English as quickly as possible.

▶ *Why are educators so concerned about culturally and linguistically diverse children?*

Culturally and linguistically diverse children are at great risk for disabilities and for low educational achievement; this risk is far greater for them than for children who come from mainstream society. Many of these families face social and economic inequities that can result in risk factors for their children. For example, poverty reduces a family's access to health care, which can lead to increased school absences and, in some cases, disabilities. Cultural differences in classroom settings require that teachers adjust their instructional techniques to match differences in learning styles. Those children whose home language is not English face additional risks and challenges. The development of second language acquisition and proficiency concurrent with academic instruction presented in English requires many accommodations. When insufficient numbers of educators who speak the family's primary language are available, the challenges of cultural differences are compounded by language dif-ferences. Schools must address the needs of children from different cultures and different languages. If they do not, students from diverse backgrounds will continue to be overrepresented in disability categories and under-represented in gifted education. They will also continue to drop out of school at alarming rates. Not finishing high school is associated with reduced employability and increased contacts with the juvenile justice system.

▶ *In what ways can biases occur in the identification and assessment process?*

One risk in the assessment and identification processes is discrimination. When testing culturally and linguistically diverse children, bias can occur for many reasons: the information (content level) being tested is not known by culturally and linguistically diverse students, minority groups are not represented in the standardization population, the administrator of the test is not trained in multicultural or bilingual techniques, or the child does not adequately comprehend the language used in the testing situation. Bias in the testing process is a major factor in the overrepresentation of culturally and linguistically diverse children in special education programs and the underrepresentation in gifted education.

▶ *How can school personnel integrate children's home cultures and languages into the educational environment and curriculum?*

Educators have the opportunity to demonstrate their cultural awareness and sensitivity to their students' diversity throughout every school day in every instructional unit by the examples and resources they integrate into their lessons. They can show their acceptance of different languages by posting signs, publishing columns in school newsletters, displaying posters from different countries, and learning welcoming phrases in their students' native languages. They can enrich their instruction by encouraging students to read literature from their home cultures, work together in study groups, and join clubs that offer common interests and additional supports. Educators can seek the assistance of parents, family members, and community volunteers to work with students as language and academic tutors, enhance instructional units with culturally relevant illustratives, connect the curriculum with students' personal experiences, and become active partners in classroom instruction.

Challenge Question

▶ *Why is there such a national debate about the issue of the overrepresentation of culturally and linguistically diverse students in disability categories and their underrepresentation in gifted education?*

Clearly, culturally and linguistically diverse children are overrepresented in disability categories and underrepresented in gifted education. Multiculturalism and bilingualism do not cause disabilities or the likelihood of being gifted, but many correlates of being diverse do. One of the main culprits here is poverty, because in the United States factors associated with poverty (e.g., access to health care) do result in a variety of disabilities. Many culturally and linguistically diverse students do not live in poverty; but for those who do, the effects of poverty are sometimes confused with the effects of diversity. Cultural and linguistic diversity can mask a child's giftedness and inappropriately suggest a cognitive disability or language impairment. Language and communication differences often challenge both the child and special education personnel, and cultural differences may raise questions about the behavior of the child and family and about the appropriateness of interventions. In addition, mobility (e.g., homelessness, migrant worker transience, and immigrant or refugee circumstances) interrupts education, aggravates educational problems, creates great disadvantages in learning and academic experience, adds stress, and causes logistical difficulties in the education of some children.

〜 *SUPPLEMENTARY RESOURCES* 〜

In this section, we have provided you with some resources to enrich your study of multicultural and bilingual special education. Although certainly not exhaustive, we included some scholarly books so you can seek additional information, more than what we can offer in one chapter in an introductory text. Over the years, culturally and linguistically diverse individuals have been included in fictional and nonfictional roles in both books and films. (We only included videos that can be rented at many large video stores.

Unfortunately, copies of many excellent television shows and movies are not readily available.) A brief listing of such creative works is included here; a more complete list is found in the *Students' Resource Manual* accompanying this text. This section concludes with a listing of a few of the organizations and agencies (a more complete list is also available in the *Students' Resource Manual*) that can be helpful with specific questions and concerns.

Scholarly Books

Baca, L. M., & Cervantes, H. T. (Eds.). (1984). The bilingual special education interface. St. Louis: Times Mirror/Mosby.

Banks, J. A. (1994). An introduction to multicultural education. Boston: Allyn and Bacon.

Banks, J. A., & Banks, C. A. M. (1993). Multicultural education: Issues and perspectives (2nd ed.). Boston: Allyn and Bacon.

Cheng, L. L. (Ed.). (1995). Integrating language and learning for inclusion: An Asian-Pacific focus. San Diego: Singular Publishing Group.

Cummins, J. (1986). Empowering minority students: A framework for intervention. Harvard Educational Review, 56, 18–36.

Gollnick, D. M., & Chinn, P. C. (1994). Multicultural education in a pluralistic society (4th ed.). New York: Macmillan Publishing Company.

Lynch, E. W., & Hanson, M. J. (1992). Developing cross-cultural competence: A guide for working with young children and their families. Baltimore: Paul H. Brookes.

Popular Books

Anaya, R. A. (1979). Tortuga. Berkeley, CA: Editorial Justa.

Dorris, M. (1989). The broken cord. New York: Harper & Row.

Kenzaburo, O. (1994). The pinch runner memorandum. London: M. E. Sharpe.

Kozol, J. (1995). Amazing grace: The lives of children and the conscience of a nation. New York: Crown.

Ng, F. M. (1993). Bone: A novel. New York: Hyperion.

Rechy, J. (1993). The miraculous day of Amalia Gomez. New York: Arcade.

Wilson, A. (1993). Two trains running. New York: NAL-Dutton.

Videos

To kill a mockingbird. (1960). United Artists.
The milagro beanfield war. (1988). Universal Films.
Stand and deliver. (1989). Warner Brothers.

Professional, Parent, and Consumer Organizations and Agencies

Division for Culturally and Linguistically Diverse Exceptional Learners (DDEL)
Council for Exceptional Children (CEC)
1920 Association Drive
Reston, VA 22091
Web site: http://www.cec.sped.org

National Association for Bilingual Education (NABE)
1220 L Street NW, Suite 605
Washington, DC 20005
Web site: http://www.nabe.org
E-mail: nabe.org
Phone: (202) 898-1829

National Association for Multicultural Education
2101A North Rolfe St.
Arlington, VA 22209-1007
Web site: donna@ncate.org
Phone: (202) 416-6157

National Clearinghouse for Bilingual Education
1118 22nd St. NW
Washington, DC 20037
Web site: http://www.ncbe.gwu.edu
Phone: (800) 321-6223

National Association for Multicultural Education (NAME)
1511 K Street NW, #430
Washington, DC 20005
E-mail: name@nicom.com
Phone: (202) 628-6263

National Indian Education Association
1819 H Street NW, Suite 800
Washington, DC 20006

P. Buckley Moss. *Sunday Afternoon.* © P. Buckley Moss, 1987.

P. Buckley Moss is a highly successful contemporary artist who faced a childhood filled with school failure and challenge. She says of her schooling, "I was totally unprepared for the discipline of school; and the reading that I knew would be so easy turned out to be a frustration I would never overcome" (Moss, 1989, p. 19). She remembers being described as inattentive, a slow learner, and even stupid. She knew she was not stupid; and when the diagnosis of learning disabilities was made, it was almost a relief. Moss is not only a well-recognized American artist; she is also a supporter of many associations concerned with learning disabilities.

Learning Disabilities

ADVANCE ORGANIZERS

OVERVIEW

Learning disabilities is the largest special education category, with over 50 percent of all students with disabilities identified as having it as their primary handicapping condition. Although these individuals comprise a heterogeneous group, they all share at least one common characteristic: difficulty mastering academic subjects, particularly reading. Partly because of the ease of identifying students as belonging to this special education category and the size of this group, much controversy surrounds these children and their educational programs. Although some have questioned whether this disability even exists, considerable evidence indicates not only that it does exist but also that it is a lifelong disability.

FOCUS QUESTIONS

SELF-TEST QUESTIONS

▶ What are the differences and similarities between the two major definitions of learning disabilities?

▶ Why can students be identified as having learning disabilities in one state or school district but not qualify for special education services elsewhere?

▶ Why is it correct to consider learning disabilities a lifelong condition?

▶ What are some learning characteristics that contribute to these students' poor academic performance?

▶ How can social competence and status affect these individuals?

CHALLENGE QUESTION

▶ What constitutes an appropriate education for these students, and in what setting should it be provided?

A *Personal Perspective*: College Students with Learning Disabilities Speak Out

College students with learning disabilities were asked a set of questions that reveal their feelings and some of the challenges they face as young adults.

Kyle Morgan Twenty-two-year-old sophomore, First identified in second grade, Major: considering athletic training

Jack Gelfand Twenty-six-year-old freshman, First identified in eleventh grade, Major: plans on business

Timothy Daniel Herron Twenty-year-old freshman, Identified in eighth grade, Major: undecided

Tanley Gress Twenty-nine-year-old sophomore, Identified when she was 10 years old, Major: preparing for economics

Chris Baca Twenty-three-year-old junior, Identified in middle school, Major: fine arts

Peter Haines Twenty-three-year-old junior, Identified while in college, Major: history

Why did you decide to come to college?

KYLE: I want to receive a better education to pursue a better job. Both of my parents are college graduates. This gave me the incentive and push to succeed.

TIMOTHY: I wanted to play college golf. Also, I know I need a four-year degree to succeed and achieve the standard of income I am used to right now.

CHRIS: I used to go with my mother to her classes when she attended college when I was 10 years old until I was 15, and this experience fueled my desire to go to college. So, to me, college was a good place that I eagerly awaited.

What are your goals?

KYLE: To finish college, get a good job in my field, and to have a family.

JACK: To graduate from college, and proceed to a well-paying job, or, I hope, start my own business.

TIMOTHY: Play four years of golf and become an All-American, and to get a four-year degree within five and a half years.

TANLEY: To be the world's greatest economist. (You think I'm joking. I can do it. No problem now.)

CHRIS: I have always enjoyed art, and I am now working toward a bachelor's degree in fine arts. And, then, the sky's the limit!

What accommodations/support do you need and use from the university?

KYLE: Tutoring, extended time for test taking, talking books, counseling, and support group.

TANLEY: Special services; it has lots of things. I did use a tape recorder, but this semester I don't need it. I take advantage of extended test time and tutoring in math.

CHRIS: The most important accommodation, one I feel has been the most helpful to me, is the support and understanding of others who can help me overcome my learning disabilities.

PETER: Extended time on tests, special LD tutors, and books on tape.

What social aspects of college do you participate in?

KYLE: I am a member of Resident Hall Student Senate, and a representative for Coronado Hall Student Government.

TIMOTHY: I am on the varsity golf team; we practice three to six hours a day.

CHRIS: I have always participated by going to theatrical and musical events. But recently, I have been participating in the political aspects of college life. I am also president of MEChA (a Chicano student group).

What would you like to say about your disability to other college students who do not have learning disabilities?

KYLE: We may have disabilities, but we are just like you. We walk, talk, feel, and dream just the same.

TIMOTHY: I am not dumb, but not highly intelligent. My disabilities give me a hard time in remembering almost everything, like reading, taking notes, and listening. It is not a cop-out. I know that I take twice as long as some of my friends to study the same subject.

CHRIS: I would like to say that no obstacle is too big. It just requires that we learn more than the average person in order to overcome the disability. We are not dumb or slow, we just learn differently. Moreover, the learning process for an LD student sometimes requires special accommodations, which is *NOT* a way to take the easy road, but a necessity.

PETER: Everybody is different. Some people have blue eyes, some brown. Some people learn differently than others. Just because I'm learning disabled doesn't mean I'm stupid. *ALWAYS* keep an open mind.

1. What support systems do these students need (that are different from your needs) to succeed in college?

2. How are these students like you?

We have all had the experience that no matter how hard we try, we have trouble understanding the information presented. In school, we might sit through lectures and not understand the messages the instructor is trying to deliver. We may not understand the reading material for a particular class. We find it impossible to organize our thoughts to write a coherent essay or report. Sometimes, we stumble over words and are unable to convey our thoughts, feelings, or knowledge. And occasionally, we are uneasy and uncomfortable with other people. For most of us, these situations are infrequent. For people with **learning disabilities**, however, one or more of these situations is commonplace.

People with learning disabilities belong to a group of very diverse individuals, but they do share one common problem: They do not learn in the same way or as efficiently as their nondisabled peers. Although most possess normal intelligence, their academic performance is significantly behind their classmates'. Some have great difficulty learning mathematics, but most find the mastery of reading and writing to be their most difficult challenge (Kavale & Forness, 1996).

In this chapter, you will come to understand learning disabilities. You will learn that because of this group's **heterogeneity,** or diversity, there is no single answer about why such otherwise normal individuals have problems learning at the same rate and in the same style as their nondisabled classmates. You will learn that professionals in this area do not agree about how best to teach these individuals. You will also learn that many individuals overcome their learning disabilities through highly specialized, intensive, individualized instructional programs. Unfortunately, for many others, a learning disability will last a lifetime.

Learning Disabilities Defined

Students who qualify for special education services because of a learning disability must meet specific criteria established by the state and school district in which they live. These criteria are based on federal or professionally adopted definitions, or their combination. However, interpretation of the definition of learning disabilities and identification of students vary considerably from state to state (Mercer, King-Sears, & Mercer, 1990). Most state and local school districts have detailed and complex eligibility requirements for educational programs designed for students with learning disabilities. Many use complicated formulas combining a student's age, intelligence quotient, achievement test results, behavioral observations, and other performance data (Reynolds, 1992). Some states also require that a test revealing the student's perceptual abilities be included in the diagnostic battery. All states, though, use a general definition as the basis for their specific criteria for identification of these students.

Nationally, two definitions of learning disabilities are the basis for many states' definitions. One is included in IDEA; the other was adopted by a coalition of professional and parent organizations concerned with learning disabilities. Here is the federal government's definition:

> "Specific learning disability" means a disorder in one or more of the basic psychological processes involved in understanding or in using language, spoken or written, that may manifest itself in an imperfect ability to listen, think, speak, read, write, spell, or to do mathematical calculations. The term includes such conditions as perceptual disabilities, brain injury, minimal brain dysfunction, dyslexia, and

learning disabilities (LD). A disability in which the individual possesses average intelligence but is substantially delayed in academic achievement.

heterogeneity. Variation among members in a group.

developmental aphasia. The term does not apply to children who have learning problems that are primarily the result of visual, of hearing, of motor disabilities, of mental retardation, of emotional disturbance, or of environmental, cultural, or economic disadvantages. (U.S. Department of Education, 1992)

The National Joint Committee on Learning Disabilities' definition is as follows:

"Learning disabilities" is a general term that refers to a *heterogeneous group of disorders* manifested by significant difficulties in the acquisition and use of *listening, speaking, reading, writing, reasoning or mathematical abilities*. These disorders are intrinsic to the individual, *presumed to be due to central nervous system dysfunction*, and may occur across the *life span*. Problems in *self-regulatory behaviors, social perception, and social interaction* may exist with learning disabilities but do not by themselves constitute a learning disability. Although learning disabilities *may occur concomitantly* with other handicapping conditions (for example, sensory impairment, mental retardation, serious emotional disturbance) or with extrinsic influences (such as cultural differences or insufficient or inappropriate instruction), they are not the result of those conditions or influences. (National Joint Committee on Learning Disabilities, 1988, p. 1; emphasis added)

Basically, the difference between these two definitions rests in orientation about the causes of the disability. The federal definition is older and reflects a medical orientation. The medical orientation, in turn, reflects the earliest work done in this field by doctors helping individuals who suffered injuries to the brain. Notice that terms like *brain injury* and **dyslexia** are included in the federal definition but not in the more recent National Joint Committee definition. The National Joint Committee definition states that an individual's learning disability may be due to a **central nervous system dysfunction** but allows for the inclusion of individuals who do not have such a documented dysfunction. There are other differences between these two definitions; see whether you can identify several more.

The more recent definition requires that the primary reason for a student's disability be learning disabilities but allows for another disability as well. Therefore we now may see educational records indicating that a student is deaf and has a learning disability or is gifted and has a learning disability. Some states insist that students be classified and served by their primary disability; that is, they will not "serve a student twice." In those states, a student is eligible for services for either the deaf or those with learning disabilities, but not both. Other states have taken a different approach and have created, for instance, classroom programs for students who, for instance, are both gifted and learning disabled. Also remember the strong relationship between early identification of language impairments and learning disabilities (Wallach & Butler, 1995). Should these students be served as having two disabilities? Or, as seems to be the practice today, should they be reclassified sometime during the middle of the elementary school years?

The National Joint Committee definition also reflects the growing awareness of problems many of these individuals have in the social domain. For over fifteen years, parents and professionals have recognized a relationship between social skills and learning disabilities, with consensus that some 75 percent of these students have difficulty achieving social competence (Kavale & Forness, 1996). This characteristic, however, may not be a defining characteristic of learning disabilities, but one more related to low achievement (Haager & Vaughn, 1995). Remember, however, the predominant problem these students face is developing academic competence.

 MAKING CONNECTIONS

See the History Section of this chapter.

 MAKING CONNECTIONS

See the section on gifted students with disabilities in Chapter 7.

 MAKING CONNECTIONS

In Chapter 5, review the sections about
- communicative competence (Types of Language Impairments),
- prevalence of preschoolers with language impairments.

dyslexia. Severely impaired ability to read; presumed to be caused by a central nervous system dysfunction.

central nervous system dysfunction. Some brain or neurological damage that impedes individuals' motor and/or learning abilities.

Considerable debate about the definition of learning disabilities has raged over the years. Thus definitions of learning disabilities abound, and the search for better ways to operationalize a definition continues (Lyon, Gray, Kavanagh, & Krasmego, 1993; Shaw, Cullen, McGuire, & Brinckerhoff, 1995). Although most resemble either the federal or the National Joint Committee definition, many states, organizations, and professionals use their own definitions. Some differences among these definitions are due to philosophical orientations about what causes the disability and how it should be treated. Some definitions are medically oriented; others are educationally based; still others seek to limit the size of this population of learners. Some key features, however, exist in almost every definition; they are summarized in Table 4.1.

Despite the ongoing debate and controversy surrounding the definition of learning disabilities and its implementation, professionals outside of special education and even children without disabilities hold common beliefs about what constitutes a learning disability (Swanson & Christie, 1994). These "nonexperts" make these statements about the condition we call learning disabilities: "specific reading/math problems, general impressions/writing, planning/attention/memory, communication/motor skills, work habits, perception, intelligence, social/affective skills, instructional support/processing, and expression of sympathy" (p. 250). They also believe that this is a diverse group. Possibly, such public opinion should be used to validate new definitions or criteria for identification as they emerge.

Types of Learning Disabilities

Because learning disabilities are manifested in different ways with different individuals, there is no uniform classification system for students with learning disabilities. Although these students have normal intelligence, they do not achieve academically as well as could be expected. Some individuals' academic problems occur in only one area, and others' are more pervasive. However, results from achievement tests do allow teachers and diagnosticians to talk about how far behind a particular student is in a certain academic area. Information about an individual's social skills, learning style, and other characteristics that might be

TABLE 4.1

Key Features of Definitions of Learning Disabilities

Intelligence scores within the normal range
A significant discrepancy between academic achievement and expected potential
Not caused by other factors, such as cultural differences, educational opportunities, poverty, or other disabilities: the exclusion clause
Often manifested in language-related areas, such as communication, written language, or reading
Problems intrinsic to the individual involving that person's central nervous system, specific deficits in information processing, or the ability to learn
Learning problems specific and confined to one or two cognitive areas

interfering with efficient learning is usually discovered only by working individually with that person.

Practitioners typically do not further divide this large group of diverse learners into specific types. Although for many years researchers have worked to identify groups of individuals with learning disabilities, definitive groups have not yet been identified. Some researchers are focusing on subtypes by academic area, and others are focusing on psychological processes (Shafrir & Siegel, 1994). Other researchers are working to identify a clear neurological basis for many learning disabilities (Rourke, 1994). Such work is still in its formative stages and so far cannot give teachers useful information about how to work effectively with specific subgroups.

We have talked about the difficulties in classifying what constitutes a learning disability. Despite the diversity in types of learning disabilities, however, professionals have observed some characteristics common to these individuals. One is their difficulty in reading and writing. Their academic achievement in reading is significantly below the levels of their nondisabled classmates and is the most common reason for referrals to special education. In fact, reading problems are the basis for referral twice as often as mathematics problems (Kavale & Reese, 1992). Reading and writing, obviously, are important skills; in school, students must be able to read information from a variety of texts (social studies, science, literature) and write in varying formats (essays, reports, creative writing, notes). As the complexity of academic tasks increases, students who are not proficient in reading and writing cannot keep pace with the academic expectations of school settings.

A small percentage of students with learning disabilities have difficulties only in mathematics; however, most find *all* areas of academics challenging. In the past, students with specific academic difficulties were grouped together. For example, those with severe reading problems were called dyslexic. Students with writing disorders were said to have **disgraphia**, and those unable to learn mathematics readily had **discalculia**. These terms imply that the individual has experienced brain injury that resulted in the disorder. Given that very few students with learning disabilities have documented brain damage, such terms should be applied cautiously.

Some youngsters with learning disabilities display behavioral problems along with poor academic performance. For example, many are **hyperactive** or **impulsive**, seem unable to control their behavior, and display excessive movement. These children are unable to sit or concentrate for very long; their parents and teachers comment that they are in constant motion. Both hyperactivity and impulsivity are characteristics frequently associated with other disabilities (traumatic brain injury, emotional disturbance) and attention deficit disorder.

Identification

Some researchers wrestle with issues of identification and implementation of the definition, whereas others try to refine the criteria for inclusion in this group. Many school districts and states rely on quantitative data such as **discrepancy scores.** Others rely on classroom observations, input from parents and teachers, and evaluations of children's academic performance on their daily schoolwork. To date, a measurable and nationally consistent method of determining whether a student has a learning disability has not been agreed on. Many different methods for iden-

MAKING CONNECTIONS

Also refer to the section on Reading found in the Interventions section of this chapter.

MAKING CONNECTIONS

For more on ADD, see the Learning Characteristics section found in the Profiles section of this chapter.

disgraphia. Severely impaired ability to write; presumed to be caused by central nervous system dysfunction.

discalculia. Severely impaired ability to calculate or perform mathematical functions; presumed to be caused by central nervous system dysfunction.

hyperactivity. Impaired ability to sit or concentrate for long periods of time.

impulsive. Impaired ability to control one's own behavior.

discrepancy scores. The scores used in some states to determine eligibility for services designed for students with learning disabilities.

tifying these youngsters are used across the country; Ysseldyke, Algozzine, and Epps (1983) found seventeen different methods when they analyzed different states' practices.

Because so many states and school districts use **discrepancy formulas** to help in the identification of students with learning disabilities, we now explain how they are used. These formulas measure the difference between a child's potential, as measured by a standardized intelligence test, and the child's actual academic achievement, as determined by a standardized achievement test. Discrepancy formulas are very complicated; some require a computer program to calculate the discrepancy score. Some states have thus developed tables for diagnosticians to use as they evaluate students' scores, and other states use a minimum discrepancy score as a cutoff point for identification. Whatever method is employed, 76 percent of the states use some version of standard scores to classify students as having a learning disability (Frankenberger & Fronzaglio, 1991). **Standard scores** represent a measure common to all tests so that the results can be compared. If students have a discrepancy (difference) of 23 or more standard score points between the scores they received on an intelligence test and on an achievement test, they qualify in many states for special education. Let us use Suzi, a 10-year-old fourth grader, as an example. Suzi is reading at the first-grade level, she is able to solve third-grade arithmetic problems, and she has difficulty writing an organized, coherent paragraph. Her intelligence quotient (IQ), or standard score on an intelligence test, is 100, which is considered average. However, her standard achievement test score is 72. Because the difference between the two scores is greater than 23 points, Suzi has been classified as having learning disabilities, and she qualifies for special education.

One way to determine whether a child's academic achievement is equal to his overall intellectual abilities is to use standardized achievement tests. Another method is to collect data on his daily academic performance.

discrepancy formulas. Formulas developed by state educational agencies or local districts to determine the difference between a child's actual achievement and expected achievement based on the student's IQ scores.

standard scores. Converted test scores that equalize scores from different tests to allow comparison.

Educators in the field of learning disabilities do not agree on the use of discrepancy formulas (Stanovich, 1991). First, they are complicated to calculate, requiring much time and effort. Second, they tend to focus solely on academic achievement and do not consider other factors such as cognitive or social abilities. Professionals know that discrepancies between intelligence and achievement are not exclusively characteristic of students with learning disabilities (Swanson, 1991). Third, the identification process is criticized because available tests lack precision and accuracy. As Robinson and Deshler (1995) point out, a student can be identified and served as having a learning disability in one school district but not in another school district just a few miles away.

Professionals currently employ alternative methods of assessment for identification purposes. Some use a standard cutoff score as an identification measure. Thus a student may be identified as having a learning disability if a standard score on an achievement test falls below a certain number. Other professionals compare the subtest scores on an IQ test or use an arbitrary, minimum cutoff score so that students with scores below a certain number cannot qualify as having a learning disability. For example, in this method, students with IQ scores below, say, 90 would not be identified as having learning disabilities. Still other professionals carefully consider observational data and input from parents, teachers, and support staff acquainted with the student. Despite their inherent subjectivity, such data can provide valuable information. Clearly, professional debate will continue on these issues.

Significance

As with other groups of individuals with disabilities, those with learning disabilities range in abilities. Some children have a mild learning disability. With assistance, they profit from the standard curriculum offered in general education and are college-bound. Children with severe disabilities, however, require intensive remediation and support throughout their schoolyears and into adulthood.

Most children with learning disabilities are not identified as having a learning disability until they have attended school for several years. And, what happens in those early schoolyears can set the stage for future success or failure. Researchers have discovered an alarming pattern: Many students with learning disabilities have experienced grade retention. Retention actually increases the probability that a student will eventually drop out of school (New Mexico Learning Disabilities Association, 1994). Those who are retained once are 30 to 40 percent more likely to drop out, and those who have been retained twice have a 100 percent chance of leaving school before graduation. Despite the fact that retaining students does not improve either academic or social adjustment, 58 percent of students with learning disabilities had repeated a grade before being referred and identified as having a learning disability (McLeskey, 1992). The students who are retained seem to have the lowest ability and achievement (McLeskey, Lancaster, & Grizzle, 1995). Because the outcomes for those who are retained are not good and because more and more of these students are being included in general education classes with fewer supports, it is important for educators and parents to change their beliefs about the effectiveness of retention.

Students with learning disabilities are different from their nondisabled classmates. These youngsters have very low scores on achievement tests and perform very poorly on academic tasks in the classroom. They tend to perform far below their expectancy (McLeskey & Waldron, 1991). Most (60 percent) are identified by third grade (Kavale & Reese, 1992) when reading and writing take on greater importance. At this time, students begin to read textbooks to gain information and are required to write reports and themes. It is a time when curriculum materials require use and comprehension of figurative and symbolic language, communication skills that are difficult for many individuals with learning disabilities (Abrahamson & Sprouse, 1995). Also, teachers expect students at this age to work at their desks independently for longer periods of time. For many students with learning disabilities, being able to work independently and concentrate on one task is a difficult, seemingly impossible requirement.

As the demands of school increase, many of these students fall further and further behind their classmates' academic achievement. Some develop behavioral problems, and many develop poor self-esteem (Kavale & Forness, 1996). It is at this point—when they are several years behind their classmates' academic achievement levels and when they do not behave according to teachers' expectations—that they are referred for special education services. Even intensive efforts from special educators do not enable some students with learning disabilities to learn at the same rate as their normal peers. Without special assistance, they usually find the increasing academic demands of school impossible to cope with. According to Schumaker, Deshler, Alley, and Warner (1983), by the time students with learning disabilities reach seventh grade, their average achievement in reading and written language is at the high third grade level. By their senior year in high school, their average academic achievement in these two areas is at the fifth grade level, with mathematics scores slightly higher.

Because of the harm that can be done to a child who is misidentified and incorrectly labeled as having a disability, educators are concerned that only those students with learning disabilities be so identified. Despite concerns like those raised in the Focus on Diversity box, bilingual children as well as low-achieving students are at risk for inappropriate referrals and identification (Algozzine & Ysseldyke, 1986; Ruiz, 1995). Unfortunately, it is fairly easy for students without disabilities to be placed in special education under this category. Why can such errors occur? How can achieving students with normal intelligence quotients who are several years behind in academic achievement also meet the criteria for learning disabilities? Some educators also maintain that classes for those with learning disabilities serve as a means for general education teachers to rid themselves of their most difficult students. How can we resolve this issue? More stringent criteria, better identification procedures, more cultural awareness, and a general education system more tolerant of individual differences should bring a reduction in the number of low-achieving and culturally and linguistically diverse students referred and ultimately incorrectly identified as having a disability.

Remember, however, that being identified as having a disability and being "labeled" as having a learning disability is not always devastating. It can bring both relief and understanding. Such was the case for P. Buckley Moss and for Joan Esposito (1995). Now an adult, Joan recalls that, for her, going to school was a form of child abuse. Every morning she awoke sick to her stomach knowing that the school day would be filled with struggle, humiliation, failure, and pain. She says that she spent hours alone in her bedroom trying to figure out ways to hide her reading problems from family and friends. As an uninformed and innocent child, the labels she gave to herself were stigmatizing and debilitating. She reports that the label of learning disabilities freed her, helped her and her teachers find an

 MAKING CONNECTIONS

In Chapter 3, review the sections about
• overrepresentation,
• prevalence.

 MAKING CONNECTIONS

See the biographical sketch of P. Buckley Moss, whose art is found at the opening of this chapter.

Language Difference or Learning Disabilities?

The overrepresentation of culturally and linguistically diverse students in programs for students with learning disabilities has raised the concerns of parents and educators across the nation (Gollnick & Chinn, 1994). This problem is particularly acute for African American students and for students who have limited English proficiency. One of the fastest growing segments of the U.S. student population comprises those who fall into the limited English proficient group (U.S. Department of Education, 1993). Because of the lack of sophistication of most educators and the difficulty in determining when an individual has gained true proficiency in the English language, the risk of misidentifying these students is great. The learning disabilities category, where the difference between potential and current achievement is a major criterion used for identification, is particularly vulnerable to incorrect disability determinations.

appropriate instructional remediation, and assisted her in becoming a productive citizen. Joan's difficulties have not disappeared, but she is able to understand and cope with them constructively.

As with Joan Esposito, most individuals with learning disabilities have a lifelong disability. Table 4.2 shows that students' learning difficulties can be present from the preschool years through adulthood. Some remedial procedures are effective, however, and Table 4.2 also describes a few treatment plans.

History of the Field

The field of learning disabilities is relatively new. The term *learning disabilities* was coined on April 6, 1963, by Professor Sam Kirk and others at a meeting of parents and professionals in Chicago. From this date, public school programs were started for elementary school children with learning disabilities. The past thirty years have seen an explosion in the number of pupils identified, teachers trained, and classroom programs offered. Services continue to expand, as we provide programs for **postsecondary** students and adults.

Investigation of learning disabilities, however, put down roots long before 1963 (Wiederholt, 1974). In 1919, Kurt Goldstein began working with young men with brain injuries who had returned to the United States after World War I. He found many of them distractible, unable to attend to relevant cues, confused, and hyperactive. They also could no longer read or write well. Some years later, Alfred Strauss and Heinz Werner expanded on Goldstein's work. Strauss and Werner worked at the Wayne County Training Center in Michigan with pupils who were thought to be brain injured. They found many similarities to the group of World War I veterans that Goldstein had studied earlier. However, there was one important difference between these two groups: Goldstein's group *lost* their abili-

MAKING CONNECTIONS

See the section on Transition Through Adulthood in this chapter for more information.

postsecondary. Education that comes after high school (e.g., community college, technical/vocational school, college, university, continuing education).

~~~
**TABLE 4.2**
Life Span View of Learning Disabilities

| | *Preschool* | *Grades K–1* | *Grades 2–6* | *Grades 7–12* | *Adult* |
|---|---|---|---|---|---|
| Problem areas | Delay in developmental milestones (e.g., walking)<br><br>Receptive language<br><br>Expressive language<br><br>Visual perception<br><br>Auditory perception<br><br>Short attention span<br><br>Hyperactivity | Academic readiness skills (e.g., alphabet knowledge, quantitative concepts, directional concepts, etc.)<br><br>Receptive language<br><br>Expressive language<br><br>Visual perception<br><br>Auditory perception<br><br>Gross and fine motor<br><br>Attention<br><br>Hyperactivity<br><br>Social skills | Reading skills<br><br>Arithmetic skills<br><br>Written expression<br><br>Verbal expression<br><br>Receptive language<br><br>Attention span<br><br>Hyperactivity<br><br>Social-emotional | Reading skills<br><br>Arithmetic skills<br><br>Written expression<br><br>Verbal expression<br><br>Listening skills<br><br>Study skills (metacognition)<br><br>Social-emotional-delinquency | Reading skills<br><br>Arithmetic skills<br><br>Written expression<br><br>Verbal expression<br><br>Listening skills<br><br>Study skills<br><br>Social-emotional |
| Assessment | Prediction of high risk for later learning problems | Prediction of high risk for later learning problems | Identification of learning disabilities | Identification of learning disabilities | Identification of learning disabilities |
| Treatment types | Preventive | Preventive | Remedial<br><br>Corrective | Remedial<br><br>Corrective<br><br>Compensatory<br><br>Learning strategies | Remedial<br><br>Corrective<br><br>Compensatory<br><br>Learning strategies |
| Treatments with most research and/or expert support | Direct instruction in language skills<br><br>Behavior management<br><br>Parent training | Direct instruction in academic and language areas<br><br>Behavior management<br><br>Parent training | Direct instruction in academic areas<br><br>Behavior management<br><br>Self-control training<br><br>Parent training | Direct instruction in academic areas<br><br>Tutoring in subject areas<br><br>Direct instruction in learning strategies (study skill)<br><br>Self-control training<br><br>Curriculum alternatives | Direct instruction in academic areas<br><br>Tutoring in subject (college) or job area<br><br>Compensatory instruction (e.g., using aids such as tape recorder, calculator, computer, dictionary)<br><br>Direct instruction in learning strategies |

*Source: Students with Learning Disabilities* (4th ed., p. 50) by C. Mercer, 1991, Columbus, OH: Merrill. Reprinted by permission.

*Sam Kirk is considered by many to be the "father" of the field of learning disabilities, in part because he helped coin the term at a meeting in 1963 of what was to become the Learning Disabilities Association of America.*

**lateral dominance.** A preference for using either the right or the left side of the body for one's motoric responses; some believe that mixed dominance or lateral confusion is associated with poor reading performance.

**direct instruction.** Specifically focusing instruction on the desired, targeted behavior.

**process/product debate.** Argument that either perceptual training or direct instruction was more effective for instruction.

ties to read, write, and speak well; Strauss and Werner's group had *never developed* these abilities. Study of learning disabilities thus originated in the work of these pioneers, and their concentration on brain injury continues to affect the field today.

During the 1920s and 1930s, Samuel Orton, a specialist in neurology, developed theories and remedial reading techniques for children with severe reading problems, whom he called "dyslexic" and believed to be brain damaged. He emphasized the importance of **lateral dominance.** In the late 1930s, Newell Kephart worked with Strauss at the Wayne County School and further studied a group of children who were considered to have mental retardation but behaved like Goldstein's brain-injured subjects. Both Kephart and Laura Lehtinen developed teaching methods for what they thought were a distinct subgroup of children with disabilities. Kephart's approach was motoric; he sought to remediate these children's difficulties through physical exercises. Lehtinen developed a set of instructional procedures similar to those used by some classroom teachers today. At about the same time, Sam Kirk, who also worked at the Wayne County School, helped to develop a set of word drills and other teaching procedures he referred to throughout his career. In 1961, the *Illinois Test of Psycholinguistic Abilities* (ITPA) was published (Kirk, McCarthy, & Kirk, 1968). Although developed to identify individuals' strengths and weaknesses and their learning styles and preferences (whether they learned better by seeing or by hearing information presented), it was used for many years to identify students with learning disabilities.

During the early years of learning disabilities programs, professionals supported visual perceptual approaches. In the 1960s, Marianne Frostig, for example, developed materials that were used to improve students' visual perceptual performance. The thought was that students with learning disabilities were unable to process information accurately through the visual channel. If their visual perceptual skills were enhanced, their reading abilities would also show improvement. This approach was popular for many years, but little research evidence was offered to support its value.

Throughout the history of learning disabilities, various fads have become popular with the press and the public. One fad suggested teaching students with learning disabilities to crawl again, regardless of their age. Others claimed that various diets improved students' academic and behavioral performances. Fluorescent lighting was blamed as the cause of learning disabilities. Plants placed on students' desks were given credit for improving academic skills. In most of these instances, people made claims about students' improvement, but offered little if any research data to support the method being advocated. Parents spent considerable money, time, and resources chasing one cure after another, but the problems did not disappear. The best tool we have for evaluating recommended programs is research. To be better consumers, parents, and advocates, we must consistently and persistently ask for data that prove the benefits of such treatments.

During the 1970s, the field of learning disabilities was embroiled in heated debate about the best approaches to use in the remediation of students' academic deficits. One camp advocated the use of perceptual training, or process, approaches. The other camp advocated **direct instruction** and behavior modification approaches. This debate, which raged for years, seriously divided the field and was known as the **process/product debate.** In the end, an analysis of the research data showed that perceptual approaches were seldom effective in teaching academic skills (Hammill & Larsen, 1974).

The 1980s saw a number of different approaches developed and researched. Learning strategies are now taught to students to help them learn to learn. Other research explored how individuals with learning disabilities acquire, retain, and transfer knowledge. This line of research follows the information-processing theory. **Metacognition,** or **cognitive behavior modification,** has students use **self-management techniques** as they learn and is proving to help students to remember what they are taught, to think, to organize their study, and to solve other problems. The research of the 1980s has provided promising preliminary results that may universally change the way these students are taught and how successful they are in school and later life.

## Prevalence

Learning disabilities has grown to be the largest category of exceptional learners in the United States. In 1976–1977, almost 25 percent of the school-age population with disabilities had a learning disability. In the 1994–1995 schoolyear, according to the *Eighteenth Annual Report to Congress on the Implementation of the Individuals with Disabilities Act* (U.S. Department of Education, 1996), over 50 percent of all children with disabilities were identified as having learning disabilities as their primary disabling condition. Since IDEA was passed in 1975 and initiated in 1977, the number and percentage of students with learning disabilities have increased dramatically (see Figure 4.1). Although the acceleration was not as great in the 1992–1993 schoolyear, it appears that the number of students included in this disability group is substantially increasing again. Over this same period of time, the prevalence of students with mental retardation and speech or language impairments has decreased substantially.

Today, there are about two and a half million children with learning disabilities served by our nation's schools, indicating that 5 percent of U.S. children are identified and served within this special education category. Thus about 5 of every 100 schoolchildren have a learning disability. As we mentioned earlier, though, some states have reported excessive numbers of students with learning disabilities. The number and percentage varies state by state and even school district by school district. In some states, more than 7 percent of the school-age population is identified as having this disability, with over 50 percent of the population with disabilities belonging to this category (U.S. Department of Education, 1996).

Recall the discussion about the different ways that students with learning disabilities are identified. Different identification systems produce different numbers of students. Some states, for example, have stricter requirements for eligibility. Thus states that require a greater discrepancy between intelligence and achievement identify fewer students. States that define normal intelligence by using a narrower range of intelligence quotients (for example, IQ scores must be greater than 90, or IQ scores must be between 95 and 110) also identify and serve fewer students.

Many teachers, administrators, and state directors of special education are concerned about the growing number of those identified as having learning disabilities. Here are some of the questions they have raised:

- Do some children not have learning disabilities but, rather, are low achievers?

MAKING CONNECTIONS

Later in this chapter, see the sections about
- Learning Characteristics in the Profiles section,
- Learning Strategies in the Interventions section.

**metacognition.** Understanding one's own learning process.

**cognitive behavior modification.** Instructional strategies that teach internal control methods (such as self-talk) in structured ways to help students learn how to learn.

**self-management technique.** A set of instructional procedures whereby the individual uses self-instruction, self-monitoring, or self-reinforcement to change behavior.

~~~~
FIGURE 4.1

Number of Children with Learning Disabilities Served under IDEA Age 6 to 21: School Years 1976–77 through 1994–95.

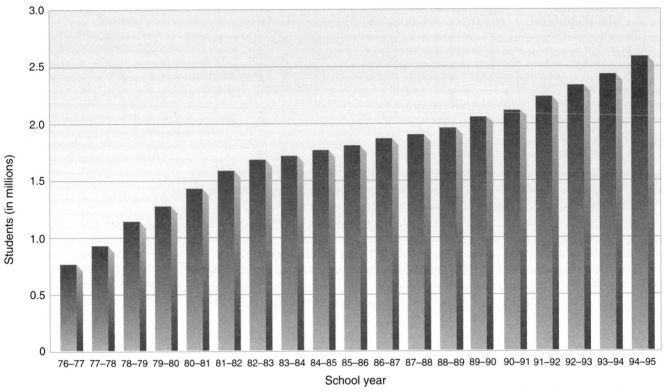

Source: Adapted from the *Thirteenth, Fourteenth, Fifteenth, and Eighteenth Annual Reports to Congress on the Implementation of the Individuals with Disabilities Education Act,* by the U.S. Department of Education, 1990, 1991, 1992, 1993, 1995, 1996. Washington, DC: Government Printing Office.

▪ Because it might be harmful to some individuals to be identified and therefore labeled as having disabilities, should fewer students now considered as having learning disabilities be included in special education?

▪ Can the states and the nation afford to serve so many students in special programs?

▪ Why are so many students not succeeding in general education programs?

▪ Is the label *learning disabilities* not as stigmatizing as other labels and therefore used for students with other more stigmatizing disabilities?

These are serious questions that professionals, parents, state legislators, educators, and the federal government need to answer. The answers are far reaching: They will affect the lives of students and their families. They will affect entire school systems because they influence how many students are served without special education supports by general educators and could alter the depth of content covered and the instructional methods used.

Causes and Prevention

People with learning disabilities comprise a heterogeneous group of individuals. Their learning disabilities are manifested in different ways and at different levels of severity. Unfortunately, researchers do not have much concrete information about the causes of learning disabilities (Bender, 1992; Hallahan, Kauffman, & Lloyd, 1996). What information is available is discussed in the following section.

Causes

As the field has wrestled with definitions of learning disabilities, so too has it argued over the causes of the problem. As we discussed earlier, some professionals maintain that learning disabilities result from injury to the brain or central nervous system. In the majority of cases of learning disabilities, however, there *is no* physical evidence or actual medical diagnosis of brain injury or damage to the central nervous system. For this reason, many special educators oppose the use of medical terms associated with brain injury. They believe that using terms like *assumed brain injury* or *presumed central nervous system dysfunction* leads to a conclusion that cannot be proven and may be misleading. They believe that the use of the term *brain injury* gives the impression that nothing can be done about the condition. This impression can lead parents, educators, and the individuals concerned to give up or not try to remediate identified educational difficulties. They might also set expectations too low. We know from research on education that when expectations and goals are set low, they are usually met but not exceeded. For a child with a learning disability, if goals are set too low, the child may never reach his or her potential.

Although we know little about the causes of learning disabilities, we can presume that students who have them are as diverse as are the types. Some students may have a central nervous system dysfunction that inhibits their learning. Some may have proven brain damage—caused by an accident or by a lack of oxygen before, during, or after birth—resulting in neurological difficulties that affect their ability to learn. Some may have inherited their disability (Decker & Defries, 1980, 1981; Oliver, Cole, & Hollingsworth, 1991). A gene has now been identified that may be responsible for reading problems (New Mexico Learning Disabilities Association, 1994). Diet and various environmental factors have also been suggested as causes of learning disabilities. Although not proposing that ear infections cause learning disabilities, Reichman and Healey (1983) did find an interesting connection between otitis media and children identified as having learning disabilities. They found that chronic and early incidence of otitis media was twice as common in children identified as having learning disabilities as in those without learning disabilities. They maintain that mild hearing losses could make these children at risk for developing delays in auditory, language, and academic skills. There does seem to be a connection between language impairments and learning disabilities (Wallace & Butler, 1995). Gibbs and Cooper (1989) found that 96 percent of their sample with learning disabilities had either a speech, a language, or a hearing problem. Yet others (Englemann, 1977; Lovitt, 1977) maintain that some of these children may have serious difficulties learning academic material because early on they were poorly taught basic academic skills.

Why do children with learning disabilities not learn as efficiently or in the same way their classmates do? Some professionals (Hallahan & Bryan, 1981)

 MAKING CONNECTIONS

For more on the relationship between learning disabilities and language impairments, see these sections in Chapter 5:
• Prevalence
• Cognitive and Academic Performance in the Children with Speech or Language Impairments section

 MAKING CONNECTIONS

In Chapter 5, review all of the sections about language impairments, particularly in these sections:
• Identification
• Causes
• Children with
In Chapter 3, see Education and the Preschool Child.

believe that individuals with one type of deficit are unable to focus their attention constructively: Their **selective attention**, or ability to attend to relevant rather than irrelevant features of a task, is faulty. Such children might have difficulty dealing with distractors in arithmetic word problems. (An example word problem is the following: Twelve children went to the beach. Each child brought $5.00 spending money. David bought three hot dogs at $1.50 each and a coke for 50 cents. Kathryn bought a bag of popcorn for 75 cents. How much money did David have left?) Some children with a selective attention deficit might have difficulty taking in information from the teacher when others are talking at the same time. Others might have trouble distinguishing important from unimportant facts presented in a lecture and remembering them.

Prevention

Providing guidelines about preventing learning disabilities is difficult because we cannot pinpoint causes. Methods of preventing or reducing the effects of this disability do exist, however. For instance, developing adequate language skills may be beneficial, as shown by apparently strong relationships between poor language development and learning disabilities (Wallach & Butler, 1995). Young children who do not develop good language skills during their early childhood years tend to be at risk for academic problems during their later schoolyears. And children who develop language very late tend to have poor cognition: They do not reason or solve problems well. Therefore children who do not develop adequate language

selective attention. Ability to attend to the crucial features of a task.

Teachers can help encourage interactive play and language development by selecting materials and activities that are interesting and appropriate for the children's ages and levels of ability.

skills early in their lives are at risk for learning disabilities. There is strong evidence that early intervention programs, such as Headstart and other well-structured preschool programs, positively influence children's language and thinking skills and their later success in school (Currie & Thomas, 1995). Children who are at risk or show developmental lags in these areas should be referred to an early intervention program, even if they have not yet been identified as having a disability.

As we mentioned earlier, professionals believe that some learning disabilities are caused by poor teaching. Englemann (1977) claims, for example, that 90 percent of this population is handicapped because of faulty instruction during the early years at school. Of course, this claim is hard to prove, but a closer look at the educational system is warranted. Traditional instruction is not always sensitive to individual differences in learning rates and styles. Yet we know that not all children learn at the same pace; individual children require different amounts of drill, practice, and review. Many experts believe that these youngsters may not process information properly or may need to *learn how to learn* (Bos & Vaughn, 1994; Deshler & Schumaker, 1986; Lerner, 1993). Those who do not receive enough repetition to master the skills being taught are left behind. Because the concept currently taught often builds on one that was just presented, lack of mastery of basic concepts could result in children falling further and further behind their peers' academic achievement.

To prevent the compounding effects of learning disabilities, these children need special assistance, either from a special educator or their general education teacher, as soon as possible. Attentive teachers will observe characteristics such as those listed in Table 4.3 and can help their students through timely referral and

TABLE 4.3

Possible Signs or Characteristics of Learning Disabilities

Significant discrepancy between potential and academic achievement

Distractibility or inability to pay attention for as long as peers do

Hyperactive behavior, exhibited through excessive movement

Inattentiveness during lectures or class discussions

Impulsiveness

Poor motor coordination and spatial relation skills

Inability to solve problems

Poor motivation and little active involvement in learning tasks

Overreliance on teacher and peers for class assignments

Evidence of poor language and/or cognitive development

Immature social skills

Disorganized approach to learning

Substantial delays in academic achievement

provision of special services. Remember, though, that not all students with learning disabilities have all the characteristics listed in the table; as always, caution should be exercised when applying theory.

Children with Learning Disabilities

Providing a profile for children with learning disabilities is difficult because the most cited characteristic of this group is their individual differences. Time after time, reference is made to the group's heterogeneity (Haager & Vaughn, 1995). Wallace and McLoughlin (1988) believe that the term *learning disabilities* refers to a variety of specific disorders, with no two individuals possessing the same patterns of skills and behaviors. Despite the diversity in this group of learners, many of these youngsters share some common characteristics and patterns of behavior that have been noted by their teachers, peers, and parents. In this section we discuss typical learning and social characteristics, and we also describe a condition—attention deficit disorder—that is often a secondary diagnosis for children with learning disabilities.

Learning Characteristics

Let's be clear. The predominant problem of *all* students with learning disabilities is learning and mastering academic tasks (Kavale & Forness, 1996). Although individuals might differ in their strengths and weaknesses, learning styles, and personalities, all have learning difficulties that result in poor academic performance. For most, the learning impairment is so severe that by the time they are in high school, they are many years behind their classmates in achievement. Many researchers feel that the following learning characteristics impede these students' abilities to learn efficiently: lack of motivation, inattention, inability to generalize, and insufficient problem-solving, information-processing, and thinking skills (Rivera & Smith, 1997). Depending on a student's learning style, altering these characteristics can lead to substantial improvement in achievement.

Motivation and Attribution. **Motivation** is usually defined as the inner stimulus that causes individuals to be energized and directed in their behavior. Motivation can be explained as a person's trait (a need to succeed, a need not to fail, a great interest in a topic) or as a temporary state of mind (a test or class presentation tomorrow, a passing interest in the topic). Differences in motivation may account for differences in the way people approach tasks and for differences in their success with those tasks. Clearly, year after year of frustration and failure at school can affect students' motivation and their approach to the task of learning. Interviews with two children with severe reading problems, presented in the accompanying box, give us some insight into the compounding effects of learning difficulties on motivation.

By the time most students are identified as having a learning disability, they have experienced many years of failure. School failure can result in both academic and motivational deficits. Therefore students are afraid to respond, take risks, or actively engage in learning. They develop a negative attitude and come to believe that their failure is a result of lack of ability, rather than a signal to work harder or ask for help. They lower their expectations and believe that success is an unat-

motivation. Internal incentives that are influenced by previous success or failure.

Middle School Students with Reading Disabilities Talk About How They Feel About School

Ben tells us about what comprises reading instruction for him and also reveals his attitudes about school as he answers some questions about his school experiences.

What do you read at school?

Ben: Read dull cards.

Cards? What kind of cards?

Ben: NFL cards and stuff like that [reading kit cards].

Do you read for the teacher individually or in groups?

Ben: By myself.

So if you come up against a word you don't know, what happens?

Ben: Nothin'.

Nothing? Do you ask?

Ben: Yeah, but it ain't worth it.

Why, what happens when you ask?

Ben: 'Cause she tells me to figure it out, and I'm like, "I can't figure it out."

Missie expresses her concerns after she learned that she will not have a special reading class next year when she moves on to high school.

So next year you're not going to have a reading class. Does that upset you?

Missie: Yeah. That's what the teachers told me, that I wasn't gonna have reading class. And that kind of upset me, 'cause when I don't have reading class, I won't get no better. Plus, when I'm in high school, how can I...I'll be embar...it really embarrass me when I read in front of people. At high school, they're gonna think, "Where'd she come from? She don't belong here! She gonna have to get more help..." you know all that kind of stuff.

Source: Adapted from "Persistence of Reading Disabilities: The Voices of Four Middle School Students" by R. Kos, 1991, *American Educational Research Journal, 28,* pp. 882, 884. Reprinted by permission.

tainable goal. They do not believe in themselves and do not try to learn. When people expect to fail, they become dependent on others—a situation referred to as **learned helplessness.** They come to believe that they are not responsible for their achievements and that luck is the reason for their successes and failures, not effort (Pearl, 1982). To overcome this pattern, students need to be shown the relationship between effort and accomplishment. How can adults help them?

Many individuals with learning disabilities need structure; they find that working in a systematic and predictable environment helps them learn more efficiently. Teachers and parents should therefore provide structure for them and organize their day carefully as well as help them learn to structure their lives themselves.

learned helplessness. A phenomenon in which individuals gradually, usually as a result of repeated failure or control by others, become less wiling to attempt tasks.

Motivation and attribution are directly related to success in school. Many students with learning disabilities become poorly motivated to accomplish educational tasks and may attribute their difficulties to external factors.

These skills are also important in later life when, as adults, they need to be able to allocate time to a variety of activities, including work and leisure.

Children with learning disabilities also must learn to handle failure. They know that they are not performing as well as the other students in their classes. Some have problems in one academic area, and others have problems in almost all their classes. These students need careful instruction. For example, they need to be told how to solve a problem, even when others seem to know how to instinctively. Tutoring from a classmate or extra assistance from the teacher often helps these students. They can also benefit from encouragement. Research findings show that many students with learning disabilities, probably because of their excessive number of failure experiences, have a greater incidence of overall negative attitudes (Yasutake & Bryan, 1995). However, when those attitudes are turned around, learning and performance improve.

Attributions, which are internal justifications that individuals use to explain why they succeed or fail at particular tasks, affect motivation in all of us, and they are particularly important in students with learning disabilities. After many and repeated experiences with failure, individuals come to expect failure. This expectation becomes outwardly directed, viewed as something beyond one's control (Pearl, 1982; Switzky & Schultz, 1988).

Students who expect academic failure tend to be passive. This trait is seen in many students with learning disabilities, who are said to be **inactive learners** (Torgesen & Licht, 1983). They do not approach the learning task purposefully and are not actively involved in their learning. They do not ask questions, seek help, or read other related material to learn more. They often attribute their success to luck rather than to their abilities or effort (Dohrn & Bryan, 1994), and 70 percent attribute poor performance to lack of ability (Kavale & Forness, 1996). These characteristics are just the opposite of those of **high achievers,** who tend to expect success and view it as an incentive to work harder. Thus students with learning disabilities tend to be **low achievers;** they expect failure and see no use in expending more effort.

attributions. The explanations individuals give themselves for their successes or failures.

inactive learners. Students who do not become involved in learning situations, do not approach the learning task purposefully, do not ask questions, do not seek help, or do not initiate learning.

high achievers. Students who expect success and view it as an incentive to work harder.

low achievers. Students who expect failure and see little use in expending effort to learn.

By comparing low-achieving students' motivation and attributions with those of high-achieving students, we can better understand the concepts of attribution and learned helplessness. Let's look at a classroom situation, such as writing a social studies term paper, to see how students' motivation affects the way they approach the task. High achievers, when given the assignment of writing a term paper on, say, the Revolutionary War, approach the task with confidence, knowing that they are capable of producing a thorough and well-written paper. They realize that if they read their textbook and other materials available at the library, they will know enough about the topic to prepare the paper. Because of past successes, they know that making an effort results in success. Therefore these students will proofread their term papers and even add extras (such as maps and diagrams) to their final products. The low-achieving students, in contrast, do not approach this assignment with much vigor. They seem overwhelmed by the assignment and complain that it is too difficult. These children believe that it is useless to ask for assistance, spend time in the library, or read extra materials. Instead, they write a short and incomplete term paper that is probably not developed with care or proofread.

Attributions and motivation can be altered (Fulk, 1996). With intensive efforts from teachers and parents, youngsters can learn that their efforts can lead to success. Students and adults need to discuss actual performance and how it can be improved. Students also need to be helped to approach learning strategically; they need to be taught strategies for approaching the learning task. For example, by breaking tasks into smaller units, students realize that many tasks are easily mastered and are not as difficult as originally perceived and that with more effort and greater persistence success can be achieved.

Attention. Another learning characteristic commonly observed by teachers and researchers is inattention, or **attention deficits** (Mercer, 1997). Children who do not focus on the task to be learned or who pay attention to the wrong features of the task are said to be distractible. Several researchers (Lenz, Alley, & Schumaker, 1987) have found that advance organizers help to focus students' attention by providing an introductory overview of the material to be presented. These introductory statements explain why the information is important and provide a key to the crucial elements of the presentation.

 MAKING CONNECTIONS

Every chapter begins with an advance organizer, which can serve as an example.

Generalization. Most students with learning disabilities also have difficulty transferring or generalizing their learning to different skills or situations (Rivera & Smith, 1988). They might apply a newly learned study skill in history class but not in English class. Or a child might master borrowing in subtraction with a zero in the units column but not apply that rule when borrowing with two zeros. Again, research has shown that some teaching methods can actually interfere with students learning the concept of generalization (Ellis, 1986). The overuse of feedback on performance (knowledge of results) reinforces dependency, learned helplessness, and learning inactivity.

 MAKING CONNECTIONS

Generalization is also discussed in Chapter 4.

Teachers help students learn to generalize by having students take more responsibility for managing their own instructional programs. For example, a special education teacher who is concerned about a student who is not applying a recently learned study skill to a general education science class might remind the student to use the study skill when preparing for the next science test. Next, the teacher might collaborate with the science teacher, explaining the strategy and asking that teacher to remind the student to apply the strategy while studying.

attention deficits. A characteristic often associated with learning disabilities in which students do not pay attention to the task or the correct features of a task to learn how to perform it well.

Then the special education teacher might ask the student to keep a record of the times the strategy was used. Finally, the teacher might reward the student for improved performance in science class.

Processing Information. Many people with learning disabilities have difficulty learning to read and write, understanding things they are told, and even expressing themselves through oral communication. To explain why, researchers are studying theories of learning and then applying them to the way students with learning disabilities actually learn. One theory, **information processing**, follows the flow of information while people learn new skills; the theory begins with the input of information, shows how information is processed, and ends with its output. Lerner (1993) helps us to understand this theory by comparing the way computers work and the way people learn (see Figure 4.2). Like the computer, the human brain takes in information, processes that information (makes associations, stores information, calls it up, acts upon it), and generates responses from it. This model is currently guiding researchers in their study of students with learning disabilities and how they learn (Swanson, 1987, 1990).

Even though research on information processing is preliminary, it provides educators with some guidelines for the instructional process. To benefit from the information they receive in class, students must pay attention and must remember the information. Educators can help by repeating important information, presenting material that is organized and grouped in a systematic fashion, and providing students with information that is meaningful to them and associated with other information they are already familiar with. In addition, educators can help students manipulate information—that is, use the information in their writings and discussions. The learning strategy approach, discussed later in "Education and the Schoolchild," incorporates these teaching practices and should be part of the educational program for students with learning disabilities.

Problem-Solving and Thinking Skills. Many researchers feel that students with learning disabilities have poor **problem-solving** and thinking skills (Rivera & Smith, 1997). They are not strategic learners. To study efficiently and remember content, students must be proficient in the following thinking skills: classifying, associating, and sequencing. **Classifying** allows the learner to categorize and group items together by common characteristics. Usually, people will remember more items in a list if they approach the task by **chunking**, or clustering, the information presented. For example, if you forget your grocery list and are already at the store, you might try to remember what items you need by thinking about groups of items. You might recall that potatoes and corn were on the list when you think of vegetables and that ice cream, pizza, and TV dinners were on the list when you think of frozen foods.

People are more strategic in their learning and remembering when they relate or associate information by some common denominator (for example, softness or hardness, style of painting). **Association** also helps individuals see the relationships that exist among and between different knowledge bases. By associating facts or ideas, the mind is able to find the relationships and connections that units of information possess. By using this thinking skill, people can relate information on different dimensions. **Sequencing** information also facilitates memory and learning. Items can be sequenced in many ways. For example, physical items can be sorted and sequenced by size, weight, or volume. Facts, events, and ideas can

information-processing theory. Suggests that learning disabilities are caused by an inability to organize thinking and approach learning tasks systematically.

problem solving. Finding answers or solutions to situations.

classifying. The ability to categorize items or concepts by their common characteristics.

chunking. Grouping information into smaller pieces so that it can be more easily remembered.

association. In thinking the ability to see relationships among different concepts or knowledge bases.

sequencing. Mentally categorizing and putting items, facts, or ideas in order according to various dimensions.

FIGURE 4.2

Information Processing Theory and its Similarities to the Computer System

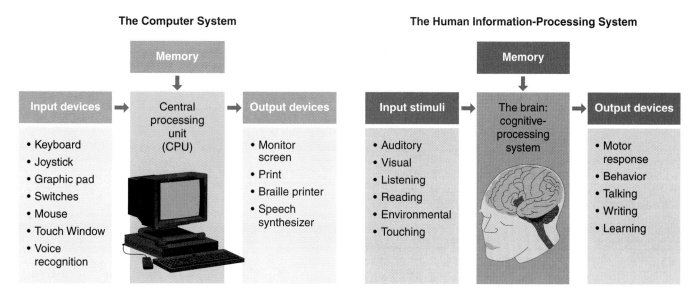

Source: *Learning disabilities: Theories, diagnosis, and teaching strategies,* (6th ed.), p. 195, by J. Lerner, 1993, Boston: Houghton Mifflin. Adapted with permission.

be sequenced by time, importance, or complexity. These thinking skills—classifying, associating, and sequencing—help students approach learning tasks more purposefully. With guided practice, these abstract skills can be learned and developed into useful tools for learning.

Social Skills Characteristics

Although deficits in social skills may not be a defining characteristic of learning disabilities, problems in this area are quite common (Haager & Vaughn, 1995). Overwhelmingly, teachers rate their students with learning disabilities significantly lower in social competence and school adjustment than their other students (Turkaspa & Bryan, 1995). Pervasive problems in the social domain, particularly when they persist into adulthood, can be devastating to both the individuals and their family members (Bryan, 1994). Because of the importance of developing friends, getting along with others, and understanding appropriate social interaction conventions, we now focus on two important areas: social competence and social status.

Social Competence. Social competence relates in some way to almost all actions and skills that people perform. It is the ability to perceive and interpret social situations, generate appropriate social responses, and interact with others. Through a comprehensive analysis of 152 independent research studies, Kavale and Forness (1996) found that almost 80 percent of students with learning disabilities are perceived to have a deficit in social competence. Their lack of social competence is due to several factors. First, their poor academic standing causes low self-esteem, which in turn can affect all social behavior. Second, communicative competence and

MAKING CONNECTIONS

Review again the Defined section in this chapter.

MAKING CONNECTIONS

Reread the Social Competence Section found in the Children with Speech or Language Impairment section of Chapter 5.

All students should have the opportunity to participate in extra curricular activities to find the ones best suited for them.

social competence are related, and many of the skills associated with understanding and using language are also associated with social abilities.

Let's take a look at how language skills affect social skills. (Recall the strong relationship between language impairments and learning disabilities.) One component of both communicative and social competence is understanding nonverbal communications. A recent study in England found that children with learning disabilities are exceptionally poor at distinguishing emotions, particularly, disgust, neutrality, and surprise (Nabuzoka & Smith, 1995). Being less proficient than their nondisabled peers in comprehending nonverbal messages could explain why many of them do not have successful social situations. Many students with learning disabilities have difficulties in a related component of communicative competence: understanding implied messages. They do not understand figurative or nonliteral language. This point was well illustrated in a study about these students' abilities to comprehend the moral messages included in fables (brief tales where animals replace human characters and relate indirect messages that have great social meaning). This study showed that students with learning disabilities do not comprehend the meaning of these stories, cannot understand even rudimentary metaphors, and are unable to create meaning from abstract language (Abrahamsen & Sprouse, 1995).

Such inability in pragmatic language skills, once again, demonstrates the relationship between communicative competence and social competence. It is important to realize the broad and negative impact the lack of communicative competence can have on an individual's overall performance: understanding of stories read in the general education class, teacher's explanations of concepts, and interactions with others. It may also affect other outcomes, such as feelings of loneliness, isolation, and victimization (Sabornie, 1994). Alert teachers must see the relationship between a student's learning disabilities and social behavior. Table 4.4, which lists some of the more common characteristics noted by parents and professionals when observing individuals with learning disabilities, may help call your attention to some of these relationships.

Social Status. Teachers note that these children often are not accepted by their classmates and have difficulties making friends. The social status of these children needs to be given greater attention by educators and parents. These concerns are borne out by research that shows that children with learning disabilities, regardless of placement, are rejected by their classmates without learning disabilities and considered by their teachers to be poorly adjusted (Kavale & Forness, 1996). They are less likely to be selected for extracurricular activities, which also reduces the likelihood of their developing leadership skills, friendships, and a sense of competence outside of academic situations (Geisthardt & Munsch, 1996). As adolescents, they do not seek the support of peers or friends as do their classmates without disabilities, leaving them with feelings of rejection and isolation. Of even more concern is their tendency to be victimized—threatened, physically assaulted, and having their belongings stolen more frequently—more than their peers (Sabornie, 1994).

TABLE 4.4

Social Skills Characteristics

Students with learning disabilities tend to

1. choose less socially acceptable behavior;

2. be less able to predict the consequences of their behaviors;

3. misinterpret social, nonverbal cues;

4. make poor decisions;

5. be unable to solve social problems;

6. use social conventions (manners) improperly;

7. adapt to the characteristics of the person they are interacting with incorrectly (do not defer or assert themselves when appropriate);

8. not pay close enough attention during classroom assignments;

9. be shy, withdrawn, distractible, or hyperactive;

10. be socially naive and unable to determine when other people are sincere, deceptive, or sarcastic;

11. be lonely;

12. experience rejection from their peers;

13. be victimized more often.

Why do these youngsters have such low social status? Peer rejection seems to be related to classroom behavior: Children who exhibited either acting out or withdrawn behavior were more likely to be rejected by their nondisabled classmates (Roberts & Zubrick, 1993). However, students with learning disabilities who did not display either behavioral excesses or deficits did not experience rejection from their peers. Teachers can play an instrumental role in reducing peer rejection by pairing these students with nondisabled classmates in areas of mutual interest (Fox, 1989). For example, teachers might plan activities for which students with common interests (sports, music, hobbies) are assigned to work together on an academic task such as a social studies report.

Attention Deficit Disorder

Sometimes called attention deficit hyperactivity disorder (ADHD), **attention deficit disorder (ADD)** has been estimated to affect between 10 and 20 percent of the school-age population (Shaywitz & Shaywitz, 1992). This condition can be confusing to parents, professionals, and people in the community. For one thing, not all students diagnosed as having ADD qualify for special education services (Lerner, Lowenthal, & Lerner, 1995). Those who do are covered by various special education categories and are considered to have a co-existing condition of learning disabilities. Hyperactivity and attention problems are common among children with learning disabilities and are characteristics of the ADD condition. Also,

attention deficit disorder (ADD). A condition that describes students who display hyperactive behaviors, have difficulty attending to the task at hand, and tend to be impulsive.

MAKING CONNECTIONS

See the section on ADD in the Children with BD/ED section of Chapter 8.

MAKING CONNECTIONS

For other groups with similar characteristics, see the section about Traumatic Brain Injury in Chapter 12.

MAKING CONNECTIONS

• See the Intervention Ladder described in the Interventions section in Chapter 8.
• Also see the Teaching Tactics boxes in each chapter of the book.

MAKING CONNECTIONS

Refer to the sections about dropping out of school found in
• Chapter 1,
• Chapter 3, Transition Section,
• Chapter 8.

children with ADD are at significant risk for academic failure, as are children with learning disabilities (Riccio, Gonzalez, & Hynd, 1994). Therefore it is not surprising that some 25 to 50 percent of children with ADD are identified as having learning disabilities as well (Shelton & Barkley, 1994). The other special education category in which a significant number of students with ADD are found is behavior disorders and emotional disturbance.

So, what is ADD? According to the DSM IV (American Psychiatric Association, 1994), ADD "is a persistent pattern of inattention and/or hyperactivity-impulsivity that is more frequent and severe than is typically observed in individuals at a comparable level of development" (p. 78). The DSM IV also established criteria for determining whether a child has ADD; those criteria are listed in Table 4.5. As you read this table, think about what ADD is and what it is not.

How does a teacher help the student with ADD? Like their counterparts who only have learning disabilities, students with ADD respond well to highly structured learning environments where topics are taught directly. Professionals suggest carefully planned educational procedures, such as giving rewards, making assignments more interesting, shortening the task, giving clear and precise instructions, and teaching students to use self-control and to reduce inappropriate behaviors (Lerner, Lowenthal, & Lerner, 1995). For those who do not qualify for special education services, general educators must accommodate their problems and differences in learning styles by providing them with instruction that meets their individual needs.

Many physicians prescribe drugs, such as Ritalin or Dexedrine, to help children with attention deficit disorder focus their attention on assigned tasks. Controversy surrounds the usefulness of behavior control drugs for these youngsters, though. Clinical evidence indicates that these drugs are effective in reducing the hyperactivity for some of these children but that the drugs do not seem to positively influence academic performance. For most, the drugs are unnecessary and can even be harmful (Armstrong, 1995). Instead behavioral techniques, direct and systematic instruction that is evaluated on a frequent basis, and highly motivating instructional materials have proven successful with many children currently identified as having ADD.

Educational Interventions

You have already learned that considerable debate surrounds the issue of properly identifying students with learning disabilities. Professionals also debate the content of educational programs and where students are best educated. In this section, you will learn about educational programs for students with learning disabilities, programs that span preschool through young adulthood. You will learn about the successes, the failures, and the work that still needs to be done. You will also learn of some alarming data about the dropout rate of students with learning disabilities and why transitional services for these youngsters are so important. The issues presented here have not been resolved and will require the attention of current and future special education professionals.

Education and the Preschool Child

Because learning disabilities primarily involve academic accomplishment, the condition is usually not diagnosed until children are 8 or 9 years old; some are identified as late as high school or even college. Therefore not many preschool

TABLE 4.5

DSM IV Diagnostic Criteria for Attention Deficit/Hyperactivity Disorder

Either inattention or hyperactivity/impulsivity must have persisted for at least six months. Either condition must be at a level that is both maladaptive and inconsistent with development and must include six (or more) of the following symptoms:

Inattention

- Often fails to give close attention to details or makes careless mistakes in schoolwork, work, or other activities
- Often has difficulty sustaining attention in tasks or play activities
- Often does not seem to listen when spoken to directly
- Often does not follow through on instructions and fails to finish schoolwork, chores, or duties in the workplace (not due to oppositional behavior or failure to understand instructions)
- Often has difficulty organizing tasks and activities
- Often avoids, dislikes, or is reluctant to engage in tasks that require sustained mental effort (such as schoolwork or homework)
- Often loses things necessary for tasks or activities (e.g., toys, school assignments, pencils, books, or tools)
- Is often easily distracted by extraneous stimuli
- Is often forgetful in daily activities

Hyperactivity/Impulsivity

- Often fidgets with hands or feet or squirms in seat
- Often leaves seat in classroom or in other situations in which remaining seated is expected
- Often runs about or climbs excessively in situations in which it is inappropriate (in adolescents or adults, may be limited to subjective feelings of restlessness)
- Often has difficulty playing or engaging in leisure activities quietly
- Is often "on the go" or often acts as if "driven by a motor"
- Often talks excessively
- Often blurts out answers before questions have been completed
- Often has difficulty awaiting turn
- Often interrupts or intrudes on others (e.g., butts into conversations or games)

Also, some hyperactive-impulsive or inattentive symptoms were present before age 7 years.

The symptoms must be present in two or more settings (e.g., at school [or work] and at home).

Clear evidence of clinically significant impairment in social, academic, or occupational functioning must be demonstrated.

The symptoms do not occur exclusively during the course of a pervasive developmental disorder, schizophrenia, or other psychotic disorder and are not better accounted for by another mental disorder (e.g., mood disorder, anxiety disorder, dissociative disorder, or a personality disorder).

Source: From *American Psychiatric Association: Diagnostic and Statistical Manual of Mental Disorders* (4th ed.) (DSM IV). (pp. 83–85), 1994, Washington, DC: American Psychiatric Association, 1994. Adapted with permission.

programs are designed specifically for these students. Although many children are identified during their preschool years as having a language impairment and are later identified as having a learning disability, many professionals are reluctant to identify children as having a learning disability in kindergarten or even first grade. The reason is that young children do not develop at exactly the same rate. Some youngsters in kindergarten are not as ready for school as their classmates. For example, a child who has been in structured day care and preschool programs may appear to be more ready for school than a child who has been at home for five years. Other children may not have developed as quickly as their peers but do not have a disability and will catch up. Still others are the youngest in their class and are not and should not be developmentally equal to their classmates.

Many characteristics of learning disabilities are similar to normal developmental patterns shown in young children. For example, it is normal to observe **reversals** of letters, numbers, or words (letters or a word written or read backward) by young children. If a child is still reversing many letters and words by third grade, though, there might be cause for concern. Most young children have difficulty paying attention for long periods of time. Young children also fidget and need to move around a lot. As we have noted before, these characteristics are common of many students with learning disabilities, but they are also *typical* of young children in general. Therefore most educators are reluctant to identify preschoolers as having learning disabilities. Educators are also concerned that labeling a young child as having disabilities could become a self-fulfilling prophecy, lowering adults' expectations of the child and resulting in damage to the child's self-concept and possibly his or her cognitive and social development (Smith & Schakel, 1986).

Many states offer preschool programs to children at risk, particularly those students below age 3. These programs are noncategorical and do not require participants to have been identified as having a specific disabling condition. However, most states require that children between the ages of 3 and 5 be identified as having a disability and assigned to a particular category in order to be eligible for special preschool programs. Although educators are reluctant to identify and label preschoolers as having a disability, there are several good reasons for doing so. First, children who can be definitely identified as having learning disabilities at an early age can receive specialized services as soon as possible. For example, children who received injury to the brain during birth or infancy or children who are not talking by age 3 are candidates for special services. Second, we now have a better understanding of who is at risk for having learning disabilities. We now know, for instance, that low-birthweight and premature babies are at risk for developing learning disabilities (American Academy of Pediatrics, 1992). Third, new early screening procedures are available that are not contingent on school failure but do predict future difficulties mastering reading (Hurford et al., 1994). These measures assess children's beginning reading skills (awareness of sounds in oral communications, ability to isolate sounds, ability to blend sounds into words, ability to identify letters). Being able to reliably identify preschoolers at risk for reading problems during their schoolyears should reduce the fears of misidentifying youngsters who do not have a disability. Preschool children who attend "literacy rich environments" can gain many prerequisite skills necessary for reading and writing (Katims, 1994). By retelling and reenacting their favorite stories, the important concept that print has meaning is understood early on and becomes a foundation to future instruction.

 MAKING CONNECTIONS

In Chapter 1, review information about
• Noncategorical vs. categorical placement options,
• Labeling.
In Chapter 2, review information about Preschool programs and IFSPs.
In Chapter 5, review information about
• Preschool programs for children at risk,
• The connection between early identification of language impairments and later identification of learning disabilities, Prevalence section.

 MAKING CONNECTIONS

• Chapter 3, Prevention section discusses the benefits of early intervention programs, particularly Headstart.
• Also, see the Prevention section of this chapter.

 MAKING CONNECTIONS

More information on early screening and detection of reading problems is found in the Reading section of Educational Interventions in this chapter.

reversals. Letters, words, or numbers written or read backward.

Education and the Schoolchild

As we discussed, most students with learning disabilities have not learned how to learn. They are not well organized and do not approach learning situations strategically. Teachers can help them become more efficient and effective by incorporating some simple principles into the classroom setting. The Tips for Teachers box lists some of these basic techniques that research and experience has shown to help students become better learners.

So many easy-to-use and proven instructional methods for use with students with learning disabilities have been verified (Lovett, 1995) that it was difficult deciding which ones to highlight in this chapter. We selected three areas to discuss: reading, learning strategies, and homework. Because becoming proficient in reading is the most prevalent problem for this population of learners and some important new research findings are available in this area, we felt it merited some focus. "Learning how to learn" is often posed as an area on which teachers must concentrate, and the learning strategies approach has proven so effective, that we devote a section to this topic. And, finally, because almost all students with learning disabilities attend general education classes and receive homework assignments, we felt that knowing about the new research in this area would be useful.

We would like to underscore two important principles: Select instructional techniques that are verified through rigorous research, and collect information about the effectiveness of the methods selected for each student. The field of learning disabilities, in particular, has a history of advocating one instructional method after another that has not been thoroughly tested first. There are many examples to cite, but let's take sensory integration as a case in point. Sensory integration is based on the importance of sensory (visual, auditory, tactile) stimulation, particularly in the context of motor activity. It is from this theory that perceptual motor training as a prerequisite to reading instruction for students with learning disabilities has its roots. Years ago, elementary-age children were taught to crawl again, engage in patterning exercises, walk balance beams, make angels in the snow, and draw lines on dittos from one pattern to another. These sensory integration activities were thought to be related to improved reading. Periodically, despite consistent evidence that these procedures are absolutely ineffective, they gain in popularity (Hoehn & Baumeister, 1994). Unfortunately, teachers do not carefully select their instructional procedures from those proven effective through carefully conducted research (Talbott, Lloyd, & Tankersley, 1994). It may not be as exciting to use **best practices** that are "tried and true" as to use those that sound new and innovative, but that may well be our obligation to the students we are responsible to teach.

Besides using instructional methods that have passed the scrutiny of research, it is very important that teachers be certain the tactics they select are actually working with each student. Remember, students with learning disabilities comprise a heterogeneous group of learners, each possessing different learning needs and styles. Therefore it is necessary to ensure that the "right" instructional method has been selected, and to do that requires that data be collected about how well the student is performing the academic task being taught. Curriculum based assessment (CBA), whereby students' performance on each learning task is evaluated directly to determine whether the intervention is effective, whether the intervention is effective enough, and whether the child's progress is sufficient to move on to other tasks. So, now let's turn our attention to the general issue of reading.

 MAKING CONNECTIONS

Reread the History section of this chapter for background information on the use of unverified techniques.

 MAKING CONNECTIONS

Curriculum based assessment is also discussed in Chapters 2 and 4.

best practices. Instructional techniques or methods proven through research to be effective.

Learning How to Learn

1 Use instructional tactics that actively involve the child in learning activities.

2 Start every lesson with advance organizers.

3 Teach students how to use and apply strategies to help them comprehend and remember academic assignments.

4 Use concrete examples, often demonstrating how to perform the instructional task correctly.

5 Help children focus their attention on the relevant features of a task.

6 Include activities in the instructional day that teach youngsters how to think and solve problems.

7 Allow children to manage some part of their instructional day (decide when they will do an academic task, pick the instructional technique you will use, determine a reward for achieving a goal).

8 Individualize instruction, allowing children to master basic academic skills at their own rate.

9 Help children understand the connection between effort and success.

10 Have children predict the consequences of their behavior.

11 Teach children to evaluate their own progress in learning and mastering academic tasks.

12 Refer to members of your school-based IEP team children who are unable to keep pace with the academic demands of your classroom, do not have the communicative competence of their peers, or have inappropriate or immature social skills (withdrawn, hyperactive).

Reading. Of this there is no doubt: Most students with learning disabilities have difficulty learning to read. Because this basic skill is used in almost all other curriculum areas, these students must receive as much *effective* instruction as possible in this area. New research findings show that students with learning disabilities do not, in general, benefit from the whole language approach (Mather, 1992). They do, however, profit from learning basic phonological skills—sound blending and decoding, for example (Moats & Lyon, 1993; O'Connor, Jenkins, Leicester, & Slocum, 1993).

The whole language approach is widely used in general education classes. It emphasizes the "wholeness" of reading and writing and seeks complete infusion into the entire curriculum. All methods that promote "natural learning" are encouraged, but direct instruction on decoding, isolated vocabulary development, or discrete skills that are components of the reading process are considered unacceptable (Mather, 1992). Teaching independent skills, such as sound–symbol associations, is also not endorsed. Reading is integrated into the entire curriculum, across the school day. "Whole language has a one-approach-fits-all quality to it" (Pressley & Rankin, 1994, p. 161), which puts this approach at the far end of the spectrum from individualized instruction. For children at risk of reading failure and those with learning disabilities, "substantial contemporary evidence documents the efficacy of explicit systematic instruction of important reading skills—that is, research supports practices explicitly inconsistent with whole language" (p. 161). In other words, for these students, in particular, whole language is an ineffective instructional method. For them, research shows that individualized instructional procedures that systematically and explicitly focus on the basic skills (phonics) and component parts (sound blending) of reading should be what comprises reading instruction at least during the acquisition process. The relationship between long-term reading achievement and early instruction that promotes phonic awareness is clear (Torgesen, Wagner, & Rashotte, 1994). This early instruction seems most effective when provided through intensive one-to-one tutoring or small groups in which all students need to work on the same skills. It is through such direct instruction that basic reading skills needed for reading mastery are acquired (Hurford et al., 1994). It seems apparent: No single instructional method can guarantee reading proficiency for all children. This may be partly why educators abandon one method for another. Because the ability to decode is important, phonics should be part of all balanced reading programs, which seems to be the position that Los Angeles and many other large school districts are promoting (Colvin, 1996).

How can we determine early enough which students are at risk for reading failure, so intervention programs can begin before children are years behind? This question could not be answered until recently. Future reading difficulties *can* be predicted with some confidence (Hurford, Schauf, Bunce, Blaich, & Moore, 1994). The link between phonological awareness and successful early reading performance is now confirmed (Majsterek & Ellenwood, 1995). Phonological awareness is the ability to identify sound segments in words (the three sounds in *cat*) and the ability to manipulate sound segments (understanding that *fall* and *wall* rhyme). Those preschoolers who cannot identify letters and cannot correctly associate sounds with their symbols should be candidates for direct instruction on such reading skills during first grade. According to Reid Lyon of the National Institute of Health's Child Health and Human Development Branch, some 20 percent of young children have difficulty with phonological awareness and about 7 to 10 percent have major problems. He is convinced that if these children do not receive direct instruction on phonics by age 9, 70 percent of them will have problems through high school (*CEC Today*, 1995).

Once students with learning disabilities acquire the fundamentals of reading, there is no guarantee that they will automatically become fluent (proficient) in reading, develop the skills needed for reading comprehension, or achieve literacy. Research shows that these skills also must be systematically taught. For example, students gain better fluency when they are able to listen to the passage read orally first before they read it aloud (Daly & Martens, 1994). And, it appears that it is best if the rate of the prereading sample is only about 25 percent faster than their own reading rate (Skinner, Adamson, Woodward, Jackson, Atchison, & Mims, 1993). So, students who are reading orally about 50 words a minute correctly will increase their speed of reading and, thereby their proficiency, by being able to listen to a reading passage read at a rate of 75 words a minute before they read the passage again independently. Teaching students with learning disabilities how to read can be an arduous task, with each component skill requiring direct instruction. The teaching tactics that are successful in teaching these skills often vary by student. For this reason, many teachers incorporate CBA into their teaching routines to ensure that their instruction continues to be as powerful as possible.

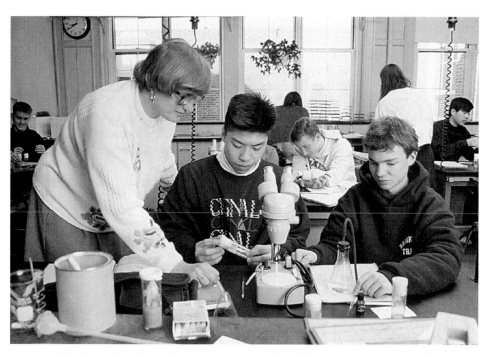

These students are learning science concepts together. By pairing a student with learning disabilities with another student, a teacher can enhance learning and limit social rejection.

MAKING CONNECTIONS

For other examples of learning strategies, see
• the Student's Resource Manual that accompanies this text for examples of notetaking using main ideas and details,
• the teaching tactic box in Chapter 2.

learning strategies. Instructional methods to help students read, comprehend, and study better by helping them organize and collect information strategically.

mnemonics. A learning strategy that promotes the remembering of names by associating the first letters of items in a list with a word, sentence, or picture.

Learning Strategies. Experts in the field of learning disabilities consistently advocate that these students receive direct instruction in learning *how* to learn. To accomplish this, specialists recommend a **learning strategies** approach. For those working with middle school and secondary students, researchers at the University of Kansas Center for Research on Learning have diligently worked for years to develop and verify the usefulness of this approach (Deshler, Ellis, & Lenz, 1996; Deshler & Schumaker, 1986). The results are impressive! The learning strategies method helps students learn and remember information more efficiently. For many years, teachers of these students practiced "crisis teaching"—that is, they tutored their students with learning disabilities to prepare for imminent academic crises, so that they might have a better chance of receiving a passing grade on tomorrow's test or term paper. The learning strategies approach goes beyond crisis teaching and helps students meet the demands of the general education secondary curriculum.

Teachers who use learning strategies receive intensive, specialized training, using the materials and the theories produced during years of research and application at the University of Kansas. The materials, which are highly structured, all use advance organizers, mnemonics, and built-in systems of evaluation. **Mnemonics** helps people remember information. For example, many people remember the names of the Great Lakes by associating them with the mnemonic HOMES (Huron, Ontario, Michigan, Erie, and Superior). Another strategy has students group activities by main ideas and details, which helps them remember a great amount of information. Youngsters are also taught how to read difficult passages in high school social studies and science texts and how to write themes and reports in systematic ways. In addition, strategies have been developed that help students study more efficiently and take tests more effectively.

Other researchers have developed teaching tactics that include many of the elements found in the Kansas learning strategies approach—advance organizers, mnemonics, systematic instruction, CBA measures. They, too, have proven to be powerful interventions with this group of learners. For example, Scruggs and Mastropieri (1992) developed the *pictorial mnemonic*, a tactic that uses a visual image to help children remember important information. Figure 4.3 shows the illustration used to help them remember that birds are warm-blooded animals. Other researchers have shown that math test scores improve when students are taught to be more strategic (organized and preparatory in the way they approached the problems). For example, they were taught to prepare for the next test by reviewing the problems they had correctly solved on the previous test. While taking the test, they were taught to do the problems they were sure of first, circle the number of each problem they were "kinda sure of" as a marker to come back to those first, and then tackle the ones they did not think they knew how to solve (Winnery & Fuchs, 1993). Another example was applied to difficult spelling words (Greene, 1994). Children are taught to use cues (like making the two o letters in the middle of the word "look" into eyes) to help them remember the correct

FIGURE 4.3

A Pictorial Mnemonic: Symbolic Reconstruction of "Bird-Warm Blooded"

Source: From "Classroom applications of mnemonic instruction: Acquisition, maintenance, and generalization" by T. E. Scruggs and M. A. Mastropieri, 1992, *Exceptional Children, 59,* p. 222. Reprinted by permission.

spelling for words they find difficult. Clearly, this group of tactics, often generally referred to as "learning strategies," have met the test. They have been proved through research to be effective tactics with many students with learning disabilities. Teachers also indicate that students enjoy creating their own mnemonics and strategies.

Homework. The word *homework* can bring horror to the minds of parents of students with learning disabilities, and probably to the children as well.

> The mere mention of the word may bring to mind memories of many long, unpleasant nights spent cajoling an LD student to complete unfinished assignments. Such nights often end up in shouting matches between parent and child, sometimes with one or both in tears. Other parents spend the year ranting and raving at their child simply trying to get homework brought home or trying to get it back to school. The problems with homework are so numerous....(Higbee-Mandlebaum, 1992/1993, p. 1)

Despite the negative situations that homework can create for the family, it appears to be gaining in popularity. Researchers have found that homework accounts for about 20 percent of the time most children spend on academic tasks (Cooper & Nye, 1994). Although many children and their parents would like to see homework "just go away," there are positive relationships between homework and achievement (Bryan, 1995). With the national concern about student achievement, it is unlikely that homework will be discontinued.

Although many children with learning disabilities believe that homework is too hard, a waste of time, and boring, general education teachers believe that it is valuable and that all students in the class should get the same amount and be graded in the same way (Bryan, Nelson, & Mathur, 1995; Bryan, 1995). Because homework is a reality of school life, some researchers are now attempting to develop methods to make this a more positive experience. Some have explored the effectiveness of cooperative homework teams (O'Melia & Rosenberg, 1994). In this system, peer teams grade and as a group make corrections to homework completed individually the previous evening. Others have created instructional materials, like *Planning for Success,* which is designed to restructure homework activities so they become positive learning experiences (Bryan & Sullivan, 1994a, 1994b). To help teachers become more consistent and fair about what and how they assign, these authors developed checklists for teachers to use as part of their overall program. A sample is shown in the Teaching Tactics box.

The purpose of teaching youngsters learning strategies and having them complete longer and longer homework assignments is to have them succeed in the traditional general education curriculum (for example, history, science, literature). But is the traditional education curriculum appropriate for all students with learning disabilities? Let's see what some parents and educators think about this issue.

Inclusion

The majority of parents of children with learning disabilities and professionals agree: Most students with learning disabilities should receive at least some of their education in general education classrooms alongside their nondisabled peers. And, their education must be supported by an array of special services and curricular options that will meet their individual needs. However a recent court decision reminds educators that there is no single answer to "What is the least restrictive environment for the education of students with learning disabilities?" In fact, in *Zumwalt School District v. Missouri State Board of Education, 24 IDELR 222* (E. D. Mo. 1996), the courts ruled that the school district should pay for the cost of a private, segregated school because the student's self-esteem, behavior, and academics were negatively affected by his association with students from whom he felt different (Kahn, 1996).

At the same time, though, many parents and professionals worry about the implementation of a full-inclusion policy for students with learning disabilities (Council for Learning Disabilities, 1993; Learning Disabilities Association, 1994; National Joint Committee on Learning Disabilities, 1993). The concerns voiced by such organizations are also articulated by individual parents (Carr, 1993). For example, they are concerned that the array of special services now available will disappear and that in the future the general education option, without sufficient supports, will be the only one available. Many fear that the teacher training necessary to support this plan will not be delivered. Among other things, they worry about the current emphasis on national assessments and high test scores. What is the underlying concern? It is that such efforts will become disincentives to include students with learning disabilities. The outcomes could be higher referrals of nonacademically competitive students to special education and ultimately a higher dropout rate for students with learning disabilities.

Does the full-inclusion movement actually mean significant changes in the educational placements for most students with learning disabilities? The answer is no. In the 1992–1993 schoolyear, almost 80 percent received either limited special education support (less than 21 percent of the school week) from specialists either within or outside of the general education class or more support (somewhere between 21 and 60 percent) from resource room specialists (U.S. Department of Education, 1995). And, the 20 percent who attended special classes for most of their school day still participated in some aspects of the general education program. If most of these students are participating in general education programs, what is the concern? Some evidence exists that the number of resource rooms is decreasing and that special supports are not as plentiful. There is also evidence that the individualized educational programs required by these students are not consistently being delivered in the general education classroom. Let's look at these issues more carefully.

Is the reduction in the number of resource rooms across the country a problem? The answer, of course, is not necessarily. It is the student's teachers and related service providers (e.g., SLPs) who deliver an appropriate education as specified on the IEP. A full and rich array of placement or service options does not guarantee an appropriate education for every child, and a more limited array does not always imply inferior educational opportunities. Innovative models are being developed that hold promise. For example, evidence shows that a team teaching model—in which a special educator and a general educator work together and are supported by a multidisciplinary team—can produce increases in the self-esteems of students with learning disabilities while fostering good academic achievement (Baneji & Dailey, 1995). Unfortunately, not all general education classrooms produce such results for these students with disabilities. The accommodations required can take teacher's time and extra planning (see the Making Accommodations box for some ideas). As you have learned, the learning strategy approach is highly effective with this group of learners. However, the findings of one study indicate that it may be more difficult to teach and implement strategy instruction in general education settings (Scanlon, Deshler, & Schumaker, 1996). Also, when compared with students who learned the strategy in a special education setting and applied it in a general education setting, these students had much poorer outcomes in strategy mastery and use.

There are other differences between the education delivered in special education settings and general education settings. For example, general education teachers use group, rather than individualized, instruction. They tend not to make special arrangements for students with special needs, even when only 40 percent of them are successfully participating in a group activity (O'Connor & Jenkins, 1996a). Possibly because of the importance of getting through an assignment and moving on to the next, little, if any, time is spent on direct reading instruction (word analysis or reading strategies) (O'Connor & Jenkins, 1996b). Other findings also show that when attending most general education settings, they do not

MAKING CONNECTIONS

More information about learning strategies is available in the Education of the Schoolchild section.

1. Provide structure and a standard set of expectations:

   Help students develop organizational skills,

   Establish sets of rules for academic and social activities and tasks.

   Adhere to a well-planned schedule.

   Match your language to the comprehension level of the student.

   Be consistent.

2. Adjust instructional materials and activities:

   Individualize instruction; be sure the reading level is appropriate.

   Break tasks down into smaller pieces (or chunks).

   Begin lessons with advance organizers.

   Supplement oral and written assignments with learning aids (computers).

   Assign a peer tutor.

   Modify tests, allowing the student to take more time or complete it in a different way (listen to a tape of the test).

   Evaluate the effectiveness of your instructional interventions and when they are not effective, change them.

3. Give students feedback and reinforcement for success:

   Tell students when they are behaving properly.

   Reward students for improvement.

   Praise students when they have done well or accomplished a goal.

   Inform students when they are not meeting expectations.

   Encourage students to develop partnerships among each other, and reinforce those who do so.

4. Make tasks interesting:

   Develop attention by making assignments interesting and novel.

   Vary the format of instruction and activities.

   Use high-interest curriculum materials.

   Encourage students to work together during extracurricular activities.

receive differentiated instruction (tailored to their individual needs), are not engaged in the learning process, participate very little, interact with their teachers and fellow students infrequently, and make few academic gains (McIntosh, Vaugh, Schumm, Haager, & Lee, 1993; Zigmond & Baker, 1994). Possibly, the years of research findings showing that there is no single answer to what comprises an appropriate or effective education for these students is what should be heeded (Roberts & Mather, 1995). These findings imply the need for a continuum or an array of special education offerings. The question then arises, "For students with learning disabilities, is special education a good or bad alternative?" When asked, these students seem to support special education classes (Guterman, 1995; Padeliadu & Zigmond, 1996). They understand that they get more academic assistance in these settings where the environment is more reinforcing and organized. Because of such results, many professionals and parents argue that a full continuum and array of educational options must be retained and be available for these students.

Some school districts may not be able to retain a rich array and variety of educational options:

> It no longer seems feasible to develop or maintain pullout programs for all students who are experiencing learning problems in the general education classroom, and yet we simply cannot overlook that some youngsters have extraordinary learning needs that are not being adequately addressed within the general education class. (McIntosh, Vaugh, Schumm, Haager, & Lee, 1993, p. 260)

So, what are the alternatives? Vaughn and Schumm (1995) define what they believe is responsible inclusion for students with learning disabilities (see Table 4.6). Here, the goal is for all students to be placed in general education settings. If a student's academic or social needs cannot be met in that setting, then an alternative experience needs to be arranged. This system puts the needs of students with disabilities first and bases decisions on the student's outcomes in the general education setting.

We believe that the type of educational and supportive programs that a student with learning disabilities receives must be determined by that child's individual needs, wherever the program is delivered. Most students with learning disabilities included in the general education classroom need at least some extra assistance. They require the adaptation and modification of commercially available textbooks and instructional materials. They may require more instructional time for explanations, drill, practice, and feedback. In many cases, these students need to learn how to apply a specific strategy to the learning process; others require some tutoring in mastering academic tasks. Some students with learning disabilities do not profit from the standard curriculum used in general education. For them, an educational experience with a life-skills, functional, or vocational emphasis is more appropriate.

Printed with permission of the Des Moines Register.

With the costs of education rising and the number of special needs students rising, many school districts are searching for ways to save money. One alternative used is to reduce the number of special education programs, particularly resource room programs.

TABLE 4.6

Components of Inclusion for Students with Learning Disabilities

Responsible Inclusion	*Irresponsible Inclusion*
Student first The first priority is the extent to which the student with disabilities is making academic and/or social progress in the general education classroom. Ongoing assessment, monitoring, and placement consideration is critical to success.	**Place first** Students' academic and social progress is second to the location in which their education occurs. If the student is in the general education classroom, there is little else to consider because place is the foremost consideration.
Teachers choose to participate in inclusive classrooms Teachers are provided opportunities to participate in inclusive classrooms and self-select their involvement.	**Teachers are mandated to participate in inclusive classrooms** Teachers are mandated to participate and feel no opportunity to provide feedback about the extent to which their skills will allow them to be successful in general education classrooms.
Adequate resources are considered and provided for inclusive classrooms Personnel understand that for inclusion to be successful, considerable resources, related to both personnel and material, are required to develop and maintain effective inclusive classrooms.	**Resources are not considered prior to the establishment of inclusive classrooms.** The inclusion model does not initially consider that additional resources are needed, and inclusive classrooms are established with little consideration of the personnel and physical resources required.
Models are developed and implemented at the school-based level School-site personnel develop inclusive models that are implemented and evaluated to meet the needs of studnts and families in their community.	**School district, state, and/or federal directives provide the guidelines for inclusion** School-based models are mandated at the district and/or state level, and key personnel in the school and community are rarely engaged in the development of the model.
A continuum of services is maintained A range of education programs are available to meet the needs of students with learning disabilities. It is not expected that the needs of all students will be met with full-time placement in the general education classroom.	**Full inclusion is the only service delivery model** All students are placed in general education classrooms full time, regardless of their needs or their successes.
Service delivery model is evaluated on an ongoing basis The success of the service delivery model is considered and fine-tuned in light of the nature of the students with learning disabilities and with consideration for the extent to which it meets their academic and social needs.	**Service delivery model is established and implemented** If problems occur, personnel are blamed rather than the model being evaluated to determine its effectiveness.
Ongoing professional development Personnel realize that for teachers and others to be effective at inclusion, ongoing professional development at the school-site level is required.	**Professional development not part of the model** Teachers and other individuals are not provided adequate time or opportunity to improve their skills and/or increase their knowledge about effectively meeting the needs of students with learning disabilities.
Teachers and other key personnel discuss and develop their own philosophy on inclusion This philosophy on inclusion guides practice at the school and sets a tone of acceptance for all students.	**A school philosophy on inclusion is not developed** Several teachers in the school may participate and understand inclusion, but it is not part of the school philosophy as a whole.
Curricula and instruction that meet the needs of all students are developed and refined Successful inclusion provides for curricula and instructional practices that meet the needs of all students.	**Curricula and instruction that meet the needs of all students are not considered** The success of average- and high-achieving students is of little interest as long as students with disabilities are included in general education classrooms. Specialized curricula and instruction for students with LD are not considered.

Source: From Responsible inclusion for students with learning disabilities by S. Vaughn & J. S. Schumm, 1995, *Journal of Learning Disabilities,* 28, p. 267. Copyright (1995) by PRO-ED, Inc. Reprinted by permission.

Transition Through Adulthood

The experiences of adults with learning disabilities are about as varied as the population itself (Patton & Blalock, 1996a). Many drop out of high school, and yet others complete graduate school; some become chronically unemployed, and others become successful professionals. Until recently, many educators believed that children would outgrow their learning disabilities, that their conditions were mild, and that they would not persist into adulthood. Maybe these are the reasons that systematic transitional services have not been available to this population of learners, as it has for those with some other disabilities. The data from longitudinal studies that describe and explain what happens to these people as adults indicate that many are in great need. Because general education is currently engaged in reform, now may well be the time to seize the moment to develop innovative transitional programs for students with learning disabilities (Bassett & Smith, 1996). So, to set the stage for this discussion, we first review studies about what happens to these individuals as adults, then use some of that information to describe what is currently available and what else might be needed. As you read along, think of what services you think need to be developed.

Follow-up Studies. Longitudinal or follow-up studies provide valuable information about how adults with learning disabilities fare in society. These studies also give us insight into the nature of this disability, the educational requirements of these individuals while in elementary, middle, and secondary schools, and the types of support they need throughout their lives.

Some highly successful adults had or have learning disabilities. For example, Hans Christian Andersen, Leonardo da Vinci, Thomas Edison, Nelson Rockefeller, and Woodrow Wilson are thought to have had a learning disability. Some present-day celebrities—Cher, Magic Johnson, Brook Theiss, Bruce Jenner, and Greg Louganis, among others—have acknowledged having a learning disability. Recently Charles Schwab, the millionaire discount broker, has revealed his lifelong reading problem (Colvin, 1996). Schwab's significant learning disability created challenges for him particularly throughout his academic career. These public figures show the gains that an individual with a learning disability can make. Such cases are not typical, however.

Follow-up studies indicate that many adults with learning disabilities do not fare well. These data should challenge educators to redesign the educational programs available to these individuals while they are elementary and high school students. Many of these adults

- left high school without a diploma (Aune & Friehe, 1996; Dunn, 1996);
- are unemployed or underemployed (Blalock, 1997);
- do not possess the basic mathematical skills necessary for daily living (Johnson & Blalock, 1987);
- are extremely dependent upon their families (White, 1992);
- have difficulties with social relationships and desperately wish to have friends (Learning Disabilities Association, 1994);
- regardless of their abilities, work in fast-food and service-related jobs that do not require them to read or write (Haring, Lovett, & Smith, 1990);
- are not satisfied with their jobs (Patton & Blalock, 1996a);

- express great concerns about having low incomes and little opportunities for job and career advancement (Learning Disabilities Association, 1994);
- (about half) are unable to live independently (Schalock, Holl, Elliott, & Ross, 1992); and
- in fact the majority, are not self-supporting (White, 1992).

Students with learning disabilities drop out of high school at a rate that is much too high. The follow-up data on these individuals (one to four years after leaving school) reveal some depressing facts about which all educators must be aware (Sitlington & Frank, 1993):

- only 56 percent of dropouts are employed (lower than the 77 percent of their special education classmates who graduated).
- Sixty-eight percent of those employed work in labor or service occupations.
- The females in the dropout group have lower-status jobs (93 percent).
- The group's average wage is $4.39 per hour.
- Thirty-seven percent have received postsecondary education or training.
- Sixty-four percent are living with their parents.
- Eighty-seven percent are involved in a leisure time activity.

The outcomes for students with learning disabilities, however, is not always bleak. For example, those who graduate from college have very positive outcomes. One study (Greenbaum, Graham, & Scales, 1996) followed up adults who had graduated from the University of Maryland between 1980 and 1992. The average age of those participating in this study was 26, and all had received support services from the Office of Disabled Student Services while attending college. Their outcomes are quite different from the information just reported about the typical young adult with learning disabilities. They were happy with their lives, employed primarily in white-collar jobs (71 percent professional/technical, 23 percent clerical/sales, and 6 percent service), and participated in recreational and community activities. What makes this group so different from their peers with learning disabilities? They may well comprise a subgroup that has greater abilities and skills. It seems that they developed the following characteristics that enabled them to succeed in school and work: understanding of their disability and their strengths and weaknesses, determination, perseverance, abilities to seek accommodations and self-advocate (Greenbaum, Graham, & Scales, 1995). Another common characteristic may well be the most important: This group also came from well-educated, middle- to upper-middle-class families who offered considerable emotional and financial support to them. Other research has shown that parents' **socioeconomic status** and educational status is an important factor in the success of adults with learning disabilities (O'Connor & Spreen, 1988).

When such support from family is unavailable, carefully designed transitional services should compensate, but what actually does the typical adolescent with learning disabilities receive? Patton and Blalock (1996b) help us better understand why adult outcomes are not as universally positive. These students

- receive inadequate vocational experiences;
- obtain little help from school personnel in finding either a job or work experience;

socioeconomic status. The status an individual or family unit holds in society, usually determined by job, level of education, and the amount of money available to spend.

A Middle School Student Considers Dropping Out of School

Will's comments help us understand why so many high school students with learning disabilities drop out of school.

When did you start skipping school or decide that skipping school was a better choice than being in school?

Will: Sixth grade.

Why?

Will: Well, I just wanted to go hunting or something, hang out with friends and it was boring in school.

How was that?

Will: Well, I'd go to class and they'd tell me to do something; I couldn't do it. But I had to do it anyway. So I figured they didn't need me here.

If they gave you things you couldn't do, how did that go?

Will: Well, I'd just mark down some answers. It didn't matter.

Did they give you help?

Will: No.

So you felt it didn't matter if you were in school?

Will: Yeah, 'cause I wasn't learning anything.

Source: "Persistence of Reading Disabilities: The Voices of Four Middle School Students" By R. Kos, 1991, *American Educational Research Journal, 28*, p. 887. Reprinted by permission.

▪ tend not to access postsecondary options within five years of leaving high school, 16 percent attending vocational schools, 12 percent attending two-year colleges, and 4 percent going to four-year colleges;

▪ are less adept in using community resources.

Now, let's see whether the programs available to these students actually meet their needs.

High School Options. Students with learning disabilities tend to follow one of three paths during their high school years: Some receive the traditional college preparatory curriculum, some receive a transitional curriculum that focuses on vocational and functional or life skills, and the majority drop out of school, although an increasing number of these individuals complete high school later through a GED option.

High school is difficult for most students with learning disabilities. Even for those who are successful, it can be fraught with frustration and failure. As a result, many high school students with learning disabilities elect to drop out. Students with disabilities drop out at a rate almost double the rate for students without disabilities; only 10 percent of them leave school with a diploma (U.S. Department of Education, 1995). And students with learning disabilities represent the group with the largest number of dropouts (the largest percentage is for students with behavior disorders and emotional disturbance). Why do students with learning disabilities leave school? According to one study, they have greater feelings of social alienation toward their classmates and teachers than those who complete school (Seidel & Vaughn, 1991). Also, there is a strong relationship between poor school performance, absenteeism, and dropping out of school. For those who do not see the importance of school, who are faced with constant failure, and who do not believe that they will graduate, dropping out may seem like the best option. (See the box, page 164, for the comments of one dissatisfied midschooler.)

However, these students may reevaluate their decision a few years after they drop out of high school. For instance, according to the American Council on Education, passing the *General Education Development (GED)* test is a popular way to earn a high school equivalency certificate (Baldwin, 1996). In 1995, more than 520,000 American adults obtained high school credentials based on these tests. Of those, 4,902 received special accommodations because of documented disabilities, a 17 percent increase over the previous year. However, passing this test is not an automatic event. Again, learning strategy instruction has proven effective by helping many attain a GED (Westberry, 1994).

Because of the high drop out rates among students with learning disabilities, more attention has recently been given to developing alternative curricular options in high school for them. One option seeks to assist students more consistently with their transition from school to the world of work (Dunn, 1996). These programs should be individually tailored for the needs of each student and should include curriculum topics beyond traditional vocational education or job placements. It should also address self-determination, understanding of one's disability, psychosocial issues, and problem solving.

 MAKING CONNECTIONS

For more information on self-determination, see that section in Chapter 8.

Using the overwhelming data from follow-up study after follow-up study, experts are beginning to question whether the high school experience provided to the majority of students with learning disabilities is appropriate. Given the data that less than half (43.9 percent graduate from high school with a diploma) (U.S. Department of Education, 1995) and only about 4 percent go immediately on to a four-year college (Aune & Friehe, 1996), there is growing support among professionals for change. For those who are college-bound, instructional programs need to provide them with even stronger academic programs that include the kind of supports they should expect from support services available at most colleges and universities. For those who are not, more time and effort should be devoted to instruction on topics centering on **life skills**. Programs should include instruction about budgeting, banking, caring for a home or apartment, cooking, comparison shopping, and independent living skills (Cronin, 1996).

Postsecondary Options. The number of students with disabilities, particularly those with learning disabilities, who are enrolled in college is on the rise. In 1978, 2.6 percent of all college students were students with a disability; in 1992, that percentage rose to 8.8 percent. The greatest growth is for students with learning disabilities; one third of all freshmen with disabilities who attend college are in this group (Henderson, 1995). Particularly considering the high dropout rate from secondary school, it is interesting that over half of high school seniors with learning disabilities aspire to a college degree.

Individuals choose to attend college for a variety of reasons. Factors affecting their decision include how successful they are in academic subjects, how secure

 MAKING CONNECTIONS

Reread the interviews of college students with learning disabilities found at the beginning of this chapter to get a better understanding of these individuals' goals and needs for accommodations.

life skills. Those skills used to manage a home, cook, shop, and organize personal living environments.

they are in their opinion of themselves, and whether they are guided toward college by their families and teachers. For those with learning disabilities, how much they participated in extracurricular activities in high school is also a predictor of whether they will choose to attend college (Geisthardt & Munsch, 1996). Perhaps being involved in extracurricular activities helps to increase students' feelings of involvement and acceptance. Unfortunately, however, students with learning disabilities have fewer opportunities for involvement in such activities because they are the least likely to be picked by their peers. In any event, knowing these factors helps educators prepare their students for college.

Students who are college-bound also need to be prepared to compete academically in postsecondary school settings. Like the college students whose interviews were given at the beginning of this chapter, many young adults with learning disabilities who attend college need supportive services (academic tutoring, readers, assistance with note taking). It is important that all students pick their college carefully, particularly those with disabilities (HEATH, 1996). For some, attending a precollege program helps prepare for college, and the number is growing steadily. In 1996, for example, HEATH identified sixteen special summer programs for high school students with learning disabilities preparing to attend college in the near future.

The past few years have also witnessed an increase in the postsecondary educational options available for students with learning disabilities. Many two-year community college and technical/vocational school programs are now designed specifically for these students. Several guides are available to help students and their parents select a college. *Peterson's Colleges with Programs for Learning Disabled Students* (Mangrum & Strichart, 1994) lists 800 colleges and universities in the United States and Canada that have special programs to support students with learning disabilities, and the *K&W Guide to Colleges for the Learning Disabled* (Kravets & Wax, 1995) provides detailed information about 200 specific programs. Many traditional colleges and universities are now offering students with learning disabilities a variety of academic supports. Trennell Smith, the leading rusher in division III football, benefited from a special program on his campus that provided him with concentrated tutoring, taped versions of class lectures, untimed tests, and enlarged print (Berkow, 1995). Such accommodations for college students with learning disabilities can mean the difference between success and failure. Such growth in programs means that students and their families now have more choices and can more carefully match a student's needs, interests, and talents with a school. Clearly, postsecondary education is a growing option for students with learning disabilities, but to succeed they must be adequately prepared.

Employment. The employment experience for adults with learning disabilities is often disappointing. For example, only 45 percent of the adult members of the Learning Disability Association of America (LDA) who responded to a questionnaire were employed fulltime, an additional 30 percent were employed on a part-time basis, and 26 percent were unemployed (Smith, 1992). Of those working, 11 percent earned over $35,000, and 45 percent earned less than $7,000 per year.

Failure to find and hold a job can have many causes. Lack of opportunity and low self-esteem and motivation are often factors. But the most frequent reason for failure is lack of the skills required to do the job. Currently, researchers explain job success in terms of four variables: job match, social acceptance, work attitude, and special services (Siegel & Gaylord-Ross, 1991). In particular, they find that individuals who are successful in job situations are those who match their skills and interests to the job. Usually, a person will require services from a trained and experienced professional to obtain this match.

Two other variables crucial to occupational success of adults with learning disabilities are vocational education and on-the-job training. Neubert, Tilson, and Ianacone (1989) found that vocational high school programs improve these students' later employability. But they also found that these individuals require additional support during their first few years of employment. Unfortunately, most individuals with learning disabilities do not seek the services of agencies that provide such supports. Furthermore, many of these agencies (for instance, vocational rehabilitation) are not prepared to deal with adults with learning disabilities (Smith & Dowdy, 1993). Clearly, vocational education and on-the-job training are two areas that need further improvement.

Families

As discussed earlier in this chapter, most children with learning disabilities are not identified until they are school age, and some are not identified until they are in college. In contrast, most deaf children, blind children, or those with severe disabilities are diagnosed when they are very young by medical professionals. The parents are aware of their children's disabilities during their early years of life. Most have prepared themselves to cope with the day-to-day challenges a disability can present, and many have become active participants in their children's educational programs during the preschool years. Many parents of children with learning disabilities, however, do not suspect that their children have a disability until difficulties at school become apparent, and it is often school personnel who have to deliver the bad news to them. This is a crucial time for parents and for the children who are diagnosed as having a learning disability. It is a time of confusion and concern—and, often, a time of anger, frustration, and stress. If the identification process were speedier and even earlier, some think, the emotional turmoil families often experience would be lessened (Dyson, 1996). Besides finances, think of some reasons that the identification process might not seem efficient to family members.

The challenges that family members of individuals with disabilities face can be great. A disability can affect every aspect of a person's life. Many family members have found that gaining support from others can be helpful. Often, educators offer considerable assistance. Because learning disabilities are academically related disabilities, many parents find that connections with teachers, school administrators, special education teachers, and whoever else can help their children accomplish realistic goals in school is crucial. And, it may be for some of these reasons that the role of teachers is expanding (O'Shea, O'Shea, & Hammitte, 1994). Let's examine two of these: parent conferencing and parent–teacher partnerships.

Parent Conferencing

Educators can develop good relationships with parents if they use good conferencing skills when meeting with them. At least, four factors contribute to successful meetings (Kroth, 1978; Kroth & Edge, 1997). First, the area selected should be comfortable and free from interruptions. A desk or table between the parents and the educator can act as a barrier to discussion; a round table might get better results. Second, the professional must be a good listener. By listening carefully, the professional can help parents solve problems, and parents can come to a better understanding of how the family and the school can develop a partnership. Third, teachers should write down significant information shared by the parents. This note helps the teacher remember and stresses to the parent the importance of the meeting. And finally, parents should know how many meetings are planned and how long the meetings will last. Time periods should be adhered to; limiting the number and the length of the meetings seems to enhance their effectiveness.

Even under the best of circumstances, where meetings are skillfully conducted, many parents report that they are overwhelmed with the amount and sophistication of the information presented (Simpson, 1996). Because of the emotionally charged nature of parent–teacher meetings, particularly the initial one, parents often indicate that they remember nothing after terms like *brain damaged* were used. To solve this problem, educators may need to schedule extra meetings to ensure the following results:

- The purpose of the meeting is specified.
- The information given is clear and precise.
- Information is restated using different words and examples.
- Jargon is not used.
- A professional attitude is maintained.
- Feedback on the child's social and academic performance is provided.
- The results of the meeting are recorded.

Home–school communications can also be improved if educators are flexible in their scheduling to better accommodate parents' other obligations (Jayanthi,

Parents can be valuable resources as their children learn skills at school that can be practiced and reinforced at home.

Sawyer, Nelson, Bursuck, & Epstein, 1995). For example, meetings can be scheduled during the day if teachers have release time. Or, if teachers could receive extra pay, meetings can be scheduled early in the morning or in the evenings.

Parent–Teacher Partnerships

Many parents of children with learning disabilities become active participants in their children's educational programs. Some also tutor their children in the skills being learned at school (Hudson & Miller, 1993). Their effectiveness is enhanced when teachers help them develop good teaching skills and provide the materials needed for appropriate instruction. For example, each day, a parent may review and practice the week's spelling words and set a reading time when parent and child read to each other. Parents can learn to observe and take notes on their children's behavior so that they can share information with the teacher about progress made at home. If parents and teachers note data on a target behavior, they will be able to compare performance at school and home and determine whether progress is being made or whether new tactics should be selected.

Let's look at an example. Tara is a third grader with learning disabilities who has great difficulty interacting positively with other children. Her mother and father keep a record of the number of times Tara fights with her sister, and Tara's teacher, Ms. Navarrete, keeps similar data at school for fights with classmates. Both at home and at school, Tara gets a mark for each fighting incident. Each day, the teacher sends a daily report card home about Tara's behavior at school. Among other notes about Tara's daily accomplishments to her parents, Ms. Navarrete includes the number of times Tara fought at school. At eight o'clock each evening, Tara's parents add the points from school and from home, and Tara is allowed to watch television for thirty minutes minus the number of fights she had during the day. So if Tara has ten marks, say, she is allowed to watch only twenty minutes of television. By working together, Ms. Navarrete and Tara's parents provide the continuity in the educational program that Tara requires. Although not always achievable, such collaboration between school and home is a goal that all parents and educators might work toward.

The development of parent–teacher partnerships reaps many benefits (Garland, 1993). For example, knowledge that might not otherwise be communicated is often shared when full partnerships exist. In addition, teachers often gain a better understanding of students' strengths and weaknesses, family values and culture, home conditions, parental attitudes, and family needs. Another benefit can be increased support from parents for school programs and the teacher's efforts. Active partnerships require considerable effort. This ongoing process encourages professionals and parents to share, disagree, solve problems, and work together to meet a mutual goal (O'Shea, 1993). Parents and educators must assume more responsibility for initiating communications when problems can be predicted (Jayanthi et al., 1995). Remember, the basis of all positive partnerships should be trust and openness.

Technology

Today, microcomputers are common in classrooms or computer labs in almost every school. About every eleven students share a computer (Carroll, 1996). But this ratio is misleading because much of the hardware is outdated and will not

"run" current software, allow access to the Internet, or have the capacity to use CD-ROM technology. Also, most computers at schools are placed in labs, so students have access to these machines for only about fifteen minutes each day (Woodward & Gersten, 1992). Nevertheless, microcomputers can assist general and special education students as they study, learn new information, and write essays and reports. For students with disabilities, computers will continue to change the content and the mode of their instruction.

As we discuss throughout this text, many applications of computer technology benefit students with disabilities and their teachers. For students with learning disabilities, we highlight the applications of computer-assisted instruction (CAI), word processing, and some new innovations in videodisc instruction.

Computer-Assisted Instruction

Breakthroughs and improvements in both hardware and software occur almost daily in the computer field. For students with learning disabilities, advances in software are the most important and far-reaching. For example, the effectiveness of **computer-assisted instruction (CAI)** to supplement or replace traditional instruction and of **computer-enhanced instruction** for drill and practice depends on the quality of the software available (Lewis, 1993). Adaptable software also lets teachers use proven instructional techniques more simply. For example, time delay (the feature found on many language tapes in which there is a pause between a foreign word and its English translation) can be more easily arranged using a computer. And, it is just about as effective in computer format as it is administer by a teacher (Koscinski & Gast, 1993). Computerized adaptations of general education textbooks that include graphic organizers, study guides, and vocabulary drill have

 MAKING CONNECTIONS

To remind yourself about how technology impacts the lives of people with disabilities, review the other technology sections in this book.

computer-assisted instruction (CAI). Self-contained instructional software programs that students use to supplement or replace traditional teacher-directed instructional methods.

computer-enhanced instruction. Software programs that students use to supplement traditional instruction, used primarily for drill and practice.

been shown to be as effective as paper-and-pencil versions of such modifications and are certainly easier for students to manage (Lovitt & Horton, 1994).

Educators need to consider many issues when thinking about using technology in their classrooms. What benefits does the technology bring to the student? the teacher? and the instructional program? One common application is to provide more interesting opportunities for drill and practice of basic skills (arithmetic facts). One research study found that individualized teacher-directed instruction is somewhat more effective than a high-quality software program (Wilson, Majsterek, & Simmons, 1996). However, the time commitment of one-to-one instruction is substantial, and those costs are important factors when deciding when technology can optimize learning by freeing the teacher for more demanding instruction.

An exciting CAI development is **Hypertext**, which uses pop-up text windows for further explanation of textbook material. For example, definitions of difficult vocabulary words, rewording of confusing or complicated text, additional detailed maps, and further explanation of concepts introduced in the text are available to the student with the simple press of a key on the computer keyboard. This feature allows teachers to adapt textbooks so that students with learning disabilities can participate in general education course content. For example, students can read on a computer screen what would usually be printed in a textbook. Using Hypertext, they can highlight on the screen words that they do not know, concepts they do not understand, or material they would like more information about; a press of a key then gives them additional explanations. Using this system, students with learning disabilities learned the content required for a course in Washington State history quickly and efficiently (Higgins, Boone, & Lovitt, 1996).

New advances in computer capabilities have allowed for improvements on the concept introduced by Hypertext. **Hypermedia** uses a variety of formats to supplement and enrich text by merging computer and media technologies. Multimedia encyclopedias on CD ROM are good examples of Hypermedia. Recent research has shown that there are many benefits of this approach for students with learning disabilities (Babbit & Miller, 1996):

- Immediate access to multiple representations of information in a variety of formats,
- Access to multiple resources in a nonsequential manner on student demand
- Adaptability to many different learning styles and preferences,
- Individually paced.

For CAI applications concentrated in the area of drill and practice, Hypermedia has proven effective in teaching problem-solving skills (Babbit & Miller, 1996). With the added possibilities of incorporating the principles of **anchored instruction**, many institutional programs and techniques to teach thinking skills are on the horizon.

Writing Technology

The writing process is difficult for students with learning disabilities because this complex task requires the application of many different skills and cognitive abilities. For example, students need to select their topic, generate and organize the content of their paper, revise it, proof and edit it, and produce a final copy

Hypertext. A computer program that can be used to modify textbook materials through rewording, defining vocabulary, and providing further explanations.

Hypermedia. Computer programs that incorporate text, graphics, sound, photographic images, and video clips.

anchored instruction. The use of video taped real-life situations to make learning more relevant and meaningful.

(MacArthur & Schwartz, 1991). However, the combination of special writing instruction and the use of a computer with a good word processing program improves both the quality and quantity of these students' writing, and now new software features provide even more assistance to students with writing problems.

The computer supports the writing process naturally. For some students, it is physically less tiring. For others, print on a computer screen is easier to see and read than print on paper. Still others like the use of a computer because the results of the word processing program can be exceptionally attractive. The computer can facilitate collaboration, making it easier for two or more students to work together and merge their components of a writing task. Cochran-Smith (1991) found other benefits in using word processing technology to teach writing to students. With word processing, for instance, students tend to make more revisions to their writing than they do with paper and pencil. Students also produce longer papers, and their writing contains fewer errors. Remember, though, that the use of word processing alone does not guarantee improvement; instruction must be combined with computer use.

A feature of many word processing programs helps some students with learning disabilities with their writing. For example, spell checkers can improve some students' written work (MacArthur, Graham, Haynes, & DeLaPaz, 1996). When the spell checker was unavailable, students corrected only 9 percent of their spelling mistakes; but when it was available, they corrected 37 percent of their errors. When a correct suggestion was given for a misspelled word, the students made the right selection 82 percent of the time. Unfortunately, the spell checkers did not produce a correct spelling of the intended word between 26 and 37 percent of the time. For those students whose writing and spelling is so deficient that standard word processing programs are insufficient, other options are now available (Hunt-Berg, Rankin, & Benkelman, 1994). For example, some programs provide speech output so that students can determine whether the word they wrote matches the word they hear. Synthesized speech also supports students' writing by allowing them to listen to the work they have generated. Many students notice incomplete parts of their work, detect errors in the meaning or intention of their writing, and identify awkward sentence structures when this option is available to them (MacArthur, 1996).

Other helpful options can also support students engaged in the writing process. **Word banks** allow students to select words suggested by the computer (MacArthur, 1996). Some word banks generate lists of words the student has used previously and the student scrolls through the list to find the word he or she is searching for; and other word banks predict the words and the student makes a choice. Clearly, improvements in software promise many benefits to students who find writing a challenging task.

Videodisc Instruction

One newly developed technology with great utility in classroom settings is the videodisc (Woodward & Gersten, 1992). **Videodisc instruction** provides high-quality visual and auditory presentations. Presently, one side of a disc holds thirty minutes of continuous motion pictures, which can include slides, video, archival film, and graphics. Students can watch such presentations and be guided through their instruction by a carefully prepared narration that uses effective, researched-based instructional methods. Designed to be used with groups, this system fits well into typical instructional situations.

word banks. Computer-generated lists of words.

videodisc instruction. An alternative to CAI; instructional discs contain narrated segments of visual images.

The videodisc is an easy-to-use system that frees the teacher for other tasks. For example, while the class is attending to the videodisc material, the teacher could work individually with a child who needs extra attention, could finish required paperwork, or could grade papers.

Although still in the experimental stage, this technology holds great promise for a wide range of academic applications. For example, Carnine (1989) reports the successful use of laser videodisc equipment in teaching earth sciences. He used an interactive format that allowed students to see experiments conducted or text content demonstrated in video segments. With videodisc instruction, students can learn at their own pace and also experience activities that are not usually available in most classroom settings.

Concepts and Controversy: Is ADD a Disability?

 MAKING CONNECTIONS

To review how IDEA is passed and reauthorized, and the outcomes of each reauthorization, see Chapter 1 again.

In 1990, Congress studied and then reauthorized the Individuals with Disabilities Education Act (IDEA) (PL 101-476). At that time, attention deficit disorder (ADD) received considerable attention. Members of Congress heard testimony from parents that their children with ADD were not being served either appropriately or adequately in public schools. Parents argued that ADD is a disabling condition that requires intensive special education services. They wanted *all* children with ADD to receive special services and the schools to receive extra federal funding so that they could meet these children's educational needs.

ADD is not a new condition (Wiederholt, 1991). It was first described by Kurt Goldstein in his observations of young men with brain injuries returning to the States after World War II. It was also described by Strauss and Werner in their studies of children attending the Wayne County Training School in the 1930s and 1940s. During the 1960s, when the field of learning disabilities actually developed, many of the behaviors that today are considered characteristics of ADD were included in the description of students with learning disabilities. And in the 1970s, many people were concerned about the use of stimulant drugs, such as Ritalin and Dexedrine, to assist in the control of hyperactivity. So you may wonder why so much attention is directed at this condition in the 1990s. The extra notice is probably due to our lack of knowledge: Neither medical nor education professionals know how to treat or serve these children well. Parents, in their frustration and concern for the well-being of their children, turned to Congress for help.

 MAKING CONNECTIONS

• For background about ADD, see the History section of this chapter.
• Also see the section on ADD found in the Children with Learning Disabilities section of this chapter.

However, the controversy about ADD was not settled with the 1990 reauthorization of IDEA. Rather, Congress agreed to study the issues surrounding ADD until the next time IDEA was to be reauthorized, but Congress did not solve the issue by making ADD a separate special education category. So, the confusion and controversy continue.

What is the controversy? Some researchers estimate that 10 to 20 percent of schoolchildren have ADD (Shaywitz & Shaywitz, 1992) and that 50 percent of them do not presently qualify for special education services. But other researchers do not believe that ADD is even a disorder, let alone a disability (Armstrong, 1995; Reid, Maag, & Vasa, 1993). Yet others believe that those with attentional problems, rather than hyperactivity, are the ones at risk for academic failure; and those children are already served under the learning disabilities category (Riccio,

Gonzalez, & Hynd, 1994). What would happen if there were a separate category for ADD? Additional children would undoubtedly become part of the special education rolls, although no one is sure just how many. Can the nation afford to serve more children in special education? Do all children with ADD have disabilities that require unique special education services? Is another category necessary if the children with ADD are already being served by special education, primarily through the learning disabilities and behavior disorders categories?

Do you think that Congress should create a new special education category for students with ADD? Do you think that ADD is a separate disability or a symptom of several already identified and being served? How would you have resolved the issue in 1990? today?

~~~ *SUMMARY* ~~~

Individuals with learning disabilities do not learn in the same way or at the same pace as their nondisabled classmates. Current research is attempting to find better methods of instruction so that these students see further improvement in academic and social performance. When taught by teachers who are well trained and knowledgeable about the newest research findings, many of these individuals should be able to compensate for their disabilities. However, without the best that education can offer, the likelihood is small that individuals with learning disabilities will succeed as they should in life.

FOCUS QUESTIONS

Self-Test Questions

▶ *What are the differences and similarities between the two major definitions of learning disabilities?*

Although many definitions have been proposed, two (or adaptations of them) are generally used to guide the field of learning disabilities: the federal definition found in IDEA and the one put forth by the National Joint Committee on Learning Disabilities. Debate about the best definition of learning disabilities has continued since this field was begun in the 1960s. Since then, almost forty definitions have been proposed, each with a slightly different orientation, philosophy, and thrust. Some definitions, particularly the older ones, are medical in nature. Some definitions address the fact that this is a lifelong disability and might result in deficits in academic and social skills. The basic difference between most of the definitions is due to the originators' beliefs about what causes this disability. The older ones, like the federal definition,

have a medical orientation, and the newer ones reflect a more educational perspective. Regardless of what definition is used, professionals recognize some common characteristics. For example, most people with learning disabilities do have normal intelligence but are significantly behind nondisabled peers in academic achievement.

▶ *Why can students be identified as having learning disabilities in one state or school district but not qualify for special education services elsewhere?*

Nationally, special educators remain concerned about the definition of learning disabilities and the criteria for identification because of inconsistencies in prevalence rates within and across school districts and states and because of the tendency to identify a large number of students as having learning disabilities; estimates range from 3 to 30 percent of the school population. Prevalence rates vary state by state as definitions and criteria for identification vary as well. Without stringent controls over the number of students served as having learning disabilities, this group of learners seems to grow in number every year. Thus educators fear that children who are not succeeding at school are being misdiagnosed. This may be due to general education teachers, concerned about students who cannot keep up with others in their classes, referring them to special education in hopes that their educational needs will be better met with different arrangements.

▶ *Why is it correct to consider learning disabilities a lifelong condition?*

Although recognized by professionals only relatively recently, it is now quite clear: Learning disabilities and their effects present lifelong challenges to these individuals and their families. Those who continue to have difficulties reading often find that their postsecondary education opportunities are limited. They also tend to make career choices based on jobs that do not require them to read or write. For those who dropped out of high school, their adult outcomes appear grim, with their employment opportunities narrow and low-paying. For many adults with learning disabilities, the greatest difficulties center on their lack of friends and social outlets. Changes in curriculum and the expansion of transitional services may alter the adult outcomes for those still in school, but there are many issues to consider (which students receive a college-bound curriculum and which do not) and services to develop.

▶ *What are some learning characteristics that contribute to these students' poor academic performance?*

Recent research findings show that many of these learners do not approach learning tasks as others do. They tend to be passive (inactive) learners. Possibly, because of a history of failure, they attribute success with academic tasks to luck or chance rather than effort and ability. These attributions are not innate personality traits but are learned characteristics that can be altered through systematic instruction. However, attributions do affect motivation and influence how hard an individual will work to succeed at a task. These youngsters also have a tendency not to focus on the task or the correct aspect of the task. These students also have difficulties transferring (generalizing) learning from one task, skill, or situation to another.

Solving problems, processing information, and applying high-level thinking skills can also present problems for many of these individuals. Children can learn to focus their attention properly, apply their newly learned skills to other situations, learn to learn, and process information more efficiently. They need to learn these skills to be able to compete successfully in basic high school courses such as history, science, and literature. For this to occur, however, requires systematic and intensive instruction. The development of learning strategies and other teaching techniques are proving to help many of these youngsters be more positive and efficient active learners.

▶ *How can social competence and status affect these individuals?*

A learning disability is a complex condition. Although the prevailing problem among this population is low academic performance, many have substantial problems in the social arena in both social competence and social status. They seem unable to understand the social contexts of various situations because of their relatively poor abilities to communicate well, reason, or solve problems. They lack the ability to perceive and interpret social situations, generate appropriate social responses, and interact with others. The result is often peer rejection, an inability to make and sustain friendships, and a susceptibility to fall victim to more sophisticated peers. However, with specific instruction in the area of social skills, some of their deficits can be remediated, but there is a great deal of work to do in this area.

Challenge Question

▶ *What constitutes an appropriate education for these students and in what setting should it be provided?*

Debate continues about where these students should be educated. The use of different options—teams of special education and general education teachers, consulting special educators collaborating with general education teachers, resource rooms, self-contained special education classes, special schools—varies state by state and school district by district. Regardless of the service delivery option used by a school district—categorical or noncategorical—services for students with learning disabilities are available across the nation. These programs vary, but most center on the general education curriculum with strategy instruction or other additional supportive services. They are available from elementary to high school. Today, debates about where these students should be educated and what that education should comprise are being held by parents, educators, and the students themselves. The practices being implemented reflect professionals' and parents' philosophies about the concepts of LRE and full inclusion, the segregation of students, the most appropriate curriculum for these students, and the appropriate roles of general and special education with these students. For this group, in particular, growing consensus is that decisions about education should be made on an individual basis and a full array of services and placements must be available to meet the educational needs of students with disabilities.

~~~ SUPPLEMENTARY RESOURCES ~~~

Scholarly Books

Bos, C. & Vaughn, S. (1994). *Strategies for teaching students with learning and behavior problems.* Boston: Allyn and Bacon.

Deshler, D. D., Ellis, E. S., & Lenz, B. K. (1996). *Teaching adolescents with learning disabilities: Strategies and methods* (2nd ed.). Denver: Love Publishing.

Hallahan, D. P., Kauffman, J. M., & Lloyd, J. W. (1996). *Introduction to learning disabilities.* Boston: Allyn and Bacon.

Lerner, J. (1997). *Learning disabilities: Theories, diagnosis, and teaching strategies* (7th ed.) Boston: Houghton Mifflin.

Lovitt, T. C. (1995). *Tactics for teaching* (2nd ed.). Columbus, OH: Merrill, an imprint of Prentice-Hall.

Lyon, G. R., Gray, D. B., Kavanagh, J. F., Krasnegor, N. A. (1993). *Better understanding learning disabilities: New views from research and their implications for education and public policies.* Baltimore: Brooks.

Rivera, D. P., & Smith, D. D. (1997). *Teaching students with learning and behavior problems.* Boston: Allyn and Bacon.

Smith, C. R. (1994). *Learning disabilities: The interaction of learner, task, and setting.* Boston: Allyn and Bacon.

Smith, T. E. C., Dowdy, C. A., Polloway, E. A. Blalock, G. E. (1997). *Children and adults with learning disabilities.* Boston: Allyn and Bacon.

Popular Books

Brown, C. (1965). *Manchild in the promised land.* New York: Macmillan.

Cummings, R. W., & Fisher, G. L. (1991). *The school survival guide for kids with learning differences.* Minneapolis: Free Spirit Publishing.

Lee, D. (1992). *Faking it: A look into the mind of a creative learner.* Portsmouth, NH: Heineman Educational Books.

Moss, P. B. (1990). *An autobiography: P. Buckley Moss: The people's artist.* Waynesboro, VA: Shenandoah Heritage.

Sacks, O. (1985). *The man who mistook his wife for a hat.* New York: Summit Books.

Troyer, P. H. (1986). *Father Bede's misfit.* Monkton, MD: York Press.

Videos

The hero who couldn't read. (1984). ABC-TV.
When words don't mean a thing. (1987). ABC.
Read between the lines. (1989). ABC Video Enterprises.

Professional, Parent, and Consumer Organizations and Agencies

Council for Learning Disabilities (CLD)
P.O. Box 40303
Overland Park, KS 66204
Phone : (913) 429-8755

Division for Learning Disabilities (DLD)
Council for Exceptional Children
1920 Association Drive
Reston, VA 22091
Phone: (800) 224-6830
Web site: http://www.cec.sped.org

Learning Disability Association of America (LDA) (formerly the Association for Children with Learning Disabilities (ACLD)
4156 Library Rd.
Pittsburgh, PA 15234
Phone: (412) 341-1515
Web site: http://www.ldanatl.org

National Center for LD (NCLD)
381 Park Ave. S. Suite 1420
New York, NY 10016
Phone: (212) 545-7510
Web site: http://www.ncld.org

National Network of Learning Disabled Adults (NNLDA)
808 N. 82nd Street Suite F2
Scottsdale, AZ 85257
(602) 941-5112

Orton Dyslexia Society
8600 LaSalle Road
Chester Building
Suite 382
Baltimore, MD 21286-2044
(410) 296-0232
(800) 222-3123
Web site: http://www.ods.org
E-mail: info@ods.org

Lewis Carroll. *Alice Liddell as a Beggar Child*. No date.

Lewis Carroll is probably best known to all of us for his timeless story of *Alice in Wonderland*. Born Charles Lutwidge Dodgson in 1832, he was one of ten children and the eldest son of an Anglican minister. He was recognized at school as possessing "a very uncommon share of genius" and particularly excelled in mathematics. He was a nervous boy who had a chronic stuttering problem and was often ridiculed by his classmates. Although he considered following in his father's footsteps as a preacher, his stuttering problem made preaching difficult, and it is suggested that this is why he developed skills as a photographer and pursued a career as a writer (Hinde, 1991). This photograph, which Carroll hand-colored, is of the girl he used as his model for the character Alice.

Speech or Language Impairments

OVERVIEW

When students' primary and secondary disabilities are considered, speech or language impairments is the largest special education category. Most people use oral language for their primary means of communication, and if the communication process is flawed, all facets of interpersonal communication are affected. The relationship between early identification of a language impairment and later identification of a learning disability is strong because language is the foundation for cognition, reading abilities, and social competence. The importance of acquiring language in the normal developmental sequence cannot be underestimated, for it influences the overall child's potential and achievements.

FOCUS QUESTIONS

SELF-TEST QUESTIONS

▶ What comprises speech impairments and language impairments?

▶ What is the prevalence of this disability?

▶ How do language delays, language differences, and language impairments differ?

▶ How can teachers enhance language development and help to remediate a language impairment?

▶ What is alternative and augmentative communication, and what are its benefits to this population of learners?

CHALLENGE QUESTION

▶ What related service provider serves the needs of students with speech or language impairments, their families, and their teachers, and what roles does this professional serve today?

A Personal Perspective:
A Parent's View of a Speech Impairment

Gloria E. Enlow is the mother of two daughters, now ages 25 and 30. Divorced when the children were 5 and 10 years of age, Ms. Enlow raised them on her own for five years, until her remarriage. The younger daughter, Samantha Reid, has cerebral palsy. Ms. Enlow tells her family's story:

Communication is not something that I was thinking about as I held my baby daughter for the first time. As she looked at me with those big, bright brown eyes, though, I knew there was something different about her. She cried a lot, had trouble sucking and chewing, was quite stiff, and startled easily. As time went on and she was not able to sit unassisted or hold objects by herself, my anxiety heightened. Finally, at 18 months of age, she was diagnosed as having cerebral palsy. Samantha's condition is the result of lack of oxygen at birth, causing brain damage, which, for her, means lack of muscle control, including the larynx and tongue. The latter translates into labored and, often, unintelligible speech.

Relieved to know just what the problem was, we launched into a regimen of physical, occupational, and speech therapy, which continued through high school. Even though Samantha had special problems, we always treated her as just another member of the family, and she fully participated in everything from sledding to religious ceremonies. She was beautiful, happy, well adjusted, and developed a positive self-image. Her own personal desire to be involved in as many normal activities as possible prompted me, her teachers, and school administrators to act as advocates to maximize her potential and tap that obvious intelligence, which was masked by her lack of spontaneous, articulate speech.

We were fortunate that stable and well-established special education programs were in place by the time Samantha was ready for first grade. Even so, I had to search constantly for the proper care, services, and equipment to help her. A major goal was to enhance her speaking capability. As a result, an administrator and speech therapist identified her first augmentative communication device. By age 10, she had learned to program and use the Autocom, which had a digital display and printout capability. This aid made it easier for her to be integrated into her first regular academic class, a major accomplishment for all of us. Although Samantha liked and appreciated her special education classmates and teachers, she did not want to operate in an isolated environment. As Samantha's integration increased, people realized that she had academic ability. This set the stage for her introduction to newer and more sophisticated communication aids and word processors. This strong support from me, classroom aides, assistive devices, and Samantha's sheer determination all contributed to her ability to accomplish work. Samantha's long-term academic goal was to attend college, and through her ability and will she earned an academic scholarship at the University of New Mexico.

Samantha is very concerned about personal appearance, and she had resisted the idea of accumulating contraptions to carry around on her wheelchair. However, by the time she was completing high school, she knew that an electronic device would be necessary in college. She was introduced to the Touchtalker, a computer with a digital display and synthesized voice. She knew it could be of great assistance to her for communicating her own thoughts in the larger, more unfamiliar environment of the university. It has taken tremendous effort and time for her to learn to use the Touchtalker effectively, but she has mastered it well enough to work it herself and to teach others how to use the equipment.

From reading this story, you may have the impression that Samantha's life and my life were ordered. But that is not the case. I have not discussed my sustained efforts to identify sources of support and necessary resources. I joined committees, councils, and advocacy groups to learn what options and programs were available and to take part in influencing their direction. For many years, I wrote Samantha's dictated answers to homework assignments, spent countless hours at the library, and was intimately involved in her progression of study to assure that she would meet college enrollment requirements. A full-time aide was authorized for high school only after many sessions with numerous levels of school officials. Samantha is considered to be a unique case because of her intelligence and accomplishments despite multiple disabilities. She is determined to earn her degree, live independently, and earn a living. She does not intend to stay dependent on federal or state support. She will require substantial support until she earns a college degree, but the return on investment will be a self-sustaining, accomplished adult.

Today, Samantha is still a college student. Like many others, she interrupted her studies with marriage and the birth of a beautiful little girl, Theresa. I only hope that the future holds a reward for her in the way of acceptance for all that she has to offer.

1. What do you think the future holds for Samantha?

2. How will Samantha's adult life be different from those of individuals with cerebral palsy and severe speech impairments who were born twenty years before her? twenty years after her?

Our society places a high value on oral communication, and for most of us, it is the primary method of interacting with others. We talk with each other to share knowledge, information, and feelings. Most of us, in fact, prefer talking to other forms of communication, such as writing. Notice the intensity of conversations in cafeterias, college dining halls, and restaurants; think about how often we choose to use the telephone instead of writing a letter. Oral communication allows us to interact with others on many dimensions. Clearly, communication is a crucial part of life. Steven Warren (1993) helps us understand the importance of communication and the group of professionals who work to remediate speech or language impairments:

> The field of communication and language intervention is truly transdisciplinary due to the fundamental role that these skills play in human functioning. Language is often noted as the most impressive attainment/invention of our species. It is the basis of our culture, of commerce (i.e., the information age), science, religion and so forth. It is what separates us from virtually every other species on this planet. Individuals' fluency and skill with this tool will to a large extent determine their opportunities and options in our society. (Warren, 1993)

This chapter will help you understand people who have difficulty communicating with others because they have either a speech or oral language impairment. We will discuss the different types of these impairments, what causes them, and how they might be prevented or corrected. You will learn how this disability affects children during their schoolyears and how speech and language specialists and classroom teachers can improve children's communicative abilities. You will learn what problems these individuals face as adults and what hope there is in technological advances. You will come away with a clearer understanding of speech or language impairments and the role professionals play in ameliorating them.

Speech or Language Impairments Defined

To understand speech or language impairments, we must first understand the communication process people use to interact with others. Think of communication in terms of a game with at least two players (the sender and the receiver) and a message (the purpose of the interaction) (Marvin, 1989). Communication occurs only when the message intended by the sender is understood by the receiver. The sender may have an idea or thought to share with someone else, but the sender's idea needs to be translated from thought to some code the other person can understand.

Coding thoughts into signals or symbols is an important part of the communication game. **Communication signals** announce some immediate event, person, action, or emotion. Signals can be gestures, a social formality, or a vocal pattern, such as a gasp or groan. The U.S. Marine Band playing "Hail to the Chief," for example, signals the appearance of the President of the United States. A teacher rapping on a desk announces an important message. Symbols are used to relay a more complex message. **Communication symbols** refer to something: a past, present, or future event; a person or object; an action; a concept or emotion.

communication signals. A variety of messages that announce some immediate event, person, action, or emotion.

communication symbols. Voice, letters of the alphabet, or gestures used to relay communication messages.

These children are engaged in the communication process. They are taking turns being receivers and senders.

Speech sounds are **vocal symbols**. Letters of the alphabet are **written symbols**. **Sign language** uses gestural symbols. Symbols are used in combination with each other and are governed by rules. Signals, symbols, and the rules that must be followed constitute language and allow language to have meaning.

Once thought is coded, the sender must select a mechanism for delivering the message. The sender chooses from a number of mechanisms: voice, sign language, gestures, writing tools. The delivery system must be useful to the receiver. For example, selecting voice via telephone to transmit a message to a deaf person is useless (unless that person has technology for a voice-decoding telephone device). Sending a written message to someone who cannot read also results in ineffective communication.

Communication messages require the receiver to use eyes, ears, or even tactile (touch) senses (for example, those who use Braille) to take the message to the brain where it is understood. Receivers must understand the code the sender uses and be able to interpret the code so that it has meaning. Figure 5.1 illustrates the communication process. As you review this diagram, think about how even a simple message, such as an order at a fast-food restaurant, follows the steps outlined in the diagram.

Communication is unsuccessful if the sender or receiver cannot use the signals or symbols adequately. And if either person has a defective mechanism for sending or receiving the information, the communication process is ineffective.

At this point, it might be helpful for us to distinguish three terms—communication, language, and speech—that are different but related to one another. **Communication** is the process of exchanging knowledge, ideas, opinions, and feelings (Owens, 1994). This transfer is usually accomplished through the use of

vocal symbols. Oral means of relaying messages, such as speech sounds.

written symbols. Graphic means, such as the written alphabet, used to relay messages.

sign language. An organized established system of manual gestures used for communication.

communication. The transfer of knowledge, ideas, opinions, and feelings.

FIGURE 5.1

The Communication Process

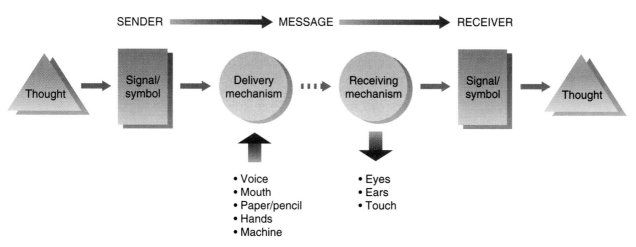

Source: "Language and Learning" (p. 148) by C. Marvin, in D. D. Smith, *Teaching Students with Learning and Behavior Problems* (2nd ed.), 1989. Englewood Cliffs, NJ: Prentice-Hall. Reprinted by permission.

language. Sometimes, however, communication can occur with the glance of an eye, a gesture, or some other nonverbal behavior. **Language** is a formalized method of communication involving the comprehension and use of the signs and symbols by which ideas are represented. Language also has rules that govern the use of signs and symbols so that the intended message has the correct meaning.

Speech is the vocal production of language. In most instances, it is the fastest and most efficient means of communicating. Understanding how we produce speech requires knowledge of the neurological, respiratory, vocal, and speech mechanisms that work together in our bodies to produce speech and language. Refer to the diagram of the head and chest cavity shown in Figure 5.2 as you read the following description of the process of generating speech.

When we want to speak, the brain sends messages that activate other mechanisms. The **respiratory system's** primary function is to take in oxygen and expel gases from our bodies. However, the diaphragm, chest, and throat muscles of the respiratory system that work to expel air also activate the **vocal system.** Voice is produced in the larynx, which sits on top of the trachea and houses the vocal folds. As air is expelled from the lungs, the flow of air causes the vocal folds to vibrate and produce sounds; the vocal folds lengthen or shorten to cause changes in pitch. The larynx and vocal folds are referred to as the **vibrating system.** As the sounds travel through the throat, mouth, and nasal cavities—the **resonating system**—the voice is shaped into speech sounds by the articulation or **speech mechanisms**, which include the tongue, soft and hard palates, teeth, lips, and jaw.

We have discussed the communication process in general terms. Let's turn now to a discussion of impairments in communication.

language. The formalized method of communication by which ideas are transmitted to others.

speech. The vocal production of language.

respiratory system. The system of organs whose primary function is to take in oxygen and expel gases.

vocal system. Parts of the respiratory system used to create voice.

vibrating system. The orderly function of the larynx and vocal folds to vibrate and produce sounds and pitch.

resonating system. Oral and nasal cavities where speech sounds are formed.

speech mechanisms. Includes the various parts of the body—tongue, lips, teeth, mandible, and palate—required for oral speech.

FIGURE 5.2

The Body's Systems for Generating Voice and Speech

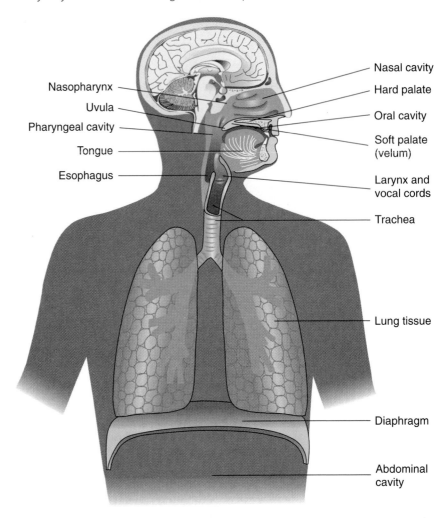

Nasopharynx

Uvula

Pharyngeal cavity

Tongue

Esophagus

Nasal cavity

Hard palate

Oral cavity

Soft palate (velum)

Larynx and vocal cords

Trachea

Lung tissue

Diaphragm

Abdominal cavity

Types of Speech or Language Impairments

People with speech or language impairments have difficulty using the communication process efficiently. Although considered one special education category, **speech impairments** and **language impairments** are really two separate, though related, disabilities. Each of these major problem areas is further broken down into more specific problems, as shown in Table 5.1. Let's look at each type to better understand how a problem with any of the areas listed in the table influences the effectiveness of communication.

Speech Impairments. Speech is abnormal when it is unintelligible, is unpleasant, or interferes with communication (Van Riper & Erickson, 1996). The three major types of speech impairments are voice, articulation, and fluency (for

speech impairment. Abnormal speech that is unintelligible, is unpleasant, or interferes with communication.

language impairment. Difficulty or inability to master the various systems of rules in language, which then interferes with communication.

TABLE 5.1

Types of Speech and Language Impairments

Impairment	Explanation
Speech	Impairment in the production of oral or spoken language
Voice	Absence or abnormal production of vocal quality, pitch, loudness, resonance, and/or duration
Articulation	Abnormal production of speech sounds
Fluency	Interruptions in the flow, rate, and/or rhythm of verbal expression
Language	Delayed or deviant development of comprehension and/or use of the signs and symbols used to express or receive ideas in a spoken, written, or other symbol system
Form	Lack of knowledge or inappropriate application of the rule systems that govern the sounds of language, word structures, and word forms that provide the basic elements of meaning, and the order and combination of words to form sentences
Content	Inability to understand or correctly transmit the intent and meaning of words and sentences
Use	Inability to apply language appropriately in social context and discourse

example, stuttering). Any one of these three speech impairments is distracting to the listener and can negatively affect the communication process.

Voice Problems. One type of speech impairment, **voice problems**, is not very common in schoolchildren, but when this speech impairment does occur it needs immediate attention from a professional. Voice is a measure of self; it is part of one's identity. We can identify many of our friends, for example, simply by hearing their voices. Voice distinguishes each person from others, and we typically do not think about how it functions. But when it does not function as usual, such as when we have laryngitis, we find it frustrating. Many famous personalities are recognized by their unique voices. Think of how impressionists create mental images of famous people through voice and gesture. Our voices also mirror our emotions; we often can tell when people we know well are happy, sad, angry, or scared merely by hearing their voices.

Two aspects of voice are important: pitch and loudness. A voice problem usually involves a problem with one or both of these aspects. **Pitch** is the perceived high or low quality of voice. Men typically have lower voice pitch than women. A man's voice whose pitch is high or a woman's pitch that is low attracts attention. If the receiver of communication pays more attention to the voice than to the message, though, communication is impaired (Van Riper & Erickson, 1996). When young boys' voice pitch changes during puberty, attention is drawn to the boys and their unintentional changes in voice. Of course, this pitch change is a normal

voice problem. An abnormal spoken language production, characterized by unusual pitch, loudness, or quality of sounds.

pitch. An aspect of voice; its perceived high or low sound quality.

Children with speech or language impairments may require extra encouragement to practice their newly acquired skills in front of their peers.

part of development and disappears as the boy's body grows and voice pitch becomes stabilized.

Loudness is the other main aspect of voice. In some cases, people are labeled with certain personality traits because of the loudness of their voices: "She is such a soft-spoken individual." "He is loud and brash." Voice can communicate much of the intended message for delivery. In some cases, if the quality of voice is so distracting that the message is misunderstood or lost, speech therapy is probably necessary.

Articulation Problems. Articulation problems are the most common speech impairments (Van Riper & Erickson, 1996). Articulation is the process of producing speech sounds. The receiver of communication must understand the sounds of the words spoken to understand the full message. If speech sounds are incorrectly produced, one sound might be confused with another, changing the meaning of the message. A child who substitutes a *t* for a *k* sound might say "titty tat" instead of "kitty cat." In such cases, if the words are different or unintelligible, the message has no meaning. Speech/language pathologists (SLPs), who specialize in correcting speech impairments, spend a considerable portion of their time remediating articulation errors. They also work with language, voice, and fluency problems.

Articulation is related to the speaker's age, culture, and environment (Boone & Plante, 1993). Compare the speech of a 3-year-old child, a 10-year-old, and an adult. Some of the most common articulation errors young children make are substitutions and distortions of the *s* and *z* sounds and substituting a *w* for an *l* and a *w* for an *r*. A 3-year-old might say, "Thee Thuzi thwim" for "See Suzi swim," and is perceived by adults as being cute and acceptable. However, the same articulation behavior in a 10-year-old child or an adult is not developmentally correct or acceptable. Articulation behavior that is developmentally normal at one age is not acceptable at another. The chart in Figure 5.3 gives the ages when various speech

loudness. An aspect of voice, referring to the intensity of the sound produced while speaking.
articulation problems. Abnormal production of speech sounds.

sounds develop. For example, most children learn to articulate *p, m, h, n, w, b* sounds from ages 2 to 3. But the range for learning to articulate *t* and *ng* can be from ages 2 to 6 (Sander, 1972). Some children are able to correctly articulate particular speech sounds earlier than the ages shown in Figure 5.3, and others develop them later.

About 2 to 3 percent of all children require professional help to overcome or compensate for their articulation errors. Teachers and others working with young children should be aware that children ages 2 to 6 generally make certain articulation mistakes as they go through a normal sequence of speech sound development. Adults should not pay too much attention to such misarticulations. However, if adults become concerned that a child is not acquiring articulation skills in a normal manner (see Figure 5.3), the child should be referred to an SLP for a speech evaluation.

Articulation, as mentioned earlier, is also related to the geographical region in which a person lives. For example, some people from certain sections of New York substitute a *d* for the *th* sound, resulting in *dese, dem,* and *dose.* Bostonians often use an *er* sound for an *a* (*idear* for *idea*), and many Southerners draw out vowels. Although these different articulations are apparent to people who do not reside in

FIGURE 5.3

Sander's Chart, Indicating When 90% of All Children Typically Produce a Specific Sound Correctly

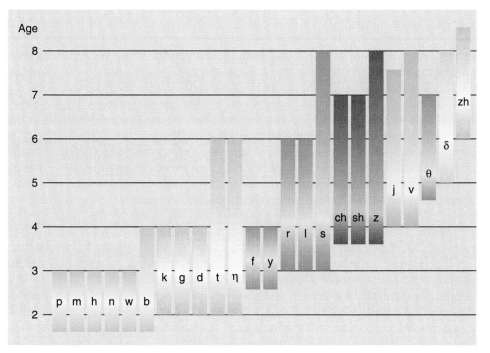

Notes: At the bottom of Sander's chart, you will find two speech symbols, The θ symbol stands for the breathed "th" sound, as in the word *bathroom.* The δ symbol stands for the voiced "th" sound, as in the word *feather.*

Average-age estimates and upper-age limits of customary consonant production. The solid bar corresponding to each sound starts at the median age of customary articulation; it stops at an age level at which 90 percent of all children are customarily producing the sound.

Source: "When Are Speech Sounds Learned?" by E. K. Sander, 1972, *Journal of Speech and Hearing Disorders, 37,* p. 62. Reprinted by permission.

 MAKING CONNECTIONS

For supporting information about language differences, see in Chapter 3
• Linguistically Diverse Students (Defined),
• Language and Communication Differences (Diverse Children).

a particular locale, they are normal in those regions. Differences in articulation due to regional dialects are *not* errors. Teachers should be careful not to refer children who have moved from one area of the country to another to an SLP solely because of dialectal differences in their speech.

Fluency Problems. Fluency difficulties are associated with the rate and flow pattern of a person's speech. A **fluency problem** usually involves hesitations or repetitions that interrupt the flow of speech. **Stuttering** is one type of fluency problem.

Some young children (ages 3 to 5) often demonstrate **dysfluencies** (nonfluencies) in the course of normal speech development, but they are not usually indicative of a fluency problem. Adult speech is not always smooth and fluent either. Even the best of speakers find times when they are dysfluent—when they hesitate in the middle of sentences, repeat parts of words, speak very quickly, or insert fillers such as "you know," "like," or "umm" in their speech. Dysfluencies are likely to occur in exciting, stressful, or uncommon situations.

As young children search for words or the rules to apply to their messages, they may become disfluent, and their manner of speech may suggest stuttering. The rate of their dysfluencies may even fit a definition of stuttering. However, in young children (below age 6), the rate of spontaneous recovery is great, possibly as high as 75 percent (Ratner, 1995). As with articulation, excessive attention to a perceived fluency problem early in a child's development can exaggerate rather than eliminate the problem. However, because of the remarkable results now being demonstrated by early intervention programs designed to remediate stuttering, it is inadvisable to delay intervention much beyond the age of 3 1/2 (Onslow, Andrews, & Lincoln, 1994). Individuals who have a stuttering problem persisting into childhood frequently experience some difficulty in speaking throughout their lives. Their ability to communicate, their interactions with other people, and their own self-concepts are affected, but their speech generally can be improved with professional help.

 MAKING CONNECTIONS

Read again the short biographical sketch of Lewis Carroll at the beginning of this chapter to see how his life and career choices were influenced by his stuttering problem.

Language Impairments. Language is the second major area within the special education category referred to as speech or language impairments. It is the complex system we use to communicate our thoughts to others. Oral language is expressed through the use of speech sounds that are combined to produce words and sentences. Other language systems, such as manual communication or sign language, use gestures or other means of communication, but not speech sounds. There are three aspects of language: form, content, and use.

Form. The rule systems used in oral language are referred to as **form**. Three rule systems characterize form in language: phonology, morphology, and syntax.

Phonology is the sound system of language; it includes the rules that govern various sound combinations. The phonology of language varies according to language. For example, the speech sounds of Hawaiian are different from those of Spanish and from those of English. The English language, for instance, uses forty-five different speech sound combinations; the Hawaiian language uses only half that number (Marvin, 1989). Swahili and some Native American languages use "clicking" sounds not found in European languages. Rules in each language govern how vowels, consonants, their combinations, and words are used.

fluency problems. Hesitations or repetitions of sounds or words that interrupt a person's flow of speech.

stuttering. The lack of fluency in an individual's speech pattern, often characterized by hesitations or repetitions of sounds or words.

dysfluencies. Aspects of speech that interrupt the pattern of speech; typical of normal speech development in young children.

form. The rule system of language; it is comprised of phonology, morphology, and syntax.

phonology. The rules within a language used to govern the combination of speech sounds to form words and sentences.

The rules that govern the parts of words that form the basic elements of meanings and the structures of words are called **morphology**. For example, prefixes and suffixes change the meanings of the roots of specific words: An *-ed* at the end of a verb changes the tense to past; a *un-* at the beginning of a word means that something is not. Notice the difference in the meanings of the following words: *cover, uncover, covered, uncovered, covers, discovered, discovering, discover, discovery, recover*. We understand the changes in these words' meanings because we understand the rules governing the structure of words.

Syntax determines where a word is placed in a sentence. Like phonology rules, syntax rules vary in different languages. Compare how a sentence is made negative in the English language, in Spanish, and in French, if you are familiar with Spanish and French. The rules within a language determine the meaning of the communication. In English, nouns generally precede verbs in a sentence; but when they do not, the construction might be a question: *It is one o'clock. Is it one o'clock?* The placement of the words in sentences can change their meaning. For example, *The car hit the boy* has a meaning very different from *The boy hit the car*. Rules also structure our placement of adverbs and other parts of speech. *I hardly studied this chapter* and *I studied this chapter hard* show different understandings of how the elements of the English language are put together. Many of these subtleties can be difficult to master.

Form is important in all language (oral, written, and sign); form comprises the rules of language where not all combinations are acceptable. Oral and written language use letters and letter combinations to produce the words and word combinations (sentences) of language. The use of these letters (symbols) and words is governed by the rules of language. What we know about speech sounds, letters, words (or vocabulary), and rules of language influences the way we speak, read, write, and spell. Games like Scrabble, Wheel of Fortune, and Hangman require knowledge about letters and their rules for combinations. Those who play such games well have mastered these rules of language.

Content. The second aspect of language, **content**, relates to the intent and meanings of spoken or written statements. The rules and form of language are important, but for communication to be effective, words must be meaningful. **Semantics** is the system that patterns the intent and meanings of words and sentences to comprise the content of the communication. The key words in a statement, the direct and implied referents to these words, and the order of the words used all affect the meaning of the message. Often, we are not clear and precise in our use of words; we use words like *these* and *those*, *here* and *there*, without being exact. When senders of messages use indirect or implied referents, the receiver might not understand the message that is intended. When a child comes home and tells his mother, for instance, that he "left it at school," she might be unclear about what the child left at school, unless he is answering a direct question like, "Where is your jacket?"

Use. The third aspect of language, **use**, concerns the application of language in various communications according to the social context of the situation. Use includes **pragmatics**, which is the study of language in context, and in part focuses on the intention of the communication. For example, an individual may request, order, or give an action or some information through a communication; the com-

 MAKING CONNECTIONS

For a review of the communication game,
- read again the opening section of this chapter,
- see also Figure 5.1.

For more about the relationship between language skills and social competence, see Social Competence in the Social Skills section in Children with Learning Disabilities (Chapter 4).

morphology. Rules that govern the structure and form of words and comprise the basic meaning of words.

syntax. Rules that govern word endings and order of words in phrases and sentences.

content. An aspect of language that governs the intent and meaning of the message delivered in a communication; includes semantics.

semantics. The system within a language that governs content, intent, and meanings of spoken and written language.

use. An aspect of language; applying language appropriately; includes pragmatics.

pragmatics. A key element of communication; the relationship among language, perception, and cognition.

munication is different depending on the intent or the social context of the communication. Thus the context of discussion between two children talking to each other during free play is quite different from the context of discussion between a teacher and a child.

The relationships among language, perception, and cognition are key factors in the development of **communicative competence**. Ruiz (1995) helps us understand this important concept: "[Communicative competence] is what a speaker needs to know to communicate appropriately—what may be said and what should not be said; when, where, and by whom; and for what purposes—in addition to the linguistic knowledge necessary to produce grammatical utterances" (p. 477). Students who are not communicatively competent have difficulties understanding teachers' instructions, their lectures, and often interactions with their peers. Ruiz likens this situation to a class being taught in a foreign language the students do not understand. Such students are unable to participate successfully in the communication process that Marvin compared to a game. Many reasons can explain the students' lack of communicative competence. It may be that they have not mastered the necessary language skills because they are still learning English, or it may be due to an actual language impairment.

Blank, Rose, and Berlin (1978) brought the importance of pragmatics to the attention of professionals. They emphasized that language cannot be considered separately from children's overall development. They pointed out that a child must know what an object is before it can be labeled meaningfully, described, or referred to in communication. For example, a child must know what a cup is—an object that holds liquid, is picked up, is used to drink from—before that child can develop a concept about cups or use it in conversation. Blank and her colleagues' pragmatics approach to language and its development provides yet another perspective of language and how children develop an ability to gain meaning from oral communication through a pragmatic approach. Language instruction that teaches words or even concepts in isolation is not as effective as instruction that allows children to build and expand on their own experiences. This pragmatic approach to language and its development is becoming widely adopted by professionals in the field.

To achieve competence in communication, a person must be able to use language correctly in a social context. Social competence and communicative competence are related. Being able to communicate effectively is an essential component of being able socially (Walker, Schwarz, Nippold, Irving, & Noell, 1994). Social conventions or rules are used to initiate conversations and to communicate with others. Thus the way we use language at home or with our friends in a casual conversation is different from the way we speak to an employer, a school principal, or people in authority. Not understanding the social rules of language can have serious consequences. For instance, perceived rudeness to a teacher can result in a trip to the principal's office. Remember, mastering the rules and the nuances of language and communication can be difficult for some children. Also, successful conversations require that all aspects of language (form, content, and use) be applied with the rules of conversation (Weiss, 1995).

MAKING CONNECTIONS

See also the Educational Interventions section of this chapter.

communication competence. Proficiency in the use of language, allowing people to participate in all aspects of communication in social and learning situations.

Identification

Although most people can tell that someone has a speech or language impairment by listening to that person, the formal assessment of speech and language impairments is complicated. Usually, SLPs conduct these assessments because they have the necessary skills, knowledge, and training in normal and abnormal speech and language development. If a hearing loss is suspected as a reason for the speech or language impairment, the SLP is joined by an audiologist.

Speech Impairments. Each of the three aspects of speech—articulation, voice, and fluency—requires a different type of assessment to determine whether the child has an impairment. Given that it is the most common problem in children, let's look at articulation first.

Articulation. These errors are very common in children, but not all occurrences represent a speech impairment. Children learn to articulate the sounds of our language throughout their early childhood. The last sound most U.S. children master at 90 percent accuracy is the *z* sound (as in wa*s*) by age 8 1/2. So the judgment about whether a child has an articulation problem must be made by considering when children typically master various speech sounds. For example, a 6-year-old who cannot produce the *z* sound correctly probably does not have a speech impairment, but a child age 12 who is still making many articulation errors probably does have an articulation problem.

 MAKING CONNECTIONS

Refer again to Figure 5.3 to review the ages when speech sounds are typically mastered.

When considering whether children have a speech impairment, SLPs must consider both age and situation. Professionals understand that children tend to simplify speech and make more articulation errors when they are excited, in an unfamiliar setting, or nervous (Boone & Plante, 1993). For example, a very young child eager for a freshly baked cupcake might say, "I dan a tutay." Under normal situations, the child would articulate the specific sounds correctly and say, "I want a cupcake." Articulation errors like these, even when made in nonstressful situations, might not represent a speech impairment for a young child but certainly would for an older child or adolescent.

Some children make articulation errors because they do not use the right motor responses to form the sounds correctly. The cause may be a physical problem, such as a **cleft palate**, where the roof of the mouth is not joined together, or an injury to the mouth. The cause may also be errors in the way the individual uses the speech mechanisms—tongue, lips, teeth, mandible (jaw), or palate—to form the speech sounds.

People can make four different kinds of articulation errors: substitutions, distortions, omissions, and additions; Table 5.2 defines and provides an example of each type. Any one of these articulation errors can affect or change the meaning of a communication; more than one error must occur before a child is diagnosed as having an articulation problem. However, no hard-and-fast rules exist regarding the number and types of articulation errors a child must make before a referral for speech therapy is appropriate. SLPs use their professional judgment and weigh a number of factors when identifying children as having an articulation problem. For example, they consider how seriously communication is negatively affected by poor articulation and the frequency, type, and consistency of errors a child makes. Most children with articulation problems, even those whose speech is almost unintelligible, have no apparent physiological reason for their articulation difficulties. In fact, some children can correctly pronounce a sound when it is found at the beginning of words but not when it is in the medial position or in some words and not in others (Rice, 1995). The functional nature of articulation problems can sometimes make it difficult to determine when therapy is actually required.

cleft palate. An opening in the roof of the mouth, causing too much air to pass through the nasal cavity when the individual is speaking.

TABLE 5.2

Four Kinds of Articulation Errors

Error Type	Definition	Example
Omission	A sound or group of sounds is left out of a word. Small children often leave off the ending of a word (sounds in the final position).	Intended: *I want a banana.* Omission: *I wanna nana.*
Substitution	A common misarticulation among small children, one sound is used for another.	Intended: *I see the rabbit.* Substitution: *I tee the wabbit.*
Distortion	A variation of the intended sound is produced in an unfamiliar manner.	Intended: *Give the pencil to Sally.* Distortion: *Give the pencil to Sally* (the /p/ is nasalized).
Addition	An extra sound is inserted or added to one already correctly produced.	Intended: *I miss her.* Addition: *I missid her.*

Voice. These problems are not common in young children. However, a significant change in voice or a voice quality that deviates substantially from those of one's peers can be a sign of a serious laryngeal disease. For this reason, even very young children with an abnormal voice quality should have a medical examination. Overall, there are two general reasons for voice problems in children: an organic cause (such as a tumor) and a functional cause. Functional causes of voice problems are usually due to individuals using their voices inappropriately. For example, screaming for long periods of time puts undue stress on the vocal folds and larynx, causing damage to the voice mechanisms: The voice will sound hoarse, too low or high in pitch, or breathy. As with articulation, SLPs measure voice by using their clinical judgment—their knowledge and experience—to determine when a child's voice is actually impaired and in need of therapy.

Fluency. The third kind of speech impairment is a fluency problem: The flow of speech breaks down because syllables are repeated or a communication includes many hesitations or extraneous words or sounds. Stuttering is a fluency problem, but there are important distinctions between stuttering and dysfluent speech. All of us, particularly young children mastering language, are dysfluent sometimes, and this is normal. Adults can distinguish between normal dysfluency and stuttering in children by noticing carefully what aspects of speech are repeated (Boone & Plante, 1993). One very important aspect is the age of the child. Children around age 3 1/2 are still hesitant in their language use. They spend a lot of energy searching for words and retrieving thoughts. At this age, children often repeat words and phrases. By age 4 1/2, one year later, repetitions of words and phrases have an entirely different purpose. They are used for emphasis.

Another difference between normal dysfluencies and stuttering is in what gets repeated. Children with normal speech often repeat whole words or phrases, like "Give me the, give me the, give me the ball." Children who stutter are more likely to say "Gi-gi-gi-give m-m-m-me the b-b-b-ball"—that is, they repeat specific sounds or syllables. Children who stutter also have a higher frequency of repetitions than do children who are dysfluent. For example, children with normal speech do not repeat more than 3 percent of what they say, whereas children who stutter repeat syllables in 7 to 14 percent of what they say (Wingate, 1962). They also tend to show nonverbal signs of struggling with their speech by blinking, grimacing, or becoming tense. SLPs measure a fluency problem by analyzing the frequency and type of an individual's involuntary dysfluencies from samples of oral language taken in various situations, such as free play and answering direct questions.

Language Impairments. Difficulties in language can result in more serious learning problems than speech impairments cause. Lack of language competence influences children's ability to learn to read and write at the pace of their classmates as well as their ability to communicate orally with others. An SLP assesses an individual's language competence through a thorough evaluation, which usually includes assessment of the three aspects of language: form, content, and use. To assess the *form* or structure of an individual's language, the SLP determines how well the child uses the rules of language. Problems with form cause errors in letter or sound formation, grammatical structure usage, or in sentence formation. Many children who have difficulty with the rules of language also have problems recognizing sounds and understanding the meaning of different grammatical constructions, sentence types, and sentence complexities. For example, a child who has not mastered the rules of language might not be able to tell the difference between these two sentences: *Go to the store. Did you go to the store?* The second aspect of language that SLPs assess to determine language competence is *content*. Children with problems in language content often do not understand the meaning of what is said to them and choose inappropriate words for their oral language communications. They might also have difficulty comprehending the written material presented in textbooks. The third aspect of language competence, *use* (pragmatics), is discussed to determine how appropriately a child uses language in social contexts and conversations.

SLPs evaluate children's language competence to determine whether the child actually has a language impairment. One part of this evaluation or assessment is a case history that documents the child's birth, development, and cognitive and physical growth. Usually, the child's doctor and the parents complete a case history form before the SLP actually sees the child. When the parents bring their child to the clinic for the evaluation, they are interviewed and the child's language is evaluated in several different situations: free play, informal testing, and formal testing. The free play situation is the primary source of the assessment of the child's spontaneous speech, which about 75 percent of SLPs incorporate into their evaluations (Johnston, Miller, Curtiss, & Tallal, 1993). When the child's use of language in a free play setting is evaluated, the parents are often asked to play with their child in a room equipped with many toys and objects, a one-way mirror (so that the SLP can observe without distracting the child or parents), and an audio system. The SLP might take data by using a standardized evaluation scale or might

 MAKING CONNECTIONS

For more information about the relationship between language impairments and learning problems, see
• Prevention section (Chapter 4),
• Prevention section (Chapter 6),
• Social Skills section (Chapter 4),
• Preschool section (Chapter 6).

take informal notes about the child's language. In informal tests, the SLP might ask a series of questions to see how well a child understands what is said. The SLP might show the child some pictures, asking the child to name and describe what is in a picture or to make up a story about several pictures. Some SLPs tape the child's language and transcribe it at a later time so that they can conduct a formal and detailed evaluation of the form, content, and use of language. The child's language is also evaluated formally with standardized tests. The number and types of tests used vary depending on the speech and language difficulties the SLP identified in the informal evaluations.

Finally, the SLP prepares an evaluation report that becomes part of the child's permanent record if the evaluation was conducted by or paid for by the school district the child attends. This report presents the status of the child's speech and language and includes a statement about whether the child has a speech or language impairment. It also presents a summary of the child's strengths and weaknesses in speech and language and an overall assessment of the child's language competence. In addition, the report usually includes a suggested remediation plan, a list of the services the child requires, and a statement about the predicted outcome of treatment and remediation. The SLP reviews this report with the parents so that they understand which specific services are being recommended and why. For a child diagnosed as having a speech or language impairment, this process is the beginning of a partnership of parents and professionals working together to remediate the child's disability.

Significance

Understanding and being able to use speech and language well influences an individual's success in school, social situations, and employment. A speech impairment affects how a person interacts with others in all kinds of settings. The story of Lewis G. Carroll is not uncommon among those who stutter. Their impairment often influences career choices, social life, and emotional well-being. It is not uncommon for children to develop emotional problems because of their stuttering. Some researchers (Shames & Ramig, 1994) believe that as listeners, and the individuals themselves, react to this nonfluent speech, feelings of embarrassment, guilt, frustration, or anger are commonly experienced. Stuttering can lead to confusion, feelings of helplessness, and diminished self-concept. The long-term effects can be quite serious. Some individuals respond by acting overly aggressive, denying their disability, and projecting their own negative reactions to their listeners. Others withdraw socially, seeking to avoid all situations in which they have to talk, and ultimately they become isolates.

A language impairment has the potential of being even more serious, for it can impact all aspects of a child's classroom experiences, including the abilities to speak, write, and comprehend what is written and spoken. Language is a complex system to master: Its rules are not consistent, and it has many subtle conventions to learn and follow. Language is an important foundation to the skills children learn at school, however. We know of the relationship between the knowledge of language and the ability to learn to read and write easily. The histories of many children with learning disabilities reveal that they were identified as having a significant language delay or impairment as preschoolers. There are many reasons for a relationship between learning disabilities and language impairment. For example, children who do not understand what is said to them do not develop language

MAKING CONNECTIONS
• See the Parents and Teachers as Partners (Family section), Chapter 4.
• See Chapter 2.

MAKING CONNECTIONS
For the impact of stuttering on an individual, reread the biographical sketch of Lewis Carroll found at the opening of this chapter.

MAKING CONNECTIONS
For more about the relationships among language abilities, cognition, and learning, see these sections in Chapter 4:
• Focus on Diversity box
• Prevention
• Learning Characteristics

at the same rate as children who do understand and benefit from communicative interchanges. Some children with delayed language also do not develop cognitive or thinking skills at the same pace as their nondisabled peers, which can influence all levels of academic achievement, particularly in reading and writing.

Clearly, people who cannot communicate well find that their impairment affects the way they interact with others and how efficiently they communicate and learn. Ultimately, it influences employment options. For example, a receptionist in an office must be able to talk on the phone, take and deliver messages to the public and to other workers in the office, and provide directions to visitors. Thus these individuals should be provided with the services they need to enable them to learn how to communicate successfully with others.

 MAKING CONNECTIONS

For supporting information about communicative competence, see
• Social Competence (Chapter 4),
• Defined, in this chapter.

History of the Field

Speech and language problems have been a part of the human condition since our ancestors began to speak. Even before 1000 B.C., individuals with disabilities were considered fools, buffoons, and sources of entertainment. During Roman times, cages were placed along the Appian Way to display individuals with disabilities. There, Balbus Balaesus the Stutterer would attempt to talk when a coin was thrown into his cage (Van Riper & Erickson, 1996).

There have been many documented cases of speech or language impairments throughout the centuries. Treatment programs also existed; they were not based in schools, and they met with mixed results. In the United States, speech correction was not available in the public schools until the twentieth century. In 1910, the Chicago public schools hired an itinerant teacher to help children who "stammered" (Moore & Kester, 1953). In 1913, the superintendent of the New York City schools began a program for speech training for children with speech impairments. The first speech clinic was opened in 1914 by Smiley Blanton at the University of Wisconsin. In 1925, the American Academy for Speech Correction (later called the American Speech and Hearing Association and now called American Speech-Language-Hearing Association) was formed by a small group of professionals to share their ideas and research. Robert West spearheaded the formation of the academy and is credited by some (Van Riper, 1981) as being the father of his field. Two other pioneers, Lee Travis and Wendell Johnson, developed the program at the University of Iowa and guided this emerging field at the organizational and national level. Through their guidance, the field of speech or language impairments became independent from medicine, psychology, and speech and debate.

In the early part of the twentieth century, public schools hired speech clinicians to work with children who had speech problems, but services were limited. During World War II, the military developed screening procedures to identify persons with speech problems and hearing losses and began their own clinical and research programs. These efforts demonstrated that speech therapy can be effective, and after the war university programs to train SLPs increased in size and number. Correspondingly, public

Robert West, one of the founders of what is now the American Speech-Language-Hearing Association, is considered by many to be the father of this field.

school programs expanded. By 1959, thirty-nine states had laws allowing or requiring school districts to provide services for students with disabilities, including those with speech or language impairments, and to receive state funding.

Throughout the history of the field, professionals who work to remediate children's speech and language problems have had many titles, partly because of their changing roles. At first they were called speech correctionists or speech teachers; these early professionals centered their efforts on remediating stuttering, voice, and articulation difficulties. During the late 1950s and 1960s, professionals began to be called speech therapists and speech clinicians. In this period, they saw more than two hundred children per week, primarily in small groups for as little as thirty minutes per day. However, many children with language problems, with moderate to severe disabilities, with multiple disabilities, or with mental retardation did not receive speech therapy because professionals thought these children were not developmentally able to profit from therapy. During the early 1970s, professionals were called speech pathologists. By the end of the decade, ASHA coined the term *speech/language pathologist* to reflect the broader view of the services they provide.

The 1970s was a period of transition. ASHA and the professionals it represents sought to further improve the quality of services provided to children. Research data indicated that many articulation problems were developmental and were corrected naturally with age. Therefore this period of time also saw a shift in the priorities of speech therapy in the schools. SLPs began to work with fewer children with mild articulation problems and concentrated on youngsters with severe speech or language problems.

Today, SLPs often consult and collaborate with general education classroom teachers to remediate minor speech or language problems. SLPs can then work intensively with twenty or thirty children who have serious speech or language impairments. Although articulation deficits are still a large part of their caseloads, SLPs serve in a variety of roles, ranging from consulting to individualized teaching. They work with children, their teachers, and their parents to remediate speech or language problems.

Prevalence

Many professionals believe that children with speech or language impairments form the largest population of students with disabilities in the schools, and some estimate that the prevalence in schoolchildren may be as high as 10 percent (Boone & Plante, 1993). However, as noted in Chapters 1 and 4, official reports show that the largest single category of exceptional learners is learning disabilities (U.S. Department of Education, 1996). How can we account for these differing opinions? Remember that children are reported by their primary disabling condition. For a large proportion of children with speech or language impairments, their primary disabling condition is learning disabilities, mental retardation, hearing impairments, or health impairments. When the children have *only* a speech or language impairment, they are counted in this group, which is the second in prevalence even using this system of counting. In the only study of its kind, the caseloads of SLPs showed that 42 percent of all the children with communicative difficulties had another primary disabling condition (Dublinski, 1981).

MAKING CONNECTIONS

For overall student disabilities rates, see Figure 1.1 (Chapter 1).

Data from the *Eighteenth Annual Report to Congress on the Implementation of IDEA* (U.S. Department of Education, 1996) indicate that during the 1994–1995 schoolyears 2.3 percent of the entire school-age population was identified as having a disability because of speech or language impairments or both. Thus more than 2 of every 100 schoolchildren, or a total of 1,019,424 students between the ages of 6 and 17, received services for speech or language impairments as their primary disability. If this comprises 58 percent of those school-age youngsters SLPs serve, then an additional 591,265 students whose primary disabling condition was not speech or language impairments received supportive services because of speech or language difficulties or both. Putting it all together, it appears that almost 5 percent of all schoolchildren receive services for speech or language impairments, whether or not this category represents their primary handicapping condition (Rice, 1995). And, of this group how many have speech impairments and how many have language impairments? Estimates indicate that 53 percent of the students seen by SLPs have speech impairments and 47 percent have language impairments (Dublinski, 1981). The percentages of students with language impairments and each type of speech impairment are shown in Figure 5.4.

Of interest to professionals in the field is the relationship between a student's age and these disabilities. Articulation problems, for example, are more common during the preschool and elementary years. Speech or language impairments is definitely the most common label used for children at the age of 6 (the first year they must be identified as belonging to a special education category). For example, over 200,000 six-year-olds were so identified in 1994–1995, and the next most prevalent category was learning disabilities at over 37,000 students (U.S.

FIGURE 5.4

The Percentage of Students Having Different Types of Speech and Language Impairments

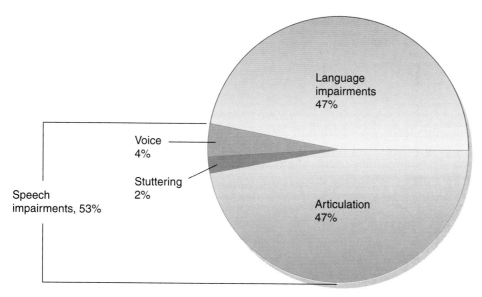

Department of Education, 1996). Compare those numbers to the prevalence of 15-year-olds with this disability, which was 12,071 in the 1994–1995 schoolyear. Why is it that this is the most common category used for young elementary-aged students? Why does this not continue throughout the school years? Do these problems disappear with age? Are early remediation efforts so successful that these impairments are corrected and do not persist through childhood? Or are these youngsters reclassified into another group (such as learning disabilities) as they become older? Certainly, this evidence supports the popular idea that the connection between early identification of speech or language impairments and later diagnosis of learning disabilities is strong (Tallal, Miller, Bedi, Byma, Wang, Nagarajan, Schreenei, Jenkins, Merzenich, 1996; Wallach & Butler, 1995).

Causes and Prevention of Speech or Language Impairments

Researchers attempt to find what factors cause certain disabilities so that they might be prevented. In this section, you will learn that although there are various theories, professionals still do not know what causes many types of speech or language impairments. You will also find that some impairments are preventable and that others are not.

Causes

As with so many disability areas, the most common cause of speech or language impairments is unknown. As you read through this section, however, you will find that many causes for some specific impairments are well known.

Speech Impairments. In general, the known causes of speech impairments are varied and include brain damage, malfunction of the respiratory or speech mechanisms, or malformation of the articulators. Some types of impairments have an organic cause, meaning that there is a physical reason for the disability. For example, many individuals with severely misaligned teeth cannot articulate well. Once their adult teeth grow in, however, their articulation will probably be fine, so they do not have a speech impairment. This example shows how a problem with an articulator can affect speech; other organic causes of speech impairments are more serious. For example, a cleft lip or palate affects the ability to produce oral speech. This incidence varies by race/ethnicity: about 1 of every 500 live births for Asian-Americans, about 1 out of 750 live births for whites, and 1 out of 2,000 for African Americans (McWilliams & Witzel, 1994). The proportions of cleft lips and palates tend to be consistent: about 25 percent involve the lip, 50 percent involve the lip and the palate, and the remaining 25 percent involve the palate. Most cleft lips can be repaired through plastic surgery and do not have a long-term effect on articulation. A cleft palate, however, can present continual problems because the opening of the palate and the roof of the mouth allows excessive air and sound waves to flow through the nasal cavities. The result is a very nasal-sounding voice and difficulties in producing some speech sounds, such as *s* and *z*. A cleft palate is one physical cause of a speech impairment that requires the intensive work of many specialists (plastic surgeons, orthodontists, and SLPs) to help the individual overcome the resulting speech disability.

MAKING CONNECTIONS

Again, for discussions about language impairments and learning disabilities, see these sections in Chapter 4:
• Defined
• Social Skills

MAKING CONNECTIONS

Read each of the sections about the causes of specific disabilities to understand that the cause of most cases of disabilities is unknown.

Too many young children are referred by their teachers to SLPs for articulation problems. These referrals are made because teachers do not remember that speech sounds are mastered at different ages and that individual children acquire specific speech sounds at different times (see Figure 5.3). Many children outgrow their inability to properly articulate sounds. Children who make consistent articulation errors that are not developmental, however, are less likely to learn to make speech sounds correctly without therapy. In other words, those who make consistent errors tend not to "outgrow" established misarticulation patterns (Van Riper & Erickson, 1996). Therefore all children who are late in acquiring correct production of specific speech sounds and make consistent articulation errors should be referred to an SLP for assessment.

Voice problems are not as common in schoolchildren, although they can be symptomatic of a medical problem. For example, conditions that interfere with muscular activity, such as juvenile arthritis, can result in a vocal disturbance. Voice problems also can be caused by the way the voice is used: Undue abuse of the voice by screaming, shouting, and straining can cause damage to the vocal folds and result in a voice disorder. Rock singers frequently strain their voices so much that they develop nodules (calluses) on the vocal folds, become chronically hoarse, and must stop singing or have the nodules removed surgically. Teachers who notice changes in children's voices that are not associated with puberty should refer the student to an SLP.

Stuttering, a lack of fluency in speaking, may be characterized by severe hesitations or the repetition of sounds and words. Although professionals can describe stuttering, they seem unable to agree on or explain a single cause (Silverman, 1996). They can, however, describe conditions when nonfluency is more likely to occur in stutterers. For example, stuttering is more likely to occur when the conversational situation is very complex or unpredictable (Weiss, 1995). It appears that stress makes its likelihood more probable.

Some factors have been eliminated as causes of stuttering. It appears that stuttering is not linked to underlying deficiencies in language knowledge or language abilities (Ratner, 1995). In other words, the language capabilities of individuals who stutter are not different from those who do not stutter. One important factor, however, may be a significant contributor to the frequency of stuttering. It appears that these individuals are less able than those who do not stutter to monitor their speech and recognize when it is not fluent (Finn & Ingham, 1994). Evidently, monitoring their speech is not a natural act and may well prove to be an important instructional target.

Language Impairments. Many problems that fall into the area of language impairments have multiple causes. As with **aphasia**, they can result from brain injury or disease that damages the central nervous system. They can result from the inability to hear well at the time language should be developing. For example, children with chronic **otitis media**, or ear infections, often have associated difficulties with language development, possibly because of the interruptions in hearing language during the typical developmental periods or because of related health problems.

Some researchers have found a family connection with language impairments (Lahey & Edwards, 1995). However, most often, poor language development is caused by various environmental factors, including the lack of stimulation and proper experiences for mental development and learning language. Environmental

aphasia. Loss or impairment of language ability due to brain injury.

otitis media. Middle ear infection that can result in hearing loss, communication impairments, or learning disabilities if it becomes a chronic condition.

MAKING CONNECTIONS

For supporting information about factors that can contribute to poor language development, see
• Causes and Prevention (Chapter 4),
• Causes and Prevention (Chapter 6).

MAKING CONNECTIONS

For more information about learning characteristics of students with mental retardation, see Chapter 6:
• Children with Mental Retardation,
• Educational Interventions.

MAKING CONNECTIONS

Information about diversity in language and culture is integrated throughout the text and in particular is found in
• Chapter 3,
• Focus on Diversity boxes throughout the text,
• Concepts and Controversies (Chapter 7).

language delay. Development of language skills that is slower than in the majority of peers; may signal language that will require assistance of a specialist to use language proficiently.

language-different. Children who are not native English speakers and those who speak nonstandard English and do not have an impairment even though their language is not typical.

factors also affect children's abilities to acquire language and become proficient in its use. Some children do not develop language because they have no appropriate role models. Some are left alone too often; others are not spoken to frequently. Some are punished for speaking or are ignored when they try to communicate. Many of these children have no reason to speak; they have nothing to talk about and few experiences to share. Such youngsters are definitely at risk for developing significant language impairments. Fortunately, early intervention programs can reduce or eliminate the probability of acquiring this disability.

As we know, language develops throughout childhood. The ability to use language and follow its rules increases with a child's age. Although individual children acquire language skills at different times, normal language seems to develop in the same sequence, even during the first 18 months of life (Stark, Bernstein, & Demorest, 1993). Children with typical language development gain skills in an orderly fashion, like the youngster whose profile is shown in Table 5.3. Note that most children after age 3 (40 months) can use some fairly sophisticated language. The child with language impairments at the same age is speaking in only two-word combinations, however.

Differences between children whose language is delayed and those whose language is impaired are apparent to those who analyze children's language development. Children with delayed language generally acquire language in the same sequence as their peers but do so more slowly. Many of these children do not have a disability and catch up with their peers. Some children acquire language in the correct sequence, do so very slowly, and never complete the acquisition of complex language structures. For example, most children with mental retardation have **language delays.** Their language development will remain below that of their peers who have normal intelligence and are developing at expected rates. Some, like Leonard, maintain that these youngsters' language is not impaired, but rather merely delayed. These children profit from intensive language instruction that can be delivered by classroom teachers with the help of SLPs. Leonard (1994) claims that children with language impairments tend to follow a common pattern of language acquisition: They develop slowly *and* differently. Review Table 5.3 again; notice that the child with disabilities uses the word ending *-ing* after her mean sentence length is two words. The normally developing child is using *-ing* at the same time that she is using two-word combinations. Many children with severe language impairments require intensive remediation efforts, usually delivered by an SLP.

What of the child who is not a native speaker? As we discussed in Chapter 3, many teachers have difficulty determining whether a child who is not a native speaker of English is merely **language-different** or has a language impairment (Langdon & Cheng, 1992). Cultural differences and family values also influence how individual children learn language skills, and it is important to understand that different interaction styles result in communicative competence (see Focus on Diversity box). Remember, children whose primary language is English can have a language impairment; so, too, can children whose primary language is not English. English being a second language does not result in a disability. And, English that reflects dialects of American English are not impairments either (Taylor & Payne, 1994). Because so many language-different children are misidentified as having a language impairment (and therefore a disability), it is crucial that educators pay close attention to these children and seek assistance from other professionals when designing the most appropriate educational programs for them (Ruiz, 1995).

TABLE 5.3

Pattern of Development Shown by a Child with Language Impairments and by a Normally Developing Child

Child with Language Impairments			Normally Developing Child		
Age	Attainment	Example	Age	Attainment	Example
27 months	First words	*this, mama, bye bye, doggie*	13 months	First words	*here, mama, bye bye, kitty*
38 months	50-word vocabulary		17 months	50-word vocabulary	
40 months	First two-word combinations	*this doggie, more apple, this mama, more play*	18 months	First two-word combinations	*more juice, here ball, more TV, here kitty*
48 months	Later two-word combinations	*Mama purse, Daddy coat, black chair, dolly table*	22 months	Later two-word combinations	*Andy shoe, Mommy ring, cup floor, keys chair*
52 months	Mean sentence length of 2.00 words		24 months	Mean sentence length of 2.00 words	
55 months	First appearance of -*ing*	*Mommy eating*		First appearance of -*ing*	*Andy sleeping*
63 months	Mean sentence length of 3.10 words		30 months	Mean sentence length of 3.10 words	
66 months	First appearance of *is*	*The doggie's mad*		First appearance of *is*	*My car's gone!*
73 months	Mean sentence length of 4.10 words		37 months	Mean sentence length of 4.10 words	
79 months	Mean sentence length of 4.50 words			Mean sentence length of 4.50 words	*Can I have some cookies?*
	First appearance of indirect requests	*Can I get the ball?*	40 months	First appearance of indirect requests	

Source: "Language Disorders in Preschool Children" (p. 147) by L. Leonard, in G. H. Shames, E. H. Wiig, and W. A. Secord (Eds.), *Human Communication Disorders: An Introduction* (4th ed.), 1994, NY: Merrill, an imprint of Macmillan. Reprinted by permission.

What is at issue for bilingual children? Remember that acquiring and mastering a second language is a long process. Many youngsters may appear to be fluent in English because they converse with their classmates on the playground and express their basic needs in the classroom. These abilities, however, are only some of the language skills acquired on the way toward communicative competence. What are the major concerns of students from diverse backgrounds? Dialects affect an individual's accent (the way spoken language sounds) and also can affect the rules for language use (Taylor & Payne, 1994). Dialects result from historical,

Just Different, Not Better

Social class and economic status contribute substantially to the quality of children's language development. Mother–child interactions among poor families, particularly from culturally and linguistically diverse backgrounds, vary considerably from those from the middle-class. Research has found that among low socioeconomic families, the frequency of mothers' vocalizations with their infants differs across racial/ethnic groups (Taylor & Payne, 1994). Hispanic mothers "talk" to their infants more than African American mothers of poverty, and Navajo mothers interact verbally very little with their babies. These cultural differences alone do not negatively influence children's language development, however. For example, Japanese mothers demonstrate a low frequency of verbal interactions with their infants. Instead, they emphasize nonverbal communication. Despite their low verbal interactions, their children are not inferior in language development. Teachers must not make assumptions and judgments about cultural styles and children's development. What is important is to understand that children need to have rich experiences, develop reasons and high desires for communication, and have opportunities for natural instruction.

social, regional, and cultural influences and are sometimes perceived by educators as inferior or nonstandard (Battle, 1996). As with bilingual children, many children from diverse backgrounds who use dialects are misidentified as having a language impairment. Professionals who can make the distinction between language difference and language impairment must be proficient in the rules of the particular child's dialect and in nondiscriminatory testing procedures.

Prevention

MAKING CONNECTIONS

See also the prevention section in Chapter 10.

Some types of speech or language impairments can be prevented today. Table 5.4 lists preventable and unpreventable causes of speech or language impairments. As you can see from the table, many problems have a medical basis. And for many problems, preventive measures are needed prior to the birth of a baby. For example, polio and rubella can have devastating effects on an unborn baby; proper immunization protects adults and children from these and other diseases. Recent research has shown that a nutritional supplement of folic acid during pregnancy can reduce the risk of cleft palates and lips by 25 to 50 percent (Maughn II, 1995).

Proper prenatal care is important to the health of babies. Good nutrition influences the strength and early development of very young children. Also, the availability of proper medical care at birth is crucial so that conditions like viral encephalitis can be avoided or treated early. Although no longer common in the general population, encephalitis is prevalent in poorer communities of our society. If left untreated, encephalitis causes brain damage, which, in turn, can result in cognitive and language disabilities. The link between poverty and language dis-

MAKING CONNECTIONS

Information about poverty and disabilities is found in the Causes and Prevention sections (Chapter 3).

TABLE 5.4

Marge's Examples of Preventable and Nonpreventable Causes of Speech and Language Impairments

Impairment	Preventable Causes	Nonpreventable Causes
Articulation	Hearing loss Dental abnormalities Chronic infections, especially 　upper respiratory infections Most types of mental retardation Injuries Infectious diseases 　(mumps, measles, encephalitis)	Developmental immaturity Neuromuscular disorders 　associated with unknown 　etiologies Some types of genetic 　disorders
Voice	Vocal abuse Upper respiratory infections Allergies Airborne irritants Smoking Hearing loss Trauma and injury Faulty respiration due to allergies, 　infections, and emphysema Drug and alcohol abuse Some genetic disorders	Constitutional factors Some cancers Viral infections Some genetic disorders
Fluency (stuttering)	Environmental factors: general 　stress, communicative stress Adverse reactions by others Cultural factors	Suspected genetic factors Suspected neurophysiological 　problems
Language	Familial factors Cultural factors Some types of mental retardation Some types of hearing loss Some genetic disorders Brain damage due to prematurity, 　anoxia, physical trauma, 　Rh blood factor, infections Malnutrition Low birthweight Fetal alcohol syndrome Prenatal drugs and smoking Strokes Environmental pollutants 　(lead poisoning)	Some types of hearing loss Some genetic disorders Developmental immaturity Autism Progressive neurological 　deficits Suspected constitutional 　factors resulting in 　psychosis (schizophrenia) Some types of mental 　retardation

Source: "The Prevention of Communication Disorders," by M. Marge, 1984, American Speech-Language-Hearing Association, 26, pp. 29–33. Reprinted by permission.

abilities is clear. Those who are poor are less likely to have access to information and medical programs, which puts them at risk for disease. Better public education programs available to the entire population inform people of the necessity of good prenatal care, nutrition, and medical care. It may be, however, that innovative

MAKING CONNECTIONS

Refer to these sections for more information about prevention:
• The Concepts and Controversy sections at the end of this chapter
• Family section (Chapter 3)

approaches to the dissemination of information about the importance of protecting children from disease may need to be implemented. For example, accessing the African American community may require different approaches. Participation in health fairs sponsored by churches, sororities, fraternities, and other community organizations may prove to be more effective ways to communicate important information than are traditional means (Terrell, 1993). These services might initially be costly in time and effort, but the positive impact on preventing and overcoming disabilities is significant.

One of the most important ways of reducing the impact of any disability is through early identification, so that treatment can begin as soon as possible. With speech and language impairments, children who receive help and support from highly trained experts can learn to either correct or compensate for their disability. For many of these youngsters, referrals and identification will not occur until their schoolyears, when speech and language are reaching their final stages of development. Alert teachers can be most helpful by referring youngsters who might have either a speech or language impairment to an SLP. Table 5.5 lists some of the signs of these disabilities. Teachers should remember, however, that many signs of these impairments are part of the normal developmental process. Teachers must balance their concern about a possible disability with the child's need to work through problems that may just be developmental and will disappear with age.

Children with Speech or Language Impairments

Children with speech or language impairments comprise a large and diverse group of youngsters. Some have a speech impairment, others have a language impairment, and still others have both a speech and a language impairment. Naturally, these chil-

TABLE 5.5

Possible Signs or Characteristics of Speech and Language Impairments

Speech

Makes consistent and age-inappropriate articulation errors

Exhibits dysfluencies (repetitions, prolongations, interruptions) in the flow or rhythm of speech

Has poor voice quality, such as distracting pitch

Is excessively loud or soft

Language

Is unable to follow oral directions

Is unable to match letters with sounds

Has an inadequate vocabulary

Demonstrates poor concept formation

Has difficulty conveying messages or conversing with others

Has difficulty expressing personal needs

dren have different learning needs. For example, a child with a voice problem will have a different remediation program than a child who has difficulty articulating speech sounds correctly. Certainly, those with speech impairments have entirely different remediation programs than children with language difficulties. Teachers must understand the differences among these types of problems so that they can make better referrals and more effectively assist with treatment programs.

Speech Impairments

Most children whose primary disability is a speech impairment (articulation, voice, or fluency impairment) attend general education classes and function well academically with their peers. Usually, their disability does not influence their academic learning. If, however, their speech impairment is severe and sustained, they might have some difficulty with their peers in social interactions. Depending on how the peer group reacts to an individual's disability, the person with a severe disability might have long-term difficulties with self-concept and independence (Van Riper & Erickson, 1996). Social difficulties are particularly common for those who stutter (Shames & Ramig, 1994). Stuttering can negatively affect a person's sense of adequacy and confidence. To avoid embarrassment, many people who stutter avoid situations in which they have to talk to others. Consequently, their disability influences the types of jobs they seek, the friends they make, their relationships with others, and their overall quality of life. Think about how you react to people with severe speech impairments. Do you look away from them? Do you try to be helpful to the stutterer by finishing his or her sentence? Do you try to avoid the person? Now think about how young children treat their peers who use different speech sounds, who have a different voice quality, or who stutter. Facing these reactions is an everyday reality for individuals with speech impairments. It is understandable that some would like to withdraw from a society that treats them as being different.

Language Impairments

Language impairments have many different outcomes. Unlike most speech impairments, however, multiple results—beyond the production of oral language—are observed. Many youngsters' social competence is affected, and a variety of their social skills are inferior to those of peers without this disability. It is also quite common to find correlated cognitive and academic difficulties in children with language impairments.

Social Competence. The relationship between communicative competence and effective social skills is clear (Walker, Schwarz, Nippold, Irvin, & Noell, 1994). Being able to understand messages and communicate well is important in interactions with peers and adults. For example, part of everyday life at school and in the community is resolving conflicts. It seems that conflict is an inevitable part of life because individuals have incompatible goals or a different understanding about an event or situation. Being able to solve misunderstandings or disagreements is an important skill that requires abilities to solve problems, understand others' points of view, and clearly present one's feelings. Language impairments, particularly in the pragmatic area, negatively influence the skills required for successful conflict resolution (Stevens & Bliss, 1995).

MAKING CONNECTIONS

Information about the relationship between language skills and social competence is also found in Social Skills section (Chapter 4).

Language impairments due to problems in the area of pragmatics can result in other difficulties that negatively impact social skills. Many of these youngsters are unable to understand ambiguity in messages (Lloyd, 1994). They seem unable to identify the features that uniquely identify specific objects. For example, they might not be able to successfully play a game in which a target photograph is to be identified by a partner. When the objective is to make as few guesses as possible, the requirement is to describe the distinguishing features of the object using as few clues as possible. How would you help a partner know that it was a photo of a zebra and not of a giraffe that was the target? (Try color of its stripes.) An example of this type of activity is included in the Teaching Tactics box found in the Language Instruction section of this chapter.

Undeveloped pragmatic skills can also influence social competence in the area of persuasion. The ability to influence other people's actions, beliefs, or attitudes is a skill that most children, except many with language impairments, have developed by age 18 (Nippold, 1994). Normal development of this aspect of language includes the following abilities (Nippold, 1994, p. 2):

- Greater tendency to adjust to the listener characteristics (age, authority, and familiarity)
- Greater tendency to state an advantage to the listener as a reason to comply
- Greater tendency to anticipate and reply to counterarguments
- Greater use of positive strategies such as politeness and bargaining
- Less use of negative strategies such as nagging and begging
- Ability to generate a greater number and variety of different arguments
- Better ability to control the interaction.

Most children with language impairments do not develop the skill of using oral language to persuade others to adopt their position on an issue. To develop this and other pragmatic skills, direct instruction and definite inclusion into the curriculum must occur. The importance of the concept of communicative competence should be becoming more apparent.

Cognitive and Academic Performance. "Cognition involves the representation and processing of knowledge about physical objects, events, and their relationships" (Stevens & Bliss, 1995, p. 599). Whether it be verbal or nonverbal (e.g., sign language), at the foundation of cognition is language. Research finding after research finding provides substantial evidence that children identified as having a language impairment during the preschool years are very likely to have difficulties mastering reading when they are in elementary school (Catts, Hu, Larrivee, & Swank, 1994). It also appears that reading comprehension is the most seriously affected (Catts, 1993).

With the knowledge about the connection between language impairments and reading difficulties, it is not surprising then that other researchers have made a definite connection between language impairments and learning disabilities. Unlike children with speech problems, children with language impairments often have related academic difficulties in school (Wallach & Butler, 1995). Some believe that 80 percent of all students with learning disabilities have a language impairment (Wiig & Secord, 1994). And, a commonly held belief among professionals is that a language impairment diagnosed in a

MAKING CONNECTIONS

See these sections on Reading (Chapter 4):
- Education and the Schoolchild
- Educational Interventions

preschooler will result in a learning disability during the schoolyears. Others draw clear connections between early language impairments and later difficulties developing literacy (Fey, Windsor, & Warren, 1995).

Some national data support this conclusion. According to the *Annual Report to Congress on the Implementation of IDEA* (U.S. Department of Education, 1995), during the 1993–1994 schoolyear 68 percent of all 6-year-olds identified as having a disability were diagnosed as having a speech or language impairment. By age 8, that percentage had dropped to 42 (with learning disabilities at 37 percent); and by age 12 almost 10 percent of all students with disabilities were identified as having a speech or language impairment (with learning disabilities at 63 percent). Although it would be nice to believe that early remediation has reduced the prevalence of language impairments by high school, it is more likely that across the schoolyears these children are relabeled or identified as having learning disabilities.

Educational Interventions

A variety of issues in education impact children with speech or language impairments. Today, almost every school in the United States has access to an SLP. In some cases, the SLP is a permanent faculty member. In other cases, the SLP works part time at several schools or is an itinerant teacher, traveling from one school to another. In all cases, the SLP is available to receive referrals, provide therapy, and consult with teachers concerned about a student's communicative abilities. As we noted earlier, the role of the SLP has changed over the last decade. Today these professionals collaborate more with teachers, provide less direct services to children (particularly those with more mild disabilities), and guide teachers in the implementation of language development and remediation programs.

General education teachers play a crucial role in children's language development. Teachers must create rich learning environments by providing a stimulating instructional setting that encourages oral language and provides the framework necessary for literacy (see the Tips for Teachers box for some ideas on how to accomplish these goals). For instance, teachers might include activity centers in their classrooms. One center could have electrical components to create circuits so that children can discover cause-and-effect relationships; another center could have magnets and containers of different types of materials. Some part of the day could be set aside for children to talk about their exploration of the materials in the activity centers. Teachers could also use this discussion time to talk about other topics of interest to the children, such as current affairs, environmental issues, or sports. In the following sections, we discuss ways in which all teachers can foster speech and language improvement in their students.

Education and the Preschool Child

Preschool programs can make a significant, positive, and long-term difference for young children and their families. Congress, aware of the potential power of preschool programs, created the federally funded program called Headstart and enacted PL 99–457, which allows special education funding to be used for infants and toddlers at risk for disabilities and those already identified as having a disability. The importance of early intervention was brought to the attention of

Congress by both clinical reports and research findings that attest to the significant impact of well-designed early childhood programs. For example, low-birthweight infants who received a customized day care program averaged 15 IQ points higher than the control group (Education of the Handicapped, 1992). Only 2 percent of these youngsters—at risk for speech or language impairments, mental retardation, and learning disabilities—were identified as having a disability later on; the control group was nine times more likely to have a disability.

To help you better understand the concept of "at risk," in the following subsections, we look at three groups of youngsters at risk for disabilities. During a child's developmental periods, the acquisition of good communication and language skills is crucial to the child's later development of academic and social skills. We therefore also look at some strategies and teaching methods used in successful early intervention programs.

At Risk. Accurately identifying infants and toddlers with disabilities is a complex task. The dangers of misidentifying children are great, but so too are the dangers of denying early intervention services to children and their families. Therefore Congress made important allowances for infants and toddlers served by IDEA funds: No special permission is required during the early preschool years (birth to age 3) for federal special education funds to be used to support educational programs for babies at risk for disabilities. Normally, IDEA funds programs for older students who have *identified* disabilities. Researchers have identified three categories of children at risk:

1. those with an established risk,

2. those whose environment places them at risk, and

3. those with a history that might place them at risk.

Many children with an established risk have a diagnosed medical condition with a known cause. For example, a medical condition, like Down syndrome, strongly suggests both speech *and* language impairments. Because the production of speech requires motor skills, many children with cerebral palsy also have an established risk for speech impairments. Children in this at-risk category should be enrolled in preschool programs as early as possible.

Children who are environmentally at risk, the second category, are born healthy but are at risk because they were abused or neglected, became ill, or failed to thrive as infants. The third category of at-risk children comprises infants who have a history (pre- or postnatal) that might lead to a disability. For example, babies born prematurely or with very low birthweight are more likely to have a language impairment than the rest of the population. These children are good candidates for preschool programs that emphasize language development.

Early Intervention Strategies. Preschool programs for children with or at risk for speech or language impairments should be in accepting and responsive environments that motivate students to communicate. Early intervention programs should foster cooperative play, encourage spontaneous talking, facilitate social interactions with peers, develop responsiveness with conversational partners, and guide parents in the creation of a home environment that fosters language development. Instruction should occur in natural settings where children are free to interact and explore. Because language—its acquisition and generalization—does not occur in isolation, Boone & Plante (1993) remind us that social interaction must be integrated into the instructional program.

Settings that promote language production are rich in objects and activities that interest and reward young children. Ostrosky & Kaiser (1991) give us some ideas about how to stimulate young children's language, encourage its development, and provide a climate where social interaction is fostered. Their strategies, which are listed and described in Table 5.6, include providing children with reasons to speak, motivating them to interact with others, and making learning interesting and fun. Adults can directly and indirectly create such environments, in which language use is necessary and part of the typical routine.

For young children with and at risk for disabilities, good language development does not happen by accident; it occurs through the deliberate actions of preschool teachers and other adults. They must create an environment that fosters language development and thereby promotes early literacy—an environment carefully arranged so that children must imitate, request objects, and obtain the attention of an adult through verbal responses (Warren, Yoder, Gazden, Kim, & Jones, 1993). Given the importance of play to preschoolers and young children, it is a key to enhanced language and social interaction skills (Clarke, 1996). Through play,

MAKING CONNECTIONS
- For more on Down syndrome, see Causes section (Chapter 6).
- For more about cerebral palsy, see Neuromuscular/Skeletal Condition in the Defined section (Chapter 9).

MAKING CONNECTIONS

Additional information about low-birthweight babies is found in the Causes section (Chapter 6).

TABLE 5.6

Strategies that Promote Preschoolers' Communication

Interesting materials	The classroom should be rich with materials and activities children are interested in, want to play with, and enjoy.
Out of reach	Some materials should be placed within view of the children but out of their reach, so that they are motivated to make a verbal request for their use.
Inadequate portions	Teachers should arrange the environment to encourage more communication from children—by providing insufficient materials (such as paper, paints, or crayons), for example.
Choice making	Teachers should create situations in which children need to make choices and to ask for the activity they want to engage in or the materials they want to use.
Assistance	Teachers should create situations in which children are likely to need help in order to increase the likelihood that they will communicate their needs to each other or an adult.
Sabotage	Teachers should arrange situations in which children do not have all the materials they need for an activity (painting without brushes, sandbox pails but no shovels) in order to encourage them to request the missing items.
Silly situations	Teachers should create absurd situations (giving them clay instead of crackers at snack time) that surprise the youngsters and encourage their responses.

children learn skills like cooperation and turn taking; they learn to explore shared concerns and to make friends—in short, they learn to communicate and interact with others. Disabilities, however, can be barriers to social interaction and communication. For example, preschoolers with disabilities play alone at a far greater rate than their nondisabled peers (Rogow, 1991); their rate of isolated play, 70 percent, is very high. Even after considerable intervention, preschoolers with disabilities engage in social and collaborative play only 30 percent of the time; their peers without disabilities do so 60 percent of the time. Consequently, teachers must prompt youngsters with disabilities to join groups and play with others. Statements like "Are you going to play with us? Do you want to be a doctor, too?" invite children to play with others, but teachers must create opportunities for them to have social interactions.

The relationship of environment to language, cognition, and reading abilities is clear (Catts, Hu, Larrivee, & Swank, 1994). Preschool environments should be rich in experiences and in literature, including books that are predictable and those that come from children's literature (picture books, storybooks, fairy tales, naming books). Many children begin the reading process by talking about what they think the story says (Katims, 1994). Many come to know every word in the

MAKING CONNECTIONS

Other sections about developing social competence are found in
- the Social Competence section in Children with Learning Disabilities (Chapter 4),
- the Social Skills section in Children with Behavior Disorders (Chapter 8).

story without being able to actually read a word. Such repetitions enhance both early literacy and language development. Language development is also enhanced by children providing oral narratives of stories (Crais & Lorch, 1994). Storytelling in itself can be a wonderful precursor to reading while expanding children's oral language abilities.

Newly developed language skills also need to be facilitated and reinforced at home. The quality of the home's language environment has significant and long-term effects in young children (Hart & Risley, 1995). Some families need guidance as they attempt to develop nurturing environments for their children. For these reasons, most preschool programs include a strong family component. Professionals who work in preschool programs for children with disabilities or those at risk should help parents implement language-learning lessons at home and help these children transfer (or generalize) their learning from school to home. The team effort of teachers and parents enriches children's learning experience and enhances their communication skills.

MAKING CONNECTIONS

Literacy is also discussed in Chapter 4 under Reading in
• Education and the Schoolchild,
• Educational Interventions.
And in Chapter 11 in these sections:
• Methods of Reading and Writing (Children with Low Vision and Blindness)
• Literacy (Educational Intervention)

Education and the Schoolchild

Teachers and parents need to be alert to substantial differences in children's speech, language use, and development. Individuals acquire communicative skills at different rates. Before becoming overly concerned about an individual's speech or language abilities, teachers should consider several factors: age, setting, and stress.

Alert teachers will refer students who *consistently* exhibit poor communication skills for special help. Once a child is identified as having a speech or language impairment and is to receive special services from an SLP, the teacher must work

Exciting classroom environments stimulate children's language and learning.

closely and collaborate with the SLP to implement individualized programs for that child. SLPs can offer guidance and practical tips to use in the general education class. For example, an SLP might suggest ways that the teacher can encourage children to expand oral language: be an attentive listener, provide more opportunities for children to talk about what they are interested in, ask open-ended questions that encourage children to talk more. Many SLPs and teachers also team-teach special units that integrate language instruction into the standard curriculum. For instance, a unit about a local environmental issue might culminate in students' preparing short position papers, letters to the editor of the local newspaper, oral presentations by a panel of experts, or a debate. SLPs and teachers find that collaborative efforts greatly improve students' speech and language disabilities. In addition, teachers often see improvement in the language skills of their other students.

Teachers' Language. The responsibility for creating and fostering a positive learning environment rests with the teacher. Gruenewald and Pollack (1984) illustrate the relationship among the student, the teacher, and the curriculum in all academic settings: Students interact with one another, the teacher, and the curriculum as they participate in classroom activities. By planning both the content and the manner of delivering the instruction, the teacher can match language with the comprehension abilities of the students. The teacher delivering a lecture is the sender; the students are the receivers of the message.

Effective teachers understand the role that language plays in learning. They know they must adjust their language and adapt written materials so that students understand the message being delivered. They make these adjustments by moderating their rate of speech, the complexity of their sentences, and their choice of questions (Gruenewald & Pollack, 1984). Almost naturally, teachers adjust their rate of speech depending on the age and level of their students (Cuda & Nelson, 1976). For instance, first grade teachers speak more slowly than fifth grade teachers. Effective teachers are also careful in their use of referents. They systematically show students the relationships among items and concepts. They expand discussions about new concepts and ideas. They show children how concepts are related. They also ask questions at graduated levels of difficulty to help students test the accuracy of their new knowledge. All these techniques facilitate teaching and learning. They are helpful to all professionals working with children with special needs, and they are particularly helpful to children with disabilities placed in general education settings.

Effective teachers also are sensitive to the individual needs of their students. Students who are not native English speakers and are from a cultural background different from their teachers' often need special adjustments from their teachers (Westby, 1995). As we discussed in Chapter 3, these youngster's mastery of English may not yet be sufficient for typical content instruction, and the teacher may need to provide several examples to illustrate a point or explain a concept. They also may need to be cautious in their use of referents and expressions. For example, "We're nearing the two-minute warning" may have no meaning to a child unfamiliar with American sports.

Language Instruction. Learning is not merely listening to lectures; it is also mastering the communication game. Students who have a language disability need to be taught how to use language effectively. Language teaching should be part of the

TEACHING TACTICS

The Shopping Spree

Ms. Lucero wanted to give her students practice associating symbols with objects and producing speech sounds. She divided her class into small groups of four to five students each and gave each group approximately thirty assorted picture cards. She told the class that they had to decide how the pictures were to be organized for a shopping spree. For example, all of the fruits could be used for a fruit stand, the clothes could become the contents of a department store. After each group of students decided what stores they would create and organized their cards, the game began. Members from another group were first told what "stores" they were "shopping" in, and they had to guess the items from clues given by members of the organizing group. A record was kept of the number of guesses made to identify each item from each "store" and credited to both groups (the guessers and the clue-givers). The group with the fewest number of guesses made to identify the items won the game.

After the game was over, Ms. Lucero had the children return to their groups to reorganize their pictures by sounds by position. For example, they were to make a stack of those pictures that used the *b* sound. That stack could have pictures of items that used each sound in the initial, medial, or final position. When the groups were done, all of the cards were placed in stacks grouped by sound and its position in the word. For example, soap and glass (*s* sound) might be in the same stack and bear and baseball (*b* sound) might be in another stack. When all of the groups were finished arranging their picture cards, they had to review their organizational scheme with the entire class, which was encouraged to talk about other ways the pictures could have been grouped.

---

curriculum throughout the elementary schoolyears. Just as time is devoted to teaching mathematics, reading, spelling, and social studies, time should be allocated to teaching the language skills that underlie these subjects. During these periods, children should be encouraged to listen, talk, and understand the language of instruction as well as the language of social interactions. All students benefit from this instruction; but for students with language impairments, it is essential.

For teachers who are not trained in oral language development, excellent instructional materials are commercially available. For example, the *Peabody Language Development Kits* (PLDK–Revised), Levels P and 1, *Developing Understanding of Self and Others* (DUSO–Revised), and *Classroom Listening and Speaking* (CLAS) include useful activities to increase language and cognitive skills for students in primary grades. *Let's Talk, Conversations, Communicative Competence,* and *Directing Discourse* provide ideas for adolescents.

Teachers can use a variety of classroom activities, including games, that encourage children's use of language (Marvin, 1989; Watkins & Rice, 1994). **Barrier games** (like the one described in the Teaching Tactics box) require children to describe objects while the other players guess what they are describing. In a simple version of this game, the teacher could create a game using picture cards, such as those found in the *Peabody Picture Collection* (PPC). The teacher asks the children to tell about a recent experience or make up stories from a set of sequential pictures.

barrier games. Drill and practice activities that require the application of verbal skills to solve problems, using a game format.

Inclusion

Where do children with speech or language impairments receive their education? Most of them receive their education and their therapy in the general education class alongside their age-mates. In the vast majority of cases, only those with severe speech impairments (those who stutter, those with cleft palates, those with severe articulation problems) receive small-group or individualized instruction from SLPs outside the general education classroom. The federal government estimates that almost 3 percent of schoolchildren have these disabilities. Therefore in a class of thirty children, teachers might expect to find at least one child with a speech or language problem. Of course, children with other disabilities, such as learning disabilities or mental retardation, who are included in that class may also have difficulties with speech and language. Hence, general education teachers may have several students with a speech or language impairment attending their classes and so will be directly involved in these IEP goals. Increasingly, SLPs work as consultants who collaborate with classroom teachers to implement remediation programs (Conner & Welsh, 1993).

Remember, language problems are often characteristics of other disabilities, such as mental retardation or learning disabilities. For example, most students with learning disabilities have a language impairment that affects their overall academic development, and they require intensive, specialized instruction. Who should deliver this instruction, and where? Currently, considerable acceptance of the notion of inclusive schools exists: All children attend the school in their neighborhood and receive most of their education in the general education classroom. However, achieving this aim *and* providing an appropriate education for students with disabilities is difficult (Rouse, 1993). Many barriers exist, such as lack of knowledge, inadequate resources, and insufficient physical space; the result is that students might not receive the individualized instruction they require.

Clearly, students with speech or language impairments should be able to hear classmates without these disabilities communicate with others. But these normal role models are typically not found in special education classroom settings. Therefore students with speech or language disabilities should be educated in the general education classroom as much as possible. They also should be included with their age-mates in extracurricular and community activities. However, successful inclusion requires special care and planning; it also requires effort from the students themselves, their classmates, their teacher, and all the specialists who support those students in the general education setting. A positive, full-time, integrated classroom experience is neither automatic nor easily accomplished. And as you will learn as you read the rest of this text, it is also not a goal set by all parents and professionals for every student with disabilities. For almost all students with speech impairments and many students with language impairments, though, the majority of their educational experiences occur in the general education classroom, so these experiences must be positive and successful. How can we make this happen? The following subsections discuss two important issues of inclusion. First, we look at what skills the student needs in order to increase the chances of success in the general education setting. Then we analyze the skills the teacher needs to accommodate students with disabilities.

Necessary Student Behaviors. All teachers have various expectations of their students, sometimes called the **setting demands**. Of course, teachers adjust their expectations according to the age, social maturity, and abilities of their stu-

MAKING CONNECTIONS

IEPs are discussed in detail in Chapter 3.

MAKING CONNECTIONS

Inclusion is discussed in
• the Inclusion sections in every chapter (Educational Interventions).
• Service Delivery Options (Chapter 2).

setting demands. The behavioral expectations for a particular place or setting.

dents. For example, kindergarten teachers do not expect their students to sit at their desks for forty-minute periods, listen to teacher lectures, take notes, and sit quietly for the whole time. These are the expectations of secondary-level teachers for high school content classes. Although the expectations may vary, once set by the teacher, they become the setting demands for that learning environment. In one study (Ellett, 1993), high school teachers were asked to list the behaviors they expect from all their students in classes that include students with disabilities. The following list shows these expectations ranked from most to least important.

1. Follows directions in class.
2. Comes to class prepared with materials.
3. Uses time wisely.
4. Makes up assignments and tests.
5. Treats teachers and peers with courtesy.
6. Completes and turns homework in on time.
7. Appears interested in subject.
8. Works cooperatively in student groups.
9. Completes tests with a passing grade.
10. Takes notes in class.
11. Scans a textbook for answers and information.
12. Volunteers to answer questions in class.
13. Writes neatly.
14. Able to give oral report and speeches. (Ellett, 1993, p. 59)

These minimal student expectations can be challenging for many students with speech or language impairments. Think about what you have learned so far about students with speech impairments. Which of these setting demands might be most challenging for them? Now think about students with language impairments. Which expectations might they find most difficult to achieve? Most likely one group of these students would find some of these expectations easy to meet, and another group would find them frustrating. For example, secondary students with speech impairments might not be comfortable speaking in front of the entire class. They probably would not volunteer to answer questions or give oral reports. Similarly, secondary students with language impairments often have difficulty taking and organizing class notes, following directions, or scanning complex material in textbooks. Thus for successful inclusion, SLPs must help teachers accommodate their assignments and expectations for students with speech or language impairments, so their expectations are reasonable for these individual students. SLPs also need to work with these students to help them achieve the basic expectations. Because each student has different abilities and needs, individualized plans must be arranged collaboratively between the SLP assigned to the student and each of his or her teachers.

Necessary Teacher Behaviors. As noted previously, teachers must adjust their teaching styles, presentation of content, and expectations for each student in their classes. Studies have shown that successful inclusion of students with disabilities, although an ideal held by most educators, is not automatic. Sirotnick and

1. Talk more slowly.
2. Create a relaxed communication environment by using short pauses in between responses.
3. Model good language; keep it simple when appropriate.
4. Accept what the child has to say rather than how it is said, particularly for stutterers.
5. Set good conversational rules whereby people do not interrupt each other and take turns.
6. Listen attentively to the students.
7. Give students more time to finish assignments and tests.
8. Shorten assignments and make them less complex.
9. Provide tutors.
10. Give students extra help with assignments.
11. Give students credit for effort.
12. Evaluate work on the basis of gain, not specific level of mastery.
13. Allow students to retake tests or redo assignments.
14. Create a variety of activities so that students can do well on at least some of the work across the course of a semester or schoolyear.
15. Reduce the probability of failure and increase the probability of success.

Lovitt's research (1992), for instance, found that high school principals were committed to meeting the needs of all students in their schools and to including all students in general education classes, but they were disappointed with the quality of the education many students with disabilities receive. The principals attributed the lack of quality to the inability of general education teachers to deal with special education students, their contrary attitudes about including these students in their classes, or both. The principals thought that special training was needed for the teachers, but in most cases no training was being planned by either the school or the district administrators. On the other hand, the teachers felt that they were not receiving adequate support and resources to accommodate these difficult-to-teach youngsters and were not allowed to create innovative and flexible programs because of school bureaucracies.

Even without special training, most teachers who have students with disabilities in their classes try to adjust their teaching routines and make adjustments to the language environment to meet these students' needs (Geluke & Lovitt, 1992; LaBlance, Steckol, & Smith, 1994). Many apply strategies like those listed in the Making Accommodations box so that these students can do general class assignments.

One common finding from research about inclusion is that general education teachers feel ill-prepared to meet the needs of students with disabilities. These teachers all wish that special training sessions were available to help them accommodate these students. They acknowledge that many essential teaching practices might be included in the training (Cannon, Idol, & West, 1992), but the one topic that most of them request is classroom and behavior management. Many teachers feel that organizing a classroom to handle a wide range of abilities is the most challenging task they face; in fact, many teachers believe that educating students with disabilities exclusively in any one setting cannot result in an appropriate education for these students (Fuchs & Fuchs, 1994/1995).

Clearly, teachers' attitudes are crucial to the success of any instructional program, but particularly so for students with disabilities, who require individualization and a variety of accommodations. Are general education teachers willing to make substantial adjustments to their educational settings, and do they believe it is feasible to do so? Several researchers found that the answers to these questions depend on the specific adaptations necessary (Schumm & Vaughn, 1991). Teachers are willing to provide reinforcement and encouragement to students with disabilities, establish personal relationships with them, and include them in class activities. In other words, teachers are willing to try to motivate these students. They do not believe, however, that they can successfully communicate with students with disabilities, adapt general education materials to their needs, use alternative instructional materials, use computers, or provide individualized instruction. In another study, these researchers found that secondary school teachers are less willing to make accommodations for students with disabilities than elementary school teachers (Schumm & Vaughn, 1992). High school teachers tend to think that making adaptations is wrong, unfair, and a disservice to these students. Clearly, we need better communication among teachers. And, general education teachers need more assistance in adjusting the learning environment to accommodate the needs of all special learners.

Transition Through Adulthood

Adults with speech or language impairments comprise several different subgroups. Some have only a speech impairment, others have only a language impairment, and some have both. Age of onset and causation, however, are what make these subgroups different from one another. Despite having great difficulties as children, the vast majority of adults experience a lifetime of using normal communication (Boone & Plante, 1993). Problems experienced by adults who were not identified as having speech or language impairments when they were children, typically, are caused by disease, accidents, or aging. Those who had some kind of speech or language impairment during childhood represent but a small percentage of this adult group. To date, very little is known about how children with these impairments fare when they are adults. In the following subsections, we look at their overall adult performance and then describe some of the skills necessary for successful employment.

Global Outcomes. In a comprehensive **follow-up study** of youth with disabilities, students with learning disabilities and speech impairments appeared to have better outcomes than other youth with disabilities (Wagner, D'Amico, Marder, Newman, & Blackorby, 1992). Although too early to know, it appears that young adults with learning disabilities or speech impairments seem to function fairly well some five years after graduation. Few are socially isolated. They are beginning to move away from home; 40 percent live independently. They also are employed at about the same rate as their peers without disabilities. Their long-term prospects, however, may not be as good. Although 86 percent are served in general education classes, only 44 percent of students with learning disabilities and speech impairments graduate with a diploma (U.S. Department of Education, 1994) and only 4 percent of students with learning disabilities and 13 percent with speech or language impairments attend four-year colleges (Wagner et al., 1992). Serious concerns about their success as adults can be raised. Changing this situ-

follow-up study. To provide later evaluation, diagnosis, or treatment of a condition.

ation might well demand different types of services while these students are in high school (Aune & Friehe, 1996). These students may require more access to tutoring to remain in academic content courses, services from guidance counselors, experience in advocating for accommodations and special services, and increased instruction on listening and speaking skills.

MAKING CONNECTIONS

• See Chapter 1 for a discussion of desired outcomes for all students with disabilities.
• Also see the Transition sections (Educational Interventions) in the other chapters in this text.

Employment Skills. We do not know how ready students with speech or language impairments are to achieve desired outcomes—integrated employment, community living, citizenship and involvement, and personal autonomy and life satisfaction. What we do know are the skills and personal abilities needed for success in the workplace (Snider, 1992). Three foundation skills are necessary (Snider, 1992):

1. *Basic skills*—reading, writing, arithmetic, mathematics, speaking, and listening
2. *Thinking skills*—the ability to learn, to reason, to think creatively, to make decisions, and to solve problems
3. *Personal qualities*—individual responsibility, self-esteem and self-management, sociability, and integrity

In addition to these foundation skills, students need to achieve competency in five areas: resource management, interpersonal skills, information processing, systems design and evaluation, and use of technology. Unfortunately, many of these skills and competencies are not part of the curriculum students with disabilities receive. Aune and Friehe (1996) suggest that educators reevaluate the instructional programs for these students to ensure that the foundation skills are mastered. Also, transition programs and students' ITPs should reflect these skills as goal areas.

Families

We now focus on two topics: on the home environment as a necessary and crucial ingredient for language development in young children and on parents as consumers of technology. As you will see, these two topics are important to children with speech or language impairments.

Language Development and the Home

The early childhood years for children with exceptionalities are crucial to their long-term development. It is at this stage of development that young children begin to develop the motor, social, cognitive, and speech and language skills they will use the rest of their lives. Children (and adults) spend less time at home with family than ever before. For example, in 1985 parents spent 40 percent less time with their children than they did in 1965, and that was only 17 hours per week (Cleminshaw, DePompei, Crais, Blosser, Gillete, & Hooper, 1996). Some evidence hints that today's parents spend even less time with their children: About 7 million children of working parents, as early as 11 weeks old, spend thirty hours per week in child care (Children's Defense Fund, 1996). Regardless, the child's parents and the home environment provide the foundation for these skills. Even for those children who spend most of their days away from home, those whose home environment is rich in language—where parents talk to their children, where children are given the opportunity to explore the use of language, and where experiences are broad—usually develop fine speech and language skills. When children do not have appropriate language models—when they do not hear language used often, when they do not have experiences to share or a reason to talk—it is not uncommon for their language to be delayed and can even become impaired. Children are individuals; so too are parents and the language environments they provide at home. It is important for educators not to make generalizations about either parents or students. For example, it is unfair and incorrect to assume that parents are responsible for their child's stuttering. Research has shown that parents of stutterers are not different in any characteristics and speech qualities from parents of nonstutterers (Nippold & Rudzinski, 1995). Generalizations about families from diverse backgrounds are inappropriate. Diversity is heterogeneous, where no assumptions are accurate.

MAKING CONNECTIONS

Review the Focus on Diversity box in this chapter.

Language is normally acquired in a rather orderly fashion (Stark, Bernstein, & Demorest, 1993). During the first year of life, infants hear language spoken around them and organize what they hear so that they can gain meaning from it. Toward the end of their first year, infants are able to respond to some of the language they hear. For example, they know their names, respond to greetings, respond to simple verbal commands, and use objects in their immediate environment. At this time, infants also seem to copy the voice patterns they hear by babbling, regardless of the language they hear. Babies begin to talk by first using one- and two-word utterances that are easy to say and have meaning to them (*mama, cookie, doggie*). Throughout their second year of life, children use a growing vocabulary, longer sentences, and more complexity. They are learning the form (the rules) of language and how to apply language rules to give meaning to their oral communications. Regardless of the language heard, children seem to develop language in much the same way across cultures—by interacting with their environment.

To make sense of the language they hear and, ultimately, to learn how to use that language, children employ various strategies. All do not use the same ones, but children who develop language normally apply some structure to make sense of what they hear (Leonard, 1994). For example, some young children, who do not yet understand oral language, might come to understand an adult's intentions by watching nonverbal clues and comprehending the context of the situation. Through such repeated experiences, they come to learn language as well. Other children attend more selectively and learn more vocabulary for objects they can act on or interact with (*ball, key, sock*) or objects that change or move (*clock, car*). Still others focus on specific characteristics of objects (*size, shape, sound*). All these children are learning to categorize and organize objects and their thoughts, skills that are necessary for learning academic tasks later.

When children do not develop language at the expected rate, intervention is needed. In almost every community, speech and language specialists are available to provide therapy and instruction to children and to assist parents in helping their children acquire language. With training and guidance from SLPs, parents can be excellent language teachers for children with language impairments. In fact, when home-based intervention is provided by parents, children's language scores improve more than when only clinic-based instruction is provided by professionals (Cleminshaw et al., 1996).

MAKING CONNECTIONS

For a comparison of children's language gains, refer to Table 5.3.

What kinds of strategies can parents use at home to improve language skills? Specialists suggest that family members specifically label or name objects in the home. They also suggest that simple words be used more often to describe the objects the child is playing with: "This ball is red. It is round. It is soft." They can encourage repetitions of correct productions of sounds and repeat the child's error to help make a comparison. They can play a game of "fill in the blank" sentences. They can ask the child questions that require expanded answers. The family should include the child in activities outside of the home, too, such as visits to the zoo, the market, or a shopping center, so that the child has more to talk about. Practicing good language skills can be incorporated into everyday events. Family members should model language and have the child imitate good language models. For example, a parent might say, "This pencil is blue. What color is this pencil?" and the child should be encouraged to respond that the pencil is blue. Crais and Lorch (1994) also suggest that parents encourage children to engage in the act of "storytelling." Through these stories, children should describe, explain, and interpret their experiences or the stories they have read. Children need a reason to talk, and the home environment can foster children's oral expression by providing many rich and diverse experiences for children to talk about and by providing good language models for children to imitate.

Parents as Consumers of Technology

MAKING CONNECTIONS

For more on the communication skills of many individuals with cerebral palsy, see
• the Defined section (Chapter 9),
• the Personal Perspective section of this chapter.

Some children are unable to develop understandable speech. For example, some children with cerebral palsy have difficulty communicating. Many of these children can understand and use language but cannot produce speech sounds correctly. Thus they will benefit from the use of assistive technology to communicate with others. An example is the **speech synthesizer**, whose development has advanced rapidly over the past years. Other devices will also become a part of these individuals' lives, even during their preschool years. As more equipment and technology becomes available, parents of the children who need it will have to become more sophisticated consumers. They will need to judge the worth of a piece of equipment against the cost of purchase and maintenance and the family budget.

Parents must resist the temptation to acquire every new version of an electronic communication device in the hopes of making their child's speech seem normal. Fishman (1987) makes an important point: "Just as an individual who is a paraplegic and given a wheelchair cannot be equal in physical ability to a person who is able to walk, a speech-impaired individual with a communication aid cannot be equal in speech ability to a person who is able to speak" (p. 13). Parents will need to obtain objective evaluations of new equipment. How can the parents make these technical judgments? In some cases, the SLP, a specialist in assistive technology, and the teacher can assist the family and the student. These professionals can help parents evaluate hardware and software and help them find knowledgeable experts to explain what equipment will be beneficial to their child. Parents must always balance their desire to give their child the best with their need to be objective. One way to do this is to analyze their goals for their child, the family's values, their financial resources, and the time commitment they are willing to make to ensure mastery and ongoing use of the equipment. They also need to judge whether the maintenance of the specific equipment will contribute to family stress. Clearly, successful outcomes in the use of technology are directly related to the support and commitment of family members over time (Parette & Angelo, 1996).

speech synthesizers. Equipment that creates voice.

Technology

Technology has had an impact on rehabilitation and the instructional programs for some children with speech or language impairments. For example, an **obturator** can be used to help create a closure between the oral and nasal cavities when the soft palate is missing or has been damaged by a congenital cleft. An artificial larynx can be implanted when the vocal folds become paralyzed or have been removed because of a disease. Because these disabilities are not common in children, however, this technology has affected only a few children with speech or language impairments. More influential to most of these children have been advances in computer technology, which also hold considerable promise for the future. Computer technology also helps the professionals who work with these students by providing a management tool to simplify their work.

Alternative and Augmentative Communication

The term **alternative and augmentative communication (AAC)** and its definition was provided by ASHA (Beukelman & Mirenda, 1992). AAC includes both low-tech devices (such as communication boards) and high-tech equipment (such as speech talkers). AAC provides alternative ways for individuals with speech or language impairments to interact and communicate with others. AAC devices can be electronic or nonelectronic, they can be constructed for a certain individual, and they can be simple or complex. The common characteristic of AAC systems is that they are used to augment oral or written language production.

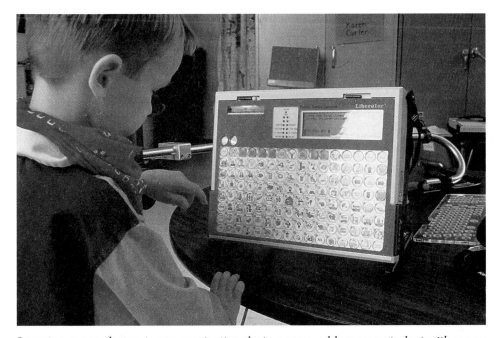

Learning to use electronic communication devices can enable even a student with severe speech or language impairments to engage in a complex interchange of ideas with others. The Liberator, once mastered, will "speak" for this child.

obturator. A device that creates a closure between the oral and nasal cavities when the soft palate is missing or damaged.

alternative and augmentative communication. Assistive technology devices that specifically help individuals communicate, including those that actually produce speech.

A variety of low-tech AAC devices have been in use for many years. For example, communication boards have long been available to persons who are unable to speak; a person wishing to communicate merely points to pictures or words that have been placed on the board. In the near future, these devices will probably be replaced almost entirely by computerized communication devices. Advances in computer technology, particularly in the area of voice synthesis, have changed and will continue to change the mode of communication for many of these individuals. With a computer, a person can type in a message and have it converted to voice or print. Some computers allow the individual to select the voice qualities the machine uses. Some are solely dedicated to speech production, and others have a voice capability as only one of its many functions. Some computerized communicative devices are even small enough to be worn on a person's wrist.

The current capabilities of electronic AAC systems are amazing, and the devices continue to improve. Review Samantha's story in both the chapter opening Personal Perspective and in this section and notice how important technology is to her personal and her school life. AAC systems vary in capability (some can serve multiple purposes) and in price. For example, the Liberator, which is produced by the Prentke Romich Company and costs under $10,000, can produce both written and oral language. This lightweight equipment can generate ten different age- and gender-appropriate voices, so the individual can select the voice he or she is most comfortable with. Because it uses an icon system, the Liberator (once mastered) is relatively quick and easy to use, and it can be accessed by touch or, for those with limited motor abilities, by switches. The system even includes a calculator and a math scratch pad. What other improvements in the AAC technology can bring more benefits to those who have significant difficulties communicating to others?

Some individuals with severe speech and language impairments and their families resist using electronic communication aids, and certainly individuals' values and those of their families must be considered when professionals recommend an assistive device (Parette & Angelo, 1996). Professionals must also consider the amount and degree of technical and informational support the family will require to ensure use of current equipment and to upgrade equipment across time. Most users and their families report great satisfaction with ACC, feeling that the child develops communication competence, increases self-esteem, and gains independence.

Emerging Technologies for Language Intervention

Advances in CD-ROM technology and its increasing accessibility at schools and at home could revolutionize therapy and treatment of speech or language impairments (Maughn II, 1996). The application of research findings, indicating that many youngsters with language impairments do not process speech sounds quickly enough to make them meaningful, to emerging technologies should prove beneficial to a great number of children with disabilities. Speech sounds can now be modified and slowed down so these children can understand them, and the results are new methods and materials for use at school and at home. In the therapy version, the altered speech is applied in a video game format whereby speech sounds are progressively shortened to approximate normal speech sounds. Amazingly, after only a few weeks of therapy, the participating children achieved near normal

MAKING CONNECTIONS

See the Technology sections in
• Chapter 9,
• Chapter 10.

Samantha Reid Tells Us What Technology Means To Her

Earlier, Gloria Enlow shared her experiences as a parent of a child with a severe speech impairment. Here Samantha Reid, her daughter, explains what technology means to her. Samantha was born with cerebral palsy, which affected her speech. Samantha has used and demonstrated different types of communication boards and devices since she began elementary school. Samantha is a student at the University of New Mexico. She is currently using a device called a Touchtalker, which has a synthesized voice; this device gives her more opportunities to interact with others.

Until I started school, I used my own speech, but my speech was not clear, and I became frustrated having to repeat myself. Eventually, I started using an electric typewriter for classwork and to communicate when people could not understand me. My speech pathologist, Claudia Pacini, also drew symbols and letters on a piece of cardboard, which I used as a communication board by pointing to symbols or spelling out words with my thumb. Then, during the late seventies and early eighties, Mrs. Pacini took me to workshops with her to view and demonstrate adaptive/assistive devices. The Autocom was one of the first major breakthroughs in adaptive devices. It helped me tremendously at school. My seventh-grade English teacher grew to hate the Autocom because it tended to break down in the middle of her English class.

When I was ready for college, I learned about two other adaptive communication devices. One of them, the Speech Pac, is simple to operate, but it is usually used by people who understand fewer words. The Touchtalker was more sophisticated but takes much more time to learn to use effectively. I have always loved challenges, but I thought college was enough of a challenge without having to learn this difficult technology. However, I soon discovered that the Speech Pac, although easy to learn, was too limited. Also the Touchtalker has a female voice, and I really did not want to use a speech synthesizer that had a man's voice. Before I knew it, I had taken on another challenge—learning how to use the Touchtalker.

Today, I use the Touchtalker not only when speaking to strangers and taking tests but also when I act in my capacity as a consultant in the state of Texas. As a consultant I am paid to demonstrate the usefulness of augmentative communication devices for parents, teachers, and administrators who work with children with speech impairments.

Assistive devices have helped me greatly in sharing my own thoughts and ideas with people, and will be a major contributor to my growing independence.

---

language capabilities. This same technology is also available on CD-ROM and audio tapes where expanded speech is available in stories for home use. One can only guess what the future will hold with the increasing use and availability of technology.

An innovative therapy now holds promise for improved language development (Merzenich, Jenkins, Johnston, Schreiner, Miller, & Tallal, 1996; Tallal et al., 1996). The training strategy incorporates computer-generated speech to teach these youngsters to process fast speech sounds, a definite deficit for many children with language impairments and learning disabilities. The experimental program, which uses a computer game format, influenced substantial gains in language comprehension and an increased ability to recognize speech sounds (Peavler, 1996).

Concepts and Controversy: Can We Afford Not To?

> When the Great Plague was devastating Russia many years ago, someone asked what was being done about it. The answer was that another thousand coffins had been ordered! To my mind, the tens of billions of tax dollars allocated to various government agencies concerned with our chronic social problems have accomplished little more than buying those coffins. (Anderson, 1972, p. 1)

Two decades ago, Camilla May Anderson called for our government to address the problems of health care. Her special concern was the prevention of diseases causing lifelong disabilities and death. In her book *Society Pays: The High Costs of Minimal Brain Damage in America,* she pointed out that diseases affecting pregnant women and young children can result in brain damage, which, even if minimal, can profoundly influence children's abilities to learn.

The health care issue is a hot topic of debate today. Let us look at the measles virus as an example. Measles is a very dangerous disease that can easily be prevented. The airborne virus can cause death and serious disabling conditions in children (blindness, deafness, brain damage, language impairments), especially if contracted by a pregnant woman or a young child. A vaccine that prevents measles has been available in this country since 1963. During the 1960s, approximately 400,000 cases of measles were reported each year; this number dropped to 1,497 in 1983, and predictions were made that the disease would soon be eradicated. However, a new epidemic of measles raged in the United States recently. Why? Major causes were the unavailability of free vaccinations for the poor, the failure of insurance companies to offer coverage, and the fact that many parents failed to make sure that their children are vaccinated. Nationally, 45 children died of measles in 1989; 40 died during the first four months of 1990. In Los Angeles County, the number of measles cases in 1986 was 42, in 1989 it was 1,202, and in the first four months of 1990 it reached 2,000 (Hilts, 1990). More than 25,000 cases of measles were reported across the nation in 1990; those cases resulted in 60 deaths, with over half of them being preschoolers (Associated Press, 1991). The epidemic predominantly affected unvaccinated African American and Hispanic preschoolers living in inner cities, but the disease also struck secondary school students, college students, migrant workers, and other adults (Bradley, 1990). Estimates indicate that while 95 percent of schoolchildren are vaccinated because it is required to attend school, only 50 percent of inner-city preschoolers were vaccinated. The disease is most devastating when it strikes young children.

Should the federal government take on the responsibility of a national immunization program? If so, how much would it cost? The cost for an individual child is small; but for all children, the cost is quite high. But what are the costs of *not* preventing diseases like measles and rubella? ASHA's Committee on the Prevention of Speech-Language and Hearing Disorders (1984) cites an excellent example of the cost effectiveness of preventive measures. In 1969, the federal Bureau for the Education of the Handicapped (BEH), now called the Office of Special Education Program, conducted a study of the impact of the rubella epidemic of the early 1960s; the findings show that if, in 1963, all young females had been vaccinated for rubella, the epidemic would not have occurred. The cost of a national immunization program in the 1960s would have been $10 million; although considered, the program was not implemented. The rubella epidemic left between 20,000 and 30,000 children with impairments. BEH estimated that the projected total expenditure for special education and related services for all the children whose illness resulted in their having a disability because of the rubella epidemic would approach $1 billion; this staggering amount is probably an underestimation of the financial costs. Wisconsin's Department of Health and Social Services developed a series of comparative cost figures for prevention versus treatment of mental retardation, mental illness, and alcoholism. It projected that $1 million could be saved for each individual whose retardation was prevented (ASHA, 1984).

Because of the concerns about the long-term and devastating effects on children, Congress passed the Vaccines for Children's Program (VFC) in 1994, and in 1995, federally purchased vaccines were available to low- and moderate-income preschoolers (and those whose health insurance providers did not cover them) in the forty-nine participating states (Alaska elected not to participate) (Children's Defense Fund, 1996). The results of this program are impressive. In 1991, only 50 percent of preschoolers were protected, now 75 percent are. In Florida the immunization rate is at 80 percent, up from 65 percent. Although the situation is greatly improved, the problem is not solved: One in four preschoolers is still not protected from preventable infections. Only 59 percent of children living below the poverty level are protected as compared to 71 percent of those living above the poverty levels. And, with federal budget cuts looming, the future is not yet secure. Is this a federal responsibility? Can the nation afford this program? Can it afford not to have it?

～～ SUMMARY ～～

Communication does not occur in isolation. It requires at least two parties and a message. Communication is impaired when either the sender or the receiver of the message cannot use the signs, symbols, or rules of language effectively. Communication occurs only when the message intended by the sender is understood by the receiver. The sender may have an idea or thought to share with someone else, but the sender's idea needs to be translated from thought to some code the other person can understand. For most of us, oral language is the primary mode of socializing, learning, and performing on the job. Therefore communicative competence—what speakers need to know about language to express their thoughts—is the most important goal for students with speech or language impairments. Because oral communication (or sign language for those who are deaf) occurs in a social context, this ability directly affects an individual's social competence as well.

FOCUS QUESTIONS

Self-Test Questions

▶ *What comprises speech impairments and language impairments?*

There are two general kinds of impairments: speech and language. A speech impairment is present when the sender's articulation, voice (pitch or loudness), or fluency patterns impair the receiver's attending to or understanding the message. When either the sender or the receiver of the message cannot use the signs, symbols, or rules of language, a language impairment exists. The three aspects of language are form, content, and use (pragmatics). Articulation problems are the most common type of speech impairment in children. Children with articulation problems make consistent errors in producing speech sounds. Articulation errors are part of the normal developmental sequence, with most children able to correctly produce individual speech sounds within the appropriate age ranges. About half of the children seen by SLPs have language impairments. Although the cause of most language impairments is unknown, the relationship between language impairment and delays in cognitive development and the development of social skills is clear.

▶ *What is the prevalence of this disability?*

Speech or language impairments is not the largest category of exceptionalities when only a primary disability is considered. Some estimate that when a student's primary and second disability area is considered, as much as 10 percent of the school-age population may be affected. The U.S. government reports that over 2 percent of all students are served with speech or language impairments as their primary disability. However, 42 percent of the youngsters seen by SLPs have another primary disabling condition (mental retardation, learning disabilities, deafness and hard of hearing). It is also important to recognize that as children progress through school, the prevalence of this disability decreases but related disabilities (i.e., learning disabilities) increase.

▶ *How do language delays, language differences, and language impairments differ?*

Teachers should be careful not to confuse dialect (regional) differences in speech with speech impairments and not to refer young children whose speech is developing normally but is not yet correct. Language differences can also occur when children are acquiring English as their second language (also review Chapter 3 for special considerations for ESL students). Children with language delays acquire language following the normal developmental sequence but do so more slowly than the typical learner. Students with language impairments do not acquire language following the sequence used naturally by children without this disability. Professionals do not consider the first two groups of youngsters as having a language impairment.

▶ *How can teachers enhance language development and help to remediate a language impairment?*

The teacher's role is important in the educational programs they make available to students with speech or language impairments. Teachers need to integrate language development into the entire curriculum and provide direct instruction about oral language. They should try to match the language they use to the language comprehension skills of their students, and they must create a language-rich environment for *all* students. Because of their role in the referral process, teachers must be sure that children with these disabilities are identified and receive the specialized services they require. They also assist in remediation programs,

collaborate with SLPs, and work to foster maintenance and generalization of skills mastered in therapy.

▶ *What is alternative and augmentative communication, and what are its benefits to this population of learners?*

Technology provides many advantages to students with speech or language impairments, and the future holds even more promise. Alternative and augmentative communication (ACC) is particularly beneficial for those with severe speech impairments. The options are many, ranging from low-tech to high-tech devices that actually speak for the user. New breakthroughs signal hope for those with language impairments as well. CD-ROM technology now allows for speech to be systematically altered so it is easier to understand. Such expanded speech, progressively shortened to the rate of normal speech, can even be delivered in game or story formats for use at both school and home.

Challenge Question

▶ *What related service provider serves the needs of students with speech or language impairments, their families, and their teachers, and what roles does this professional serve today?*

The field of speech or language impairments has grown and changed over the years. In the past, remediating speech impairments filled the large caseloads of SLPs. More recently, professionals in the field are concerned about children's abilities to communicate with others. Language needs to become a topic of substantial interest for all educators. Speech/language pathologists (SLPs), experts in the field of speech, language, and communication, serve youngsters whose speech or language impairs their ability to communicate effectively with others. Professional SLPs serve in a variety of roles, ranging from consultative services to classroom instruction. They work with families, teachers, small groups of children, and individuals. Depending on the individual's difficulties, SLPs assess and remediate deficits that prevent efficient and effective participation in communication. The most common problems they address are speech impairments; the second most common problem involves language development. SLPs provide both supportive and direct services. They work not only with students whose primary disability is either a speech or language problem but also with individuals who have a primary disability other than a speech or language impairment.

∿ SUPPLEMENTARY RESOURCES ∿

Scholarly Books

Boone, D. R., & Plante, E. (1993). *Human communication and its disorders* (2nd ed.). Englewood Cliffs, NJ: Prentice-Hall.

Fey, M. E., Windsor, J., & Warren, S. F. (Eds). (1995). *Language interventions preschool through the elementary years.* Baltimore: Paul H. Brookes.

Shames, G. H., Wiig, E. H., & Secord, W. A. (Eds.). (1994). *Human communication disorders: An Introduction* (4th ed). NY: Merrill, an imprint of Macmillan.

Watkins, R. V., & Rice, M. L. (1994). *Specific language impairments in children.* Baltimore: Paul H. Brookes.

Popular Books

Butler, S. (1936). *The way of all flesh.* New York: Limited Editions Club.

Byars, B. (1970). *The summer of the swans.* New York: Viking.

Caldwell, E. (1948). *Tobacco Road.* New York: Grosset and Dunlap.

Johnson, W. (1930). *Because I stutter.* New York: Appleton.

Melville, H. (1962). *Billy Budd.* Chicago: University of Chicago.

Videos

World according to Garp. (1982). Twentieth Century Fox.

This side is good. (1983). Filmmakers Library.

The pain of shyness. (1985). ABC News 20/20—Filmmakers Library.

Life is but a dream. (1985). Filmmakers Library.

A fish called Wanda. (1987). Thames.

Primal fear. (1996). Paramount.

Professional, Parent, and Consumer Organizations and Agencies

American Speech-Language and Hearing Association
National Institute of Communication
10801 Rockville Pike
Rockville, MD 20852
Phone: (301) 897-5700
Web site: http://www.asha.org

National Institute on Deafness and Other Communication Disorders (NIDCD)
National Institute of Health
Bethesda, MD 20892
Phone: (800) 241-1044
Web site: http://www.nih.gov/nidcd/
E-mail: nidcd@aerie.com

Division for Children with Communication Disorders
The Council for Exceptional Children
1920 Association Drive
Reston, VA 22091
Phone: (800) 224-6830, (703) 620-3660
Web site: http://www.cec.sped.org

Stuttering Foundation of America
3100 Walnut Grove Rd. Suite 603
P.O. Box 11749
Memphis, TN 38111-0749
Phone: (800) 992-9392
E-mail: stuttersfa@aol.com

William Britt. *Winter Cityscape.* 1990.

Although **William Britt**, now in his fifties, has mental retardation, he has been a practicing artist for many years. At first self-taught, Britt became a student of Professor Tom Halsall at Westchester Community College in Valhalla, New York in 1983 where he was included on the Dean's List for his artistic accomplishments. Under the guidance of Professor Halsall, Britt's natural talent has developed rapidly to an extraordinarily professional level. Britt works in a studio, which is on the grounds of The Margaret Chapman School in Hawthorne, where he has lived for 16 years. His professional recognition began in May 1976 at the first annual New York State Southern Regional Very Special Arts Festival. Since then his work has been featured in local, state, and national art exhibitions, including the New York State Special Olympics Bicentennial Arts Showcase in Albany; the Manhattanville College Art Show in Purchase; the National Very Special Arts Festival in Niagara Falls; and the Very Special Arts Gallery in Washington, D.C. He is a recipient of the Kennedy International Award for his exemplary role in raising public awareness to the valuable contributions that people with mental disabilities make to society through their creative talents.

Mental Retardation

ADVANCE ORGANIZERS

OVERVIEW

Mental retardation is a cognitive disability, with about 1 percent of all schoolchildren being identified as having this disability. It is defined by reduced cognitive (intellectual) ability, limited adaptive behavior, and the need for support to participate fully in the community. Over the last twenty years, people with mental retardation have been gaining greater access to education, society, and independence. However, these students still have one of the lowest rates of integration in general education classes.

FOCUS QUESTIONS

SELF-TEST QUESTIONS

▶ What are the key differences between the two AAMR definitions of mental retardation?
▶ How are the causes of mental retardation organized, and what are some of the specific causes within each group?
▶ Why is it important to identify more causes of mental retardation?

▶ What are the learning characteristics of students with mental retardation?
▶ How can educators be more effective when working with families of students with mental retardation?

CHALLENGE QUESTION

▶ What are some examples of the four levels of support, and how do they make a difference in the lives of people with mental retardation?

A Personal Perspective:
An Older Brother with Mental Retardation

Maurice Pasternack is over 50 years old. He has Down syndrome and mental retardation. He has actually lived through many of the changes you will read about in this chapter.

When Maurice was born in 1942, the doctors recognized his Down syndrome immediately. They also diagnosed an obstruction in his intestine (common in infants with Down syndrome) that prevented him from digesting foods properly. The intestinal obstruction could be easily repaired by surgery, but because Maurice had Down syndrome, the doctors made a recommendation to his parents that was typical then: to let Maurice die by not giving him the surgery.

Maurice's mother opposed the doctors and rejected the advice they gave. Her defiant attitude was to her a simple decision: her firstborn son *was* going to live. This was an unusual action for a parent to take in 1942.

Maurice's childhood was indeed difficult. The 1940s were a long way from the 1970s. It was an era before IDEA, "normalization," integration, community living, or family support, and before people with mental retardation were recognized as having the rights of citizens. So Maurice was not permitted to attend his neighborhood school, and no programs existed in his community.

Maurice was eventually institutionalized in a large facility, a four-hour drive from his home. It was the only place he could live and perhaps get some of the services he needed. Although his family drove to see him on many weekends, he spent most of his time alone. In the facility, he was forced to sleep on a dirty mattress on the floor, never got enough to eat, and received almost none of the programs he needed.

Maurice's younger brother Bob was born ten years after Maurice. Bob did not have a disability, and so he lived at home with their mother and father. His only contact with his older brother for many years was on those weekend visits, which he admits frightened him. Later, the family moved to Florida, and Maurice was transferred to a private residential facility in Miami. Bob went to college and began working in special education. Bob became the president of a firm that provided diagnostic services for students with disabilities and directed a summer camp for children with severe disabilities and their families.

Bob speaks about Maurice's life now:

In 1980, after my mother died, I decided to drive to Florida to bring Maurice back to the Southwest to live closer to me. Although he lived in a segregated facility in Florida, he now lives in a six-person **group home** in our community. For the first time in his life, Maurice has a job—in fact, he has two jobs. He helps other adults with disabilities make weavings and he grows bedding plants at a greenhouse. Maurice loves to go to work and he loves the group home. We go places together. We have a tradition that every year we go to the Dallas Cowboys/Washington Redskins football game. Sometimes on the weekend, we go to a bar or out to dinner at a restaurant. I am his guardian, and I take care of him. I have for a long time and I guess I always will.

When we were young, the thing he used to do that embarrassed me the most was to hug and kiss me in public. It took a long time before I could accept that. The funniest thing I remember was trying to fix the zipper on his pants in the men's room at the New York World's Fair in 1966. The expressions on the faces of the men in that bathroom have stayed with me for thirty years!

I wish my mother could have lived long enough to see the way special education has changed. Attitudes toward people with mental retardation have changed so much: She could not have imagined that the day would come when parents would be able to have their sons and daughters with mental retardation live at home; when there would be family support groups, wide availability of services, the trend toward independent living, normalization, and integration.

Maurice has always been a strong influence in my life. He affected my choice of a career in special education. But very early, I had to face the fact that he would never be the ideal of the big brother that every boy wants—Maurice would not be able to fight my fights, take care of me, or help me with my homework. But he has done something else for me that an extraordinary big brother can sometimes do: He has helped me learn what things are important in life, and he has loved me unconditionally for my entire life.

1. In what ways might Maurice's life be different if he had been born in 1980 instead of 1942?

2. What do you think would have happened to Maurice if Bob had not moved him from the segregated facility to his home community?

group homes. Apartments or homes in which a small number of individuals with disabilities live with the assistance of service providers.

Children and adults with mental retardation are people first. Their mental retardation is only one of many attributes that make up who they are. It is important to remember that they are members of families, they have relationships with friends and neighbors, and they have personalities shaped by their innate characteristics as well as by their life experiences. Youngsters with mental retardation go to school, plan for the future, hope for a good job, wonder whom they will marry, and anticipate adulthood. These people have hopes and dreams like everyone else. They experience joy, sadness, disappointment, pride, love, and all the other emotions that are a part of living.

All disabilities are serious, even when they are considered mild. Those with mental retardation have impaired intellectual abilities. These differences in abilities and the way society reacts to those differences create obstacles for these individuals and their families. People with this disability must make special efforts to learn, and many need considerable special assistance from teachers and others. Some of the challenges these individuals face, however, are aggravated by prejudice, lack of information, and discrimination. Through persistence and courage, and with support from their families, friends, teachers, and others, people with mental retardation can overcome some of these obstacles.

Mental Retardation Defined

Over the years, many definitions of **mental retardation** have been developed, but they are all very similar. Most refer in some way to intelligence and an impaired ability to learn. Some definitions also refer to limitations in the everyday behaviors necessary to function independently. Still others stress a certain age by which the condition must have begun, and some require that the disability be incurable. Some definitions require physical proof of the disability or a physical origin for the mental retardation. Let's look at two widely recognized definitions.

The 1983 American Association on Mental Retardation (AAMR) definition of mental retardation appeared in *Classification in Mental Retardation* (Grossman, 1983). (AAMR was formerly called the American Association on Mental Deficiency.) Although considered outdated, this definition is still used by many groups and is the basis for the definitions developed by many states.

> Mental retardation refers to significantly subaverage general intellectual functioning existing concurrently with deficits in adaptive behavior, and manifested during the developmental period. (p. 1)

The definition is implemented by applying criteria to its three major components: intellectual functioning, **adaptive behavior**, and developmental period. Deficits in intellectual functioning means that individuals must score below 70–75 on a standardized test of intelligence. Adaptive behavior is defined by how well an individual meets society's expectations for social responsibility and personal independence in accordance with that person's age and cultural group. The third component, developmental period, requires that the disability occur before age 18. In 1992, AAMR supported the development of a new definition of mental retardation. This one is less rigid; it is not as dependent on scores from, now often criticized, tests of intelligence, and is more modern by reflecting society's changing attitudes about the needs of people with this disability. This definition was pub-

mental retardation. A disability characterized by cognitive impairment, limited adapted behavior, need for support, and initial occurrence before age 18.

adaptive behavior. Performance of everyday life skills expected of adults.

lished in *Mental Retardation: Definition, Classification, and Systems of Supports* (Luckasson, Coulter, Polloway, Reiss, Schalock, Snell, Spitalnik, & Stark, 1992):

> *Mental retardation* refers to substantial limitations in present functioning. It is characterized by significantly subaverage intellectual functioning, existing concurrently with related limitations in two or more of the following applicable adaptive skill areas: communication, self-care, home living, social skills, community use, self-direction, health and safety, functional academics, leisure, and work. Mental retardation manifests before age 18. (p. 1)

The orientation of this definition is radically different from previous definitions. Let's examine it more closely to better understand some of these differences. It is a functional definition that looks at the relationship among the individual, the environment, and the types of supports the individual needs to function maximally. These relationships are illustrated in Figure 6.1. There are other differences as well. For example, adaptive behavior is put into the context of the community in relation to the person's age. It is also related to the amount and type of support the individual requires. The concept of support, as part of a definition, is probably the most innovative. Unlike any previous definition, individuals are classified on the basis of how much support and assistance they require to live in the community rather than on the score they received on a test. It is also assumed that the condition and individual's performance will improve when appropriate supports are provided over a sustained period of time. Another important feature is the co-

FIGURE 6.1

The Relationships Between Individuals, Their Environment, and Supports

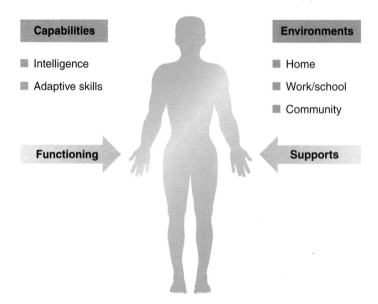

Source: Adapted from Mental Retardation: Definition, Classification, and Systems of Supports (p. 10) by R. Luckasson, D. Coulter, E. Polloway, S. Reis, R. Schalock, M. Snell, D. Spitalnik, and J. Stark, 1992, Washington, DC: American Association on Mental Retardation. Copyright 1992 by American Association on Mental Retardation. Reprinted by permission.

existence of subaverage intellectual functioning and problems in adaptive skill areas. If a person has problems in only one area, mental retardation does not exist. What does this mean? Someone who functions independently at home, at work, and in the community does not have mental retardation even if the IQ score received met the criterion. The intent of this definition is to focus on the person and his or her individual needs rather than on deficits often found in the group.

It is important to recognize, however, how this definition is similar to the previous, 1983, AAMR definition. Just like the older definition, the 1992 one requires the individual to have substantial limitations in intellectual functioning, and the guidelines for a ceiling (a maximum score on a standardized test of intelligence between 70 and 75) are the same. Although the adaptive skill areas are more clearly described than those in the 1983 definition and these problems must exist along with low intellectual ability, the determination of problems with adaptive behavior is a requirement in both definitions. And, both definitions require that the disability exist before the individual's eighteenth birthday. Unlike many disabilities (deafness and hard of hearing, low vision and blindness), mental retardation does not increase its likelihood with age (dementia and strokes in adults are not causes of mental retardation).

Types

Regardless of the definition used, mental retardation varies along a continuum. Most individuals with mental retardation score near the 70–75 cutoff score on IQ tests, have mild cognitive impairments, and usually require few supports. Typically, those individuals with lower IQ scores require considerable supports.

Older Classification Systems. Since the development of the intelligence (IQ) test, around the turn of the century, people have been grouped, classified, and served on the basis of the score they received on one of these tests. One classification method, popular among educators in the 1960s and 1970s, distinguished educable mental retardation (EMR) from trainable mental retardation (TMR). These subgroups were directly linked to IQ scores. The EMR label was reserved for those individuals who scored between 50 and 80 (the ceiling was higher in those days), and the TMR label was used for those individuals who scored between 25 and 50. The use of EMR and TMR came into disfavor, possibly because educators knew that *all* people can learn and that education and training should not be separated. Also, perhaps they realized that suggesting that certain human beings were merely trainable sounded like an unfortunate comparison to animals. Since passage of IDEA in 1975, distinctions between education and training has blurred. Today, we understand that all children are capable of learning and have the right to education.

The 1983 AAMR definition attempted to address these problems by dividing mental retardation into four levels: mild, moderate, severe, and profound (Grossman, 1983). These subclassifications were used to compare an individual with others who had mental retardation. Mild mental retardation, as for those in the EMR group, referred to a disability that was less severe. Notice that this classification system has two more groups: severe and profound. Before IDEA, these children were not likely to find their place in public schools, but since its passage in 1975, educators recognize their responsibility to educate all children, and these two new groups were added to the 1983 definition.

Sensitive and well-prepared teachers can help all children learn and have successful experiences at school.

Emerging Classification Systems. The 1992 AAMR definition provides a new classification system based on an individual's needs for supports. Unlike the older systems, individuals were no longer classified by their IQ scores. This might be one of the most significant differences between this definition and all previous ones. The 1992 definition describes a profile and intensities of needed supports on levels from least intense to most intense: intermittent (I), limited (L), extensive (E), and pervasive (P). These levels refer to the services and supports the individual, whatever his or her IQ, needs in order to function in the environment. Table 6.1 provides more details about this system. Remember, the levels of intensities are not a substitute for the older scheme in which the levels of mild, moderate, severe, and profound were based on IQ scores.

Identification

The new system contains three steps: diagnosis, classification, and proposed systems of supports. In step 1, if the individual has an IQ score of approximately 70–75 or below, existing concurrently with impairments in at least two applicable skill areas, and manifested before age 18, the diagnosis of mental retardation is made. In step 2, the individual's functioning is analyzed in four dimensions: intellectual functioning and adaptive skills; psychological and emotional considerations; physical, health, and etiology considerations; and environments. In step 3, a profile and intensities of needed supports are developed.

Fundamental Concepts. To understand mental retardation, it is helpful to know about the basic theories and principles of intelligence and adaptive behavior and how those concepts relate to an individual's age. First, let's consider intelligence and its measurement.

theoretical construct. A model based on theory, not practice or experience.

normal curve. A theoretical construct of the normal distribution of human traits such as intelligence.

Intelligence Quotient. The question of what intelligence is has challenged philosophers, scientists, educators, and others for centuries. Because intelligence is a **theoretical construct**, it has been defined in many ways, but the simplest way is to classify according to IQ scores. On IQ tests, intelligence is regarded as a human trait that is distributed among humans in a predictable manner. This statistical distribution can be represented as a bell-shaped curve, called the **normal curve.** As shown in Figure 6.2, in this curve the majority of a population falls in the middle of the bell, at or around an intelligence quotient (IQ) score of 100, and fewer and fewer people fall to either end of the distribution, having very low or very high intelligence. IQ level is then determined by the distance a score is from the mean, or average, score. The IQ level of approximately 70–75 or below for mental retardation is also shown in Figure 6.2. Using this system, approximately 2 to 2.5 percent of the population can be classified as having mental retardation.

TABLE 6.1

The 1992 AAMR Definition and Examples of Intensities of Supports

Intermittent	Supports on an "as needed basis." Characterized by episodic nature; person not always needing the support(s), or short-term supports needed during life span transitions (e.g., job loss or an acute medical crisis). Intermittent supports may be high or low intensity when provided.
Limited	An intensity of supports characterized by consistency over time; time-limited but not of an intermittent nature; may require fewer staff members and less cost than more intense levels of support (e.g., time-limited employment training or transitional supports during the school to adult period provided).
Extensive	Supports characterized by regular involvement (e.g., daily) in at least some environments (such as work or home) and not time-limited (e.g., long-term support and long-term home living support).
Pervasive	Supports characterized by their constancy, high intensity; provided across environments; potential life-sustaining nature. Pervasive supports typically involve more staff members and intrusiveness than do extensive or time-limited supports.

Source: Adapted from *Mental Retardation: Definition, Classification, and Systems of Supports* (p. 26) by R. Luckasson, D. Coulter, E. Polloway, S. Reiss, R. Schalock, M. Snell, D. Spitalnik, and J. Stark, 1992, Washington, DC: American Association on Mental Retardation. Copyright 1992 by American Association on Mental Retardation. Reprinted by permission.

FIGURE 6.2

The Normal Curve, IQ, and Mental Retardation

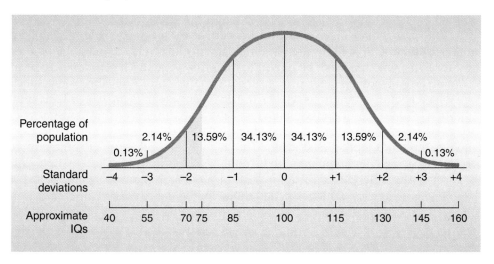

Mental Age. Professionals generally prefer not to refer to mental age when referring to people with disabilities. However, it is a construct that still is used occasionally; therefore we explain it here. Sometimes, the concept of mental age is used to describe the **intellectual functioning** of an individual. **Mental age (MA)** is defined as developmental level—or level of acquired ability or knowledge—compared with the age of the individual. Mental age is calculated as the chronological age (CA) of children without mental retardation whose average IQ test performance is equivalent to that of the individual with mental retardation. For example, a man of 35 who has an IQ of 57 might be said to have a mental age of 9 years 5 months. Such a comparison is imprecise and inaccurate because adults have the physical attributes, interests, and experiences of their nondisabled adult peers. Describing them by mental age underestimates these characteristics. At the same time, the mental age comparison can overestimate certain intellectual skills such as the use of logic and foresight in solving problems.

Adaptive Behavior. For over four decades, professionals have agreed that IQ scores alone are not enough to either qualify individuals for services or assist in the development of an IEP. Adaptive behavior must also be considered (see Table 6.2 for the ten adaptive skill areas, as defined from the 1992 AAMR definition). Measures of adaptive skill areas attempt to determine whether the individual actually performs the everyday skills expected of an individual of that age in a typical environment.

Measures. Given that mental retardation is an impairment of intelligence and the ability to learn socially expected behaviors, measuring the disability centers on attempting to assess intelligence and adaptive behavior. Judgments in these areas can be subjective, with standards often varying by cultural group. Disagreements over the definition of intelligence and the delineation of socially expected behaviors have prevented universal acceptance of any measurement tool or procedure. Regardless, the use of standardized tests remains popular, even for intelligence. Although tests of intelligence have been criticized for cultural bias and resulting discrimination, they remain one way to systematically assess cognitive abilities across a large number of people.

Many practitioners have expressed concern about judging individuals' abilities in the adaptive skill area because such judgments are typically made by parents and teachers, who may well be biased in their assessment. The tendency to overestimate an individual's skills or to assess them inaccurately against a nonspecified age-relevant standard is great. A new instrument is now available that specifically assesses adaptive behavior. Developed in 1996, the *Assessment of Adaptive Areas (AAA)* allows the examiner to convert scores to age equivalents in each of the ten adaptive skill areas. This highly useful instrument brings more objectivity to the determination of individuals' abilities in this important area. This is particularly important with the increased weight of adaptive behavior in the identification of cases of mental retardation.

Significance

People with mental retardation often experience the negative effects of unpleasant and unfair stereotypes. For example, many people think of individuals with Down

MAKING CONNECTIONS

Also see related sections about adaptive behavior in this chapter in
- History of the Field,
- Children with Mental Retardation (adaptive behavior section),
- Educational Interventions (functional curriculum, community based instruction, and transition sections).

MAKING CONNECTIONS

See sections about overrepresentation of culturally and linguistically diverse groups found in the Identification section of Chapter 3.

MAKING CONNECTIONS

Also see related sections about adaptive behavior in this chapter in
- Table 6.3,
- History of the Field,
- Children with Mental Retardation (adaptive behavior section),
- Educational Interventions (functional curriculum, community based instruction, and transition sections).

intellectual functioning. The actual performance of tasks believed to represent intelligence, such as observing, problem solving, and communicating.

mental age (MA). An age estimate of an individual's mental ability, derived from a comparison of the individual's IQ score and chronological age.

~~~~

TABLE 6.2

The AAMR Adaptive Skills

Adaptive Skill Area	Explanation
Communication	Understanding and expressing messages through either symbolic or nonsymbolic behaviors.
Self-care	Toileting, eating, dressing, and grooming skills.
Home-living	Home environment skills relating to housekeeping, property maintenance, cooking, budgeting, home safety, and scheduling.
Social	Skills related to social exchanges, including interaction with others, as well as the initiation and termination of this interaction.
Community use	Use of appropriate community resources, such as traveling in the community, shopping, purchasing services, and using public transportation.
Self-direction	Skills related to making choices, completing tasks, seeking assistance, and resolving problems.
Health and safety	First aid, physical fitness, illness identification, and safety skills.
Functional academics	Skills related to learning in school, such as basic reading, writing, and practical mathematics.
Leisure	Recreational interests and activities that may involve social interaction, mobility skills, taking turns, and playing appropriately.
Work	Employment (job) skills, such as task completion and money management.

Source: From *Assessment of Adaptive Areas (AAA): Examiner's Manual* (pp. 2–3) by B. R. Bryant, R. L. Taylor, and D. P. Rivera, 1996, Austin, TX: Pro-Ed. Reprinted by permission.

syndrome as "happy, affectionate, music loving, but none-too-bright," despite the wide variation in ability and personality among those who comprise this group (Thomson, Ward, & Wishart, 1995). Stereotypes exist among the public and, surprisingly, among professionals as well.

Lowered Expectations. Just as it is wrong to minimize the effects of mental retardation, it is wrong to assume that any individual can achieve only to a certain level or will not be able to master a specific task. It is undeniable: The learning difficulties faced by students with mental retardation are great, particularly because they are compounded by communication problems. However, lowering expecta-

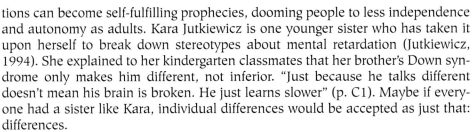

The Standardized Intelligence Test

Disputes about discriminatory testing and placement sometimes arise when culturally and linguistically diverse students are identified as having mental retardation and placed in segregated classes. Traditionally, these challenges assert that a school or state has used inappropriate IQ tests or procedures and has, as a result, misidentified culturally and linguistically diverse students as having mental retardation. IQ testing to identify culturally and linguistically diverse students is forbidden in at least one state. Recently, however, a few parents have made the opposite argument—that denying their children the right to take an IQ test has deprived the children of identification as having a disability and eligibility for important special education services.

MAKING CONNECTIONS

• Refer to the sections about communicative competence in Chapter 5.
• Also see the section about prevention in Chapter 4.

MAKING CONNECTIONS

• See the history section in this chapter for more information about the horrible treatment and discrimination people with mental retardation have experienced across time.
• Chapter 1 also gives background information about the stigma associated with disabilities and with mental retardation in particular.

tions can become self-fulfilling prophecies, dooming people to less independence and autonomy as adults. Kara Jutkiewicz is one younger sister who has taken it upon herself to break down stereotypes about mental retardation (Jutkiewicz, 1994). She explained to her kindergarten classmates that her brother's Down syndrome only makes him different, not inferior. "Just because he talks different doesn't mean his brain is broken. He just learns slower" (p. C1). Maybe if everyone had a sister like Kara, individual differences would be accepted as just that: differences.

Rosario Marin—a California councilwoman, mother of a child with Down syndrome, and recipient of the Rose Fitzgerald Kennedy Award—is helping other parents understand and overcome their feelings of embarrassment and shame about their children with disabilities. By sharing her own personal experiences, she has changed the negative attitudes of other parents. "We still get hung up on the disability. It's just plain ignorance." (Hernandez Jr., 1995, p. B2)

The Stigma of Mental Retardation. Our society places a high value on intelligence. Just think about the comments you hear when someone is being criticized or insulted. Many of these insults—*stupid, dummy, moron, retarded,* or *village idiot*—accuse the person of not being smart. It is not surprising, then, that people whose intelligence is impaired often suffer severe criticism. They may become the victims of prejudice and discrimination solely because of their limited intelligence.

The stigma that often accompanies mental retardation is thus an additional layer of disability for these individuals (Szivos & Griffiths, 1990). Sometimes, the fear of rejection and stigma leads individuals with mental retardation to pretend that they do not have mental retardation. Or it may cause them to be shy or especially reserved. Some people have even lied about their stay in a mental retardation institution, claiming to have been in psychiatric institutions or even prisons (Edgerton, 1967). It should give all of us pause to think that some people place higher value on prison than institutions for mental retardation.

History of the Field

Although mental retardation has always been a part of human history, it was only in the late 1700s that it became the focus of sustained study by professionals. Jean-Marc-Gaspard Itard (1806), a French physician, began working in 1798 with the boy Victor, who had lived all his life in the wild with animals. Itard's work and the progress reports he published provided tangible evidence that it was possible to improve mental disability through skilled teaching.

Residential institutions appeared throughout Europe and Great Britain by the mid-nineteenth century. In the United States, Samuel Gridley Howe, the first director of the Perkins Institute for the Blind in Boston, developed the first U.S. mental retardation institution in 1848. Initially part of the Perkins Institute, it later became a separate institution known as the Walter E. Fernald State School. Ironically, Howe clearly saw the dangers of residential institutions that isolated people with disabilities both geographically and socially. He wrote that there should be only a few residential institutions and they should remain small in size:

> Grave errors were incorporated into the very organic principles of our institutions, which make them already too much like asylums; which threaten to cause real asylums to grow out of them, and to engender other evils...all such institutions are unnatural, undesirable, and very liable to abuse. We should have as few of them as possible, and those few should be kept as small as possible. (Howe, 1866, p. 39)

Despite warnings to keep the number down and to keep them small, institutions spread over the United States. By 1917, all but four states had institutions for people with mental retardation, and many of them were large. The rise in number and size of institutions for people with mental retardation was based on unjustified fear of these people and their negative effect on society (Winzer, 1993). In 1877, Richard Dugdale, a member of the New York Prison Association, put forth a story about the Jukes family to illustrate that people with mental retardation were a danger to society. Dugdale believed that mental retardation was a hereditary condition and that people with it were the source of crime, poverty, and other social ills found in the country at that time. The logic worked this way: the Jukes, and families like them, were the source of poverty, immorality, crime, and more "feeblemindedness." They also overpopulated. They were a menace to society, and good people should be protected from them. Members of such families therefore should be cast away, put in institutions, and not be allowed to have further offspring. Dugdale was not the only propagator of such theories and reasoning. Henry Goddard, in 1912, released the story of Deborah Kallikak who came from a family of "feebleminded" people. This condition, Goddard maintained, was passed on by heredity, and nothing could be done to correct the situation. Because of the likelihood that these people would become criminal, and because they were the reason for all of society's ills, they should be removed from society and their population controlled. Reinforcing the notion that feeblemindedness and criminality were related surrounded the attempted assassination of presidential candidate Teddy Roosevelt in 1912. Although they had not personally examined the assailant, three psychiatrists suggested in the press that he was feebleminded (Gelf, 1995). It is quite likely that such inaccurate accounts contributed to factors allowing the terrible state found in institutions for people with mental retardation. It was not until the 1970s and 1980s that abuses came to the public's attention

MAKING CONNECTIONS

For more information about Itard and the Wild Boy, see Chapter 1.

MAKING CONNECTIONS

Later in this chapter, see the Concepts and Controversy section.

through many exposés. Citing inhumane conditions and standards far below minimum, the courts ordered many closed because they violated residents' constitutional rights.

At about the same time that residential institutions were started, organizations of professionals and parents sprang up to call attention to the needs of these citizens. The American Association on Mental Retardation (AAMR), the largest and oldest interdisciplinary organization of professionals in the field of mental retardation, was founded in 1876 as the Association of Medical Officers of American Institutions. In 1919, the AAMR formed a committee to develop a definition and classification system for mental retardation (Bryant, Taylor, & Rivera, 1996). Its first manual appeared in 1921. Across time, as more has become known about the condition and attitudes have changed, the AAMR has refined its definitions and classification systems of this disability. For example, the 1959 manual was the first to include limited adaptive behavior skills as part of the condition, and the 1992 version includes the concept of needed support. Founded in 1954, The Arc (formerly the Association for Retarded Citizens) also advocates for people with mental retardation. It was founded by parents to advocate for educational opportunities for these children.

During the 1960s and 1970s, researchers developed and refined new systems of instruction. Behavioral approaches that included token economies, positive reinforcement, direct instruction, and task analysis (breaking tasks down into small teachable units) proved to be highly effective, teaching students with mental retardation skills never mastered with instructional procedures used previously (Ayllon & Azrin, 1964, 1968; Birnbrauer, Wolf, Kidder, & Tague, 1965). Jim Lent and his colleagues at the **Mimosa Cottage Project** analyzed many complex tasks and skills found in daily life and on the job (Lent & McLean, 1976). They then taught these complex skills—which some thought students with mental retardation could never learn—to their pupils, residents with mental retardation of a state-funded residential school in Parsons, Kansas. They pioneered work with this population of learners by applying behavioral principles that included systematic instruction, carefully controlled instructional materials, reinforcement for correct responses, and daily evaluation of student progress; these procedures have become commonplace in special education programs.

Also in the 1960s, a new philosophy was stimulated by Benjt Nirje in Sweden (Nirje, 1969). The normalization movement had influence all over the world, including here. Normalization emphasizes that people with mental retardation should have available to them "patterns of life and conditions of everyday living which are as close as possible to the regular circumstances and ways of life of society" (Nirje, 1976). In this country, the principle of normalization as well as the principle of dignity of risk (Perske, 1972; Wolfensberger, 1972) helped provide a foundation for civil rights court cases that brought to people with mental retardation more access to society, schools, and the community. Court actions also subsequently led to widespread **deinstitutionalization** of people with mental retardation.

Although residential programs in the United States were developed by the middle of the 1800s, the first special class for "defective children" was not opened until 1896 (in Providence, Rhode Island). It was soon followed by others in large cities, and by the early 1900s special classes dotted the country. These early classes were few in number and were generally segregated: The students spent their entire day with other students with mental retardation. Most of these classes had rules

Mimosa Cottage Project. One of the earliest demonstration and research sites, located at a state-funded institution in Kansas, where institutionalized individuals were shown to be able to learn a variety of tasks.

deinstitutionalization. Decreasing the number of individuals with mental retardation living in large congregate facilities.

about who could attend and usually excluded those who could not walk or were not toilet-trained. Because of court cases, laws passed by some state legislatures, and the passage of IDEA, it was in the middle 1970s that all children with mental retardation were allowed to attend public schools. Today, most of these children attend their neighborhood schools and classes alongside their peers without disabilities.

The civil rights struggle for people with disabilities, begun somewhat after the civil rights movement of the 1960s, brought attention to these issues for people from diverse backgrounds. Part of this movement for people with disabilities, and an outgrowth of the normalization movement begun in Sweden in the late 1960s, was the birth of self-advocacy groups. These self-help groups were formed to assist people with mental retardation learn about and gain access to their rights as U.S. citizens. The first self-advocacy group began in the 1970s and was stimulated by annual People First Conferences held in Oregon. One purpose of these meetings was to teach people with mental retardation how to form other groups across the United States and to advocate for one another. The growth of self-advocacy groups is astounding. A year after the first meeting in Oregon, 16 groups were reported to exist. The results of a 1994 study revealed a total of 505 such groups in forty-three states alone (Longhurst, 1994).

Prevalence

Estimates about the prevalence of mental retardation vary from 1 to 3 percent of the total population. According to the federal government, slightly more than 1 percent (that is, 1 out of every 100) of our nation's schoolchildren are identified and served as having mental retardation as their primary handicapping condition (U.S. Department of Education, 1996). During the 1994–1995 schoolyear, approximately 570,855 children with mental retardation were served across the country. By far, most of these students have mental retardation at higher IQ levels and need fewer supports.

Some propose that the criterion for inclusion in this group should change and only include those with lower IQs (MacMillan, Siperstein, & Gresham, 1996). If this should happen, the prevalence rate for mental retardation will certainly change. Why would experts suggest that this disability area exclude those with mild cases? They maintain that prevalence rates for students with IQs over 50 fluctuate by state, school district, and economic advantage. To illustrate their point, they cite figures showing that 75 percent of the group in the mild range is from economically poor backgrounds, but that the rate for those with more severe cognitive impairments tends to be quite stable. They also remind educators that these two groups of youngsters require very different educational interventions: more of a life skills curriculum with many supports for those with more severe disabilities. Also, at the lower IQ levels, more causes of mental retardation are known, and many of those include syndromes and diseases. What are some other reasons for suggesting that mild mental retardation be classified separately from those cases that require more support? Is it because of concerns about serving too many youngsters from diverse backgrounds in special education? Is it because general education is assuming more responsibility for mild conditions? Only time will tell whether a new classification system will be devised, but understand that the discussions are beginning.

 MAKING CONNECTIONS

Information about the civil rights movement for people with disabilities is also given in Chapter 1 in these sections:
• Advocacy Movements in the History of the Field section
• Legislation

 MAKING CONNECTIONS

Self-advocacy and self-help groups are discussed in the transition section of this chapter.

 MAKING CONNECTIONS

Figures and discussion about the normal curve are found in
• the Fundamental Concepts section of the Defined section of this chapter,
• the Defined section of Chapter 7.

Causes and Prevention

Mental retardation is caused by many factors. Understanding a few facts related to causes of mental retardation can be helpful:

1. Specific causes can be associated with treatable health-related problems.

2. The cause itself may be treatable, preventing or minimizing mental retardation.

3. Information about causes is necessary for effective prevention programs.

4. Some research, leading to more effective educational interventions, is more useful if the research subjects can be grouped by the cause of their mental retardation.

The link between identifying specific causes of mental retardation and the development and implementation of preventive measures is clear (Coulter, 1996). When a cause is identified, ways to prevent the debilitating effects of cognitive impairments have often followed soon after. However, the cause in many cases is unknown. In 25 to 40 percent of individuals with IQs below 50 and in 45 to 62 percent of the individuals with IQs between 50 and 70, the cause cannot be identified (Coulter, 1996). Therefore the call for more funding for research targeted toward identifying the causes of mental retardation has been made (Stevenson, Massey, Schroer, McDermott, & Richter, 1996). Unfortunately, with the present federal funding crisis, whether this call will be answered is doubtful.

Causes

Today, it is impossible to single out *every* cause of mental retardation. Typically, factors interact in complex ways to cause mental retardation. The major causes can be organized in several ways. Sometimes, they are divided into four groups: socioeconomic and environmental factors, injury, infections and toxins, and biological causes. However, the dividing lines between these groups are not always clear. For example, lead is a **toxin,** but it is also a socioeconomic and environmental factor because few toxins have been eliminated where poor people live. Similarly, malnutrition of a pregnant woman is a socioeconomic factor, but the damage to the baby is biological.

In the 1992 AAMR manual that includes the new definition of mental retardation, another grouping system is proposed (Luckasson et al., 1992). There, the authors suggested that the causes of mental retardation be grouped according to the **time of onset.** Using this system, the causes of mental retardation are organized into three groups:

1. **Prenatal** causes, including chromosomal disorders, syndromes, inborn errors of metabolism, developmental disorders of brain formation, and environmental influences;

2. **Perinatal** causes, including intrauterine disorders and neonatal disorders; and

3. **Postnatal** causes, including head injuries, infections, toxic-metabolic disorders, malnutrition, environmental deprivation, and any other conditions causing mental retardation after birth.

MAKING CONNECTIONS

The 1992 AAMR definition of mental retardation is found in the Defined section of this chapter.

toxin. A poisonous substance that can cause immediate or long-term harm to the body.
time of onset. When the disability occurred.
prenatal. Before birth.
perinatal. At the time of birth.
postnatal. After birth.

We decided to organize our discussion about causes by using the newer system suggested by AAMR. Let's examine the major causes of mental retardation organized by time of onset.

Prenatal Causes. Many cases of mental retardation have their onset before birth, during the prenatal period. The origin of some cases are genetic, others are not. For example, maternal infections and toxins ingested by pregnant women can seriously affect their unborn babies, and many of these cases are preventable. Let's first turn our attention to genetic causes.

Genetic Causes. Down syndrome is an example of retardation with a biological cause. In England, Down syndrome occurs at a rate of 12.6 per 10,000 live births, and in the United States that rate is 7.63 per 10,000 births (Thomson, Ward, & Wishart, 1995). In England, it accounts for one-third of all children with severe learning difficulties, but here Down syndrome accounts for less than 10 percent of all individuals with mental retardation. It is, however, the most common specifically identified genetic cause of mental retardation (Jutkiewicz, 1994). Down syndrome is a chromosomal abnormality. Each human cell normally contains 23 pairs of chromosomes (a total of 46) in its nucleus. In the most common type of Down syndrome, trisomy 21, the 21st pair of chromosomes has three rather than the normal two. Certain identifiable physical characteristics, such as an extra flap of skin over the innermost corners of the eyes (an **epicanthic fold**), are usually present when the individual has Down syndrome. In Down syndrome, the child's degree of mental retardation varies, in part depending on the speed with which the disability is identified, the adequacy of the supporting medical care, and the timing of the early intervention.

Fragile X syndrome is a recently identified inherited genetic disorder associated with mental retardation (Hagerman & Silverman, 1991; Schopmeyer & Lowe, 1992). Now that doctors know about this syndrome, it may prove to be the most common genetic form of mental retardation. The degree of cognitive, physical, and behavioral impairment in an affected individual may range from mild to severe. Fragile X syndrome may also be implicated in other disabilities, such as learning disabilities, attention deficit disorders, autism, and behavior and emotional disturbance (Santos, 1992).

Phenylketonuria (PKU), also hereditary, occurs when a person is unable to metabolize phenylalanine, which builds up in the body to toxic levels that damage the brain. If untreated, PKU eventually causes mental retardation. Changes in diet (eliminating certain amino acid proteins such as milk) can control PKU and prevent mental retardation. So, here is a condition rooted in genetics, but it is the chemicals in milk which become toxins to the individuals affected that cause the mental retardation. Now, let's look at other toxins that do not have a hereditary link.

Toxins. Alcohol, cigarettes, and other drugs taken by mothers during pregnancy can cause mental retardation in their children. Mothers who drink, smoke, or take drugs place their unborn children at serious risk for premature birth, low birthweight, and mental retardation. For example, one study found that women who smoked heavily during the last six months of pregnancy were 60 percent more likely to have children with mental retardation (Bergstein, 1996). The connections in these cases can be compounded by a combination of smoking and drinking alcohol during pregnancy.

 MAKING CONNECTIONS

For more about PKU see the Prevention section of this chapter.

Down syndrome. A chromosomal disorder that causes identifiable physical characteristics and usually causes delays in physical and intellectual development.

epicanthic fold. A flap of skin over the innermost corners of the eye.

Fragile X syndrome. An inherited genetic disorder associated with disabilities and is particularly linked to mental retardation.

One of the top three known causes of birth defects is **fetal alcohol syndrome (FAS)** (Griego, 1994). FAS—a condition that manifests with mental impairments, behavior problems, and usually some physical differences, particularly facial features—is caused by the mother's drinking alcohol during pregnancy (March of Dimes, 1993). The children afflicted with this preventable condition and their families are often devastated (Dorris, 1989). About 5,000 babies per year are born with documented cases of FAS (Griego, 1994). The incidence rate in some communities is higher than in others. For example, in New Mexico, the FAS rates for all of the American Indian tribes in the state is two to five times higher than the national average. The number of these unnecessary cases of mental retardation may be as high as 3.7 out of every 10,000 live births. FAS occurs when alcohol in the mother's bloodstream crosses the placenta and enters the baby's bloodstream. Does it matter what the mother drinks or how much she has consumed? It does not matter whether it is beer, wine, or hard liquor, but whether enough alcohol reaches the baby to cause damage. Is any amount safe? No one really knows, and it is risky for expectant mothers to experiment. That is why professionals advise pregnant women not to drink any liquor.

Expectant mothers' use of drugs places infants at risk for mental retardation in many ways, all dangerous for the baby. Although longitudinal research has not yet definitively identified the long-term effects of prenatal drug exposure, the risks are great (Mandell & Stewart, 1994). The first danger is with the toxin she is exposing her child to. For example, when a pregnant woman uses cocaine, crack, or heroin, the infant also experiences the drug. As with alcohol, these drugs can damage the developing baby and can result in serious mental, physical, and social problems. Many of them are born addicted to the drug and must go through the agony of withdrawal. In addition, drug-using parents are often unable to provide the care and nurturing required for healthy infant development after birth.

MAKING CONNECTIONS

Immunizations and the prevention of disabilities is discussed in Chapter 5 in these sections:
• Prevention
• Concepts and Controversy

fetal alcohol syndrome (FAS). Congenital mental impairments, behavior problems, and perhaps some physical disabilities, caused by the mother's drinking alcohol during pregnancy.

HIV infection. Human immunodeficiency virus; a microorganism that infects the immune system, impairing the body's ability to fight infections.

Disease. Viruses such as rubella, meningitis, and measles can cause mental retardation, although programs of immunization have decreased the incidence of mental retardation from these infections. However, immunization programs are still not provided for all children. For example, some families do not have access to immunizations, because a health care facility is unavailable or too far from home or because the immunizations are too expensive. Some families ignore or are uninformed about the risks of skipping vaccinations, and other families avoid immunizations for religious reasons or believe that the risk of getting the disease from the vaccination is greater than being unprotected. As a result, easily preventable cases of mental retardation due to infection still occur.

We just discussed some of the dangers of drugs to unborn babies, but there are others. The needle sharing that often accompanies some drug use is one of the culprits in the spread of AIDS, and that spread can be to unborn babies as well. Sexually transmitted diseases such as syphilis, gonorrhea, and **HIV infection** (AIDS) can cause mental retardation in the unborn child. The HIV virus has been found in blood and other bodily fluids, especially semen and vaginal secretions, and in rare instances in breast milk. HIV infection is transmitted most frequently through needle sharing or unprotected sexual intercourse with an infected person. Many pregnant women who are HIV-positive pass the infection to their unborn children, who are then born with a variety of disabilities, including mental retardation. The consequences of HIV infection for infants are devastating. The central nervous system is damaged, opportunistic infections cause progressive disability requiring prolonged hospitalization, and psychosocial factors and nutritional deficiencies lead to a chaotic and painful time before early death.

Neural Tube Defects. Anencephaly—where most of the child's brain is missing at birth—and spina bifida—an incomplete closure of the spinal column—can result from the health and condition of the expectant mother. For example, obese mothers are twice as likely as thinner mothers to have babies with neural tube birth defects (Tanner, 1996). With the recent rise in obesity, an estimated 10 percent of women in the childbearing years are at risk.

 MAKING CONNECTIONS

Information about spina bifida is found in Chapter 9.

Perinatal Causes. Although not as common a cause as prenatal and postnatal factors, problems can develop at the actual time of birth. The birth process can be dangerous to both mother and child and can result in a variety of disabilities, including mental retardation. Let's look at a few of these.

Birth Injuries. Deprivation of sufficient oxygen (**anoxia** or **asphyxia**), umbilical cord accidents, obstetrical trauma, and head trauma can result in serious and permanent damage to the baby. The brain requires a certain amount of oxygen in order to function. Deprivation of oxygen will lead to death in a relatively short period of time. An even shorter period of oxygen deprivation or oxygen saturation can cause damage to the brain, often resulting in cerebral palsy (which may or may not result in mental retardation).

Low Birthweight. The survival of very tiny premature infants has led to a new cause and increased numbers of individuals with mental retardation (Haney, 1994). Medical advances of the 1980s now make the probability of infants born under two pounds surviving quite commonplace. The medical costs of these babies' first few months of life can run into the hundreds of thousand dollars, but for many of these infants and their families the greater cost is the resulting disabilities. Fortunately, not all of these infants grow up to have a disability. For the others, their disabilities vary greatly. Some have visual problems; others have motor problems; some have subtle learning problems; and many have substantial cognitive impairments. Here are some specific results for children who had an average birthweight of 1½ pounds. While only 15 percent of the general population has IQs under 85, half of these children did. While 2 percent of full-term babies have mental retardation, 21 percent of these children did. While only 2 percent of full-term babies have exceptionally poor eyesight, 25 percent of this group of children had significant visual problems.

Why do some of these children have substantial and continuing problems? There must be many reasons, but it appears that one answer may lie in a lack of strong parental support (Bates, 1996). On the average, children and teenagers who were low-birthweight babies lag behind their peers on every academic measure, and these problems persist. However, in one sample of these 7-year-olds from middle-class backgrounds, half did not require special education. The researchers attributed family support as one reason for the difference. It is now time for researchers to determine the causes for such differences in the outcomes for low-birthweight babies and improve the outcomes for all of these youngsters.

 MAKING CONNECTIONS

Low birthweight babies are also discussed in the Preschool section of this chapter.

anoxia. Inadequate supply of oxygen to the body, usually at birth.
asphyxia. Deprivation of oxygen, often through near drowning or smoke inhalation.

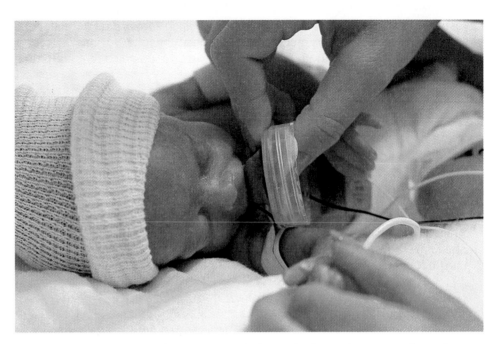

Advances in medical technology can save the lives of infants who previously might not have survived, can prevent disabilities, or can lessen the impact of disabilities.

Postnatal Causes. Many cases of mental retardation begin after birth but during the early years of life, during the developmental period. The preschool years are crucial to the development of every child, and the events—experiences, illnesses, and accidents—that occur in this period can seriously impact the youngster.

Child Abuse and Neglect. Abused children have lower IQs and reduced response rates to cognitive stimuli (*Youth Record,* 1995). In a recent study conducted in Canada that compared abused children with nonabused children, the results of abuse become clear. The verbal IQ scores and the pulse rate changes between the two groups of otherwise matched peers were very different: The abused children had an average total IQ score of 88, whereas their nonabused peers' average overall IQ was 101; and the more abuse, the lower was the IQ score. The link between child abuse and impaired intellectual functioning is now definite, but the reasons for the damage are not. Rather than the result of brain damage, the disruption in language development caused by the abusive situation may be the cause of permanent and profound effects on language ability and cognition. This idea is supported by similar findings of another study of children who were neglected but not physically abused. They also experienced significant impairments in language and cognitive skills. Recall the story of Victor the Wild Child; the connection between neglect and mental retardation is part of the early history and documentation of this field.

Toxins. Toxins abound in our environment. All kinds of hazardous wastes are hidden in neighborhoods and communities. In many cases, the environment was polluted before the dangers of chemicals and poisons were known. In some cases,

MAKING CONNECTIONS

Review in Chapter 8 the sections about child abuse and neglect and juvenile justice and delinquency
• Causes and Prevention
• Children with Behavior Disorders and Emotional Disturbance
In Chapter 1, see
• the story about Itard and Victor the Wild Boy.

the environment was polluted because of carelessness. And, unfortunately, in some instances greedy business leaders did not want to spend the money necessary to properly dispose of or clean up waste products.

One toxin now known to cause mental retardation is lead. Two major sources of lead poisoning can be pinpointed. One was exhaust fumes from leaded gasoline, which is no longer sold in the United States. Before it was outlawed, children who lived near freeways and city streets were at great risk (as were unborn children whose mothers breathed high levels of lead in the air). The other source is lead-based paint, which is no longer manufactured. Unfortunately, it remains on the walls of older apartments and houses. Children can get lead poisoning from a paint source by breathing lead directly from the air or eating paint chips. For example, if children touch paint chips or household dust that contains lead particles and then put their fingers in their mouths or touch their food with their hands, they ingest the lead. Regardless, some landlords run the risk of significant lawsuits and fail to expend the funds necessary to remove the paint (Torres, 1995). Low-income 1- to 5-year-olds are four times more likely than their peers from high-income families to have harmful levels of lead in their blood (Sherman, 1994).

Accidents. Injury, **trauma**, and accidents are major causes of many types of disabilities, including mental retardation. Children under the age of 18 who suffer brain injuries—in automobile or cycle accidents, falls, near drownings—may acquire mental retardation.

 MAKING CONNECTIONS

In Chapter 12, see the section about Traumatic Brain Injury.

Prevention

As you can see from the discussion about causes, many cases of mental retardation in this country are preventable. The President's Committee on Mental Retardation (n.d.) reports that *more than 50 percent of all cases* of mental retardation could have been prevented through known intervention strategies. Most of these strategies (see Table 6.3) are simple and obvious, but the effects can be significant. For example, in the case of child abuse, teachers have a legal (and many believe moral) responsibility to report suspected cases so that further damage to the child might be avoided (Lowenthal, 1996).

As you can see by studying Table 6.3, many preventive measures are available. Possibly, the most important for all pregnant women is to stay healthy. Other prevention strategies involve testing the expectant mother, analyzing the risk factors of the family (genetic history of disabilities or various conditions), and taking action when necessary; screening infants; protecting children from disease through vaccinations; creating positive, nurturing, and rich home and school environments; and implementing safety measures. Notice that not all of these strategies are biological or medical. It is important to use a broad concept that looks at all aspects of the child and the environment for the prevention of mental retardation (Coulter, 1996). Let's look at a few examples of a few preventive strategies.

People should not underestimate the importance of prenatal care. Staying healthy means taking proper vitamins and eating well, and there are good examples of why this is important. For example, folic acid reduces the incidence of neural tube defects (except in obese women). By eating citrus fruits and dark, leafy vegetables (or taking vitamin supplements), one receives the benefits of folic acid—a trace B vitamin—that contributes to the prevention of conditions like spina bifida (Tanner, 1996).

 MAKING CONNECTIONS

Immunizations and the prevention of disabilities are discussed in Chapter 5 in these sections:
• Prevention
• Concepts and Controversy

trauma. An injury.

TABLE 6.3

Prevention of Mental Retardation

For Women Who Are Pregnant	For Children	For Society
Obtain prenatal medical care.	Ensure proper nutrition.	Eliminate child poverty.
Maintain good health.	Place household chemicals out of reach.	Create appropriate education and habilitation programs for children with retardation.
Avoid alcohol drinking.	Use automobile seatbelts, safety seats, and cycle helmets.	Educate parents, and provide support for good parenting skills.
Avoid drugs.		
Avoid smoking (fetal tobacco syndrome).	Provide immunizations.	Protect children from abuse and neglect.
Obtain good nutrition.	Prevent infections.	Improve sanitation and safety.
Prevent premature births.	Provide medical care to treat existing infections.	Provide family planning services; support spacing of children.
Take precautions against injuries and accidents.	Prevent lead intake (from paint and automobile exhaust).	Screen at birth for PKU and other conditions that can lead to retardation if untreated.
Prevent or immediately treat infections.	Routinely test lead levels.	
Avoid sexually transmitted diseases.	Shunt (drain) excess fluid around the brain.	Provide systematic state prevention programs.
Plan and space pregnancies.	Provide neonatal intensive care services.	Provide public education on fetal alcohol syndrome.
Seek genetic counseling and prenatal tests.	Guarantee proper medical care for all children.	Provide public education on HIV prevention.
	Offer early education programs.	Eliminate environmental toxins such as lead.
	Eliminate child abuse.	Assure proper nutrition for pregnant women.
	Eliminate child neglect.	Assure proper health care for pregnant women.
		Assure proper health care for children.

MAKING CONNECTIONS

See the discussion of PKU in the Causes section of this chapter.

Infant screening has proven effective in preventing PKU. Using a procedure developed by Robert Guthrie in 1957, a few drops of the newborn's blood are taken from the heel to determine whether the infant has the inherited genetic disorder that prevents metabolizing phenylalanine, a naturally occurring amino acid found in milk. This test, which costs 3 cents, prevents mental retardation because the baby's diet can be changed before the effects of PKU can begin. It also saves over $1 million per PKU victim, the estimated cost for an untreated individual and a lifetime of care (NY Times News Service, 1995). Guthrie developed the test because his son and his niece had PKU, and he wanted to prevent the condition from affecting others. Early screening of mothers and their newborns prevents other causes of mental retardation as well. For example, the blood condition of RH incompatibility can be prevented through screening methods.

Couples can take certain actions before the woman becomes pregnant to reduce the risk of biologically caused mental retardation. Some couples have medical tests before deciding to conceive a child. These tests, combined with genetic counseling, help couples determine whether future children are at risk for certain causes of mental retardation. Tay-Sachs disease, for example, is a cause of mental retardation that can be predicted through genetic testing. Other couples take tests that search for defects after they find out that the woman is pregnant (see Table 6.4 for a listing of prenatal tests). These tests can determine, in utero, the presence of approximately 270 defects.

TABLE 6.4

Prenatal Tests for Abnormalities

Test	Approximate Cost	Substance Tested	Earliest Time of Test	Approximate Risk of Miscarriage	Abnormalities Tested
Multiple marker screen (MMS)	$70	Woman's blood	15th week	None	Down syndrome, spina bifida, and others
Amniocentesis	$1,500	Amniotic fluid	12th week	0.5%	Approximately 270 defects, including Down syndrome, sickle-cell anemia, muscular dystrophy, and cystic fibrosis
Chorionic villi sampling	$1,500	Hairlike strands on the placenta	9th week	1%	Approximately 270 defects, including Down syndrome, sickle-cell anemia, muscular dystrophy, and cystic fibrosis
DNA analysis	$100–$500	Blood or cells	Varies according to sample	1% if fetal blood or cells	Many possibilities, including hereditary disabilities
Fetal echo cardiogram (doppler)	$100–$500	Imaging of heart	21st week	None	Structural abnormalities of heart
Genetic counseling	$100/hour	History of family	Any time	None	Varies
Percutaneous umbilical blood sampling (PUBS)	$150–$500	Analysis of umbilical cord blood	18th week	1%	Many possibilities, including viruses such as CMV and parasites such as toxoplasmosis
Ultrasound image	$300	Noninvasive view of structure of fetus	Any time	None	Structural abnormalities such as spina bifida, small size

FIGURE 6.3

How a Shunt Draws Fluid from the Brain

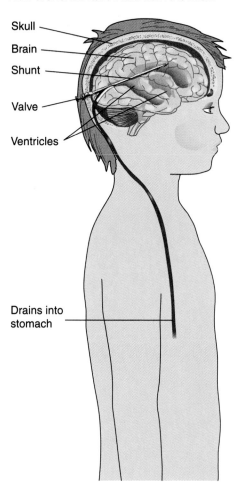

Skull
Brain
Shunt
Valve
Ventricles
Drains into stomach

Let's look at another preventive technique that has saved children from mental retardation. Hydrocephaly is the buildup of fluids in the brain ventricles that causes them to expand. This in turn stretches the child's head outward and squeezes and compresses the brain and nerves. After some time, the result is brain damage. Medical procedures can now avoid the damage. Figure 6.3 shows how a **shunt**, or tube, drains excess spinal fluid from the child's brain to another place in the child's body (e.g., the abdomen), where the body can safely absorb, process, and eliminate the fluid. Before this technique was available, children with this condition had irreversible medical problems and mental retardation.

Remember, not all conditions or factors that cause mental retardation can be prevented. In over half the cases of severe mental retardation, the cause is unknown (Stevenson et al., 1996). Genetic causes account for about 20 percent of the causes, infections about 11 percent, trauma another 11 percent, prematurity about 4 percent, and other individual causes making up the total. Until more causes are identified, we will wait for new preventive measures to be developed.

Children with Mental Retardation

Every person with mental retardation is an individual, and stereotypes can be unfair and inaccurate when applied to individual people. Regardless, it is helpful to understand some of the common characteristics that educators frequently encounter when working with students with mental retardation and their families. Recall that three of the defining characteristics of mental retardation are problems with cognition, adaptive behavior, and the need for supports to sustain independence.

Cognitive Impairments

The most common, and perhaps the most defining characteristic of people with mental retardation, is impaired cognitive ability. This trait has pervasive effects, whether the disability is mild or severe. It makes simple tasks difficult to learn. It can interfere with communicative competence because the content of the message is harder to deliver and comprehend. It influences how well one can remember and how flexible a person is with already learned knowledge and skills. Ultimately, the degree of cognitive impairment determines the types of curriculum content these individuals are taught: academic or life skills.

Learning new skills, storing and retrieving information (memory), and transferring knowledge to either new situations or slightly different skills are challenges for individuals with mental retardation. Memory, especially short-term memory, is often impaired. The student may also have trouble with long-term memory—correctly remembering events or the proper sequence of events, particularly when the events are not clearly identified as important. Even when something is remembered, it may be remembered incorrectly, inefficiently, too slowly, or in insufficient detail. Teachers can assist students in developing memory strategies and help them compensate for their lack of abilities in this area in many ways. For example, the student can learn to create picture notebooks that sequence the steps in a task they need to perform, a job that needs to get done, a task to be accomplished, or a checklist of things to do before leaving the house. Sometimes enhancing stu-

MAKING CONNECTIONS

See the sections about learning strategies found in Chapter 4:
• Learning Strategies
• Generalization

shunt. A tube used in a medical procedure that draws excess fluid from the brain and head area and disposes it in a safe area in the body.

dents' attention improves memory. A student, for instance, may have a short attention span for certain tasks; that student needs special help focusing or selecting the appropriate tasks on which to focus attention. By responding to students' leads in attention (Yoder, Kaiser, & Alpert, 1993) and preferences in learning materials, activities, and environments, teachers can enhance students' learning.

One limitation of mental retardation is that the individuals with this disability are frequently less able than their peers to acquire knowledge through incidental learning—that is, accomplish learning that is an unplanned result of their ordinary daily experiences. For some, it seems that direct instruction is required for almost every task to be learned. Teachers must plan for the generalization (transfer of learning) so newly learned skills are applied in a variety of settings (school, home, neighborhood), performed with and for different people, and expanded to similar but different skills. See the Tips for Teachers box for some ways to improve generalization.

Problems with communication are also associated with impaired cognition. Delayed language is common, as are speech problems (Drew, Logan, & Hardman, 1992). This situation is compounded because many children with mental retardation have fewer experiences and less exposure to ordinary activities. Remember, language development is inhibited when children have restricted experiences during the preschool years when language is developing.

Students with mental retardation benefit from the services of SLPs. Because most of these children do not begin speaking at the typical age, an SLP should begin working with the child and the family as soon as possible. For those identified at birth, it may mean that some SLP services may begin before the child's first birthday. For those identified about at age 3 (because they are not yet talking), services should begin immediately. It is helpful for educators to know what kind of speech and language services a child has received across the years as IEPs are developed and instructional programs are implemented.

 MAKING CONNECTIONS

Refer to the section about cognitive and academic performance in the Language Impairment section in Chapter 5.

 MAKING CONNECTIONS

- See the discussion in Chapter 1 about the related service professionals who assist children with special needs.
- Refer to Chapter 2 and the section about IEPs.

Early intervention and appropriate education enhance the abilities of students with mental retardation. These early experiences will allow for this boy's successful integration into a general education setting.

MAKING CONNECTIONS

• See Chapter 5 for more information about assistive communication devices (Technology section).
• Sections about manual communication and American Sign Language (ASL) in Chapter 10 explain more about the use of nonverbal communication systems.

MAKING CONNECTIONS

Also see related sections about adaptive behavior in this chapter:
• Defined
• Table 6.3
• History of the Field
• Educational Interventions (functional curriculum, community based instruction, and transition sections)

augmentative communication systems. Alternative methods of communicating, such as communication boards, communication books, sign language, and computerized voices.

communication board. A flat device on which words, pictures, or other symbols are used to expand the verbal interactions of people with limited vocal abilities.

Some children with mental retardation do not acquire speech at all or do not acquire speech that can be understood by most of the people around them (Parette & Angelo, 1996). This does not mean that these students cannot communicate. Even children without speech are able to learn other methods of communication. For example, a student may use eye blinks, touches, movement, technology, or sign language to indicate needs and desires. Some children use **augmentative communication systems**, **communication boards**, to express their needs and feelings. In the simple systems, words and/or pictures are placed on a flat surface or in books. The student communicates by pointing to the appropriate symbols. Symbols are customized to the individual; the words or symbols on the board reflect the individual and the needs of the environments in which he or she operates. Some boards are simple homemade projects; others use quite sophisticated technology. The teacher's job is to encourage and shape these techniques into a reliable system of communication for the student. With reliable communication, learning and social interaction can take place.

Adaptive Behavior

Think about some people you know who are very smart, get great grades in school, but cannot manage daily life. These individuals probably have difficulties with some adaptive skill areas. Now think about people you know who are highly successful on the job but have no social skills. Or, those who have great personal hygiene and grooming skills but are unable to balance their personal budgets. All of these people have problems in at least one adaptive skill area. They also are bright (or at least average in intellectual ability), so they do not have mental retardation, just as those people who do not score high on an IQ test but have adequate adaptive skills do not have mental retardation. Review Table 6.2 again, and think about the independence of many of the ten adaptive skill areas. Also think about how important each is to independent functioning in the community. The point here is that mastery of adaptive skills is vital to an individual's successful functioning as an adult in the community. They are not skills that people, regardless of ability or disability, always master without instruction. However, for students with mental retardation, each of these areas should be goals on their IEPs and effort to attain mastery of each should be vigorous.

Support

Everyone needs and uses supports. We ask our friends for advice. We form study teams before a difficult test. We expect help from city services when there is a crime or a fire. We join together for a neighborhood crime watch to help each other be safe. And, we share the excitement and joys of accomplishments with family, friends, and colleagues. For all of us, life is a network of supports. Some of us need more support than others, and some need more support at different times of their lives.

Recently, the *types of support* needed by people with mental retardation have gained the attention of researchers and scholars (McDonnel, Mathot-Buckner, & Ferguson, 1996). The 1992 AAMR definition includes support as a defining characteristic of this disability and specifies four types. **Natural supports** are the individual's own resources, family, friends, and neighbors (Bradley, Ashbough, & Blaney, 1993). These natural, supportive relationships exist among people in almost every setting and in almost every aspect of life. People help each other in simple and complex day-to-day tasks. **Nonpaid supports** are ordinary neighborhood and community supports. Examples of these kinds of supports include clubs, recreational leagues and groups, or private organizations. **Generic supports** are the type that everyone has access to, such as public transportation or the state human services system. **Specialized supports** are those that are disability-specific, like human services delivered to families of children with disabilities or even special education. The *amount of support* needed can vary for each individual and change at different periods of time. Think of *support* as a fluid concept that is responsive by providing only as much assistance as needed when necessary. Remember, the four levels of support (intermittent, limited, extensive, and pervasive) can be delivered to the same person, at the same time, for different behaviors.

One creative way of helping people with mental retardation receive the support they need was an innovation of Anthony K. Shriver (nephew of the late President Kennedy). **Best Buddies** is a program that links college students with individuals with mental retardation. The goal is for these people to become friends through which support and companionship are natural outcomes. Many of these relationships exist for years, with the pairs going to movies, sporting events, concerts together. The Best Buddy also helps when the need arises (Best Buddies, n.d.).

Educational Interventions

Students with cognitive impairments require special and intensive instruction, and this instruction needs to begin early. Whether the target of instruction is a life skill, such as making change or cooking a meal, an academic task, or a vocational skill, sound instructional principles must be followed (see the Making

 MAKING CONNECTIONS

Also see related sections about support in this chapter:
• Defined
• Table 6.1
• Transition (Educational Interventions)

natural supports. Supports that occur as a natural result of typical family and community living.

nonpaid supports. Ordinary assistance given by friends and neighbors.

generic supports. Nondisability-specific public benefits to which all eligible people have access.

specialized supports. Disability-specific benefits.

Best Buddies. A program that pairs college students with people with mental retardation to build relationships, friendships, and opportunities for support.

Specify the Instructional Objectives

List the objectives in observable terms such that they will communicate to others.

Focus the objectives on what is directly the instructional target.

Plan how the objectives will be evaluated to ensure continued student progress.

Sequence Skills

Be sure prerequisite skills are mastered first.

Sequence easy skills before more difficult ones.

Plan to teach confusing concepts separately.

Match Instructional Tactic with Topic or Skill to Be Taught

Select a tactic that has been proven through rigorous research.

Monitor its effectiveness continuously.

Change tactics when it is no longer effective.

Provide Many Opportunities for Practice

Have students apply their learning in different settings.

Have students apply their learning with slightly different or expanded tasks or skills.

Be Certain That the Skill Is Truly Mastered

Have the student demonstrate mastery when performing the skill independently.

Have the student demonstrate mastery in a variety of settings.

Accommodations box). When the target of instruction is specifically identified and is taught directly, and progress is evaluated systematically and consistently, students with mental retardation achieve well (Jitendra & Nolet, 1995).

In these sections, we decided to describe some special curriculum and instructional areas that these students are more likely to need than other students with disabilities or their peers without disabilities need. For example, we spend some time discussing what comprises a functional curriculum, community based instruction, choice making, supported employment, and self-advocacy. At the end, we hope you will come to appreciate what gains can be made, what effort it takes, and what accomplishment is felt when adults with mental retardation take their places in the community.

Education and the Preschool Child

Early identification and intervention are important to children with mental retardation and their families. Early intervention can limit the severity of the mental retardation, provide the foundation for the development of important skills later in school and in life, and is a time when the family begins its long involvement in the education of their child with a disability. Let's look first at the positive effects of early intervention, then at some different types of preschool settings.

The Power of Early Intervention. Early childhood education programs are essential for young children with disabilities and young children who are at risk for developmental delay. Children at risk are those whose medical needs or whose

MAKING CONNECTIONS

Information about the three at-risk categories is found in Chapter 5 (Language section).

Children need opportunites to have exciting and varied experiences, so they have reasons to develop their language and thinking skills.

environment make it likely that they will have developmental delays if early intervention is not provided. Ramey and his colleagues (Ramey, Bryant, Wasik, Sparling, Fendt, & LaVange, 1992)—in a pioneering, multisite, randomized study of 985 low-birthweight, premature infants—found that young children at risk who received a comprehensive and intensive early intervention program showed significantly increased IQ scores and decreased behavior problems. In fact, the odds of having an IQ score below 70 were 2.7 times greater in the control group that did not receive the early intervention program.

Other studies have achieved similar findings (Blair, Ramey, & Hardin, 1995). Low-birthweight babies are at high risk for cognitive impairments. These children could be considered doubly at risk because of the likelihood that they come from low socioeconomic backgrounds. Finding ways to improve the outcomes for these children is very important, and it may be that data now show us how. The intellectual development of children who receive three years of early intervention services that included home visits, attendance at child care centers, and parent involvement had IQs higher than children who did not participate consistently in all three types of services for at least three years. These gains were only made by those fully participating in the early intervention services. Policymakers, parents, and educators must recognize the importance of comprehensive and sustained services for these children while they are toddlers and preschoolers.

Preschool and Peer Relationships. Perhaps it is during the preschool years that children with mental retardation have the greatest opportunities for integration in educational settings. Many integrated preschool experiences are available for young children with and without disabilities to attend school together.

 MAKING CONNECTIONS

Review the information about low birthweight in the Causes section of this chapter.

 MAKING CONNECTIONS

The relationship between poverty and disabilities is discussed throughout this text, but in particular reread these sections in Chapter 3:
• Causes
• Prevention
• Education and the Preschool Child
Overall outcome data for individuals with disabilities are found in
• Chapter 1,
• in the Transition sections found in
  every chapter in this book.

These, along with segregated settings, allow for new studies and comparisons of preschool options for these youngsters (Guralnick, Connor, & Hammond, 1995).

Mothers of young children with mental retardation are concerned about their youngsters' relationships with peers and with their ability to make friends. It is nice to report that young children with mental retardation, regardless of the type of preschool they attend, have friends at school and that these friendships extend into the community. Children who attend integrated settings seem to have high levels of social interaction, particularly with nondisabled peers, but they also experience more rejection and less overall acceptance than children attending segregated settings. This seems to be due to both the behavior of the child with disabilities and the attitudes of the children without disabilities. Regardless of setting, preschoolers with mental retardation seem less able to resolve conflicts in social situations than their peers without disabilities. These findings clearly point to some important instructional targets that need to be incorporated into these young children's educational programs.

Some distressing findings have also come to light and need the attention of educators (Guralnick, Connor, & Hammond, 1995). Students in integrated settings are less likely to have completed IEPs. They are also less likely to have special accommodations made for them or to receive special services (e.g., speech and language services). Quality services require that all the special needs of the child be met, not "traded off" for a particular type of placement. On a more positive note, mothers of preschoolers with mental retardation seem pleased with the services their children receive, whether in a segregated or an integrated setting.

Education and the Schoolchild

Most students with mental retardation have mild disabilities. Increasingly, these students are included in general education classes. Frequently, these students' learning goals are similar to or identical with those of their peers without disabilities. Of course, teachers have to adapt their techniques and adjust the curriculum somewhat to accommodate these students' special learning needs. Many students with mental retardation, however, have very complex learning needs. They might require intensive, specialized instruction from a variety of professionals in settings away from the traditional school building—for example, learning how to ride a bus by using public transportation. They might even require a different curriculum that includes daily living skills, so that their long-term goal of independent living can be met. And, some of these youngsters might need a "balanced curriculum" in which both traditional academics are taught along with more functional skills (Hicksom, Blackman, & Reis, 1995).

Functional Curriculum. A functional curriculum focuses on **life skills**. This type of curriculum answers the needs of those students who have particular difficulties with adaptive behavior. A functional curriculum teaches skills that are used in everyday life or that prepare students for life after graduation. Those skills should include those required for personal maintenance and development, homemaking and community life, work and career, recreational activities, and travel within the community (Hicksom, Blackman, & Reis, 1995). Teachers must remember that their lessons should relate to skills that students need for independence.

Many teachers have begun to emphasize **functional academics** (Drew, Logan, & Hardman, 1992). Students' reading, writing, and mathematics instruction focuses

MAKING CONNECTIONS
For detailed information about IEPs, see Chapter 2.

life skills. Skills used in daily life and independent living.

functional academics. Using life skills as the means to teach academic tasks.

on practical skills. The reading program would include reading for protection and information. Here, survival words (street signs: walk, don't walk, stop; safety words: danger, poison, keep out) might be the topics of instruction. Writing instruction could center on taking phone messages, writing directions for getting to a restaurant, or taking notes on how to do a job. Mathematics instruction would include such topics as: time-telling, making change, money skills, cooking measures. All instruction using this system is practical. For example, counting is taught by asking students to count the number of books in the room rather than by absentmindedly reciting numbers from 1 to 20. A unit on measurement becomes an opportunity to teach cooking, rather than having the students measure lines in a workbook.

When teaching functional or life skills, teachers often find that they need to create their own instructional programs because they are not available from commercial publishing houses. In these circumstances, teachers find that **task analysis** is helpful when breaking skills down into teachable units. Simple, linear tasks are easily applied to this system. For example, buttoning a shirt, zipping a jacket, tying shoes, cooking, using public transportation, making change, and telling time are all examples of skills that are often part of these students' IEPs and that are easily submitted to task analyses. The Teaching Tactics box gives you an example of a skill, zipping a jacket, that was task analyzed and taught to a young child with mental retardation through direct instruction techniques. To complete their instruction, teachers make certain that their students can apply their newly learned skills in real-life situations. For example, the teacher would be sure that the student zips his jacket when going outside to play on a cold day. In some cases, these practical applications should occur away from the school setting, and this is why the concept of community based instruction was developed.

Community Based Instruction. We mentioned earlier that **community based instruction (CBI)** is the strategy of teaching functional skills and adaptive behaviors in the environments in which they should occur naturally. Remember, generalization abilities are problem areas for many students with a disability, and CBI is designed to help students learn to apply skills in all appropriate settings. Like task analysis, CBI is a crucial teaching tool for many students with mental retardation. Let's look at some examples. Learning how to make change is more natural when using real coins at the neighborhood store than when using paper cutouts of coins in the classroom. Learning how to use public transportation to get from home to work is more effective when actually making such trips on a city bus than when pretending to do so at school. Also, rather than addressing a specific curriculum area such as self-help or language skills in artificial settings, CBI allows for these skills to be taught in at least four important situations: vocational, community, recreation and leisure, and home and family.

CBI also assists students with transferring learning across situations, people, and places by teaching skills in the environment where the behavior is typically expected. Students have the opportunity to learn and practice generalizing their learning from one person to the next. Of what use is it to be able to make change with the teacher if the students forget the skill and cannot make change with the local shopkeeper? a stranger? Generalizing from one place to another can be enhanced by purchasing items in a store rather than from an old refrigerator carton on which the teacher has painted the word *STORE*. Think of more examples about how incidental learning can occur in natural settings through the application of CBI. For example, a trip to the store can include crossing streets, reading road signs,

 MAKING CONNECTIONS

See the sections about generalization in this chapter and in Chapter 4.

task analysis. Breaking down problems and tasks into smaller, sequenced components.

community based instruction (CBI). A strategy of teaching functional skills in the environments in which they occur; for example, shopping skills should be taught in the local market rather than a classroom "store."

Task Analysis and Chaining

Teachers often use a task analysis of the skill they wish to teach as a guide for their instruction. When using these systems, teachers may elect to teach a skill in two different orders of **chaining**. In forward chaining, students are taught to perform the first step in the chain first. In the task of zipping a jacket, for example, students would be taught to engage the tab first. Each step up the chain of steps is taught and mastered before the next step in the chain is taught and mastered. In some cases, the teacher might elect to teach the steps in reverse order, which is called *backward or reverse chaining*. Mrs. VanEtten elected to use this approach when teaching Ted how to zip his coat.

Ted is a 5-year-old youngster with mental retardation and extensive needs for supports in most areas. His fine and gross motor skills are not yet well developed, but he does have the ability to use both of his index fingers and thumb to pinch and grasp with sufficient strength to be able to pull up a tab of a zipper. Winter is coming, and Mrs. VanEtten has decided that Ted must learn to put on and zip up his jacket by himself now. Until now, Mrs. VanEtten or the class paraprofessional has prepared Ted to go outside for recess or to go home after school. At home, Ted's mother dresses him.

Mrs. VanEtten decides to use task analysis for zipping, with backward chaining of the instructional sequence. Ten minutes before recess, Mrs. VanEtten schedules time to work with Ted alone on the skill of zipping. On the first day of instruction, Mrs. VanEtten tells Ted that he is going to learn to zip up his jacket by himself. She tells him that for several days she will help him do the task, but fairly soon, he will be responsible for doing the job himself. She also tells him that he will learn how to zip in small steps. Each day, they will work on a different step. If he can show her that he can do the step being taught that day correctly three times, he can go out to recess early. Mrs. VanEtten stands behind Ted with her arms around him. She slides the tab into the slider and pulls the zipper up about halfway. She then tells Ted to finish zipping the jacket. He does not respond, so she takes his right hand, helping him grasp the tab, and guides his hand as they finish the zipping task together. Mrs. VanEtten then unzips Ted's jacket. She repeats the process, zips Ted's jacket about halfway up, and asks him to finish zipping his jacket. This time, he completes the task. She repeats this step three times. Ted correctly finished zipping his jacket three times and leaves for recess early.

On the next day ten minutes before recess, Mrs. VanEtten works with Ted again. Standing behind him and putting her arms around him, she tells Ted to watch her as she zips his jacket. Mrs. VanEtten slides the tab into the zipper and moves it up approximately an inch. She then tells Ted to finish zipping his jacket, which he does. She unzips his jacket and repeats the process until Ted has completed the task correctly three times. Again, he goes to recess early.

On the third day, Mrs. VanEtten asks Ted if he is ready for the hard part. She repeats the steps she has followed on the two previous days, and for the first time, she helps Ted slide the tab into the slider. She guides him several times; each time, he finishes the last steps by himself. She then asks Ted to zip his coat by himself. She offers him some assistance by holding the sides of his jacket firmly. Ted then zips his jacket. When he does so three times correctly, she praises him for his good work and excuses him to go to recess. Mrs. VanEtten plans to begin instruction on putting on his jacket next week.

chaining. A strategy to teach the steps of skills that have been task analyzed either first step first (forward chaining) or last step first (backward chaining).

locating the store, finding the items, purchasing them, and interacting politely with the clerk. For those trips outside walking distance, students learn about bus routes, change for the bus, locating the stop, and similar tasks.

We have made the case that CBI is most effective with students who need to learn adaptive behaviors and have generalization difficulties. However, CBI provides a dilemma for some educators because it is not compatible with inclusive education in age-appropriate general education placements. When a student is learning in the community while age-peers are learning in the school building, the student with mental retardation is deprived of inclusion opportunities with peers. How can the benefits of CBI be weighed against the benefits of inclusive settings? How should this dilemma be resolved?

Making Choices. Learning how to make decisions is a life skill and should be part of a functional curriculum (Wehmeyer, Kilchner, & Richards, 1996). Once acquired, for students with mental retardation to generalize this skill and apply it when appropriate requires application with guided practice in a variety of settings. Learning how to make choices while in community settings increases the probability of being able to use these skills when independent and in the community. Therefore it is also a perfect instructional topic to include in a community based instructional program.

People with mental retardation are allowed fewer choices than other people with disabilities and their nondisabled peers (Wehmeyer & Metzler, 1995). Everyday, people make choices for themselves. They decide where to sit, where to eat, what to eat, how long to stay, where to go, and with whom to interact. For people with mental retardation, particularly those who were allowed to make few choices while growing up, the ability to make decisions is unfamiliar. Other people make even the simplest decisions for them. It is not uncommon for people who are paid to be escorts for people with mental retardation to make all of the choices, like what movie to see, at what restaurant to eat, or in what recreational event to participate (Belfiore & Toro-Zambrana, 1994). To avoid such situations, educators may have to teach decision-making skills and be sure these individuals can apply them in a variety of community and home settings.

Teachers can help their students get a head start on decision- and choice-making skills by ensuring that such opportunities exist in the classroom. For example, students could be allowed to choose from an assortment of snacks, from a variety of activities, or whether to work alone or with a partner. This component of education, which will eventually lead to independence and autonomy as adults, can begin during the preschool years. Young children can be encouraged to decide which toys to play with, rather than having someone else pick them out. They can also decide what activities to engage in during different time periods. Although this tactic may seem simple, because the tendency is to make choices for children with mental retardation and because making choices is such an important part of adult life, education and experience with this skill must begin early.

Merely choosing an option is not enough. People must also be able to *express* the choice. How do students with mental retardation express their choices? Like their peers without disabilities, most *say* what they want. But students with severe disabilities often cannot express themselves easily. So they must learn to use other creative means to make their choices known. These techniques range from pointing with a finger or arm, to using different gestures for yes and no, to using certain facial expressions, to pointing with a light or stick attached to a headband. Some must also learn to truly express their choice, rather than telling the adult or other person what they think they want to hear.

Inclusion

Participation of people with mental retardation at school and in society is not always achieved at desirable levels. Many of these people are not allowed to interact with others who do not have disabilities, work alongside nondisabled peers, or participate in recreational activities because they do not have access to typical activities that each of us is involved in on a daily basis. These opportunities may not exist because the general public finds the concept novel or even uncomfortable. Why might this be so? Maybe this is because children with mental retardation have a low participation rate in general education programs at school and in recreational activities after school and because people without cognitive impairments are not experienced in dealing with these differences.

Let's look at the school situation first. Only about 7 percent of students with mental retardation use the general education classroom as their primary educational placement option. Although some 27 percent attend resource rooms, almost 57 percent attend special education classes and almost 8 percent attend separate schools (U.S. Department of Education, 1995). Inclusion can be a successful experience for many individuals with mental retardation and their peers. Luke Zimmerman has shown everyone how he can be an important part of the school and the football team (Associated Press, 1995). Luke plays football for Beverly Hills High School. Although this tailback with Down syndrome has never touched a ball in play, his teammates say that it is his spirit and rousing speeches in the locker room that inspired them to an 8–1 season. Successful inclusion, however, requires planning and learning on the part of all participants, not just the student with mental retardation. It also takes coordination across many professionals representing many different disciplines: speech and language, occupational therapy, physical therapy, and nursing.

Luke Zimmerman is an important member of his high school football team.

Some parents, however, are deciding that full inclusion for their sons and daughters with mental retardation may not be the best option across all of the school years (Tobin, 1996). Jesse is a preschool student who has done very well in fully inclusive settings. Jesse, who has Down syndrome, has thrived socially and gotten along well with his peers without disabilities. Jesse will attend a general education kindergarten next year. Robert, who also has Down syndrome, has attended an integrated kindergarten this year, but his father decided that Robert's educational needs would be better met next year in a special education class. Although Robert has profited from socializing with peers in the general education setting, his father feels that he needs a curriculum and instructional procedures tailored to functional life and academic skills. Having an array of options available for students allows families and educators to make decisions for all individuals based on their own unique needs and abilities.

Inclusion and integration in school settings are important goals for students with disabilities and for their classmates. It is equally important for students with and without disabilities to work and play side by side outside the school setting. One group working to include youngsters with disabilities is 4-H for All, a community club in Cook County. Through this program, over two thousand youth with disabilities are included in 4-H activities in the Chicago area (Cook County Cooperative Extension Service, 1990). Alongside their nondisabled peers, these students learn valuable life skills, such as how to grow vegetables and cook nutritious meals. They also learn skills that might be applied to a vocation or career, such as making jewelry, sewing leather items, and even incubating chicken eggs and raising the chicks. The 4-H for All is a unique and special program that meets the needs of all the youngsters who participate by accommodating everybody's needs.

In another model program offered by 4-H, youngsters with disabilities work with nondisabled peers to plant and maintain garden sites (*Urban Update*, 1992). On Saturday mornings throughout the spring and summer, 4-H participants plant and tend to flowers and vegetables. What began as a rocky and weedy area has become a wonderful children's garden where some of the most important life skills are learned by all. Betty Greenwood Houbion, the creator of the award-winning Children's Garden of Vernon Hills near Chicago, states that the goal of her program is to enable children to participate in building community inclusively and expansively while empowering themselves and other children to grow and learn (Sullivan, 1992).

When educators speak of inclusive programs, they must expand their vision to include not only traditional classroom settings but also community programs where students with disabilities have not traditionally been part of the group. The Chicago area 4-H club is an exemplar community program that includes many activities for youngsters with and without disabilities to work and learn together.

Transition Through Adulthood

The transition from school to life as an independent adult can be a difficult accomplishment for individuals with mental retardation and their families. Unfortunately, it is not successfully achieved for many of these individuals. For example, a substantial proportion of adults with Down syndrome remain dependent on their own parents as caregivers (Thorin, Yovanoff, & Irvin, 1996). Although out-of-home placements do increase with age, some 85 percent of children and adults with mental retardation live at home (Krauss, Seltzer, Gordon, & Friedman, 1996). As expectations for people with disabilities have changed and they live in the community and experience integration into society, transition goals assume greater importance.

What does transition mean? It is a time when the outcomes of the learning process at school become actualized and the supports required by the individual to function in the community become more apparent. And, it is a time when the learning process continues. Important goals need to center on making decisions and becoming an advocate for oneself and on developing the skills needed in the workplace. It is also a time when dilemmas appear to families, dilemmas that are complex and often have no "right" solutions (Thorin, Yovanoff, & Irvin, 1996). Study Table 6.5, and think about how you might address each of these issues if you were the parent of a young adult with mental retardation.

TABLE 6.5

Transition Dilemmas

Wanting to:

Create opportunities for independence for the young adult, and wanting to assure that health and safety needs are met.

Have a life separate from the young adult, and wanting to do whatever is necessary to assure a good life for him or her.

Provide stability and predictability in the family life, and wanting to meet the changing needs of the young adult and family.

Create a separate social life for the young adult, and wanting to have less involvement in his or her life.

Avoid burn-out, and wanting to do everything possible for the young adult.

Maximize the young adult's growth and potential, and wanting to accept the young adult as he or she is.

Source: Adapted from "Dilemmas faced by families during their young adults' transitions to adulthood: A brief report" by E. Thorin, P. Yovanoff, and L. Irvin, 1996, *Mental Retardation, 34,* pp. 118–119. Reprinted by permission.

What are the indicators of successful transition for people with mental retardation? Some research conducted in England helps us better understand what targets should become part of the curriculum for these youngsters (Thomson, Ward, & Wishart, 1995). The following are at least some of those achievements:

- Employment
- Economic self-sufficiency
- Personal independence
- Social competence
- Adult role-taking at home and in society
- Postsecondary education

Let's look at two important targets that help individuals achieve these goals: self-advocacy abilities and vocational skills.

Self-Advocacy. Many adults with mental retardation, particularly those who were not trained as young children to make choices, continue to find that they need help in making decisions for themselves and assuming control of their own lives. In fact, although they might need it most, this group of people has been among the last to have **self-determination** become a target of instruction (Wehmeyer & Metzler, 1995). Self-determination refers to the attitudes and abilities required to act on one's own behalf, make decisions for oneself, and make choices. Although the normalization movement is well over two decades old, people with mental retardation typically do not have the experience or opportunity to

 MAKING CONNECTIONS

A section about self-determination can be found in Chapter 8.

self-determination. A set of behaviors that include making decisions, choosing preferences, and practicing self-advocacy.

make their own decisions or be independent. They often do not even get the chance to make simple decisions, like what movie to see, what restaurant to eat at, whether to go to church, or whom to visit—even when the person making the decision was hired to assist the person with mental retardation accomplish his or her needs (Wehmeyer & Metzler, 1995).

Many adults with mental retardation have found that they can achieve more independence and control of their lives if they receive support through the **self-advocacy movement**, which is comprised of self-help groups. The major goal of self-advocacy groups, which are located in almost every state, is to help individuals with mental retardation achieve equality, independence, and recognition as full citizens in society (Longhurst, 1994). These groups help one another solve individual problems, create leisure time activities, and develop friendships and supportive networks. These groups educate people with disabilities about their rights and help them address issues of personal concern. They are clearly one important support needed by many people with mental retardation and help them gain greater access to society.

 MAKING CONNECTIONS

Self-advocacy groups are also mentioned in the History section of this chapter.

Supported Employment. One question often asked by policymakers who are evaluating how government funding should be spent is: Can these adults financially support themselves? Or must they always depend on government or family aid? Jobs have become an increasingly important issue for these people, for many reasons. Jobs give them the opportunity to earn money, the opportunity for friendships, the opportunity to engage in the social activities of the community, and the opportunity to develop a sense of self-satisfaction and feelings of making a contribution. Unfortunately, jobs are not easy to find or to hold. People with disabilities have higher rates of unemployment than their peers, and individuals with mental retardation have higher unemployment rates than those with learning disabilities, emotional disturbance, or speech impairments (SRI, 1991). Females with disabilities suffer employment discrimination based not only on their disabilities but also on their gender. Young women with mental retardation have significantly lower rates of employment than young men with mental retardation (SRI, 1992). This may be partly due to the types of jobs available and the skills the applicants have for these positions.

One way to gain important vocational skills is through **supported employment** experiences. Through this system students are helped in locating jobs and also with developing the skills needed to be successful in that position. Many students with mental retardation may need the help of a **job developer** to discover or even design work that they can accomplish. A **job coach** might also be necessary to work alongside the individual, helping the person to learn all parts of the job.

Remember that individuals with mental retardation can lead satisfying lives as adults. They can work in jobs, establish close relationships with friends and family, live in their home communities, and pursue desired activities. Adults with a mild disability may require assistance only from time to time during their lives. Other individuals with mental retardation will always need assistance and support. Transition periods, especially transition to adulthood, appear to be times of increased stress for individuals with mental retardation and their families. Families, however, can play a crucial role in successful transitions for their sons and daughters (McNair & Rusch, 1991).

self-advocacy movement. A social and political movement started by and for people with mental retardation to speak for themselves on important issues such as housing, employment, legal rights, and personal relationships.

supported employment. Used in job training, whereby students are placed in paying jobs for which they receive significant assistance and support and the employer is helped with the compensation.

job developer. An individual who seeks out, shapes, and designs employment opportunities in the community for people with disabilities.

job coach. An individual who works alongside people with disabilities, helping them to learn all parts of a job.

Families

The families of individuals with mental retardation face special challenges. Most of these families require additional services and supports at some time, especially during times of transition, to effectively address the needs of the child with mental retardation and their own needs. These supports might include personal care, family support, respite care, financial allowances, subsidies, and in-home assistance (Birenbaum & Cohen, 1993). Many families also gain strength and information from organizations such as The Arc or other parent support and advocacy groups. However, it is the families themselves who provide the required day-to-day supports (Bradley, Knoll, & Agosta, 1992). Educators must recognize that these families provide long-lasting and sustaining life connections with their family members with disabilities long after the schooling years are over. Most individuals with disabilities receive considerable, vital support from their immediate and extended families throughout their lives. Often, educators only acknowledge the mother and her role in childrearing and caregiving (Beach Center, 1995a). This orientation must be broadened. The dilemmas faced by families of individuals with mental retardation can be complex and confusing, and their resolution requires the efforts of the entire family (Thorin, Yovanoff, & Irvin, 1996). So, in this section we draw your attention to the support given to family members with disabilities from fathers, grandparents, and siblings.

Family Support: Dads

Fathers are very important in the lives of their children, and this is true for children with and those without disabilities. Fathers of children with disabilities are as involved and spend about the same amount of time with their children as fathers who do not have children with disabilities (Beach Center, 1995b). They just do things differently. These fathers spend more time doing child care. They watch more TV and spend more time at home than other fathers. Those fathers who do help with the rearing of their children with disabilities also tend to have a higher level of satisfaction with their marriage (Willoughby & Glidden, 1995).

Fathers of these children, however, have a serious complaint about service providers: They believe that they are treated like second-class citizens (Beach Center, 1995b). They get the message that mothers are the "experts" about their children. One father even reports that a social worker thanked him for his cooperation and that the worker would check the accuracy of his answers with his wife. Some fathers believe that the predominately female fields that work with children with disabilities are not sensitive to the differences in fathers' emotional perspectives about their children with disabilities. Most fathers seem to understand the importance of their roles. They, more than service providers, know that it takes "two of us to handle all that was happening; service providers would just have to get to know me and learn to accept, if not like, the fact that I was involved with my daughter's life" (p. 4). Children who have positive relationships with their fathers tend to have higher achievement, are more motivated, and have better social skills than those who do not have a dad active in their lives (Beach Center, 1996c). Educators need to remember that fathers are an important part of the family support team. They need to be involved and included in their children's educational programs.

Family Support: Grandparents

Grandparents can be important members of the family support team, particularly if they live close to their grandchild with disabilities. The same can be said about the roles of extended family members in some cultures. When planning educational programs and collaborative activities with the home, educators should remember the entire family network. Grandparents, although often overlooked, often provide considerable assistance through babysitting, shopping, and financial support (Sandler, Warren, & Raver, 1995). Although there are some reports about grandparents who have difficulties accepting their grandchild's disabilities (even casting blame), there is more evidence that they can be a valuable resource and source of considerable support to their own children, the parents of the child with problems. Professionals should develop better strategies to involve grandparents, as they help build a strong family support system for each child with disabilities.

Family Support: Brothers and Sisters

Siblings of people with disabilities have not received much attention from researchers or policymakers. However, recent research shows that siblings play an important role in the lives of their brothers and sisters with disabilities, particularly those with mental retardation (Krauss, Seltzer, Gordon, & Friedman, 1996). When a family's children are all adults, siblings without disabilities maintain regular and personal contact with their brothers or sisters with mental retardation. Most nondisabled siblings provide emotional support and are very familiar with the needs of their siblings with mental retardation. For those whose brother or sister is still living at home, they stand ready to assume the care of their sibling when situations make it necessary. Many, 36 percent in one study, even intend to co-reside when their parents' health or status prevents their continuing to care for their son or daughter with disabilities. This is particularly true when the adult with mental retardation is in poor health. It is interesting that in most of these cases, their parents are making plans for their adult child with disabilities to live in publicly supported residential services, not co-reside with a sibling. The remainder of the siblings plan on living apart from their brother or sister but maintain an impressive degree of contact and involvement, most on a weekly basis. Policymakers and community service providers must come to understand and better appreciate the roles that siblings intend to take regarding the care of their brothers and sisters with disabilities.

 MAKING CONNECTIONS

In Chapter 3, review
• the Family section.
• the Tips for Teachers box.
Re-read the Personal Perspective in this chapter.

Technology

Modern technology can make a tremendous difference in the lives of individuals with mental retardation, and the range of technology that has made a difference is wide. Technology can be as simple as letting students with mental retardation use a calculator to perform arithmetic tasks, allowing them to compensate successfully for the difficulties they often face when having to solve mathematical problems used in important life skills like balancing a checkbook (Horton, Lovitt, & White, 1992). Technology benefiting this group of individuals can also be complex. For example, medical technology has provided interventions and techniques that lessen the impact of some causes and has *prevented* others. For example, the development of

MAKING CONNECTIONS

Medical technology used to prevent mental retardation is found in that section of this chapter.

MAKING CONNECTIONS

For more information about assistive technology and augmentative devices, see the Technology section in Chapter 5.

MAKING CONNECTIONS

Computer assisted instruction is discussed in the Technology section of Chapter 4.

shunt technology has prevented thousands of cases of mental retardation that were inevitable with the onset of hydrocephaly. Some medical techniques can now be performed in utero, before the baby is born. Recent advances in fetal tissue transplantation, fetal gene implant therapy, fetal corrective surgery, and fetal therapy are effective today and hold great promise for the future (Kolata, 1993). But, when we think of technology, we usually do not think of medical technology. We think of computers, and the applications of computer technology to individuals with disabilities and to classroom settings are far reaching as well.

The ready availability of computer technology has opened up communication possibilities for many students with mental retardation who are unable to communicate with others through speech (Parette & Angelo, 1996). The ability to communicate is essential to life satisfaction. It can make the difference between a sad, depressed, isolated child and a child who is an enthusiastic participant in the world. Computer technology allows many individuals with severe disabilities to communicate. Computers can be used as communication boards and to synthesize speech, to write, and to communicate with others who have computers. Computer technology has also empowered individuals with disabilities by putting their environment within their control. Modern computers can drive gadgets and toys and can perform complex functions that will make life better for all persons with disabilities. Touching a keyboard is no longer required; eye contact with the machine can cause the production of text or speech. Researchers are even developing ways to control a computer by merely thinking commands (Pollack, 1993).

When people think of technology and school, they usually think of computer-assisted or enhanced instruction. As time goes on, the availability and use of computers in all classrooms will increase. Teachers will need to possess considerable skills about when to use computers to assist instruction, to teach new skills, to serve as an information resource, and for drill and practice. And more importantly, they will need to become sophisticated in how to evaluate software for classroom use (Hickson, Blackman, & Reis, 1995). Table 6.6 gives a form helpful to teachers when analyzing the benefits of computer applications for classroom use.

Let's look at different types of applications and their potential benefits. Computer-assisted instruction can be grouped by different functions: drill and practice, tutorial instruction, games, simulations, and programming (Hickson, Blackman, & Reis, 1995). Drill and practice allows students to master and become proficient at tasks. Although little different from traditional workbooks, they allow students to progress at their own pace, giving fewer items if they are not needed and more if mastery is not achieved in typical time. Tutorial instruction allows for students to skip items they have mastered on their own or receive more practice and instruction on segments of skills where instruction is still required. Games offer interesting formats for drill and practice. They often provide fast-paced activities, immediate feedback, and built-in evaluation. Many students find them fun and highly motivating, certainly more so than the traditional sets of dittoed worksheets. Simulation technology is developing, so students will be able to learn skills in close to real-life contexts. By using interactive video technology, skills like banking, safety, shopping, and navigating communities can be taught in classroom settings. Finally, teachers are now able to program for individual students' needs, and students with disabilities can create their own graphics and computer programs. There is no question that the future holds exciting new applications for technology in classroom settings. Teachers' challenge will be to remain current about what is available and clever in making decisions about what hardware and which software will benefit their students.

TABLE 6.6

Sample Computer Software Review/Analysis Form

1. Clearly identify the software being reviewed. Specify the name of the program, the publisher, the address of the publisher, and the hardware and memory requirements of the software.

2. Clearly specify the overall goals and/or instructional objectives of the software. Is this information explicitly provided?

3. What type of educational software does this program represent? Check one of the following:

_____ drill and practice   _____ simulation

_____ tutorial instruction   _____ programming tool

_____ game   _____ other (describe)

4. Clearly specify the target population(s) for whom this software was developed. Is this information explicitly provided? Was it developed for individuals with disabilities? Type? Specify the targeted age and/or functioning level.

5. Estimate the approximate reading grade level required for use of this program.

6. Estimate the approximate arithmetic grade level required for use of this program.

7. Are the instructions clear and easy to follow? Provide examples.

8. Are the activities appropriately sequenced? Provide examples.

9. Is appropriate feedback and reinforcement provided? Give examples.

10. Does the program appear to be technically adequate (i.e., free of "bugs")?

11. Are data available on the effectiveness of this program? (Response to this question may require a search of the literature.)

12. Overall, would you recommend the use of this software with individuals with mental retardation? In light of the above criteria, specify the range of age and functioning levels for which it might be appropriate (if any).

Source: From *Mental retardation: Foundations of educational programming* (p. 139) by L. Hickson, L. S. Blackman, & E. M Reis, 1995, Boston: Allyn & Bacon.

Concepts and Controversy: Eugenics and Its Logical Extension

In 1927, under a Supreme Court approved law, Virginia had Virginia Carrie Buck sterilized after her diagnosis as being "feebleminded" and the birth of her illegitimate child. She was also committed to an institution for people with mental retardation. It is estimated that following this precedent, some 50,000 people were sterilized in the United States (Smith, 1994, 1995). In 1933, the German government, using the Virginia law as its model, passed a sterilization law that sanctioned Nazi sterilization of some 2 million people who were considered defective between 1933 and 1945. The justification for this action (as explained in Hitler's

 MAKING CONNECTIONS

Review the History section of this chapter for more information about the eugenics movement and people with mental retardation.

book *Mein Kampf*) was that the "race" needed to be preserved and protected: Defective people should not be allowed to propagate equally defective offspring. The eugenics movement—which was extremely popular in the United States, France, and Germany throughout the beginning of the twentieth century—supported the position that *all* human characteristics were attributed to heredity and genetic determination. The only way to stop the destruction of society because of an overpopulation of incompetent people was to prohibit their "breeding." The one way to guarantee this event was sterilization.

Of course, support for the eugenics movement diminished after World War II and the atrocities of the Nazi government were revealed. However, some of the attitudes from this movement remain. For example, a survey of obstetricians conducted in 1972 found that 97 percent of them supported the sterilization of welfare mothers who had illegitimate children (Rodriguez-Trias, 1982). In a 1991 issue of Mensa's Eugenics Special Interest Group's (ESIG) publication, *ESIG Bulletin*, it is recommended that people with Down syndrome not be allowed to reproduce. Herrnstein and Murray (1994), in their book *The Bell Curve*, revive the notion that intelligence is more closely related to heredity than to factors in the environment. Are these isolated and rare examples? Rock (1996) points out that such attitudes are not restricted to birth, but also to death. For example, in discussions about providing life-sustaining medical treatments to individuals with mental retardation, quality-of-life issues qualitatively different from those for people without disabilities are often topics of concern. Who has the right to make decisions about whether specific individuals should become mothers and fathers? How should medical decisions be made? Should benefits to society enter into the decision-making process?

~~ SUMMARY ~~

People with mental retardation have significantly impaired intellectual functioning, have problems with adaptive skills, and require a variety of supports to achieve independence as adults and assume their places in modern society. Their disability must have been manifested during the developmental period, from birth to age 18. But people with mental retardation are people first with all the emotions, motivations, and complexities of any human being. Thus attempts to provide education and habilitation to students with mental retardation must be based on the realization of the fundamental similarities of all people.

FOCUS QUESTIONS

Self-Test Questions

▶ *What are the key differences between the two AAMR definitions of mental retardation?*

The American Association on Mental Retardation (AAMR) has offered definitions of this disability since 1921 and since 1959 has included problems with adaptive behavior as a characteristic of the condition. The organization's two most recent definitions were developed in 1983 and in 1992. The 1983 definition has three major components: significant subaverage general intellectual functioning, concurrent deficits in adaptive behavior, and origination before the age of 18. It also divides people with this disability by four levels that are defined by scores individuals receive on standardized tests of intelligence: mild, moderate, severe, and profound. This definition is driven by IQ scores. The 1992 AAMR definition is more flexible, although it still requires that individuals identified as having this disability obtain scores on tests of intelligence somewhere below 70 and 75. It is more specific about the areas that comprise adaptive behavior and requires that an individual have problems in at least two of these areas. In addition, the AAMR does not allow individuals to qualify for mental retardation services who have low IQ scores but no difficulties with adaptive behavior. The most unique aspect of the newer definition focuses on individuals' needs for support to function independently at home, at work, and in the community.

▶ *How are the causes of mental retardation organized, and what are some of the specific causes within each group?*

The 1992 AAMR definition classifies causes of mental retardation into three major groups that relate to the time of onset of the disability: prenatal, perinatal, and postnatal. Prenatal causes happen before the child is born and may be caused by factors such as genetic errors, toxins, disease, or neural tube defects. Some examples of genetic causes are Down syndrome and Fragile X syndrome. Other genetic causes create predispositions to mental retardation from toxins. PKU is such an example. Toxins are very dangerous to unborn babies. Expectant mothers drinking alcohol can cause fetal alcohol syndrome (FAS). Other drugs taken by expectant mothers, including tobacco, can also cause mental retardation. Diseases—like meningitis, rubella, and measles—can cause retardation, depending on which prenatal period the mother contracted them. Most of these causes of mental retardation can be prevented by vaccines. Other diseases, like AIDS, that are passed on to the unborn child can be devastating as well. Injuries at birth or during the birth process (perinatal causes) often result from oxygen deprivation. Low birthweight is also associated with cognitive impairments that affect these children throughout their lives. Postnatal causes can include child abuse and neglect, accidents, and toxins in the environment.

▶ *Why is it important to identify additional causes of mental retardation?*

Many of the causes of mental retardation can be prevented, and more causes need to be discovered so preventive measures can be developed. It is important to recognize that about 50 percent of the cases of mental retardation could have been prevented by screening pregnant women and their babies for risk factors, protecting children from disease through vaccinations, providing positive and nurturing home and school environments, and implementing safety measures. Most of the effective preventive measures now commonly applied were developed in response to a known cause. For example, mental retardation from PKU is prevented because researchers discovered that the amino acid in milk harms those children who are genetically predisposed to this problem. Shunts and the operations that allow for the safe drainage of excess fluid from the brain were developed when hydrocephaly was understood. History has shown that when a cause is identified, preventive measures soon follow. Increasing the research dollars invested in identifying the causes of mental retardation would greatly decrease the number of cases of this disability.

▶ *What are the learning characteristics of students with mental retardation?*

The most common characteristic of students with mental retardation is limited cognitive ability. Cognitive impairments manifest themselves in many ways. Clearly, it makes learning more difficult. It also affects memory and the ability to generalize learning to different settings, similar skills, or to different individuals. A common, associated problem is in the area of communication. Both delayed language and speech problems are common among this group of learners. It is also important to recognize that cognitive impairments in these individuals result in difficulties with the ten adaptive skill areas: communication, self-care, home-living, social community use, self-direction, health and safety, functional academics, leisure, and work. Difficulties in adaptive behavior can result in limitations in independence as adults, and for this reason many of these individuals need some support in some adaptive skill areas.

▶ *How can educators be more effective when working with families of students with mental retardation?*

Educators who develop meaningful partnerships with their students' families find that they are better able to meet their students' educational needs. Unfortunately, many educators do not recognize all significant members of the family unit. For many students with disabilities, the immediate and extended family provide significant support. Family involvement should include not just the mother, but also the father, brothers and sisters, and grandparents. In some cases, it would also include aunts and uncles if they are involved in the student's life on a frequent basis. The support that family members provide extend far beyond the school day and extend to the years after school is completed. Members of the family unit should be included in informational and planning meetings about a student's educational programs, respected as valuable members of the student's support network, and involved in evaluating the effectiveness of school.

Challenge Question

▶ *What are some examples of the four levels of support, and how do they make a difference in the lives of people with mental retardation?*

The primary goal for most individuals with mental retardation is to achieve a life of autonomy and self-direction. Opportunities to live in normalized living arrangements in communities, to work, and to have satisfying personal relationships are extremely impor-

tant. Achieving these aims requires support for many of these people, some of which are naturally available and others needing to be arranged. Types of support include natural (from family, friends, and neighbors), nonpaid (neighborhood and community groups), generic (supports everyone has access to), and specialized (disability-specific). The four levels of support identified in the 1992 AAMR definition are intermittent, limited, extensive, and pervasive. Some individuals need only intermittent (or short-term) support during times of crisis or transition, for example, when they are moving or finding a new job. Others need limited support that is consistent over time (not intermittent) when they are learning new job skills. Extensive and pervasive support includes regular involvement in the person's life and may include supervised living arrangements, money management, and leisure time activities. Support for any individual can be provided on a pervasive basis for some skills and on an intermittent basis for other skills. The intent is to create a flexible and responsive support system that allows the person to live, work, and play in the community with as much independence as possible.

～～ *SUPPLEMENTARY RESOURCES* ～～

Scholarly Books

Drew, C. J., Logan, D. R., & Hardman, M. L. (1992). *Mental retardation: A life cycle approach.* New York: Merrill, an imprint of Macmillan.

Hickson, L., Blackman, L. S., & Reis, E. M. (1995). *Mental retardation: Foundations of educational programming.* Boston: Allyn and Bacon.

Polloway, E., & Patton, J. (1996). *Strategies for teaching learners with special needs.* Upper Saddle River: Merrill, an imprint of Macmillan.

Popular Books

Bérubé, M. (1996). *Life as we know it: A father, a family, and an exceptional child.* New York: Pantheon Books.

Hunt, N. (1967). *The world of Nigel Hunt: The diary of a mongoloid youth.* New York: Garrett.

Keyes, D. (1966). *Flowers for Algernon.* New York: Bantam.

Meyers, R. (1978). *Like normal people.* New York: McGraw-Hill.

Perske, R. (1986). *Don't stop the music.* Nashville: Abingdon Press.

Sachs, O. (1987). *The man who mistook his wife for a hat and other clinical tales.* New York: Harper & Row.

Steinbeck, J. (1937). *Of mice and men.* New York: Viking Press.

Videos

Charly. (1968). ABC—Selmur Pictures—CBS/Fox.

L'Enfant Sauvage (The wild child). (1969). F. Truffaut (Director).

Being there. (1979). Lorimar/CBS/Fox.

Of mice and men. (1992). MGM/United Artists.

What's eating Gilbert Grape? (1993). Paramount.

Professional, Parent, and Consumer Organizations and Agencies

American Association on Mental Retardation (AAMR)
1719 Kalorama Road NW
Washington, DC 20009
Phone: (800) 424-3688
E-mail: aamr@access.digex.net
Web site: http://www.aamr.org

The Arc (formerly the Association for Retarded Citizens of the United States, ARC-US)
P.O. Box 6109
Arlington, TX 76005
Phone: (800) 433-5255
E-mail: thearc@metronet.com
Web site: http://TheArc.org/welcome .html

American Association of University Affiliated Programs for Persons with Developmental Disabilities
8605 Cameron Street, Suite 406
Silver Spring, MD 20910
Phone: (301) 588-8252
E-mail: aaupjones@aol.com
Web site: http://www.waisman.wisc.edu/aauap/index.html

Division on Mental Retardation Council for Exceptional Children
1920 Association Drive
Reston,VA 22091
Phone: (703) 620-3660
Web site: http://www.cec.sped.org

Michelangelo Buonarroti. *Pieta* (detail). 1499.

Michelangelo Buonarroti "was probably the greatest artistic genius who ever lived. He has left imperishable work in sculpture, painting, architecture and poetry: no one else has mastered at his level of attainment all four means of esthetic communication" (Coughlan, 1966, p. 6). No one can account for or explain such genius; it is merely for people to marvel. His talent was recognized when he was a very young child, although his father would have preferred his assuming a more noble career. The *Pietà* was unveiled in 1499 at the Vatican when Michelangelo was 24. This photograph shows a detail of the *Pietà*. In 1501, in Florence, he began work on the magnificent and personal sculpture, the *David*. Although he spent many years in Rome painting the ceiling of the Sistine Chapel, he always considered himself first a Florentine and a sculptor (Reynal and Company, 1966).

Giftedness and Talent Development

ADVANCE ORGANIZERS

▼ OVERVIEW

Although educational services for gifted students are neither protected nor funded by IDEA, many of the basic principles of special education are applied to this population. In most states, these services are considered part of special education. Currently, professionals in gifted education are questioning the basic tenets of their field: who they serve, what education should comprise, and where services are delivered. Current discussions focus education attention on the development of talent (skills and achievement) with youngsters who possess high potential and abilities.

▼ FOCUS QUESTIONS

SELF-TEST QUESTIONS

▶ Regardless of the definition used, what descriptors can be used for gifted and talented individuals?

▶ What factors can inhibit giftedness and talent development?

▶ Why are educators concerned about issues related to underrepresentation and the various subgroups of gifted learners?

▶ What are three gifted education approaches, and how do they differ from one another?

▶ What are the four service delivery models often used in gifted education, and how do they differ from one another?

CHALLENGE QUESTION

▶ Why, throughout the history of the United States, has there been such an inconsistent commitment to gifted education?

A *Personal Perspective*: Students Attending a Class for Gifted Children Share Their Thoughts

Gifted middle school students were interviewed by their teacher. Their responses reveal their feelings about their education and what it is like to be identified as gifted. These children are sixth and seventh graders, attend the same school, and have the same teacher of the gifted for their special education classes.

How does it make you feel to be called gifted?

ROBERT MONTANO: It doesn't really feel any different than how I used to feel, but it makes me feel like good and happy when people say I'm smart and gifted.

KIMBERLY SILVER: It feels strange because I'm the same as everybody else—like everybody's gifted somehow.

JOSHUA BARNARD: Kinda funny because the other kids make fun of you. I guess they are kinda jealous.

ROY BERNALES: I don't know—normal. Just feels like when someone calls me by my name—no different, too.

MICHELLE GOMEZ: It feels neat because you're in higher classes and sometimes you have more fun than in general classes.

DECTRA DIXON: Sometimes it makes you feel like you're ahead of other students. Sometimes they call you nerds, but I like the word GIFTED even if they do call me a nerd.

MARTY FREDERICKSON: I feel singled out. I feel pressured.

JESSICA LUCERO: It feels nice because you have a gift and you should be proud of it.

CHRISTY OLLOWAY: Like everybody thinks you're smart and they ask you to do stuff. Sometimes it bugs me because you don't want to answer the questions, but you're expected to.

What do you like best about your time in gifted class?

GUADALUPE VELASQUEZ: I like it because we dissect things, and it's fun in here, and I think that they teach you more.

KIMBERLY SILVER: I can get more help if I need it, and the teacher explains better.

JOSHUA BARNARD: I like being with only a few people, and I like the teacher. It's nice to be with other people who understand you.

ALIMA MILLS: Things you do in this class are interesting and fun, but still learning.

ROY BERNALES: I like it because there aren't a lot of people—it's not noisy.

DECTRA DIXON: You learn more stuff than in your general classes because in the other one they mess around and in the gifted you have to be serious about what you're doing.

JEREMY CORDOVA: Work is challenging, but more fun. Also, I like working in a small group.

CHRISTY OLLOWAY: You have to try to work extra hard and you feel good about being here.

What does it mean to you to be gifted?

GUADALUPE VELASQUEZ: It means you're more educated. You know more in that subject.

KIMBERLY SILVER: Smart in a different way. Like a different way of learning.

ALIMA MILLS: It's easier for you to learn things, and you are a little smarter than others.

ROY BERNALES: You're special. People think you're all smart and stuff.

MICHELLE GOMEZ: It's like you're smarter in some sections than other people, and you get to show it in higher classes instead of hiding it.

DECTRA DIXON: That you have a faster learning ability than other students.

MARTY FREDERICKSON: Being smarter. Being able to do more. Being singled out.

1. What are the differences between what the children think the term *gifted* means and what it feels like to them to be called gifted?

2. What do these children perceive to be the differences between general and special education?

3. What do you think being called gifted means?

Across time, people living in different periods of history have sometimes exhibited extraordinary levels of particular skills, abilities, or talents. For example, the Indus civilization in North Africa between 2400 and 1800 B.C. demonstrated advanced concepts of city planning and architecture. Indus cities were built on a regular grid with major streets running north and south. A drainage system served an entire city, and each home had a bathroom and toilet connected to a sewer system. During the time of the ancient Greeks, athletic prowess and excellence in the fine arts reached peak levels, obvious in the legacies of their civilization: their philosophical writings, dramas, architecture, and sculpture. During the time of the ancient Chinese, literary works, architecture, music, and art far surpassed the standards of other cultures. During the second century B.C., the Chinese wrote books, using silk for paper, on topics such as astronomy, medicine, and pharmacology. By the first century B.C., books on mathematics and other topics were produced on paper. Similarly, the temples of the ancient Egyptians stand as testimony to the skills of architects, engineers, and artisans.

A concentration of particular abilities and outstanding achievement can be observed during other segments of history as well. During the height of the Roman civilization, the number of great orators far surpassed the numbers found in many other periods of history. Between A.D. 300 and 750, the Teotihuacan culture in Mexico developed a sophisticated craft industry that produced figurines, pottery, and tools for export throughout the region. During the Renaissance in Europe, a great number of fine artists—Michelangelo, Leonardo da Vinci, Raphael, and others—created beautiful paintings, sculpture, scientific inventions, homes, palaces, churches, and public buildings. Almost two hundred years ago a concentration of musical protégés (Handel, Haydn, Mozart, Chopin, Liszt) created work that is still valued and enjoyed. Today, computer developers, software designers, and Internet innovators amaze us with their brilliance and technical aptitude.

Why have there been periods in history when particular talents are displayed in abundance? One answer is that periods of brilliance result from a combination of excellent early opportunities, early and continuing guidance, and instruction for the individual (Morelock & Feldman, 1997; Simonton, 1997). These features must be coupled with a major interest of society in that particular ability, opportunities to continually practice and progress, close association and interchange with others with similar abilities, and strong success experiences. Certainly, individuals who demonstrate superiority in a particular area must also have innate talent, but it seems that traits valued by a culture emerge with some frequency when importance is placed on them. The discussions in this chapter will lead to a better understanding of gifted individuals and the conditions necessary for them to develop their talents and make significant contributions to society.

Giftedness and Talents Defined

Individuals who have high levels of intelligence, are high achievers academically, are extremely creative, or have unique talents are not handicapped in the sense of having a disability. Certainly, they do not face the limitations or the difficulties that most children who receive special education services do. However, many of these individuals, because of their differences, are handicapped by society and our educational systems. They can be stifled by educational approaches that do not challenge or develop their cognitive abilities or that do not allow them to learn

MAKING CONNECTIONS

For a review of IDEA, special
education services, and gifted
education, see Special Education
Defined and Legislation sections
(Chapter 1).

MAKING CONNECTIONS

For more information about inclusion
and other debates about educational
placement options, see

- the inclusions sections (Educational
  Interventions) in every chapter about
  disabilities,
- History of Special Education section
  (Chapter 1),
- Education Environments (Special
  Education Services) (Chapter 2),
- Concepts and Controversy section
  (Chapters 1 & 2).

MAKING CONNECTIONS

For another discussion on IQ, see
Fundamental Concepts in the
Identification section (Chapter 6).

gifted. A term describing individuals with high levels of intelligence, outstanding abilities, and capacity for high performance.

academic content at an accelerated pace. Sometimes directly and sometimes indirectly, peers, teachers, and parents discourage them from developing their abilities maximally. Some believe that the result is a significant loss to the individuals and to society in general (Gallagher, 1985).

> Failure to help handicapped children reach their potential is a personal tragedy for them and their families; failure to help gifted children reach their potential is a societal tragedy, the extent of which is difficult to measure but which is surely great. How can we measure the loss of the sonata unwritten, the curative drug undiscovered, the absence of political insight? They are the difference between what we are and what we could be as a society. (Gallagher, 1985, p. 4)

Types of Giftedness and Talents

The field of gifted education is currently experiencing a time of transition (Coleman, 1996; Feldhusen, 1995). Accepted philosophies, beliefs about what the concept of "giftedness" means, and the value of gifted education are being challenged. The basic foundations of this educational system are being questioned by education professionals. Gallagher (1996, p. 234) distilled the fundamental issues into the following questions that this field must address:

- Is there such a thing as giftedness?
- If there is such an entity, can we find students who possess it or them?
- If we can find such children, can we provide them with quality differentiated services?
- Is it morally right or correct that we put such programs or services into action?

Throughout this chapter, we address these questions and hope that you will develop your own answers. Remember, at the present time the professionals working in gifted education are not in agreement, so there is no "right" answer. Let's start by coming to an understanding of how concepts of "gifted" and "talented" have been defined across this century. Such definitions are important because they reflect beliefs about who qualifies and what services they should receive. Across time, the definitions of giftedness have ranged from a narrow view based exclusively on cognition, reasoning, and the score a person receives on a test of intelligence to a multidimensional view of intelligence, aptitudes, abilities, and talent development.

Traditional Perspectives. As early as 1925, Terman studied individuals with exceptionally high cognitive aptitude. He considered children **gifted** who score in the highest 1 percent (having scores over 140) on an intelligence (IQ) test. Terman's definition reflects a narrow view of giftedness in which high intelligence is closely associated with high academic achievement. In addition to tying giftedness to a score on an IQ test, Terman also believed that intelligence is a fixed characteristic, one people are born with and one that does not change positively or negatively across time. From his perspective, intelligence is determined solely by heredity; it is a trait inherited from your parents. Lastly, this view of giftedness reflects many biases about women and people of underrepresented ethnic groups that were prevalent in his time.

Today's professional educators are much less confident than Terman was in the results from standardized tests, believing that such tests can bias against individuals who are not from the dominant American culture. Some tests identify as gifted only persons who have received a strong educational foundation, and this is

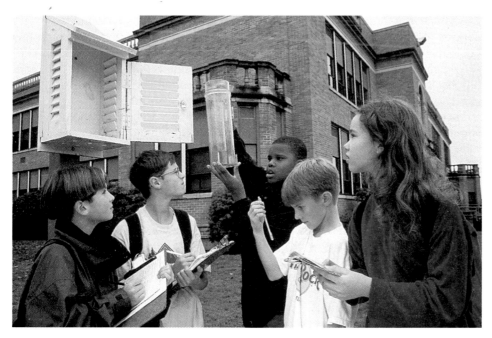

Learning new skills and solving problems does not always have to happen inside the walls of a traditional classroom.

only one bias that standardized tests present to culturally and linguistically diverse children and youngsters with disabilities. Our understanding of intelligence has changed since Terman's time. In contrast to Terman's view, researchers now believe that intelligence, like any other trait, is influenced by both genetics and environment (Hunsaker, 1995). It is no longer thought that IQ is a fixed characteristic of the individual. Even though his definition is often criticized, Terman's longitudinal research with gifted individuals continues to be referred to and respected in the professional literature.

In a move toward a less restrictive perspective of giftedness, Sidney Marland, then U.S. Commissioner of Education, offered the nation a definition of the gifted and talented to supplant the Terman definition. The 1972 Marland definition, with minor variations, is still the most widely accepted and is used as the basis for most states' current definitions (Marland, 1972, p. 10):

> Gifted and talented children are those identified by professionally qualified persons who by virtue of outstanding abilities are capable of high performance. These are children who require differentiated educational programs and services beyond those normally provided by the regular school program in order to realize their contribution to self and society. Children capable of high performance include those with demonstrated achievement and/or potential ability in any of the following areas singly or in combination:
>
> 1. General intellectual aptitude.
> 2. Specific academic aptitude.
> 3. Creative or productive thinking.
> 4. Leadership ability.
> 5. Visual and performing arts.

Notice that there is no reference to a minimal IQ score in this definition of giftedness. In addition, this definition, unlike most presented in the chapters in this book about disabilities, includes a statement that these youngsters should be educated differently from their classmates. The assumption is that under the right conditions (good instructional programs, student motivation, and interest), these students will show overall accelerated performance. This suggestion about a difference between potential and performance implies that if the educational system is not responsive to students' individual needs, achievement will not reflect aptitude and underachievement will occur. Also note that Marland's definition includes discussion of two other issues: (1) who should receive special education services and (2) what that education should comprise.

Broadened Concepts. Most researchers today believe that giftedness is multidimensional, with high academic aptitude or intelligence being only one factor. For example, Renzulli (1978; Renzulli & Reis, 1997) suggested that those who have three clusters of characteristics—above-average intelligence, high **creativity**, and substantial task commitment—should be considered gifted. Certainly, Renzulli's view of giftedness is broader than Terman's. As you can see from Renzulli's graphic illustration shown in Figure 7.1, though, some individuals who have obtained high scores on tests of intelligence might not meet his other qualifications for giftedness. However, Renzulli's approach to gifted education is more inclusive than others, for he advocates that 15 to 20 percent of U.S. schoolchildren

~~~

FIGURE 7.1

Renzulli's Three-Ring Concept Of Giftedness

The ingredients of giftedness

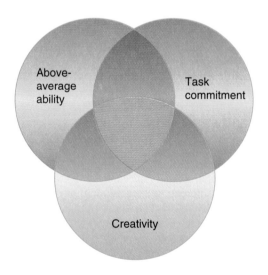

Above-average general ability

creativity. A form of intelligence characterized by advanced divergent thought, the production of many original ideas, and the ability to develop flexible and detailed responses and ideas.

Source: "What Makes Giftedness: Reexamining A Definition" by J. S. Renzulli, 1978, *Phi Delta Kappan, 60,* p. 182. Reprinted by permission.

should receive enhanced educational services that include many opportunities to develop creativity, critical-thinking, and problem-solving skills.

Now let's look at an even more multidimensional view of abilities. Gardner, in 1983, proposed an even broader view of intelligence and giftedness. Although he first proposed his theory of multiple intelligences over fifteen years ago, in a book entitled *Frames of Mind* (Gardner, 1983), it is now receiving considerable attention. According to his multidimensional approach to intelligence, which provides an alternative view to the traditional one of IQ, "human cognitive competence is better described as a set of abilities, talents, or mental skills that we have chosen to call intelligences" (Ramos-Ford & Gardner, 1991, p. 56). Through careful study of human behavior and performance, Gardner concludes that there are seven dimensions of intelligence and that a person can be gifted in any one or more of these areas. A summary of the seven intelligence areas is presented in Table 7.1. By studying this table, you should be able to see how some gifted youngsters are excluded when traditional views of giftedness are applied, resulting in their not receiving the educational services they need to develop their unique abilities and talents.

TABLE 7.1

Gardner's Seven Intelligences

Intelligence	Explanation*	Components	Adult Roles
1. Verbal-linguistic	The ability to use language in a number of ways	Syntax, semantics, pragmatics, written and oral language	Novelist, lecturer, lawyer, lyricist
2. Logical-mathematical	The ability to reason and recognize patterns	Deductive reasoning, inductive reasoning, computation	Mathematician, physicist
3. Visual-spatial	The ability to see the world and re-create it	Ability to represent and manipulate spatial configurations, interrelationship of parts	Architect, engineer, mechanic, navigator, sculptor, chess player
4. Body-kinesthetic	The ability to use the body and hands skillfully	Ability to use all or part of one's body	Dancer, athlete, mime, surgeon
5. Musical-rhythmic	The ability to perceive the world through its rhythm	Pitch discrimination; ability to hear themes in music; sensitivity to rhythm, texture, and timbre; production of music through performance or composition	Musician, composer, singer
6. Interpersonal	The ability to notice and respond to other people's needs	Ability to understand and act productively on others' actions and motivations	Teacher, therapist, clergy, politician, salesperson
7. Intrapersonal	The ability to understand one's own feelings	Understanding of self	

*Source: "Opportunities to Learn through Multiple Intelligences," (p. 1) by A. D. Morgan, Fall 1994, *School Renewal Update*, Effective Schools Unit, New Mexico State Department of Education.

MAKING CONNECTIONS

For more about the debates about special education services and where they should be delivered, see
• the Inclusion sections (Educational Interventions) in every chapter about disabilities,
• History of Special Education section (Chapter 1),
• Education Environments in the Special Education Services section (Chapter 2),
• Concepts and Controversy section (Chapters 1 & 2).
To review how many experts in gifted education feel about this debate, reread Gallagher's questions at the beginning of this section (Defined).

Paradigm Shifts. As we mentioned at the beginning of this section, gifted education is in a state of transition, self-analysis, and challenge. Some (Magolin, 1996; Sapon-Shevin, 1996) believe that gifted education should be eliminated because it represents a form of legalized tracking that could be a way to disguise racial segregation in school settings. (See the Focus on Diversity box for suggestions about ways to minimized such bias.) Critics also argue that gifted education is elitist, morally incorrect, unfair, and damaging to general education students who would benefit from more access to these peers. They also maintain that the general education environment and curriculum will be enhanced when more of the gifted instructional methodology is incorporated into these classrooms' educational programs.

Although such issues are not yet resolved, important considerations have been raised that support special education and an array of services for gifted students (Borland, 1996; Gallagher, 1996). Consider these provocative questions and reach your own conclusions:

■ Is gifted education and the removal of gifted students from the general education classroom for any time during the school day racist? Or, is not providing differentiated services to those students whose families cannot afford private schooling racist?

■ Is gifted education merely a form of tracking? Or, is it feasible to expect one setting, one broadly prepared teacher, and one curriculum to accept the primary educational needs of a heterogeneous group of students who have a great disparity of learning styles and achievement performance?

■ Is it necessary to eliminate gifted education services to bring quality to general education? Or, can the school reform movement be orchestrated along with gifted education services to blend with general education where appropriate and meet the individual needs of students when such specialization is appropriate?

■ Is gifted education (which singles out children of affluence, prepares them for leadership, and provides them with differentiated instruction) morally wrong, a philosophy contributing to inequality, evil social outcomes, and societal oppression? Or, are such points of view misplaced interpretations of equity and equality.

■ Is gifted education unfair to typical learners, making them feel bad because they were not selected as being special or because they were made aware that they could not perform a task (playing a violin, throwing a football, solving calculus problems) as well as someone else? Or, is it unfair to gifted learners not to challenge and accelerate them through an enriched and diversified instructional program that is deep in content and thinking skills?

So, what is the likely future of gifted education? Of course, no one knows for sure, and, most likely, some different options will be implemented in specific locales. If history is any judge of the future, even in states or school districts where gifted education has been eliminated, it will return. Here, the most important question is, "when?" not "if?" Support for educational services for gifted youngsters have waxed and waned since this nation's founding. It is likely that a new conceptual framework for gifted education will be adopted. At least one framework is emerging and gaining considerable support although specific models and interpretations are still developing and being proposed.

 MAKING CONNECTIONS

See also the History section of this chapter for more information about the U.S.'s inconsistent commitment to gifted education.

paradigm shifts. A change in conceptual framework that is a basic understanding or explanation for a field of study.

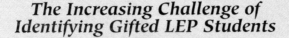
The Increasing Challenge of Identifying Gifted LEP Students

"In the next few decades, it will be virtually impossible for a professional educator to serve in a public school setting, or even any private school context, in which the students are not racially, culturally, or linguistically diverse" (Garcia, 1994, p. 13). By the year 2000, our nation's schools will serve 6 million students with limited English proficiency (LEP); by 2026, estimates place that figure at 15 million or 25 percent of the school population. In California today, the native language of about 40 percent of those children entering school is not English, and in Southern California schools, as an example, over ninety different languages are spoken. Although many of these students are gifted, it is difficult to assess their potential and few guidelines are available, and the challenge is increased by the diversity of languages and cultures present. Being more responsive to these children's needs will require teacher training, improvement in assessment tools and procedures (tests, rating scales, checklists, inventories), the use of subjective measures (parent ratings, teaching ratings, community nominations), and authentic forms of talent demonstration (Kitano & Espinosa, 1995).

 MAKING CONNECTIONS

Information about multicultural assessment is also found in
- Identification (Defined) (Chapter 3),
- most of the Focus on the Diversity boxes found in each chapter of this text.

The concept of **talent development** is gaining acceptance and may well be the focus of new innovative efforts for able youngsters. Feldhusen (1995) believes that the development of talent is the responsibility of the home, school, and community. It is for family members, stimulating teachers, peers who value developing abilities, and experts who are successful in a variety of fields who serve as mentors to help students develop their aptitudes into outstanding abilities and achievements. The Purdue Pyramid (see Figure 7.2) shows one way to think of talent development. Acceptance is the foundation all children need to develop their abilities; the vertical rays represent the wide array of learning experiences required to develop talent; these experiences lead to the necessary self-understanding of the talents and abilities possessed by gifted individuals; and finally the importance of commitment from individuals to develop their abilities into skills and talents is stressed.

According to experts like Treffinger and Feldhusen (1996), this new orientation toward talent development will shift and broaden the focus of gifted education. The goal will no longer be solely the development of intellect and academic achievement, but will also include all areas of human activity (e.g., vocational and career domains, art, social-interpersonal skills). Feldhusen (1992) proposed four basic domains that schools can address: academic, artistic, vocational, and personal-social. What might the areas of focus be under this new endeavor toward talent development? Gagné (1996) proposed talent fields relevant to schoolchildren for development: academics, games of strategy (chess, puzzles, video games), technology, arts, social action, business, and athletics. Gardner (Ramos-Ford &

 MAKING CONNECTIONS

For more information about multiple intelligences theory, review Table 7.1.

talent development. The process of translating ability into achievement.

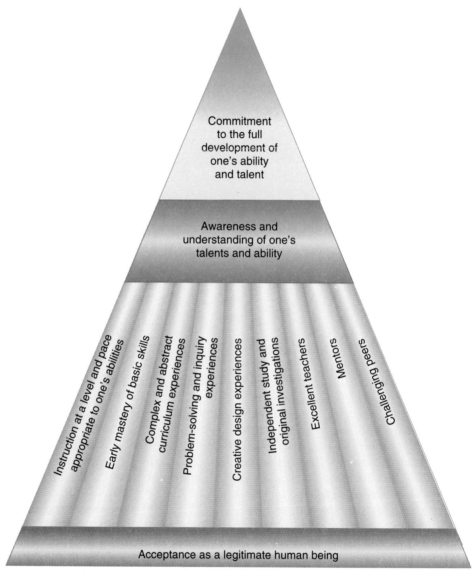

FIGURE 7.2

The Purdue Pyramid

Commitment to the full development of one's ability and talent

Awareness and understanding of one's talents and ability

Instruction at a level and pace appropriate to one's abilities

Early mastery of basic skills

Complex and abstract curriculum experiences

Problem-solving and inquiry experiences

Creative design experiences

Independent study and original investigations

Excellent teachers

Mentors

Challenging peers

Acceptance as a legitimate human being

Source: "Talent Development: The New Direction in Gifted Education" by J. F. Feldhusen, 1995, *Roeper Review, 18,* p. 92. Reprinted by permission.

Gardner, 1991) would probably propose focusing on talent development for each of his seven multiple intelligences. Van Tassel-Baska (1995) advocated an integrated curriculum for talent development that includes the following dimensions: advanced content knowledge, higher-order thinking and processing skills, learning experiences developed along themes and ideas relevant to real-world issues.

Will the term *gifted* be replaced by the term *talent*? Gagné (1996) thinks this unlikely. He believes that gifted education is so much a part of everyday language that it will be retained. However, he believes, as do many other experts in gifted education (Feldhusen, 1995; Van Tassel-Baska, 1995), that the terms *giftedness* and *talent* need to be differentiated. Giftedness would be used to describe high, natural abilities, but not for a single dimension or trait. Talent would refer to a high level of performance and well-developed skills. Giftedness or aptitude without the work, effort, and unique experiences does not lead to superior mastery or talent development in a particular field of human activity. In other words, for Gagné, gift-edness refers to measures of potential and talent is reserved for achievement. For these bright and able students to reach their potential, to turn aptitude into talent and achievement, is not a simple feat. Gallagher (1996) believes that such accom-plishments require an array of educational services delivered to gifted students by specialists, highly prepared for the responsibility of instructing these students.

 MAKING CONNECTIONS

For other discussion about the array of services, see
• Special Education Services (Chapter 2),
• Figure 2.2,
• Educational Interventions section (Chapter 6).

Identification

As you have just learned, the field of gifted education is experiencing a paradigm shift, a time of change. Once giftedness is reconceptualized and agreement about the conceptual framework is achieved, new identification procedures might be developed and implemented. For example, we might one day not use IQ scores to identify students, but might instead use other methods, such as portfolio assess-ments, to replace that process. For the time being, however, most states and school districts will continue to use traditional identification procedures that use stan-dardized tests.

 MAKING CONNECTIONS

• Additional information about portfolio assessments is found in Individualized Special Educational Programs (Chapter 2),
• For another discussion of alternative assessment procedures, see Gifted Culturally and Linguistically Diverse Students (Subgroups section) in this chapter.

Although most definitions of giftedness do not include precise criteria to deter-mine eligibility for special programs, the use of IQ scores is still prevalent today to identify students who are gifted. Therefore you should know what these scores mean. Let's look at how intelligence scores are distributed. The assumption is that if measurements of intelligence were given to a large sample of people, the scores obtained would approximate a normal (bell) curve. The scores would cluster around the mean, or average, in a predictable way. Two commonly used tests of intelligence, the *Stanford-Binet* and the *Wechsler Intelligence Scale for Children III (WISC III)* (Wechsler, 1991), use the score of 100 as the mean. Each of these tests break scores into groups called a **standard deviation (SD)**. On the Stanford-Binet, 16 points from the mean equals one standard deviation. On the *WISC III*, 15 points from the mean equals one SD. So a score of 130 on the *WISC III* is two SDs from the mean. Figure 7.3 shows a normal curve that has been divided by SDs and the percentage of the population that falls within each SD grouping. Notice that slightly more than 68 percent of the population fall within one SD below and above the mean (of 100). For a criterion of two SDs higher than the mean, slightly more than 2 percent of the population should fall above the score of 130 on the *WISC III*. Thus you often hear that gifted students have IQ scores above 130. Remember, though, that this unidimensional (using a single IQ score) approach to identify gifted students is becoming outdated as theories, like Gardner's multiple intelligences, are becoming more widely adopted.

 MAKING CONNECTIONS

For another discussion about the normal curve and the distribution of intelligence scores, see Chapter 6.

The methods used to identify students and ultimately to determine which ones are selected for gifted education programs relate directly to the definition and relat-ed selection criteria used for this special education category. Although Marland's

standard deviation (SD). A sta-tistical measure that expresses the variability and the distribution from the mean of a set of scores.

FIGURE 7.3

Distribution of Intelligence Scores

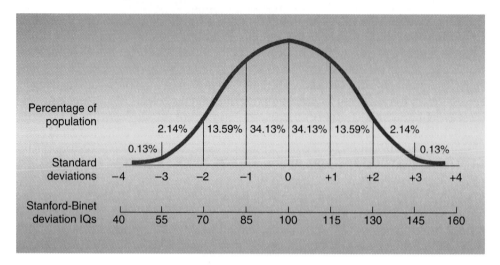

 MAKING CONNECTIONS

See these sections in this chapter:
• Subgroups (Gifted Children)
• Concepts and Controversy

definition is used in many states, it is not universally accepted or it is modified because it does not provide specific criteria for identifying gifted students. States concerned about how many children they either desire to serve or can afford to serve in special programs often use specific cutoff scores when they identify and qualify students. Unfortunately, this method often excludes many children, particularly members of certain subgroups who would qualify if more flexible criteria were applied.

Let's look at how states actually identify gifted students. The Gifted Education Policy Studies Program at the University of North Carolina at Chapel Hill helps us understand such practices at the state level (Coleman & Gallagher, 1994). A comprehensive study about how students are selected for gifted education services surveyed all fifty states. These researchers found that forty-nine of the states had regulations in place to guide school districts and that every one of those states uses scores from standardized tests of intelligence and achievement in the identification process. Some states included additional information such as teacher nominations (forty-six states), parent nominations (forty-five states), and student products or work samples (forty-four states). They also found that in their definitions of gifted, forty states also included creativity, thirty-four artistic ability, and twenty-eight leadership skills. So, you can see that even though this field is experiencing a paradigm shift, where scholars are debating crucial issues, practitioners are still using traditional methods for identification.

Significance

 MAKING CONNECTIONS

Read again the Gallagher quotation in the Defined section of this chapter about the importance of developing the talent of gifted students.

Gifted individuals are not handicapped by any lack of ability. Rather, the challenge to educators is to provide a stimulating educational environment and a broad curriculum to help these individuals reach their full potential and develop their talents. Unfortunately, gifted education has not received the full commitment of policymakers during this century. It is not funded by IDEA, as is education for those who have disabilities. Funding for school-based programs for gifted children comes from state funds, and it is not consistent across time or locales.

Certain attitudes about giftedness—that education of the gifted is elitist, is socially incorrect, should be merged with general education or even eliminated (Margolin, 1996; Sapon-Shevin, 1996)—place this field in a precarious position. Negative attitudes about gifted education most likely stem from myths about the field and the individuals it serves. For example, many people think that these children will thrive without special programs, that they can make it on their own. Others think that programs for the gifted are elitist. As a result of these attitudes, programs for the gifted have been sporadic since this nation's founding.

Of course, some gifted children do achieve their potential without the benefits of special education; however, many do not. Data clearly support the need for special services and a differentiated educational experience for these youngsters (Cornell, Delcourt, Goldberg, & Bland, 1995; Pendarvis & Howley, 1996). For example, gifted education approaches, such as acceleration, are powerfully effective and are almost impossible to implement in general education classes with age-peers. Also, some instructional interventions purported to help gifted students profit from general education placements—for example, cooperative learning—can obstruct learning for the brightest student. In addition, developing talent—that is, translating aptitude into ability—requires special instruction, fostering, guidance, and practice. All children need to develop the motivation to grow and expand. For many gifted children, the general education classroom alone cannot provide the challenges they require to remain motivated or learn at an accelerated and comfortable pace.

MAKING CONNECTIONS

To better understand the roots of these attitudes, read the History section of this chapter.

MAKING CONNECTIONS

See the Educational Interventions section of this chapter for information about different approaches to gifted education.

History of the Field

Emphasis on educating those with exceptional abilities has been sporadic in human history. Confucius, a Chinese philosopher who lived around 500 B.C., believed that all children should be educated but that education should be tailored to their abilities. His views were implemented during the Tang dynasty in A.D. 618 when gifted and talented children were brought to the imperial court for special education. Because the Chinese valued literacy, leadership, imagination, memory, and reasoning, these topics were part of the curriculum. The Japanese also provided differential educational opportunities to their children. For example, during the Tokugawa society (1604–1868), children born of the samurai nobility were educated in Confucian classics, martial arts, history, moral values, calligraphy, and composition. The children of the poor, however, were educated about the value of loyalty, obedience, humility, and diligence (Davis & Rimm, 1994). In western African cultures, specialized education was provided to children based on the children's status, recognized characteristics, or cleverness. And, as early as 3000 B.C., the Egyptians sent the best students (along with royalty) to court schools or assigned mentors to work in intensive internships to develop their special talents (Hunsaker, 1995).

In Western cultures, attention to people's innate and superior abilities can be attributed to the work of Charles Darwin and Sir Francis Galton in the middle 1800s. Charles Darwin is most famous for his theories about natural selection and the evolution of species. Before his time, no one had studied, on a broad scale, individual differences among people or issues relating to intelligence and heredity (Clark, 1992). In 1869, Galton proposed his theory that genius is solely attributed to heredity and that **eminence** is due to two factors: (1) an internal motivation to excel and (2) intellect, both of which were thought to be genetically inherited. The notion that genetic factors contribute greatly to giftedness is still adhered to today, but the important contributions of the environment are also recognized.

In the United States, our wavering commitment to the education of the gifted reflects our national philosophy about equity and social justice. During the eighteenth century, many leaders of the country leaned toward the view that education was best for the elite. Thomas Jefferson, however, argued against elitism, believing that the purpose of education was to foster democracy. During the nineteenth century, egalitarianism—the notion that no one should get special treatment—became popular. The egalitarian position was extreme, holding that no individual could be considered better than anyone else regardless of innate abilities, status, or education. Gardner (1984) suggested that it was from this social philosophy that the concept of equal opportunity was developed.

One legacy of egalitarianism is the attitude that special education for gifted children is undemocratic, elitist, unnecessary, and wasteful. Some researchers believe that special programs for gifted youngsters in this country were not advocated "for fear that any attention to their abilities would give rise to a dangerous aristocracy" (Silverman, 1988, p. 136). Similarly, Sapon-Shevin (1996) maintained that although most Americans believe in individual opportunity and the notion of excellence, a concern about elitism, she specified, is the reason that the same education programs should be offered to all children. But this view does not account for individual differences, nor does it recognize equality of opportunity. If, as a nation, we foster, develop, and even treasure extraordinary talents in athletics, music, and art, then it is inconsistent to claim that identification and special education for gifted children is elitist.

Most chroniclers of gifted education in the United States (Clark, 1992; Gallagher, 1988) stress the importance of the development of the Binet Intelligence Test in 1905. Although not originally developed to identify students who are gifted, this test nonetheless marks the beginning of interest in this country about such individuals. Some programs for the gifted were established as early as 1866, but real development and growth in educational services for these individuals did not come until the 1920s. Leta Hollingworth, one of the early pioneers in the field of gifted education, who joined the faculty at Teachers College, Columbia University, in 1916, taught the first course and wrote the first textbook in this area. One of Hollingworth's major contributions to the field was her proposal that giftedness is affected by both heredity and environment, a concept widely held today (Silverman, 1992).

Another pioneer, Lewis Terman, conducted a classic study in 1925 of individuals who were gifted, both as children and as adults. Although dated, it is still highly respected as one of the most comprehensive studies of eminent individuals. This study stimulated interest in gifted education, but efforts were halted by the Great Depression of the 1930s and World War II in the 1940s. Terman did more than draw attention to gifted individuals; he also set a priority for gifted education that is still important today. Terman was most interested in identifying gifted individuals, not in intervening or enhancing giftedness. Callahan (1996) believes this orientation has left an unfortunate legacy for gifted education in which too much attention is paid to identification and too little to developing best practices for instruction.

The 1960s saw a renewed interest in gifted children. The promotion of unique

MAKING CONNECTIONS

Review again the questions about the merits of gifted education found in the Paradigm Shift section (Defined) of this chapter.

eminence. Superiority in ability.

Leta Hollingworth, here working in 1938 with students at the Speyer School (the laboratory school of Teachers College of Columbia University), provided the foundation for many of the methods used today in gifted education.

educational services can be linked to a specific historical event: the 1957 Russian launching of the space satellite **Sputnik**. The launch was viewed as a risk to national security and a blow to national pride, and the United States vowed to catch up and surpass the competition. Hence, federal funding was appropriated to establish programs, develop ways to identify students with high academic achievement, particularly in math and science, and conduct research to find effective methods for providing excellent educational experiences. Gifted students were now seen as a great national resource, the persons who would make the United States the leader once again.

During the late 1960s and 1970s, the nation turned its attention to the civil rights movement, to the needs of the culturally and linguistically diverse and poor, and to gifted education. It was thought to be one more advantage for the already advantaged youth of our society, and some of the nation's policymakers adopted the position that these youngsters could make it on their own (Maker, 1986). June Maker, however, continued the research in this field with her pioneering work on behalf of gifted students with learning disabilities. In 1977, she published the results of her research, shedding light on a previously ignored group of learners.

The late 1980s saw the situation change once again, with renewed interest in gifted education. In 1988, for example, more than $200 million was spent by the fifty states for special programs for students who are gifted (Gallagher, 1988). Also, in 1988, Congress passed the Jacob K. Javits Gifted and Talented Students

Sputnik. The name of the Russian spaceship that was launched in 1957 and caused a renewed interest in the education of the gifted in this country.

Education Act. This landmark legislation stressed Congress's belief that "unless the special abilities of gifted and talented students are recognized and developed during their elementary and secondary school years, much of their special potential for contributing to the national interest will be lost" (Clark, 1992, p. 163). Enacted in 1990, the act provided $11 million in 1993 in federal funding for research, demonstration, and personnel preparation in this area. The act also reestablished a separate administrative unit in the U.S. Department of Education to serve as a focal point of national leadership and information on the educational needs of gifted and talented students and on the availability and types of educational services designed to meet these needs. Thus, as a nation, we once again have become concerned about the quality of our education and the development of our talented youngsters. However, in the federal budget crisis of 1996, funding was once again in jeopardy. In the end, only $10 million was appropriated in 1996.

Prevalence

The number of children identified as gifted in the United States depends on the definition and concept of giftedness used. For example, if we consider only those who score in the highest 1 percent on an intelligence test, then 1 in every 100 children qualifies for special services. If we consider those who score in the highest 2 percent, then 2 in every group of 100 children qualify. Some educators estimate, however, that as many as 3 to 5 percent of the school population should receive specialized services for the gifted (Davis & Rimm, 1994); others place the percentage higher, at 10 to 15 percent (Renzulli & Reis, 1997). When a score from a test of intelligence is the sole means for identifying gifted students, the number who qualify for services is much smaller than when other exceptional characteristics are also considered. For example, under the criterion of IQ score only, children whose primary language is not English who obtain an IQ score of 120 but demonstrate outstanding spatial and interpersonal skills would not qualify for special services.

Gifted students are not mandated or funded by IDEA, and their prevalence data are not reported in the *Annual Reports to Congress on the Implementation of the Individuals with Disabilities Education Act*. Only twenty-five states mandate that gifted education be offered to those students who qualify (National Center for Educational Statistics, 1994). Thus estimates of the total number of students with IQ scores above a certain level, based on percentages, overrepresent the number of children actually being served. Table 7.2 shows how many children should be identified per units of children by bands of IQ scores. Using this table, you can identify how many children might be provided special services in a school district of 50,000 students, in an elementary school of 400, or in a high school of 2000. These calculations, though, are based solely on the criterion of the scores obtained on an intelligence test. If other factors, such as leadership abilities, were considered, or alternative forms of assessment applied, more children would be identified. Another factor to consider is that giftedness is not evenly distributed across locales; some communities, particularly those with a high proportion of educated parents, have more children with IQ scores above 130 attending their schools.

A long-standing problem in gifted education is that the number of students who receive special services is much lower than it should be. Marland (1972) found that a relatively small percentage of the estimated 1.5 to 2 million children who should qualify for services actually received special services. Ten years later, the situation had improved, and only two states did not have programs for these

MAKING CONNECTIONS

To compare prevalence rates for gifted students with students with specific disabilities, see the Prevalence sections in the other chapters in this text.

MAKING CONNECTIONS

To review again the multiple intelligences theory, see in this chapter
• Table 7.1,
• Broadened concepts section (Defined).
For other views about what constitutes giftedness, see in this chapter
• Concepts and Controversies,
• Defined section.
For a review about what IDEA funds, see Legislation (Chapter 1).

TABLE 7.2

Prevalence of Individuals Who Are Gifted, Depending on the IQ Cutoff Score Used

IQ Score	Approximate Incidence
130	2 in 100
140	1 in 1000
150	1 in 10,000
160 and above	1 in 100,000

Source: Educating Special Learners (3rd ed., p. 322) by G. P. Cartwright, C. A. Cartwright, and M. A. Ward, 1988, Belmont, CA: Wadsworth. Reprinted by permission.

children (Mitchell, 1982). About twenty years after Marland's study, thirty states had mandated services for gifted students (Schmidt, 1993). It is unlikely, however, that all the school districts in those states that permit but do not require special programs actually provided special education for gifted students. In fact, the number of children served may be declining; with many school districts in financial crisis, gifted education programs are being challenged and eliminated.

Even if all states and school districts provided services, they would still not serve all the children they should. Considerably less than 3 percent of children receive gifted education, and culturally and linguistically diverse students are particularly underrepresented. Although Asian Americans are underrepresented in disabilities categories, they are twice as likely to be identified as gifted (U.S. Department of Education, 1993). Recall the statistics about Native American students in Alaska, Montana, South Dakota, and Arizona presented in Chapter 3; these students are overwhelmingly identified as having disabilities. In Alaska, for example, Native Americans comprise 25 percent of the population but only 15 percent of those students receiving gifted education (Harry, 1994).

MAKING CONNECTIONS

For a discussion about nontraditional identification procedures, see the Concepts and Controversy section in this chapter.

Causes: Factors That Enhance or Inhibit Giftedness

Throughout the history of gifted education, people believed that genetics is the primary factor. The work of Terman, in the 1920s, also reflected this view. Today, however, researchers recognize the important roles that both the environment and heredity play in the development of the intellect (Hunsaker, 1995; Simonton, 1997).

Research has shown that factors such as cultural values and expectations, socioeconomic level, birth position (for example, firstborn), and number of children in the family are related to giftedness (Terman, 1925). Environmental stimulation also correlates with gifted abilities. But environmental factors can also diminish giftedness. For example, children whose early experiences are not rich or diverse often do not develop outstanding cognitive skills, and children who are not challenged in school do not develop their potential. Today, superior abilities are generally recognized as developing from an interrelationship between heredity and the environment. Therefore special programs that help gifted individuals achieve their potential should be available.

Many factors enhance or inhibit giftedness. For example, boredom can inhibit giftedness, a point well made by a 9-year-old gifted child:

MAKING CONNECTIONS

For a review of Galton's position on genetics and the beliefs of many living during the mid-nineteenth century, see the History section in this chapter.

MAKING CONNECTIONS

For a reminder of the influence of poverty on cognitive development, see the Causes sections in
• Chapter 3,
• Chapter 6.

Oh what a bore to sit and listen,
To stuff we already know.
Do everything we've done and done again,
But we still must sit and listen.
Over and over read one more page
Oh bore, oh bore, oh bore.
Sometimes I feel if we do one more page
My head will explode with boreness rage
I wish I could get up right there and march right out the door.*

Gifted Children Speak Out (p. 72) by J. R. Delisle, 1984, New York: Walker. Reprinted by permission.

Enthusiasm and creativity should never be discouraged.

MAKING CONNECTIONS

See all of the Prevention sections in this text, and in particular reread the one found in Chapter 6.

Intelligence and talent are not fixed. Although heredity plays a crucial, perhaps even dominant, role in an individual's intellectual abilities and developed talent, other factors are also important, including the environment, the individual's life experiences, and others' expectations. Major environmental factors—wars, famines, social upheavals—can affect the potential of any individual. Certainly, prenatal malnutrition, isolation, neglect, abuse, insufficient infant stimulation, and poor medical treatment can have devastating effects on development of the intellect.

Another factor that can inhibit some aspects of giftedness is the way children grow up. As Renzulli (1978) observed, many young children are inherently creative, yet relatively few adults are. What happens to these children during their preschool and early elementary years? Were they really not creative in the first place? Or is creativity discouraged by our society? Teachers favor highly intelligent students who do well academically but are not able in other areas. Even children's peer groups criticize divergent, independent, and imaginative behavior among their creative friends. Many educators tend to encourage realism instead of imagination: Dolls talk and act like real children; computerized toys teach children the correct answers to arithmetic problems and the correct way to spell words. College students are advised to select majors that will lead to high-paying jobs. Krippner (1967) makes the point that the United States is an achievement-oriented society that rewards individuals merely for being competent. Qualities valued are ability to get along with others, ability to work toward a goal, and ability to adapt, not creativity and individual differences. In fact, the need for acceptance causes many people to repress giftedness.

Gifted Children

As with any group of people, it is unfair to generalize group characteristics to individual members. On the other hand, it is easier to understand a group if some commonly observed features are described. Research findings presented in Table 7.3

TABLE 7.3

Common Characteristics of the Gifted Child

Intellectual/Academic	Social/Emotional
Reasons abstractly	Criticizes self
Conceptualizes and synthesizes	Empathizes
Manages and processes information quickly and meaningfully	Plays with older friends
Solves problems	Persists
Learns quickly	Is intense
Shows intellectual curiosity	Exhibits individualism
Has wide interests	Has strength of character
Dislikes drill and routine	Demonstrates leadership abilities
May show unevenness	Is concerned about ethical issues
Generalizes learning	Takes risks
Remembers great amount of material	Is independent and autonomous
Displays high level of verbal ability	Is highly sensitive to others and self
Prefers learning in a quiet environment	Has mature sense of humor
Adapts to new learning situations	Is nonconforming
Applies varied reasoning and thinking skills	Uses different modes of expression
Uses nonstandard pools of information	Strives for perfection
Is highly motivated by academic tasks	Experiences great stress from failure
Focuses and concentrates on topic or idea for long periods of time	

provide us with some common characteristics of gifted people (Clark, 1992; Jenkins-Friedman & Nielsen, 1990; Roberts & Lovett, 1994; Van Tassel-Baska, 1996; Yong & McIntyre, 1992).

In this section, we discuss two very important issues: the social behavior of gifted learners and four subgroups that require very special attention. Because of the misconceptions about gifted individuals, we felt it is important to share some research about their social skills and behavior. Then, we turn our attention to often neglected subgroups of this population of learners.

Social Behavior

Gifted learners are often victims of stereotypes and sometimes of negative descriptors: "thin, nervous, brash, snobbish, difficult to tolerate, and concerned only with books, ideas, and self" (Laycock, 1979, p. 57). Hollingworth (1942) pop-

 MAKING CONNECTIONS

For rationales for using classifications systems, see these sections in Chapter 1:
• Disabilities Defined
• Classification and Labeling

Reprinted with special permission of North American Syndicate.

ularized the belief that gifted individuals are likely to develop personality problems. However, research has consistently shown that these negative characteristics do not exist for the group, that these people are not necessarily anxious, nor do they exhibit discipline problems. In general, gifted individuals are better adjusted than the general population (Davis, 1996; Terman, 1925). Remember, however, that many people at different periods of their lives are in need of counseling, and this holds true for everyone, gifted or not.

Current comprehensive research studies consistently show that gifted youngsters are no more likely to exhibit disruptive or problem behaviors in classroom settings than typical learners (Freeman, 1994). Gifted students do, however, complain about being bored at school, which might explain some of the behavior problems noted by some teachers. Certainly, keeping these students engaged can be a challenging experience for educators, particularly those who have a class of students who exhibit a wide range of abilities and achievement levels.

Educators should be aware of some common characteristics often seen in these youngsters: sensitivity, perfectionism, and intensity (Piechowski, 1997). For example, they tend to be highly sensitive (Freeman, 1994). This characteristic may lead some of them to overreact to even modest criticism. This coupled with a need for perfection causes many gifted students to experience more negative reactions to what they perceive as failure (Roberts & Lovett, 1994). These tendencies may well contribute to underachievement in some gifted students.

Another characteristic that deserves attention is these students' intensity. Van Tassel-Baska (1995) notes that this characteristic can manifest itself both socially and academically. For example, she has observed that these students often react strongly to the death of a pet or the perceived injustice of a teacher. It is also this characteristic that causes these students to become highly focused on an activity they find fascinating, enabling them to concentrate on an intriguing idea for long periods of time. It is also because of this high intensity that they become disinterested in busywork or frustrated when not allowed to explore curriculum content in depth. Knowledge of these characteristics and learning styles can help the keen educator understand these students' educational needs and keep them motivated.

Subgroups Requiring Special Attention

As with any group of people, subgroups of those who are highly intelligent or highly creative face unique or specific problems. In this section, we discuss four subgroups: females who are gifted, culturally and linguistically diverse students, gifted persons with disabilities, and underachievers who are gifted. Throughout these discussions, remember how society's values and expectations can influence all of us.

We might all agree that it is important to identify and serve all children who are gifted. However, many subgroups in this category are not currently served or even identified as gifted or uniquely talented, which is a loss to these individuals and to the nation.

> If we do not provide for these underserved children, we will never know how many Franklin D. Roosevelts or Helen Kellers, or George Shearings or Nelson Rockefellers, or Count Basies are hiding, never to be discovered in the next generation. If we do not start in the beginning of their school career, we may lose in them the fragile desire to do well in school and to pursue knowledge vigorously. (Gallagher, 1988, p. 110)

Gifted Females. As early as the 1920s, Hollingworth raised issues regarding bias toward gifted females. She argued that the prevailing notion that women were intellectually inferior to men was incorrect; rather, women did not have equal opportunities to excel and achieve to their potential. Concurrently with Hollingworth's work, Terman studied many individuals identified as gifted; the number of men in his study outnumbered the women. Even today, the number of men considered gifted or talented exceeds the number of women who have achieved such status (AAUW, 1992), even though the numbers of preschool boys and girls identified as gifted are about equal (Silverman, 1995). What are the reasons for this difference in numbers? Are there innate differences between the genders that cause giftedness to occur more frequently in men than in women? Innate differences have never been proven in research. Rather, are society's expectations for people and the roles they assume the crucial factors in the achievement levels of either gender?

The answers to these questions reveal some major flaws in the educational system in the United States. The findings of a comprehensive study about girls in school found that the lack of gender equity in our nation's elementary and secondary schools was the primary reason for girls' underachievement (AAUW, 1992). Many teachers tend to favor boys, encourage them more, pay them more attention, and focus instructional activities toward their interests. Teachers' and parents' expectations can affect how well girls do in certain subjects, what courses they take in high school, and, ultimately, what careers they choose. Such bias may be the contributing factor in girls' poor self-concepts about their mathematics abilities (Dickens & Cornell, 1993). Thus, even though girls' and boys' scores on mathematics achievement tests are about the same, girls are less likely to take advanced courses. Their performance in science is far inferior to boys', and they are less likely to pursue careers in science or technology (AAUW, 1992).

Some researchers (Eccles, 1985; Rand & Gibb, 1989) believe that females who are gifted need a different kind of educational programming to achieve their potential, especially in mathematics and the sciences. Because of lowered expectations and the way girls are treated in school, girls think they cannot do well in the sciences and mathematics. Fortunately, attitudes can be changed. In one study, after an eighteen-week program that included problem-solving activities, math-related career opportunities, and self-esteem issues, gifted girls changed their attitudes, becoming more positive about mathematics (Lamb & Daniels, 1993). Given this knowledge, we must actively involve all children in the instructional topics presented in school. Silverman (1995) suggests that gifted girls must be identified early in their schooling, provided with a challenging curriculum, counseled to achieve in areas not traditionally pursued by women, and be given many examples and role models to follow.

Culturally and Linguistically Diverse Gifted Students.

Culturally and linguistically diverse students, particularly the gifted subgroup, face many challenges. They tend to be overrepresented in disability categories and underrepresented in gifted education programs. Why do these youngsters frequently not qualify for gifted special services? A number of reasons have been offered (Callahan & McIntire, 1994; Davis & Rimm, 1994; Ford & Harris, 1994; Gallagher & Gallagher, 1994; Hunsaker, 1994). First, let's categorize the different explanations given for these students not being identified as gifted at the rate that should be expected:

- Cultural values at variance with mainstream society
- Barriers presented because of poverty
- Bias in traditional methods used for testing and identification
- Educator's attitudes about culturally and linguistically diverse students

Now, let's examine these issues more carefully.

Students from some ethnic groups (African American, Hispanic, Pacific Islanders, Native Americans, and others) often do not perform as well as their peers from other groups on standardized tests or on classroom academic tasks. One reason for their poor performance may be their families' different cultural values and different emphasis on cognitive development (Gallagher & Gallagher, 1994; Maker & Schiever, 1989). As an example, Table 7.4 compares the absolute characteristics of giftedness with cultural values generally found in and valued by the Hispanic culture. The differences noted in the table mean that sometimes the culture of the school clashes with the culture of the home. This clash can cause great difficulties for the youngster who cannot discriminate between the expectations of home and those of the school. In many cases, students who are not from the dominant culture mask their giftedness in the school environment because they do not believe it is appropriate to demonstrate unique abilities or talents. Each culture has different values and norms, of course, and it is impossible to generalize from one culture to another. But it is possible to note differences between the cultures of school and of home. These differences should be considered not only when identifying youngsters for services, but also when planning their educational programs. For example, supportive services, like counseling, can help some students bridge the gap between the cultures of home and school (Ford, 1995).

Unfortunately, one fact of American life is that culturally and linguistically diverse children are more at risk to grow up in poverty than other groups of American children. Poverty is associated with many factors that can result in barriers to school success. How is this so? Borland (1996) helps us understand that socioeconomic status is a variable that should never be underestimated. He notes that students from affluent families are five times more likely to be identified as gifted than are students from poor families. This could be because poor culturally and linguistically diverse children are less likely to have access to health care, and the relationship between good health and intellectual development is clear.

MAKING CONNECTIONS

For issues related to under- and overrepresentation, see Prevalence (Chapter 3).

MAKING CONNECTIONS

For more information about the influence of culture on the understanding of giftedness, see
• many of the Focus on Diversity boxes found in every chapter in this text,
• all of Chapter 3,
• this chapter's Concepts and Controversy section.

MAKING CONNECTIONS

See Causes and Prevention sections in
• Chapter 3,
• Chapter 6.

TABLE 7.4

Characteristics of Giftedness and Cultural Values of Hispanics and the Behaviors Resulting from Their Interactive Influence

Absolute Aspects of Giftedness	Cultural Values Often Characteristic of Hispanics	Behavioral Differences
High level of verbal ability	Traditional language of family	Communicates fluently with peers and within community, even if using non-standard English
Emotional depth and intensity	*Abrazo*, a physical or spiritual index of personal support	Requires touching, eye contact, feeling of support to achieve maximum academic productivity
Unusual sensitivity to feelings and expectations of others	Family structure and dynamic-male dominance	Personal initiative, independent thought, and verbal aggressiveness often inhibited in females
Ability to conceptualize solutions to social and environmental problems	Nuclear and extended family closeness	Often assumes responsibility for family and/or younger siblings
Unusual retentiveness; unusual capacity for processing information	Traditional culture	Adapts to successful functioning in two cultures
Leadership	Collaborative rather than competitive dynamic	Accomplishes more, works better in small groups than individually

Source: "Defining the Hispanic Population" by C. J. Maker and S. W. Schiever (Eds.), 1989, in *Critical Issues in Gifted Education: Defensible Programs for Cultural and Ethnic Minorities* (Vol. 2) (p. 4), Austin, TX: Pro-Ed. Copyright 1989 by Pro-Ed. Reprinted by permission.

Children who do not get proper nutrition, are not inoculated for disease, or do not get appropriate medical treatment for illness are at risk for impaired mental development. Another factor associated with poverty is the instability of the home environment. Many of these children come from families that move frequently and so are not at one school long enough for either identification or services. Finally, underrepresentation related to poverty may be the result of the poor educational levels of parents, the deficiencies of inner-city schools, and lack of exposure to mainstream society.

Clearly, a primary reason for culturally and linguistically diverse children not being identified as gifted is their not meeting stringently applied cutoff scores on standardized tests. Providing the kinds of educational services these underserved gifted students need may require the use of flexible identification procedures. Earlier in this text, we discussed portfolio assessments, a new assessment procedure that is often advocated for students biased against by traditional testing procedures (Ford & Harris, 1994). Portfolio assessment procedures can be implemented in many ways. For gifted youngsters this system is beneficial because it matches well with Gardner's theory of multiple intelligences. Maker, Nielson, and Rogers (1994) also believe that culturally and linguistically diverse students can benefit from a multidimensional identification system based on Gardner's theory. Maker, who is working with Native American students living on

 MAKING CONNECTIONS

For more on alternative assessment procedures, see
• Individualized Special Education Programs (Chapter 2),
• Identification section (Defined) in this chapter,
To review Multiple Intelligences, see
• Defined section in this chapter,
• Identified (Chapter 3).

a rural reservation, has verified a new method to identify gifted students who have limited proficiency in English. Rejecting the use of standardized tests of intelligence, she is using Gardner's framework and a process in which children solve ever-increasingly complex problems. Most certainly, the process used to identify gifted youngsters from diverse backgrounds itself calls for greater imagination and creativity.

Many educators advocate that alternative assessment procedures be implemented for these students. Peer nominations, teacher nominations, authentic assessments (frequent evaluations of students' classroom work), and curriculum based assessments have all been suggested. Unfortunately, some recent data indicate that alternative assessments may not offer the solution to this problem as many have hoped (Hunsaker, 1994). Reports from many educators working in local school districts indicate disappointment with alternative assessment procedures because they believe that they do not result in increased placements for culturally and linguistically diverse students: The underrepresented population remains underrepresented. Hunsaker's findings indicate that many educators believe that at the heart of the problem is rigid policies and narrow testing practices. Unfortunately, this is not the only source of the problem. He also found that many educators do not believe that giftedness exists across all groups of students regardless of their ethnic background or economic level. In this case what needs to change is educators' attitudes.

Now let's shift the discussion from identification to services. Educational opportunities make a great difference for these students, but only a few special programs can be found across the country. What special considerations should be included in programs designed specifically for culturally and linguistically diverse students who are gifted? Besides gifted education methods, teachers must be sensitive to their students' cultural differences (review again Table 7.4). Patton and Baytops (1995) provided some specific suggestions for African American students (see Table 7.5 for a framework). They maintained that the heritage, culture, and worldviews of this group demand instruction that both nurtures these students' unique backgrounds and empowers them. To these experts, exemplary programs allow students to explore topics of significance and interest to the individual learner, to respond to real-world issues and problems, to learn advanced content in core curriculum areas (math, language arts, science), and to be challenged by interdisciplinary study that cuts across curriculum areas.

Examples of developed programs illustrate the diversity and differences of the opportunities that could be available to all of these students. In one exciting program, the New York Theater Ballet School offers a special arts program for children in homeless shelters (Morgan, 1991). Another ballet program is offered by a public middle school in New York City, the Professional Performing Arts School (Dunning, 1991). Here, an equal mix of children from different cultures expand their talents in music and dance. Without such special programs, children from lower-income families typically do not have the opportunity to discover and develop their creativity and giftedness.

Gifted students who are singled out for special programs face peer pressure, however. Consider Crane High School in Chicago, which is situated in a neighborhood surrounded by low-income housing projects. Teachers at Crane offer special classes in logic, philosophy, reasoning, advanced mathematics, and writing. The educational program also enriches these students' lives through exposure to

TABLE 7.5

Methods of Accentuating Selective Strengths and Learning Modes of African
American Gifted Learners

Selective Strengths and Learning Modes	Responsive Teaching-Learning Methodologies
Verbal fluency; stylistic, charismatic use of language	Emphasize creative writing, poetry, public speaking, oral discussion, debating, drama, literature
Expressive movement, advanced kinesthetic ability	Emphasize hands-on learning strategies and allow flexible classroom organization
Advanced aesthetic sensibilities	Integration of arts with core instruction
Resourcefulness, inventiveness, advanced creative abilities	Utilize problem-based learning: opportunities for experimentation with ideas, and seeking solutions to real problems
Preference for person-to-person (over person-to-object) interactions	Emphasize development of social interaction and leadership skills, attention to world affairs, and current issues
Sensitivity for the interconnectedness of humankind with nature	Focus on science, ecology, outdoor field experience, anthropology, and social sciences
Expressed spirituality related to sense of power of external forces of nature, existence of a supreme being, and a heightened sense of responsibility for others within primary reference group	Use of moral, affective overarching themes as base for instructional experiences: study use of parables and proverbs of varying cultures; examine life experiences of selected leaders (those characterized by intense spirituality, individualization, and moral responsibility)

Note: This table represents selective strengths and learning modes most often noted by scholars
as characteristics of African American gifted/high-ability learners (Baytops, Sims, & Patton, 1993;
Hale-Benson, 1986; Hilliard, 1976; Shade, 1990; Torrance, 1977). The concomitant methodologies
were developed from work of Baytops, et al. 1993).

Source: Effective Education of African American Exceptional Learners: New Perspectives (p. 43) by B. A.
Ford, F. E. Obiakor, and J. M. Patton (Eds.), 1995, Austin, TX: Pro-Ed. Reprinted by
permission.

opera, museums, and retreats, experiences that youngsters from their background
do not usually have. The price for their education is high, though: These students
are greatly resented by neighborhood gang members because they go to this special
school (Wilkerson, 1990); in fact, some of the gifted students have been
assaulted on their way to the school. But to them, their special program is worth
the cost. It is also worth its cost to society: All the students have been accepted at
colleges.

Gifted Individuals with Disabilities. When you think of people with disabilities who are also gifted and have developed outstanding talents, you might think of people like Steven Hawkins, the renowned scientist, Ludwig van Beethoven, Thomas Edison, Helen Keller, Franklin D. Roosevelt, Stevie Wonder, Itzhak Perlman, and others. Despite their severe disabilities, their genius and major contributions to their respective fields have brought them considerable recognition. However, it is not only those with physical and sensory disabilities who are intellectually gifted; it occurs in all other special education categories, except for those with mental retardation or severe developmental disabilities (as you can see in the art shown at the beginning of Chapters 6 and 12, talent development does occur in some of these individuals).

Unfortunately, students with disabilities often are not included in educational programs for the gifted because their disabilities may mask their potential; and frequently, the scores they receive on ability and achievement tests are falsely low (Silverman, 1995). Davis and Rimm (1994) believe that this subgroup of gifted learners are underidentified and underserved. They estimate that approximately 188,000 students should fall into this category; yet many school districts offer no services for them. Furthermore, people with disabilities are seldom perceived by their families or teachers as possessing gifted abilities. Davis and Rimm found that when teacher and peer nomination systems were used to identify gifted students, not one student with a disability was nominated. Clearly, society's biases about people with disabilities can overshadow the individuals' strengths. For example, a student with a severe physical disability might require more time to answer questions on a timed, standardized test. Students with disabilities might need to use special equipment such as a print enlarger or a computer to function in a traditional testing situation. Modifications to the testing situation are seldom provided when qualifying a youngster for classes for the gifted. In the 1970s, Maker (1977) began to raise the awareness of educators about the needs of gifted learners with disabilities. In her research, Maker (1986) found one key variable leading to these individuals' success: motivation to succeed. She maintains that in addition to the special educational content usually found in programs for the gifted, these students need guidance to become more self-confident and develop a strong, internally driven motivation to achieve.

Currently, attention is being focused on gifted students with learning disabilities. Historically, a large number of underserved students come from this group. For example, research conducted in a large school district found that 66 percent of the **twice-exceptional students** identified were gifted and also had a learning disability (Nielsen, Higgins, & Hammond, 1993; Nielsen, Higgins, Hammond, & Williams, 1993). These students, also sometimes called "crossover children," are extremely bright, but because of their learning disability, many do not achieve to their potential. Often, these students are caught in the middle and receive no special services. In many states, because of their high IQ scores, they do not qualify for educational programs for those with learning disabilities; and because of their low achievement test scores, they do not qualify for educational programs for the gifted.

Carefully designed educational programs can meet the individual needs of gifted students with learning disabilities and can make a significant difference in their lives. The dilemma is whether to teach to their learning disabilities, to their giftedness, or to both. These students are individuals, of course, but as a group, they show some patterns in their learning style. They are often distractible, highly sensitive to criticism, and extremely curious and questioning; they have difficulty getting to the

MAKING CONNECTIONS

For specific tips about modifying the educational environment for students with disabilities, see the Making Accommodations boxes found in every chapter of this text.

MAKING CONNECTIONS

For a review of learning disabilities, see Chapter 4.

twice-exceptional students. Students who have a disability and who are gifted.

TIPS FOR TEACHERS

Considerations for Twice-Exceptional Children

1 Look beyond the student's disability.

2 Be flexible and encourage flexibility in your colleagues to ensure that these students' special learning needs are met.

3 Involve or develop a support team that includes other educators at your school and other resource personnel from the school district (experts in learning disabilities and in gifted education).

4 Find a community mentor to serve as an adult role model for the student.

5 Assess whether social skills instruction or strategies to build self-esteem are required by the individual student.

6 Consider providing additional structure in scheduling and work space.

7 Implement behavior management programs to reduce problem areas that may be the result of attention deficits.

8 Encourage independent learning.

9 Allow for special arrangements in testing situations.

10 Watch for signs of depression.

11 Be understanding and sensitive to parental frustration.

12 Involve parents as part of the educational team.

13 Remember, there is no one answer.

point, and they seem to be interested in the whole picture rather than in the details (Nielsen et al., 1993). They also tend to have inefficient learning strategies, memory problems, and poor relationships with their peers; and often they experience social rejection and lack friends (Davis & Rimm, 1994). These characteristics reflect their learning disabilities. They also have learning characteristics that reflect their giftedness. These students are bright and inquisitive learners who can experience rapid gains in achievement when placed in an educational program that fosters the development of higher-level thinking (Bireley, 1995). Gifted students with disabilities can present unique challenges to their teachers and their families. The Tips for Teachers box lists some special considerations that experts in this area believe are beneficial to twice-exceptional students (Bireley, 1995; Davis & Rimm, 1994).

A good educational program for these students should include direct instruction in areas in need of remediation, as in any educational program for students with learning disabilities. The educational program must also incorporate gifted education methods. Thus the program would allow students to compensate for their weaker areas and yet fosters their development of critical thinking, reasoning, problem-solving, and compensatory skills. For example, students might be encouraged to use a broad array of technologies (word processing, spell checkers, calculators, database software, and other assistive devices) to compensate for their deficits. Some students might use audio-recorded literature for their reading assignments or tape recorders to take class notes. They would also use technology when

 MAKING CONNECTIONS

- For information about the different approaches used in gifted education, see Education and the Schoolchild (Educational Interventions) in this chapter.
- For how technology applies to all students with special needs, read the technology sections found in Chapters 3 through 12.

they study complex problems, such as the water quality of the local river. To conduct their environmental study, they might tape record interviews with people who live along the river. They might also conduct a variety of tests assessing the water's quality at various points along the river. The students could also visit state and local government offices to determine the policies and regulations regarding pollution and visit businesses that have been cited for polluting the river to better understand their perspectives as well. The blending of instructional procedures for students with learning disabilities and procedures for gifted students is obviously important for these students' development. Because of these students' unique learning needs, some school districts have developed special programs just for these youngsters.

Gifted Underachievers. Gifted children who are underachievers demonstrate high intelligence but also low academic achievement. Depending on the discrepancy between these individuals' scores on intelligence and achievement tests, these students may be confused with gifted students who have learning disabilities. Teachers and parents often recognize these students' true capabilities, but the students do not do well in school or perform up to their abilities, sometimes for unexplainable reasons. They have been described as disorganized, unmotivated, lacking interest in school, having poor study skills, and lacking in self-confidence (Davis & Rimm, 1994). Remember the characteristics discussed in the section about gifted students' social behavior patterns. Their frustration with boring assignments, difficulties in accepting criticism, and need to be challenged may be contributing factors to the underachievement noted in some of these learners (Freeman, 1994; Van Tassel-Baska, 1995). Clearly, these students, like those with disabilities and who are gifted, need a strong motivation to succeed. In fact, it may be motivation that makes the difference between achievers and underachievers. Although these students do not achieve to the levels they should, they understand the relationship between effort and success. Unfortunately, they do not make the effort to excel at a task, a finding that appears to be particularly true for students who are African Americans (Ford, Obiakor, & Patton, 1995). Therefore these youngsters need specialized educational services to teach them how to achieve in school, how to approach learning tasks more meaningfully, and how to use their talents in a directed fashion.

Educational Interventions

Enhanced educational opportunities for gifted individuals have been available, but inconsistently, across time and across the nation. For instance, gifted education is part of special education in some but not all states, since no federal law requires that these students be guaranteed special instructional programs. Remember, gifted education is not part of IDEA and therefore does not receive federal funding for school-based programs. Also, remember that this inconsistent commitment to gifted education stems from differing philosophical beliefs about society, elitism, and educational opportunities rooted in our national history. One argument centers on the notion that these children are already advantaged and do not need more benefits. But as you have learned in this chapter, gifted youngsters are atypical learners who need specialized services to make full use of their extraordinary talents. Their potential, if wasted, represents a significant loss. For many years,

MAKING CONNECTIONS

- The long-term commitment of the United States to gifted education is summarized in the History section of this chapter.
- For a review of IDEA, see the Legislation section (Chapter 1).

educators have discussed the educational options that could be made available to students who are gifted. For example, over sixty years ago, Scheidemann in her 1931 text about exceptional children wrote:

> Enrichment of curriculum, rapid progress, or segregation in special classes for only gifted children are advocated by modern educators. The arguments extended by early objectors for these special methods, namely, that attainments of the bright children are needed to stimulate the progress of normal children, or that an IQ aristocracy would be encouraged among school children, are groundless. Even the objections on the basis of the discrepancy between physical and intellectual maturity that would result in permitting the superior child to progress at his individual rate are no longer tenable . . . . Some specialists urge time-saving by rapid promotions in precollege education, and regular or longer attendance in professional schools, because the gifted mind can spend unlimited time in specialization.
>
> Rapid promotion is urged by many educators because it is easy and inexpensive. The more thoughtful are more inclined to encourage an enrichment program for gifted children, thus keeping their intellectual powers active in association with children who are mentally and physically their equal. Social ostracism, which is the usual fate of the very young high-school child, is thus avoided. Many suggestions in regard to the specific ways in which the curriculum may be enriched are offered. (Scheidemann, 1931, pp. 261–262)

Education and the Preschool Child

What can we do for the preschool child who is gifted? As we know, early stimulation is crucial to the development of *all* young children. Research has shown that early childhood programs are also helpful for gifted children. Studies of eminent people (Terman, 1925; Goertzel & Goertzel, 1962) show that these individuals had enriched experiences early in their lives. In many instances, parents shared a talent or aptitude with their precocious offspring and provided role models as well as substantial encouragement as the child began to develop (Yewchuk, 1995). With the rise of the two-parent working family and the single-parent household, more and more children attend day care and preschool programs. For a variety of reasons, children sometimes receive their primary stimulation from these programs. Thus the quality of these early education programs should be of the highest level.

Teachers should be aware of differences between gifted and nongifted preschoolers. For example, at a young age, gifted children show higher levels of curiosity, concentration, memory, and a sense of humor (Lewis & Louis, 1991). They are likely to be healthier, quicker to learn, larger, emotionally better adjusted, and socially more mature; they persist longer at tasks, resist rules, and enjoy competition (Karnes, Shwedel, & Linnemeyer, 1982). Although different in many ways from their classmates, these youngsters tend to associate with the most popular youngsters in the preschool class, rather than playing alone or with others of their intellectual abilities (Schneider & Daniels, 1992). And, recent research has identified another important difference between these youngsters and their more typically learning peers: They gain phonological awareness and the ability to discriminate speech sounds very early. This ability is a predictor of early reading mastery, a skill highly related to school success (McBride-Chang, Manis, & Wagner, 1996).

Gifted preschoolers seem to function well in typical preschool settings. They build things, engage in pretend and dramatic play, and converse with others at the

 MAKING CONNECTIONS

To review the importance of mastering basic phonics skills, see the Reading section (Educational Interventions) in Chapter 4.

These young preschoolers are already demonstrating advanced reading and conceptual abilities. Teachers must be alert to continually challenge and support children with giftedness and creativity.

same rate as their nongifted classmates. However, those who show signs of accelerated development must be challenged so that their motivation to learn is not dulled. Educators must also understand that sometimes these young children's cognitive abilities far surpass their motor skills (Gallagher & Gallagher, 1994). For example, even those able to read may not be able to write well enough to capture their creative ideas. Researchers also caution that no child should be forced to relearn what is already mastered. Time after time, stories are told about children who come to kindergarten already reading but instead of being allowed to continue developing their reading skills are forced to engage in readiness activities with classmates. Instructional time might be better spent on different activities, such as teaching students to classify and organize information or to think critically. The development of critical-thinking skills can begin early in children's education. Units specifically aimed at developing critical thinking can be incorporated as enrichment activities. McDowell (1989) demonstrates that critical thinking can be taught to very young children through an experiential approach. The example provided in the Teaching Tactics box demonstrates how teachers can foster critical-thinking skills even in very young children.

Education and the Schoolchild

Today, a variety of educational services, varying by locale and in philosophy and orientation, are available to gifted students. In this section, we discuss several instructional models for and approaches to gifted education. Some approaches are

~~ Critical-Thinking Skills

Ms. McDowell (1989) used an apple as the basis for lessons designed to develop vocabulary, oral language, reading, and thinking abilities (cognition). The following example, using the apple model, illustrates how critical-thinking skills can be integrated into educational programs for even very young children. It involves a slight modification of typical teaching routines, more involvement of the children, and some good questioning from the teacher.

Mrs. Peterson, a preschool teacher, teaches a group of bright children. Because of their young age, their experiential backgrounds are still very limited. On the first day of her unit about apples, she reads the story of Johnny Appleseed to her class. During her reading, she stresses important concepts and language (words) presented in the story. After reading the story, she engages the children in a discussion about the story and their own experiences with apples. How do you get apples? Where do they come from? Are they all alike? What do you do with them?

On ensuing days, Mrs. Peterson creates different lessons to help the children to think about and experience a food they all have eaten. She has the children reenact the story of Johnny Appleseed, with each child taking a turn playing the main character. Then she rereads the story. She stops several times and asks the children to predict what is going to happen next. On another day the children discuss where apples come from, how they grow on trees, and when they are picked.

Later, the class takes a trip to the store. One by one, Mrs. Peterson tells them to go find the apples. The children meet in the produce section, compare different types of apples, and discuss how they differ (in color, size, texture, taste). The class then goes to find other products in the store that are made of apples. The children identify the following items: cereal, pies, cookies, applesauce, and juice. Before leaving the store, the children and Mrs. Peterson buy several sacks of apples to use at school later in the week. At school the next day, the class studies the apples they purchased. They slice one open and talk about the various parts (seeds, stem, peel). The children create a story about apples through a language experience approach and then role-play their story.

One day, Mrs. Peterson writes "Food with Apples" on the board. The children have to think of all the foods they can that are made with apples. They talk about how these foods were packaged (in boxes, bottles, jars). They discuss how many apples it would take to make these foods. Because the children seem to have no concept of the number of apples it takes to make various foods, the next day Mrs. Peterson helps them make applesauce. Beforehand, the children take turns guessing how many apples it will take to fill the two jars that Mrs. Peterson has brought to school. They all participate fully in making the applesauce, and they enjoy eating their culinary creation the next day during snack time.

comprehensive and influence the entire school day; others modify a portion of the school day; still others can be easily integrated into any ongoing instructional program. Regardless, all seek to develop the unique talents of gifted individuals and serve as illustrative examples of educational systems that are responsive to individual needs by altering traditional educational programs.

Although professionals do not agree on a best educational approach for gifted students, a number of models and instructional practices are used independently and in various combinations across the nation. Many experts advocate the use of a differentiated curriculum for these students (Clark, 1992; Van Tassel-Baska, 1992; Yong & McIntyre, 1992). A **differentiated curriculum** provides an instructional program that is flexible enough to meet individual learning needs. This program emphasizes cognitive processing, abstract thinking, reasoning, creative problem solving, and self-monitoring (Yong & McIntyre, 1992). Some researchers believe that three additional dimensions must be included (Van Tassel-Baska, 1995): content mastery, in-depth and independent learning, and the exploration of issues, themes, and ideas across all curriculum areas. Clark (1992) added that the curriculum must be flexible enough to be "increasingly difficult, interdisciplinary, broad based, and comprehensive and should provide for any needed acceleration" (p. 258). Notice that her interpretation of a differentiated curriculum combines a variety of curriculum targets with different instructional models and practices. Although many school districts still select only one approach, the current recommended practice is to combine them as appropriate. In other words, a differentiated curriculum might combine the enrichment model (which we discuss next) and the acceleration model. Table 7.6 summarizes the models and practices we discuss in the following subsections. For clarity, they are presented independently, but remember that they are best applied in combination.

Enrichment Approach. **Enrichment** can include the addition of curricular topics or the development of skills not usually included in the traditional curriculum. For example, a group of students might spend a small portion of time each week working with instructional materials that enhance creativity or critical-thinking skills. Or enrichment may be the study of a particular academic subject in more depth and detail. Some teachers, when using enrichment in this way, guide students to select a character or an event for research and study. The student's product might be an oral or written report that could become part of a class play or short story, or a nonverbal product such as a painting, construction, or model.

The enrichment approach is often used in general classroom settings to meet the needs of advanced learners. To use this approach successfully, however, teachers must be prepared to guide children as they learn and apply skills like critical thinking, problem solving, advanced reasoning, and research. Renzulli (1994/1995) gives an example of how the enrichment approach was used with a third grader, Elaine, who read at the adult level and was highly interested in biographies about women scientists. Elaine's teacher substituted challenging books in her area of interest for the third grade texts. She arranged for Elaine to spend the afternoons on early dismissal days with a local journalist who specialized in gender issues and to meet with female scientists and faculty members at a nearby university. Teachers, like Elaine's, who apply such creativity to the development of individualized programs for their students also allow these students to integrate information gained through their enrichment activities into their other academic tasks like their writing assignments.

To better understand the enrichment process, let us look at an example from a history lesson. This lesson involves **interdisciplinary instruction**, which encourages students to study a subject by using different perspectives. As one application of this instructional technique that incorporates multicultural education, Banks (1994) provides this example. The students play a game, Banks calls *Star Power,* in

differentiated curriculum. The flexible application of curriculum targets that ensures content mastery, in-depth and independent learning, and exploration of issues and themes and allows for acceleration when needed.

enrichment. Adding topics or skills to the traditional curriculum or presenting a particular topic in more depth.

interdisciplinary instruction. An approach to the education of the gifted that involves studying a topic and its issues in the context of several different disciplines.

TABLE 7.6

Approaches to Gifted Education

Approach	Explanation
1. Enrichment	
Interdisciplinary instruction	Teaching a topic by presenting different disciplines' perspectives about the issues involved
Independent study	Examining a topic in more depth than is usual in a general education class
Mentorship programs	Pairing students with adults who guide them in applying knowledge to real-life situations
Internship	Programs that allow gifted students, usually during their senior year in high school, to be placed in a job setting that matches their career goals
Enrichment triad/revolving door model	An inclusive and flexible model for gifted education that changes the entire educational system; exposes students to planned activities that seek to develop thinking skills, problem solving, and creativity
Curriculum compacting	Making additional time available for enrichment activities by reducing time spent on traditional instructional topics
2. Acceleration	
Advanced placement	Courses that students take during their high school years resulting in college credit
Honors sections	A form of ability grouping where gifted and nongifted students who demonstrate high achievement in a particular subject are placed together in advanced classes
Ability grouping	Clustering students in courses where all classmates have comparable achievement and skill levels
Individualized instruction	Instruction delivered on a one-to-one basis, with students moving through the curriculum at their own pace independently
3. Eclectic	
Purdue secondary model for gifted gifted and talented youth	A comprehensive high school curriculum for students that incorporates counseling into the standard program for all students

which the class is divided into three groups: the stars (who have the most points), the triangles, and the circles (those with the least points). The teacher designs the games so the stars are always in a dominant position, with the point being that highly stratified societies provide little opportunity for mobility. Students study historical examples of groups in positions like the stars, triangles, and circles. Some choices might include the Pilgrims of seventeenth-century England, American colonists in the late 1700s upset with English taxation policies, the Cherokee Indians in the Southeast in the 1830s, the Jews in Germany during the 1940s, and African Americans in the South during the 1950s and 1960s. One question students are to answer is how history might have been different if the target group had acted differently. Throughout this process, students learn about history from a sociological perspective. They advance their knowledge of a particular historical period while sharpening their critical-thinking skills.

Another option used in some schools is **independent study** (Sisk, 1987). As an enrichment option, independent study is usually used within a traditional course. It allows a student to study a topic in more depth, to enrich the traditional curriculum, or to explore a topic that is not part of the general education. Independent study does not mean working alone but, rather, learning to be self-directed and to work on problems in which the individual has an interest. Such a program, if guided by the teacher, can provide youngsters with experiences that stress independence, problem solving, critical analysis of a topic, research skills, and the development of a product. Table 7.7 shows a sample independent study project for a ninth grade English honors student.

MAKING CONNECTIONS

To review information about multicultural education, reread in Chapter 3
• Defined,
• Exceptional Culturally and Linguistically Diverse Students,
• Educational Interventions.

independent study. A common approach to the education of the gifted that allows a student to pursue and study a topic in depth on an individual basis.

TABLE 7.7

Sisk's Independent Study Worksheet

Content to Be Studied	*Resources/Materials*	*Learning Process/Product*
1. Charles Dickens: personality, beliefs, attitudes	1. *A Tale of Two Cities*, Charles Dickens	1. Prepare videotape discussion on findings
2. People's relationship to time	2. Interview English professor at UCLA, a specialist in Dickens	2. Conduct short sessions of Dickens with Pi Lambda Theta
3. Our inhumanity to one another	3. Examine history of French Revolution through history text	3. Write article for school literary magazine
	4. Attend *A Tale of Two Cities* play in Los Angeles	
	5. Examine history books for history of England during Dickens's life	

Source: Creative Thinking of the Gifted (p. 43) by D. Sisk, 1987, New York: McGraw-Hill. Reprinted with permission.

This girl has been matched with a woman journalist at the local newspaper, whose specialty is feminist literature, for her senior year mentorship.

Educators of the gifted have developed other approaches to enrich youngsters' growth and development. In **mentorship** programs, students with special interests are paired with adults who have expertise in that special area. For example, a student who is interested in engineering might be matched with an engineer who will help with a special project or invite the student to participate in some activity at work. Mentors can be college students, retired persons, or professionals in the community; and the experiences and knowledge they share can include almost any topic (ecology, medicine, psychology, archeology, farming, management of endangered species).

Internship is an option used with many gifted high school students who have expressed interest in a particular career. The Illinois Government Internship Program, for example, allows high school students to explore careers in law or government (Cox, Daniel, & Boston, 1985). In this program, students spend a semester at the state capitol in one of many offices: the U.S. Attorney's office, the governor's office, the department of conservation, the department of transportation, the state board of education, the auditor general's office, or the attorney general's office. Professionals in the office serve as sponsors, helping students learn about careers associated with that office. Although credit is given for the internship assignment, students who qualify for the program typically have all the credits necessary to graduate from high school at midterm. This program is part of a national internship program, the Executive High School Internship Association. These programs generally follow a standard schedule whereby students report to work during business hours four days per week. On the fifth day, all students in the program located in a particular city meet for an internship seminar. Many different students can benefit from an internship experience. For example, Hirsch (1979), the developer of the national internship program, found that gifted stu-

mentorship. A program in which a gifted student is paired with an adult in order to learn to apply knowledge in real-life situations.

internship. Programs that place gifted students, usually high school seniors, in job settings related to their career goals in order to challenge them and apply knowledge in real-life skills.

MAKING CONNECTIONS

Renzulli's model is summarized in the Defined section of this chapter.

dents with disabilities participated successfully in internships. Some needed additional support to overcome barriers caused by their physical disabilities, but these students performed as well as their peers without disabilities.

The **enrichment triad/revolving door model** seeks to modify the entire educational system (Renzulli & Reis, 1997). This model offers a different view of education for all children by allowing students to move into advanced activities on the basis of their performance in general enrichment offerings. Recall that Renzulli believes that three traits—above-average ability, creativity, and task commitment—constitute giftedness. In support of this flexible definition, Renzulli and Reis developed a model for gifted education in which enrichment activities are **infused** into the general education classroom. In addition to providing enrichment for all students, the enrichment triad model directly serves from 15 to 20 percent of the school population, rather than limiting it to the top 2 to 3 percent. This highly successful program has been adopted in many school districts across the country, and its supporters maintain that it includes students with high potential for creative production. They also believe that this larger pool will include more students from culturally and linguistically diverse backgrounds. How does the program work? Students "revolve" into and out of different levels of their program. In type 1, enrichment activities expose students to new exciting topics of study carried out through a variety of instructional approaches (speakers, field trips, demonstrations, videotapes and films, and interest centers). For many of these enrichment activities, the entire class is encouraged to participate. In type 2, activities center on the development of cognitive and affective abilities; they are also available to the entire general education class. Type 3 activities develop advanced investigative and creative skills. At this point, students who are motivated and show great interest are provided with specialized instruction and activities to explore particular topics, issues, or ideas.

How do teachers find time in the busy school day to enrich students' curriculum? Instructional time can be recaptured by applying a concept called **curriculum compacting**. Using this instructional strategy, teachers can modify or eliminate topics that gifted students have mastered or can master in a fraction of the time that their peers need. Research has shown that mathematics and language arts are areas where teachers can learn how to apply curriculum compacting easily and without any reduction in students' achievements (Reis & Purcell, 1993). This study also found that between 24 and 70 percent of the content across curriculum areas can be eliminated by using this technique. Thus a significant amount of time is left for challenging replacement activities like the enrichment practices discussed in this section.

Acceleration Approach. Considerable evidence exists that gifted students are quantitatively different from many of their age-peers. These high achievers make great gains when they are accelerated (Pendarvis & Howley, 1996). Despite this research evidence, only 17 percent of this group have participated in accelerated programs.

What does this approach include and what are its advantages? Through **acceleration**, which comes in many different forms, students can move through several years of school in a shorter period of time. For instance, an accelerated student might complete three years of school in two years by skipping a grade or taking advanced placement courses. A student could also move through academic material more quickly, completing a traditional sixth grade mathematics book in

enrichment triad/revolving door model. A model for gifted education where 15 to 20 percent rather than 3 percent of a school's students periodically participate in advanced activities planned to develop thinking skills, problem solving, and creativity.

infused. The incorporation of enrichment activities into the general education curriculum.

curriculum compacting. Reducing instructional time spent on typical academic subjects so that enrichment activities can be included in the curriculum.

acceleration. Moving students through a curriculum or years of schooling in a shorter period of time than usual.

one semester, say, instead of two. Researchers have described many positive aspects of acceleration for gifted students (Kulik & Kulik, 1997). First, these students are able to handle the academic challenges of acceleration. Second, when grouped with students of comparable abilities, they make greater achievement gains. Third, many of them develop better self-concepts and more positive attitudes about course content and school in general (Southern & Jones, 1991). Fourth, acceleration solves the criticism that gifted education segregates these students from more typical learners, because although they are not placed with students of the same age, they are participating in general education programs (Pendarvis & Howley, 1996). Some potentially negative aspects of this approach, however, cause some educators to be concerned. Children should not be pushed beyond their capabilities, which may not be consistently developed. Educators must carefully monitor students' social and academic performance and be prepared to modify programs when necessary.

Acceleration can be provided in a variety of ways. One application is through **advanced placement courses**, courses students take while in high school that earn college credit. One older study of advanced placement showed that in only ten states, more than $19 million in college costs was saved in one year alone (Gallagher, Weiss, Oglesby, & Thomas, 1983). Consider inflation and what those savings would be in today's dollars! Advanced placement allows gifted students and those who are high achievers to experience enrichment and acceleration by studying course content in more depth. A side benefit is that they do not have to retake these courses in college.

Another form of acceleration, individualized instruction, provides one-to-one instruction (Bloom & Sosniak, 1981). In this approach, teachers serve in tutorial roles, monitor student progress, provide corrective feedback, and reward students as they move through the curriculum at their own pace.

Another option, **ability grouping**, has gained considerable support from educators of the gifted. In this approach, youngsters are grouped for specific activities or courses in which they excel. These groups are easily arranged in middle and high schools, where most students travel from class to class. In this approach, gifted students can attend more advanced classes. For example, a ninth grader might attend sophomore- or junior-level mathematics classes; a high school senior might take several classes at a local college. Many high schools provide **honors sections** of academic courses as a form of ability grouping. The criterion for entrance into these classes is outstanding academic achievement in specific subject matters. Ability grouping and honors sections allow gifted students to attend classes with students who are not identified as gifted.

Ability grouping, which can be used in elementary, middle, and high schools, has advantages. It allows children who have demonstrated exceptional capabilities to excel in some areas yet remain with their general education classmates in areas where they are closer to grade level. Although used today in many schools as one option for gifted students, ability grouping was struck down in a decision by the Washington, D.C. District Court in 1967. Ability grouping was deemed discriminatory and a form of racial segregation because so few students from minority groups were included in higher track programs (*Hobson v. Hansen*, 1967).

Eclectic Approaches. Other approaches to the education of gifted students are broader. One example is the **Purdue Secondary Model for Gifted and Talented Youth** (Feldhusen & Robinson, 1986). This comprehensive program,

 MAKING CONNECTIONS

Many gifted educators consider advanced placement a transitional experience; therefore it is also discussed in the Transition section of this chapter.

advanced placement courses. High school courses that carry college credit.

ability grouping. Placing students with comparable achievement and skill levels in the same classes or courses.

honors sections. Advanced classes for any student who shows high achievement in specific subject areas.

Purdue Secondary Model for Gifted and Talented Youth. A high school curriculum for gifted students that combines enrichment and acceleration.

intended to meet all the educational needs of high school youngsters who are gifted, has many components. It combines enrichment as well as accelerated features into students' education programs and includes counseling services. Another unique feature of the Purdue model is the use of seminars to expand on topics studied in other classes or to develop library and research skills. A summary of the model is shown in Figure 7.4. Feldhusen and Robinson believe that the counseling included in the program is crucial to gifted students. Because of their superior abilities, some of these youngsters are too challenging to their teachers and classmates; others exhibit adjustment problems because they are bored with school. The school districts that have adopted this approach have found that counseling helps these students cope with the often difficult situations adolescents face at school. Counseling also guides students toward particular areas of study and careers, develops self-awareness, and promotes self-acceptance of their abilities, interests, and needs.

Another method used in gifted education to enhance creativity is the **Future Problem Solving Program**, a national project developed by Torrance and his colleagues during the late 1970s that continues today (Torrance & Torrance, 1978). In this program, students are asked to solve global problems—such as the nuclear arms race, the destruction of rain forests, or the predicted future shortages of safe drinking water. Each year, in a national competition, classes of students are presented with three problems to study and solve, to which they submit their solutions for evaluation by a panel of judges. Through this program, students learn many critical-thinking skills and are encouraged to develop positive solutions to real-world problems.

Another approach provides instruction and experiences at different levels to students (Treffinger, 1986). Regardless of the topic, students first receive basic experiences that encourage them to generalize their knowledge and analyze concepts and ideas. Next, they learn to develop divergent (or creative) thinking skills through exercises that include **brainstorming** (how many different ways a brick can be used, changes that can be made to eliminate litter on the playground, ways that the amount of garbage being sent to landfills can be reduced), listing **attributes** (the characteristics of plants, of animals, of people), and determining the relationships or associations among items and concepts (the common features of houses and school buildings, of plants and animals, of Mayan and Polynesian cultures). Students' convergent (or critical) thinking skills can be enhanced by having them make **inferences** and **deductions**, decide what information is relevant, practice with analogies, use evidence to come to conclusions, and **categorize** information.

Some important factors, however, must be in place before effective instruction can occur (Davis & Rimm, 1994). First, a learning environment that allows students to feel safe and free to explore and develop their talents must be prepared. That environment must be noncritical, nonevaluative, and receptive to novel and even wild ideas. Students must be allowed to apply different types of thinking even in traditional lessons or units.

Inclusion

You have learned throughout this text that issues relating to the concept of inclusion are currently discussed and debated in the education community, and you have learned that these issues are now facing educators of the gifted. For students with disabilities and for gifted students, the main issues are *where* they will receive

Future Problem Solving Program. A national competition and instructional program to teach creative problem solving, in which students attempt to find positive solutions to real issues such as the nuclear arms race and water conservation.

brainstorming. An instructional technique in which students quickly generate as many ideas as they can.

attributes. Common characteristics or features of a group.

inferences. Incomplete decisions or opinions, based on assumptions or reasoning.

deduction. Coming to a logical conclusion from facts or general principles that are known to be true.

categorize. Classify or group concepts or items; a thinking skill.

FIGURE 7.4

Components of the Purdue Secondary Model For Gifted And Talented Youth

1 Counseling Services

1. Talent identification
2. Education counseling
3. Career counseling
4. Personal counseling

6 Foreign Languages

1. Latin or Greek
2. French or Spanish
3. German or Asian
4. Russian

2 Seminar

1. In-depth study
2. Self-selected topics
3. Career education
4. Affective activities
5. Thinking, research, and library skills
6. Presentations

7 The Arts

1. Art
2. Drama
3. Music
4. Dance

3 Advanced Placement Classes

Open to students in grades 9–12
All subject matter areas

8 Cultural Experiences

1. Concepts, plays, exhibits
2. Field trips
3. Tours abroad
4. Museum program

4 Honors Classes

1. English
2. Social studies
3. Biology
4. Language
5. Humanities

9 Career Education

1. Mentors
2. Seminar experience
   a. study of careers
   b. study of self
   c. educational planning

5 Math-Science Acceleration

1. Begin algebra in 7th grade
2. Continue acceleration and fast-paced math
3. Open science courses to earlier admission

10 Vocational Programs

1. Home economics
2. Agriculture
3. Business
4. Industrial arts

11 Extra-School Instruction

1. Saturday school
2. Summer classes
3. Correspondence study
4. College classes

Source: "The Purdue Secondary Model For Gifted And Talented Youth" (p. 158) by J. Feldhusen and A. Robinson, in *Systems and Models for Developing Programs for the Gifted and Talented*, J. S. Renzulli (Ed.), 1986, Mansfield Center, CT: Creative Learning Press. Reprinted by permission.

their education and *who* will deliver it. There is considerable discussion and little agreement on these topics for gifted students. But before we explore the topic of inclusion and gifted education, let's first identify the range of service delivery options available across the nation. Renzulli (1994/1995) helps us understand the wide array of services that should be available in his scheme for a Continuum of Services for Total Talent Development (see Figure 7.5).

Because of inconsistent educational opportunities for students who are gifted and creative, there is no uniformity in the types of educational services available. Some districts provide a vast range of educational services; others do not offer enhanced or even different curricular options. Some school districts offer a variety of educational placements (ability grouping, resource rooms, special classes, special schools); some offer only a few; others provide no differential services.

Enrichment and acceleration can occur in a variety of settings and administrative arrangements. **Cluster programs** use the general classroom and the general classroom teacher for the delivery of special instructional opportunities. Under this plan, gifted students spend some portion of their school day engaged in enriched or accelerated activities but in the general education classroom setting. For example, these students might be assigned special independent study activities that support and extend topics that are part of the general education curriculum. Sixth graders, studying state history in social studies, might thus prepare a "Who's Who" book of the historical figures in their state's history. Or they might prepare a position paper on a current issue, like water rights, including the historical reasons for the controversy and concluding with solutions to the problem.

Although probably still the most common settings and administrative arrangements for gifted students, **pull-out programs** are decreasing in number (Van Tassel-Baska, 1995). In this service delivery option, students leave the general education class for a portion of their school day to attend a special class. Such programs provide services for either several days per week or an hour or so each day. Some schools combine cluster and pull-out programs. Both cluster and pull-out programs rely heavily on the general education classroom for the majority of a child's education.

Other educational options are available to gifted students. For example, students might receive the majority of their instruction in a special class, possibly at their neighborhood school, where they are educated in a homogeneous environment in which all the other students have comparable abilities. Some advantaged youngsters receive their education at exclusive private schools. Today, many of these schools, like Andover, offer scholarships so that students whose families cannot pay the tuition can be included in their educational communities. Some students attend special public schools exclusively for students who are gifted. Hunter Elementary, for instance, administered by Hunter College of the City University of New York, is a public elementary school exclusively for these students; but these schools are usually at the high school level and stress special areas of education. In New York and other cities, for example, schools specializing in the performing arts, math, or science are available to students who pass qualifying exams or auditions. Students attending these programs have outstanding skills and potential in particular areas that their school district administrators have determined need further development. Such special schools have been implemented in several states, often as **magnet schools** emphasizing a theme (such as the arts, science, technology). Finally, there is a growing national trend for the development of state-supported, special, residential high schools for students who are gifted and/or

MAKING CONNECTIONS

To review the various educational placement options available in special education, particularly the resource room, see Educational Environments (Chapter 2).

cluster programs. A plan whereby gifted students spend a part of their day in the general classroom on enriched or accelerated activities.

pull-out programs. The most common educational placement for gifted students, who spend part of the school day in a special class.

magnet schools. Center schools that serve children who do not live in the immediate neighborhood; some magnet schools are designed to serve children whose parents work in a nearby area; other magnet schools emphasize a particular theme (such as theater arts, math, and science).

FIGURE 7.5

The Continuum of Services for Total Talent Development

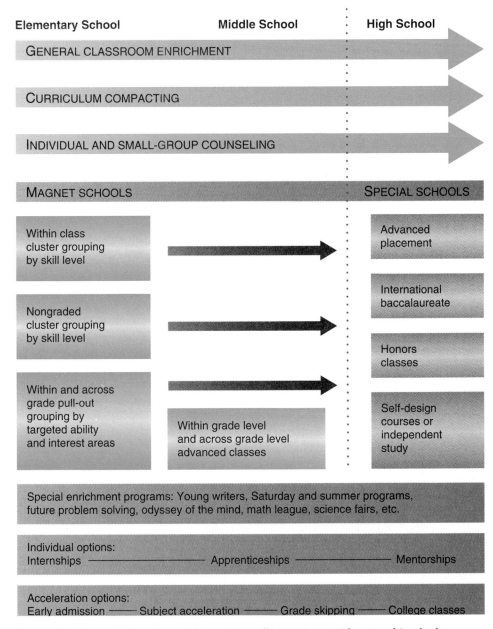

Elementary School   Middle School   High School

GENERAL CLASSROOM ENRICHMENT

CURRICULUM COMPACTING

INDIVIDUAL AND SMALL-GROUP COUNSELING

MAGNET SCHOOLS   SPECIAL SCHOOLS

Within class cluster grouping by skill level

Nongraded cluster grouping by skill level

Within and across grade pull-out grouping by targeted ability and interest areas

Within grade level and across grade level advanced classes

Advanced placement

International baccalaureate

Honors classes

Self-design courses or independent study

Special enrichment programs: Young writers, Saturday and summer programs, future problem solving, odyssey of the mind, math league, science fairs, etc.

Individual options:
Internships ———————— Apprenticeships ———————— Mentorships

Acceleration options:
Early admission ——— Subject acceleration ——— Grade skipping ——— College classes

Source: "Teachers as Talent Scouts" by J. S. Renzulli, 1994/1995, *Educational Leadership, 52,* p. 78. Reprinted by permission.

creative (Kolloff, 1997). Six states have already established residential schools for students who require a curriculum different from that offered by most schools, and other states are in the planning stages.

MAKING CONNECTIONS

• Review again the Defined and History sections of this chapter.

Although not all of these educational options exist in every state or local district, a full array of curriculum, instructional approaches, and service delivery systems are available across the nation to students who are gifted and talented. But the debate continues about where these students should receive their education, what their education should comprise, and who their classmates should be. On one side of the debate are those who contend that gifted students should receive their education exclusively in the general education classroom from the general education teacher (McDaniel, 1993; Sapon-Shevin, 1996). As in earlier periods of time, equity, elitism, democracy, and fear of an intellectual aristocracy are focal points of this side of the debate. In addition, proponents of this view say that the U.S. classroom should reflect U.S. society: one that is diverse, heterogeneous, and multicultural.

On the other side of the debate, people argue that students who are gifted require a unique and challenging educational program in which their classmates comprise a homogeneous ability group (Gallagher, 1996). They believe that most general education classroom settings cannot offer gifted students an appropriate education, since, as Schiever and Maker (1991) suggest, the current organizational structure of general education is geared to the average learner. Schiever and Maker maintain that few gifted students receive accommodations and that there is great reluctance among teachers and school officials to provide them. Research studies support their observations (Archambault, Westberg, Brown, Hallmark, Zhang, Emmons, 1993). For example, Cornell, Delcourt, Goldberg, and Bland (1995) found that culturally and linguistically diverse students, as well as their classmates, who attended gifted education classes achieved far more academically than those who did not have gifted education available to them. Despite these findings, many economically strapped school districts are discontinuing the few special programs they had offered for gifted children and these students are left with teachers unprepared to meet their educational needs (Archambault et al., 1993). General classroom teachers must and do provide educational experiences that are at grade level or at the average achievement level of their students. (See the Making Accommodations box for some suggestions.) However, giftedness is fostered through unique offerings and experiences.

Of course, as with any debate, most educators and researchers find their beliefs and opinions falling somewhere in the middle. Some, like Clark (1992), feel that educational programs for children who are gifted should be arranged on an individual basis, with careful consideration of each child's needs. Others, like Slavin (1990), maintain that mixed ability groups can be more effective than homogeneous groupings of children, particularly when **cooperative learning**—groups of children working on assignments—is combined with individualized instruction. Research findings, however, do not support the effectiveness of cooperative learning for the brightest students when they are maintained in age-grade appropriate classrooms (Pendarvis & Howley, 1996). Those who do argue for general education class placement for students who are gifted tend to agree: A successful placement for these students requires considerable adjustments to the typical general education class (Maker, 1993). What is important to remember is that no administrative arrangement or instructional program guarantees an appropriate or excellent education. The real difference comes from well-prepared teachers who can adjust their instructional practices to meet the educational needs of each individual child in their class. Gallagher (1996) offers some

cooperative learning. Groups of more than two students collaborating as they learn the same material.

1. Teach a full range of content areas in considerable depth.

2. Vary your instructional approaches.

3. Encourage students to become independent learners.

4. Enrich topics of study with additional activities, such as guest speakers, field trips, demonstrations, videotapes, and interest centers.

5. Allow students to move through the curriculum at their own pace.

6. Watch for signs of boredom.

7. Encourage lively class discussions.

8. Create a safe environment where novel ideas are accepted.

9. Pose important problems to solve so that thinking about present and future dilemmas is considered.

10. Teach and foster the use of library and research skills.

11. Develop instructional activities, and use questions that generate the application of different types of thinking skills.

12. Integrate the use of technology into your instruction.

interesting points to consider when individuals formulate their own position on this debate:

> But to argue for educational services for bright children is not an argument for inequity but rather a recognition that inequity will be unlikely to be cured by forcing a false equity upon people. Instead it would seem to be useful to give massive opportunities for those who lack them and encourage their increased level of performance in whatever area they wish to excel. (p. 246)

Transition Through Adulthood

One way to understand the transitional needs of any group of people is to study what happens to members of that group as adults. The most comprehensive study ever done was conducted by Terman (1925) and is still considered a classic follow-up study in the education of the gifted. As we mentioned earlier, there have been many criticisms of Terman's work, now over seventy years old (Hughes & Converse, 1962). Changes in cultural values, different concepts of giftedness, and the times can all influence who is considered gifted, what educational options are selected for them, and their ultimate career choices.

Even though Terman's follow-up studies are dated, many findings still are valid. For example, highly intelligent children tend to excel as adults (Terman & Oden, 1959; Oden, 1968). At midlife, 77 of the 800 men in Terman's survey were listed in *American Men of Science* and 33 were found in *Who's Who of America*. These men were also highly productive, producing 67 books, more than 400 short stories and plays, and over 1,400 professional and scientific papers. Of Terman's sample, 47 percent of the men were in professional occupations with another 40 percent in office, managerial, and semiprofessional work. Of the women, 45 percent were housewives. More recent follow-up studies also show that individuals identified as gifted

 MAKING CONNECTIONS

For a review of Terman's work, see in this chapter
• Traditional Perspectives (Defined),
• History.

during childhood are more likely to be successful adults whose giftedness has translated and developed into outstanding talents (Subotnik & Arnold, 1994).

Individuals identified as creative during their schoolyears became productive, creative adults (Torrance, 1972). They tended to select unusual occupations that involved various combinations of training and experience, including work or study in foreign countries. The creative, more often than noncreative persons, select careers in categories like the following: explorer, inventor, writer, entertainer, artist, dancer, and product designer.

Although a college education is one key to entering most professions, many individuals who are gifted do not avail themselves of higher education. In fact, a disproportionate number of these individuals drop out of high school. Davis and Rimm (1994) indicate that between 10 and 20 percent of all dropouts are gifted individuals. Students who are bored or are not challenged in high school often feel that college is a terribly long time away, so they leave school prematurely. Advanced placement provides an excellent acceleration option for such students. This approach is extremely cost-effective, saving parents millions of dollars in college tuition. For example, one recent Colorado high school graduate was able to enter college with 45 credit hours, enough to qualify him as a second-semester sophomore, and his local school district paid for his tuition (Walsh, 1991). Colorado's postsecondary options program allows high school students to take courses at public two- and four-year colleges and receive both high school and college credit for their work. Some students participating in this program take one or two college courses; others attend college full-time.

There are many variations in advanced placement. For example, Boston University opened a private four-year high school in 1993 offering a rigorous college curriculum (Sommerfield, 1992). Juniors at this school may also take biology and foreign language courses at the university, and seniors may take all their courses there. Other universities, rather than provide transition, simply admit students early. One such program, supported by counseling, is offered by California State College–Los Angeles (Gray, 1991). Enrollment there has increased by 41 percent, and the program's popularity continues to increase. The most famous early admittance program was offered by the University of Chicago, which has since discontinued the program. Administrators felt that the advanced students were not ready for graduate school or the world of work at the age of 19 or 20 when they graduated from college. Now students remain at the University of Chicago Laboratory School for their high school education and take some courses at the university. Critics of acceleration programs agree with the decision of the University of Chicago administrators. They also cite problems of adjustment, of pushing children too hard, and of not making decisions carefully on a case-by-case basis as reasons to approach acceleration programs cautiously (Wernick, 1992).

The probability for success is high for gifted individuals. In greater proportions, they are productive and contributing members of society. However, the positive outcome for many gifted individuals does not convince all experts that these students need special programs. Gallagher (1996) argues that society needs productive and contributing members; therefore the talents of gifted children need to be fostered and developed. Gifted people are needed to lead society and to keep the United States competitive in business, technology, and science. Thus more gifted individuals need to be accurately identified, educated to potential, encouraged to attend and complete postsecondary and graduate schools, and, ultimately, assume leadership roles.

MAKING CONNECTIONS

Advanced placement is also discussed in the Approaches found earlier in this section.

Families

The importance of the family cannot be underestimated for any child. Studies of eminent adults clearly show how powerful the influence of family is on gifted children (Subotnik, Kassan, Summers, Wasser, 1993; Yewchuk, 1995). Definitive and common threads run through each of these eminent adults. For example, regardless of the father's occupation, learning was valued for its own sake. The family was prepared to commit whatever time and resources necessary to foster achievement and talent development. These families arranged for instruction, encouraged and supervised practice and study, and were involved in their children's education. Perhaps most importantly, these parents served as role models by living an achieving lifestyle. It should be noted, however, that not all of the eminent adults studied came from stable homes. It is interesting that, in particular, the home backgrounds of some creative talents (writers, composers) were marked by chaos and turbulence (Albert, 1991). Regardless of this last finding, one thing is clear: The support of the family is crucial to the translation of ability (giftedness) to achievement (talent).

Parents of gifted children sometimes are confused about what constitutes support. Many of these parents, not unlike most parents, do not have a realistic perspective on their children's abilities. Some deny their child's special abilities in an attempt to keep them normal or well adjusted. Others take the opposite tack and magnify their children's abilities, putting excessive pressure on them to achieve and excel in all areas. All parents, and especially parents of gifted children, need to learn what is realistic for their child and to develop appropriate standards and expectations.

Parents of gifted children need to have positive expectations of their children and send clear, consistent, and positive messages about their expectations. Children who are expected to achieve and engage in constructive activities, and are rewarded for those actions, tend to internalize these expectations. When parents' expectations are low, children can internalize those as well. For example, Dickens and Cornell (1993) found definite relationships between parents' expectations and their daughters' performance in mathematics. They also found a relationship between parents' confidence in their own abilities in science and math and their offsprings'. If parents had a high self-concept about their mathematical abilities, their children did as well. However, those parents who believed that they did not have abilities in this area had children who held similar beliefs. Parents' expectations for themselves and their children are influential. The result can be either high or low achievement depending on the beliefs passed on to children.

Reprinted with special permission of North American Syndicate.

Lastly, many gifted children are extremely verbal and have unusual abstract-thinking skills; they also seem to be more mature than other children of their age (Davis & Rimm, 1994). Such characteristics can be deceptive. These children, like others of their age, are not capable of making complex decisions or setting their own goals and directions. Of course, their interests and feelings should be considered, but parents and teachers must not abdicate responsibility for guidance. According to Davis and Rimm, successful gifted achievers felt confident throughout their schoolyears that adults were concerned about them and made appropriate decisions about their education. They also felt that it was a wise decision to follow the lead of these adults.

Technology

For gifted people and for people with disabilities, technology can change the quality of their lives, improve the chances for more successful integration in the community, and enhance employment opportunities. The infusion of microcomputer technology into educational settings has been especially beneficial, since it allows for more applications of individualized instruction. Thus, a class of gifted students can work on a variety of instructional tasks at the same time. For example, one student can work on a tutorial in chemistry or physics while a classmate can be learning how to program the computer to develop an environmental monitoring and control system. As more software becomes available, the opportunities multiply for children to master academic tasks more quickly and efficiently, practice problem-solving skills, and work independently. For gifted students bored by instruction paced too slowly for them or on topics they have already mastered, technology can allow them to study advanced topics more in depth. For gifted students, technology needs to become an essential tool for wide applications in daily life. Technology also has great advantages for these students who live in rural and remote areas. Let's look at these two issues.

Technology as a Functional Skill

Computer technology has almost unlimited applications. Computers have become tools of modern life for many Americans, and the likelihood is that the technology that computers bring to daily life will continue to expand and develop. For today's students, mastering this tool is just as important as mastering other basic academic skills such as reading, writing, and mathematics. For example, even very young children can learn and apply word processing to their writing assignments. As they become more sophisticated in its use, they can use **desktop publishing** to produce a variety of written products.

Teachers at many schools, like Central Virginia Governor's School for Science and Technology, have infused technology into the curriculum and no longer teach these skills and applications as discrete course content (Morgan, 1993). Here, technology is viewed as falling into three categories: increased productivity, awareness of emerging technologies, and enhanced the instructional environment. In the first category, students must demonstrate proficiency using software applications in their assignments. For example, they use word processing—along with database, statistical, graphics, and literature search—applications to generate research papers. They also use computers for multimedia presentations of their final reports. In the second category, students come to an awareness of the emerging

desktop publishing. Using a microcomputer and special software to prepare written and graphic material in publication format and quality.

applications of technology to better understand what is on the horizon. For example, students are given the opportunities to explore robotics, holography, telecommunications, biotechnology, and other developing scientific applications of computer technology. In the last category, the instructional environment is enhanced through the capabilities of technology. In laboratory settings students explore "what if" scenarios to expand on classroom learning. For example, in the study of motion, students can hypothesize what will happen to a velocity or an acceleration curve when a variable (mass, friction, or air resistance) is altered.

Students who have the opportunity to enhance their learning by using technology as a tool rather than an isolated curriculum topic should be enabled to evolve as the practical applications of technology develop. By integrating technology into the instruction of other disciplines, the computer becomes an intellectual tool used to facilitate learning and its generalization to other settings and skills. Such integration also helps extend the standard curriculum. For example, students could construct a database to keep records for a science project on air quality. The database could be used to compare different variables—such as the time of day, temperature, wind conditions, cloud cover, and season of the year—with the amount of air pollution. By using telecommunications (the next topic in this section), students could share the database and the results of various comparisons with other students across the nation.

Electronic Outreach

Almost all of us can attest to the benefits of **telecommunications** in our daily lives. We are now able to communicate with friends efficiently and economically through **e-mail** systems. We are able to do literature searches and find important or interesting information through the **World Wide Web**. Most likely, many of you searched out information about prospective colleges to attend by using the Internet to access different schools' home pages. It is amazing how quickly this technological application has become popular and in high demand. Its practical benefits to all students, particularly gifted students, have become vital components of their instructional programs.

Telecommunications allows students who live miles apart, and maybe have not even met, to work together on joint projects. Students who live in remote areas can access major library facilities and computers that have capabilities to analyze complicated sets of data. They can link up scientists who work at research laboratories to ask for help in solving a scientific or mathematical question. Telecommunications can also provide opportunities for dialogue between students and practitioners from all across the nation on real issues and problems.

At the Louisiana School for Math, Science and the Arts, a unique outreach program has been developed that allows students who live long distances from the school to participate in many courses not available at their home schools (McBride & Lewis, 1993). This distance learning application provides opportunities for gifted students living in rural areas to take advanced courses in math, foreign languages, science, and the arts. And, they can do so without leaving their home schools. Data indicate that this method of delivering instruction is highly effective. First, participating students' scores on national examinations show significant gains. Second, students living across the state in isolated areas become connected, not only for the common courses they are taking but also for other activities of mutual interest. Third, this system can provide important benefits to

telecommunications. Various electronic devices that allow students and teachers to access and send materials and information using a computer network system.

e-mail. Uses telecommunications and technology to allow individuals to communicate using computers.

World Wide Web. Using the Internet, the Web allows the accessing of information through a personal computer.

individual students. For example, one student, attending the state's smallest school, would not have been able to take a physics course required for admission to Louisiana's Engineering School if this telecommunications option were not available. He would also not have been eligible for a $10,000 state-sponsored scholarship. Lastly, these students became so computer literate due to familiarity with the hardware and software used for the distance education component that they were able to solve technical problems when they arose.

Concepts and Controversy: Do We Need a Different Way to Identify and Provide Gifted Education to Native American Students?

 MAKING CONNECTIONS

For more about the special needs of students from historically underrepresented ethnic groups, in particular see
• Chapter 3,
• The Focus on Diversity boxes found in every chapter.

Although somewhere between 3 and 5 percent of U.S. schoolchildren should qualify for gifted education, culturally and linguistically diverse children are not proportionally represented in those classes. As we mentioned in the Defined section of this chapter, most states determine eligibility for programs for gifted students by using scores on tests of intelligence and achievement as a minimum criterion for selection (Coleman & Gallagher, 1994). Typically, to be eligible for gifted education, a child must score at least 130 on a test of intelligence and demonstrate excellence in academics. Unfortunately, these criteria mean that proportionally fewer children from culturally and linguistically diverse groups qualify for gifted education.

Intelligence tests have been criticized for years by political and social leaders as being culturally biased and fostering discrimination practices. Children from African American, Native American, and Hispanic communities tend not to score over 130 on these tests. Thus it appears that these tests favor the experiential backgrounds of the dominant culture and hinder the performance of children from minority backgrounds (Banks, 1994). While these children are typically overrepresented in disability categories, they are seriously underrepresented in gifted education (Harry, 1994; U.S. Department of Education, 1993).

Relatively little attention has been paid to Native American children who might be eligible for educational programs for gifted students. Underrepresentation of these students is significant. Recall that in Alaska, Native Americans comprise 25 percent of the population but only 15 percent of those receiving gifted educational services (Harry, 1994). How should eligibility criteria be modified to accommodate these students? Can one identification system be used for all Native American children? Standard systems are used to determine whether youngsters have disabilities and therefore qualify for special education. Should nationally normed standardized tests of intelligence and achievement *not* be included in the assessment batteries for Native American children? One problem with developing uniform criteria for these youngsters is that they do not come from a homogeneous group. The U.S. government recognizes 177 different tribes in this country, and 187 native languages are spoken. The poverty rate among this population is exceptionally high, moreover.

Are there really fewer Native American children who should receive specialized educational services for the gifted? Or should the process used and the criteria for entrance in such programs be different for Native Americans? If the criteria for selection is determined by the local community, should the number of students included be limited? Definitions and criteria developed at each reservation might exclude some children who would be considered gifted by the dominant culture, and they might include children who would not be typically identified as gifted but who possess certain traits valued by the local culture (Callahan & McIntire, 1994). Maker and her colleagues (Maker, Nielson, & Rogers, 1994) believe that traditional methods should be adapted by applying a flexible interpretation of Gardner's theory of multiple intelligences.

A different plan for Native American students leaves us with many questions, however. For example, should the size of these programs be limited to some percentage of the school population? Should a consistent way of identifying students be used across all tribes, or should each local community devise its own system for qualifying youngsters? What would the content taught in these classes be? If a local community decided to emphasize its culture in these classes rather than academic achievement, creativity, and problem solving, would that content be acceptable to the professional community of educators of the gifted? Who should pay for these programs? Would reimbursement (possibly from the Bureau of Indian Affairs or the state educational agency in the state where the tribe is located) be contingent on a curriculum deemed acceptable by an outside community or agency?

Certainly, these issues leave considerable room for debate and discussion. How would you assist a Native American community in identifying students who should participate in specialized programs for the gifted?

~~ *SUMMARY* ~~

Gifted individuals do not have a disability that presents obstacles to their learning and participating in society. However, they can be handicapped by our social and educational systems, which present barriers to achieving to their potential. Gifted individuals possess unique intellectual abilities that can be developed into talents. One challenge facing educators is to develop and put into place a consistent array of educational options that will facilitate these individuals' development.

FOCUS QUESTIONS

Self-Test Questions

▶ *Regardless of the definition used, what descriptors can be used for gifted and talented individuals?*

Although each person is an individual, possessing unique abilities, some common descriptors apply to the group of learners who are called gifted. Under the most common definitions, these individuals are very bright and demonstrate their high intellectual abilities by scoring well on tests of intelligence, learning more quickly than their peers, and applying complex thinking skills. Their academic achievement is significantly higher than their classmates'. These individuals also tend to become leaders. Three common characteristics tend to mark this group: sensitivity, perfectionism, and intensity. Possibly, because of these characteristics, many of them become successful adults.

▶ *What factors can inhibit giftedness and talent development?*

Educators are interested in identifying the factors that enhance or inhibit giftedness and talent development. Clearly, a strong interplay between heredity and the environment contributes to the intellectual and talent outcomes for all individuals. For example, environmental variables, such as deprivation and lack of stimulation, can impede normal child development.

Other factors—like cultural values and expectations, the family's socioeconomic level, the individual's birth position—also are related to giftedness. Also, educational opportunities can be very important to many youngsters with great potential. For them, more educational and social service programs need to be developed and consistently available to enable these youngsters achieve their potential.

▶ *Why are educators concerned about issues related to underrepresentation and the various subgroups of gifted learners?*

The nation serves fewer children as gifted than it should. Estimates indicate that between 3 and 5 percent of U.S. children should qualify for gifted education. However, substantially less than 3 percent of children from culturally and linguistically diverse groups in this country receive services. Programs for those who are gifted are not equally available to all students who demonstrate unique and outstanding abilities. Because standardized tests of intelligence and achievement tend to favor children who come from the dominant culture, fewer African American, Hispanic, and Native American children receive educational services for gifted students. These students are underrepresented in gifted education services. Also, individuals from other subgroups—those with disabilities, underachievers, and females—have less access to these programs. Programs need to be put into place that support these subgroups and meet their individual needs.

▶ *What are three gifted education approaches, and how do they differ from one another?*

Different types of educational programs are used with gifted students. Some school districts provide a variety of different services, whereas others provide no special services. Few early education programs are specifically designed or available for these children. At the school level, the most common educational arrangement is the pull-out program, which functions like a special education resource room. In general, three approaches are used in gifted education: enrichment (interdisciplinary instruction, independent study, mentorships, internships, enrichment triad/revolving door model, curriculum compacting), acceleration (advanced placement, honors sections, ability grouping, individualized instruction), and eclectic (e.g., Purdue Secondary Model for Gifted and Talented Youth). The approach most commonly used in high school is acceleration, through honors programs or advanced placement options.

▶ *What are the four service delivery models often used in gifted education, and how do they differ from one another?*

Considerable debate about where gifted students should be educated is occurring at the present time. Some educators maintain that they should remain in general education classes and be offered enriched instruction by general education teachers. By enriching the entire general education curriculum, some believe that gifted education will become unnecessary. Many professionals and teachers of gifted students do not agree; believing strongly that these students must spend significant portions of their educational programs with others of comparable abilities engaging in an accelerated and enriched program. Still, the most common arrangement is the pull-out program, in which students spend several hours a day working with a specially trained teacher. Some school districts offer special classes for gifted education. Here, students receive almost all of the education with peers who are also highly gifted, and, although not common, some special residential schools are available.

Challenge Question

▶ *Why, across the history of the United States, has there been such an inconsistent commitment to gifted education?*

Gifted education has experienced periods of great interest and periods of neglect across our nation's history. When leaders sense threats to the country's national security, education of the gifted becomes a priority. For example, education of the gifted flourished after the Russians launched the space satellite *Sputnik* in 1957, and so during the 1960s programs for gifted students were developed and expanded. The 1970s were marked by a diminishing of educational services for students who were gifted. In the 1980s, U.S. leaders again saw external threats to our economy, as standardized test scores revealed that our students were not achieving at levels of students from other nations. As a result, a national interest in gifted education was renewed. The 1990s has seen a paradigm shift where fundamental questions about gifted education, its merits, its equity, and its value are being asked. Partly because programs for those who are gifted are not mandated by the federal laws that ensure educational programs for those with disabilities, gifted education is subject to such changes in priorities.

Scholarly Books

Gallagher, J. J., & Gallagher, S. A. (1994). *Teaching the gifted child* (4th ed.). Boston: Allyn and Bacon.

Davis, G. A., & Rimm, S. B. (1994). *Education of the gifted and talented* (2nd ed.). Englewood Cliffs, NJ: Prentice-Hall.

Clark, B. (1992). *Growing up gifted.* New York: Merrill-Macmillan.

Colangelo, N., & Davis, G. A. (Eds.). (1997). Handbook of gifted education (2nd ed.). Boston: Allyn and Bacon.

Popular Books

Eberstadt, F. (1991). *Isaac and his devils.* New York: Knopf.

Fitzgerald, J. D. (1985). *The great brain.* New York: Dell.

Kanigel, R. (1991). *The man who knew infinity: A life of the genius Ramanujan.* New York: Scribner.

Kerr, B. A. (1985). *Smart girls, gifted women.* Columbus: Ohio Psychology Publishing.

L'Engle, M. (1962). *A wrinkle in time.* New York: Farrar, Straus, & Giroux.

Videos

Goonies. (1985). Warner Brothers/Amblin Entertainment.

Weird science. (1985). Universal Pictures.

Class act. (1992). Warner Brothers.

Little man Tate. (1991). Orion.

Searching for Bobby Fischer. (1993). Paramount Pictures.

Professional, Parent, and Consumer Organizations and Agencies

Gifted Child Society
190 Rock Rd.
Glen Rock, NJ 07452
Web site: http://www.gifted.org
Phone: (210) 444-6530

National Association for Gifted Children
1707 L. Street N.W.
Suite 550
Washington, DC 20036
Web site: http://www.nagc.org
Phone: (202) 785-4268

Mensa, Gifted Children Program
201 Main Street
Suite 1101
Fort Worth, TX 76102
Web site: http://www.us.mensa.org
Phone: (817) 332-7299

The Association for the Gifted (TAG) Council for Exceptional Children
1920 Association Drive
Reston, VA 22091
Web site: http://www.cec.sped.org
Phone: (703) 620-3660

The World Council for Gifted and Talented Children, Inc.
210 Lindquist Center
The University of Iowa
Iowa City, IA 53342
Web site: http://www.uiowa.edu/~belinctr
Phone: (319) 3356-6248

National Research Center on the Gifted and Talented
362 Fairfield Road, U-7
Storrs, CT 06269-2007
Web: http://www.uconn.edu/~wwwgt
Phone: (860) 486-4678

Edvard Munch. *Melancholy.* n.d.

Edvard Munch, the Norwegian painter who is probably best known for the highly emotional and tormented images in his paintings, himself had a tragic childhood and troubled life. Leaving behind what he thought were the emotionless subjects of the impressionists, he sought to record the anguish of modern humanity's psyche. The result was stark and terrifying images of alienation and despair, emotions that Munch himself experienced. For many years, Munch was plagued by nervous disorders and depression. His first documented hospitalization was at a Swiss clinic in 1900 (Bischoff, 1988). During that decade, Munch had long periods of depression and a series of nervous breakdowns. In 1908, after a nervous breakdown in Copenhagen, he spent half a year in a clinic and recovered after electroshock treatment (Grolier, 1993). Many of his paintings during this period were of the nurses and doctors who took care of him (Messer, 1985). Possibly, his most famous painting in America is the *Screamer*.

Behavior Disorders and Emotional Disturbance

8

ADVANCE ORGANIZERS

OVERVIEW

Children with behavior disorders and emotional disturbance typically fall into one of two categories: externalizing behavior problems or internalizing behavior problems. Aggressive and hostile children have externalizing problems, have the poorest outcome probabilities, are identified at a greater rate, and experience more social rejection than those with withdrawn or internalizing problems. Only 1 percent of all schoolchildren are identified as having this disability, but this probably reflects the underidentification of youngsters with internalizing problems.

FOCUS QUESTIONS

SELF-TEST QUESTIONS

▶ By identifying the components of two definitions—the one in IDEA and the one offered by the National Mental Health and Special Education Coalition—how would you compare them?

▶ What are the two major subgroups of this disability, and how would you compare the conditions that fall into each subgroup?

▶ What are the major causes of this disability, and how can it be prevented?

▶ What are the long-term prospects for these children?

▶ How can teachers help children with this disability?

CHALLENGE QUESTION

▶ Why does an array of educational placement options need to be available for students with behavior disorders and emotional disturbance?

A *Personal Perspective*: A Mother Discusses Stigma

Rebecca Viers is the mother of a teenager classified by special educators as having "behavior disorders and emotional disturbance." Rebecca is the founder of Parents for Behaviorally Different Children. Her experiences of the past seventeen years can teach us a great deal about how to improve services for these children and their families. Here is how she describes her experiences.

Stigma. I know it well. I know stigma intimately as the mother of a 17-year-old daughter with a severe brain disorder. This is our story.

I celebrated the birth of my first and only child as any other young mother would. Jessica was so beautiful and looked so healthy. The first days of her life seemed "average" enough. It would be thirteen difficult years before I was to learn that Jessica was born with a severely abnormal brain structure.

Uncontrolled seizures began when she was 10 months old. By the age of 2, Jessica's behaviors had become quite aggressive, noncompliant, and more difficult than any day care staff cared to handle. She began to talk of "Satchuwa," an imaginary playmate whom she held responsible for the deep scratches on her arms and the handfuls of hair pulled from her head.

I made an appointment with a child specialist, the first in a long line of specialists we consulted across the country. A team of professionals evaluated Jessica and declared that she, in fact, was fine—it was her mother who needed help. Well, I won't pretend that I didn't need help by then. My daughter's behaviors were becoming a greater struggle each day. No one made a connection between the seizures and abnormal behavior.

I was still young and insecure, and I gave in to the professionals' theory that I must be doing something wrong. Within a year, I had tried every behavior management plan, token economy system, and time-out procedure known. All with little success. Her behavior did not improve but, instead, grew steadily worse. As a single working parent, I found myself financially drained and socially isolated. It was difficult to find baby-sitters for Jessica. Most went out the backdoor as quickly as they came in the front. I had no extended family to rely on. The behavior became more bizarre, and our situation seemed hopeless.

She was expelled from six or seven day care centers. Finally, she was old enough to begin public school, and I was so relieved. But Jessica lasted less than a week that first year in kindergarten. So I found a private religious preschool that would take her. But Jessica came home and told me that her teacher stood her in a circle of tape

on the floor. Jessica asked me, "Mommy, how did the devil get inside of me? My teacher said that's why I'm bad. I don't want to be bad."

We endured, and when fall rolled around, I enrolled her in public kindergarten again but had her tested before classes began. She was placed in special education and then in a hospital program where I was told that her problems were a result of my own relationship with my mother and life stressors, and had nothing to do with her neurological makeup.

I began searching for other parents who had similar experiences with their children, and I attended a "families as allies" conference that changed my life. As I sat in that room and listened to the parents and professionals speak about how families were not responsible for these illnesses and how families have a valuable role in planning the treatment for their children, tears streamed down my face. Unlike previous tears, this time they were tears of liberation. I had been freed of my guilt and pain. Other parents had similar experiences. I clearly remember an older farmer from Idaho who, for the first time in his life, told about his daughter who became ill with schizophrenia at the age of 16. He described the pain and guilt that he and his wife had endured silently all those years. My maternal instinct, that unconditional love for Jessica, had been right all along. I felt empowered when I left the conference.

My story has a somewhat happy ending. I have found great healing in my advocacy work and in freeing other parents from the prison of blame. No parent should be blamed for biologically based disorders. In Jessica's case, her behavior and emotional problems had more to do with her in-utero environment than they ever had to do with her home environment. Programs should be family-centered, with parents considered the experts on their children. I wonder how different these past seventeen years might have been for Jessica and me if such a philosophy and program had been available to us.

I would like to say that we all lived happily ever after, but Jessica still experiences many problems. She did not attend her high school football game last Saturday evening, nor was she invited to the teenage slumber party down the street. But she is getting better. The future is brighter for Jessica and for us as a family.

1. For Rebecca Viers and Jessica, what forms did stigma against behavior disorders and emotional disturbance take?

2. Transition to adulthood will hold challenges for Jessica. Think about ways in which an individualized transition plan could be helpful. What should be included?

*E*very day we are asked, both subtly and explicitly, to comply with mainstream society's norms and expectations. Most of us find ways to express our individuality and creativity while keeping our behavior within the boundaries of what is considered appropriate. Most children learn very early that life is easier and more pleasant when they conform to certain standards of behavior. Although these standards are rooted in a long history and tend to be rather inflexible, they do vary by situations. Judgments about the appropriateness of someone's actions are made in terms of the parameters of behavior expectations with respect to an individual's age or the setting in which the behavior occurs. Let's look at these two situations a little more closely.

Standards for normal behavior change as children grow up and move through the stages of their lives. Infants, for example, are expected to be messy and dependent and to communicate through gurgles, facial expressions, and crying. Toddlers, in turn, go through routine stages when temper tantrums and resistance are tolerantly interpreted as the predictable "terrible twos." As children progress through childhood and adolescence, accepted stages of development, including even rebelliousness, are usually viewed as predictable and appropriate for the age of the child.

But some children behave contrary to the predicted stages of child development in our society. An 8-year-old who suddenly begins to wet the bed, clings to his mother, and stops talking creates great concern about his behavior. Even though almost identical behavior would be totally accepted in an infant, an 8-year-old who acts in that way is perceived as having a problem. We can cite many examples of behavior that draw concerns about children of one age but, if demonstrated by a child of a different age, do not raise questions at all. Consider Christy, a teenager who throws "kicking and screaming" temper tantrums. If she were 2 years old instead of 16, she would probably be regarded as normal. Because she is now at an age when such behavior is no longer developmentally appropriate, her behavior is seen as a serious problem.

Just as society provides norms of behavior for different stages of development, it also provides norms of behavior for specific environments. Children in school, for example, are expected to be generally quiet, orderly, cooperative with other children, and attentive to learning. Children at home are expected to be cheerful, loving, helpful, and obedient to their parents. In their communities, children are expected to respect their neighbors' property, to abide by curfews and traffic rules, and generally to grow into their roles as the new generation of adult leaders of society. Children whose behavior is inconsistent with expectations of normal behavior in these environments are regarded as having problems.

We have highlighted behavior problems that in rather obvious ways do not fit with societal standards for the age or environment of the child. Sometimes, however, the problems are not so obvious. For instance, the individual's behaviors may be hidden. Or perhaps behaviors that at first glance appear to conform actually exaggerate certain societal standards. What are we to think of the teenage girl who constantly diets, starving herself to the point of endangering her health, in an exaggerated effort to be fashion model slim? or of the boy who hides his suicidal depression behind a facade of perfect behavior? These hidden disorders are also serious problems, but their signs are often ignored and the conditions untreated.

We do not want to leave you with the impression that all disorders are simple violations of age or societal norms. Some behavior disorders and emotional distur-

Children in school are expected to pay attention to their schoolwork, but this expectation can be difficult for students with behavior disorders and emotional disturbance to meet.

bance appear to be unrelated to either norm. These disorders are obvious at any age or in any culture. For example, psychosis—a major departure from normal acting, thinking, and feeling, sometimes expressed in unprovoked physical aggression toward self or others—would be considered disordered behavior at any age or in any society.

The fact that many behavior and emotional problems can be described, and even defined, in terms of differences from developmental stages and societal norms does not diminish the problems. When these problems reach a certain level of severity and when they persist, they are undeniably serious problems—for the child, for the family, for the school, and for the community. Teachers and other professionals can play an important part in helping children with this disability learn in school, have more satisfying relationships with friends and family, and assume adult responsibilities in their communities. Let's see how this might be accomplished.

Behavior Disorders and Emotional Disturbance Defined

As the introduction makes clear, **behavior disorders** and **emotional disturbance** are difficult to define. In fact, some think that people are identified as having this disability "whenever an adult authority said so" (Hallahan & Kauffman, 1997, p. 212). In other words, in many cases the application of the definition is subjective. Until recently, most definitions of this disability, including the one used in IDEA, are based on the one developed by Bower (1960,

1982). Let's first look at the federal definition and then at a more recent one that is gaining in popularity.

IDEA uses the term **serious emotional disturbance (SED)** to describe children with behavior disorders and emotional disturbance, defining it as follows:

> The term means a condition exhibiting one or more of the following characteristics over a long period of time and to a marked degree that adversely affects a child's educational performance:
>
> - An inability to learn that cannot be explained by intellectual, sensory, or health factors;
> - An inability to build or maintain satisfactory interpersonal relationships with peers and teachers;
> - Inappropriate types of behavior or feelings under normal circumstances;
> - A general pervasive mood of unhappiness or depression; or
> - A tendency to develop physical symptoms of fears associated with personal or school problems.
>
> The term includes children who are schizophrenic. The term does not include children who are socially maladjusted, unless it is determined that they have a serious emotional disturbance. (U.S. Department of Education, 1992)

The IDEA definition includes some additional requirements as well. For example, although only one of the characteristics listed in the IDEA definition needs to be present, for the student to qualify for special education, those behaviors must adversely affect the child's educational performance. Because almost everyone has some periods of mild maladjustment for short periods of their lives, the definition also requires that the child exhibit the characteristic for a long time and to a marked degree or significant level of intensity.

The IDEA term and definition have been criticized by many professionals (Kauffman, 1997). They assert that the term *serious emotional disturbance* and its IDEA definition contribute to misunderstandings and underidentification of these students. For example, no other disability category uses the modifier *serious*, which seems to suggest that students with emotional disturbance must have more severe problems than those of other students with disabilities in order to get help. The use of the word *emotional* in the term seems to exclude students whose disability is interpreted as behavior. In the definition, the exclusion of students who are "socially maladjusted," which is not defined, contributes to this misunderstanding. And the reference to "school performance" has been narrowly interpreted to mean only academic performance, not behavioral or social performances, not functional or life skills, and not vocational skills.

Responding to these criticisms, a coalition of seventeen organizations, which calls itself the National Mental Health and Special Education Coalition, has drafted another definition in hopes that the federal and state governments will adopt it instead (Forness & Knitzer, 1992). Here is the proposed definition in its current form.

> The term emotional or behavioral disorder means a disability characterized by behavioral or emotional responses in school so different from appropriate age, cultural, or ethnic norms that they adversely affect educational performance. Educational performance includes academic, social, vocational, and personal skills. Such a disability:
>
> - is more than a temporary, expected response to stressful events in the environment;

serious emotional disturbance. The term used in IDEA to classify students with behavior disorders and emotional disturbance.

- is consistently exhibited in two different settings, at least one of which is school-related; and
- is unresponsive to direct intervention in general education, or the child's condition is such that general education interventions would be insufficient.

Emotional and behavioral disorders can co-exist with other disabilities.

This category may include children or youths with schizophrenic disorders, affective disorders, anxiety disorder, or other sustained disorders of conduct or adjustment when they adversely affect educational performance in accordance with [the opening part of the definition]. (p. 13)

In this chapter, we focus on the educational needs of these children and the ways teachers and other professionals can enhance their success in school. But we must keep in mind that peers and adults frequently respond negatively to students who have these characteristics. It is clear that the potential for psychological pain is always present for these children and their families. Therefore their needs almost always extend into other areas of their lives and require multidisciplinary team efforts whereby many professionals, including psychologists, psychiatrists, physicians, social workers, family counselors, and others, collaborate to meet the individual needs of each specific child.

MAKING CONNECTIONS

Review the section on multidisciplinary teams in Chapter 2.

Types

Behavior disorders and emotional disturbance are often categorized by whether they are primarily externalizing (typically aggressive) behavior problems, internalizing (typically withdrawn) behavior problems, and low-incidence disorders (e.g., schizophrenia). Of course, there are other ways of classifying these disorders. For example, the *DSM IV* (American Psychiatric Association, 1994) provides a section for disorders usually first diagnosed in children. Some of these disorders are considered as disabilities (mental retardation, learning disabilities) by the federal government and the special education community, and others are not (motor skills disorders, tic disorders, mood disorder, oppositional defiant disorder). We find this system confusing and not easily applied to school settings. To us, using the classification scheme of externalizing behaviors and internalizing behaviors is both practical and of educational value. Table 8.1 defines and explains some of the common behaviors and disorders observed using this organization system.

Regardless of the classification scheme used, some of these conditions are more disturbing to other people—though not necessarily more serious—resulting in some disorders not being identified early enough or being left untreated. Here's the point: Because externalizing behavior disorders are so obviously disruptive to other people in the environment, they are often identified more quickly in school settings than internalizing behavior problems (Landrum, Singh, Nemil, Ellis, & Best, 1995). As a result, children with internalizing disorders are not always identified and therefore do not always receive appropriate special educational services. School personnel must try to be alert not only to externalizing disorders but also to the equally serious, although less disruptive, internalizing disorders.

Externalizing Behavior Problems. **Externalizing behaviors** are aggressive behaviors expressed outwardly, usually toward other persons. Some typical examples are hyperactivity, a high level of irritating behavior that is impulsive and distractible, and persistent **aggression**. Table 8.1 lists some examples of external-

externalizing behaviors. Behaviors, especially aggressive behaviors, that seem to be directed toward others.

aggression. Hostile and attacking behavior, which can include verbal communication, directed toward self, others, or the physical environment.

TABLE 8.1

Examples of Externalizing and Internalizing Behavior Problems

Externalizing Behaviors	*Internalizing Behaviors*
Violates basic rights of others	Exhibits painful shyness
Violates societal norms or rules	Is teased by peers
Has tantrums	Is neglected by peers
Causes property loss or damage	Is depressed
Is hostile	Is anorexic
Argues	Is bulimic
Is defiant	Is socially withdrawn
Is physically aggressive	Tends to be suicidal
Ignores teachers' reprimands	Has unfounded fears and phobias
Steals	Tends to have low self-esteem
Damages others' property	Has excessive worries
Demonstrates obsessive/compulsive behaviors	Panics
Causes or threatens physical harm to people or animals	
Uses lewd or obscene gestures	
Is hyperactive	

izing behavior problems. Here, we discuss three common problems: hyperactivity, aggression, and delinquency.

Hyperactivity is probably one of the most common complaints about children referred for evaluations as having behavior disorders and emotional disturbance. Hyperactivity is difficult to define, however, because any definition must consider both the nature and type of activity. Judgment about whether a certain level of a specific activity is too much or "hyper" is often subjective. If, for example, the activity is admired, the child might be described as energetic or enthusiastic rather than hyperactive. Nevertheless, the *DSM IV* gives some good examples about which there is considerable consensus. Use their illustratives and see whether you can arrive at a definition of hyperactivity:

> Hyperactivity may be manifested by fidgetiness or squirming in one's seat, by not remaining seated when expected to do so, by excessive running or climbing in situations where it is inappropriate, by having difficulty playing or engaging quietly in leisure activities, by appearing to be often "on the go" or as if "driven by a motor," or by talking excessively. (American Psychiatric Association, 1994, p. 79)

Aggression may be turned toward objects, toward the self, or toward others. The *DSM IV* does not directly define aggression, but it does include elements of

MAKING CONNECTIONS

• Review the section on ADD in Chapter 4.

MAKING CONNECTIONS

In this chapter, review the sections about aggression found in
• Peer Perceptions (Children with Behavior Disorders and Emotional Disturbance),
• Juvenile Justice and Delinquency (Children with Behavior Disorders and Emotional Disturbance),
• Curriculum Based Assessment (in Educational Interventions).

 MAKING CONNECTIONS

See section about Juvenile Justice and Delinquency (in Educational Interventions).

MAKING CONNECTIONS

See Defined section for definitions of this disability.

social maladjustment. Referring to a group of children who do not act within society's norms but are excluded from the definition of children with serious emotional disturbance.

conduct disorders. Behavior patterns that are externalizing and include "acting out" and hyperactivity, but this condition alone does not qualify as a disability according to IDEA.

internalizing behaviors. Behavior that is withdrawn, into the individual.

anorexia. Intense fear of gaining weight, disturbed body image, chronic absence or refusal of appetite for food, causing severe weight loss (25 percent of body weight).

bulimia. Chronically causing oneself to vomit, limiting weight gain.

aggression in two of the disorders it describes: conduct disorders and oppositional defiant disorder. Of the latter, they identify:

> a recurrent pattern of negativistic, defiant, disobedient, and hostile behavior toward authority figures... and is characterized by the frequent occurrence of at least four of the following behaviors: losing temper, arguing with adults, actively defying or refusing to comply with the requests or rules of adults, deliberately doing things that will annoy other people, blaming others for his or her mistakes or misbehavior, being touched or easily annoyed by others, being angry and resentful, or being spiteful or vindictive. (American Psychiatric Association, 1994, p. 91)

Aggressive behavior, particularly when observed in very young children, is particularly worrisome. This is not just because of the behavior itself—which should not be minimized—but because of its strong correlation to long-term problems (dropping out of school, delinquency).

Delinquency, or juvenile delinquency, is defined by the criminal justice system rather than the medical or educational system. Delinquency refers to illegal acts committed by juveniles, which could include crimes such as theft or assault. Remember, some children who are delinquent have behavior disorders and emotional disturbance, but many do not—just as some children with behavior disorders and emotional disturbance are delinquent and many are not. However, it is very important to understand that children with emotional disturbance and behavior disorders are at great risk for being involved with the criminal justice system. Their rates of contact are disproportionately high. While still in high school, 20 percent have been arrested, as compared to 9 percent of all students with disabilities. By the time they are two years out of school, 35 percent have been arrested (2 1/2 times higher than the general population) (Koyanagi & Gaines, 1993).

Two groups of children who exhibit disturbing behavior are not eligible for special education services (unless they have another qualifying condition as well): Children who are **socially maladjusted** and those with **conduct disorders.** *Neither* group is included in the IDEA definition, although social maladjustment is widely discussed, particularly as politicians and educators talk about discipline and violence in the schools. There is no generally agreed-on definition of social maladjustment, although many people simply refer to these students as "naughty." Conduct disorders are not part of the IDEA definition, but they are defined in the *DSM IV.* According to that manual, the essential feature of this disorder is "a repetitive and persistent pattern of behavior in which the basic rights of others or major age-appropriate societal norms or rules are violated" (American Psychiatric Association, 1994, p. 85). Considerable debate surrounds this group of students. Many experts are afraid that they will cause an explosion in the special education enrollment, increasing their numbers to beyond tolerance and acceptability. Others strongly feel that they should be included in this special education category so that their needs can better be met (Kauffman, 1997). Because they are not included in IDEA, we do not provide any further discussion of them in this chapter. What do you think about this issue? Should these additional children be included in special education? Why? Why not?

Internalizing Behavior Problems. **Internalizing behaviors** are typically expressed through social withdrawal. **Anorexia** and **bulimia** are two examples of internalizing behaviors. In this section, we discuss depression and anxiety, which also fall into the internalizing category.

Depression is often difficult to recognize in children. Its components—such as guilt, self-blame, feelings of rejection, lethargy, low self-esteem, and negative self-image—are often overlooked or may be expressed by behaviors that look like a different problem entirely. Children's behavior when they are depressed may appear so different from the depressed behavior of adults that teachers and parents may have difficulty recognizing the depression. For example, a severely depressed child might attempt to harm himself by running into a busy street or hurling himself off a ledge. An adult might assume this child's behavior was normal because many children accidentally do those things. Furthermore, adults often misinterpret or undervalue children's pain, believing that children have easy lives and should always be happy. In addition, children usually do not have the vocabulary, personal insight, or experience to be able to recognize and label feelings of depression.

Anxiety disorders may be demonstrated as intense anxiety or separation from family, friends, or a familiar environment, excessive shrinking from contact with strangers, or unfocused, excessive worry and fear. Anxiety disorders are difficult to recognize in children. Because withdrawn children engage in very low levels of positive interactions with their peers, peer-rating scales may help educators with identification. Children with internalizing behavior problems, regardless of type, tend to be underidentified, leaving many of them at risk for being untreated or receiving needed services later than they should.

Low-Incidence Behavior and Emotional Disorders. Some disorders occur very infrequently but are quite serious when they do occur. For example, schizophrenia, Tourette's syndrome, and autism can have tragic consequences for the individuals involved and their families, and thankfully they do not have high prevalence rates. Notice that we only mention autism here. The federal government has decided that autism belongs in a separate disability category, so we have included it in another chapter. Regardless it is important to understand that this issue is not resolved, and many professionals believe that autism does belong in this disability category.

Schizophrenia, sometimes considered a form of psychosis or a type of pervasive developmental disability (American Psychological Association, 1994), is an extremely rare disorder in children, although approximately 1 percent of the general population over the age of 18 has been diagnosed as having schizophrenia. When it occurs, it places great demands on service systems. It usually involves bizarre delusions (such as believing thoughts are controlled by the police), hallucinations (such as voices telling the person what to think), "loosening" of associations (disconnected thoughts), and incoherence. Schizophrenia is most prevalent between the ages of 15 and 45, and experts agree that the earlier the onset, the more severe the disturbance in adulthood (Newcomer, 1993). Children with schizophrenia have serious difficulties with schoolwork and often must live in special hospital and education settings during part of their childhood. Their IEPs are complex and require the collaboration of members from a multidisciplinary team.

Another low-incidence disorder, occurring in about 4 to 5 individuals per 1,000, is **Tourette's syndrome**. This disorder is characterized by multiple tics (sudden, rapid, recurrent, and stereotyped motor movements or vocalizations). These individuals might engage in uncontrollable movements at different locations in the body. Or, they may make strange noises or say inappropriate words or phrases. Or, they may have both motor and verbal tics. The verbal tics may be

MAKING CONNECTIONS

See Table 8.1 for examples of externalizing behaviors.

MAKING CONNECTIONS

Chapter 12 provides full coverage of autism.

MAKING CONNECTIONS

For a review of IEPs and of multidisciplinary teams, see Chapter 2.

depression. A state of despair and dejected mood.

anxiety disorders. Conditions causing painful uneasiness, emotional tension, or emotional confusion.

schizophrenia. A rare disorder in children that includes bizarre delusions and dissociation with reality.

Tourette's syndrome. A low-incidence disability that is characterized by multiple and uncontrollable motor and/or verbal tics.

sounds like grunts, yelps, snorts, barks, or obscenities. This disorder causes considerable distress to the individual involved and impairs all aspects of the person's life (American Psychiatric Association, 1994).

Identification

In part because there has been little consensus about the definition of behavior disorders and emotional disturbance or the criteria associated with it, a single method for identifying these children does not exist. Assessment usually takes one or more of the following forms: collection of behavioral data and information, psychodynamic analysis using projective tests or self-reports, or **ecological assessments**. For an individual child, some or all of the following methods might be used:

- Behavior rating scales completed by parents or teachers
- Rating scales completed by the child
- Ratings of peer acceptance or rejection
- Classroom observations, including direct and frequent measures of behavior
- ABC analyses
- Interviews
- Projective tests, in which a clinician uses clinical judgment to attempt to determine (project) the individual's thoughts from pictures or an interview
- Intelligence tests
- Neurological evaluations
- Psychiatric analysis (for example, Freudian analysis)
- Social work evaluations of the individual's environments
- Physical evaluations

As you can see, these methods can be used by parents, teachers, psychologists, psychiatrists, and other professionals.

In addition to determining the presence of problems, educators may also want to measure the intensity or degree of the problems' disturbance for several reasons. First, the definition requires that the characteristics exist to a "marked degree." Generally, the greater the intensity of the problem, the higher the priority to ameliorate it. Second, pre- and postmeasurements of intensity can be used to assess the effectiveness of an intervention. Table 8.2 lists some criteria for determining problems' intensity.

Research continues in an effort to develop more precise assessment instruments. One test is proving to be reliable, efficient, and inexpensive. The *Systematic Screening for Behavior Disorders (SSBD)* is designed for systematic screening of all students in an elementary school (Walker, Severson, Nicholson, Kehle, Jenson, & Clarke, 1994). This instrument uses the conceptual model of externalizing and internalizing behaviors as the organizing system for this disability area. Professionals believe that by screening all students in a school, early identification and early treatment can prevent some problems from becoming more serious and get services to those who need them as quickly as possible. Another benefit is that groups of students with this disability who have a high probability of being underidentified have a better chance of getting the services they need.

MAKING CONNECTIONS

For more on ABC analysis or the ABC model, see
• Prevention section in this chapter.

MAKING CONNECTIONS

Table 8.1 provides examples of externalizing and internalizing behaviors.

ecological assessment. A procedure that includes observational data collected in the student's natural environments for the purpose of identifying the antecedent events that cause a problem behavior or consequent events that maintain or increase the target behavior.

~~~~
TABLE 8.2

Criteria for Determining the Degree of Disturbance

| | Degree of Disturbance | | |
Criteria	Mild	Moderate	Severe
Precipitating events	Highly stressful	Moderately stressful	Not stressful
Destructiveness	Not destructive	Occasionally destructive	Usually destructive
Maturational appropriateness	Behavior typical for age	Some behavior untypical for age	Behavior too young or too old
Personal functioning	Cares for own needs	Usually cares for own needs	Unable to care for own needs
Social functioning	Usually able to relate to others	Usually unable to relate to others	Not able to care for own needs
Reality index	Usually sees events as they are	Occasionally sees events as they are	Little contact with reality
Insight index	Aware of behavior	Usually aware of behavior	Usually not aware of behavior
Conscious control	Usually can control behavior	Occasionally can control behavior	Little control over behavior
Social responsiveness	Usually acts appropriately	Occasionally acts appropriately	Rarely acts appropriately

Source: *Understanding and Teaching Emotionally Disturbed Children and Adolescents* (2nd ed., p. 139) by P. L. Newcomer, 1993, Austin, TX: Pro-Ed. Copyright 1993 by Pro-Ed. Reprinted by permission.

Significance

These students present unique challenges to themselves, their families, their teachers, and the educational system as a whole. Some of them require supports that are far beyond what the typical classroom is designed to provide. Because of the complexity of problems these children usually present, many experience little continuity in programs or interventions. This fragmented situation can eventually lead to very expensive (often residential) educational services that are sometimes too late to be of much benefit (U.S. Department of Education, 1994).

This group of special education students can be set apart from their peers with disabilities (U.S. Department of Education, 1994). They have lower grades than any other group. They are more likely (77 percent of them) to fail at least one class during high school. They often experience grade retention. Probably because of their lack of success academically, half of them drop out of school, often by tenth grade—the highest dropout rate of all groups of students with disabilities. And, they have a high probability of encountering the juvenile justice system (Oswald & Coutinho, 1996a). Their educational programs are also different from those of their peers with and without disabilities. Possibly because of the excessive number of

 MAKING CONNECTIONS

For more on the educational placement options, see
- in Chapter 2, the section on the array of educational services,
- the Inclusions sections found in every chapter about a disability in this text.

 MAKING CONNECTIONS

In Chapter 4, review the Significance section for more information about grade retention.
The effects of dropping out of school are also discussed in the Transition sections of
- Chapter 4,
- Chapter 3.

Appropriate services help students with behavior disorders and emotional disturbance enjoy improved self-concepts and satisfying school experiences.

externalizing behaviors they present, their educational programs focus almost exclusively on behavior management and social adjustment. Unfortunately, a balance of these features with either academic or vocational components is typically not achieved (U.S. Department of Education, 1994).

Obviously, behavior disorders and emotional disturbance have grave impacts on the life of the individual, whether child or adult, who has the disability. Without intervention, the person is likely to live with emotional pain and isolation, perhaps even engage in ever-increasing antisocial activity. Once students with behavior and emotional problems are identified and receive appropriate services, they generally improve their academic skills, enhance their personal relations, and enjoy more satisfying relations with other people. This disability also affects relationships with family members, adults, friendships with peers, and the individual's academic success. Let's take their teachers as an example. Because of the stress of working with such challenging children, these professionals are more likely to seek reassignment or leave their positions (Ahearn, 1995). One study asked teachers of students with behavior disorders and emotional disturbance about their career intentions, and the results were alarming (George, George, Gersten, & Grosenick, 1995). Over 36 percent of the teachers questioned intended to leave the field during the upcoming year, and an additional 10 percent were uncertain of their plans. Let's put this into a frame of reference: Only 9 percent of all special education teachers intended to leave the field. Why the disparity? Teachers intending to make a career change believed that they had far less support from their supervisor and far less assistance from their colleagues. We must also recognize that these teachers are working with some of the most difficult children in school systems.

History of the Field

Throughout history, people have recognized behavior disorders and emotional disturbance particularly in adults, but this disability was often confused with other disorders (Safford & Safford, 1996). It was probably Leo Kanner's 1935 book, entitled *Child Psychiatry,* that stimulated the development of services for children in the United States. In ancient times, people believed that individuals who had behavior disorders or emotional disturbance were possessed by the devil or evil spirits. During some periods—for example, when Egypt reigned supreme—treatment was enlightened and humane (Deutsch, 1949). However, the mystery surrounding mental illness often resulted in negative assumptions about the causes and in horrible treatment. Some societies, believing that these disorders were contagious, removed these people from the community so others would be protected. Treatments in those days reflected such beliefs and commonly included excessive punishment, imprisonment, placement in poorhouses, beatings, chainings, straitjacketing, and other cruel actions.

The first institution for people with mental disorders was established in London in 1547. Officially titled St. Mary of Bethlehem, it became known as Bedlam, a term that now means a place of noise and uproar. Individuals in this institution were chained, starved, and beaten. A popular form of London entertainment was to take the family, including children, for an outing to view the "lunatics" at Bedlam.

By the eighteenth century, changes began to occur through the efforts of reform-minded individuals. For instance, Philippe Pinel, a French psychiatrist, in 1792 ordered humanitarian reform, including unchaining, for mental patients at

Philippe Pinel, chief physician at Salpêtrière, freeing patients with mental disorders from their chains.

Dorothea Dix, the social policy activist, changed the course of treatment for people with mental disorders across the United States.

MAKING CONNECTIONS

For more about Samuel Gridley Howe, see the History sections in
• Chapter 6,
• Chapter 11.

MAKING CONNECTIONS

• For more on multidisciplinary services, review that section in Chapter 2.
• Also see the Family section at the end of this chapter.

the Salpêtrière, a Paris asylum for the "insane" (Brigham, 1847). In the United States, major reform in the identification and treatment of children and adults with behavior disorders and emotional disturbance began with the efforts of reformers in the 1800s. Benjamin Rush (1745–1813), considered the father of American psychiatry, proposed more humane methods of caring for children with these problems. Rush, a signer of the Declaration of Independence, was also a leader in the U.S. independence movement and a founder of the first U.S. antislavery society.

Samuel Gridley Howe, in addition to his work in blindness and mental retardation, worked to improve the treatment of people with mental disorders. Dorothea Dix influenced the founding of state institutions for people with mental disorders. By 1844, many states had institutions for people with mental disorders, and the Association of Medical Superintendents of American Institutions for the Insane (now the American Psychiatric Association) was founded. But the hope with which early institutions were founded soon gave way to pessimism as the institutions became primarily custodial.

Before the late 1800s and the initiation of public school classes for children with behavior disorders and emotional disturbance, most of these children received no services at all. The passage of compulsory education laws toward the end of the century caused educational services for these students to be developed, even though many attended ungraded classes along with other students who did not adapt well to general education settings. In 1871, a class for students who were regarded as troublemakers was opened in New Haven, Connecticut. It is interesting that many of the early public school classes provided many noneducational services to these students. These multidisciplinary services often included mental health, health care, and other social services, much like the "wraparound" services being proposed today. In 1909, William Healy founded the Juvenile Psychopathic Institute in Chicago, where he and Augusta Bronner conducted studies of juvenile offenders (Healy & Bronner, 1926). At about this same time, the theoretical work of Sigmund Freud (1856–1939), the founder of psychoanalysis, and his daughter Anna Freud began to influence the education and treatment of children with behavior disorders and emotional disturbance in Europe and in the United States.

By the twentieth century, professionals realized that children needed special programs, teachers, and teaching techniques. Around 1935, Lauretta Bender at Bellevue Hospital pioneered the development of educational services for children with behavior disorders and emotional disturbance. She even convinced the local public schools to provide teachers for students living on the wards of the hospital, an exceptionally innovative concept for the times. Meanwhile, Karl Menninger, his father, and his brother revolutionized U.S. psychiatry by stressing a "total environment" of kindness and treatment for patients with mental disorders. Bruno Bettelheim began his work with children with severe emotional disturbance at the

University of Chicago in 1944. His ideas about the value of a "therapeutic milieu" continue to be used in many classrooms.

The 1960s and 1970s saw many advances for children with behavior disorders and emotional disturbance, as many researchers, scholars, and educational developers created new ways to teach these students. In 1962, Norris Haring and Lakin Phillips published *Educating Emotionally Disturbed Children*, a book that described their experimental work in the public schools of Arlington, Virginia. Their approach stressed behavior principles, a structured environment, and interactions between the child and home and school environments. Meanwhile, Eli Bower, working in California, developed a definition of behavior disorders that is the basis for the federal definition and those used in many states today (Bower & Lambert, 1962).

MAKING CONNECTIONS
Review again the Defined section for definitions of this disability.

Two highly successful programs were developed in the 1960s. Project Re-Ed was begun in the 1960s by Nicholas Hobbs. This landmark effort, conducted in Tennessee and North Carolina, clearly showed that an ecological approach, whereby children attended residential schools for short periods of time and returned to a restructured community and family environments, could effect major changes in the lives of very troubled children. Another major demonstration effort was being conducted in California about the same time. In the Santa Monica Project, Frank Hewett developed the engineered classroom, a highly structured classroom environment that was based on behavior management principles.

The 1970s saw the expansion of many of the pilot programs already described. In the 1980s and 1990s, scientific work on biological causes—such as genetic indicators, chemical imbalances, and brain abnormalities—has been producing breakthroughs in diagnosis and treatment. Progress continues in efforts to educate children with behavior disorders and emotional disturbance, but continued work needs to be aimed at resolving definitional issues and problems surrounding who should be included in this special education category (conduct disordered, socially maladjusted, autistic). It is also now apparent that although the educational system is very important, it alone cannot solve the problems of these students and their families. Rather, real partnerships that produce coordinated, **wraparound services**, services that meet all of the needs of these children and their families from educational and mental health systems must be the goal (Koyangi & Gaines, 1993).

Prevalence

It is difficult to accurately estimate the prevalence of behavior disorders and emotional disturbance for two major reasons. First, the definition remains unclear and subjective. Second, because the "serious emotional disturbance" label is so stigmatizing, many educators and school districts are reluctant to identify many children as having this disability. Only 1 percent of all schoolchildren are identified as having this disability. Many believe that this is not due to an actually lower prevalence rate for these youngsters, but rather to a reluctance of educators to so label and identify children (Oswald & Coutinho, 1996a). Some conservatively estimate that approximately 3 to 6 percent of all students have this disability (Kauffman, 1997). Clearly, the number of students with behavior disorders and emotional disturbance who receive special education services in the schools is much smaller than the total number of children in this country with these disorders.

wraparound services. A service delivery model whereby all of the child's needs are met through the coordination of the education system, mental health agencies, social services, and community agencies.

Too Many When There Are Too Few

According to the Office of Civil Rights, the demographics of the U.S. elementary and secondary student body is 68 percent white, 16 percent African American, and 12 percent Hispanic. According to data collected by the U.S. Department of Education (1994), the demographics of students identified as having behavior disorders and emotional disturbance is 67 percent white, 25 percent African American, and 6 percent Hispanic. They also reported that the rate of overrepresentation varies by locale. For example, one state identified African American students for this category 400 times more than what would be expected by the overall state's demographics. In one inner-city school district (in another state), African American children accounted for 37 percent of the total school population and 56 percent of the students enrolled in programs for behavior disorders and emotional disturbance. Although it appears that overall students are underrepresented in this category, some groups of students have a higher probability of being so identified.

An important factor in prevalence is gender. Clear gender differences show up in the identification of this exceptionality: Most children who are identified as having behavior disorders and emotional disturbance are male. *The Sixteenth Annual Report to Congress on the Implementation of the Individuals with Disabilities Education Act* (U.S. Department of Education, 1994) reported some interesting data: 68 percent of all high school students with disabilities are male and 76 percent of those identified as having behavior disorders and emotional disturbance are male. This is the highest ratio of boys to girls in special education categories. We do not know the reason for this gender difference, but it is probably linked to boys' higher propensity of being troublesome and violating school rules. Another factor in the prevalence data appears to be race (see Focus on Diversity box). It appears that, particularly in some locales, African American children are overrepresented in this special education category, and many believe that bias and cultural misunderstanding are significant contributors to this problem (Peterson & Ishii-Jordan, 1994).

MAKING CONNECTIONS

In Chapter 3, review the sections about
• overrepresentation,
• prevalence.

Causes and Prevention

The causes of behavior disorders and emotional disturbance in an individual are usually unknown; therefore how to prevent this disability also remains elusive. Children are so unique, our scientific study of biological causes so young, the interactions of children and youth with their families and environments so complex, and the interactions with society so individual that we can almost never point to any one variable with certainty as the cause of behavior disorders and emotional disturbance. We do know, however, that children who experience abuse and turmoil in their daily lives are at great risk for developing this disability. So, how substantial is the problem? Everyday, it seems we hear from politicians and the media that more of our nation's families are in crisis. Child abuse and neglect are major threats to children's well-being. They clearly affect children's mental health and are on the increase (Children's Defense Fund, 1995). In 1993, over one million cases were documented. Figure 8.1 shows more information about how these children were mistreated. Also, between 3.3 million and 10 million children are exposed to domestic violence every year. Possibly, the most tragic victims of such situations are the children.

Causes

At least three general areas can contribute to behavior disorders and emotional disturbance: biology, home and community, and school. Again, the reasons for problems in a particular child are difficult to identify, and the disability is likely to be the result of multiple and overlapping factors.

Biology. As researchers have discovered and continue to look for biological causes for some types of disorders (e.g., fetal alcohol syndrome [FAS], Down syndrome, autism, Tourette's syndrome), they are seeking biological causes for behavior disorders and emotional disturbance. Their efforts are beginning to yield some

 MAKING CONNECTIONS

- For a review of Down syndrome and FAS, see Chapter 6.
- For more on autism, see Chapter 12.

FIGURE 8.1

Abuse and Neglect

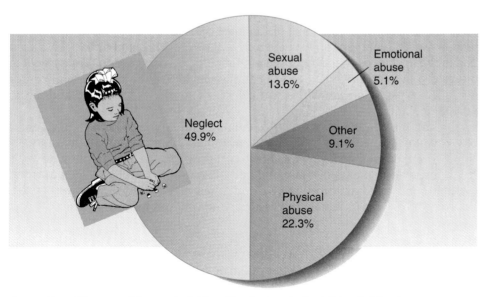

Source: From *The state of America's children: Yearbook 1995* (p. 73) by Children's Defense Fund, 1995, Washington, DC: Author and U.S. Department of Health and Human Services, National Center on Child Abuse and Neglect. Reprinted by permission.

results. For example, there may be a biological dimension to a psychological disorder such as anorexia or bulimia. Mood disorders, depression, schizophrenia, and attention deficit disorder may have a genetic foundation (American Psychiatric Association, 1994). Knowing whether biological reasons are part of the cause of a disorder can play a role in treatment. For example, knowing that depression has a biological cause allows for the development and use of medications. In fact, antidepressants are now an important component in many treatment programs for depression. As researchers continue to find biological causes, more medical treatments will become available.

Home and Community. Children, like older people, do not live in a social vacuum. They are members of an immediate family, an extended family, and a variety of communities (neighborhood, church, clubs). All of these units comprise the environments that shape and influence each individual's growth and development—whether positive or negative. No single negative experience can lead to or aggravate emotional problems, but combinations of abuse, neglect, inconsistent expectations and rules, confusion, and turmoil over long periods of time can. So, too, can lack of supervision, erratic and punitive discipline, low rate of positive interactions, high rate of negative interactions, lack of interest and concern, and poor adult role models. For example, children whose parents are violent and have arrest records also tend to become violent and find themselves in trouble with the law (Hallahan & Kauffman, 1997). On the other hand, healthy interactions, such as warmth and responsiveness, consistent discipline, demand for responsible behavior, along with modeling, teaching, and rewarding desired behaviors can promote positive behaviors in children.

Many children who might otherwise be able to avoid emotional disturbance become vulnerable when faced with stressors such as family disruption, poverty, death, illness, and violence. But we all know of examples of youngsters who have survived horrible situations and grown into healthy adults. These especially resilient individuals teach us that adverse circumstances do not lead inevitably to behavior disorders and emotional disturbance (Werner & Smith, 1992). Other children, however, seem especially vulnerable to life's problems and develop disorders under circumstances that do not seem as serious, by comparison. Thus teachers must keep in mind that each child is an individual; there are no general cause-and-effect explanations for why a particular person develops a particular disorder at a particular time.

Just as it is important to recognize the powerful influence home and community environments can have on child development, it is also important to understand that there is not always a direct correlation between parents' and their child's behavior. Parents of these children often are wrongfully blamed for their children's misconduct, unruliness, and disruptive actions (Ahearn, 1995). Educators must always remain professional and cautious in casting blame or judging fault.

School. Teachers have tremendous influence in their interactions with students. Teachers' expectations influence the questions they ask students, the feedback they give, and the number and character of interactions with students. Problems can get better because of teachers' actions, and they can get worse. In other words, what educators do makes a difference. For example, a teacher who is

MAKING CONNECTIONS
- Figure 8.1, in this chapter, shows the impact of abuse and neglect on children.
- Also see the Causes sections (Chapters 3 and 6).

unskilled in managing the classroom or insensitive to students' individual differences may create an environment in which aggression, frustration, or withdrawal are common responses to the environment or teacher. And, teachers who are skilled at managing classroom behavior, systematically select interventions that match the students' behavior, and are consistent in their application of those interventions can improve students' outcomes (Rivera & Smith, 1997; Smith & Rivera, 1993). Good teachers are able to analyze their relationships with their students and the learning environment, and they keep close watch on problems and potential problems.

 MAKING CONNECTIONS

In this chapter, refer to these sections in Educational Interventions:
• Effective Discipline
• The Intervention Ladder (Teaching Tactics box)

Prevention

Prevention of behavior disorders and emotional disturbance can be accomplished in two ways. In some cases, techniques can be directed toward eliminating the major causes of these disorders. For example, the behavioral effects of fetal alcohol syndrome can be prevented if pregnant women do not drink. In other cases, prevention consists of eliminating or ameliorating the symptoms of the disability at its initial onset.

The choice of prevention strategies often depends on the theoretical orientation of the teacher or therapist. Let's consider an example. Tod is beginning to disrupt his fourth grade classroom immediately before school dismisses. How might his teacher, Ellen Brudos, prevent this from developing into a serious problem? The answer depends in part on the theoretical orientation of the teacher. Teachers who are trained to think about behavior disorders and emotional disturbance in strictly behavioral terms would likely select prevention strategies that include **functional assessments** (Tobin, Sugai, & Colvin, 1996). Functional assessments help to determine what events cause the behavior to occur and what other events contribute to the behavior's increase or maintenance. One system that helps accomplish this goal is a model based on the antecedent, behavior, and consequence events to the target behavior—an approach called the **ABC model**. Using the ABC model, Ms. Brudos analyzes three stages: the circumstances prior to the behavior, the behavior itself, and the circumstances after the behavior. She intervenes either prior or subsequent to the target behavior. Ms. Brudos might decide to institute a more structured and predictable class dismissal, or she might arrange for Tod to receive verbal praise when he remained orderly during dismissal. A teacher with a strong background in clinical psychology might address the problem differently. That teacher might determine that Tod and his family need therapy, and she might urge the school to assist with arranging it. Alternatively, she might institute a teaching program for the family to help them improve their interactions with Tod. She might also specifically teach Tod to monitor his own behavior and to control himself when he anticipated the disrupting behaviors.

Usually, prevention strategies are not as sharply differentiated as those just described. In practice, many other variables contribute to the selection of a strategy, including the cause of the behavior, the educator's experience with strategies that succeeded in the past, recommendations from other professionals, the preferences of the child and family, and the overall orientation of the program. Sometimes, a combination of strategies is used.

functional assessments. Similar to ecological assessment except that behaviors are manipulated (where they are not in the other system) to determine those events that cause and maintain target behaviors.

ABC model. A behavioral way to analyze and select interventions by looking at whether they occur antecedent to (before), concurrent with (during), or consequent to (after) the target behavior.

TABLE 8.3

Possible Signs or Characteristics of Behavior Disorders and Emotional Disturbance

Has problems with

    Adults, particularly those in authority

    Family relationships

    Peers

    Social skills

Demonstrates

    Hyperactivity

    Aggression toward self or others

    Impulsivity

    Distractibility

    Depression and unhappiness

    Suicidal tendencies

    Withdrawal into self

    Anxiety or fearfulness

Children with Behavior Disorders and Emotional Disturbance

Behavior disorders and emotional disturbance can affect a student's functioning beyond behavior problems or inappropriate emotional expression. The student will likely exhibit learning impairments that affect both academic performance and social interactions with peers and the teacher. Table 8.3 lists typical signs or characteristics that these children often exhibit.

Social Skills

MAKING CONNECTIONS

For a review of IEPs, see Chapter 2.

Students with behavior disorders and emotional disturbance, possibly more than any other group of children with disabilities, present problems with social skills to themselves, their families, their peers, and their teachers. Whether their problems are externalizing or internalizing, developing social competence and appropriate behavior are usually major goals on these children's IEPs. Deficits in social skills, rather than academic difficulties, may be the actual reason these students are removed from the academic mainstream. Being able to use appropriate social skills makes it possible to achieve three important goals (Walker, Schwarz, Nippold, Irvin, & Noell, 1994, pp. 70–71):

1. They allow an individual to initiate and develop positive social relationships with others.

Cardinal Rules for Conducting Social Skills Training

1 Social validation of social skills by target consumer groups is a critical step in both the selection and training of social skills.

2 Social skills should be taught as academic subject matter using instructional procedures similar to those for teaching basic subjects (e.g., reading, mathematics).

3 Whenever possible, social skills should be taught directly along with possible variations in their appropriate application.

4 The social context and situational factors both mediate the use of social skills and must be taken into account systematically in facilitating students' use of them.

5 The instructional acquisition of social skills does not guarantee either their application or topographic proficiency within natural settings.

6 There is considerable inertia operating against the behavioral integration of newly taught social skills into a student's ongoing behavioral repertoire, as is the case with any newly acquired skill.

7 To be effective, social skills training must be accompanied by the provision of response opportunities, feedback, and incentive systems within natural settings to provide for their actual demonstration and mastery.

8 The critical test of the efficacy of social skills training is the integration of newly taught skills into a student's behavioral repertoire and their use in natural settings.

9 Social skills training procedures are not an effective intervention for complex behavior disorders or problems. They represent only a partial solution and should not be used by themselves to mediate highly aggressive or disruptive behavior patterns.

10 Social skills training can be an important complement to the use of behavior reduction techniques in that it teaches adaptive alternatives to maladaptive or problematic behavior.

11 There are two types of deficits in social-behavior adjustment: skill deficits (can't do) and performance deficits (won't do). These deficits should be assessed and treated differently, as they require different forms of intervention for effective remediation.

Source: From "Social skills in school-age children and youth: Issues and best practices in assessment and intervention" by H. M. Walker, I. E. Schwarz, M. A. Nippold, L. K Irvin, & J. W. Noell, 1994, *Topics in Language Disorders, 14,* p. 79. Reprinted with permission.

2. They facilitate the individual's ability to cope effectively with the behavioral demands and expectations of specific settings.

3. They provide for the appropriate communication and assertion of one's needs, desires, and preferences.

Social skills are the foundation for practically all human activities in all contexts (academic, personal, vocational, and community). We use social skills to interact with others and perform most daily tasks. We believe that they should be considered functional life skills that are monitored by educators, just as academic skills are.

Those who are deficient in social skills, and will not be able to develop social competence independently, should receive instruction in this target area. Overwhelming evidence now exists to show that students can profit greatly from instruction in social skills (Locke & Fuchs, 1995; Walker et al., 1994). However, when social skills are taught, teachers must be aware of some important considerations. The Tips for Teachers box (p. 345) provides some guidance to those implementing such instructional programs in classroom settings.

Peer Perceptions

What do classmates of students with behavior disorders and emotional disturbance think about these peers? The answers to this question are important because they influence educators' integration efforts. Unfortunately, the answers are not favorable for youngsters with this disability (Safran, 1995). First, educators should recognize that young children without disabilities can clearly discriminate externalizing behavior disorders from nondisordered behavior. They do so by the age of 7. Second, they have exceptionally negative feelings about peers who act out, exhibit aggressive behavior, or are antisocial. Interestingly, girls have stricter standards than boys and are more sensitive to aggressive behavior. Third, children with externalizing behaviors are considered less desirable for friendship. Fourth, children without disabilities do not recognize internalizing behavior problems—like being socially withdrawn—until about seventh grade. But when they do, the depressed child is less liked, considered less attractive as a friend, and thought to need therapy. During these later schoolyears, externalizing and antisocial behaviors are considered most problematic by their peers and clearly lead to social rejection of these peers. Children without disabilities have much more compassion and understanding for peers with medical problems than for those with psychological disorders.

Juvenile Justice and Delinquency

Lack of discipline and increasing violence in our nation's schools have been topics of great concern for some time. However, growing alarm is now focusing on violent acts committed by very young children (Montgomery, 1996). Take Robert as an example. His record of crime began two years ago when he set a neighbor's garage on fire. He has been arrested twice since: once for burglarizing a neighbor's home and another time for stealing a $150 CD player from a store. Robert is now 7 years old. What does the future hold for him, his family, and his teachers? The answer is probably: Nothing very good. Robert is not an isolated case. In 1994, 110,000 children under age 13 were arrested for acts of felonies, and 39 of those were for murder. The statistics show increasing numbers of violent crimes being committed by young children. Some research now shows that children arrested before the age of 12 are likely to have histories of neglect and abuse. And, these children are also more likely to join gangs and commit very serious crimes later in their lives.

MAKING CONNECTIONS

Reread the Social Competence section found in the Children with... sections of
• Chapter 4,
• Chapter 5.

MAKING CONNECTIONS

For a list of externalizing behaviors, see Table 8.1 again.

MAKING CONNECTIONS

For a review of the debate about discipline in U.S. schools and what should be done about it, see in Chapter 1
• Legislation,
• Concepts and Controversy.

MAKING CONNECTIONS

For a review of the influence of abuse and neglect, see these features in this chapter:
• Figure 8.1
• section on Home and Community (Causes section)
• Juvenile Justice and Delinquency

Walker and Sylvester (1994) make this frightening observation by asking and answering a question important in the lives of many of these children: "Where is school along the road for those who are bound for prison? It's merely a way-station for most." Schools need to take more preventive measures to avoid the predictable, and unfortunate, outcome for many of these youngsters.

So, how do we predict which children are at the greatest risk for juvenile delinquency? Research indicates that this child will have the following characteristics (Day & Hunt, 1996, p. 66):

- displays problem behavior beginning at ages 4 to 5;
- engages in a range of antisocial activities (e.g., both overt and covert);
- is a problem at home, school, and in the community;
- is overactive and inattentive; and
- demonstrates extreme aggression.

Children with these characteristics are likely candidates for other negative outcomes: substance abuse, school dropout, teen pregnancy, suicide, AIDS, poor marital relations, chronic unemployment, and psychiatric disorders (depression and personality disorders). Of these five characteristics, the single best predictor of problems is aggression, which appears to be quite stable over time. Aggressive tendencies and delinquency seem to be strongly related to each other, moreover, so it is crucial to get early intervention services to youngsters who display aggressive behaviors as preschoolers.

As children grow up, the peer group takes on more importance. This may be even more so for youngsters who were (or are) abused or neglected. Figure 8.2 displays some of the reasons teens believe young people join gangs. Notice that the great majority (62 percent) believe that gangs give youngsters a sense of belonging, a sense of family (Hackett, 1995a). In contrast to the support that gang members gain from one another, other adolescents fear for their safety, and probably for good reason. Overwhelmingly, even young children are afraid of violence and physical harm from gang members. And, they have good reasons for their concerns. Gangs are present in schools across the nation, in urban, rural, and suburban areas; they victimize fellow students regardless of race or ethnicity; and their numbers are increasing (Hackett, 1995b). At schools where gangs are present, students report increased victimization and fear. Students' fears are real. Where gangs are present, there is an increase in the numbers of guns and weapons at school. Students are three times more likely to have something forcibly taken away from

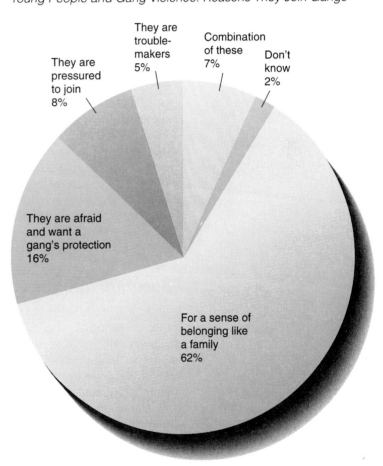

FIGURE 8.2

Young People and Gang Violence: Reasons They Join Gangs

Source: From "New national pool finds majority of young children fear they might die young; Youth exposed to serious health and safety threats" by *Youth Record* (December 31, 1995) 7, p. 2. Reprinted by permission.

Children with Behavior Disorders and Emotional Disturbance 〜〜 **347**

them and more than twice as likely of being physically attacked. Of course, not all gang members have behavior disorders or emotional disturbance, but clearly some do. Regardless, the presence of gangs at school affects the learning environment, negatively impacting on feelings of security and safety. They present a challenge to the entire educational community.

Academic Performance

MAKING CONNECTIONS

For other discussions of underachievement, see
• Gifted Underachievers in the Gifted Children section (Chapter 7),
• Motivation and Attribution section in Children with Learning Disabilities section (Chapter 4).

Students with behavior disorders and emotional disturbance typically do not perform well academically, regardless of their intellectual potential (Kauffman, 1997). They could be referred to as underachievers. Many of them lack basic reading and math skills. Of course, the more severe the disability, the greater overall performance is affected. Clearly, being in personal turmoil affects one's ability to attend to school tasks and learning in general. Thus a teacher must, in addition to helping the child with behavior, teach academic skills.

Educational Interventions

Education is extremely important for children with behavior and emotional disorders. As you will learn, most students with this disability have poor educational outcomes. The blame for such dismal results must rest, in part, with the educational system (Chesapeake Institute, 1994). Through what has come to be called *The National Agenda for Better Results for Children and Youth with SED*, a team of experts attempted to focus the nation's attention on the problems faced by these students and their teachers, and they offered some suggestions on how they should be solved. Briefly, the team's findings include the following: The instructional programs offered these children should be positive and accountable, increase the capacity (personnel preparation, support personnel, reduced teacher–pupil ratios) of the neighborhood school to better meet the needs of these students, value diversity, increase collaboration with families, and include ongoing assessments to monitor students' progress. As you think about the sections you have read and integrate that information with what you will read next, consider how these goals could be met in classroom settings.

MAKING CONNECTIONS

For other information about poor educational outcomes, see these sections in this chapter:
• Significance (in Defined section)
• Transition

Education and the Preschool Child

It is difficult to identify some types of behavior disorders and emotional disturbance in young children. For example, internalizing behavior problems are not usually identified until children are school age. However, extreme externalizing behaviors are often obvious by age 4 or 5. Sometimes, severe disabilities, such as a psychosis, manifest themselves during the early developmental period as well. Regardless, it is unusual for preschoolers to be identified as having this disability, even though it is advantageous to identify a child's behavior disorder and emotional disturbance as early as possible.

The early identification and management of young children with this disability has many benefits (Feil, Walker, & Severson, 1995). First, problem behaviors seen in preschoolers tend to be very stable over time. In other words, they do not go away without intervention, and they even worsen. The behavior problems seem to follow a progression like the following: disobedient at home, having temper tantrums, teacher reports of fighting or stealing. Second, they are predictive of future learning problems. Third, children with early onset of antisocial behavior account for only 3 to 5 percent of this population, but they account for 50 percent of all crimes committed by children and youth. Fourth, if children's disorders can be identified early, professionals might be able to intervene with the family at an early stage, assist these children with environmental stresses such as extreme poverty, or help them in other ways without removing them from their natural environment. Early intervention may rectify problems before they become more serious or develop into well-established patterns, help avoid a later need for psychotropic medication to control behavior, reduce stress in the family, and allow for changes in the young child's behavior when the possibility for change is strongest.

Education and the Schoolchild

Many different approaches are used in the education and treatment of schoolchildren with behavior disorders and emotional disturbance. Which approach selected depends on the conceptual model the professional uses for teaching these children. Table 8.4 lists seven major conceptual models of treatment and education. This quick overview is meant only to illustrate the range of options and orientations available—from clinical to behavioral to holistic to eclectic. Generally, educators incorporate various elements of many of these approaches into their education programs for these children. Because a major focus of school programs is to increase the child's academic success in school, many teachers find the behavioral approach in combination with elements from one or two others most useful for educating these children.

In this section, we are only able to highlight some important features and best practices that educators should incorporate into their instructional programs. Because it is essential that teachers evaluate the effectiveness of their instruction, we first discuss measuring student progress by using curriculum based assessment techniques. Then, we focus your attention on effective discipline techniques. We do so here because externalizing behavior problems are of great concern to many of these students' teachers, peers, and families. It is crucial that teachers systematically match the best tactic with the specific target behavior; the principles of effective discipline help educators accomplish this goal. Third, because students with this disability are prime candidates for corporal punishment, we decided that all of us needed to be reminded of some cautions and concerns, and some data, about its application in school settings. And, finally, we share information from a newly developing curricular area that holds great promise for students with behavior disorders and emotional disturbance: self-determination.

 MAKING CONNECTIONS

For a definition of best practices, see the marginal terms in Chapter 4.

Curriculum Based Assessment (CBA). Teachers often use curriculum based assessment (CBA) to measure a child's academic gains and thereby evaluate the effectiveness of their instruction. For example, teachers use CBA to measure the percentage of correct spelling words, the number of new arithmetic facts memorized, reading fluency (how quickly the child reads), and the ability to write topic sentences in their writing assignments. They also use this method to measure social behaviors of individual children, to see whether they improve with the application of various interventions.

To measure progress in complex areas, the teacher first breaks down those

 MAKING CONNECTIONS

For another section about curriculum based instruction, see Chapter 2 (Steps to an IEP, Program Evaluation).

TABLE 8.4

Conceptual Models in the Treatment of Children with Behavior Disorders and Emotional Disturbance

Behavioral approach	Based on the work of B. F. Skinner and other behaviorists, this model focuses on providing children with highly structured learning environments and teaching materials. The student's behaviors are precisely measured, interventions are designed to increase or decrease behaviors, and progress toward goals is measured carefully and frequently.
Psychoanalytic (psychodynamic) view	Based on the work of Sigmund Freud and other psychoanalysts, this model views the problems of the child as having a basis in unconscious conflicts and motivations: based not on the behavior itself, but on the pathology of one's personality. Treatment is generally individual psychotherapy, long term, and designed to uncover and resolve these deep-seated problems.
Psychoeducational approach	The psychoanalytic view is combined with principles of teaching, with treatment measured primarily in terms of learning. Meeting the individual needs of the youngster is emphasized, often through projects and creative arts, through everyday functioning at school and home.
Ecological approach	The problems of the child are seen as a result of interactions with the family, the school, and the community. The child or youth is not the sole focus of treatment, but the family, school, neighborhood, and community also are changed in order to improve the interactions.
Social–cognitive approach	The interactions between the effects of the environment and the youngster's behavior are taught to the child. This approach seeks to integrate and reconceptualize behavioral and cognitive psychology. The result is a view that behavior is the result of interactions in a person's physical and social environments, personal factors (thoughts, feelings, and perceptions), and the behavior itself.
Humanistic education	Love and trust, in teaching and learning, are emphasized; and children are encouraged to be open and free individuals. The approach emphasizes self-direction, self-fulfillment, and self-evaluation. A nonauthoritarian atmosphere in a nontraditional educational setting is developed.
Biogenic approach	Physiological interventions such as diet, medications, and biofeedback are used, based on biological theories of causation and treatment.

Source: Schema is borrowed from *Characteristics of Behavioral Disorders of Children and Youth* (6th ed., pp. 111–124) by J. M. Kauffman, 1997, Columbus, OH: Merrill.

areas into precise behaviors. It is important that the behavior specifically of concern is the one targeted for intervention and measurement. Then, the appropriate data collection system is selected. Among the many simple choices for such record keeping are tallies (or sheer counts of the frequency of the target behavior's occurrence during a consistent observation period), duration (how long the target behavior lasts during a constant time period), percentage (the proportion of the day the target behavior occurs), or rate (how many times the behavior occurs per minute). The measurement of the specific target behavior occurs daily and across enough time to allow comparisons under different treatments. In other words, how well did the student behave before the teacher implemented a reward system, how well did the student behave while the intervention was in effect, and does that behavior change maintain?

Let us look at an example. Terrell is a kindergartner who has exhibited extreme externalizing behaviors since coming to school. In particular, the multidisciplinary team—which includes the district's school psychologist; a family therapist; a social worker; the school nurse; Ms. Kea, Terrell's, special education teacher; Ms. Steppe-Jones, his general education teacher, and members of his family—is concerned about his aggressive behavior. The team discusses what constitutes aggression for Terrell, and these are the behaviors they identified: physically attacking others, bullying, and hitting. They also decide that the setting to begin intervention is the lunch recess, where the problems seem to be the worst. They also decide that after a short assessment phase (to be sure they have targeted the right behaviors and to have a set of data to compare future progress to), the first intervention they will try is contingent instructions ("Don't hit!" after each act) paired with criterion-specific rewards (five minutes of freetime at the end of the day for "beating" yesterday's score). Every lunch period, Ms. Kea counted the number of aggressive acts committed by Terrell and noted them on the evaluation chart, which is shown in Figure 8.3. As you, and the members of the multidisciplinary team, can see, systematic and careful intervention planning caused remarkable improvement in Terrell's behavior.

Learning to take turns is a crucial skill for children to learn. For some it is a difficult learning experience.

 MAKING CONNECTIONS

In this chapter, review the sections about aggression found in
• Types (in Defined),
• Peer Perceptions (Children with behavior disorders and emotional disturbance),
• Juvenile Justice and Delinquency (Children with behavior disorders and emotional disturbance).

Effective Discipline. Of this there is no question: The public's concern about violence at schools and discipline in the classroom is growing. Unfortunately, and inaccurately, students with disabilities are being blamed for this situation (Voyles, 1994). Rather than casting blame, however, it might be best for all educators to work diligently to create safe school settings in which violence and abuse have been eliminated.

 MAKING CONNECTIONS

See Chapter 1 again for the nation's reaction to increased violence in the schools.

Educators are charged with the responsibility of helping students learn maximally, whether the topic of concern is basic academic skills, general or specific knowledge, or social skills. Effective and efficient instruction cannot occur in chaos or in a repressive environment. What is required is a positive learning climate in which children can learn, create, discover, explore, expand their knowledge, and apply new skills. When the amount of disruption is high, causing educators to spend time and energy addressing conduct problems, students do not learn either effectively or efficiently. Disruption—whether from several individuals or most of the class—can be held to a minimum without destroying the climate

FIGURE 8.3

Terrell's Evaluation Chart

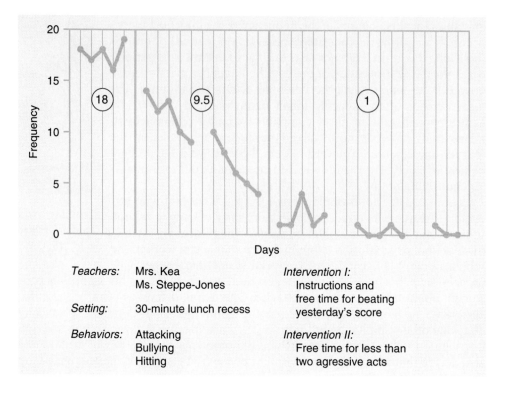

Teachers:	Mrs. Kea Ms. Steppe-Jones	*Intervention I:*	Instructions and free time for beating yesterday's score
Setting:	30-minute lunch recess		
Behaviors:	Attacking Bullying Hitting	*Intervention II:*	Free time for less than two agressive acts

needed for learning. To accomplish this goal, teachers need to be armed with an array of proven interventions and know when they are most appropriately applied.

To help teachers better understand how to match interventions with the level and severity of disruptive behavior, Smith and Rivera (1993) use the **Intervention Ladder** (see the Teaching Tactics box). This ladder's foundation includes basic preventive measures that good teachers incorporate into all of their instruction. For example, educators are encouraged to make school challenging and exciting so that all students are actively engaged in learning and less likely to be disruptive (Nelson, Johnson, & Marchand-Martella, 1996). Also, all members of the school community must be aware of the basic rules or standards of behavior, and everyone must consistently apply the same consequences when the standards are violated. The Intervention Ladder illustrates the hierarchy of interventions, starting from the simplest and least intrusive to the most complex and punitive. Only after evaluation procedures indicate that a mild intervention is not successful are more drastic procedures implemented.

Many students with behavior disorders and emotional disturbance need special help to maintain self-discipline. For example, the teacher may have to spend much more time discussing the school and classroom rules so that these students

the Intervention Ladder. A hierarchy of disciplinary tactics organized from the least intrusive and least complex to the most intrusive and most complicated.

The Intervention Ladder

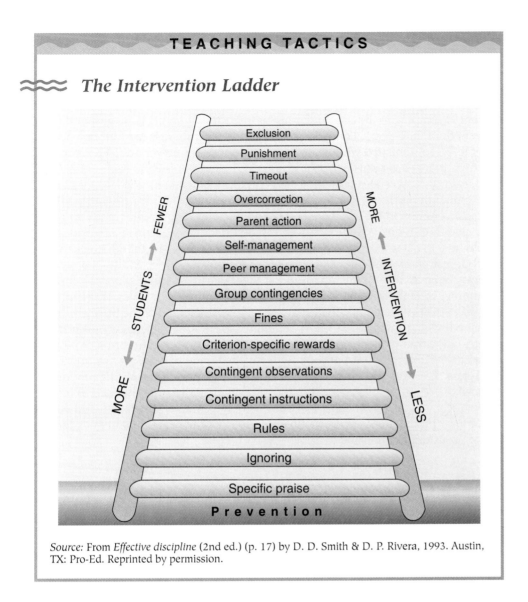

Source: From *Effective discipline* (2nd ed.) (p. 17) by D. D. Smith & D. P. Rivera, 1993. Austin, TX: Pro-Ed. Reprinted by permission.

have a clear idea of the behaviors required. Some of the requirements students must meet in academic environments are obvious, such as keeping quiet when the teacher is talking or joining the other students in the line to go to the lunchroom. But some **setting demands** are more subtle, and for students with this disability direct and concise instructions are often required so they understand how they are supposed to behave. For example, the student is expected to make eye contact with the teacher when speaking in the hallway, take turns in group games, or sit with good posture when school administrators visit the classroom. Violations of setting demands such as these can lead to students' being perceived as lacking in discipline. Problems can be prevented, however, by specifically teaching the child to meet the demands of the environment. When the rules are broken, however, the teacher must ensure that the consequences are consistently and fairly applied.

setting demands. The behavioral requirements, both obvious and subtle, of an environment.

Corporal Punishment. Corporal punishment is high on the Intervention Ladder, but we decided to spend a little time discussing this intervention because of its overall negative impact on students and the school environment. All educators should be aware of the potentially devastating effects corporal punishment can have on children. And, they should know that students with disabilities and students from poverty have a much higher probability of receiving corporal punishment than their peers. For example, African American boys are four times more likely to be so punished when compared to their white peers. And, 12 percent of Hispanic males are punished, whereas only 8 percent of white males are. As of 1995, twenty-seven states had abolished corporal punishment as a legal or acceptable form of punishment in school settings (Evans & Richardson, 1995). Paddlings are most common in the southern states and in a few states in the Southwest. It is estimated that in one year alone, over 160,000 paddlings occurred in Texas.

As you just learned in the previous section, there are many alternatives to corporal punishment. But first, let's review what punishment is. Many people mistakenly believe that punishment must necessarily involve physical hitting, screaming, or embarrassment for the child. Punishment, however, is technically defined as any consequence that reduces the rate or strength of the behavior being punished, which means that many different tactics—including corporal punishment—fall within this category. Some teachers find that certain forms of punishment can be an important part of an effective teaching plan to change unwanted behaviors. For example, mild reprimands, temporary withdrawal of attention, or the loss of certain privileges are all punishing tactics (they are intended to reduce the frequency of the target behavior) but do not have the negative long-term effects of corporal punishment (Smith & Rivera, 1993). Some general guidelines for the use of punishment are listed in Table 8.5.

~~~~

TABLE 8.5

Guidelines for Using Punishment

1. Punishment should be used only when the behavior is very serious or dangerous.

2. Other tactics should be tried first.

3. Although parental permission is not required for most forms of punishment, Repp and Dietz (1978) suggested that it be granted in writing before the technique occurs so the student will understand why and when punishment will be used.

4. If the behavior does occur, no threats or warnings should be given.

5. The behavior should be stopped as soon as it is noticed.

6. The behavior should be punished each and every time it occurs.

7. The punishment should be of substantial and uniform intensity (it is best not to use mild forms and then gradually increase the intensity).

8. Other positive behaviors of the student should be reinforced. When punishment is used, it should not be the only intervention in effect; there also should be positive elements of the program.

Source: From *Effective Discipline* (pp. 144–145) by D. D. Smith and D. P. Rivera, 1993, Austin, TX: Pro-Ed. Reprinted with permission.

Corporal punishment should be *avoided* in school settings. It may temporarily stop undesired behaviors, but it certainly does not teach new skills that students can use to achieve their goals. It may also cause the teacher to become engaged in a power struggle with the student, an unhealthy negative interaction that the youngster has, in effect, dictated. Excessive use of harsh punishment by a teacher can change the classroom to a battleground where the focus is on power and coercion. When a teacher uses corporal punishment, the teacher is modeling a negative style of interaction that other students, as well as the one being punished, may copy in their interactions with others. Remember, any form of punishment should always be accompanied by teaching a new behavior. All classrooms must be safe and orderly environments where students can feel secure to attempt the difficult tasks of learning and trust the educators charged with this important responsibility.

Self-Determination. What is **self-determination**? Because this area is so new, the definition is evolving. However, here are some of the outcomes researchers believe should occur when students have mastered a self-determination curriculum (Martin & Marshall, 1995). After studying these outcomes, even without a proper definition, you should have an understanding of what self-determination is and why gaining these skills is important to individuals with disabilities, particularly those with behavior disorders and emotional disturbance. Successful individuals

- know how to choose,
- know what they want and how to get it,
- choose goals and persistently pursue them,
- make their needs known,
- evaluate progress toward meeting their goals,
- adjust their performance and create unique approaches to solve problems,
- become their best advocates.

How did researchers arrive at these outcomes? They studied successful people and identified some common characteristics that probably contributed to their achievements. The conclusions they reached also should help you further understand this curriculum area better.

> Successful people know what they want and persistently go after it. They decide upon major goals, set a timeline, develop specific plans to attain their goals, determine the benefits that reaching the goals will bring, close off discouraging influences and thought, and build coalitions with others who share similar goals and who encourage each other in reaching those goals... When peak performers make decisions, they (a) choose a mission leading to an action; (b) envision and communicate a clear mission; and (c) develop an action plan consisting of specific goals and benchmarks to evaluate the timing, quality, and quantity of the results. (Martin & Marshall, 1995, p. 147)

Many individuals with disabilities do not develop the characteristics you just read about. Instead of becoming increasingly independent as they gain years and experience, many become more dependent. Some do not feel comfortable making choices for themselves, and others make inappropriate choices because they do not possess the skills or strategies necessary to make wise decisions. Some

self-determination. A set of behaviors that include making decisions, choosing preferences, and practicing self-advocacy.

researchers suggest that this situation may be due in part to the special education experience (Wall & Dattilo, 1995). Students are not given sufficient opportunities to make choices or decisions. When the opportunities do arise, they are not systematically guided in making decisions. Some believe that instructional environments should be restructured to become more "option-rich, responsive, and informational environments" (Wall & Dattilo, 1995, p. 289) in which self-determination opportunities are infused into the school day. Others believe that a more direct approach is necessary, where self-determination becomes a topic for instruction.

Several researchers have been working to develop a set of materials or procedures teachers can use to help their students become proficient in the behaviors that comprise self-determination (Serna & Lau-Smith, 1995). By using the list found in Table 8.6, teachers could develop activities that would help students learn skills that comprise self-determination.

Inclusion

Children with behavior disorders and emotional disturbance receive their education in a variety of settings. While many are included in the general classroom, many others can be found in special education classrooms, special schools, community-based residential group homes, halfway houses, institutions, and hospitals. Regardless of placement, these students need many accommodations (see Making Accommodations box). Coutinho and Oswald (1996b) conducted a four-year study of the educational placement patterns of children with behavior disorders and emotional disturbance. Their findings reveal some interesting information about these students and how their needs are met in the U.S. educational system. First, they found that despite the movement toward inclusion and more integration of special education students into general education classes, the placement rates of students with behavior disorders and emotional disturbance changed little

Although being included in sporting events and learning how to be a member of a team are instructional topics for some students, these important social skills are usually mastered with the aid of systematic instruction.

TABLE 8.6

Self-Determination Skills List

Prerequisite Social Skills
 Giving positive feedback
 Giving criticism
 Accepting criticism
 Resisting peer pressure
 Negotiation
 Following instruction
 Conversation
 Problem solving

Self-Evaluation Skills
 Evaluating present skills
 Evaluating skills needed for future goals

Self-Direction Skills
 Goal setting
 Goal planning
 Self-management

Networking Skills
 Informal Networking
  Seeking information (trusted adult)
  Seeking advice (trusted adult)
  Initiating activities and joining activities
  Dealing with rejection
 Formal Networking
  Enlisting help of others to achieve goals
  Formal meeting behaviors with network mentors
  Developing strategies to achieve goals
  Evaluating outcomes

Collaborative Skills
 Determining team needs
 Teaming to develop goals
 Planning strategies for goal attainment
 Implementing strategies
 Evaluating outcomes

Persistence and Risk-Taking Skills
 Persistence through problem solving
 Risk taking through decision making

Dealing with Stress
 Recognizing feelings
 Expressing feelings appropriately
 Stress reduction skills
 Time-management skills

Source: From "Learning with purpose: Self-determination skills for students who are at risk for school and community failure" by L. A. Serna and J. Lau-Smith, 1995, *Intervention in School and Clinic, 30,* p. 144. Reprinted by permission.

MAKING ACCOMMODATIONS	
Collaborate with others to create a positive school climate	Encourage success
Exert your influence	Plan for transitions
Communicate carefully	Match intervention to infraction
Establish classroom expectations	Use the Intervention Ladder
Anticipate problems	Avoid power struggles
Maintain consistency	Give students choices
Be positive	Avoid grudges
Reduce boredom and frustration	Evaluate the effectiveness of your interventions
Make learning fun and exciting	Use curriculum based assessment and systematic measurement techniques
Motivate students	

across the time period they studied. Second, the placement pattern for this group of students differs from those of other students with disabilities: They are included less in general education classrooms. Let's take a closer look at these placement rates.

- Almost 20 percent of students with behavior disorders and emotional disturbance (as compared to 6 percent of their peers with disabilities) attend school at segregated settings, either at separate schools or facilities.

- Less than 16 percent of them receive services in general education classes (as compared to 35 percent of all students with disabilities).

- About 50 percent of all students with disabilities in residential programs are identified as having this disability.

- For these students, separate special education classes are the most common educational placement option used.

MAKING CONNECTIONS

- See other Inclusion sections in this book for information about the debate and discussion generated for each disability area.
- As a reminder of the problems surrounding the reauthorization of IDEA and discipline, review the Legislation section (Chapter 1).

Issues about inclusion spark controversy in special education. For the group of students with behavior disorders and emotional disturbance, it is no different. In fact, the arguments may even be more contentious, with heated debates raging about the Stay-Put Provision and inclusive settings for students who are very disruptive. Particularly for those who have externalizing behaviors that are aggressive, general educators seem to agree: They are neither trained nor equipped to handle these children (Cheney & Barringer, 1995). In addition, some experts question the benefits experienced by these students when placed in general education classrooms (Hallenbeck & Kauffman, 1995). Although many educators and parents of students with disabilities presume that students benefit from being exposed to socially appropriate peer role models, this may not hold true for students with behavior disorders and emotional disturbance. It is only through intensive direct instruction that these children learn correct social behaviors (Walker, Colvin, & Ramsey, 1995).

So it may be that inclusion may not be desirable in some cases and may not be a possibility in others. Students who are being detained by the legal and criminal justice system, for example, are unable to participate in inclusion classes. During the time of their incarceration, it is especially important that their educational needs not be neglected. Students have a right to receive appropriate and individualized special education even if they are in correctional settings such as halfway houses, jails, or prisons. Unfortunately, children in these settings often do not receive the education they need. Nelson, Rutherford, and Wolford (1987) recommend techniques to address the special needs of this group of students, for example, developing a functional curriculum, teaching prosocial skills, and implementing transition plans.

Transition Through Adulthood

The outcomes for students with this disability are not good. In fact, they are some of the worst for all students with disabilities (Chesapeake Institute, 1994). Although some of these data were presented in earlier sections of this chapter, the impact of grouping them in the following information points is dramatic. Students with behavior disorders and emotional disturbance

- have lower grades than any other groups of students with disabilities,

- fail more courses than other students with disabilities,

- fail more minimal competence tests than other students with disabilities,

- are retained more often,

- do not graduate from high school with a diploma at a rate that should be expected (42 percent as compared to 50 percent for all students with disabilities and 76 percent for all students in the general population),

- miss more days (eighteen per year) of school due to absenteeism than their peers with disabilities,

- have a high dropout rate (48 percent), particularly when compared to other students with disabilities (30 percent) or peers without disabilities (24 percent),

- experience a high rate (20 percent) of arrest while still in high school (compared to 9 percent of students with disabilities and 6 percent of those without),

- are very likely (58 percent of them) to be arrested within five years of leaving school (as opposed to 30 percent for all students with disabilities).

Although some students with behavior disorders and emotional disturbance do graduate from high school and go on to higher education, the vast majority do not. Before they leave the educational system, educators should assist these students in developing the skills needed to manage their lives independently. Because of the terrible results shown for most of these students, many educators are now advocating a life skills curriculum for them where functional skills are the focus of much of the instruction (Frank, Sitlington, & Carson, 1995). What do you think ought to comprise the educational programs of these youngsters?

 MAKING CONNECTIONS

For more about the array of curricular options and functional life skills, review
- Individualized Transition Plan, Chapter 2,
- Education and the Schoolchild, Chapter 6.

"Sam, neither your father nor I consider your response appropriate."

Drawing by Koren, © 1983 The New Yorker Magazine, Inc.

MAKING CONNECTIONS

Rebecca Viers, in the Personal Perspective section at the beginning of this chapter, shares the extra commitments she has made because of her daughter's disability.

Families

Parenting a child with behavior disorders and emotional disturbance is usually quite difficult. These families are most likely to be blamed for their children's problems and are also more likely to make significant financial sacrifices to secure services for their children (Ahearn, 1995). Increasingly, though, teachers are paying more attention to both the contributions and the needs of family members and are listening more carefully to parents' concerns. In this section, we decided to call your attention to two common elements in the lives of these children and their families: negotiating the mental health care system and foster home placement.

Negotiating the Mental Health Care System

In 1994, Congress provided funds that support community-based services for children with behavior disorders and emotional disturbance and their families. The intent is that these children's multiple health and mental health care needs will be met through a coordinated network of service providers (Children's Defense Fund, 1995). Although these services are now available, they are not being used at the rate they should. Let's look at some reasons why and how the problem can be solved.

Accessing our nation's mental health care system can be a daunting experience even for the most capable and most affluent. For those who have limited resources, the barriers can be so great that needed services are not sought or received. Those barriers include lack of transportation, lack of child care for other children, lack of information about what services are available and where they can be received, and emotional support. One innovative project is now lowering those barriers, and the result is more families and children with behavior disorders and emotional disturbance are accessing the mental health care services they so desperately need (Koroloff, Elliott, Koren, & Friesen, 1996). This project uses parents who had negotiated the mental health care system for themselves and their children. These experienced parents are hired as paraprofessionals, and the results are spectacular. Although they cannot help with respite or child care, their assistance in providing transportation, information, and emotional support resulted in a very low dropout rate and a very high contact rate with health care providers. This project is just one example of how challenging problems, even working within the most complex of the social service systems, can be met when positive thinking, creativity, and people-resources are applied.

Foster Home Placements

The number of our nation's children placed in foster care settings is increasing each year. The Children's Defense Fund (1996) estimates that each day during 1994, 462,000 children were living in a foster home placement, an increase of almost 20,000 children per day over the previous year. More surprising is the number of infants and toddlers who experience foster care. In a five-state survey, one out of every four children in foster care had entered the system before the age of 1, many of them as newborns. The proportion of these children who have disabilities is great, in part due to the large number of them prenatally exposed to cocaine and other drugs. In fact, it is estimated that the prevalence of disabilities among children in foster care is about double that in the school-age population (Smucker, Kauffman, & Ball, 1996).

Let's look more closely at children with disabilities who live in foster care placements. In one state, Illinois, 30 percent of children in foster care also receive special education, and almost half of them have been identified as having behavior disorders and emotional disturbance (Smucker, Kauffman, & Ball, 1996). This is the situation when about 10 percent of the school population is identified as having disabilities and only 1 percent of this group has behavior disorders and emotional disturbance. This disproportionate representation of students with this disability living in foster care placements is most apparent when two groups are compared: (1) those who attend special education and live in foster care settings, and (2) those who attend special education but are not living in foster care placements. They experience more difficulties in both the academic and behavioral areas. They are more likely to move from school to school, have higher grade retention rates, and be perceived as more negative by school staffs. It appears that it is the combination of foster care and this disability that so exacerbates these problems. In fact, for these students longer stays in foster care seem to cause increases in school-related problems. And, some maintain that the likelihood is great that many of these individuals will spend a great portion of their adult lives in jail (Sherman, 1994).

Educators need to be aware of the poor outcomes of these students. What can be done to improve this situation? One thing educators can do is create a positive and consistent classroom environment, where students understand the consequences for their actions, both positive and negative.

 MAKING CONNECTIONS

- ISee the Transition section of this chapter for a summary of the poor outcomes often made by children with this disability.
- Also see Chapter 4 to review the negative effects of grade retention.

Technology

Throughout this text, we have shown how advancements in computerized technology augment and expand students' physical and academic skills. The computer can be especially helpful to a student with behavior disorders and emotional disturbance (Rivera & Smith, 1997). It can serve as an emotionally neutral system with which to interact, have fun, achieve success, and even develop job skills.

Computers assist learning without the pressure of subjective judgments; a computer does not criticize or impose feelings about the child who is using it. Answers are simply right or wrong. Thus a computer serves as a safe environment in which to practice and improve skills. When a teacher incorporates computer-assisted instruction for an individualized learning activity for a child, the computer mirrors many of the attributes of a good teacher:

 MAKING CONNECTIONS

See other Technology sections in this book to understand the broad range of applications and benefits technology is making to children with disabilities and their families.

- It provides immediate attention and feedback.
- It individualizes to the particular skill level.
- It allows students to work at their own pace.
- It makes corrections quickly.
- It produces a professional-looking product.

- It keeps accurate records on correct and error rates.
- It ignores inappropriate behavior.
- It focuses on the particular response.
- It is nonjudgmental.

Using a computer is not a substitute for learning to interact appropriately with other people, however, and a teacher should not rely solely on computer interactions with children with behavior disorders and emotional disturbance. In arithmetic, for example, a teacher might introduce the instruction, allow drill and practice on the computer, and return periodically to check the student's progress. Many computer learning programs are available at different levels. By consulting with computer specialists, teachers can ensure that their judgments about the learning needs of the students are translated into the appropriate computer materials.

Concepts and Controversy: Behavior Control Through Medication—Is It Necessary?

More than one million American children take Ritalin to help them control externalizing behaviors. This represents an increase of over two and a half times the number of children on this behavior control medication since 1990, and a rate five times higher than the rest of the world (Hancock, 1996). And, it appears that students with behavior disorders and emotional disturbance are more likely to have this drug prescribed than are their peers. In one research sample, 56 percent of the students with behavior disorders and emotional disturbance were using this drug (Landrum, Singh, Nemil, Ellis, & Best, 1995). It is also interesting to note that across the entire sample, white students (48 percent) were more likely to be using Ritalin than African American students (33 percent).

Why are so many children being placed on behavior control medication? Are doctors better today in diagnosing conditions and prescribing proper medical treatment? Is it that parents and educators are less tolerant of disruptive behavior? Are adults less effective at controlling inappropriate behavior through their actions? Does the medication actually improve learning and behavior? These are some of the questions that professionals in the fields of education and medicine are asking. These are some of the same questions asked during the 1970s when medical management of behavior problems was also popular. In studies conducted then, findings indicated that for the vast majority of students receiving stimulant drugs (e.g., Ritalin, Dexedrine) to control hyperactivity, behavior management techniques were as effective as the drugs (Sulzbacher, 1972; Carpenter & Sells, 1974). The drugs were the same; maybe the children were different thirty years ago?

The controversy over the use of behavior-controlling medication is growing. Some experts believe that the drugs do not improve learning and only improve behavior when paired with behavior modification techniques (Hoff, 1993). Some say they are not effective with all children, while others believe they are a modern miracle (Hancock, 1996). Some are very concerned about side effects such as weight loss and sleeplessness and feel that the medication is not effective enough to justify its use (Armstrong, 1995). How should these issues be resolved?

Precise definitions and criteria for identification of behavior disorders and emotional disturbance have not yet been written. This disability reflects, in part, societal standards for behavior and expectations about the development of children. Many of the behaviors that our society labels as disordered in a particular individual might be acceptable if that person were a different age, lived in a different society, came from a different culture, or exhibited the behaviors under different circumstances. Of course, some conditions are considered disturbed despite age or society's standards.

It is difficult to identify most behavior disorders and emotional disturbance in young children, and there is great reluctance from some professionals to identify preschoolers because of the damage that misidentification can do. However, it is now recognized that this disability has considerable stability over time, particularly for individuals who exhibit severe aggressive behaviors by the time they are 4 years old. For these people, the benefits of early identification can be great. Some problems can be treated before they become serious; interventions can be developed for the home and community environments; school settings and educational programs can be tailor-made to meet the needs of the youngster from the time of school entrance; and the dismal adult outcomes experienced by many individuals belonging to this group can be avoided.

FOCUS QUESTIONS

Self-Test Questions

▶ *By identifying the components of two definitions—as in IDEA and as offered by the National Mental Health and Special Education Coalition—how would you compare them?*

The IDEA definition of severe emotional disturbance (SED)—the term used in law—describes these children as unable to develop or sustain positive relationships with peers or teachers, having difficulties with academic tasks, exhibiting inappropriate behaviors, experiencing considerable unhappiness or depression, developing physical symptoms relating to fears about personal or school problems, and having no other (intellectual, sensory, health) reason for the condition. This definition also requires that the condition be severe and long-lasting. The National Mental Health and Special Education Coalition's definition also requires that the condition be extreme and long-lasting and adds that it also consist of inappropriate behaviors and negatively affects educational performance. This definition also specifies that the behaviors of concern are observed across settings (both school and home), are unresponsive to direct intervention in general education, and can co-exist with other conditions. The federal definition has been criticized because of its narrow focus. The label used, SED, places too much emphasis on emotional problems without mentioning behavior problems. It also is the only label that uses the word *serious*, implying that mild or moderate difficulties are not to be included in this special education category. This definition also provides an older view of schooling that focuses exclusively on academics, rather than incorporating social behavior into a more complete concept of education. The National Coalition's definition attempts to correct these problems.

▶ *What are the two major subgroups of this disability, and how would you compare the conditions that fall into each subgroup?*

Behavior disorders and emotional disturbance can be divided into two groups: externalizing behavior problems and internalizing behavior problems. Some have argued that schools dwell too much on externalizing disruptive behaviors, ignoring the equally serious problems of children and youth with internalizing problems, such as depression. This may be the case because aggression, hostility, and defiance disturb others more than internalizing behaviors, for example, being extremely shy, withdrawn, or depressed.

▶ *What are the major causes of this disability, and how can it be prevented?*

The specific causes of a behavior disorder or emotional disturbance in a particular individual are almost always unknown. However, in general three basic areas are often the root of the problem: biology, home and community, and school. As with other disability areas, more and more biological causes are being identified. For example, Tourette's syndrome appears to have a biological basis, and the genetic links for schizophrenia and even for depression are becoming clear. The powerful impact of environment on individuals cannot be denied, particularly on the developing child. The concept of environment must include the home, extended family, and community. Certainly, the family's situation cannot be minimized. The devastation caused by abuse and neglect on young children is an American tragedy and is certainly a major cause of behavior disorders and emotional disturbance in children today. Although probably more of a reason for the continuation (maintenance of) problems, poorly managed classrooms that provide little consistency and structure and do not produce a positive learning environment can result in students' exhibiting externalizing behavior problems. When educators provide safe, positive, and exciting learning environments that actively engage children in learning, many problems are prevented.

▶ *What are the long-term prospects for these children?*

Without direct intervention, the long-term prospects for students with externalizing or internalizing behaviors are not promising. Both groups of children are recognized by their peers as different, and they are often rejected. The outcomes for the entire group include high dropout rates, low academic achievement, failing grades, low high school graduation rates, and contact with the criminal justice system. Those with externalizing behavior problems, particularly those with severe problems with aggression when they were preschoolers, are at risk for even more significant problems as adults. The likelihood is that they will be arrested at rates much higher than other students with disabilities.

▶ *How can teachers help children with this disability?*

Research findings are clear: Direct and systematic instruction that includes on-going evaluation to ensure the continued effectiveness of selected interventions produces achievement in these children. Whether the instructional target is in the academic, vocational, or social areas, these procedures and array of teaching tactics are powerful. For example, when behavior is of concern, the tactics found on the Intervention Ladder (specific praise, ignoring, rules, contingent instructions, contingent observation, criterion-specific rewards, fines, group contingencies, peer management, self-management, parent action, overcorrection, timeout, punishment, exclusion) are paired with curriculum based assessment (CBA) and systematic measurement techniques to assist in determining whether a tactic is sufficiently effective or another one needs to be tried; disruption can therefore be held to a minimum and a positive learning environment fostered. Likewise, when direct instruction (e.g., phonics instruction for acquisition of reading skills, rewards for increased reading rate or fluency) are paired with CBA, academic performance improves dramatically as well. New curriculum areas are also being developed. A good example is the work currently being conducted in the area of self-determination, where students are learning to make choices and decisions.

Challenge Question

▶ *Why does an array of educational placement options need to be available for students with behavior disorders and emotional disturbance?*

Education for children and youth with behavior disorders and emotional disturbance is provided in a variety of environments, including general education classrooms, special education classrooms, community-based residential group homes or halfway houses, and even institutions or hospitals. This group of students has the highest rate of placements in segregated settings and the lowest rates of inclusive placements of any other group of students with disabilities. Of children and youth with disabilities who are placed in residential programs, about 50 percent of them have this disability. For those able to participate in programs offered by their local public schools, many do not participate in general education classes because of their aggressive and threatening behavior patterns. General education teachers do not feel prepared to deal with dangerous behaviors in their students, and the settings in which they work are usually not prepared to handle such situations either. Clearly, a fluid and full array of service delivery options must be available for these students and the educators who work with them.

~~~ *SUPPLEMENTARY RESOURCES* ~~~

Scholarly Books

Coleman, M. C. (1996). *Emotional & behavior disorders: Theory and practice* (3rd ed.). Boston: Allyn and Bacon.

Kauffman, J. M. (1997). *Characteristics of behavioral disorders of children and youth* (6th ed.). Columbus, OH: Merrill.

Newcomer, P. L. (1993). *Understanding and teaching emotionally disturbed children and adolescents* (2nd ed.). Austin, TX: Pro-Ed.

Peterson, R. L., & Ishii-Jordon, S. (1994). *Multicultural issues in the education of students with behavioral disorders.* Cambridge, MA: Brookline.

Rosenberg, M. S., Wilson, R., Maheady, L., & Sindelar, P. T. (1997). *Educating students with behavior disorders* (2nd ed.). Boston: Allyn and Bacon.

Walker, H. M., Colvin, G., & Ramsey, E. (1995). *Antisocial behavior in school: Strategies and best practices.* Pacific Grove, CA: Brooks/Cole.

Popular Books

Atwood, M. (1996). *Alias Grace.* New York: Doubleday.

Duke, P. (1987). *Call me Anna: The autobiography of Patty Duke.* New York: Bantam.

Kesey, K. (1977). *One flew over the cuckoo's nest.* New York: Penguin.

Plath, S. (1971). *The bell jar.* New York: Harper & Row.

Styron, W. (1990). *Darkness visible: A memoir of madness.* New York: Random House.

Videos

One flew over the cuckoo's nest. (1975). United Artists.
Camille Claudel. (1989). Orion.
Fisherking. (1991). Columbia Pictures.
The piano. (1993). Miramax.

Twelve monkeys. (1995). Universal Studios.
Primal fear. (1996). Paramount.
Shine. (1996). Pandora Films.
Sling Blade. (1996). Miramax.

Professional, Parent, and Consumer Organizations and Agencies

Council for Children with Behavioral Disorders (CCBD)
Council for Exceptional Children
1920 Association Dr.
Reston, VA 22091
Phone: (703) 620-3660
Web site: http://www.cec.sped.org

American Psychiatric Association
1400 K St. N.W.
Washington, DC 20036
Phone: (202) 682-6000
Web site: http://www.psych.org

National Alliance for the Mentally Ill
Children's and Adolescent's Network (NAMICAN)
2101 Wilson Blvd., Suite 302
Arlington, VA 22314
Phone: (800) 950-6264
Web site: http://www.cais.com/vikings.nami

American Psychological Association (APA)
1200 17th St. N.W.
Washington, DC 20036
Phone: (800) 374-2721
Web site: http://www.apa.org

National Mental Health Association
1800 N. Kent St.
Arlington, VA 22209
Phone: (703) 684-7722
Web site: http://www.nmha.org

National Mental Health Services
Knowledge Exchange Network
P.O. Box 42490
Washington, DC 20015
Phone: (800) 789-2647
Web site: http://www.mentalhealth.org

Henriette Wyeth. *Doña Nestorita*. 1940.

Henriette Wyeth, an extremely prominent artist in her own right, came from a family of very successful and well-known artists. Her father was the famous artist and illustrator, N. C. Wyeth; her brother, Andrew, and her sister, Carolyn, also became well-known artists; and her husband was Peter Hurd, the renowned western painter. Henriette Wyeth faced many challenges during her young life, including growing up in a high-achieving family that had exceptional expectations for her. She spoke of the path she took to find the right outlet for her own creativity and talents and how her own special physical challenge helped to shape her future: "I wanted to be a singer. Due to polio at 3, I couldn't play the piano. I wanted to be an actress, too. By the age of 16, I was hooked on painting. I thought everyone drew—like having salt and pepper on the table" (Horgan, 1994, p. 30). The very special piece shown here was painted in 1940. Doña Nestorita, a 90-year-old Mexican woman, was blind and had lived most of her simple life in the rural Southwest. Wyeth described her as "charming, of great dignity, in a pitiful, tiny, blind person" (p. 58).

Physical Impairments and Special Health Care Needs

9

ADVANCE ORGANIZERS

OVERVIEW

Physical impairments and special health care needs are disability categories that comprise hundreds of conditions and diseases, yet even combined, in children they are low-incidence disabilities (comprising approximately 2 percent of all schoolchildren with disabilities). Today, most children with physical impairments attend their neighborhood school, but they require modifications in the physical environment. Those with special health care needs tend to have high rates of absenteeism, and they require flexibility and modifications in their instructional programs. Some of these children may present crises to their teachers and require emergency techniques.

FOCUS QUESTIONS

SELF-TEST QUESTIONS

▶ Why are there so many different ways to organize and classify these disabilities?
▶ What are some steps teachers should follow to assist a child who is having a seizure?
▶ What are the five general causes of physical impairments and special health care needs, and how can they be prevented?

▶ How can the learning environment be modified to accommodate students with physical impairments and special health care needs?
▶ Why is the multidisciplinary team approach necessary for these children, and how can educators improve collaboration across diverse professionals?

CHALLENGE QUESTION

▶ What are the barriers to these individuals' full participation in society, and how can they be minimized?

A *Personal Perspective*: The People Who Make Special Education Special

Karen Canellas-U'Ren was a highly successful teacher of students with disabilities. She is now an administrator who is assisting an entire middle school community accommodate for every student's special learning needs. This dedicated professional continues to be excited about her work.

As I examine how I started my career and compare it to now when I am an advocate for children with special needs, I recognize that several key people and experiences influenced me. In the beginning of my career, I was an elective teacher in a small rural community. That experience taught me that every student has unique qualities and can make a significant contribution to a class or school. Like most first-year teachers, I was open to almost all situations and requests. I am so glad now that my administrator asked me to take some students in my classes who were not successful with some other teachers. Some of my senior colleagues told me that I was being "dumped on," but I did not see it that way. No special education classroom or teacher was available at the school. Intuitively, I knew that another option was needed for many children at my school.

Looking back, I guess I became that option, that special education teacher who helps meet individual students' needs. I provided a classroom that was open to every student at that school. "My" students from that year will always be in my heart. I never worried about what they could or could not do. Rather, I encouraged them to be who they were and to be proud of the talents they possessed. Mary was about at the end of her high school experience and much older than her peers. She spent almost all day with me. I couldn't have been prouder when Mary graduated from high school and went on to become a mechanic.

My experience with Mary and students like her sparked my interest in special education and students with disabilities. I decided to pursue a master's degree and prepare myself to work with these students and their families. I was hired by the school district near the university on a waiver while I attended school. I learned a lot on the job and at the university. My special education career had begun.

Later, I became a teacher-trainer, and taught other teachers about students with disabilities and their families. I found that most teachers want to know more about special learners but are afraid of the unknown. As an administrator, I once again am educating a school community about students with special needs, particularly those who are being integrated into general education classes for a great part of their school day.

I often wonder what makes me so committed to these students. Maybe it is what I see in their eyes, in their faces, as they struggle to take a breath, utter a response, lift their heads, and participate in their education programs. Maybe it is because they struggle so hard and use every bit of their strength to make their body work. I think the reason for my commitment is basic: It is a result of *their courage*.

The students with severe medical and physical disabilities are, in my opinion, brave beyond words. Their families display unbelievable courage when they entrust their children to us, the teachers and administrators at their neighborhood school, knowing how involved or medically fragile their children are. Whenever I feel frustrated with the discipline problems we have to deal with on a daily basis at school or when I have to deal with difficult people, I "escape" to "my" children and become an active participant in a classroom. There, I can re-establish myself with the children who are the real purpose of my work. Just watching and working with children like Matt and Jason, who really have to struggle to do ordinary tasks, who smile and reach out to me with limbs that are stiff or spastic or weak, reminds me again of their true strength and courage. I can actually feel their psychological strength, despite their physical weaknesses. I get the same feelings as I watch Carissa, another student with severe physical disabilities, sing in a chorus with her peers without disabilities. It is these experiences that restore my faith in children and youth because I can visibly see their compassion and vigor. There is nothing more special than hearing the laughter of children who are so medically fragile that no one knows whether they will survive to adulthood. It is that laughter that makes my job of being their advocate, their facilitator, so important and worthwhile.

I have been fortunate to experience the strength of character of these students and their parents and the tolerance, acceptance, and tenderness of adolescents without disabilities who are these students' peers. Most of these classmates have developed a caring attitude toward others who are different from them, an attitude which I hope will carry with them throughout their lives. Everyday, children and adults in our learning community interact with special learners and, most importantly, embrace them as important individuals in their lives.

1. Why do you think that special educators like Karen Canellas-U'Ren are so dedicated to their profession?

2. How has the field of special education changed since she selected it as a career?

Our society seems obsessed with youth, beauty, and physical fitness. The advertising industry urges us to purchase certain styles of clothes, special cosmetics and hair products, new exercise equipment, and even cars to make ourselves more attractive. Have you noticed messages about physical perfection in television shows, commercials, music videos, and movies? Have you or your friends assigned popularity ratings to others on the basis of physical appearance? Sometimes, we even equate physical perfection with virtue or goodness, imperfection and deformities with evil. Think, for example, of the villain, the deformed Darth Vader, always dressed in black in *The Star Wars Trilogy.* This symbolism has been repeated in many books and movies, including *The Hunchback of Notre Dame, Dark Crystal, Lion King,* and *The Wizard of Oz.*

Children whose health is precarious often do not conform to the standards of strength and energy emphasized by the fashion, advertising, sports, and entertainment industries so admired by our society. Unfortunately, the prejudices of society frequently are reflected in schools as well. These children—whose appearance is unusual because of deformities or muscle problems or those whose walking ability, not to mention their athletic prowess, is challenged by wheelchairs or braces—may suffer prejudice and discrimination in school. How can educators eliminate these prejudices in order to provide appropriate learning environments for all children? How can educators address the individual learning needs of children who face physical challenges and require special accommodations because of their health care needs? These are some of the questions and related issues discussed in this chapter.

Organizing the information found here, however, challenged us because there are so many different diseases, impairments, and conditions that can significantly affect children, their lives at school, and those who educate them.[1] It is impossible to describe in any detail every condition leading to a physical impairment or special health care need that educators might encounter at schools. Also, these two disability areas are not mutually exclusive. For example, some impairments are typically grouped under a physical disability or an orthopedic impairment and also result in a long-term health problem. And, one more point: Possibly more than any other disability category, many children with physical impairments or health problems do not require special education services. We are also not convinced it is necessary for you to master all the information about each specific condition, illness, or disease at this point in your educational career. If you intend to concentrate your studies on people with physical impairments and special health care needs, courses to follow will provide you with the detailed content you will need as a professional. For the rest of you, we trust that when confronted with a condition rarely seen in children, you will be certain to learn all about it by seeking out specific information from the many resources available to you: local physicians, the child's multidisciplinary IEP team, and some of the agencies found in the *Student's Resource Book* that accompanies this

---

[1] The content of this chapter also reflects current understanding about various disabilities, their causes and effects, along with how perspectives and knowledge change across time. For example, at one time autism was thought to be a form of mental retardation, at another time a type of emotional disturbance, later a subcategory of physical disabilities, but is now considered an independent disability category. The content here also reflects how prevention and treatment have diminished the long-term effects of many diseases and conditions. For example, medical technology can now prevent the mental retardation once associated with spina bifida, so spina bifida is discussed in this chapter rather than in Chapter 6.

Physical disabilities and health impairments should not cause individuals to be shut out of experiences and opportunities.

text. In this chapter, we discuss the most common physical disabilities and health impairments that occur in children. More importantly, later in the chapter we stress ways that these children's educational needs can be best met through accommodations in physical and learning environments.

Physical Impairments and Special Health Care Needs Defined

One confusing aspect about these disability areas is the multiple ways the overall area is organized and defined. For example, in IDEA the federal government gives two overarching definitions for students with physical impairments and special health care needs. Children with physical impairments—those youngsters who have a problem with the structure or the functioning of their bodies—are referred to as having **orthopedic impairments**, defined in IDEA as a condition

> that adversely affects a child's educational performance. The term includes impairments caused by congenital anomaly (e.g., clubfoot, absence of some member, etc.), impairments caused by disease (e.g., poliomyelitis, bone tuberculosis, etc.), and impairments from other causes (e.g., cerebral palsy, amputations, and fractures or burns that cause contractures). (U.S. Department of Education, 1992)

Many children with health impairments—who have limitations in their physical well-being and require ongoing medical attention—also have special needs at school. The federal government in IDEA defines **other health impairments** as

> having limited strength, vitality or alertness, due to chronic or acute health problems such as a heart condition, tuberculosis, rheumatic fever, nephritis, asthma, sickle cell anemia, hemophilia, epilepsy, lead poisoning, leukemia, or diabetes, that adversely affects a child's educational performance. (U.S. Department of Education, 1992)

orthopedic impairments. Conditions related to a physical deformity or disability of the skeletal system and associated motor function.

other health impairments. Chronic or acute health problems resulting in limited strength, vitality, or alertness.

Other experts in the field group these disabilities differently, and even use other terms to describe them. Some use a variety of terms—"orthopedic and neurological impairments" (Sirvis & Caldwell, 1995), "orthopedic and muscular impairments" (Best, Bigge, & Sirvis, 1994), "physical disabilities" (Hallahan and Kauffman, 1994), and "physical impairments" (Heller, Alberto, Forney, & Schwartzman, 1996)—to describe what IDEA calls severe orthopedic impairments. Some experts further cluster specific conditions into major groups, such as neuromotor impairments, degenerative diseases, muscular-skeletal disorders, and major health impairments (Heller et al., 1996), while others talk about all of these children having special health care needs and do not assign them to any group (Urbano, 1992). Probably, the primary reason for the differences in the ways professionals discuss these conditions is that there is no simple organizational scheme that uniformly applies. For example, one child with cerebral palsy may face some physical challenges and need considerable assistance from a physical therapist to learn how to control movement and yet have no special health care needs, while another child with the same condition may have both physical limitations and serious health care needs. Students with either disability might require flexible schedules because they are not physically able to participate in six straight hours of school or might need special arrangements (e.g., peer tutors) so they do not fall behind in their studies due to frequent absences. And, remember, some of these children may not require any special education services or accommodations.

Types of Physical Impairments and Special Health Care Needs

We approached this section with two fundamental beliefs: It is important for educators to know about (1) the conditions that lead to physical impairments and special health care needs, and (2) the common *childhood* conditions that fall into each group. These beliefs yielded two important outcomes: Those conditions and diseases now prevented in the United States (e.g., polio) and those found in adults but seldom seen in children (e.g, multiple sclerosis) would not receive much coverage. Our experience also told us that it is easier for most college students to learn and understand information new to them when they have some organizational scheme that helps them group the topics presented. So, although there is no nationally adopted way to organize and describe the conditions, impairments, disorders, illnesses, and diseases educators might see at school, we dared to create a scheme (see Figure 9.1) to help you in your study and mastery of the material presented in this chapter. Notice that Figure 9.1 lists many different conditions that can result in physical and health impairments found in classroom settings but does not include the much less common conditions. Also, space limitations required us to reserve chapter coverage for the most prevalent among schoolchildren. Remember, these conditions, even when grouped, are "low-incidence" disabilities. The number of children who pertain to this discussion is small, particularly when compared to those with other disabilities, such as learning disabilities. After we provide this introductory information about the conditions educators are likely to confront in classroom settings, we focus on how to modify learning and physical environments to best meet the educational needs of these students.

 MAKING CONNECTIONS

- Refer to Chapter 1 for a review of the overall prevalence of different disabilities and later in this chapter for specific prevalence information.
- Read remaining chapters of this text to learn more about "low-incidence disabilities."
- For a division of special education categories into high- and low-incidence disabilities, see this text's table of contents.

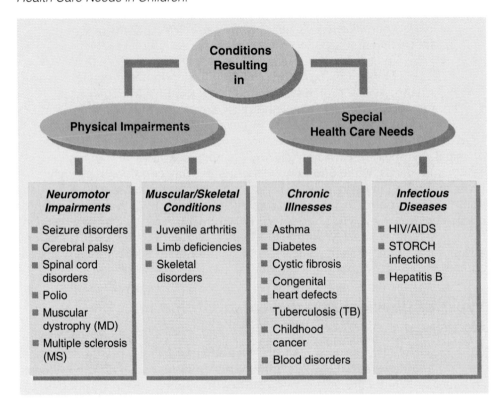

~~~

FIGURE 9.1

An Organizational Scheme for the Conditions, Disorders, Impairments, Illnesses, and Diseases That Can Result in Physical Challenges and Special Health Care Needs in Children.

Neuromuscular/Skeletal Conditions. Look again at Figure 9.1 to see the names of many of the conditions and impairments that can lead to a physical disability. This organizational scheme created two major groupings: **neuromotor impairments** and **muscular/skeletal conditions**. In Table 9.1, we define each of these conditions, but in the text we discuss only those with the highest prevalence. We do not discuss muscular dystrophy because of its low prevalence or multiple sclerosis because it is an adult disease. Polio is not discussed because it is almost eradicated; in 1994, there were only eight new cases in the United States (Neergaard, 1995). These diseases are, however, described in Table 9.1.

Neuromotor Impairments. When the central nervous system (the brain and the spinal cord) is damaged, a serious neurological impairment that limits muscular control and movement often results. It is likely that all educators sometime during their careers will work with children who have some type of neuromuscular impairment; probably either epilepsy or cerebral palsy. Although less likely, they might also work with students who have spinal cord (neural tube) disorders. So, these three conditions are discussed in this section.

neuromotor impairment.
Condition involving both the nerves, muscles, and motor functioning.
muscular/skeletal conditions.
Conditions affecting muscles or bones and resulting in limited functioning.

~~~
**TABLE 9.1**

Types of Neuromuscular/Skeletal Conditions

| Condition | Description |
|---|---|
| **Neuromotor Impairments** | |
| Seizure disorders | *Epilepsy,* the most common type of neuromotor impairment in children, is a condition of recurrent convulsions or seizures caused by abnormal brain electrical activity. It is treated with medications and frequently is well controlled without any effect on learning or motor skills. |
| Cerebral palsy (CP) | *Cerebral palsy* is an incurable and nonprogressive condition caused by brain injury that sometimes limits the individual's ability to control muscle groups or motor functioning in specific areas of the body or, infrequently, the entire body. It may be associated with multiple disabilities. Orthopedic and physical therapy offer benefits. |
| Spinal cord disorders | A neural tube birth defect, *spina bifida* is the improper closure of the protective tissue surrounding the spinal cord. It results in limited neurological control for organs and muscles controlled by nerves that originate below the level of the lesion. Increasing numbers of children have suffered traumatic head or spinal cord injuries resulting in permanent disabilities. Health care needs for both groups include good skin care, management of bladder and bowel care, and orthopedic and physical therapy.<br><br>Typically, the result of injuries from accidents or abuse, *spinal cord injuries* can cause severe motor impairments and even paralysis. |
| Polio | Caused by a viral infection, almost totally prevented in children immunized in the United States, *polio* attacks the spinal cord and can result in paralysis and motor disabilities. Health care needs parallel those for spinal cord disorders. |
| Muscular dystrophy (MD) | An exceptionally rare, incurable, and progressive disease, *muscular dystrophy* weakens and then destroys the affected individual's muscles. Health care needs center on lung function support, prevention of pneumonia, and physical therapy. |
| Multiple sclerosis (MS) | A chronic disease typically occurring in adults, *multiple sclerosis* causes the myelin covering the nerve fibers of the brain and spinal cord to deteriorate, impeding the transmission of electrical signals from the brain to other parts of the body. Health care needs parallel those for MD. |
| **Muscular/Skeletal Conditions** | |
| Juvenile arthritis | *Juvenile arthritis* is a disease caused by an autoimmune process resulting in swelling, immobility, and pain in joints. Health care needs include medication to suppress the process and orthopedic and physical therapy to maintain function in small and large joints. |
| Limb deficiencies | Skeletal problems in which the individual's limb(s) are shortened, absent, or malformed. They may occur from congenital conditions or from injuries. Health care needs focus on adaptive interventions to support or improve functioning of the missing limb(s). |
| Skeletal disorders | *Dwarfism,* a condition caused by abnormal development of long bones, may result in varying degrees of motor disabilities. Health care needs may include human growth hormone to improve height.<br><br>*Osteogenesis imperfecta,* sometimes known as brittle bone disease, is a condition in which normal calcification of the bone does not occur, leading to breakage and abnormal healing of bones with accompanying loss of height. Health care interventions include physical therapy and medical care.<br><br>*Scoliosis,* a curvature of the spine that occurs in children during puberty, may in severe form limit mobility of the trunk. Health care needs include monitoring of the amount of curvature of the spine and appropriate interventions to arrest the process. |

Although ranging in severity from mild to severe, these disabilities are usually very serious and affect these individuals in significant ways throughout their lives.

The most common neuromotor impairment encountered at school is epilepsy, also called a seizure disorder or a convulsive disorder. A person with **epilepsy** often has recurrent seizures resulting from sudden, excessive, spontaneous, and abnormal discharge of neurons in the brain. This can be accompanied by changes in the person's motor or sensory functioning and can also result in loss of consciousness (Epilepsy Foundation of America, 1994a). **Seizures** may involve the entire brain (generalized seizures) or only a portion of the brain (partial seizures). The frequency of seizures may vary from a single isolated incident to hundreds in a day. Some children actually anticipate their seizures because they experience a preictal stage, or an **aura**, and have heightened sensory signals of an impending seizure such as a peculiar smell, taste, vision, sound, or action. Others might experience a change in their behavior. Knowing about an aura pattern is helpful, as an individual can assume a safe position or warn companions before a seizure begins.

The Epilepsy Foundation of America (1994a) identifies four main types of seizures: (1) generalized tonic-clonic, (2) absence, (3) simple partial, and (4) complex partial (psychomotor). Generalized **tonic-clonic seizures** (formerly referred to as grand mal seizures) are the most serious type of seizure and are characterized by convulsions and loss of consciousness. The dramatic behaviors exhibited during a tonic-clonic seizure may, at first, be frightening to the teacher and to other students in the class. The child may fall to the floor and usually experiences a stiff (tonic) phase, in which the muscles become rigid, followed by a clonic phase, in which the arms and legs jerk. Other behaviors may accompany the seizure, including teeth grinding, frothing due to inefficient saliva swallowing, and loss of bladder control. These seizures usually last less than five minutes, after which the individual enters the resting stage (postictal) and becomes relaxed, very sleepy, and disoriented. Teachers can help students during and after such a seizure episode; for some guidelines, see Table 9.2.

**Absence seizures** (also called petit mal seizures) are characterized by short lapses in consciousness. It may even be difficult to determine that the person is experiencing anything out of the ordinary, and, in fact, the person may not even realize a seizure has occurred after it is over. Typically, someone experiencing an absence seizure simply stares or shows small eye movements like fluttering of the eyelids. Because absence seizures are not dramatic, a teacher might wrongly assume that the child is merely daydreaming or not paying attention.

Not all seizures are obvious to those around the individual having this experience. Such is often the case with **simple partial seizures**, where children may think their environments are distorted and strange, that inexplicable events and feelings have occurred. With these seizures, teachers might incorrectly believe that the child is acting out or exhibiting bizarre behavior patterns. **Complex partial seizures** (psychomotor seizures) are the result of a unique electrical dysfunction, localized in a specific part of the brain. For this reason, they are sometimes called *focal seizures*. After a short period, the child returns to normal activities. Sometimes, teachers interpret the child's behavior during a complex partial seizure as misbehavior or clowning. This mistake can lead to confusion on the part of the child, who is not aware of his or her behavior during a psychomotor seizure, and on the part of the teacher who does not recognize the misbehavior as a seizure.

MAKING CONNECTIONS

See the "Tips for Teachers" box found in the Prevention section of this chapter for more about dealing with seizures in classroom settings.

**epilepsy.** A tendency to recurrent seizures.

**seizure.** A spontaneous abnormal discharge of the electrical impulses of the brain, sometimes referred to as a *convulsive disorder.*

**aura.** A signal of an impending seizure, sometimes called the *preictal stage.*

**tonic-clonic seizures.** Seizures characterized by a stiff (tonic) phase in which the muscles become rigid, followed by a jerking (clonic) phase in which the arms and legs will snap (formerly referred to as *grand mal seizures*).

**absence seizures.** Seizures with a short lapse in consciousness (also called *petit mal seizures*).

**simple partial seizures.** Not always apparent; often affect behavior and feelings.

**complex partial seizures.** Periods of automatic behavior resulting from discharge in a localized area of the brain (sometimes called psychomotor or focal seizures).

~~
**TABLE 9.2**

Seizure Recognition

| Seizure Type | What It Looks Like | What It Is Not |
|---|---|---|
| Generalized tonic-clonic (also called grand mal) | Sudden cry, fall, rigidity, followed by muscle jerks, shallow breathing or temporarily suspended breathing, bluish skin, possible loss of bladder or bowel control, usually lasts a couple of minutes. Normal breathing then starts again. There may be some confusion and/or fatigue, followed by return to full consciousness. | Heart attack<br>Stroke |
| Absence (also called petit mal) | A blank stare, beginning and ending abruptly, lasting only a few seconds, most common in children. May be accompanied by rapid blinking, some chewing movements of the mouth. Child or adult is unaware of what's going on during the seizure, but quickly returns to full awareness once it has stopped. May result in learning difficulties if not recognized and treated. | Daydreaming<br>Lack of attention<br>Deliberate ignoring of adult instructions |
| Simple partial | Jerking may begin in one area of the body, arm, leg, or face. Can't be stopped, but patient stays awake and aware. Jerking may proceed from one area of the body to another and sometimes spreads to become a convulsive seizure. | Acting out, bizarre behavior |
| | Partial sensory seizures may not be obvious to an onlooker. Patient experiences a distorted environment. May see or hear things that aren't there, may feel unexplained fear, sadness, anger, or joy. May have nausea, experience odd smells, and have a generally "funny" feeling in the stomach. | Hysteria<br>Mental illness<br>Psychosomatic illness<br>Parapsychological or mystical experience |
| Complex partial (also called psychomotor or temporal lobe) | Usually starts with blank stare, followed by chewing, followed by random activity. Person appears unaware of surroundings, may seem dazed and mumble. Unresponsive. Actions clumsy, not directed. May pick at clothing, pick up objects, try to take clothes off. May run, appear afraid. May struggle or flail at restraint. Once pattern established, same set of actions usually occur with each seizure. Lasts a few minutes, but post-seizure confusion can last substantially longer. No memory of what happened during seizure period. | Drunkenness<br>Intoxication on drugs<br>Mental illness<br>Disorderly conduct |

*Source:* From *Seizure recognition and first aid*. Epilepsy Foundation of America, 1994b. Landover, MD: Author. Reprinted with permission.

Another neuromotor impairment frequently encountered in schoolchildren is **cerebral palsy**. Cerebral palsy comprises a family of syndromes associated with disordered movement and posture. This condition is a result of damage, usually because of insufficient oxygen getting to the brain during its developmental period

**cerebral palsy.** A disorder of movement and posture caused by damage to the developing brain.

MAKING CONNECTIONS

For more about the challenges of
cerebral palsy, see Sam's story in the
Technology section of Chapter 5.

**spastic.** A type of cerebral palsy
characterized by uncontrolled
tightening or pulling of muscles.

**athetoid.** A type of cerebral palsy
characterized by purposeless and
uncontrolled involuntary
movements.

**ataxia.** A type of cerebral palsy
characterized by movement disrupted by impaired balance and
depth perception.

**contractures.** Joint stiffening,
often because of muscle shortening, to the point that the joint can
no longer move through its normal
range.

**spinal cord disorders.** Always
involve the spinal column, usually
both the nerves and muscles.

**neural tube disorders.** Another
name for spinal cord disorders,
which always involve the spinal
column and usually the spinal
cord.

**spina bifida.** A developmental
defect whereby the spinal column
fails to close properly.

(United Cerebral Palsy Association, 1993). Cerebral palsy is most often congenital, with damage occurring either before (prenatally), during (perinatally), or immediately after (postnatally) the child's birth. Some individuals, however, acquire cerebral palsy later, during the first three years of life. Acquired cerebral palsy is usually caused by brain damage resulting from accidents, brain infections, or child abuse. Cerebral palsy is not a disease, but rather a nonprogressive and noninfectious condition. Regrettably, once acquired, it cannot be cured (at least today).

The severity of the condition depends on the precise location of brain damage, the degree of brain damage, and the extent of involvement of the central nervous system. Individuals with cerebral palsy whose motor functioning is affected show these characteristics alone or in combination: jerky movements, spasms, involuntary movements, and lack of muscle tone. Often, individuals with cerebral palsy have multiple disabilities, probably caused by the same damage to the brain that caused the cerebral palsy. For example, many individuals who have severe difficulties in motor functioning also have difficulties mastering oral speech. These individuals have a speech impairment and a physical disability. Other disabilities that sometimes accompany cerebral palsy include seizures, sensory deficits such as abnormal sensation and perception, visual impairments, hearing loss, speech or language impairments, and learning problems. Although some degree of mental retardation is present in about half of the children with cerebral palsy, others are intellectually gifted. It is a tragic mistake to assume that cerebral palsy and mental retardation always occur in combination.

Cerebral palsy is usually described in two ways: by mobility or by the affected area. The three main types of cerebral palsy defined by movement are (1) **spastic**, in which the movements are very stiff; (2) **athetoid**, in which involuntary movements are purposeless and uncontrolled and purposeful movements are contorted; and (3) **ataxia**, in which movements such as walking are disrupted by impairments of balance and depth perception. Many individuals with cerebral palsy have impaired mobility and poor muscle development. Even if they can walk, their efforts may require such exertion and be so inefficient that they need canes, crutches, or a wheelchair to get around. Students with cerebral palsy may also need braces to help support the affected limbs and make them more functional or to prevent **contractures** that would eventually lead to bone deformities and further mobility limitations. Proper positioning of the body also must be considered. Many children need wedges, pillows, and individually designed chairs and worktables so they can be comfortable; breathe easier; avoid injuries, contractures, and deformities; as well as participate in group activities. The classifications of cerebral palsy according to the areas of the body affected are shown in Figure 9.2.

The last neuromotor impairment we discuss is **spinal cord disorders**, also called **neural tube disorders**. These conditions involve both the nerves and the muscles of the spinal column. Spinal cord injuries and **spina bifida** are the two most common conditions in this group and may be the result of accidents or abuse. In younger children, spinal cord injuries often result from child abuse or car accidents. In older youngsters, many such injuries are caused by sports accidents. In both spinal cord injuries and spina bifida, the defect's seriousness depends on how high the defect is along the spinal column (the closer to the neck, the more serious the impairment) and how much of the spinal cord material is damaged.

Spina bifida, a neural tube birth defect, is caused when the spinal column fails to close properly. The spinal column is the protected area through which nerves transmit messages from the brain to other parts of the body. This bony tube of ver-

*FIGURE 9.2*

*Areas of the Body Affected by Cerebral Palsy*

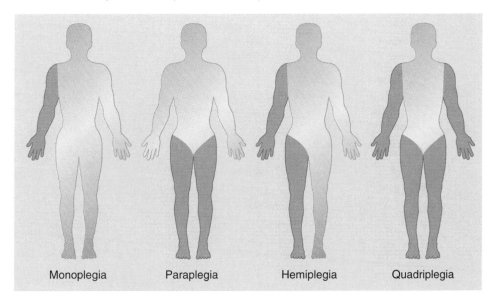

Monoplegia    Paraplegia    Hemiplegia    Quadriplegia

tebrae in the back encases and protects the nervous tissue of the **spinal cord** and its covering, the **meninges**. The spinal cord is connected to the brain. Neural tube birth defects occur along the spinal column anywhere from the tailbone (coccyx) to the neck. The defect may range from absence of protective vertebrae to actual protrusion of the spinal cord and its covering. Because of the importance of the spinal cord and the brain, the risks to the infant who has a defect in the spinal column can be grave. Risks include the possibility of infection and further damage to the delicate nervous system, brain damage such as hydrocephaly (expansion of the brain ventricles as spinal fluid collects and does not drain properly), and paralysis. Figure 9.3 shows how the body is affected by the types of spina bifida.

The portion of the central nervous system damaged by spina bifida generally would have controlled the sensations and muscles of the body areas below the location of the lesion. The parts of the body that would have been supplied by sensory and motor nerves branching from the spinal cord at this point or lower are likely to be paralyzed and deprived of sensations. The higher the lesion, the more areas of the body are affected by the damaged nerves. When the lesion is very low on the spine, the child may not be paralyzed but might have some nerve loss or weakness in the legs and feet.

**Muscular/Skeletal Conditions.** Like those individuals with spina bifida that affects their mobility, individuals with muscular/skeletal conditions usually have difficulties controlling their movements, but the cause is not neurological. Some need to use special devices and technology to do many of the simple tasks—like walking, eating, or writing—most of us take for granted. We discuss two of these conditions here: limb deficiencies and juvenile arthritis.

**Limb deficiencies** can be the result of a missing or nonfunctioning arm or leg and is either acquired or congenital. Regardless of when the impairment occurred,

 MAKING CONNECTIONS

For a review of hydrocephaly and shunt technology, see Chapter 6:
• Causes and Prevention
• Figure 6.3

**spinal cord.** The cord of nervous tissue that extends through the bony spinal column to the brain.

**meninges.** Membranes that cover the spinal cord and brain.

**limb deficiencies.** Resulting from missing or nonfunctioning arms or legs.

~~
FIGURE 9.3

How the Body Is Affected by the Types of Spina Bifida

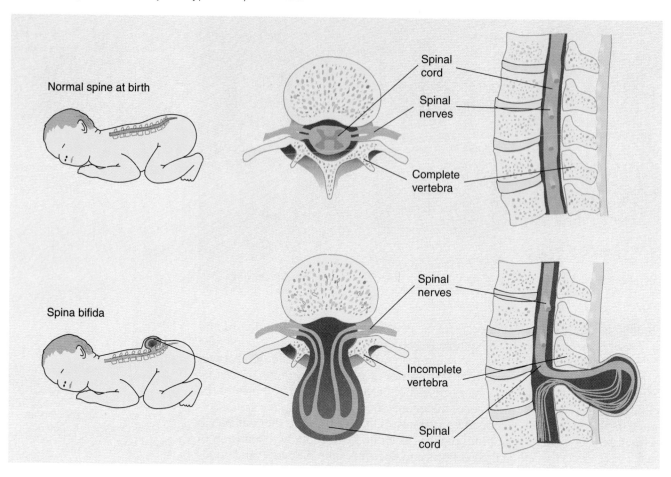

MAKING CONNECTIONS

Robotics is discussed in the Technology section of this chapter.

**juvenile arthritis.** Chronic and painful muscular condition seen in children.

the result is a major impediment to normal physical activity and functioning. Although the root of the disability is physical, many individuals with a limb deficiency have difficulties adjusting to their situation. The attitudes of those who work with these youngsters and of course the support given by family members, can be major contributors to their psychological health. Emerging technology (particularly robotics) now provides great assistance to those with missing limbs. Artificial limbs now enable movement that only a few years ago was thought to be impossible. However, learning to use these devices is a challenge, requiring dedication, extensive therapy, and considerable effort by the individual and professionals in the field of rehabilitation. Many people with physical disabilities find that sports and recreational activities are an important part of their lives. Teachers can be instrumental in encouraging participation in individual sports (wheelchair racing, tennis) and team sports (basketball, rugby).

A relatively common condition affecting joints and the function of muscles is **juvenile arthritis.** Although there are many different forms of this disease, it is typically chronic and painful. Juvenile arthritis usually develops in early childhood and can cause many absences from school. These children often need help keeping up with their classmates because they miss so much class instruction. Teachers must understand that their ability to move may be inconsistent—being better at different times of the day—and that sitting for extended periods of time can cause them to become stiff and experience considerable pain. These children need to be allowed to move around a lot. Those who have a high rate of absences probably need tutoring and extra help to master their academic subjects and keep up with their peers. Fortunately, for many of these youngsters, the disease often shows considerable improvement and may even go into remission by the age of 18 (Best, Bigge, & Servis, 1994). Unfortunately, this is after their elementary and high school years are over. Promising medical treatments reduce the amount of disability from the disease. However, some medications can have side effects that alter some aspect of personality and physical appearance.

*Health Impairments.* Many of us have experienced a serious illness sometime during our childhood; some illnesses, like appendicitis, even require surgery and hospitalization. In most cases, the illness is not long term and does not affect a substantial portion of our childhood or education. For some of us, the illness is serious and chronic. Some children do not require special education, and if they do (e.g., home-bound instruction), it is usually for only a short period of time. Refer to Table 9.3 to find the definitions of different types of health impairments.

MAKING CONNECTIONS

Review Figure 9.1 for names of common health impairments and their groupings.

**Chronic Illnesses.** For a small number of children, their illnesses are chronic, lasting for years, even a lifetime. Children with **chronic illnesses** often do not feel well enough to focus their attention on the instruction being presented. They also experience many absences, causing them to miss a substantial part of their education. We discuss two chronic illnesses here: asthma and the blood disorder, sickle cell anemia.

**Asthma** is a pulmonary disease and is the most common chronic illness of children. It is the leading cause of school absences among all the chronic diseases (Altman, 1993). A person with asthma usually has labored breathing that is sometimes accompanied by shortness of breath, wheezing, and a cough. A combination of three events causes the wheezing: (1) tightening of the muscles around the bronchial tubes, (2) swelling of the tissues in these tubes, and (3) an increase of secretions in these tubes. Years ago, many people held a common belief that asthma is a psychological disorder. It is not; its origin is physical. Many factors (e.g., chalk dust, dirt in the environment) can trigger an asthma attack, including physical activity or exertion. Many of these students are unable to participate in sports or even in physical education activities. Teachers can fill a very special role by helping these individuals find other fulfilling activities in which to participate.

**Sickle cell anemia** is a hereditary, life-threatening blood disorder. Although prevalent among African Americans and others whose ancestors are from the Mediterranean basin, it is not restricted to these groups of people. This condition causes the red blood cells to become rigid and take on a crescent, or sickle, shape. During what is called a "sickling crisis," this rigidity and shape of the cells do not allow blood to flow through the vessels, depriving some tissues of oxygen and resulting in extreme pain, swollen joints, high fever, and even strokes. Some information about this condition is particularly important to educators who have students with sickle cell anemia. First, there seems to be a correlation between the

**chronic illness.** Being sick for long periods of time.
**asthma.** A common, chronic condition resulting in difficulty in breathing.
**sickle cell anemia.** A hereditary blood disorder that inhibits blood flow.

~~~
TABLE 9.3

Types of Health Impairments

Condition	Description
Chronic Illnesses	
Asthma	*Asthma,* a condition caused by narrowing of airways accompanied by inflammatory changes in the lining of the airways, may result in severe difficulty in breathing with chronic coughing. Health care needs include appropriate medications, environmental modifications, and monitoring and frequently result in no limitation of activities.
Cystic fibrosis	*Cystic fibrosis* is a genetic birth defect that results in chronic lung infections and digestive difficulties. Health care interventions include replacement of required enzymes for aiding digestion and aggressive care of lung infections and function.
Diabetes	*Diabetes* is the loss of the ability of the pancreas to produce enough insulin, resulting in problems with sugar metabolism. Health care needs include the monitoring of blood sugar levels, appropriate diet and exercise regimens, and knowledgeable response for insulin reactions.
Congenital heart defects	*Congenital heart conditions* can result in high rates of school absences for specialized health care. Most have had surgical intervention and medical monitoring by specialists. Health care needs include taking medications during the school day.
Tuberculosis (TB)	A disease caused by bacterial infection, *tuberculosis* rarely causes severe disease in children older than infancy. Most often the bacteria remain sequestered and harmless until late adulthood or when the body's immune system fails. The rates of infection are on the rise in many parts of the United States.
Childhood cancer	*Cancer* is the abnormal growth of cells that can affect any organ. The most common types of cancer in children are leukemia and lymphomas. While going through treatment, children may feel too ill to profit from classroom instruction.
	Leukemia causes an abnormal increase in the white blood cells, which are important in the body's defenses against infection. It often results in anemia and enlargement of the lymph glands, spleen, and liver.
	Lymphomas are malignant and cause enlargement of the lymph nodes.
Blood disorders	*Hemophilia,* a genetic condition typically linked with males, is characterized by poor blood clotting, which can result in massive bleeding from cuts and internal hemorrhaging from bruises.
	Sickle cell anemia, a hereditary disorder, causes a distortion in the red blood cells that restricts their passage through the blood vessels.
Infectious Diseases	
HIV and AIDS	*Human immunodeficiency virus (HIV),* a potentially fatal viral infection that in school-aged children results from transmission from a mother infected with the virus to her newborn child or from transfusion with blood or blood products carrying the virus, causes *acquired immunodeficiency syndrome (AIDS).* Health care needs include careful monitoring of general health, specialists to care for potentially overwhelming lung infections, and medications that slow or cure infections. The infection is primarily acquired through the exchange of body fluids in older children, through sexual abuse in younger children, through sexual activity in adolescents, and through intravenous drug use. Health care needs include sources of confidential care, counseling, and health education.
STORCH infections	*STORCH* is the acronym for a group of congenital infections that have the potential of causing severe, multiple impairments. It stands for syphilis, toxoplasmosis, other, rubella, cytomegalovirus, and herpes.
Hepatitis B	A viral disease, *hepatitis B* is infectious and causes inflammation of the liver and is characterized by jaundice and fever. Cases of this dangerous virus are on the increase.

sickling crisis and emotional stress and strenuous exercise (Best et al., 1994; Heller et al., 1996). Teachers should work with the family so they understand what health care management may be required during the school day. For example, teachers may need to carefully supervise and monitor both their students' physical activity and the difficulty level of the work assigned. Second, many of these children may be absent from school often. To reduce the stress these students experience when they return to school knowing that they have missed assignments and instruction, teachers need to develop strategies with the students and their families to compensate for missed school days. For example, a neighborhood child could serve as a peer tutor who brings assignments home to the student and explains important instruction for the school day.

Infectious Diseases. The second type of health impairment is **infectious diseases.** Many different diseases are contracted by schoolchildren. Most, like the common cold or the flu, are relatively short in duration and result in only a few days of missed school. The majority of infectious diseases that children contract at school are not life-threatening or especially serious. Regardless, teachers can help to reduce the spread of these diseases by practicing easy preventive measures. Most of these diseases, however, cannot be avoided for a variety of reasons. For example, some diseases are not contracted at school but are passed on to classmates before the child became sick. We discuss two, serious and preventable, infectious diseases here.

Human immunodeficiency virus (HIV) is a potentially fatal viral infection transmitted primarily through exchange of bodily fluids in unprotected sex or by contaminated needles. It is the virus responsible for the deadly **acquired immunodeficiency syndrome (AIDS)** and can be communicated to a child by an infected mother. Before blood-screening procedures were instituted, the virus was also transmitted in blood transfusions. The effects of the infection in children include central nervous system damage, additional infections, developmental delay, motor problems, psychosocial stresses, and death.

STORCH infections are congenital and include many different viruses. Cytomegalovirus (CMV), a virus of the herpes group, is extremely common in children. Approximately 40 percent of children and most adults have been infected with the virus (Taylor & Taylor, 1989). Although usually harmless, infection from this virus in a fetus can lead to brain damage, blindness, and hearing loss. Therefore pregnant women who do not have antibodies to the disease must protect themselves and their unborn children from CMV and other STORCH infections (syphilis, rubella, herpes, hepatitis).

Identification

Multidisciplinary teams are required by IDEA as part of the assessment process for all children suspected of having a disability. However, for children with physical impairments and special health care needs, these teams represent the broadest array of professionals from a wide variety of disciplines. The assessment process for these individual students may be extremely complex, involving various professionals and the child's parents throughout the IEP development and implementation process. Each professional uses a wide variety of assessment tools and techniques. A complete evaluation for a child with cerebral palsy, for example, includes many professionals, all seeking input and consultation from the parents.

 MAKING CONNECTIONS

For other discussions about preventing infectious diseases, see
• Causes and Prevention section in Chapter 6,
• Concepts and Controversy, Chapter 5.

For more about CMV, see Prevalence and Causes and Prevention sections in this chapter.

 MAKING CONNECTIONS

Multidisciplinary teams are discussed throughout this text, and in particular review Personal Perspective section in Chapter 2.

infectious diseases. Contagious diseases.

acquired immunodeficiency syndrome (AIDS). A usually fatal medical syndrome caused by infection from the human immunodeficiency virus.

STORCH infections. Includes many different congenital viruses.

The Professional as Healer

Many traditional Native Americans go to their medicine men or women when they are ill; others seek help from a combination of traditional and Western medicine. This second group has learned to "walk in two cultures" and to benefit from the lessons that each has to offer. If the professional is to assume the role of healer, a person who Native Americans seek for treatment, assuming some of the customs of healers could prove to be beneficial. Healers always leave something tangible like herbs or a prayer. Ponchillia (1993) believes that many traditional people expect tangible services, and he suggests that professionals leave concrete examples of the "treatment" to be followed or leave something (e.g., an adapted spoon or pencil) at the end of a lesson.

The report from the multidisciplinary team for this child will include a physician's evaluation; an evaluation by adapted physical educators, PTs, and OTs; assessments by other professionals such as SLPs and technology experts (depending on the nature and severity of the disability); as well as a thorough academic, vocational, and intellectual evaluation by teachers and diagnosticians. Parent involvement throughout the process is crucial, and as illustrated in the Focus on Diversity box, the family's culture must also be appreciated and considered.

Physicians are often the first involved with the diagnosis of a physical or health impairment. For these youngsters in particular, doctors (or professionals from the health care community) frequently remain integrally involved in an ongoing way during treatment. They can be of great assistance to educators as instructional programs are planned and appropriate learning environments are designed. Physicians can also be invaluable resources as educators improve their understanding of the individual child's particular condition, resulting limitations, and the accommodations required to provide an appropriate education for the student.

Each discipline and its professionals have unique roles in the assessment of these students' needs and the implementation of their IEPs. For example, PTs evaluate the quality of the person's movement and later teach the student how to compensate and change inefficient motor patterns. OTs work closely with PTs as they assess and later work with upper-body movement, fine motor skills, and daily living activities. Together, PTs and OTs determine the student's physical characteristics and the assistive devices that will benefit the individual (Best et al., 1994). Rehabilitation engineers and assistive technologists recommend and devise mobility and special seating systems and are able to create equipment that will attach other devices (e.g., communication devices) to wheelchairs.

The number of experts who participate in the assessment and planning phases of these students' educational programs seems to expand continually, as new technology and knowledge is developed. Perhaps more than any other special education area, an array of professionals from many disciplines participate in these

MAKING CONNECTIONS

• For a review of the special education and related services professionals who comprise special education, see the Personal Perspective section in Chapter 2.

• For an overview of the variety of technology now available to students with disabilities, see the Technology sections in every chapter about a disability.

students' educational programs, because their needs demand ongoing collaboration by multidisciplinary teams not only for proper assessment, but also for the delivery of a truly appropriate education.

Significance

Think about how you have reacted in the past to people you have met who look different. The reactions of others have been and continue to be a major problem for students with physical and health impairments and only compound the challenges they face because of their disabilities. Physical differences and health impairments are often obvious, even at first meeting. As a consequence, individuals with these disabilities are forced to deal with the often negative or stereotypical reactions of others in addition to their own feelings about their appearance. They must also address the actual physical and medical requirements of their disabilities and accomplish the tasks of school and daily life. Educators can play an important role in helping these youngsters meet these important challenges and shape satisfying lives for themselves. And, the time might now be right as these students enter a changing society with a much more positive outlook for people with disabilities.

Before the ADA law was passed by Congress, and still today, many individuals who face physical impairments were not allowed the opportunity to participate in many aspects of daily life because of physical barriers (e.g., curbs and stairs) and discrimination. Unfortunately, physical barriers still exist in many schools (Briand, 1995). The Office of Civil Rights reports that because many schools are old and have not been renovated, many school doors are too heavy for many students with disabilities to open, school entrances are too steep to maneuver, and many bathrooms are still unsuitable. Although all problems are not yet resolved, important changes signal a better future of access and inclusion in mainstream society. For example, people with disabilities are now being featured in commercial advertisements. Paula Jean Nicholson-Klimin is the first woman who uses a wheelchair to work for a major modeling agency and was the first woman with a disability to appear on a New York fashion runway (Barry, 1994). Although she was the first and that was only a few years ago, it appears that she is part of a growing trend. Many major stores and manufacturers are now including people with disabilities in their advertisements. It is also part of a larger climate of overall acceptance and participation of people with disabilities in everyday life.

Resorts and vacation planners are now seeking out and planning to meet the needs of travelers with disabilities. For example, Miami now offers visitors with disabilities a variety of activities and is actively promoting the area's accessibility and vacation opportunities (Samuels, 1995). They offer a range of usually inaccessible activities, for example, sailing in small boats. Shake-a-Leg, a nonprofit organization, supports a free three-hour ride and even helps in transferring people from wheelchairs to a special boat seat. Some parks have special "surfchairs," specialized chairs with "puffy" wheels that allow

 MAKING CONNECTIONS

For discussions about the biases in U.S. society toward those who do not meet the standards of physical strength or beauty, see in this chapter
• the opening section,
• History.

 MAKING CONNECTIONS

The advocacy movement and reasons for it are also discussed in these sections:
• The ADA section (Legislation) (Chapter 1)
• The History section of this chapter

Joe has waited 20 years for this bus.

Now, thanks to your support of the Americans with Disabilities Act, all public buses ordered after August 1990 must be wheelchair accessible. So for Joe, and others with disabilities, the wait will soon be over. Because public transportation is for everyone.

Source: National Easter Seal Society

 MAKING CONNECTIONS

Travel accessibility is also discussed
in the Legislation section in Chapter 1.

movement on soft sand. Even the Everglades National Park has an accessible monorail so that visitors with disabilities can visit the park and see all of the wildlife. This is only a sampling of the special accommodations Miami has created to lure more tourists to their city. Many other sites are seeking out the potentially lucrative tourist business of a previously untapped group of potential travelers. Many business are now also finding that people with disabilities provide a large and profitable market for the travel industry.

As we mentioned earlier, athletics is playing a more important role in the lives of many people with disabilities. Wheelchair events are now an integral part of many marathons, with these athletes being as dedicated as those who win typical events. In addition to wheelchair basketball, tennis, and soccer, special divisions for sports for youngsters with disabilities are being organized in many cities across the nation (Woods, 1994). Special Challenger Division is often where children with disabilities get their start. These special athletic programs allow participation in what are typically very competitive youth programs. Most sports programs for children are focused on winning, so, for many students with physical impairments, extracurricular soccer, baseball, and football leagues are not an option. Designed exclusively for youngsters with disabilities, Special Challenger Divisions provide an opportunity for physical activity when it might otherwise be denied. Early access to sports and team activities can set the stage for an adult life that includes physical activity and social involvement in community events.

 MAKING CONNECTIONS

Michela Alioto is also discussed in
Chapter 1.

People with physical disabilities are also taking their place in other aspects of American life. Michela Alioto, despite losing her first congressional race, has shown to everyone that a young California woman who uses a wheelchair can give an incumbent a tough campaign. People with disabilities are more visible everywhere. For example, comedians with disabilities have now found audiences, when only a few years ago they were not generally accepted by the public. Their message is important: Laugh at us like you laugh at others; it's OK (Farrell, 1994). Some, like R. J. Johnson, are using this forum to normalize disabilities, while others view their new opportunity to deliver potentially funny material regardless of their disabilities. This discussion is not meant to minimize these serious disabilities, but rather to show that one element of their challenge—societal rejection and discrimination—may well be lessening. People with physical disabilities are gaining access to daily American life. Even without the discrimination of the past (and present), the challenges these individuals face are significant.

History of the Field

The history of physical and health impairments is as long as human history. Anthropologists have discovered skeletons with physical disabilities in grave sites over eleven thousand years old (Frayer, Horton, Macchiarelli, & Mussi, 1987). The history of treatment is as long. Records of treatment for spinal cord injuries go back to prehistoric times as well (Maddox, 1987). The earliest documented treatment was the application of meat and honey to the neck. Beginning with Hippocrates (400 B.C.), treatment usually included traction or even a stretching rack to attempt to straighten the back or push in the deformity. Spinal surgery was performed around A.D. 600, even though it was not until the mid-1800s that anesthesia became available and sterile techniques were used. Even with these medical advances, people with spinal cord injuries generally died soon after their injuries occurred. New techniques of treatment and rehabilitation developed after World War II helped many more people survive their spinal cord injuries and their medical treatment.

Descriptions of conditions such as hemophilia, cerebral palsy, and epilepsy can be found in written records from the past. For example, hemophilia, the most common bleeding disorder, was described as early as 200 B.C. Rabbis noted that its transmission was from mothers to sons (Heller et al., 1996). This hereditary condition was traced through royal and noble families in Spain, Germany, Russia, and England. William J. Little, an English surgeon, described the condition now known as cerebral palsy in well-researched case studies in 1861. Hippocrates recognized that epilepsy originated in the brain but believed that it was caused by several factors: blockage of the normal passage of "phlegm" from the brain, the discharge of cold phlegm into warm blood, and unequal heat distribution in the brain by sitting too long in the sun (Scheerenberger, 1983). Epilepsy continued to receive attention through the Middle Ages. It was frequently linked to mental retardation, and individuals who exhibited epileptic seizures were treated in the same manner as those who exhibited mental retardation. Like mental retardation and behavior disorders, epilepsy was often wrongly believed to have been caused by immoral conduct by the mother or by evil possession of the individual.

The first U.S. educational institution for children with physical disabilities was established in Boston in 1893: the Industrial School for Crippled and Deformed Children (Eberle, 1922). The first public school classes for "crippled children" were established in Chicago at the turn of the century (La Vor, 1976). Later, schools were established in New York City, Philadelphia, and Cleveland. Special schools for students with disabilities resulted from well-intended motives and reasons. They provided a centralized place where expensive equipment (e.g., therapy swimming pools) and highly skilled professionals could work with all the children with very special physical needs from the area. Such treatment, education, and facilities were not feasible when these youngsters were not in a central place. However, they were segregated, where students with disabilities were educated together with no classroom interaction with their neighborhood friends. Advocates with disabilities have called for the closure of all of these special schools, many speaking from their own school experiences in segregated settings (Winzer, 1993).

While children with physical disabilities and special health care needs have always been part of the human experience, the causes of these disabilities and the teachers' responsibilities have changed over the years. Concerns about these children have differed because factors relating to them have differed, factors such as the overall health status of children in society, the ability of medicine and science to address certain health problems, and general views toward children and health. For example, a text published in 1948, *Helping Handicapped Children in School* (Dolch, 1948), included chapters titled "Crippled Children" and "Health Handicaps." The chapter on "crippled children" focused primarily on heart trouble caused by rheumatic fever, measles, scarlet fever, and diphtheria. These diseases, once common, are now rare. Even when children contract them today, the damage can usually be limited by the use of antibiotics and other medical advances. But other causes of these disabilities now demand our attention. Dolch's 1948 chapter on "crippled children" closes by urging prevention by decreasing the accident rate and by providing prenatal and obstetrical care for all mothers and medical care for all children—pleas that continue to be heard today. The chapter on health disabilities also addressed issues that were a sign of their time: infected and decayed teeth, chronic cold and bronchitis, glandular problems, tuberculosis, and malnutrition. Although some of these problems are now less frequent in children, others may again be on the rise as more children live in poverty and unsafe circumstances.

The U.S. Congress passed significant legislation concerning these disabilities after World War I and World War II. The Soldiers' Rehabilitation Act was passed in 1918 to offer vocational rehabilitation services to wounded soldiers. Two years later, a similar law for civilians with physical disabilities was passed: the Citizens Vocational Rehabilitation Act (La Vor, 1976). (People with mental illness and mental retardation were not added to this law until 1943.) Additional laws were passed following the Vietnam War and other wars. Soldiers returned with war injuries so serious that employers, family members, friends, and the individuals forced major changes in order to reintegrate them into society. Thus in 1965, the National Commission on Architectural Barriers was established to study the problems facing people with physical disabilities.

In the past thirty years, disability has come to be understood in political terms (Kriegel, 1969). People with physical disabilities have played an important part in changing the political, legal, and social climate for all individuals with disabilities. For example, although Section 504 of the Rehabilitation Act (prohibiting discrimination) was passed in 1973, it was not until a wheelchair sit-in in the office of Secretary Califano at the Department of Health, Education and Welfare (now Health and Human Services) four years later that the implementing regulations were passed. The passage of ADA in 1990 is another example of the important role people with physical disabilities have played in improving society's response to all people with disabilities.

MAKING CONNECTIONS

For an overview of disability legislation, see the Legislation section of Chapter 1.

Ed Roberts was a leader in the civil rights movement for people with disabilities. He aggressively advocated for changes in public policy that would promote participation of people with disabilities in an accessible society.

As with many underrepresented groups, the disability community needed a catalyst to begin an organized civil rights movement. In the view of many, Ed Roberts was just that catalyst (Shaw, 1995; Stone, 1995). In 1984, with the monetary award he received from being honored as a MacArthur fellow, Roberts co-founded the World Institute on Disability, which many mark as the formal beginning of the civil rights movement for people with disabilities. At the age of 14, Roberts almost died from polio. After considerable struggle and persistence, in the early 1960s he was ready to attend college, but the University of California (UC) at Berkeley declared that he was too disabled for the campus to accommodate and the California Department of Vocational Rehabilitation would not pay for his education because he was too handicapped. Despite this rejection, he paid for the personal care attendants he needed to attend UC, and he became known as one of the "Rolling Quads" on campus. After receiving his bachelor's and master's degrees, he became the director of the agency that had previously refused to support his education. In 1995, at the age of 56, he died; but his movement has not, and the voices of people with disabilities are heard across the nation, still demanding acceptance, access, and inclusion.

Prevalence

According to the *Eighteenth Annual Report to Congress on the Implementation of the Individuals with Disabilities Education Act* (U.S. Department of Education, 1996), only .22 percent (167,113) of all children between the ages of 6 to 21 have physical impairments and special health care needs. Using this terminology and data, approximately 1.2 percent (60,604) of all children receiving special education services are categorized as having orthopedic impairments; another 2.2 percent (106,509) as having other health impairments. Thus only some 3 percent of all children receiving special education services fall within the categories discussed in this chapter. Remember, some of these children have coexisting disabilities that may cause them to be categorized and reported as having multiple disabilities rather than orthopedic or health problems.

Although the low prevalence rates of physical and health impairments are meaningless to children and their families who are affected, educators should keep these numbers and percentages in perspective. For example, although approximately 6 percent of all children have asthma, a small percentage have special education needs. About 1 percent of all fetuses contract CMV, but only 10 to 15 percent of the 1 percent of these babies develop a disability. About 1 percent of the general population has epilepsy, but substantially less than 1 percent of the school population has the condition, with 85 percent of the cases controlled by medication (Epilepsy Education Department of Neurology, University of Minnesota, 1993). About .03 percent of all children have cerebral palsy, and some of them do not require special education services (United Cerebral Palsy, 1993). Spina bifida in its mild form is very common, and most people who have it do not even realize they have the condition (March of Dimes, 1992). About four million children are born each year (about .05 per 1,000 live births) with spina bifida (Rowley-Kelly & Reigel, 1993). Prevalence varies by race and by country, with Northern Ireland having a rate of 4 to 5 per every 1,000 children and Columbia having a rate of .1 per 1,000. No one knows why rates of spina bifida vary so widely. Sickle cell anemia, although seen across ethnic groups, is more prevalent in African Americans. A startling 8 percent of this ethnic group has inherited the condition (Heller et al., 1996). For many, however, the degree and nature of their disability is significant, requiring the fullest efforts of multidisciplinary teams to develop and implement their therapy and educational programs.

The diseases and conditions that seriously affect children continue to change across time. In some cases, this is good news; in others, it is not. For example, polio, a viral infection that attacks the nerve cells in the spinal cord that control muscle function, is a serious disease that ravaged this country in the 1950s and 1960s, leaving many people with a significant, permanent disability. Hundreds of thousands of Americans contracted the disease, with the worst epidemic, some 56,000 new cases, being in 1952. Many of the senior advocates with disabilities today were disabled by polio. Jonas Salk developed a vaccine, and by the end of the 1960s polio was almost eradicated in the United States. In 1994, only eight cases were reported in the entire nation, though the disease is still prevalent in developing countries.

Some conditions are on the decline, though not yet eliminated and may never be entirely. For example, the number of young children with cerebral palsy is decreasing slightly, reflecting medical advances to prevent the condition. Balancing

MAKING CONNECTIONS

For other discussions about low-birthweight babies and prenatal care, see these sections:
• Causes and Prevention section in this chapter
• Causes and Prevention, Chapters 3, 5, and 6

decreases due to improved obstetrical and prenatal care, however, are increases due to more low-birthweight babies surviving (Kuban & Leviton, 1994). Cerebral palsy has an incidence rate of approximately 1.5 to 2.5 per 1,000 live births (Kuban & Leviton, 1994), and estimates are that about 5,000 infants are born with this condition each year (United Cerebral Palsy Association, 1993). An additional 1,200 to 1,500 preschool children acquire the condition annually. Prevalence estimates are that approximately 500,000 children and adults in this country have cerebral palsy. As the medical profession determines the exact cause of the disease, and then discovers vaccines or develops other preventive techniques, the prevalence of many of the conditions we discuss in this chapter may disappear.

Unfortunately, as the prevalence lessens for some conditions, others increase, and new conditions seem to appear unexpectedly. For example, the incidence of asthma is increasing sharply, making it one of only three chronic diseases on the rise throughout the world (the others are AIDS and tuberculosis). Some fifteen years ago, HIV infection was almost never found in children. In 1988, the Centers for Disease Control reported 1,065 cases of pediatric AIDS in the United States; 839 were infants and 226 were adolescents. By December 1994, 6,245 cases of pediatric AIDS (below the age of 13) had been reported (Lesar, Gerber, & Semmel, 1995). Its prevalence in infants and children now increases every year, but fortunately current levels have not reached predictions. Children with AIDS currently represent less than 2 percent of the total number of persons with AIDS. But clearly, an increasing number of children and adults will be infected by HIV until a cure is found and until more people refrain from high-risk behaviors or use preventive techniques.

Causes and Prevention

Just as there are many different illnesses, diseases, and conditions that result in disabilities, there are as many different causes, preventions, and treatments. Instead of discussing these specifically for each condition, we will focus on some common themes and use the conditions as examples. For children with physical impairments and special health care needs, their educational programs must be determined individually. These programs must reflect the impact of the disability on the individual, the student's and family's priorities, and the skills that must be mastered to achieve independent living as an adult. The summary in Table 9.4 was designed to help in your understanding of these children's disabilities, what caused them, and how they might have been prevented.

Causes

There are almost as many causes for the conditions that result in physical impairments and special health care needs as there are conditions. They can be grouped into some general areas: infections, heredity, accidents and injuries, multiple factors, and "unknown."

Infections. The causes of some disabling conditions are clearly known and understood, although at this time they still cannot be cured. One such case is HIV infections. In children under age 13, the cause of HIV infection can be traced primarily to the risk behaviors of their parents. A few years ago, approximately 75

TABLE 9.4

Causes and Prevention of Physical Disabilities and Health Impairments

Causes	Prevention
Motor vehicle accidents	Child restraints Safety belts Auto air bags Motorcycle helmets
Water and diving accidents	Diving safety Swimming safety
Gunshot wounds	Gun control Weapons training Locked storage of ammunition
Sports injuries (boxing, skiing, football)	Headgear and protective equipment Safe fields and slopes Conditioning/training
Child abuse	Family support services Parenting training
Poisoning/toxins	Knowledge of resources in emergencies Safe storage of poisons
Diseases such as polio, measles	Vaccinations
Premature birth	Prenatal care
Infectious diseases	Vaccinations Good hygiene
HIV infection	Abstinence or safe sex Avoidance of drugs Drug equipment not shared Screening of blood and plasma supplies
Genetic disabilities	Genetic screening
Seizures	Medication
Hydrocephaly	Surgery and medical technology
Asthma	Elimination of allergens from the environment

percent acquired the infection from their mothers before or at the time of birth and 20 percent acquired the infection from blood transfusions. In the 1970s and 1980s, the nation's blood supply was contaminated with the HIV virus and many hemophiliacs, unfortunately, became infected through blood transfusion. In 1982, three cases of AIDS in people with hemophilia could be documented as being caused by blood transfusion. By June 1990, 1,546 people with hemophilia were diagnosed with AIDS. Fortunately, today the blood supply is free from AIDS and hepatitis B viruses (Heller et al., 1996). (Today, it is highly unlikely that new cases are caused from blood transfusion.) In contrast, the HIV infections of adolescents are caused primarily by their own risk behaviors.

Like HIV, the causes for CMV are understood. The virus is transmitted through bodily fluids. It appears that pregnant women who work in child care settings may have an increased risk of infection. Prenatal testing can determine whether CMV infection has occurred, but a vaccine is not yet available.

Heredity. Genetic profiles are the cause of many disabling conditions. As we learn more about many of the conditions thought to have unknown causes, many cases appear to have a genetic link. Hemophilia, which occurs in only 1 in every 10,000 births, seems to be linked to the X chromosome because it is carried by the mother and passed on to the son. Muscular dystrophy, a relatively rare disease (with an incidence of about 2 in every 10,000 people) is another hereditary condition. It is a neuromotor disease in which muscle tissue is replaced by fat tissue, thus decreasing the strength and muscle use of the individual. In most cases of Duchene muscular dystrophy, the condition is carried by the mother and exhibited by some of her children.

Accidents or Injuries. Americans must improve their vigilance against child abuse because the resulting injuries can lead to cerebral palsy, seizure disorders, spinal cord injuries, brain damage, and even death. For example, spinal cord injury in young children, often caused by automobile accidents, can also be the result of child abuse. (A common site of spinal cord dislocation is in the lower back, due to the effects of spanking.) In older children, the most common causes of spinal cord injury are car accidents, falls and jumps, gunshot wounds, and diving accidents. In these cases, the importance of safety equipment (e.g., seat belts, helmets, protective gear) and caution are vitally important.

Multiple Factors. Seizure disorders can be the result of many conditions and circumstances. Dividing them into two groups—primary epilepsies (usually congenital) and secondary epilepsies (acquired)—can help in sorting out some of the common causes of this condition. **Primary epilepsy** appears at a young age, usually in families with some history of epilepsy. Often there is a stereotypical pattern of the seizure and a predictable response to specific medications. **Secondary (lesional) epilepsy** may appear at any age and can result from accidents or child abuse; degenerative diseases (e.g., Sturge-Weber syndrome); brain tumors and abscesses; lesions, head injury; lead poisoning, infections, like meningitis or encephalitis; or alcohol or drug withdrawal (Epilepsy Foundation of America, 1994a).

Recall that cerebral palsy is caused by damage to the brain, whether by impaired development, injury, or disease. It may be congenital (present at birth) or acquired within the first three years of life. Let us look at these categories a little more closely. In congenital cerebral palsy, a developing infant may have been deprived of necessary amounts of oxygen when something went wrong during birth. Circumstances such as a placenta separating from the wall of the uterus too early, a twisted birth position, knotting or kinking of the umbilical cord, or other problems of labor and delivery may cause brain damage. Cerebral palsy may also result from the effects of

MAKING CONNECTIONS

For a review of prenatal testing, see the Prevention section (Chapter 6).

MAKING CONNECTIONS

Review the History section of this chapter for a reminder of the hereditary condition, hemophilia, that has been documented almost from the beginning of human records.

MAKING CONNECTIONS

Information about traumatic brain injury is found in Chapter 12.

primary epilepsy. Predictable seizure disorders that appear at a young age and appear to be hereditary.

secondary (lesional) epilepsy. Seizure disorders that appear at any age and seem to occur in response to particular damage.

premature birth; blood type (Rh) incompatibility; the mother's infection with rubella, CMV, or other viral diseases; and attacks by other dangerous microorganisms. The later onset of cerebral palsy typically results from vehicle accidents, brain infections such as meningitis, poisoning through toxins such as lead (ingested in paint chips from walls), serious falls, or injuries from child abuse.

Unknown Causes. With some unknown causes, the medical profession has some good ideas about why the condition exists. Such is the case with asthma: The basic causes of asthma are unknown, but it is believed to be the result of an allergic reaction to certain substances (allergens) in individuals who have a physical predisposition to the condition. The substances that can trigger allergic reactions vary by individual; for some people it may be foods, for others plants, environmental pollutants, chemicals, cigarette smoke, dust mites, cockroaches, viruses, or by daily activity of heightened periods of exercise.

The medical profession is working hard to pinpoint some of these unknown causes. For example, the causes of neural tube, or spinal column, defects (like spina bifida) are not yet clear, although folic acid deficiencies and genetic factors are suspected. The defect occurs very early in the development of a fetus, between the twentieth and thirtieth day of fetal development, before a woman even knows she is pregnant. Past experience indicates that when medical researchers can pinpoint the cause of a condition, they are then much closer to finding a way to treat or prevent the condition. A good case in point is polio: The cause was pinpointed as a virus and a vaccine was soon developed to protect individuals from contracting the disease, but for those already affected they faced a lifetime disability requiring extensive supports.

Prevention

Some physical disabilities and health impairments are relatively easy to prevent, but others are not. Remember, many disabilities are caused through no one's fault and cannot be avoided. For most conditions that cannot be prevented, however, the disabling effects can be lessened through treatment. This section is organized with five themes about prevention: prenatal care, vaccinations, avoidance of injuries, prevention of infectious diseases, and treatment. Within these five sections, we talk about specific conditions that can be eliminated or lessened by implementing these measures.

Prenatal Care. We have stressed throughout this text the importance of pregnant women taking good care of themselves and their unborn babies. Women who follow some simple measures have a better chance of having healthy babies. Women should be sure they are in good health before they become pregnant and obtain early prenatal care from a physician while pregnant. Prenatal care can ensure access to intensive medical care for the mother and infant if problems occur; provide diagnosis and treatment for diseases in the mother, such as diabetes, that can damage developing infants; and help prevent exposure of the fetus to infections, viruses, drugs, alcohol, and other toxins. Prenatal care also can protect the health of pregnant women so that their babies are born well nourished, healthy, and at full-term.

 MAKING CONNECTIONS

See the following sections for a review of the impact of low-birthweight and prematurity on cognition and various disabilities:
- Prevalence section in this chapter
- Causes and Prevention, Chapters 3, 5, and 6

MAKING CONNECTIONS

Immunizations and the prevention of
disabilities are discussed in Chapter 5
(Speech and Language Problems) in
these sections:
• Prevention
• Concepts and Controversy

Vaccinations. Vaccines can safeguard our children from infectious diseases and avoid millions of dollars in health care costs and millions of lives confronted with unnecessary risks and disabilities. Vaccines have eradicated some diseases. No doubt the medical profession is well on the way toward the discovery of many other vaccines to protect us from potentially devastating diseases.

Small pox once devastated people all over the world, but today only limited and geographically isolated incidents occur. Vaccines have all but eliminated polio in the United States, with the last naturally occurring case in 1979 (Neergaard, 1995). Each year, only about eight American children get polio from the vaccine that is intended to keep them safe. This news has led some parents, incorrectly, to believe that it is safer not to immunize their children, a situation that has led to unnecessary cases of dangerous diseases. For example, failure to inoculate is the reason for two cases of measles within one week in New Mexico (*Albuquerque Journal*, 1995a) and for a raging epidemic of measles in many inner cities in this country several years ago (Associated Press, 1991). The Children's Defense Fund reports that in 1993 only 67 percent of all U.S. 2-year-olds were appropriately immunized (Finlay, 1995). This dangerous situation is not necessary. With the passage of the Vaccines for Children Program in 1993, high-cost vaccines are now free to the uninsured and poor children. The remaining barrier is educating parents to understand the importance of protecting their children.

Despite the debate and the confusion over vaccines for practically eliminated diseases, it is important to protect children. The Center of Disease Control and Prevention published guidelines and a schedule for children's immunizations (see Table 9.5).

TABLE 9.5

Center for Disease Control and Prevention: Guidelines for Child Vaccinations

Age	Immunization
Birth to 2 months	Hepatitis B
2 months	Polio; diphtheria, tetanus, pertussis (DTP); haemophilus B (Hib.)
2–4 months	Hepatitis B
4 months	Polio, DTP, Hib.
6–18 months	Hepatitis B, polio
6 months	DTP, Hib.
12–15 months	Hib; measles, mumps, rubella (MMR)
12–18 months	DTP
4–6 years	Polio, DTP, MMR (final dose of MMR may be given instead at 11–12 years)
11–12 years	Diphtheria, tetanus

Source: From Center for Disease Control and Prevention's Guidelines for Child Vaccinations. *Albuquerque Journal* (HEALTH), January 16, 1995, p. B1. Reprinted with permission.

Avoidance of Injuries. Prevention programs designed to promote the protection of children from injury can decrease the number of children subjected to brain damage and serious physical injury. It is important that as many accidents be prevented as possible and that when accidents do occur the individual is protected. The use of seat belts, air bags, helmets, and other protective devices can reduce injuries from motor vehicle and sports-related accidents. Proper child care, child supervision, and family support can help families avoid household accidents and family stresses that can lead to child injury. Family support services and training in effective parenting techniques can help parents understand the harmful physical and emotional effects of physical punishment.

Prevention of Infectious Diseases. As already mentioned, teachers cannot prevent many cases of infectious diseases. Children can become infected outside of the school setting and infect other children before they become sick themselves. However, teachers must become more aware and use preventive techniques in their classrooms so that children do not contract infectious diseases. Teachers can play an important role in this regard. For example, when they suspect that a child is sick, they should inform the school nurse and the parents. The longer infected children are playing and learning with their peers, the more the likelihood increases that the classmates will become infected. Diseases can be transmitted from unclean objects in the classroom as well, so everyone must learn to wash their hands frequently, keep toys and play areas clean and disinfected, and use some commonsense hygienic precautions at school.

It is advisable that educators and others working at schools use disposable gloves. The need for this precaution stems from the increased rates of hepatitis-B and HIV among schoolchildren. The Centers for Disease Control and physicians stress the importance of universal precautions of sanitation and hygiene, especially with all blood and bodily fluids. Gloves should be worn when helping a child who is bleeding from a fall on the playground or perhaps cut using a pair of scissors in an art activity. One common mistake of teachers is forgetting to dispose of the gloves and using a new pair whenever the next situation arises. Teachers must be sure not to work with another child while still wearing the used gloves and, after removing the soiled gloves, must be sure to wash their hands. Disposable gloves are inexpensive and should be readily available at every school. All young children tend to have accidents at school; teachers in particular should have a sufficient supply of gloves on hand to handle those small emergencies common in most classrooms.

Treatment. A variety of treatment services are available for children with physical impairments and special health care needs. The treatment must be customized to each child's needs and available family supports. The range of treatment options is great. Some treatments must be conducted by medical professionals; others are provided by health related service providers (e.g., SLPs, OTs, PTs); and still others can be conducted by educators, related service providers, and paraprofessionals at schools. At the heart of the multidisciplinary treatment efforts are educators coordinating, delivering, and ensuring an appropriate education and health maintenance program to all of these youngsters.

Medical Management. The range of medical treatments for children with physical and health impairments is great. Because treatment by physicians is not covered by IDEA (Rapport, 1996), we only provide one example for this issue. It is now common practice for infants born with spinal column (neural tube) defects to have surgery to repair the back and to avoid infection. If infection is not treated or if the infant contracts meningitis, the effects can be devastating and can include mental retardation. Surgical closure of the defect protects the infant's motor, sensory, and intellectual functioning from further damage and allows for a suitable environment for the child's neural tissue development to continue. Some children with spina bifida have hydrocephaly (a buildup of excess fluid in the brain), and to avoid mental retardation a shunt must be surgically implanted to drain excess spinal fluid from the child's brain. A shunt has greatly improved the outcome for children with spina bifida. Early medical treatment has great benefits: intellectual development is normal in about two-thirds of the children, urinary continence is achievable for greater than 85 percent, few use wheelchairs, and survival to adulthood is about 85 percent (as compared to a 10 percent survival rate noted during the 1950s) (Charney, 1992).

Classroom Management. Let's look at a few treatment measures. First, teachers need to know what to do when a child has a seizure. The Epilepsy Foundation of America (1994b) provides some excellent guidelines that teachers can follow (see the Tips for Teachers box). Second, teachers need to know that treatment for epilepsy usually involves medication. The medication must be monitored so that the proper dose is prescribed for the child and the medication is administered on a specific and regular schedule. Too much, too little, or the wrong medication can have serious effects. But even at the proper dose, medication can have side effects such as drowsiness, lethargy, intellectual dullness, coarsening of facial features, behavioral changes, or sleep disturbances (Epilepsy Foundation of America, 1992). The teacher, who is aware of the child's condition and the possible side effects of medication, is an important member of the treatment team in observing, recording, and reporting behavior patterns that may be the result of medication. Today, there is another option when medication does not control seizures. Surgery, when the damaged area in the brain is small, now provides some with an excellent chance for recovery (Epilepsy Foundation of America, 1995).

Many of these students with physical impairments profit greatly from services from related services professionals. For example, an SLP may assist the child in being understood verbally or in using an assistive device to communicate with peers, teachers, family members, and neighbors. Tools such as language boards, computers, and voice synthesizers can help many students who are not able to develop understandable speech communicate with others.

Many students with physical impairments have motor impairments that limit their mobility and dexterity. This is particularly true for many students with cerebral palsy, spina bifida, or muscular dystrophy. Although these conditions cannot be cured, proper management or treatment, with the assistance of PTs and OTs, can avoid further physical damage, increase strength, improve the child's functional skills, and offer opportunities for increased independence and autonomy.

Treatment does not guarantee a "cure" or an improved situation for all individuals with disabilities. For example, many students with cerebral palsy will face significant challenges their entire lives. Only about 85 percent of those with epilepsy have their seizures controlled through medication (Epilepsy Foundation of America, 1994a). Although asthma cannot be cured, the factors that stimulate episodes can be eliminated or substantially reduced. For example, a major aspect in the treatment of asthma is to eliminate the allergens from the child's environ-

MAKING CONNECTIONS

For a review of hydrocephaly and the shunt procedure, see in Chapter 6
• Causes and Prevention,
• Figure 6.3.

MAKING CONNECTIONS

See Chapter 5 for more about speech and language development.

Treatment Guidelines for Epileptic Seizure

Seizure Type	What to Do	What Not to Do
Generalized tonic-clonic (also called grand mal)	Look for medical identification. Protect from nearby hazards. Loosen ties or shirt collars. Protect head from injury. Turn on side to keep airway clear; reassure when consciousness returns. If single seizure lasted less than 5 minutes, ask if hospital evaluation wanted. If multiple seizures, or if one seizure lasts longer than 5 minutes, call an ambulance. If person is pregnant, injured, or diabetic, call for aid at once.	Don't put any hard implement in the mouth. Don't try to hold tongue; it can't be swallowed. Don't try to give liquids during or just after seizure. Don't use artificial respiration unless breathing is absent after muscle jerks subside, or unless water has been inhaled. Don't restrain.
Absence (also called petit mal)	No first aid necessary, but if this is the first observation of the seizure(s), medical evaluation should be recommended.	
Simple partial	No first aid necessary unless seizure becomes convulsive, then first aid as above. No immediate action needed other than reassurance and emotional support. Medical evaluation should be recommended.	
Complex partial (also called psychomotor or temporal lobe)	Speak calmly and reassuringly to patient and others. Guide gently away from obvious hazards. Stay with person until completely aware of environment. Offer to help getting home.	Don't grab hold unless sudden danger (such as a cliff edge or an approaching car) threatens. Don't try to restrain. Don't shout. Don't expect verbal instructions to be obeyed.

Source: From *Seizure recognition and first aid*, Epilepsy Foundation of America, 1994b. Landover, MD: Author. Reprinted with permission.

ment. Thus the student may require special precautions concerning the air in the classroom (frequent vacuuming, air filtration, and daily wiping of surfaces) and restrictions on playing outdoors during recess, playing with classroom pets, eating certain foods (chocolate is an allergen for many people), and handling certain teaching materials. Teachers also must know what to do for the child during an asthma attack. Consultation with the student, the family, and the physician is necessary to monitor medications, to administer breathing treatment, and to plan procedures for assisting the child during an attack.

MAKING CONNECTIONS

HIV and AIDS are also discussed in the Prevalence section of this chapter.

Lastly, let's turn to the HIV infection and AIDS. This disease was not seen in children some fifteen years ago. Unfortunately, because of the reckless behavior of their parents, pediatric AIDS, although not to levels previously predicted, is increasing steadily. Also, the rate of AIDS is quickly rising among adolescents. Teenagers need to be educated about this deadly disease and how they can protect themselves. Lerro (1994) suggests that education be direct. Youngsters need to know that AIDS is deadly, is caused by behavior, and can be prevented. Lerro also suggests that educators develop partnerships with parents as they design AIDS education programs. The treatment of children with HIV infection includes medical care, education, and developmental services. Because many professionals are concerned about the risk to themselves as they work with children with HIV infection, Kelker, Hecimovic, and LeRoy (1994) offer the following recommendations.

1. Observe guidelines for confidentiality of information.

2. Assess the student's eligibility for services under IDEA for Section 504 and other state and federal laws.

3. Design ways to modify the instructional program as needed, including ways to integrate the student into typical classroom activities and providing materials when the child is absent.

4. Create a flexible program that will allow for hospitalizations, frequent absences, and a progressive loss of stamina.

5. Improve your attention to good hygienic practices, including wearing surgical gloves when providing personal care and treating bleeding injuries, covering wounds to protect others from contact, cleaning surfaces that have been in contact with blood with a bleach solution, and increasing frequency and duration of hand washing.

6. Educate classmates' parents about the nature of the disease.

7. Be available to answer students' questions about terminal illnesses and related issues including death.

8. Seek help from school counselors and others.

Children with Physical Impairments and Special Health Care Needs

In this section, we review the characteristics that many of these disabilities present to educators, regardless of their specific condition. It is not uncommon that the health care needs of some of these children are so consuming that everything else becomes a secondary priority. Others require substantial accommodations to the physical environment so that learning is accessible to them but their learning characteristics are quite similar to their typical classmates. To meet the specific needs of each individual child, educators must seek the assistance of the entire multidisciplinary team who assisted in the assessment process and the development of that child's IEP. In each case, different professionals will be able to assume the primary resource role. For example, the teacher with a student who has a severe physical impairment will need to collaborate closely with the PT; and for the child who also presents a speech impairment, the SLP must be significantly involved in the child's educational program. However, for many children with special health care needs, these professionals might not be as crucial to the implementation of an appropriate education as the child's physician and the school nurse. What is very important is that educators seek the help of the family and those professionals who can help design the best instructional environment for each child who presents one of these special needs.

In that regard, we divided the discussion about the characteristics of these children into two major sections: Characteristics Affecting Learning and Characteristics Affecting the Classroom and School. Table 9.6 summarizes some of the characteristics typically seen in children with physical and health impairments. In many respects, you will find the following discussions rather general in nature. Our hope is that these global discussions about the characteristics presented by these students will help you understand how to design better learning environments for all children in classroom settings.

Characteristics Affecting Learning

The treatment goal for many of these youngsters is for them to stay strong, healthy, and active and to lead as normal lives as possible. Accomplishing this goal requires considerable attention to many components, including medical management. As with all children, education is also a major component of their childhood, but unlike most of their peers, they face many barriers to efficient learning. For example, fatigue may be a major obstacle for some students because of their weakened physical condition. Let's first consider some of the common barriers to learning faced by many of these students. After that we consider a special status, being medically fragile, that educators must confront. Then, we'll turn our attention to ways in which teachers can be instrumental in providing health care assistance to these students.

Barriers to Learning. We know that students learn best when they are actively involved in their instructional programs. When students are active participants in instruction, they have a heightened level of attention, have the prerequisite knowledge and skills to learn new information and skills, and have the motivation and interest to work hard. Although for many of these students intelligence is not affected, other symptoms of their conditions or illness may affect their ability to participate fully in a particular lesson or in their entire educational experience for some period of time. Depending on the student, these barriers may be temporary or they may be permanent.

Some symptoms that cut across specific conditions include muscle weakness, loss of physical coordination, tremors, paralysis, spasticity, visual impairments, and fatigue. Some of these symptoms are directly related to medications and treatment, and others are a function of the disease, illness, or condition. For example,

TABLE 9.6

Signs or Characteristics of Physical and Health Impairments

Limited vitality and energy

Many school absences

Need for physical accommodations to participate in school activities

Lack of concentration

Short attention span

Poor motor coordination

Frequent falls

Inarticulate speech

children who are receiving cancer treatment go through periods of feeling too sick to profit from much of the instructional day and during this time may have frequent absences. Some may require periods of home-bound instruction.

Teachers can help these youngsters by using some measures. First, they need to be sensitive to the student's changing condition of wellness. Attentive teachers will be able to notice when the child needs a break. Instructional units might be broken into small, concise elements with key terms and facts emphasized. Remember that long and difficult reading assignments can be shortened. For example, when studying a history unit, classmates often find that summarizing content from a chapter in the textbook, developing timelines, and preparing study notes are good learning exercises for them and a great help to their classmate with a special health care need. Teachers can also prepare summary notes and outlines of the information being presented in the history unit as handouts for all students but with particular thought to the learning characteristics of the child with special needs.

Medically Fragile Children. For many years the term **medically fragile** was used to describe all children with special health care needs. It is now usually used to describe those children, regardless of their specific condition, who have complex health care requirements including technological assistance to support their lives (Sirvis & Caldwell, 1995). Medically fragile is a status and is not assigned to any specific condition but rather reflects the individual's health situation. Students can move in and out of fragile status, but depending on the progression of the student's condition, illness or disease may present special concerns to the teacher and classmates. For example, counselors can be most helpful in helping peers deal with the progressively debilitating condition or impending death of their classmate.

It is important to understand that because of medical technology a greater number of medically fragile children are surviving medical crises. In the past, many of these youngsters would not have lived long enough to go to school. Others would have been too sick to attend their neighborhood school and would have received most of their schooling through home-based instruction. Even though many are now stable enough to attend school, they require ongoing medical management. For most, procedures must be planned for in case of emergencies. The "if, thens" must be carefully outlined and planned in collaboration with doctors and the medical profession. Although the contingencies for the "worst-case scenarios" must be arranged, in most cases the accommodations required for these children are not terribly dramatic. However, not having backup power for a child's ventilator could have disastrous results.

When planning for the needs of medically fragile children, educators should know about the child's status. Prendergast (1995) developed some intake questions that can yield some useful information to assist in the development of an educational profile to use in the design of an appropriate educational program for an individual student. Those questions are listed in Table 9.7.

Health Care Assistance. Teachers are being called on to assume more responsibilities for the medical management of their students. This is due to several factors. First, more and more of these children are receiving their education alongside their neighborhood peers in the general education classroom. Second, local education budgetary cuts are making a school nurse at every school a rare resource.

MAKING CONNECTIONS

For more on technology support for medically fragile children, see the Technology section in this chapter.

medically fragile. Used to describe children with special health care needs.

TABLE 9.7

Program Planning Questions Regarding Medically Fragile Children

1. Does the child have a medical diagnosis of a chronic health program (e.g., diabetes, asthma, cystic fibrosis, seizure disorder, tuberculosis)?

2. Does the child receive medical treatments during or outside of the school day (oxygen, injections, gastrostomy, or tracheostomy care, etc.)?

3. Is the child frequently absent because of illness?

4. Is the child frequently hospitalized because of illnesses?

5. Does the child receive ongoing medication for health problems (seizure medication, heart medication, allergy medication, chemotherapy, inhalation therapy, etc.)?

6. Does the child require adjustment of the classroom schedule for health reasons (rest following seizure, limited physical activity, breaks, naps, part-time school)?

7. Does the child require environmental adjustments to the classroom (temperature, decreased light, small class, running water)?

8. Does the child require major safety considerations (special lifting, special transportation, emergency, play, safety equipment, special handling, special feeding)?

Source: From Preparing for children who are medically fragile in educational programs by D. E. Prendergast, 1995, *Teaching Exceptional Children, 27*, pp. 38–39. Reprinted with permission.

Teachers are now called on to perform some simple tasks that help children with special health care needs. For example, some children may need assistance with their medication while at school. Coordination among the child, the child's physician, the family, and the school nurse will be necessary so that the child takes the proper dose at the proper times and so the effects of the type of medication and the dosage can be monitored and changed when necessary.

Teachers can also be called on to perform duties that historically have not been considered part of their role at school. Although it is generally understood that all children should attend school, children with fragile health may spend some of their education time at home or in a hospital. When children are in school, teachers may need to provide personal assistance. For example, while older children with paralysis generally are able to accomplish their bathroom needs independently—through the use of self-administered clean intermittent catheterization (CIC)—many younger children need the teacher's assistance. In these cases, it is important to encourage personal privacy when helping a child with hygiene needs, and it is important to maintain the highest of sanitary conditions possible in a school setting. A good start is to have everybody wash their hands often. Other children may need extra rest or support devices such as ventilators, feeding tubes, and ostomy supplies, all of which need careful monitoring by the teacher.

Many accommodations required by children who are medically fragile or chronically ill are rather simple. Remember, for many of these children education may not be their personal priority; they are more preoccupied by their health situation. This is both understandable and natural. Being sensitive to their physical

 MAKING CONNECTIONS

For information about the Supreme Court case that clarified CIC as a service to be provided under IDEA, see the Litigation section of Chapter 1.

condition is probably the most important consideration you can have. These are some issues to keep in mind for some particular students: Arrange times for naps or rests, monitor medical equipment, keep the child safe, plan for tutors, work with the parents, consider the complexity and length of homework assignments, accommodate the physical requirements of the student, collaborate with others, and keep a sense of perspective as you balance the needs of all of your students.

Characteristics Affecting the Classroom and School

The challenges facing students with physical limitations and special health care needs and their teachers are great. All schools must meet the special architectural codes required by the ADA law and must be "barrier free." Regardless, these students' world is often filled with physical and social barriers that must be accommodated and overcome before they can achieve independence and a "normal" life. Because of its importance, we turn our attention to physical barriers in this section and in the Educational Interventions section of this chapter. We have discussed social barriers earlier in this chapter, but we emphasize this issue here as well.

Physical Barriers. When considering ways to make an educational environment accessible to a child with a physical problem, educators need to consider *all* of the places the child needs to go: the bathroom, the lunchroom, the playground, the gymnasium, the music room, the library, the bus, and so on. Remember, the child's educational activities should be chosen on the basis of individual learning needs, not where a wheelchair can and cannot fit.

Every school should have bathroom stalls that accommodate wheelchairs and braces and should have accessible sinks, mirrors, towel dispensers, and door handles. The concept of **accessibility** has many interpretations. It means elevators large enough to hold wheelchairs, handrails along the corridors, chalkboards placed low enough so that children in wheelchairs can write on them, seating arrangements that can accommodate children with a variety of equipment, standing tables so that children can spend time out of wheelchairs, and playground equipment adapted to hold a child with leg braces or in a wheelchair. It also means being able to participate in school activities to the fullest extent.

Integration may require accommodations beyond those required by law (e.g., curb cuts, ramps, elevators, and bathroom alterations). In some cases, it means extra help. For example, teachers of children with spinal cord defects or severe cerebral palsy may need special training to learn how to physically move these children from place to place or to position them for class participation. The PT can provide significant help in this regard and also instruct the teacher on the safest and most appropriate manner to transfer a particular child.

Barriers to Personal Relationships. The quality of the educational environment for these children may be particularly important, since they may not be able to move easily between environments, as children usually can. Their personal relationships also require attention. Because they may not have a large number of other children in their environment, they may need extra assistance establishing and maintaining friendships. When they are hospitalized, the professional faces they see may change daily, so continuity at school is crucial.

MAKING CONNECTIONS

For more information about the physical and social barriers affecting people with physical and health impairments, see
• the Significance (Defined) section in this chapter,
• the History section of this chapter,
• the Designing Learning Environments (Educational Interventions) section in this chapter,
• the ADA section, Legislation, Chapter 1.

accessibility. Barrier-free environments allowing maximal participation by individuals with disabilities.

Mealtimes are an important social event for most people, but for students with physical impairments they may present a missed opportunity. Mealtimes must also be considered when professionals plan the educational program for these students. Some children are unable to chew or to swallow, require tube feeding, or lose their appetite because of medication. The school nurse or a nutritionist can help the teacher in these cases (Crump, 1987), but when these instances occur they limit social access and the opportunity for making friends and interacting with peers. Those students who need special utensils such as a large-handled spoon or a plate held firmly to the table by suction cups can participate in typical lunch time activities, but extra sensitivity on the part of peers and adults is important. Remember, children who have difficulty eating may be self-conscious about the problem, and their classmates may also be uncomfortable at the beginning. The teacher should look for opportunities to create a comfortable, accepting atmosphere for eating, possibly alongside their classmates. The important thing to remember is that in addition to providing the child with essential nutrients, the mealtime experience should be a healthy, happy opportunity for social exchange.

Educational Interventions

Educators must be aware of the wide variety of potential obstacles to students' education and learning. For students with physical problems and special health care needs, many of these obstacles are different from other "difficult to teach" students. To facilitate an appropriate education for some of these youngsters, teachers need to learn how to assist a child with health care needs, how to deal with frequent absences, how to assist a child who is having a seizure, how to make scheduling accommodations, how to address special issues relating to movement in the classroom, how to adapt the class activities, how to adapt teaching techniques, and how to promote social integration. Even more important is the creation of an exciting learning environment where children are free, both physically and psychologically, to experiment, take risks, interact with one another, and learn.

Education and the Preschool Child

Whether the impairment is physical or health-related, early intervention programs provide a strong foundation for the child and family. At the center of this phase of the child's educational career is the IFSP. Parents play an especially crucial educational role during these early years (Urbano, 1992). Many young children receive most of their education at home, where they and their family are supported by a multidisciplinary team comprised of experts who assist in the development of a wide range of skills. If the child's intervention program is to be successful, the parents' efforts and enthusiasm must be supported by the other members of the team. In this section, we discuss two areas that often are concerns for parents and the team of professionals working with them: motor development and positioning and developing communication skills.

 MAKING CONNECTIONS

• For a review of IFSPs, see the Individualized Special Education Programs section of Chapter 2.

• For suggestions about how to work more effectively with families from different cultures, refer again to the Focus on Diversity box in this chapter.

Motor Development and Positioning. For some children, early intervention programs focus primarily on motor development. For example, children born with cerebral palsy may have reflex patterns that interfere with typical motor development that sets the stage for maximum independence, including body schema, body awareness, purposeful motor use, and mobility. In many cases, direct instruction is necessary, but before teachers and parents become involved in the educational program they must be trained and supervised to be sure that they do not put the child at risk for injury. Enlisting multidisciplinary team members like the OT, PT, and nurse can ensure the development of an effective program and also help properly prepare those who will carry out the program. The student's program usually includes a regimen of special exercises to develop motor skills. The purpose may be to strengthen weak muscle groups through the use of weights or to adapt to and use artificial limbs or orthopedic devices. Once teachers and family members know how to assist the child with the exercises, they should not be afraid and should encourage the youngster to move, play, and interact with the environment.

Because this is a time of tremendous physical and sensorimotor growth, normal motor patterns must be established as early as possible. For those children who already have abnormal motor patterns, repeating those patterns should not be encouraged (Campbell, 1987a, 1987b). For example, the child should always be positioned properly so that alignment, muscle tone, and stability are correct during all activities (Orelove & Sobsey, 1987). If the child is not properly positioned, abnormal patterns can remain and possibly worsen. Positioning must be

Using a supine stander, this boy shares his science project with his class.

carried out at school and at home. Specific equipment, such as foam rubber wedges, Velcro straps, and comfortable mats are used to properly position children with physical disabilities. Although some of this equipment is expensive, other items can be made rather inexpensively. Parents and teachers need to keep in touch with therapists to be certain that they are working properly with their children.

After the child is properly positioned, parents and teachers should design and encourage activities that motivate the child to move in functional ways. Simply positioning a child on a wedge or bolster and then neglecting the child's learning is not good enough. Placing a rattle at the infant's eye level motivates the infant to swat it in order to hear the sound. The teacher can encourage stretching by placing a favorite food or toy at the limit of the child's reach so that the child must stretch in order to get it. This simple activity accomplishes three goals: (1) the child learns appropriate motor patterns, (2) the child's body is properly positioned, and (3) the child learns the relationship between movement and obtaining a desired object. Also, teachers must remember that children should not remain in the same position for too long. They should be repositioned every twenty minutes or so.

Developing Communication Skills. For some students, establishing communication is difficult. Parents and professionals should acknowledge and reinforce every attempt at communication. Although determining how a child with severe disabilities is attempting to communicate can be difficult, an observant person can learn a great deal about the child's communication abilities, even when others believe that the child cannot communicate at all. A good observer will be able to answer questions like these: In what specific ways does the child react to sounds? How does the child respond to certain smells? Does the child have different facial movements when different people enter the room? Does the child gaze at certain objects more than others? How is anger expressed to the family? Through careful observation and experience, parents, teachers, and family members can recognize meaningful communication even when others believe there is none. Parents and professionals should also remember that communication is a two-way street. Children learn to communicate with others by being communicated with: Talk to the child, express feelings with face and body, play games together, and encourage the child to listen to tapes and the radio.

 MAKING CONNECTIONS

To review communication abilities, see Chapter 5.

Education and the Schoolchild

Recall that each child with a physical or a health impairment has individualized needs, even those whose diagnoses seem to be the same. Many of these needs are similar to those of children with other types of disabilities; some, however, require different adjustments to the learning environment. For example, many students with disabilities need flexible schedules, more time to learn academic tasks, and extra assistance. This is also the case for many students with special physical and health care needs. So, we spend some time discussing ways instruction can be modified to meet these special learning requirements. Unlike many of their classmates, some of these students demand a unique learning environment, free from physical barriers that inhibit their movement and their interactions with their peers. Although educators often do not consider the importance of the ways classroom space is designed and its effect on instruction, we believe that this is a very important element of the learning environment and should receive more attention. Therefore we have devoted a section to designing exciting and interesting space and environments conducive to all children's learning.

Instructional Accommodations. When the child is ready to enter school, both the child and the child's family become crucial members of the IEP team, providing recommendations for a program. Sometimes, simple schedule flexibility is all that is needed. For example, here is how a teenager with the rheumatic disease lupus described one of the accommodations she needed at school: "Still, school is difficult for me. Because my knees are weak, I can't carry a lot of books at one time. I have to have extra time between my classes so I can go back to my locker and get different books" (Krementz, 1989, p. 51). Here's a tip: Ask students to describe their difficulties and what accommodations they need. They are often the best resource when teachers are planning instruction and the individualized accommodations the student needs.

Some of these students may often be absent from school because they need medical care or because they are too sick or fragile to come to school on certain days. Asthma is the leading cause of school absences, accounting for about one in five hospitalizations of children (Hannaway, 1992). Other conditions associated with excessive absences are hemophilia, cystic fibrosis, nephrosis, leukemia, and sickle cell anemia. To help these children keep up with their classmates, schools can provide a home or hospital teacher; use television, computer, or telephone hookups between the child and the classroom; make videotapes of special classroom activities; and allow classmates to take turns acting as a neighborhood peer to tutor after school. These methods not only help the child's academic progress

MAKING CONNECTIONS

Many strategies for accommodating students with disabilities are included in the Making Accommodations boxes found throughout this text.

but also maintain a social connection to the teacher and other students. They help the child feel more comfortable about returning to the classroom later when the physical condition or illness has improved.

We often look for complex answers to difficulties when only simple solutions are required. Such is often the case when adapting instruction. The keys are to anticipate accommodations and to apply your own problem-solving skills. For children who cannot write as fast and efficiently as others, the teacher could allow extra time for completing written assignments. Some students find that they can increase their speed and produce pleasing documents when allowed to use a computer for their written work. To assist students who cannot write, the teacher could ask a classmate to make an extra copy by using carbon paper or photocopying a set of class notes. Something as simple as taping children's work papers to their desks and providing extra thick pencils might allow them to accomplish the task. Some students could tape record instead of writing their assignments. These simple adjustments give a threefold message: (1) You are willing to give the student a chance, (2) the student is important to you, and (3) even with adjustments, you have high expectations for the student to produce acceptable schoolwork.

Test taking is another area in which teachers can make adjustments. Imagine trying to take a timed test while your body goes through uncontrollable jerky movements. This is just one of the difficulties testing presents to children with physical problems. The risk is that, without accommodations, the test will merely measure the degree of physical difficulty experienced by the individual rather than actual intellectual or academic abilities. How can a teacher give a fair test? Oral testing is one way to obtain an accurate reading of the student's skill level. There are many ways teachers can adapt their instruction to meet the needs of these students, yet not simplify instruction as to significantly impair the amount of information presented to the youngster. Remember, ask the student with special needs to help in solving problems presented during instruction. Besides your own thinking skills, they are often the best resource to involve because they know what accommodations have been successful in the past.

Designing Learning Environments. "Our surroundings affect our moods and temperaments; certain buildings, parks, plazas, and streets lift our spirits; others diminish them" (Sandler, 1989, p. 13). Teachers and children spend a substantial portion of their day in classrooms. Unfortunately, in many classrooms the space and its design restrict learning. For students with physical challenges, poorly designed classroom space can inhibit both academic and social learning. This situation can be remedied and in the process can become an excellent learning opportunity for the entire class.

Buildings and classrooms need to be safe and accessible. Compliance with various construction codes provides basic safety and accessibility, but those codes do not ensure an environment that is functional, scaled to the size and needs of children, and aesthetically pleasing. The physical environment is often overlooked, ignored, and misused (Taylor, 1990). Although teachers

Sharing the excitement of a good book is an activity everyone enjoys.

and students cannot alter the structure of the school building, they can redesign the space within a classroom. Students can collect data by using simple frequency counts to study the traffic patterns they use in the classroom. They can redesign the organization of desks, tables, work areas, storage space, and learning centers. They can generate visual design alternatives to their environment as it is currently structured through drawings and models. They can work together as a class to evaluate the functionality of these potential recreations of their learning environment, and as a unit decide how to best use the space allocated to them in what is referred to as a classroom. This experience can help to create a more exciting and useful learning environment for every class member and can be particularly helpful to students who face physical challenges.

As the entire class works to create a better learning environment, everyone's learning styles and needs must be considered. Students with physical problems provide a special opportunity for creativity. The class must become sensitive to the physical environment and how it can create unnecessary barriers to learning and social interaction. Students with physical problems may require specially fitted chairs, desks, and worktables and perhaps extra space for maneuvering bulky equipment like crutches or wheelchairs. These factors need to be considered when redesigning physical space. Many students with severe physical impairments require bulky language boards or computers for communication, which present challenges not only during instruction and small-group work activities but also for storage and security. Space must be allocated so that everybody can interact with the child using assistive technology.

As the class seeks to improve other learning environments, keeping everyone's needs in mind, there are many "consultants" who can provide assistance. Architects and design engineers can serve as valuable resources to the class. How do you find such experts to help? Check with the student's parents and school administrators. Call your local college or university to see whether some architecture, engineering, or interior design students would work with the class for several hours. Explore some options with a local construction company. You might be surprised how willing people from the community are to volunteer their time and expertise to this activity. Also consider professionals who are already working with your students. For example, the OT and PT providing direct instruction or itinerant services to the student with physical challenges can also serve as excellent resources to the entire class as they rethink their classroom space. For this activity to meet its potential as an excellent, integrated learning experience, be sure that all of the students remain actively involved. Refer to the Teaching Tactics box to see a practical application of a classroom's new design.

The benefits of having children participate in creating their classroom learning environment can be great. In addition to designing space conducive to each class member's learning style and physical requirements, the activity itself is a wonderful learning experience that uses many different types of thinking skills as well as integrates many academic areas (e.g., math, reading, and even history). Taylor and Warden (1994, p. 13) believe that this practical application of knowledge helps prepare students who can

- Think critically,
- Know basic skills but can creatively problem solve and apply their knowledge,
- Think visually,

≈≈ *Designing a Learning Environment*

Ms. Bessant-Byrd's fifth grade class is housed in a school that was built in the 1950s. The room is rather large and is shaped like a rectangle with windows all along the south side. On the opposite wall, two doors, one at the front of the room and one at the back, open out to the hallway. At the front of the room, blackboards are attached to the wall, and at the back of the room are storage and coat closets. On the first day of school, the classroom was organized as the previous teacher had left it. The twenty-eight desks were in four rows facing the blackboard. Several tables, which had been used for workstations, were placed along the walls. One of these held a computer and printer.

Ms. Bessant-Byrd's class is comprised of twenty-seven students, several of whom have special learning needs. Becky has a learning disability; John has a moderate visual impairment; and Alexander uses a wheelchair. Delfin, who will not be at school for another three weeks because he is recuperating from surgery, has a special health care need. Marta does not qualify for special education, but because of an attention deficit disorder requires a structured learning program. Ms. Bessant-Byrd likes to have the children spend a good portion of their day working in small groups, has planned for many hands-on science and math activities, but also knows that her students need their own space for independent work. The way the classroom is organized currently presents many difficulties. The aisles are not wide enough for Alexander to get his wheelchair everywhere in the classroom he needs to be. John uses a bulky print enlarger to read the print in the textbooks, and when Ms. Bessant-Byrd is using the blackboard he needs to be in close range. The current arrangement also inhibits both movement and small-group work.

Instead of rearranging the room sometime before the first day of school, Ms. Bessant-Byrd decided to let the class experience the restraints of this classroom design and then create their own environment. The children decided first to assess their own learning and space needs. They studied their traffic patterns, analyzed how much space Alexander's wheelchair needed for free movement anywhere in the classroom, and determined the best position for John to see the board and assigned a place for his print enlarger. The students sketched out some sample floor plans, and once they picked the best two they constructed models of their classroom, its furniture, and equipment. All along they included

- Work cooperatively,
- Interact globally,
- Participate in real-life education,
- Are responsible to community and responsible for the consequences of their actions,
- Develop a sense of stewardship and caring for themselves, each other and the planet,
- Use technology with ease, as a means to an end,
- Move through the learning environment, returning information, taking responsibility for their own learning, and self-assessing their knowledge.

Delfin in their work. Delfin was able to make a brief visit to the class as the project was beginning, so he could visualize the current design and help in its restructuring. Ms. Bessant-Bryd borrowed a speaker phone from the school's administration so the class could include Delfin in discussions about elements needed in the new design. Several neighborhood children visited Delfin at home once the sketches and models were made both to share their progress and to include his input to the final plans. When Delfin returned to school, he was part of the team and helped with the design's finalization.

The class faced several specific problems and decided they needed a consultant. The children had particular concerns about the safety and storage of equipment (the class's computer and John's print enlarger). They decided that if they could be quickly stored and retrieved, they would have more space for group work and provide security for the expensive equipment. The children called a local architect, Mr. Olion, who volunteered to help advise the class. Mr. Olion asked the children questions about how their space was to be used, he studied their plans and models, and he helped them think about some minor modifications on issues they had not considered. For example, he suggested that they were not making the best use of the southern exposure of their classroom windows and had them think about conducting some passive solar heating experiments during the winter. He also sketched out two designs for special tables. One would be suspended from the ceiling and would allow for John's printer to be raised and lowered; the other allowed the computer to be secured in one of the underutilized storage closets at the back of the room and slide out into open space when in use. Several of the students' parents came to class to help the children construct the special tables but were sure that they only guided the building process.

Now it was time for aesthetics. Some students designed a mural for the wall alongside the hallway. Others chose warm colors and repainted the beige walls. Several built mobiles, while others created a small greenhouse along one of those southern windows. When they were all done they had learned a lot about measurement, design, construction, art, ways people interact, individuals' special learning needs and how they can be accommodated, and much about environments and space. All these children shared with each other, worked together to solve problems, and completed an important task. Ms. Bessant-Byrd's students were actively involved in learning, have ownership in their classroom, and are proud of their accomplishment.

Inclusion

Perhaps no other group of students use the full array of educational placements and professionals more than students with physical impairments and special health care needs, with many experiencing considerable movement among these placements. Some require instruction while hospitalized for extensive time periods; some need home-bound schooling for a while. Many require pull-out services from a PT for some portion of their education, and most receive their entire educational program in the general education classroom. Although there still are some special schools for students with physical impairments, the appropriateness of these placements is being questioned, particularly by adults who attended separate schools when they were children.

 MAKING CONNECTIONS

For issues relating to inclusion and educational placement, see
• the Inclusion sections, Chapters 3–12,
• the Concepts and Controversies sections in this chapter and in Chapter 2.

Accessibility remains an important issue and correlates with effective integration and inclusion, not only at school, but also in everyday life. Remember, children with physical problems have a right to schools that are accessible. So, too, do all people with disabilities who might want to access a school: teachers, other employees, parents and grandparents, and guest speakers. Teachers of students with physical problems and health impairments, like teachers of all children with special needs, must make particular efforts to ensure that students do not become isolated and segregated because of their disabilities.

Inclusion in recreation has many benefits, including activities where social integration is likely to occur naturally. In addition to all the health benefits of recreation and exercise, recreational skills can allow children with physical disabilities to have fun with their classmates and can provide opportunities for enjoyment with their families. Many adapted recreational toys and games are available for people with physical disabilities. A Frisbee, for example, has been specially adapted with two adjustable clips on the top so that people with limited hand movements can play. Special sports and fitness programs are also available for individuals with physical disabilities. Recall, for instance, Little League baseball's Special Challenger Division for children with physical and mental disabilities, with a division in most cities (Woods, 1994). This program allows a wonderful opportunity for children who otherwise would not be able to participate in team sports. Workout tapes for individuals with a variety of disabilities, including people who use a wheelchair, have also been developed. Today, the opportunity to participate in team sports is not restricted to special leagues. For example, Doug Dormu, a Washington, D.C., high school senior is the star of his school's basketball team. Doug can only use one arm, but his record (40 points with four 3-pointers in one game) shows that he is a definite asset to his team (Schultz, 1994). Jesse Mutz was born with arms ending at his elbows, but that has not stopped him from playing baseball. This 13-year-old outfielder attends baseball camp in Florida with his nondisabled peers and is outstanding at bat and in the field (Associated Press, 1995). Only a few years ago, Doug and Jesse would not have had the chance to play sports with youngsters without disabilities. These are only two examples of a changing society where individuals with disabilities can participate fully.

Attitudes are changing. More students with physical challenges (35 percent) and those with special health care needs (40 percent) are receiving their education primarily in general education classes (U.S. Department of Education, 1995). Particularly in some parts of the United States, this number could increase. Successful integration and inclusion for increasing numbers of children, however, requires considerable supports from multidisciplinary teams. In some cases, it requires considerable effort from teachers, who must make adaptations and accommodations for these students (see the Making Accommodations box for some ideas).

Transition Through Adulthood

Students with physical impairments and special health care needs have among the highest graduation rates of all students in special education (U.S. Department of Education, 1996). As a result, many have a greater chance of gaining a college education. An increasing number of colleges are accessible to people with disabilities, and many have special programs to assist these students. In addition to

MAKING CONNECTIONS

Social accessibility and leisure time activities are also discussed in the Significance (Defined) and History sections of this chapter.

MAKING ACCOMMODATIONS

Adapt the Physical Environment

- Remove hazards
- Create more workspace
- Provide storage space for equipment
- Make furniture accessible
- Widen aisles
- Use positioning devices
- Change seating arrangements
- Rearrange furniture

Change Student Response Mode

- Allow speaking instead of writing
- Use a speech synthesizer
- Allow writing instead of speaking
- Allow computer-print output

Alter Materials and Equipment

- Give handouts
- Adapt writing tools
- Use special eating utensils
- Explore assistive and adaptive technology

Modify the Activity

- Allow more time to complete assignments
- Abbreviate assignments
- Create a flexible schedule

Provide Extra Assistance

- Arrange peer tutors
- Have parents or family members help
- Find volunteers to assist
- Video or audiotape lessons
- Use E-mail for help-sessions

providing physical accommodations, colleges should allow these students extra time to take tests and to provide assisted methods for taking class notes and transcribing class tape recordings. The key is for colleges to provide individualized means for these students to accomplish college work.

Independent living is the goal for adults with physical disabilities and health impairments. The "independent living movement," people helping themselves to live on their own, has had a great influence on the lives of people with disabilities. Increasingly, adults with physical disabilities and health impairments take control of their lives and their jobs, establish friendships, have families, and exercise political power. Legislation such as the Americans with Disabilities Act (ADA) has had a tremendous impact on the ability of adults with disabilities to pursue their rights and end discrimination.

Independence is important to all people but is of vital importance to most adolescents and adults with physical impairments or special health care needs. As time goes on, it appears that more and more types of assistance are becoming available. For example, specially trained animals sometimes assist individuals with physical disabilities. Service dogs have been trained to pull a wheelchair, pick up things, open doors, push elevator buttons, turn lights off and on, and bring a telephone receiver. Many Capuchin monkeys, chosen for their small size and ability to perform tasks, were bred and trained at Disney World to assist people with physical challenges and are used as service assistants. These monkeys can feed the individual; dial a speakerphone; get food out of the refrigerator; turn papers of the newspaper; and turn on the television, stereo, and even a VCR (Ferrer, 1996).

 MAKING CONNECTIONS

- For the origins of the independent living movement, review the History section of this chapter.
- See the Legislation section for a review of ADA and the civil rights of persons with disabilities of Chapter 1.

What is the life like for an adult with physical disabilities? Let us look at one person's story. Independent living and return to an active lifestyle are goals for Christopher Reeve, the actor who played Superman in the movies and who broke his neck in an accident with his horse in May 1995. Although paralyzed from the neck down, he now uses a ventilator to assist his breathing and also a motorized wheelchair which he directs by puffing air through a straw. He has attended gala charity events, but his most important accomplishment is that on December 13, some seven months after his accident, he spent his first night at home. His college friend, Robin Williams, predicts that Reeve's continued progress will astonish everyone (Koltick, 1995/1996). And, Reeve, himself, is quite anxious to begin a new phase of his career, which would include being a director (Smith, 1996).

Families

The families of children with severe physical and health impairments face special issues as they raise their children (Davis, 1993). Martin, Brady, and Kotarba (1992) document the demands that a child's chronic illness can place on a family, including fatigue and low vitality, restricted social life, and preoccupation with decisions related to the child's illness. Often, the costs of the child's health care are staggering. Thus parents' own career decisions may be driven by questions about maintaining family health insurance. Even when health insurance is available, financial record keeping and filing for reimbursements can be complicated and cause a strain. If the child is eligible for government medical benefits, eligibility regulations may be complex. Finally, some families find it necessary to move to a larger city in order to obtain necessary health care and therapies, leaving behind a community in which they have long-term social ties and extended family.

If the child's treatment or health problems require absences from school, the family's routine may be disrupted when one adult has to stay home with the child. Similarly, special planning and complicated arrangements may be necessary to accommodate a weekend away, a family vacation, time spent with other children, or time for the parents alone.

Many homes and apartments are not yet designed for the range of physical needs of the entire population. If a child needs large equipment, a special bathtub, ramps, or other accommodations typical for an individual with physical disabilities, the family may have to move to an accessible apartment or home. Another option for those who are financially able is to remodel their home.

The burdens on families of children with physical problems and health impairments are great. As we have just discussed, life with a child who has severe physical challenges or who has a chronic illness is very complex, and the stress can be overwhelming. However, many of these parents have difficulties accepting their child's disability. So, in addition to dealing with hospitals, insurance companies, an inaccessible world, financial costs, and a sick child, many have to come to grips with their own situation and personal feelings. Smith (1993) helps us better understand the common reactions of many parents when they discover their child has a severe disability. From her experience as the Executive Director of the National Parent Network on Disabilities and the parent of a child with multiple disabilities, she believes that it is typical for parents to pass through the following emotional stages: denial, anger, grief, loss, fear, guilt, confusion, feeling powerless, disappointment, and rejection. Some even feel a "death wish" for the child. Recognize that not all parents experience all of these emotions, but it is most important that they understand that they are not alone. Smith suggests that as parents of children with disabilities face their individual challenges, they take the following constructive actions as they come to accept and deal with their personal, their child, and their family situation:

- Seek the assistance of another parent.
- Rely on positive sources in your life.
- Take one day at a time.
- Learn the terminology.
- Seek information.
- Do not be intimidated.
- Do not be afraid to show emotion.
- Learn to deal with natural feelings of bitterness and anger.
- Remember that this is your child.
- Maintain a positive outlook.
- Keep in touch with reality.
- Remember that time is on your side.
- Find programs for your child.
- Take care of yourself.
- Avoid pity.
- Decide how to deal with others.
- Keep daily routines as normal as possible.
- Recognize that you are not alone.
- Talk with your mate, family, and significant others.

Keeping Smith's advice in mind, some parents have found that seeking out others who also have a child with a severe physical or health problem is helpful in many ways. Around the country, these families have joined together in support groups to address common problems and help one another. Often, families share creative ideas for helping the child with the disability to join in the activities of the family, such as inexpensive adaptations of toys, shared baby-sitting, and information exchanges about helpful medical personnel.

Technology

Modern technology can dramatically improve the ability of people with physical impairments and special health needs gain access to and control the world around them, communicate with others, and benefit from health care. The 1990 reauthorization of IDEA and the courts have clarified the role of assistive technology and the schools: It is a related service that is provided so a student with disabilities can profit from special education. It does not, however, include medical services provided by physicians (Weiss & Dykes, 1995). The adaptations that technology provides these individuals include not only **high-tech devices,** such as computers that control the environment or assist in flying airplanes, but also **low-tech devices,** such as simple built-up spoons and communication booklets. Not all technology is expensive or even sophisticated. In many cases, creativity and individualization are the keys to solving problems.

high-tech devices. Complex technical devices such as computers.

low-tech devices. Simple technical devices such as home-made cushions or a classroom railing.

Deciding what should be considered technology was difficult. Is a wheelchair a piece of technology? What about specially designed chairs for racing or for use in the wilderness? Does a wheelchair become technology if it is motorized or computerized? What if the chair has an electronic switch to permit the persons with only partial head or neck control or finger or foot control to move about independently? We also could not decide whether medical advances should be considered technology. Certainly, technology is changing the way we think and act. It might even be the cause of a new special education category: **technology-dependent children** (students who use **ventilators** or other medical equipment to survive). And, what about **rehabilitation engineering**, which has brought the benefits of science and engineering to movement, seating, and walking problems, such as those created by cerebral palsy? **Gait training** laboratories (special laboratories for walking) help many children by analyzing their weight-bearing patterns and their normal and abnormal movements. With the aid of PTs and other specialists, these laboratories help to improve children's posture and balance. In the end, we decided to focus on two types of technology used by people with these disabilities: computers and bionics and robotics.

Computers

What is possible today seemed impossible only a few years ago. What we might have thought were wild visions for science-fiction movies are today's reality. Mike Ward has Lou Gehrig's disease and can only move his eyes (Ramstad, 1995). But Mike goes to work four days a week and with the help of the new computer software called *Eyegaze*, he is a productive member of a research group at Intel. How is this so? His computer has a camera that follows his eyes and "types" the letters he looks at on the screen. When he is finished with a sentence, he looks at "enter." He uses regular word processing and e-mail software. Right now the cost of this high-tech computer application is high, at $25,000, but think about it: It is this technology that lets him work, be productive, and interact with co-workers and friends.

One of the most commonly used technological advances is the personal computer. "When used by a person with a disability, the computer has been likened to the six gun of western mythology—the great equalizer between people of different ability or strength" (Maddox, 1987, p. 223). Computers are used for many skills, including augmentative communication, writing and printing, practicing mathematics, and creating "smart rooms" where the thermostat, lights, music, and doors are controlled by a central computer panel. Many adaptations are available for computers so that people with severe physical disabilities can use them. For example, computers can be operated by voice, the gaze of an eye, a mouthstick, a sip-and-puff breath stick, a single finger, a toe, a headstick, or other creative method suitable to an individual's abilities.

Computers allow access to other environments and people. This technology can be turned into a great advantage for students who must stay at home for any length of time. Whether an illness requires one day at home or a month, students can use the Internet and **e-mail** to talk to classmates, get tomorrow's homework assignments, or work with their science group on their project. They can also conduct library research by connecting to an information system and even communicate with students around the country about information they are gathering from a central database.

technology-dependent children. Children who probably could not survive without high-tech devices such as ventilators.

ventilators. Machines to assist with breathing.

rehabilitation engineering. Application of mechanical and engineering principles to improve human physical functioning.

gait training. Analysis and instruction of walking.

e-mail. A computerized mail system allowing people using personal computers, the phone system, and a host mainframe computer to communicate.

Bionics and Robotics

Mobility is an area where the benefits of technology are obvious. Such technology thus allows freedom of movement, increased privacy, and personal independence. Today, individuals can select artificial limbs that are bionic and resemble human limbs. **Myoelectric (bionic) limbs** are battery-powered and aesthetically pleasing. They are hollow but contain a sensor that picks up electrical signals transmitted from the individual's brain through the limb. Although not yet like the **bionic artificial limbs** popularized in the television shows "The Bionic Man" and "The Bionic Woman," they do allow the individual to control movement and function.

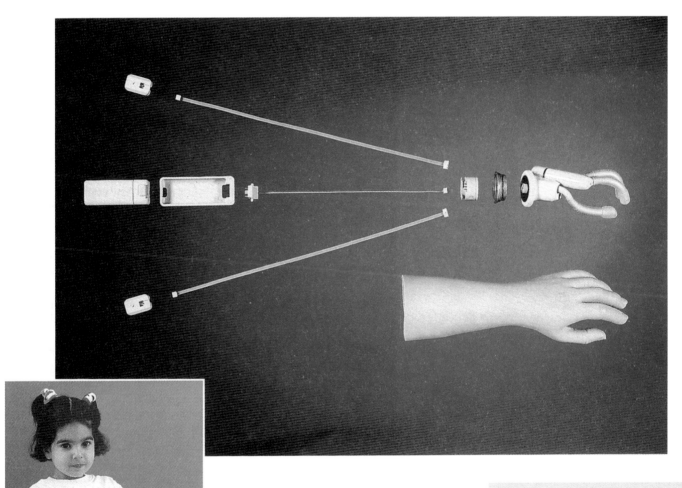

This girl's myloelectric hand allows her to play and learn almost like everyone else.

myoelectric limbs. Artificial limbs, powered by batteries and controlled by electric signals transmitted by the individual's brain (sometimes called bionic).

bionic artificial limbs. Artificial arms and legs that replace full functioning of nonfunctional limbs.

Robotics is another area that holds promise for the future of people with physical disabilities. Robotics is the use of sophisticated devices to accomplish motor skills such as grasping. For example, robotic arms can manipulate objects in at least three directional movements: extension/retraction, swinging/rotating, and elevation/depression. Voice-activated robots are in the developmental stages but offer a promise of great assistance in independent daily living. Manipulator robots have been successfully used in assisting children in such self-help activities as dialing a telephone, turning book pages, and drinking from a cup. Costs, transportability, repairs, and training are currently roadblocks to the wide use of this type of technology, but popular demand for robots that can do household chores is likely in the future and would make robotic technology more economical and widely used.

Concepts and Controversy: Inclusion Versus Segregation

MAKING CONNECTIONS

For various positions related to educational placements and students with different types of disabilities, see
• the Inclusion sections in Chapters 3–12,
• Concepts and Controversies section, Chapter 2.

Are separate special education classrooms or schools for children with physical disabilities and health impairments necessary? As we have discussed throughout this text, students with disabilities should be educated in the least restrictive environment. Sometimes, however, the need for separate classrooms and even separate schools for students with physical disabilities and health impairments is defended. Are they justified? Think about these questions in the context of what you have learned about physical disabilities and health impairments.

According to the U.S. Department of Education (1995), a considerable number of students with physical and health problems do attend general education classes for a substantial portion of their school day. When combining general and resource room placements, over 55 percent of students with physical disabilities and 67 percent of those with health problems spend most of their time attending class with their nondisabled peers. However, this placement rate is not consistent across the nation. In some states over 80 percent of the students attend general education classes most of the time, whereas in others only 16 percent do. Why would there be such differences?

Clearly, it must be differences in attitudes and philosophy. Perhaps in some states, general education teachers are uncomfortable teaching children with physical disabilities because they lack the training. Some believe that it is more efficient and cost effective to locate in one place all of the special equipment and furniture needed by children with physical disabilities. Others argue that because it would be too expensive to make every school totally accessible (beyond ADA codes), only one school in the district should be equipped with the state-of-the-art physical accommodations. And others feel that students with very special health care and nursing needs require full-time medical personnel on-site, which cannot be accomplished at every school in the district.

Do they have so much in common that they need to be in one place? Are there other reasons to explain why different states use different placement standards? Do you think these students should be separated from their nondisabled peers? Why? Why not?

robotics. Use of high-tech devices to perform motor skills.

Children with physical impairments and special health care needs can present special difficulties to their parents and teachers. Even when these two special education categories are combined, the number of students involved is small, affecting about 2 percent of all schoolchildren with disabilities. Therefore they are considered low-incidence disabilities. Many of these youngsters require substantial adjustments and modifications to their learning environments, but their relatively good high school graduation rates indicate that they are capable of competing in the standard curriculum. For many, independent living remains their greatest challenge.

FOCUS QUESTIONS

Self-Test Questions

▶ *Why are there so many different ways to organize and classify these disabilities?*

Many different systems have been proposed to organize these two special education categories. On one hand, there is great diversity among the disabilities caused by the hundreds of conditions, illnesses, and diseases that lead to physical impairments and special health care needs. On the other hand, students with physical and health problems share many special educational needs, regardless of the specific condition that caused the disability. To benefit the most from their educational opportunities, every special education student requires an individualized educational program tailored specifically to his or her individual needs. For many of these students, such programs include an array of related services and many accommodations to the physical and learning environments provided at school. This necessitates a multidisciplinary team working collaboratively on behalf of the child and with the family.

▶ *What are some steps teachers should follow to assist a child who is having a seizure?*

Teachers can serve a vital role when assisting a child who is having a seizure. Following these simple steps can avoid injury and harm to the student involved. Look for medical identification; create a safe place free from hazards; loosen clothing, particularly around the neck; protect the head from injury; turn the person sideways to ensure free air passage; if the seizure lasts longer than five minutes, call for an ambulance; upon return of consciousness, keep the individual calm; stay with the person until full consciousness is achieved; offer further assistance.

▶ *What are the five general causes of physical impairments and special health care needs, and how can they be prevented?*

The five general causes of physical impairments and special health care needs are infection, heredity, accidents or injuries, multiple factors (e.g., brain injury that was hereditary, a combination of injury and illness), and unknown causes (many of which are probably yet undiscovered hereditary conditions). Clearly, the following preventive measures might have lessened or avoided some of the physical and health impairments seen in schools today: prenatal care, vaccines, safety measures to prevent injuries and infectious diseases, and medical treatment. Many of the preventive techniques require access to health care, which, unfortunately, many families with young children do not have.

▶ *How can the learning environment be modified to accommodate students with physical impairments and special health care needs?*

The learning environment—classroom space and instructional activities—can be easily modified to better accommodate students with disabilities related to their physical and health conditions. First, the physical environment can be adapted by creating more space, widening aisles, removing hazards, changing seating arrangements, making classroom furniture accessible, and creating room for positioning devices. Second, the demands for the student's response can be changed. The student can speak instead of writing, use a speech synthesizer, write instead of speaking, or have a computer print a response. Third, materials and equipment can be altered. Handouts can be used instead of or to accompany transparencies, or audio versions of books can be assigned. Adaptive equipment such as special writing tools and adapted eating utensils can be provided. Fourth, instructional activities can be modified by allowing more time to complete assignments, abbreviating assignments, or allowing for a flexible schedule. And finally, extra assistance can be given. The student can be assigned tutors (peers, parents, volunteers). Lectures can be audio or videotaped. The teacher or a classmate can answer questions using e-mail at specific times each day.

▶ *Why is the multidisciplinary team approach necessary for these children, and how can educators improve collaboration across diverse professionals?*

The multidisciplinary team approach is important for all students with disabilities, but for those with physical impairments and special health care needs it is a necessity. By bringing together professionals from many different disciplines, the complex needs of these youngsters can be met. Most of these youngsters have difficulties across several areas (e.g., motor, communication, health, mental health), areas in which educators have not received comprehensive training. It is important that parents and educators seek the advice, support, consultation, and training from experts in every field where the student needs special education and related services assistance.

Challenge Question

▶ *What are the barriers to the full participation of these individuals in society, and how can they be minimized?*

People with physical disabilities, in particular, face considerable barriers throughout their lives. They face the physical challenge of coping with inaccessible environments, where their impaired mobility hinders their participation in mainstream society. They also face bias, discrimination, and other barriers. Because some of them cannot live independently, it is assumed that they cannot be productive employees either. Although attitudes are changing, people with physical disabilities and those with special health care needs still find rejection in the workplace, difficulties finding jobs, and social rejection by people without disabilities.

These students may require special teaching, scheduling, counseling, therapies, equipment, and technology. They may frequently be absent from school because of fragile health or medical treatments. They may need special leg braces or wheelchairs; they may need adaptive equipment such as swivel spoons or pencils with extra grips; they may have physical needs such as assistance with medications, assistance with bladder catheterization, or seizure assistance. Some may present potential emergencies and thus require a teacher familiar with emergency techniques. Some may also face powerful emotional issues, such as their impending death or continuous physical dependence, many years before their young friends must face such issues. With accommodations in their instructional programs, the development of new and different learning environments, and the opportunity for full participation in all aspects of school, the lives of the next generation of students with physical impairments and special health care needs will be different.

~~~ SUPPLEMENTARY RESOURCES ~~~

Scholarly Books

Accardo, P. J., & Whitman, B. Y. (1996). *Dictionary of developmental disabilities terminology*. Baltimore: Paul H. Brookes.

Haslam, R. H. A., & Valletutti, P. J. (1996). *Medical problems in the classroom: The teacher's role in diagnosis and management* (3rd ed.). Austin, TX: Pro-Ed.

Heller, K. W., Alberto, P. A., Forney, P. E., & Schwartzman, M. N. (1996). *Understanding physical, sensory, & health impairments*. Pacific Grove: Brooks/Cole.

Urbano, M. T. (1992). *Preschool children with special health care needs*. San Diego: Singular Press.

Popular Books

Brown, C. (1955). *My left foot*. New York: Simon & Schuster.

Gallagher, H. G. (1994). *FDR's splendid deception*. New York: Dodd Mead.

Mathews, J. (1992). *A mother's touch: The Tiffany Callo story*. New York: Holt.

Pechinpah, S. E. (1993). *Chester: The imperfect all-star*. Agoura Hills, CA: Dasan Publishing.

Stewart, J. (1989). *The body's memory: A novel*. New York: St. Martin's Press.

Videos

Mask. (1985). MCA Home Video.
Gaby: A true story. (1987). Tri-Star Pictures.
Born on the Fourth of July. (1989). Universal.

My left foot. (1989). Miramax Pictures.
Forrest Gump. (1994). Paramount Pictures.

Professional, Parent, and Consumer Organizations and Agencies

Asthma and Allergy Foundation of America
1717 Massachusetts Avenue, Suite 305
Washington, DC 20036
E-mail: info@aafa.org
Phone: (800) 7-ASTHMA
(202) 466-7643

Council for Exceptional Children
Division on the Physically Handicapped
1920 Association Drive
Reston, VA 22091-11589
Web site: http://www.cec.sped.org
Phone: (705) 620-3660

National Easter Seal Society for Crippled Children and Adults
2023 W. Ogden Avenue
Chicago, IL 60612
Web site: http://www.seals.com
Phone: (708) 238-4202

Epilepsy Foundation of America
4351 Garden City Drive, Suite 406
Landover, MD 20785
Web site: http://www.efa.org
E-mail: postmaster@efa.org
Phone: (800) 332-1000

The National Foundation–March of Dimes
1275 Mamaroneck
White Plains, NY 10602
Web site: http://www.grove.ufl.edu.kryto/mod.html
Phone: (800) 367-6630

United Cerebral Palsy Association
7 Penn Plaza
New York, NY 10016
E-mail: ucpnatl@acpa.org
Phone: (800) 872-5827
(202) 842-1266

Dorothy Brett. *Deer Dancers*. 1951.

Dorothy Brett was born of a noble British family. Although her childhood was quite sheltered, as a young adult she became entranced with the Bloomsbury Group, an English avant-garde collection of intellectuals, artists, and writers that included economist Maynard Keynes, writers Virginia Woolf and Lytton Strachey, and artist Dora Carrington. In 1924, Brett followed D. H. Lawrence to New Mexico to be part of a utopian colony. Lawrence returned to England, but Brett remained in America and became part of an artists' colony, often referred to as the Taos Artists. Brett was "partially deaf" almost her entire life; a self-portrait she completed in 1924 shows her with an ear trumpet, which she named Toby, the hearing aid of the day (Hignett, 1983).

Deafness and Hard of Hearing

ADVANCE ORGANIZERS

▼

OVERVIEW

Hearing, like vision, is a distance sense and provides us with information from outside our bodies. When hearing is limited, it affects the individual in significant ways: limiting communication, access to orally presented information, and independent living. More so than for any other group of people with disabilities, the Deaf comprise a community united by a rich culture and a unique communication system. Deafness and hard of hearing is a low-incidence disability for children, affecting about 0.13 percent of all schoolchildren.

▼

FOCUS QUESTIONS

SELF-TEST QUESTIONS

▶ What variables are used to create different subgroups of students who are deaf or hard of hearing?

▶ What is meant by the concept of Deaf culture?

▶ What are the major causes of hearing loss?

▶ What educational support services do many of these students require?

▶ How do the major instructional methods for deaf children differ, and how should an individual child's communication style affect the choice of instructional method?

CHALLENGE QUESTION

▶ What types of technology are available to assist the deaf and what advances might the future hold?

A *Personal Perspective*: A Hearing Mom of a Deaf Middle Schooler Talks About Her Son's Deafness

Ann Park, Ian's mother, shares her story about how she discovered her son was deaf and how her family's life has changed since this discovery:

In February 1984, I learned that my 17-month-old son was deaf. He had been playing with the stereo controls and inadvertently turned them on. It was so loud that the windows rattled in their casements. Even though Ian was only inches away from the stereo speakers, he did not flinch, blink, startle, or cry. We knew at that moment he did not hear like he should, confirming what we had suspected for almost a year. A couple of weeks later our fears were confirmed. Ian was profoundly deaf!

Sitting in the audiology booth with him, I saw the audiologist shaking her head no with each presentation of a pure tone that Ian did not respond to. I knew it was bad then. All of my dreams and hopes for him—being a doctor, a pilot, anything—disintegrated. I remember a sudden feeling of relief, almost overwhelming in its magnitude, when the audiologist told us Ian was profoundly deaf. At last, we knew what was wrong! Our suspicions were confirmed. At that moment, I knew what I could do. I would do everything I possibly could to give my son language and a means to communicate. As we left the audiology booth, I started signing, "Let us go down the hall. Then go home," my son watching my hands as we went.

It has become a family joke of sorts, the irony of life. I had wanted to be a teacher of the deaf since childhood. So every opportunity I could find, I learned or used the sign language I knew. I remember commenting to the SLP and audiologist working with Ian of the desire, but adding, "I also wanted to send the kids home at three in the afternoon, and get paid every other week. Now, he is all mine, twenty-four hours a day and no pay!" But I still would not change what has happened. I do get paid! Every time he succeeds at a sports event, academically, or in his daily life.

Ian went to a special preschool for deaf children. When he was 6 years old, he attended a class for deaf and hard of hearing students in our local public school. Since second grade, he has been fully mainstreamed. He has had a certified interpreter and been given preferential seating, and his classrooms have been specially adapted with acoustical treatments and special carpeting. He has had support services from an audiologist and an SLP who is fluent in sign language. Ian has also had special equipment such as hearing aids and auditory trainers with an FM microphone worn by his teachers.

Ian has been raised to be independent, to know what his rights are—like having an interpreter. But there are areas not covered by the Americans with Disabilities Act. So when he goes to soccer or baseball practices or games, either his father or myself are always there to interpret for him. We try to teach his team members and coaches the appropriate signs for the sport and those basic for general communication. Regardless, the responsibility of communication rests on our shoulders. Ian's oral speech is often intelligible, especially when the content of the topic is known by those who are listening to him. He tries very hard to speak clearly and slowly for people. But the best of situations would be if others knew how to sign. It is getting better. Ian is not bashful to call up his deaf and hearing friends on his TTY. Having one of those telephones has given him a new sense of freedom.

In our home, we sign so that Ian is included in all of our family time together. We also get the benefit of reading the TV as well as hearing it by using closed captions. We have a flashing-light system attached to various lights throughout the house that flash in different sequences to tell us when the doorbell or phone is ringing.

It is my deepest hope that Ian will be a self-sufficient, contributing member of society. Ian is a positive example of what children who are deaf can attain, and I know he will always be a positive example for others. I want Ian to bridge the gap between the hearing and the deaf worlds.

The future for deaf and hard of hearing children is so much better than in the past. Children can remain in their homes, and they and their families can receive support services to help them. Early intervention services are now available as soon as the disability is diagnosed, and language development work can begin much sooner. This is important. The disability, and its effects, cannot be erased; but with knowledge, understanding, effort and support for the child and the family, people with this disability can experience a much better future and life together. Ian is an example of what can be accomplished.

1. What do you think are some of the frustrations and challenges Ian faces because he attends a general education class?

2. What different frustrations and challenges do you think he would face if he attended a special school for deaf students?

3. How does technology help Ian and his family?

*T*he process of hearing is remarkable. Sound waves pass through the air, water, or some other medium. They cause the eardrum to vibrate. These vibrations are carried to the inner ear, where they pass through receptor cells that send impulses to the brain. The brain translates these impulses into sound. The content or associations of sound affect us in different ways. We are warmed by the sound of an old friend's voice, startled by a loud clap of thunder, fascinated by the sound of the wind rushing through trees, lulled by the ocean, excited by the roar of a crowd, consumed by the music of a rock group, and relaxed by the soothing sounds of a symphony. One important way that most of us learn about the thoughts, ideas, and feelings of others is by listening to people tell us their experiences. Through this exchange, we expand our knowledge, share ideas, express emotions, and function in typical workplaces and social settings. Many people who are deaf and hard of hearing participate fully in mainstream society in part because of advances in education and technology such as hearing aids. However, some people cannot be helped by hearing aids and thus have a much more restricted ability to communicate with their nondisabled counterparts.

Deafness and Hard of Hearing Defined

People who are **deaf**,[*] or profoundly hard of hearing, have hearing abilities that provide them with little useful hearing even if they use hearing aids. Although almost all persons who are deaf perceive some sound, they cannot use hearing as their primary way to gain information. People who are **hard of hearing** can process information from sound, usually with the help of a hearing aid.

Although the degree of hearing loss is important, the age when the hearing loss occurs is also important. Individuals who become deaf *before* they learn to speak and understand language are referred to as **prelingually deaf**. They either are born deaf or lose their hearing as infants. Approximately 95 percent of all deaf children and youth are prelingually deaf. Their inability to hear language seriously affects their abilities to communicate with others and to learn academic subjects taught later in school. One in ten of those who are prelingually deaf have at least one deaf parent. Children in this group typically learn to communicate during the normal developmental period. However, instead of learning oral communication skills, many learn through a combination of manual communication (sign language) and oral language. Those whose severe hearing loss occurs after they have learned to speak and understand language are called **postlingually deaf**. Many are able to retain their abilities to use speech and communicate with others orally.

What makes learning even more difficult for many deaf and hard of hearing students is that 25 percent of them have additional disabilities (Schildroth & Hotto, 1994). Additional disabilities may include visual impairments, mental retardation, learning disabilities, behavior disorders, or cerebral palsy. These accompanying disabilities are often caused by the same disease or accident that caused the hearing loss. For example, rubella (German measles), blood type (Rh) incompatibility between mother and child, and trauma at birth often result in more than one disability. Students whose deafness is inherited tend *not* to have multiple disabilities.

 MAKING CONNECTIONS

For more information, see the section on Deaf culture (Deaf and Hard of Hearing Children) later in this chapter.

 MAKING CONNECTIONS

- For a review of specific disabilities that may co-exist with deafness, see those chapters in this text.
- To review the causes of various disabilities, read the Causes sections in Chapters 3 through 12.

deafness. Inability to usefully perceive sounds in the environment with or without the use of a hearing aid; inability to use hearing as the primary way to gain information.

hard of hearing. Having sufficient residual hearing to be able, with a hearing aid, to comprehend others' speech and oral communication.

prelingually deaf. Having lost the ability to hear before developing language.

postlingually deaf. Having lost the ability to hear after developing language.

---

[*] In this chapter, we refer to children with severe hearing losses in different ways. Sometimes, we refer to them as "children who are deaf," and other times, we call them "deaf children." The latter referent is preferred by many people in the Deaf community because they believe it better reflects their Deaf culture and identity. The use of the capital letter *D* signifies affiliation with Deaf culture; a small *d* refers to deafness.

What is hearing loss? Hearing loss results when the ear and hearing mechanism are damaged or obstructed. To better understand the definition of hearing loss, we need to understand the process of hearing. Refer to Figure 10.1, a picture of the ear, to trace how sound moves through the ear to produce normal hearing.

FIGURE 10.1

The Structure of the Human Ear

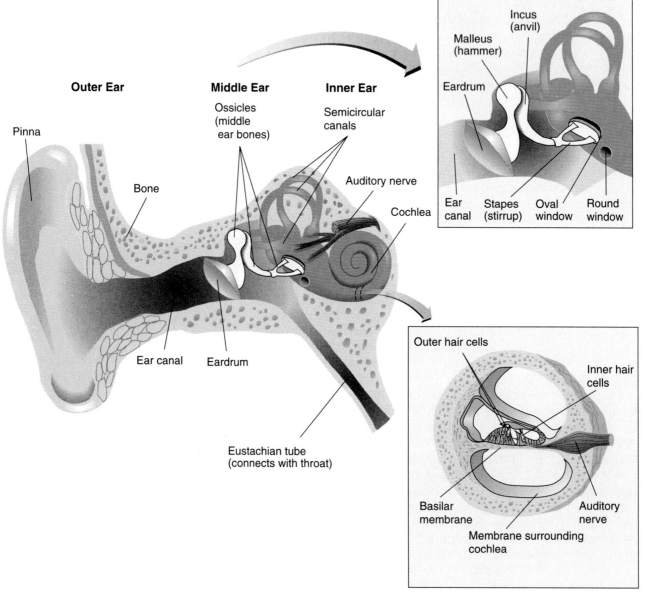

Cross section of the cochlea

Source: Physiology of Behavior, 5th ed., by N. R. Carlson, 1994, Boston: Allyn and Bacon. Adapted by permission.

A person speaks and the sound waves from the words pass through the air or some other medium. The sound waves are caught by the pinna or auricle (what we commonly call the ear) and funneled down the auditory canal of the listener; the pinna and the auditory canal are the two parts of the *outer ear.* Sound waves then travel to the *middle ear,* which is an air-filled chamber. This chamber contains the eardrum and is connected to the Eustachian tube, which equalizes the pressure on the two sides of the eardrum. Sound waves cause the **eardrum (tympanic membrane)** to vibrate. Those vibrations cause the **hammer (malleus)** and **anvil (incus)** to move and the **stirrup (stapes)** to oscillate. These three tiny bones together are called the **ossicles** and are also part of the middle ear. The stirrup converts pressure variations to mechanical vibrations, which are then transmitted to the fluid contained in the compartments of the **cochlea.**

The *inner ear* includes the semicircular canals and the cochlea, which is a hollow, spiral-shaped bone that actually contains the organs of hearing. The mechanical variations produced by the stirrup on the fluid are transmitted to the basement membrane of the cochlea that lines the inside of the hollow chamber. This membrane supports the **hair cells.** Changes in the frequency and amplitude of sound cause different zones of the basement membrane to vibrate, activating different groups of hair cells. Each hair cell has about a hundred tiny, rigid spines at its top. The hair cells vary in length, like the pipes of an organ, and are arranged in a zigzag pattern. Researchers believe that the lengths of the spines correspond to different vibrations, frequencies, or tones; the longer spines produce lower tones. When a spine is bent back and forth by alterations of the basement membrane, it produces electrochemical signals, which are sent through nerve cells along the **auditory nerve** (eighth cranial nerve) to the brain, where the signals are perceived as tones.

Hearing losses range in severity, vary in type, and influence each person differently. Let's look first at the various aspects of hearing losses and then at the way they affect the individual.

Types of Hearing Loss

There are two general types of hearing loss: *conductive* and *sensorineural.* **Conductive hearing losses** are due to blockage or damage to the outer or middle ear that prevents sound waves from traveling (being conducted) to the inner ear. Generally, someone with a conductive hearing loss has a mild to moderate disability. Some conductive hearing losses are temporary; in fact, we have all probably experienced a conductive hearing loss at some point in our lives. For example, you may have experienced a temporary loss of hearing due to change of air pressure when flying in an airplane or riding in a car in the mountains. Preschoolers often experience a conductive hearing loss when they have head colds. Because of the high frequency of head colds among children, at any one time, between 50 and 80 percent of youngsters attending kindergarten through fifth grade may have a mild hearing loss. The infection causes excessive fluid to accumulate in the middle ear, interfering with the conduction of sound waves there. With a mild loss, the individual can still hear almost all speech sounds and can hear most conversations (Moores, 1996). If the hearing loss was caused by a head cold, once the ear infection clears up, the hearing difficulties also disappear. Most conductive hearing losses can be corrected through surgery or other medical techniques.

 MAKING CONNECTIONS

Study the illustration in Figure 10.1 to see what these hair cells look like and how they are aligned.

eardrum (tympanic membrane). Part of the ear upon which sound waves and their vibrations fall and cause the ossicles to move; separates the outer and middle ear.

hammer (malleus). One of the three tiny bones (ossicles) in the middle ear.

anvil (incus). One of the three tiny bones (ossicles) in the middle ear.

stirrup (stapes). One of the three tiny bones (ossicles) in the middle ear.

ossicles. Three tiny bones in the middle ear that transmit sound waves from the eardrum through the middle ear to the cochlea.

cochlea. Part of the inner ear that contains fluid and hairlike nerve cells that transmit information to the brain.

hair cells. The structures in the inner ear that produce the electrochemical signals that pass through the auditory nerve to the brain, where these signals, which originated as sound waves, are perceived as tones.

auditory nerve. Nerve that carries messages received through the ear to the brain; known in neurology as the eighth cranial nerve.

conductive hearing loss. Hearing loss caused by damage or obstruction to the outer or middle ear that prevents transfer of sound to the inner ear.

The second type of hearing loss, **sensorineural hearing loss,** occurs when there is damage to the inner ear or the auditory nerve and usually cannot be improved medically or surgically. Individuals affected by a sensorineural loss are able to hear different frequencies at different intensity levels; their hearing losses are not flat or even. Sensorineural losses are less common in young children than the conductive types.

Identification

To understand how hearing is measured, let's review some terms and concepts about sound. Sound is produced by the vibration of molecules through air, water, wires, or some other medium. The number of vibrations per second determines the **frequency of the sound.** High frequencies are perceived through our ears as high pitch or tone; low frequencies are perceived as low pitch. Frequency is measured in a unit called **hertz (Hz).** The normal ear hears sounds that range from approximately 20 Hz to 20,000 Hz; speech sounds fall approximately in the middle of the human hearing range (between 250 Hz and 4,000 Hz). There are sounds, however, that humans cannot perceive, regardless of hearing abilities. For example, some dog whistles use high frequencies that are beyond humans' hearing range.

Intensity, or loudness, of sound is measured in **decibels (dB).** Softer, quieter sounds have lower decibel measurements; louder sounds have higher decibel numbers. A decibel level of 125 or louder is painful to the average person. Decibel levels ranging from 0 to 120 dB are used to test how well an individual can hear different frequencies; a child with normal hearing should be able to perceive sounds at 0 dB. The scale used to assess hearing has been adjusted so that 0 indicates no loss and numbers greater than 0 indicate the degree or amount of loss. Small numbers indicate mild losses; large numbers indicate moderate to severe or profound losses.

When audiologists test people's hearing abilities, they use soundproof rooms so that distractions like those found in classrooms are eliminated. They also use **pure sounds**—sound waves of specific frequencies—at various combinations of hertz and decibels. Hearing is tested also at various bands of pitch and loudness. By using an **audiometer**—an instrument that produces sounds at precise frequencies and intensities—audiologists can assess hearing in each ear independently. The results of this audiological assessment are plotted on an **audiogram,** which is a grid or graph. Along the top of the graph are hertz levels; the vertical lines represent different levels of sound frequency or hertz. Each ear is tested separately. A **hearing threshold** is determined by noting when the person first perceives the softest sound at each frequency level. Sometimes, hearing threshold is reported only for the better ear, and sometimes an average of an individual's scores at three different frequencies (500, 1,000, 2,000 Hz) is used. Any score falling below the 0 dB line on an audiogram represents some degree of hearing loss because the audiometer is set to indicate that a person has no hearing loss at 0 dB for various hertz levels. Those of you who have some knowledge of music might find Lowenbraun's (1995) explanation of hertz helpful. The frequency of middle C on the piano is approximately 250 Hz. The next vertical line on the audiogram, 500 Hz, is approximately one octave above middle C; 1,000 is two octaves above middle C; and so on. (See the scale in Figure 10.2.)

Now let us review the audiograms of two children—Travis and Heather. Most children's hearing is assessed by the **air conduction audiometry method,** which uses pure-tone sounds generated by an audiometer. Earphones are placed over the child's ears, and the child raises his or her hand when hearing a sound. Such testing is usually done by a pediatrician at a well-child checkup or by a school nurse.

sensorineural hearing loss. Hearing loss caused by damage to the inner ear or the auditory nerve.

frequency of sound. The number of vibrations per second of molecules through some medium like air, water, or wires.

hertz (Hz). Unit of measure for sound frequency.

decibel (dB). Unit of measure for intensity of sound.

pure sounds. Sound waves of specific frequencies used to test an individual's hearing ability.

audiometer. An electrical instrument for measuring the threshold of hearing tests using an audiometer; it charts individuals' thresholds of hearing at various frequencies against sound intensities in decibels.

audiogram. The grid or graph used to display a person's hearing abilities.

hearing threshold. The point at which a person can perceive the softest sound at each frequency level.

air conduction audiometry method. A method to test hearing that uses a pure-tone sound generated by an audiometer.

~~
FIGURE 10.2

Travis's Audiogram

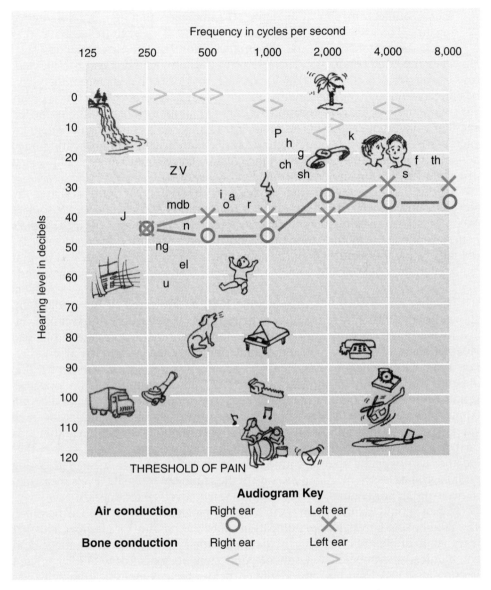

Source: Hearing in Children (p. 7) by J. L. Northern and M. P. Downs, 1984, Baltimore:
Williams & Wilkins. Used by permission.

Because Travis and Heather were suspected of having hearing losses, the audiologist testing them used two procedures: first, the air conduction method and,
second, the bone conduction method. It was apparent from the first test that the
children had hearing losses, so the audiologist needed to know whether the loss
was due to damage in the outer, middle, or inner ear. To determine the location of
the damage, the audiologist used the **bone conduction audiometry method**, in

**bone conduction audiometry
method.** A test for conductive
hearing loss in which a vibrator is
placed on a person's forehead so
that sound bypasses the outer and
middle ear and goes directly to the
inner ear; tests for conductive
hearing losses.

which a vibrator is placed on the forehead so that sound can bypass the outer and middle ear and go directly to the inner ear. When the bone conduction thresholds are normal (near 0 dB) and the air conduction thresholds are abnormal, the hearing loss is conductive.

Travis's audiogram, shown in Figure 10.2, indicates that he has a conductive hearing loss. The loss, of about 40 dB, is in the mild range with the amplification of hearing aids. Notice how flat the profile is for Travis's air conduction test. However, the bone conduction test reveals that when the middle ear is bypassed, his hearing is much closer to 0 dB. Travis's hearing loss either is temporary or can be corrected through surgery or other medical treatment. Notice also that a different code is used for Travis's right and left ears—O for the right ear and X for the left ear. Remember that each ear is tested independently. Travis's hearing threshold for each ear is marked on his audiogram. Most children with normal hearing have auditory thresholds (the points when they first perceive sound) at approximately 0 dB, while Travis's thresholds are considerably below 0.

Travis's hearing abilities are plotted on an audiogram form designed by Northern and Downs (1984) to show where various speech and other sounds occur. This form uses pictures to show where different sounds fall. If the child's pattern is above the picture, then the sound should be heard. If the child's threshold falls below the picture, then the sound pictured cannot be perceived by that child. Without a hearing aid, Travis, for example, can perceive only a few sounds (*ng*, *el*, and *u*).

Heather has a sensorineural hearing loss, as indicated in her audiogram, shown in Figure 10.3. A sensorineural hearing loss is caused by a defect or damage to the inner ear and can be more serious than conductive hearing losses. Heather has a 30 dB loss. Notice the similarity of her scores from the air conduction and bone conduction tests. Heather's hearing was also tested with her hearing aids on. Notice that with the use of aids, Heather's hearing loss is no longer as serious; it is now at a mild functional level. The shaded area on this audiogram (sometimes called the "speech banana" because of its shape) marks the area where speech sounds fall. Because Heather's hearing abilities lie above this area on her audiogram (see the top of the audiogram), the audiologist knows that Heather can hear the speech sounds at the sound intensities measured during audiological assessment. Along the side of the graph are intensity levels measured in decibels, so horizontal lines represent different levels of loudness.

When should identification occur? The simple answer is, As soon as possible. The relationship between communication skills and hearing loss is clear. The first three years of life are crucial in the development of good speech, language, and communicative competence. Of those youngsters born deaf or with a significant hearing loss, less than half are identified before their communication skills are compromised (Leary, 1993). Why is this so? Babies are not screened for hearing loss, despite simple, nonintrusive, and relatively inexpensive (about $25) procedures that can be done before babies leave the hospital.

Significance

Experts vary on their definitions of hearing loss and on the point at which it has educational significance. Of course, all hearing losses are serious, but at some point, a hearing loss substantially influences the way in which a child needs to be taught and how well the individual can use the communication modes of nondis-

MAKING CONNECTIONS

For a review of communicative competence and speech and language development, see Chapter 5.

FIGURE 10.3

Heather's Audiogram

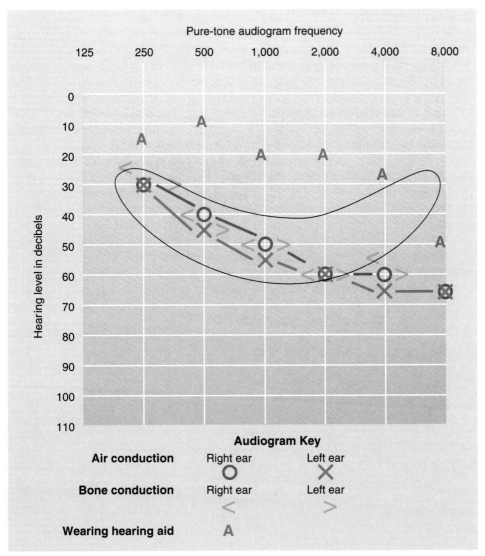

abled peers. The amount and type of an individual's hearing loss are related to the ability to understand information presented orally. These two factors also affect how a student might be taught and the types of services needed. For example, a student with a moderate loss might not profit from typical instructional methods (lectures, oral directions) alone.

But what constitutes a mild, a moderate, or a severe hearing loss? Lowenbraun and Thompson (1994) consider losses from 20 to 60 dB mild to moderate, losses from 60 to 90 dB severe, and those greater than 90 dB profound. Conductive

MAKING CONNECTIONS

Review the Communication Game in the Defined section of Chapter 5.

losses of 30 to 50 dB are relatively common and fall in Lowenbraun and Thompson's mild-to-moderate range. Persons with this level of conductive hearing loss cannot hear typical conversations without amplification. Clearly, levels of hearing loss have considerable significance for how people communicate and learn from others. Table 10.1 provides another set of definitions and levels of hearing loss. This table also gives explanations of how well individuals can hear for each level of loss, as well as the educational implications for each level.

Possibly because of their difficulty mastering oral speech and language-based academic subjects (reading, written communication), many deaf individuals have been misidentified as having mental retardation along with their deafness (Lowenbraun & Thompson, 1994). It is important for diagnosticians not to confuse linguistic deprivation with intellectual impairment or any other disability. Unfortunately, such care and concern was not taken in the case of Junius Wilson. After spending sixty-eight years locked in a North Carolina state mental hospital, Junius finally got some of the freedom he deserves (Wright, 1994). From 1925 until 1994, Wilson spent his life in a locked ward where his undeveloped sign language skills made him unable to communicate with others. Because of an alert guardian appointed by the social services agency, Wilson is now living in a three-bedroom cottage on the hospital grounds, is learning more sign language, and looks forward to rides in the car and eating at fast-food restaurants. At the age of 96, he can only look back on his life's tragedy and hope that it doesn't happen to others in similar positions.

TABLE 10.1

Educational Placement Categories of Deafness

Level	Hearing Loss	Ability to Comprehend Speech	Special Education and Related Service Requirements
I	35–54 dB	Usually has difficulty with whispered speech or faint speech	Requires special speech and hearing assistance
II	55–69 dB	Frequent difficulty with normal speech	Needs special speech, hearing, and language assistance
III	70–89 dB	Understands only shouted or amplified speech	Requires special speech, hearing, language, and educational assistance, often necessitating intensive special education services such as special classes
IV	90 dB and beyond	Cannot hear and usually cannot understand even amplified speech	Also requires special speech, hearing, language, and educational assistance; intensive special education and related services are necessary

Sources: Adapted from *Educating the deaf: Psychology, principles, and practices* (4th ed.) (p. 11) by D. Moores, 1996, Boston: Houghton Mifflin; and adapted from "Characteristics of hearing impaired youth in the general population and of students in special educational programs for the hearing impaired," by P. Pies, 1986, A. N. Schildroth and M. A. Karchmer, *Deaf children in America* (p.12), Austin, TX: Pro-Ed. Reprinted and adapted by permission.

History of the Field

As long ago as the days of ancient Greeks and the early Roman Empire, social leaders like Aristotle, Plato, and the Emperor Justinian wrote about issues facing deaf people of their time. Over the history of Western civilization, attitudes toward people who were deaf have varied. Some societies protected them; others ridiculed, persecuted, and even put them to death. Even in America, attitudes and acceptance of the deaf have changed greatly across time.

Documents dating back to the 1500s report of physicians in Europe who worked with people who were deaf. Pedro Ponce de Leon (1520–1584), a Spanish monk credited with being the first teacher of students who were deaf, had remarkable success teaching his students to read, write, and speak. William Holder and John Wallis, who lived during the 1600s, are credited with beginning educational programs in England for individuals who were deaf. Like the Spanish before, they advocated using writing and manual communication to teach speech. By the 1700s, schools for the deaf were established by Henry Baker in England, Thomas Braidwood in Edinburgh, Abbé Charles Michel de l'Epée in France, and Samuel Heinicke in Germany.

In 1817, the first school in the United States for students who were deaf was started in Hartford, Connecticut. The American Asylum for the Education of the Deaf and Dumb (now the American School for the Deaf) was begun through the efforts of Thomas Hopkins Gallaudet, a young divinity student who was sent to England and France to study about deafness so that a school could be opened in this country. At this time, the French at the school begun by l'Epée were experimenting with methods of manual communication, mainly sign language. Gallaudet was greatly influenced by the effectiveness of these methods, and he brought Laurent Clerc, a Deaf Frenchman and a well-known educator of the Deaf, to the United States. Clerc is often credited with being the father of education for the deaf in the United States. Other Americans interested in deaf education also went to Europe and were impressed by the oral approaches in deaf education used in Germany. In most oral approaches of that day, the use of any form of manual communication or sign language was greatly discouraged.

The roots of the debate about whether the oral or the manual method of instruction and communication are over 100 years old (Winefield, 1987). The battles were initiated and fueled through the debates of Edward Gallaudet, Thomas Gallaudet's son, and Alexander Graham Bell (Alby, 1962; Adams, 1929). Each of these men had a deaf mother and a highly successful father. Bell invented the telephone and the audiometer and worked on the phonograph. Gallaudet was the president of the nation's college for the deaf and was a renowned legal scholar. These two men clashed. In 1883 and 1884, Bell wrote two papers critical of policies and practices that contributed to segregation of deaf individuals from the rest of society. He believed that residential schools and the use of sign language fostered segregation. Bell proposed legislation that would prevent two adults who were deaf from marrying, eliminate residential schools, ban the use of manual communication, and prohibit the deaf from becoming teachers of students who were also deaf. Gallaudet strongly opposed these positions in both his writings and in public debates. The battle between these two strong individuals and their opposing positions carried over into Congress and even influenced federal funding of teacher preparation programs. Gallaudet's position was supported by Congress,

MAKING CONNECTIONS

Compare the story about the deaf communities on Martha's Vineyard in the Defined section of Chapter 1 with the history of deaf people recounted in this section.

MAKING CONNECTIONS

The *D* in Deaf has been capitalized here to reflect that deafness here is associated with Deaf culture; for more information, see that section in the Deaf and Hard of Hearing Children section of this chapter.

MAKING CONNECTIONS

For more about Gallaudet University, the world's only university for the Deaf, and its importance to the Deaf community, see in this chapter
• the sections about Thomas and Edward Gallaudet and the university earlier in the History section.
• Deaf Culture in the Deaf and Hard of Hearing Children section.
• Overcoming Barriers in the Educational Interventions section.

MAKING CONNECTIONS

• For a picture of an ear trumpet, see the photo of Dorothy Brett in the Technology section.
• For the importance of the hearing aid technology to hard of hearing individuals, even before modern hearing aids, see the reference to Dorothy Brett's ear trumpet in the artist's biography section at the beginning of this chapter.

MAKING CONNECTIONS

The advocacy movement and reasons for it is also discussed in these sections:
• Legislation section of Chapter 1
• The History section of this chapter

Gallaudet University. The United States's federally funded university serving Deaf undergraduate and graduate students.

Deaf pride. A term used to signify the accomplishments and achievements of members of the Deaf community.

and he received an appropriation to establish a teacher preparation program that emphasized both the oral and manual approach to education of these students. Although Gallaudet won support from Congress, the conflicts were not settled. In fact, for many years the oralist position was more popular, and the use of manual communication in any form was discouraged in classes for deaf and hard of hearing students.

Horace Mann, a leader in education and social reform during the late 1800s, sided with the oral-only camp because the signing system of the manual method did not match English in grammar and structure. Throughout the late nineteenth century and for most of the twentieth century, the oral-only position was commonly followed. It was not until the 1970s that a combined approach—called total communication—was adopted. Total communication uses oral and manual communication systems for the instruction of deaf students. The debate about oralism and a combined oral and sign language method for communicating and instruction continues today, however.

Formal education for the deaf in the United States in the nineteenth century took place primarily in residential schools. Deaf students were sent to boarding schools, as were many students without disabilities in that day. From 1817, when the first school was started, to the eve of the Civil War in 1864, twenty-four schools for the deaf were in operation. **Gallaudet University** (first called the National Deaf Mute College) was founded in 1864 on the principle of the right of all deaf students to an education. Educators at Gallaudet believed that these students can achieve and learn when expectations are high and a high-quality education is available to them.

Day schools gained in popularity later in the nineteenth century, partly because residential schools were selective and would not serve all students who were deaf (students from different ethnic backgrounds, students with multiple disabilities). However, because most U.S. cities did not have enough deaf students to fill day schools, and because many parents assumed that living and learning with others with similar hearing losses was best for these students, residential schools continued. They remain quite popular with many Deaf high school students who use ASL because they do not feel isolated, are included in extracurricular activities, and have friends with common interests.

The development of the hearing aid had a significant impact on the lives of people who are deaf or hard of hearing, particularly those with conductive hearing losses. The hearing trumpet, as it was called when first developed, before World War II, made sounds a little louder. At the end of World War II, battery-operated hearing aids were developed, but these devices were difficult to use because they were bulky. Behind-the-ear (BTE) hearing aids were created after the development of the transistor in the 1950s and, with refinements, continue in use today. Researchers continue to work to develop a new generation of hearing aids that will block out background noise, adjust to each individual's hearing profile, and amplify sounds across the entire range of frequencies used in speech.

Since the late 1980s, **Deaf pride** and Deaf culture have gained in numbers and in visibility: The Deaf community is now seen as a significant advocacy group. The Deaf President Now Movement, which galvanized the Deaf community (Gannon, 1989), began in 1988 when a hearing president was appointed to lead Gallaudet University. After protests from Deaf Gallaudet students and the Deaf community, which closed the campus and included a march on the nation's Capitol, the newly appointed president (who could not sign) resigned and I. King

I. King Jordan, the first Deaf President of Gallaudet University, has become a symbol of Deaf advocacy and Deaf culture.

Jordan became the first Deaf college president for Gallaudet and the nation. In 1994, a similar protest occurred at the Lexington Center, New York City's only public day school for the Deaf. In this case, a hearing chief executive was appointed without input or approval from the Deaf community (Soloman, 1994). Deaf leaders are now taking their proper places in society and in the workplace. One example is Dr. Robert Davila, one of eight children from a migrant farm worker's family. He was the first Deaf person to become a vice president at Gallaudet University, was the assistant secretary of education from 1989–1993, and is now president of Rochester Institute of Technology and director of the National Technical Institute for the Deaf. Most clearly, the 1988 protest at Gallaudet was a historical landmark, initiating a new period in the history of Deaf advocacy and activism.

Prevalence

Approximately two million people in the United States were reported as being profoundly deaf (Soloman, 1994). The vast majority of deaf and hard of hearing people are adults, with the greatest number over age 65. Educators, of course, are most concerned with how statistics are gathered on children, but these numbers are very difficult to obtain. Some states have carefully defined criteria for counting who is deaf, is hard of hearing, and/or has multiple disabilities. But not all states use the same criteria. In addition, the U.S. Department of Education reports children by their primary disability. So students with mental retardation who also have a hearing loss may be reported only in the mental retardation category or possibly in the multiple disabilities category, but usually not in the deafness and hard of

MAKING CONNECTIONS

Also see the discussion about prevalence rates when students have multiple disabilities in the Prevalence section of Chapter 11.

hearing category. Also, those hard of hearing students who do not need special education because hearing aids allow them to hear well enough to participate in typical classroom activities without additional assistance are not included in these counts.

Considering these factors, the number of deaf and hard of hearing students is probably underestimated. Thus according to the *Annual Report to Congress on Implementation of the Individuals with Disabilities Education Act* (U.S. Department of Education, 1996) during the 1994–1995 schoolyear, 0.14 percent of the resident population between the ages of 6 to 17, or 61,211 students, were classified as deaf or hard of hearing. The Center for Assessment and Demographic Studies at Gallaudet University also collects prevalence information (Schildroth & Hotto, 1996). Their data indicate that the number of deaf and hard of hearing children has decreased by about 12 percent over a ten-year period. They noted a decline of some 3,000 students, which they attribute to the last of those who were affected by the rubella epidemic leaving school. Other reasons for this decline include improved health care, vaccinations preventing rubella and meningitis, and better protections for mother–child blood incompatibility. Another reason might lie with the improved hearing aid technology that allows more youngsters to profit from orally dominant classroom instruction without special education supports.

However, as the overall number seems to be decreasing, the prevalence of deafness among members of ethnic minorities in this country is not. These data, shown in Table 10.2, show that enrollment in programs for deaf and hard of hearing children serve fewer white and African American students but substantially more Hispanic and Asian/Pacific Islanders. This disparity, of course, is due in part to the increased representation of these ethnic groups in the overall American demographic picture over the last ten years.

TABLE 10.2

Changes in Enrollment by Racial and Ethnic Status, 1984–1985, 1994–1995

Racial/Ethnic Status	1984–1985		1994–1995		Change	
	Number	Percentage	Number	Percentage	Number	Percentage
White	33,438	67	27,034	59	6,449	−19
Black	8,995	18	7,789	17	1,206	−13
Hispanic	5,497	11	7,789	17	2,292	+42
Asian/Pacific	999	2	1,833	4	834	+83
Other	999	2	1,375	3	376	+38
Total	49,973	100	45,820	100	4,153	−8

Source: From *Educating the Deaf: Psychology, principles, and practices* (4th ed.) (p. 23) by D. Moores, 1996, Boston: Houghton Mifflin; using data provided by A. Schildroth, Center for Assessment and Demographic Studies, Gallaudet University, Washington, DC, March 1995. Reprinted by permission.

Causes and Prevention

It is not a surprise to learn that hearing loss can result from illness or injury. For example, sustained loud noise can cause a hearing loss. Furthermore, some types of deafness are the result of heredity. It was for this reason that Alexander Graham Bell, in the late 1800s, proposed legislation to ban two deaf people from marrying; fortunately, he was unsuccessful. For educators, understanding the causes of hearing loss is useful. Teachers need this knowledge to plan educational programs for specific youngsters. For example, if a child has a conductive hearing loss, hearing aids might be able to amplify sound sufficiently that the student can profit from oral instruction in the typical classroom. In this section, we also look at some ways to prevent hearing loss.

Causes

It appears that heredity accounts for about 50 percent of childhood deafness in the United States today (Moores, 1996). However, as Table 10.3 indicates, the cause is unknown for a great many deaf and hard of hearing people. Even in these unknown cases, it is likely that heredity and genetics account for many of the hearing losses. Table 10.3 compares the percentages of students with hearing loss across a fifteen-year period. The 1992–1993 data, not given in Table 10.3, show little change from the 1987–1988 schoolyear (Schildroth, 1993). Otitis media, meningitis, and heredity are causes that have increased over time. Maternal rubella has decreased dramatically but unfortunately is still a contributing factor in the number of cases of children with hearing loss today. There are five major causes. We examine each cause in turn.

MAKING CONNECTIONS

See the Concepts and Controversy section in Chapter 5 for a discussion regarding whether the federal government has a responsibility to implement a national immunization program.

Maternal Rubella. Rubella (German measles) contracted by a pregnant woman is a devastating disease for an unborn child. Depending on when the expectant mother contracts the virus, the child may be born with a profound hearing loss, a visual impairment, or other disabilities alone or in combinations. As with other congenital hearing losses (those present at birth), those caused by maternal rubella are typically sensorineural with damage to the inner ear or the auditory nerve. The children affected are prelingually deaf. Vaccines are available to prevent women of childbearing age from contracting this disease; therefore the incidence of deafness caused by maternal rubella has declined and should be eliminated.

MAKING CONNECTIONS

For a review of prelingual deafness, see the Types of Hearing Loss in the Defined section of this chapter.

Meningitis. **Meningitis** is a disease that affects the central nervous system (specifically the meninges, the coverings of the brain and spinal cord, and its circulating fluid). Most cases that involve a hearing loss are bacterial infections rather than the more lethal viral meningitis. This disease often results in a profound hearing loss and is often associated with other disabilities. Meningitis is the most common cause of postnatal deafness in schoolchildren and is one major cause of sensorineural hearing losses that are not present at birth. These individuals' hearing losses are acquired, and they may have developed some speech and language before they developed the hearing loss. Vaccines do exist that will prevent the disease, but at present there is no national immunization program for meningitis.

meningitis. A disease that affects the central nervous system and often causes hearing loss.

TABLE 10.3

Percentage Distribution of Causes of Hearing Loss

Cause[a]	Schoolyear			
	1972–1973	1982–1983	1987–1988	1995–1996
Total, all causes	100.0	100.0	100.0	100.0
Cause unknown	48.6	39.5	48.8	35.6
Cause reported	51.4	60.5	51.2	64.4
Causes at birth				
Maternal rubella	17.6	16.3	5.2	3.3
Heredity	8.5	11.6	12.9	27.8
Prematurity	5.2	4.0	4.8	9.9
Pregnancy complications	3.2	3.4	2.9	4.8
Trauma	2.3	2.4	2.4	5.1
Rh incompatibility	3.1	1.4	0.6	0.8
Cytomegalovirus (CMV)				3.4
Causes after birth				
Meningitis	5.3	7.3	8.8	14.8
Otitis media	1.6	3.0	3.4	0.5
High fever	2.3	3.1	2.9	4.5
Infection	1.5	2.7	2.5	4.6
Trauma	0.9	0.8	0.7	1.3
Measles	2.1	0.8	0.4	0.3
Mumps	0.6	0.2	0.1	0.1
Other causes after birth				6.6
Other causes	2.5	8.0	7.2	—

[a]Because some students had more than one reported etiology, the sum of the cause-specific percentages exceeds the total percentage of cases with known causes.

Sources: Demographic Aspects of Hearing Impairment: Questions and Answers (2nd ed. p. 7) by D. Hotchkiss, 1989, Washington, DC: Center for Assessment and Demographic Studies, Gallaudet University and 1995–1996 Annual Survey Summary, Gallaudet Research Institute, Center for Assessment and Demographic Studies. Reprinted by permission.

Otitis Media. Infection of the middle ear and accumulation of fluid behind the eardrum is called otitis media. The condition can be corrected and treated with antibiotics and other medical procedures. If sustained for long periods of time or not detected in very young children, the condition may result in a language impairment that could affect future academic learning. Chronic otitis media can result in a conductive hearing loss by damaging the eardrum and in about 84 percent of the cases results in a mild to moderate hearing loss. Typically these youngsters are hard of hearing, and they profit from hearing aids because their hearing loss is conductive.

Heredity. More than 150 different types of genetic deafness have been identified, and most likely the unknown causes of deafness are genetic. Genetic causes are congenital and sensorineural. Most children whose deafness is inherited are less likely to have multiple disabilities. Look at Table 10.3 again. Notice that the percentage of cases that can now be documented as being caused by heredity is on the rise.

Noise. Although noise has not traditionally been included as a major cause of hearing loss, employers, federal agencies, and researchers are becoming more aware of its dangers. Some believe that noise is *the* major cause of hearing loss in this country (Holthouser, 1994). While European countries take legal steps to ensure noise abatement, the United States seems to be getting noisier (Browne, 1992). Information gathered on the space shuttle *Columbia* shows that even sustained levels of noise at about 70 dB can cause some sensorineural hearing loss. Imagine the damage caused by the sound levels of a rock concert (which often reaches 125 dB), a car stereo, or a personal tape player. Indications are that young males are more likely to acquire noise-induced hearing losses because they frequently engage in activities such as mowing the lawn, firing a gun, riding a motorcycle, or fixing a car engine. Even infants and toddlers can sustain irreversible noise-induced hearing losses. Of the 28 million Americans with permanent hearing loss, about a third are victims of exposure to loud sounds (Marcotty, 1996). The loss can occur without pain or any notice; and although it usually takes years of exposure, noise can cause damage that can be detected early. For example, in one study of first-year college students, 61 percent had detectable hearing losses, probably from exposure to noise. Figure 10.4 shows what sounds are considered in the danger zone.

Other Causes. As we eliminate or reduce the incidence of some causes of hearing loss, other causes are discovered. For example, high-impact aerobics is now thought to cause damage to the delicate structures of the inner ear (Rosenthal, 1990). Researchers believe that extended periods of arduous jumping and bobbing may displace the tiny granules called otoliths inside the inner ear. They float in a gel and transmit information to the hairlike stalks linked to nerve fibers, a part of the system that turns sound impulses into nerve signals for transmission to the brain. When the otoliths are displaced, both balance and hearing can be affected.

More specific causes of hearing loss continue to be discovered. We now know that congenital cytomegalovirus (CMV) infection, a herpes virus, affects about 1 percent of all newborns and can cause mild to profound sensorineural hearing losses and other disabilities as well. At present, no vaccine or cure is available to prevent or treat CMV; however, avoiding persons affected with the virus, ensuring the safety of blood used in transfusions, and good hygiene are important preventive measures (Heller, Alberto, Forney, & Schwartzman, 1996). As advances in medical technology continue, many of the unknown causes will be identified. Of course, the hope is that once a cause is identified, a cure or preventive technique will be discovered.

MAKING CONNECTIONS

For a review of language impairments, see these sections in Chapter 5:
- Speech or Language Impairments Defined
- Causes and Prevention of Speech or Language Impairments
- Children with Speech or Language Impairments

MAKING CONNECTIONS

CMV is also discussed in Prevalence; Causes and Prevention in Chapter 9.

FIGURE 10.4

Decibel Levels of Noise in U.S. Environments

Hearing Level in Decibels	Examples of Common Sounds
30	Soft whisper, quiet library
40	Leaves rustling
50	Rainfall, refrigerator
60	Normal conversation, air conditioner
70	City or freeway traffic, sewing machine
80	Hair dryer, alarm clock
90*	Lawn mower, motorcycle
100	Garbage truck, snowmobile
110	Shouting at close range, dance club, race car
120	Jet plane taking off, car stereo turned all the way up
130	Live rock music, jackhammer
140	Firecracker, nearby gunshot blast, jet engine

*Levels 85 decibels and above are considered hazardous.

Source: U.S. Congress Select Committee on Children, Youth, and Families.

Prevention

Can some hearing losses be corrected or prevented? The answer, of course, is yes. In some cases, the steps needed for prevention are simple; in other cases, complicated medical technology is required. In many cases, no preventive measures exist today. One cause that can be prevented—noise—requires only some simple measures. People can wear ear protectors when they are around loud sounds. Another preventive measure is to have makers of personal stereos, power lawn mowers, and other noisy equipment install noise-limiting devices or graphic warning lights on their products. Although many preventive measures are simple and seem to be "common sense," other measures are complicated and costly. In the following sections, you will learn how medical technology, early detection, and public awareness can contribute to reducing the number of individuals with hearing loss.

Medical Technology. Medical technology can play an important role in the prevention and treatment of hearing problems. As we have discussed, infection can cause hearing loss. But some infections, if diagnosed and treated early, do not have to result in deafness or significant loss. Today, most conductive hearing losses that involve the middle ear can be treated either medically or surgically (Lowenbraun & Thompson, 1994). Delicate surgical procedures can repair or replace poorly functioning small bones in the middle ear.

Other medical advances applied today include **cochlear implants**. This technology is currently at the center of great controversy between the Deaf and hearing communities. Because cochlear implants bring only a crude awareness of sound to some deaf people, many in the Deaf community question whether this technology should be applied, particularly to prelingually deaf children. Although it is not beneficial for some, it does improve the hearing of others. For instance, Dorothy Sorkin, who began losing her hearing when she was in her 20s and was deaf in her 40s, has profited greatly from cochlear implants. Sorkin says that the implant gives her close to natural sounds, allows her to use a regular telephone, and "I can recognize voices I heard before" (Ubell, 1995). A typical cochlear implant, shown in Figure 10.5, converts acoustic information to electrical signals that stimulate the remaining auditory nerve fibers.

Very few American children have received a cochlear implant, which costs between $25,000 and $30,000. In a 1995 survey of deaf and hard of hearing children, only 1,081 were identified who had a cochlear implant (Schildroth & Hotto, 1996). Although small in number, it still represents a substantial increase over a two-year period: an increase of 418 (64 percent). Most (83 percent) of these children are white, and 90 percent have severe to profound hearing losses. The procedure involves an incision made behind the ear; when that heals, a wire is wound through the cochlea. The wire is connected to a very small receiver that is placed under the skin behind the ear; then wire and receiver are connected to a small computer, which can be worn on a belt. In the hearing process, the computer detects sound and sends electrical signals to the implanted receiver, which stimulates the auditory nerve, creating sound. Whether that sound is interpreted as noise or as words seems to depend on many factors (how long the person has been deaf, how long the implant has been worn, whether the person knew speech before becoming deaf). In other words, implants do not guarantee the proficient use of oral language in deaf children (Fryauf-Bertschy & Gantz, 1994). Researchers are attempting to determine the predictive characteristics of success. One major factor is the age of onset of the person's deafness. Many, like Dorothy Sorkin, who become deaf long after speech and language is developed, are able to recognize words, using hearing as their primary mode of listening to others, and even use a standard telephone. Some postlingually deaf children, whose hearing loss came early in life, tend to develop moderate ability to perceive sounds and develop some intelligible speech. For those born deaf, cochlear implants seem to have the least positive effect. In one research study with children who had used a

MAKING CONNECTIONS

For more information about the debate over cochlear implants, see Concepts and Controversy at the end of this chapter.

cochlear implant. Electronic microprocessor that replaces the cochlea and allows some people who are deaf to process sounds.

FIGURE 10.5

Cochlear Implant

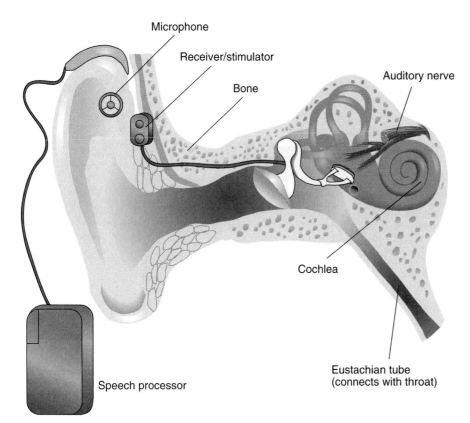

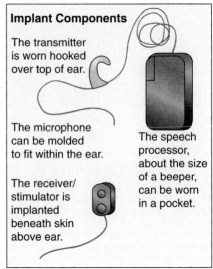

Implant Components

The transmitter is worn hooked over top of ear.

The microphone can be molded to fit within the ear.

The receiver/ stimulator is implanted beneath skin above ear.

The speech processor, about the size of a beeper, can be worn in a pocket.

Microphone

Receiver/stimulator

Bone

Auditory nerve

Cochlea

Eustachian tube (connects with throat)

Speech processor

cochlear implant for at least two years (an average of three years), only some ability to understand information presented orally and little development of intelligible speech occurred (Tye-Murray, Spencer, & Woodworth, 1995). In that study, the children could repeat only 22 percent of the words correctly when retelling a story, their speech intelligibility was very low, they learned speech at a much slower rate than hearing peers, and they continued to use sign language. The successful use of a cochlear implant in everyday communication seems to require a prior knowledge and mastery of spoken language (Lane, 1995).

If the outcomes of cochlear implants are not good with prelingually deaf children (recall that 95 percent of deaf children are prelingually deaf and have a hearing parent), why is this surgery performed? This, of course, is the central question asked by members of the Deaf community. Cochlear implants are done for many reasons. Encouraged by reports that some children begin to show marked improvement several years after they receive an implant, many hearing parents of deaf children hope that it is their child who might develop oral speech and communicate in an auditory environment well. Many hope that if given an implant immediately upon the detection of deafness, their child will learn how to interpret information coming from the implant as hearing children do with normally processed auditory information.

What's next? In its experimental stages, the Auditory Brainstem Implant (ABI) is a revolutionary technology that will allow people who do not have functioning hearing nerves to perceive sounds (Alexander Graham Bell Association for the Deaf, 1993a). This system transmits hearing signals directly to the brain and will allow those with nonoperative auditory nerves to perceive sound. Also on the horizon may be the possibility of regenerating the hair cells in the cochlea. Successful in the laboratory with animals, human trials should begin at the beginning of the next century (Soloman, 1994). If successful, deafness could practically be eliminated.

Early Detection. For hearing losses that can be prevented, early detection is a key factor. Once a hearing problem is identified and diagnosed, medical treatment and educational services can be provided. Particularly for students with hearing loss, teachers can play an important role in early identification. The Tips for Teachers box lists many of the common characteristics that could alert preschool and general education teachers to make a referral to the school nurse.

Efforts at early detection, however, are not currently sufficient. Approximately 1 in every 1,000 children is born deaf, and more than 50 percent of them are not identified until they are close to 3 years old (Goldberg, 1993). Most states do not require infants' hearing to be tested, and those that do only require it for infants who are at risk for hearing loss because of family history, low birthweight, or mother's health during pregnancy. The situation is improving, though. In 1992, Rhode Island became the first state to pass a bill requiring hospitals to test *all* newborns for hearing loss, not just those at risk; the cost of the tests are to be covered by health insurance or the hospital if the family cannot pay (Alexander Graham Bell Association for the Deaf, 1992). In 1993, a National Institute of Health panel recommended that universal hearing screening of infants be done before babies leave the hospital or no later than the first three months (Alexander Graham Bell Association for the Deaf, 1993a). These recent changes are due in part to advances in testing methods; today, the procedures are less expensive, more accurate, and easier to administer.

Increased Public Awareness. A more knowledgeable public, availability of good health care for all children, and better-prepared preschool teachers can prevent some hearing losses and provide treatment for others. Another way to prevent hearing loss is to make the public aware of the importance of proper immunization. For example, although the number of children who are deaf because of maternal rubella has been reduced drastically, this disease has not been eliminated. The public needs to be continually reminded of the importance of immunizations. For this reason, you might have noticed an increased number of public service advertisements on television reminding parents of the importance of protecting young children from disease. In addition to raising public awareness, we need to make vaccinations available to all children, even those without the ability to pay for them.

Deaf and Hard of Hearing Children

Deaf and hard of hearing children cannot be stereotyped. They are individuals with different learning styles and abilities, but they do share one common characteristic: Their ability to hear is limited. As we have mentioned earlier, the severity of the hearing loss and the age that the loss occurred determine how well a person will be able to interact with others orally. Clearly, students who cannot hear the communications of others well have a more difficult time learning through traditional instructional methods.

Deaf Culture

As detailed in a footnote in the Defined section, the word *deaf* is begun with a capital letter when the Deaf refers to something or someone associated with **Deaf culture**. When the word is begun with a small letter, deaf primarily refers to an

MAKING CONNECTIONS

For other disabilities that have known hereditary origins, see the Causes and Prevention sections of these chapters:
• Chapter 4
• Chapter 6
• Chapter 9

Deaf culture. The structures of social relationships, language (ASL), dance, theater, and other cultural activities that bind the Deaf community.

The Deaf, Another Minority Group

Usually, when the term *minority group* is used, we think of ethnic or racial minorities. However, the Deaf community is forcing Americans to broaden their thinking about what constitutes a group and what defines minority group status. Lane (1995) points out that children are considered members of a language minority when their language is not that of the majority. Other defining points for many groups include a common and often unifying history or heritage; a culture comprised of shared values, attitudes, and beliefs; and a sense of community that includes clubs, theater, and various forms of entertainment. So, if language, heritage, culture, and community that are not of the majority or dominant group are what makes a minority group, do the Deaf meet the criterion?

audiological condition or disability. Hard of hearing and deaf persons may be Deaf or deaf, depending on whether they use ASL and associate with the Deaf community. Many consider the Deaf a minority group (also see the Focus on Diversity box), much like ethnic and racial minorities in this country (Dolnick, 1993; Lane, 1995). There are many concepts and nuances to understand when learning about the culture of the Deaf; it is important that teachers understand and respect their students' home cultures.

Deafness is viewed in different ways by different individuals and groups. Many hearing people consider deafness a disability, a pathological condition. To many Deaf people, deafness is one aspect binding a minority group together, a minority group rich in culture, history, language, and the arts. The language of the Deaf community is **American Sign Language (ASL)**, a language that uses signs, has all of the elements (grammar, syntax, idioms) of other languages, and is *not* parallel to English in either structure or word order. ASL is not a mere translation of oral speech or the English language; it is a fully developed language. In fact, many states allow ASL as an option to meet the high school foreign language requirement, and the same is true at many colleges and universities. As the language of the Deaf community, ASL is used in all aspects of their culture. For example, plays are written in ASL and performed by deaf theater groups around the world, and a base of folk literature has also developed over the years. This community unites in many ways by coming together socially and for the purpose of advocacy, like when they began the Deaf President Now Movement in 1988.

For many deaf people, being Deaf of Deaf (being born Deaf of Deaf parents) is a source of considerable pride (Soloman, 1994). Although clearly a minority within in a minority, life can be substantially easier for these individuals. They learn sign language as their native language, which they develop naturally just as hearing babies develop oral language. For these individuals, their deafness is a language-difference, not a disability (Lane, 1995). Most of these individuals consider themselves part of the Deaf community and are active in its activities and clubs, attend Deaf Theater, travel in groups, use ASL as their language, and believe that it is

 MAKING CONNECTIONS

For other sections of this text that discuss issues related to diversity, see
• Focus on Diversity boxes throughout this text,
• Chapter 3.

 MAKING CONNECTIONS

For a review of the differences between being handicapped and having a disability, see Disabilities Defined section of Chapter 1.

 MAKING CONNECTIONS

For a review of the Deaf President Now Movement, see in this chapter
• the History section,
• Overcoming Barriers in the Educational Interventions section.

American Sign Language (ASL). The sign language or manual communication system preferred by many adults who are deaf in this country.

Deaf theater groups perform throughout America. Many of these productions express Deaf culture and are performed using American Sign Language.

important to learn about their culture. Of course, for those who became deaf later in life, do not know ASL, and live in the hearing world, deafness is a disability; one that disconnects them from friends and family. For these people, there is no debate: Deafness is a disability.

What is different in the situation of the Deaf is that only about 10 percent of these individuals were born of Deaf parents and learn ASL as their native language. The vast majority of others are assimilated into the culture later in life, often at residential schools for the Deaf (Fletcher, 1994). What about the majority of the prelingually deaf? Recall that 95 percent of deaf children are born of hearing parents. Many of these youngsters do not develop language (either aural or manual) when they should developmentally, which can be devastating to the individual's cognitive and social skills development. The challenges for these youngsters and their families are great. Many parents are afraid that if their children learn ASL as their first language, they will be excluded from mainstream society, seek out the Deaf community, and be lost to their natural family (Goldberg, 1995).

Academic Achievement

The academic achievement levels of students who are deaf are substantially lower than those of their peers without disabilities (Moores, 1996). By age 20, half of the students tested read below the mid–fourth grade level. Keep in mind that most newspapers are written at least at the fifth grade level. Allen (1986) compared the reading and mathematics achievement test scores of two comparable groups of deaf students—one in 1974 and one in 1983—with those of hearing students who were tested in 1982. The Gallaudet Research Institute (1994) studied the 1991 reading achievement scores of deaf students, and we did a similar analysis for mathematical computation abilities of students in Gallaudet's large, national sample. We were able to obtain the national norms for hearing students who took the test in 1991. Although hearing students show substantially higher academic achievement scores, the results indicate steady improvement in deaf students' reading and mathematics performance over time. These data are shown on two graphs in Figure 10.6: one for reading and one for mathematics. The graph for reading scores shows that the performance of deaf students in reading is substantially below their mathematical abilities. These graphs tell us that substantial improvement in deaf children's reading performance has been achieved since the first studies were conducted some twenty years ago. Still, more emphasis needs to be placed on reading for these students, particularly since reading is an important

~~~

FIGURE 10.6

Median Math and Comprehension Scores for Three Groups of Deaf and Hard of Hearing Students: 1974, 1983, and 1991 and Two Groups of Hearing Students: 1982 and 1991

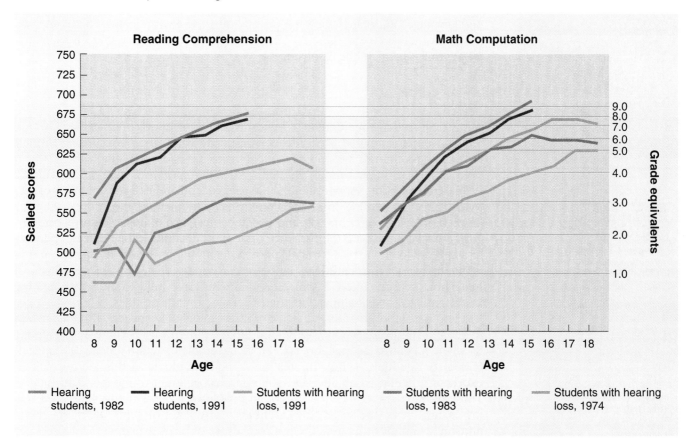

Sources: Patterns of academic achievement among hearing impaired students: 1974–1983, by T. E. Allen in *Deaf children in America*, pp. 164–165, by A. N. Schildroth and M. A. Karchmer (Eds.), 1986, Austin, TX, Pro-Ed, Inc., Gallaudet Research Institute, 1994. Reprinted by permission.

MAKING CONNECTIONS

For more about technology that assists deaf and hard of hearing people, see the Technology section of this chapter.

means of acquiring information. Many technological advances developed to benefit people with hearing loss, such as captioned television and films, require an ability to read well, for instance. These technological improvements might provide the motivation to learn to read.

Professionals identify two major educational goals for deaf children (Moores, 1996): (1) to reduce the achievement gap between students without disabilities and deaf students and (2) to develop the speech and language skills to these individuals' potential. These goals are often in competition with each other. For example, programs for deaf children spend a good deal of time developing speech and language. As a result, considerably less time is spent on academic subjects, which contributes to the lower achievement scores noted for these youngsters. Educators of the deaf need to discuss these issues openly and devote as much classtime as possible to academic instruction. Some educators have found that carefully designed group activities, for example, the Puzzle Technique described in the Teaching Tactics box, can help youngsters focus their learning, practice concepts being mastered, and incorporate peer tutoring into one activity. There are many issues for educators to discuss and solve. For example, should the school day be lengthened or the schoolyear extended to devote sufficient time to all aspects of the curriculum? Should academic subjects be given a higher priority and should more time be devoted to these topics, thereby reducing the time spent on speech and language? Because there is a high relationship between instructional time and academic achievement (Good & Brophy, 1986; Rieth, Polsgrove, & Semmel, 1979), this issue must be resolved.

Speech Ability

Many deaf students are unable to hear the communications of others well, which relates to their impaired ability to communicate with others. According to their teachers, less than 45 percent of students who are deaf have intelligible speech, even though it might sound "different" from the speech of hearing individuals (Wolk & Schildroth, 1986). Intelligibility of speech is related to a number of factors: degree of hearing loss, the communication method the individual uses (speech only, sign only, speech and sign together), age of onset, cultural and linguistic background, and the presence of another disability. The degree of hearing loss appears to be the most crucial factor in determining whether a person's speech is intelligible. Of those students who are profoundly deaf, only 25 percent have intelligible speech (Allen, 1988). Students who have mild to moderate hearing losses typically speak almost like their peers without disabilities.

Another important factor that determines intelligible speech is the age when the hearing loss occurs. One study found that children who became deaf after age 8, when language acquisition is relatively complete, retain intelligible speech (Goehl & Kaufman, 1984). Interestingly, the individuals in this study retained excellent articulation abilities but still sounded different to independent judges. These researchers suggest that although people with moderate to severe hearing losses can speak intelligibly, they still have patterns of rhythm, rate of speaking, and voice qualities that are different from those of hearing people.

Learning to speak is a difficult and arduous task for children who are deaf, requiring years of effort and systematic instruction. Only a handful of oral-only programs exist in the United States and Canada, and at these schools no signing

The Puzzle Technique

Learning how to write is a very important skill that all students, including those with hearing losses, need to become proficient at executing. By spending more time directly instructing students how to write more efficiently and accurately, teachers help students acquire these skills. The puzzle technique is well suited to group writing and language arts instruction.

Marcia Bassett teaches language arts at Jefferson Middle School. She has been worried about the writing skills of her seventh graders. Other teachers have told her that homework, in-class essays, and various assignments that require writing are unsatisfactory from this group of students. Ms. Bassett has twenty-eight students in this section with varying writing abilities. Some students have moderately acceptable writing skills; others have marginal skills, at best. Mark, a member of the class who has a moderate hearing loss, needs special help in this area.

To tackle the problems, Ms. Bassett has devised a special teaching unit that she calls "Solve the Puzzle." First, she clusters her students into seven groups of four students each. Then she assigns to each group at least one student who is more capable in writing. She assigned Mark to the group that includes the class' best writer.

To prepare for the unit, Ms. Bassett wrote a number of short essays on different topics from the students' other courses: ecology, American explorers, food chains, land purchases from Spain, and social issues like apartheid. She then rewrote each essay, deliberately incorporating a substantial number of errors in spelling, punctuation, grammar, and capitalization. She duplicated copies of each essay for each class member plus seven extras. These essays will serve as the materials the students use in their group activities.

Ms. Bassett begins each class session of this teaching unit by reminding the students of the importance of spelling, punctuation, grammar, and capitalization. She gives examples of each of these aspects of writing by showing the class errors they made in the previous day's class. The entire class works on the same essay during this period. In groups of four, they work to "solve the puzzle" of finding all the errors in one of the essays Ms. Bassett has prepared. Each student in a group has a different assignment: One student corrects all the spelling errors, another looks for all the punctuation errors, another the grammatical errors, and another the capitalization errors. After the four students have found errors of the types they were assigned, one student in the group then makes all the corrections on a clean copy of the essay. As each student reports the errors that he or she found, the others verify the corrections and look to see if others were missed.

Each day, the error-hunting assignments rotate. In this way, each student has a chance to look for different types of errors on different days.

Ms. Bassett finds that the students' writing abilities improve greatly over the course of several weeks; they all profit by helping one another proofread written material. Mark's progress has been remarkable: He has learned how to proofread written assignments and to find all four types of writing errors. Perhaps more importantly, he has developed a nice relationship with the other students in his small group. Ms. Bassett has also observed comparable, supporting relationships develop among other students in other groups. This teaching tactic has had two results: The students' writing skills have improved, and their interpersonal relationships have developed and increased.

is allowed. Since the advent of cochlear implants on children in the last few years, programs have been developed to serve these youngsters. Teachers in these programs select and sequence speech targets based on normal language development, and they incorporate considerable drill and practice. Equally important, parents must be committed and able to follow through with the instructional program at home.

Remember, hard of hearing children develop a fine ability to use speech as their means of communication. As you have just learned, however, the development of speech for those who are deaf is a great challenge; for many, it is an impossible task. And, even for those who are capable of developing speech, it requires intensive instruction and effort.

The preceding discussion concerns deaf students. Those who have mild to moderate hearing losses are able to communicate more readily with the use of a hearing aid. Hearing aids, commonly available in America for almost forty years, also help students who are hard of hearing function in general education classes. Most, however, need supportive services from SLPs as well. With extra assistance from special educators, these students can learn in general education classes and achieve as well as most of their nondisabled classmates.

Educational Interventions

Like all children with disabilities, deaf and hard of hearing children need to receive an intensive educational experience as early as possible. Professionals in this field may debate about where education should be delivered or about how much speech and language development should be stressed in the curriculum. Nevertheless, they all agree on two points: Education should begin at birth or at the time the hearing loss was discovered, and the entire family needs to be involved. In this section, we discuss just what makes first-rate educational programs for deaf and hard of hearing children. We also include some suggestions for teachers and other professionals for teaching these students more effectively. Throughout these children's schoolyears, an array of professionals and services must be available and individually arranged for each of these students.

Education and the Preschool Child

Preschool programs are especially important for children with severe to profound hearing losses. Equally important are programs for the families of these children. Parents need to know how to help their child acquire language and communication skills and develop a positive self-concept. They are primarily responsible for the child's integration into the family, neighborhood, school, and community. Finally, the family needs to learn how this disability affects the individual members of the family. The training families require best comes from the professionals at an infant or preschool program, who can help parents cope with a range of issues.

It is apparently clear: Children need to develop language at the right developmental period. Evidence connecting language and cognitive development specifically regarding deaf children is mounting. The outcome is that deaf children's academic achievement is far below their hearing peers. However, deaf children of deaf parents who learned sign language during their infancy read two grade levels above deaf children of hearing parents (Marschark, 1993). This difference occurs

MAKING CONNECTIONS

For more about hearing aids, see the Technology section in this chapter.

MAKING CONNECTIONS

For a review of the array of professionals who work with special education students, see the Special Educational Services of Chapter 2.

MAKING CONNECTIONS

Reread these sections for a review of the connections between language and cognitive development: Educational Interventions in Chapters 4 and 5.

because these children of deaf parents learned language during the proper developmental period, while most deaf children of hearing parents are not identified until age 3—an age when language development should be well underway (McIntire, 1994). Deaf children who learn sign language during infancy and the early childhood years seem to interact with others socially and behave linguistically much like their age-mates (Williams, 1994). However, deaf children who are born of deaf parents are a very small proportion of the total population. The vast majority are born of hearing parents who do not know any form of sign language.

Many hearing families, once their child's deafness is identified, choose to learn and use some combination of oral language and a manual communication system so that they can communicate more fully with their child. Some professionals (Soloman, 1994) propose that infants and their families be taught ASL, the manual language widely used in the Deaf community. They also suggest that individuals who live in the Deaf community and are proficient in ASL help these children to acquire ASL as their "native" language. Other experts suggest that parents of deaf infants and preschoolers use both manual and oral communication methods (total communication) to provide multichannel information as they interact with their children (Lowenbraun, 1995). Specialists also recommend this procedure for all family members (grandparents, brothers, sisters) and family friends, but learning a new system for communicating can be difficult and time consuming. Because the identification of deaf children not born of deaf parents can be as late as age 3, there is no time to waste. It is vital that effective communication between the family and the deaf children begin as early as possible, and it is here that early intervention specialists can be of great assistance.

Education and the Schoolchild

The educational needs of students who are hard of hearing differ from those of deaf students. There are differences in the way they are taught, in what they are taught, and, for some of these students, in where they are taught. In this section, we discuss some of those differences along with specific educational options for both deaf and hard of hearing students. In addition, we discuss some important issues related to working with educational interpreters.

Instructional Considerations for Hard of Hearing Students. Since the advent of PL 94-142 in 1975, more and more deaf and hard of hearing students have been educated in general education classes with generally positive results, particularly for hard of hearing students (Johnson & Cohen, 1994). Remember that most students with hearing loss can hear satisfactorily with amplification (that is, a hearing aid) and therefore can attend school and function well with their nondisabled classmates. In most schools, information is presented orally, and students learn through a combination of textbooks, lectures, and class discussions. Hard of hearing children can cope quite well with these methods as long as an array of supplemental services are available.

Along with acquiring educational benefits, many students learn important social skills in general classroom settings. Educators believe that when children with disabilities participate in classes with their nondisabled peers, they are more fully accepted socially, and all the children learn to interact positively. Unfortunately, some data indicate that these social interactions do not always occur naturally (Rasing & Duker, 1992). Many of these youngsters need to learn how to wait for their turn, initiate interactions, reinforce others, help others, and engage in shared conversations. Such skills can be taught and developed, though. To do so, teachers need to encourage, support, and create opportunities for interactions to occur.

With certain modifications to the environment, deaf and hard of hearing students benefit from general education class placements. A number of simple techniques and procedures can help students profit in oral communication situations; some of these methods are listed in the Making Accommodations box. Another modification to the classroom routine uses handouts listing important points from lectures, films, or movies. Also, a classmate can be asked to help by using carbon paper to make an extra set of lecture notes.

Teachers should seek the help of specialists and others who can provide guidance so that the learning environment is most efficient for all students in the class. For example, classroom teachers have found that the SLP assigned to their school can offer many good ideas about activities that foster better speech and language. The specialist can also provide suggestions about classroom organizers that will assist these students gain more from traditional classroom settings. Parents are another important source of information. The child's parents can help teachers come to a quicker understanding of their child's preferred learning styles and special need. For instance, one child might profit from having a classmate serve as a resource to ensure that homework and other assignments are correctly understood. Another child might prefer to tape lectures and listen to them carefully in a quiet setting at home in the evening. Yet another student might benefit by being able to do extra outside reading on specific topics. Teachers need to remember that each child is unique and to capitalize on each child's strengths, not just attend to that student's disabilities.

Instructional Methods for Deaf Students. Best educational practices for deaf students are still developing. As you noticed on the two achievement graphs in Figure 10.6, deaf students' academic achievement is improving, but more progress must be made. You have also learned that tension exists within the deaf education curriculum: whether to emphasize language development or academic performance. However, the communication mode of the learner and the one chosen for instruction directly relates to how instruction is delivered and what is taught. Let's look at the different methods used for deaf children:

- In the speech or **oral-only approach**, children are taught to use as much of their residual hearing as possible. This method was the most popular until the 1970s, but a few programs still use it. Using amplification, children learn how to speech-read (lip-read) and how to speak. The oral approach does not allow children to use any form of manual communication such as finger spelling or signing. In fact, even natural signing, such as using gestures, is discouraged. Those who follow the oral approach believe that individuals who are deaf must live and work in a world where most people hear normally and communicate through oral expression. They therefore believe that individuals who are deaf should learn to communicate as the majority do so that they can become part of mainstream society.

- The **total communication approach** incorporates aspects of oral speech *and* **manual communication** (signing). Total communication allows the child to communicate through whatever mode is easiest and most effective.

oral-only approach. One method of instruction advocated for students who are deaf, whereby they learn to communicate (both receiving and sending information) orally, not using sign language.

total communication approach. A system of instruction for deaf students that employs any and all methods of communication (oral speech, manual communication, ASL, gestures) that is easy, efficient, and preferred by the student for communication.

manual communication. Using the hands, not the voice, as the means of communication, as in sign language or finger spelling.

1. Place the child as close to the speaker as possible.

2. Make certain the child's hearing aid is turned on and functioning properly by listening through it.

3. Reduce the background noise as much as possible.

4. Articulate clearly, but do not talk louder unless you have an unusually soft voice.

5. Make certain to have the student's attention before talking or starting a lesson.

6. Do not exaggerate your lip movements.

7. Do not chew gum or cover your mouth when talking.

8. Do not turn your back on the class.

9. Use an overhead projector instead of a blackboard, so that the student can see your mouth.

10. Avoid moving around the classroom while talking.

11. Speak slowly.

12. Repeat and restate information by paraphrasing.

13. Spend time talking to the child alone so that you become accustomed to each other's speech.

14. Avoid glare when talking or signing by not standing near a light source such as a window.

15. Do not bounce or move around while talking.

16. Bend down so that you are at students' eye level when you talk to individuals or small groups.

17. Consult with a certified teacher of the deaf.

The philosophy behind this approach is that every child should be able to use whatever channels are available to learn and comprehend messages. About 72 percent of deaf students are now taught using this method (Moores, 1996).

- **Cued speech**, used only in a few schools today, uses hand signals to accompany oral speech (Dolnick, 1993). These hand signals help deaf people read lips to determine, for example, whether the word said was *pan* or *bat*, which look alike to the person reading lips. It is popular with hearing parents because it is easy to learn and follows the English language format and structure (which ASL does not).

- The **bilingual-bicultural approach** is still developing. Here, students are taught using ASL and, once the language is mastered, learn to read and write English as a second language (Paul & Quigley, 1994). Data from the new approach seems to indicate that the achievement levels for at least some Deaf youngsters are close to their hearing peers (Mahshie, 1995).

Why has the popularity of the oral approach diminished? Although some children in these programs develop excellent speech and can be educated in traditional settings, most do not. The development of oral speech is nearly impossible for most prelingually deaf. Even for those who do attain intelligible speech, the process is arduous, slow, and difficult. The oral approach, however, is used with almost all students who are hard of hearing.

 MAKING CONNECTIONS

For a review of bilingual special education approaches, see these sections in Chapter 3:
- Multicultural and Bilingual Special Education Defined
- History of the Field
- Educational Interventions

cued speech. Hand signals for difficult to see speech sounds that accompany oral speech to assist in lip-reading.

bilingual-bicultural approach. The application of ESL and bilingual techniques to deaf education where ASL is the native language and reading and writing in English are taught as a second language.

MAKING CONNECTIONS

For reminders about ASL and the Deaf community, see these sections of this chapter:
• History
• Deaf Culture in the Deaf and Hard of Hearing Children section
• Overcoming Barriers in the Educational Interventions section

Several kinds of manual communication are used in this country. ASL, which is a structured and formal language with its own linguistic rules and patterns, is used in the Deaf community. Because of advances in technology, a two-way dictionary is now available to individuals learning ASL or refining their skills. Sherman Wilcox has developed the *Multimedia Dictionary of American Sign,* a CD-ROM program that provides full-motion digitized video so the viewer can actually watch the ASL signs in motion (Maurer, 1995). Because ASL is not a written language, CD-ROM provides a perfect format for this dictionary, by allowing the user to search for a sign by using English words or by "describing" an unknown sign to the computer (Stiger, 1996). The need for this resource is great among members of the Deaf community, their families, and friends partly because of the recent acceptance of ASL as a language. Unfortunately, the acceptance of ASL is not complete.

Most elementary and secondary teachers of the deaf do not use ASL. Only 3 percent of teachers for the deaf use ASL in their school classes (Woodward, Allen, & Schildroth, 1985). In integrated public school classes in general education, about 60 percent of the hard of hearing or deaf students receive their education delivered orally (Johnson & Cohen, 1994). Another type of manual communication more closely matching the grammatical form and structure of standard English is available. **Finger spelling**, a form of manual communication, assigns each letter of the alphabet a sign. This system is efficient and has been used for centuries; an accomplished person can finger-spell at a rate equivalent to typical speech. Finger spelling represents English. Words are spelled out, but the rules of grammar and language are the same as for English speech.

Teaming with Educational Interpreters. One essential service needed by many deaf students enrolled in general education programs is delivered by **educational interpreters**. These professionals convert spoken messages to the student's preferred communication system, which may be a signed system like ASL or signed English. For many teachers, working with the assistance of an interpreter is a novel experience, one that might occur only once in their teaching career. For the

finger spelling. A form of manual communication that assigns to each letter of the alphabet a sign.

educational interpreters. Related service providers who translate or convert spoken messages to the deaf person's preferred mode of manual communication.

Interpreters and classroom teachers work side-by-side in integrated educational settings.

teacher inexperienced in working with students who use sign language, there is much to learn, plan for, and coordinate. The smooth inclusion of this related service provider as part of the educational team can require considerable communication and teamwork.

The teacher and the interpreter need to coordinate efforts to ensure they understand each other's roles. As responsibilities and duties are defined, it should be clear that the teacher has the primary responsibility and the interpreter serves in supporting roles (Salend & Longo, 1994). In other words, the teacher should deliver instruction and remediation (when necessary), and the interpreter should be present to facilitate communication. Because the interpreter may not be an expert in the content of the curriculum, the teacher should give the interpreter copies of lesson plans, lists of key terms, and textbooks to ensure clear and accurate translation of the teacher's lectures and instructions. The teacher and interpreter must also work together on a number of issues, many of which are minor but quite important. For example, the interpreter should sit in a glare-free, well-lit, solid-colored background location that does not block the blackboard or view of the teacher. Some other guidelines for inclusion of interpreters into classroom settings are found in Table 10.4. Possibly, the most difficult part of building a team involving the teacher, the school community, the deaf student, and the interpreter is using some good common sense and finding the time for sufficient and ongoing communications.

Inclusion

At the national level, a full array of educational services and placements are available for deaf and hard of hearing elementary and secondary students. These educational programs typically include the services of audiologists, SLPs, interpreters, teachers of the deaf, and, if required, OTs and PTs. Nationally, placement options include general education classrooms, resource rooms, special classes, special day schools, and residential center schools. When thinking about school placements for these students, remember that the needs of hard of hearing students differ from the

 MAKING CONNECTIONS

For a review of the array of related service providers who comprise special education, see Special Educational Services in Chapter 2.

TABLE 10.4

Roles and Responsibilities of Educational Interpreters, Teachers, and Deaf Students

The Interpreter	*The Teacher*	*The Deaf Student*
Holds long conversations with the student after class	Introduces the interpreter to the class	Makes certain the interpreter uses preferred mode of communication
Asks for clarification when the teacher speaks too fast or was not heard	Talks to the student, not to the interpreter	Notifies the interpreter when there is going to be a change in schedules or when that person will not be needed
Considers teaching hearing students some basic signs	Adjusts pace of speech to allow for the translation	Is clear about whether the interpreter should speak for the student
Only interprets; does not tutor or provide assistance with assignments	Arranges for peers to take notes for their deaf peer	Determines desired role with peers
Maintains confidentiality of personal and private information	Seeks assistance of interpreter when working with others (e.g., SLPs)	Meets with the interpreter on a regular basis to provide feedback, resolve problems, and evaluate progress

needs of most deaf students. And, most importantly, the decision must be based on the requirements of individual students and their families.

In the 1994–1995 schoolyear, over half of all deaf and hard of hearing students served by special education attended either a general education or resource room program (U.S. Department of Education, 1996). Although these students' use of segregated facilities, at 19 percent, is the second highest among disability groups (only the use by students who are deaf/blind is higher), these numbers and percentages have been decreasing across time (Johnson & Cohen, 1994). For example, in 1975–1976, 42 percent of all deaf and hard of hearing students attended residential schools, but in 1993–1994 only 14 percent did. These data include both deaf and hard of hearing students, but what about just the deaf? Residential schools are used most often by students who have severe and profound hearing losses, and those integrated into classes with hearing students have mild losses (Schildroth & Hotto, 1994). Of those enrolled in residential schools, 89 percent are deaf while less than 5 percent have either moderate or mild hearing losses. Attendance at all-deaf schools is on the decrease. Research conducted by Gallaudet University makes this fact clear. Between 1985 and 1995, the enrollment at 57 all-deaf schools decreased from 18,105 to 15,234, while integrated high school placements increased from 10,134 to 14,374 (Cardenas, 1996).

In recent years, educators, parents, and the Deaf community have engaged in many serious discussions about the "best" educational placement options for deaf students. Most tend to agree that hard of hearing students should attend general education classes with as much supports as they need. What is at issue? At the same time that advocacy groups for people with mental retardation fought to close or reduce the number and size of institutions, the Deaf community fought to keep residential center schools for Deaf students open and fully funded. Issues about the best placement for each deaf child are complex, and parents are faced with difficult decisions. Remember that deafness in children is a low-incidence disability area; in the general school-age population, there are few children with this disability. In 1993, there were 1,006 schools or program sites with only one deaf or hard of hearing student (Schildroth & Hotto, 1994). Without a critical mass of these youngsters, they are often left with feelings of isolation and rejection where few others use or understand their method of communication. This situation leads the Deaf community, some educators, and many parents to conclude that "inclusion far too often becomes exclusion for our children" (Harvey, 1993, p. 1).

IDEA requires all students with disabilities to receive a free appropriate education (FAPE) in the least restrictive environment (LRE). What is the least restrictive environment for deaf children? The law states that what comprises an appropriate education and what environment is the least restrictive must be individually determined. Many parents and members of the Deaf community believe that the general education classroom is *not* the least restrictive setting for deaf children (Lane, 1995). "Deaf children deserve to be in an environment where they can communicate with peers, teachers, and staff; to be in an environment that meets their academic, social, emotional and cultural needs; and to be in an environment where they are truly included in every aspect of school" (Hawkins, 1993, p. 7). For students who rely on sign language as their primary means of communication, the general school environment where administrators, teachers, and classmates are not fluent in sign language can result in considerable isolation. It is important to recognize that 60 percent of general education classes where deaf students attend use an auditory/oral-only approach (Schildroth & Hotto, 1994).

MAKING CONNECTIONS

For a review of FAPE and LRE, see Special Educational Services in Chapter 2.

Research supports parent concerns about general education placements for deaf students (Lee & Antia, 1992). For instance, these students who attend general education classes are not included in nonacademic activities by their hearing classmates; the major reason for exclusion is difficulty with communication. Innovative experiments with integration, however, are showing promise. Isolation does not have to be the outcome of general education placements. For example, at the Granada Hills/CSUN Science and Math Technology Magnet School in California, deaf and hearing students are taught by deaf and hearing teachers a rigorous curriculum that will prepare them for science majors in college. The results are excellent academic achievement and increased interactions across the two groups of students (Cardenas, 1996).

Another problem is that these youngsters receive inconsistent services in general classroom settings (Lowenbraun, 1992). For example, in one large urban high school, interpreter services were cut from the budget, so that students with severe hearing losses had no one who could communicate with them. In another high school, eighteen deaf students shared six interpreters, leaving them and their general education teachers without continual and consistent assistance.

Determining LRE for students with disabilities can be difficult, particularly for deaf students. A team of professionals and the student's parents come together to create a team that solves this problem. How does the team decide which is the most appropriate service for a deaf student? The team makes the decision on the basis of answers to the following questions:

MAKING CONNECTIONS

- For a review of inclusion and other disability areas, see the Inclusion sections in every chapter.
- For a review of IEPs, see that section in Chapter 2.

- How severe is the student's hearing loss?
- Is the student able to use speech?
- Can appropriate educational services be made available locally?
- Are the necessary support services available?

Clearly, many factors must be considered when professionals make decisions about a child's educational placement program and develop an IEP (Cohen, 1994; Schildroth & Hotto, 1994). Some of the factors concerning placement are given in Table 10.5. Meeting these goals requires that a full array of educational services and placements be available.

Transition Through Adulthood

The purpose of school-to-work transition programs for students who are deaf or hard of hearing is to improve the adult outcomes for these individuals. Of crucial importance are obtaining equitable employment, being able to obtain and hold a job commensurate with the person's abilities, earning a fair wage, and being satisfied with the job. Deaf and hard of hearing people must also be able to participate in their community and in society. We consider these issues of transition in the following subsections.

Employment Outcomes. Establishing an employment history is an important factor in starting a successful career for all young people. Researchers agree that holding summer and after-school jobs while in high school is particularly important for students who are deaf (Allen, Rawlings, & Schildroth, 1989). Unfortunately, 41 percent of these students have no work experience while in high school. Nearly all of those (97 percent) who did not hold jobs cited school

TABLE 10.5

Placement and IEP Considerations

	Type of Hearing Loss	
	Hard of Hearing	*Deaf*
Severity of loss	Youngsters with mild to moderate hearing loss can remain in the general education curriculum with consultative or supportive services from various experts such as SLPs and audiologists.	Students with severe to profound hearing loss require intensive instruction in communication skills and need assistance from an array of related services.
Potential for using residual hearing	Most of these students profit from hearing aids, thereby allowing them to benefit, with some adaptations, from typical oral methods of instruction.	Most deaf students have little useful residual hearing and require considerable accommodations to benefit from oral instructions.
Academic achievement	The academic achievement levels of deaf and hard of hearing students tend to be lower than levels of their hearing peers. Students with less hearing loss and no multiple disabilities are usually close to grade level but might need some additional academic instruction.	The academic achievement levels of deaf students are considerably below their hearing peers'. These students need considerable instruction in basic language and communication skills, as well as intensive academic remediation.
Communicative needs	Many of these students go undetected for a long time. If the loss occurred before or while the youngsters were developing language, it is likely that they will require SLP services as well as academic assistance.	Total communication is the most commonly used approach with deaf youngsters, but the help of educational assistants is necessary, and in many rural regions this expertise is not available.
Preferred mode of communication	Most of these students should be expected to become proficient using oral language.	Most postlingually deaf students learn (or retain) their use of oral language. Intelligible speech and lip-reading are typically unattainable goals for most prelingually deaf children, so for them manual communication is preferred.
Placement preference	The vast majority of these students attend their neighborhood schools with their hearing peers.	Many deaf students also attend their neighborhood schools. However, a significant number of them prefer center schools where their classmates share their deafness and their mode of communication.

responsibilities as the reason they did not seek employment. Possibly, the high school curriculum should be adjusted to include some work experience for these students.

Like you, many deaf people wonder whether college experience and graduation is worth the effort and expense. The answer is a resounding yes. Although still somewhat underemployed and underpaid, Deaf graduates of Gallaudet University could, in general, be considered relatively well educated and affluent (Rawlings, King, Skilton, & Rose, 1993). The median annual income of those who attended Gallaudet but did not graduate was $26,000 per year, $31,000 for those with bachelor's degrees, and $34,000 for those with graduate degrees. Males in these categories earned substantially more than the average ($44,000 for graduate degree holders). While 17 percent of U.S. families had incomes in excess of $100,000, 17 percent of Gallaudet graduates have incomes in excess of $75,000.

Postsecondary Options. Higher education makes a great difference in the lives of people, particularly those who are deaf or hard or hearing. For these students to benefit from higher education, special programs must be available, the students themselves must be ready to participate in these programs, and they must take advantage of these programs. We'll look first at some experiences that prepare these students for postsecondary education. Then we'll look at postsecondary education options and how they are accessed by deaf students.

Explore Your Future is a program that helps high school students who are deaf learn about colleges and how to select a curriculum that best fits their needs and interests (*Counterpoint,* 1992). Another option, available from the National Technical Institute for the Deaf in Rochester, New York, offers a one-week summer program for 120 high school students to explore careers in business, science, engineering, computer science, and visual communication. The students live on campus and can participate in social and academic activities. They learn about Deaf culture and about the wide array of college programs available to them, which helps them select the right college. This short experience in college life helps these students begin the transition adjustment and lessens their fears about moving from home and having to become more independent at a college or university.

MAKING CONNECTIONS

For other examples of precollegiate experiences for students with disabilities, see the Transition Through Adulthood sections of Chapters 4, 7, and 8.

Many deaf students use sign language as their primary means of communication; others use oral communication. Those who use spoken language and who are also prepared for college must have sufficient receptive language to understand college lectures. One study shows that not all do (Flexer, Wray, Millin, & Leavitt, 1993). One-fourth of deaf students had vocabularies as good as their hearing classmates', but three-fourths did not. No relationship was found between the amount of hearing loss and vocabulary skills. What did make a difference was the effort spent on vocabulary development in high school programs. Unfortunately, many high school teachers do not address this skill, believing that vocabulary is developed during the elementary schoolyears. For students who are deaf, more attention needs to be paid to vocabulary development.

The federal government supports various types of postsecondary schools with programs for deaf and hard of hearing students. Gallaudet University serves both undergraduate and graduate students and receives federal funding. The National Technical Institute for the Deaf (NTID) at the Rochester Institute of Technology in New York began offering technical and vocational degrees in 1968. Gallaudet and NTID serve a total of about 2,900 students. Four regional, federally funded postsecondary schools—Seattle Community College, California State University–Northridge, St. Paul Technical College, and the University of Tennessee Consortium—serve a total of 534 students.

State and privately funded universities and colleges also offer special programs for deaf and hard of hearing students. The *College Guide for Deaf Students* (Rawlings, Karchmer, DeCaro, & Allen, 1995) lists about 150 postsecondary accredited programs designed specifically for deaf students. These programs serve almost 7,000 students with hearing loss, and all have support services, including a coordinator. In 1964, there were only 6 college programs (excluding those that were federally funded) for these students (Rawlings & King, 1986). Over a three-year period from 1982 to 1985, 37 colleges added programs for students who are deaf (Rawlings, Karchmer, & DeCaro, 1987). By 1995, 200 college programs were serving over 8,000 students (Cardenas, 1996).

Not all students who are deaf complete higher education. Schroedel and Watson (1991) found that 20 percent drop out, and the dropout rate seems to be higher at schools that do not have a broad array of support services for these students. For example, less than half of the programs for students who are deaf provided counseling assistance, tutoring, or remedial help. Culturally or linguistically diverse youth who are deaf are at particular risk. They are less likely to seek postsecondary education, and those who do are more likely to enter technical-vocational rather than four-year college programs.

What makes a postsecondary program successful? Programs with the highest graduation rates have many features specifically designed for deaf students (Schroedel & Watson, 1991). They have a large support staff, including note takers and interpreters, who facilitate the academic integration of the students. At the federally funded programs, many professors are proficient in American Sign Language and use it in their lectures; at these schools, counselors also communicate through ASL. However, the majority of programs across the nation are offered at schools that do not serve a predominant enrollment of deaf students. The typical program is small, serving about forty-two full-time and part-time students; most have a coordinator and five full-time faculty members devoted to the students who are deaf. Smaller programs, even those at large universities, are often organized within a unit supporting all students with disabilities. Successful smaller programs do provide counselors, note takers, tutors, and interpreters who work with the students after class to be sure that they have understood the content of the class lecture. These programs also have active career placement advisers.

Overcoming Barriers. Although many signs indicate that the situation is improving, some experience significant barriers in their adult lives. As with most other groups of people with disabilities, deaf adults often do not hold jobs commensurate with their education, skills, and experience (Jacobs, 1989). Many find themselves in a situation similar to that of Stephen Bielik, a computer expert who has difficulty holding a job. He believes that his deafness makes some supervisors uncomfortable. When this happens, people with disabilities often get laid off, and finding a comparable job is not easy (Forbath, 1990).

Many Deaf adults and the professionals who work with them believe that people who are deaf face considerable discrimination, and that hearing people's negative attitudes are the real handicap associated with deafness (Matlin, 1995). Discrimination and bias can affect individuals' livelihood. Federal laws such as the Americans with Disabilities Act of 1990 attempt to eliminate bias and encourage better access to mainstream society. And attitudes are changing. Total communication is being used in homes of children who are deaf but whose parents are not. We now see interpreters at most public meetings. There have been television shows created by persons who are deaf for an audience of persons who

MAKING CONNECTIONS

For specific information about meeting the needs of culturally and linguistically diverse students with disabilities, see
• Focus on Diversity boxes,
• Concepts and Controversies in Chapters 5 and 7,
• Chapter 3.

are deaf (for example, "Deaf Mosaic"), and the Theater of the Deaf increases in popularity each year. For over twenty years, the Miss Deaf America has been an integral part of the Deaf community (Quintanilla, 1994). Only deaf women are eligible to enter this popular contest, and the winner's primary responsibility is to promote public awareness of issues important to the Deaf community. The Deaf community saw a milestone in 1994 when Heather Whitestone became the first deaf woman to win the Miss America pageant (Manning & Briggs, 1994). Betsy Bahtel, a deaf social worker, expressed for many Deaf people the importance of Ms. Whitestone's accomplishment: "It's always a great joy to see a deaf person move on and be treated like others" (p. D1). These are all positive signs, but more changes need to be made.

The Deaf community itself is working on effecting changes so that others do not have to face discrimination and bias. Deaf adults have learned that they can fight for their rights, and they have found power in working together in various advocacy groups to protect their rights as individuals and citizens (Rose & Kiger, 1995). They are calling for more involvement of deaf adults on school boards and boards of trustees, particularly at schools for the deaf. They also want to be included as parent trainers, teachers, and members of IEP committies. And they are making headway. For example, in 1960, not one superintendent at a school for the deaf was deaf. In 1990, nine of the sixty-five superintendents were people who are deaf, and all of them had been hired since 1985; and today, half of all of these superintendents are deaf (Moores, 1996; Sulzberger, 1990).

Recall the widely publicized example of the new power and cohesiveness of deaf adults, the protest at Gallaudet University in 1988 that drew international attention. The student body protested against the selection of a hearing president who did not know sign language. The students wanted I. King Jordan, who is deaf, installed as president, and through their protest, he was. Their actions also brought about the recall of several members of the college's board of trustees. Since the protest, I. King Jordan has become more than a university president; he is a hero and a role model for other deaf people. According to Jack Gannon, a noted scholar and an administrator at Gallaudet, "When he walks into a room to speak, he usually gets a standing ovation. He's the living symbol of the revolution" (Ayres, 1990). The advocacy movement within the Deaf community is still as strong as it was in the days of the protest, and great gains have been made.

There are still many barriers to be overcome, however. For example, Kevin DeFrancisco knows that the public does not yet recognize deafness when they should, and he has the scars to prove it (Associated Press, 1994). In a misunderstanding about the proper fare, a bus driver thought DeFrancisco was threatening her. The result was 50 stitches and a scar much more than skin deep. Others have experienced difficulties because of their deafness as well. Kenny Walker, who is deaf, was an outstanding football player for the University of Nebraska and, in his senior year, was Big Eight defensive player of the year. Still, he was not picked in the early rounds of the 1991 NFL draft (Wojciechowski, 1991); the Denver Broncos finally chose him on the 228th pick. Other people who are deaf may be completely denied their chance. Both Julie Rems and Lynn Lochrie, contestants in two separate California beauty pageants, were refused sign language interpreters because of a policy forbidding contestants to be assisted by anyone (Shaw, 1991).

Families

All children have a great number of skills and amount of knowledge to learn, but this is particularly true of a deaf child who is a member of a hearing family. The hearing members of this child's family must also gain a tremendous amount of knowledge about language, communication systems, and deafness. The addition of a family member can add stress to the household, particularly if it is a child who is an atypical learner.

Language Development

As we have stressed throughout this chapter and this text, children need to develop language as close to the proper developmental periods as possible. Faulty or incomplete language development can lead to cognitive and learning problems that become apparent during the schoolyears and also later in life. As with all other children, language development for the deaf is crucial, but these children are at greater risk for more problems in this area. The family's role in their child's language development is vital, often beginning with their choice of communication method for use during the early childhood period. As you know, families have a number of choices: oral-only, total communication, cued speech, or manual communication.

The choice should be made on an individual basis considering the needs of the child and the family. Professionals from the state's residential school, a statewide outreach center, local preschools for the deaf, and the public schools can assist families in selecting the best method for the individual child and help family members learn the special techniques they need to use. There are many examples of such programs, but one of the best known is available from the Kendall School, part of Gallaudet University in Washington, D.C., which provides a model program for infants. This home-based program stresses total communication, using manual communication simultaneously with oral speech. In this approach it is important that family members learn sign language or manual communication as early as possible in the child's life.

Including manual communication in deaf children's early language development experiences capitalizes on their typical developmental process. Research shows that deaf babies babble with their hands, and their manual babbling has many similarities with hearing babies' vocalizations (Angier, 1991; Gallaudet Research Institute, 1991). Both groups of babies begin babbling at about the same age, 10 months old. Hearing babies repeat noises and syllables, while deaf babies repeat hand motions. The deaf babies' gestures seem to be systematic and deliberate, although they have no more intent or meaning than hearing babies' babbles do. Hearing babies' babbling becomes more and more sophisticated. Eventually, after hearing their parents' spoken words and being reinforced for their attempts at imitation, hearing children begin to say their first words at about 12 months of age. A similar process occurs with deaf babies. For those whose parents use sign language, modeling, imitation, and reinforcement play the same important roles in language acquisition as they do for hearing youngsters. Thus deaf children born to deaf parents who use sign language learn this system of communication as effortlessly as hearing children learn oral language from their parents (McIntire, 1994), but a total communication approach, begun early enough, also can capitalize on this early natural behavior.

Although language, social and emotional development, and technology are important to the overall development of deaf and hard of hearing children, possibly the most important factor in these children's lives is acceptance by their families. Some parents and other family members (grandparents, siblings, extended family members) adjust quickly to the demands presented by a child with hearing loss, but others struggle with a wide range of emotions such as grief, guilt, and anger (Proctor, n.d.). Support groups that include professionals, family, friends, and other parents of children with hearing loss provide a healthy way to deal with these emotions. Somers (1984) stated a useful objective for these parents and families: "Think of the child as a normal child who has a hearing loss, not a hearing handicap" (p. 186). Family members must also find the proper balance between nurturing, developing independence, setting limits, and disciplining the child. The result will be the development of a healthy self-concept in the child.

Family Stress

To Deaf parents, the birth of a Deaf child is a great celebration and great relief (Blade, 1994). However, the birth of a deaf child to hearing parents can be frightening, and even devastating to some. In this latter situation, extreme cases of stress often occur (*Research at Gallaudet*, 1995). Moores (1996) has developed a four-stage theory about the extreme stresses that the birth of a deaf child can generate: identification of hearing loss, entrance into formal school, beginning adolescence, early adulthood. The actual identification of deafness usually comes at the end of a long and emotionally difficult process. Often the mother has long suspected that something was wrong with the child. It is not uncommon that many doctors have been consulted and have offered conflicting diagnoses. When the final diagnosis of deafness occurs, it is frequently followed first by a period of relief, followed by concerns about lack of knowledge about deafness, the long-term outcomes for the child, financial obligations, and whether their child will ultimately select the hearing or Deaf world in which to live. Another difficult decision for many families during this early childhood period is about which communication mode to use. Will they use ASL, a language the family will have to learn? Will they use total communication, which can combine signed English with oral language? Will they use an oral-only approach? The answers to these questions will have a significant impact on both the family and the deaf child.

The second stage of stress occurs when the child enters school. The family has to choose the educational program they think will be best for their child. Choices about residential school or day schools, totally integrated programs or clustered programs, often are made over and over again across each deaf child's educational career. The third stage occurs at adolescence. Of course, this can be a time when any child, with or without a disability, adds stress to the family, but for deaf children and their families, some unique situations often occur. According to Moores, the deaf child's socialization patterns tend to differ from those of his or her hearing siblings. Also, the deaf child's speech most likely falls short of the levels the parents had hoped for. The number of hearing friends often begins to diminish, and the child seeks out other deaf youngsters whether in church or social groups. For parents who were misled about their child's possible speech and social outcome, feelings of anger and outrage emerge at the professionals who many years previously had let them hear what they wanted to instead of what they needed to about deafness and their child. This is also a time when many deaf children ask to attend the residential school for the deaf, a signal to the family that their child, although integrated throughout elementary school, may well choose a life in the Deaf community.

The fourth and last point of family stress comes when the individual leaves the immediate family to become an independent adult. Moores points out that though deaf adults tend to marry later than the national average, they do marry and most of them marry other deaf people. For hearing parents, this may signal the final break from mainstream society. For some families, this may be seen as a natural progression; for others, it may not.

Technology

A variety of electronic devices have been available to deaf people for some time. **Assistive devices** can improve communication and enhance awareness of environmental sounds. Lights and vibrators signal a crying baby, a ringing doorbell or telephone, or a fire alarm. And technology has dramatically affected the lives of persons with hearing loss, as the following story illustrates.

> Lynn, a first-year law student, wakes up when her special alarm clock shakes her bed. She turns off the alarm, climbs out of bed, goes downstairs, puts some bread in the toaster, and turns on the television and closed captioned decoder so she can read the morning news subtitles. A few minutes later, a light in the kitchen begins to flash wildly. She knows this means her visual smoke detector has gone off—burnt toast again (Compton & Kaplan, 1988, p. 19).

Such innovations have changed the way people with hearing loss live their lives, and as other uses of technology are developed, their lives will continue to change. Assistive devices are important to these individuals, as demonstrated by their increased spending for such items. In 1992, $48.3 million was spent on assistive hearing devices, and, in 1993 that amount increased to $53.4 million (Stang & Stacey, 1994). Unfortunately, finances limit access to these helpful devices for most. Although the cost of many individual technological devices has decreased over the years, the overall cost to a person with hearing loss increases as more equipment is developed. For example, a speech synthesizer costs about $150, but it requires the use of a microcomputer. A decoder for captioned television sets costs $200. A TTY costs between $220 to $850, and clocks and wake-up devices cost between $50 and $100 each. Visual alerting systems for doorbells or personal signalers cost around $40 each, and smoke detectors cost around $225. A hearing aid costs about $500, and cochlear implants cost about $25,000. The overall cost of being completely technologically assisted is difficult for many deaf adults, who tend to be underemployed because of their disability. For those who can afford them, assistive devices are most helpful. For hard of hearing and deaf people assistive devices include four categories of equipment: assistive listening devices, telecommunication devices, computerized speech-to-text translations, and alerting devices.

Assistive Listening Devices

Hearing aids and other equipment that help people make better use of their residual hearing are called **assistive listening devices (ALDs).** For those with hearing loss, the **hearing aid** is the most commonly used electronic device; it amplifies sound so that the person can hear more easily. For some individuals, hearing aids

assistive devices. Any equipment or technology that facilitates people's work, communication, mobility, or any aspect of daily life.

assistive listening devices (ALDs). Equipment such as hearing aids that helps deaf and hard of hearing individuals use their residual hearing.

hearing aid. A device that intensifies sound to help hard of hearing people process information presented orally.

Dorothy Brett is shown here with her trumpet, "Toby," which is an early version of a hearing aid.

allow them to hear well within the normal range. They have therefore enabled many individuals who are hard of hearing to attend and profit from general education classes and to participate fully in mainstream society. For example, legendary track star Jim Ryun, who held the world record for the mile run for nine years and won a silver medal at the 1968 Olympics, has had a hearing loss since childhood (Alexander Graham Bell Association for the Deaf, 1993c). After years of being told that hearing aids would not help him, he was fitted for one in 1992. Ryun reports, "I know what it has meant to me to be able to hear... A whole new world has opened up to me" (p. 1). Ryun has devoted himself to increasing public awareness about hearing losses, and volunteers with many groups of deaf and hard of hearing children (Anderson, 1995). For many hard of hearing people, however, hearing aids do not sufficiently correct their disability, and more work is necessary to improve this technology even more.

Hearing aids were designed to solve the problem of reduced hearing acuity by amplifying sounds. They are typically used by people with sensorineural hearing loss, because conductive losses can usually be corrected with medicine or surgery. Hearing aids are to be used in quiet places, where speech is the dominant sound in the environment. Even in classroom settings, however, background noise competes with sounds a student might want to focus on. In other settings (lecture halls, auditoriums, and recreational centers), background noise can mask all other sounds. Typical hearing aids amplify all sounds, so everything becomes louder, including background noise. For individuals with sensorineural hearing losses, sounds perceived well without a hearing aid are amplified at the same level as those that are heard only faintly. Thus most current versions of hearing aids are often of little help to many people with hearing loss and can even be distracting. Most conventional hearing aids use analog components, and three types of these aids are most common: **behind the ear (BTE)**, **in the ear (ITE)**, and **in the canal (ITC)**. ITEs and

behind the ear (BTE). A hearing aid that cups behind the ear with a cord that runs into the person's ear canal.

in the ear (ITE). A hearing aid that fits inside the person's outer ear.

in the canal (ITC). A hearing aid that is worn inside the person's ear canal.

ITCs together represent about 80 percent of all hearing aid sales in the United States (Preves, 1994). Hearing aids are an essential tool for many students with hearing loss. Because it is a sensitive electronic device, it needs special care. Teachers can help students who use hearing aids by helping them master the care and handling of these devices:

■ Avoid dust, dirt, and humidity.

■ Do not drop the hearing aid.

■ Keep the ear mold clean.

■ Avoid hair spray.

■ Do not leave the hearing aid in a hot place.

■ Have the aid checked frequently by an audiologist.

Effective planning for instruction for hard of hearing students means that teachers need to understand the benefits and limitations of hearing aids. Remember, hearing aids do not cure hearing losses; they help people use their residual hearing better. Here are some of the major problems with common hearing aids used today (Bakke, 1995):

■ If a person does not have hearing at a specific frequency, no matter how much it is amplified, hearing cannot be restored.

■ Sound amplification does not work well in noise because both speech and background noise are made louder.

■ Hearing aids can create their own noise by making acoustic feedback, whistling, or crackling sounds.

Developers of assistive listening devices are working hard to create selective amplification systems that are self-adjusting, are individually tailored to each person's hearing profile, can restore fading high-frequency consonants, tune out background noise, and are small enough to wear behind or in the ear. The answer lies in digital systems (Robinson, 1993) that can filter out some sounds and amplify others by working much like digital stereo graphic equalizers. The system works, but size is a problem with current experimental digital systems, which are about the size of a Sony Walkman. To be commercially viable, this new generation of hearing aids will need to be no larger than the size of a BTE.

For the present, one solution to the problems of environmental noise and acoustic feedback faced by hearing aid wearers is the **telecoil** (also called *induction coils*). Telecoils are an optional device in some BTE and ITE hearing aids but cannot yet

Reprinted with permission from Tribune Media Services.

telecoil. Also called induction coils, an added option on many hearing aids that allows access to telephones, audio loops, and other assistive listening devices.

To have access to information, deaf children who use ASL need interpreters for every instructional activity, whether in a classroom or on a field trip.

be used with ITC aids. Telecoils allow sounds to be brought into hearing aids from telephones and **FM** (frequency-modulated) **transmission devices**. One version of an FM transmission device, auditory trainers, has been used by teachers and students in classrooms for many years. In this system, the teacher speaks into a microphone, and the sound is received directly by each student's receiver or hearing aid. Background noise is reduced, and teachers may move freely around the classroom without worrying about having their faces in full view of all their students.

Another FM transmission device, the **audio loop,** is an ALD that directs sound from its source directly to the listener's ear through a specially equipped hearing aid or earphone. Sound may travel through a wire connection or through radio waves. Audio loops are inexpensive and easy to install in rooms that seat up to 100 persons (Cutler & Boone, 1996). Gallaudet University uses audio loops in many of its classrooms, as illustrated in Figure 10.7. Since passage of the Americans with Disabilities Act, audio loops are being installed in many public buildings. Concert halls, theaters, and churches across the nation now use this system to give people with hearing losses greater access to events. Even airports, like Logan Airport in Boston, are installing looped areas that are tied into public address systems, so those who use hearing aids can hear public announcements (Ross, 1994). However, access by hard of hearing and deaf people to FM transmission devices is being challenged (Olson, 1994). Because of the great public demand for paging systems and other devices that use FM bands, the ten bands designated for use by these people could be reduced.

Telecommunication Devices

Telecommunication equipment includes assistive devices that take advantage of sight and hearing to improve communication and television listening. We discuss several of these devices here.

Captions, which have been available for many years, are printed words that appear at the bottom of a TV screen, like subtitles that translate foreign films. There are two kinds of captions: open and closed. **Open captions** can be seen by

 MAKING CONNECTIONS

For a review of the ADA law, see the Legislative section of Chapter 1.

FM transmission device. Equipment used in many classes for students with severe hearing loss that allows direct oral transmissions from the teacher to each individual student.

audio loop. A device that directs sound from the source directly to the listener's ear through a specially designed hearing aid.

captions. Subtitles that print the words spoken in film or video; can be either closed or open.

open captions. Captions that appear on the television screen for all viewers to see.

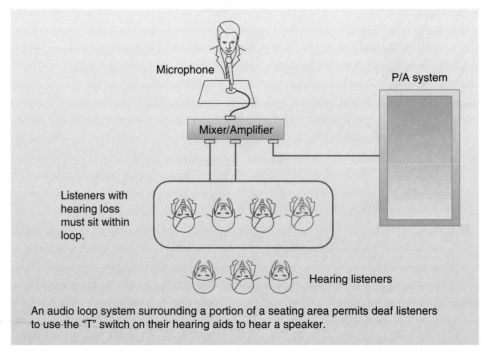

FIGURE 10.7

Diagram of an Auditorium with an Audio Loop

Microphone

P/A system

Mixer/Amplifier

Listeners with
hearing loss
must sit within
loop.

Hearing listeners

An audio loop system surrounding a portion of a seating area permits deaf listeners
to use the "T" switch on their hearing aids to hear a speaker.

Source: "Up Close and Personal: Assistive Devices Increase Access to Speech and
Sound," by C. L. Compton and H. Kaplan, 1988, *Gallaudet Today, 18,* p. 22. Reprinted
by permission.

all viewers and were used with certain television programs in the 1970s. The
"French Chef" with Julia Child was the first captioned television show, appearing
on public television in 1972. Because open captions were unpopular with the general public, **closed captions** (which need an assistive device to be seen) became
available in the 1980s.

Captioning is an important tool for deaf people because it allows them to have
equal access to public information and entertainment. The Television Decoder
Circuitry Act, introduced in 1990 and signed into law in July 1993, requires all new
television sets sold in the United States to be equipped with an internal, micro-
sized **decoder** that allows captions to be placed anywhere on the screen (to avoid
interfering with on-screen titles or other important information in the program) and
to appear in different colors (LaSasso & King, 1992). Because of mass production,
only $3 is added to the price of these newer sets. Eventually, as old television sets
are replaced with newer versions, everyone will have access to closed captions.
Before 1993, use of closed-caption technology required the purchase of a separate
decoder; because of the cost ($200), only 10 percent of people with hearing loss
had access to closed captions (Sulzberger, 1990).

Since the introduction of closed captions, their use has steadily increased. In
1993, for instance, the major broadcast networks (ABC, CBS, and NBC) captioned
100 percent of their prime-time shows, children's programming, and national news

closed captions. Captions that
can be seen on the television
screen only with the use of a
decoder.

decoder. A device that allows
closed captions to appear on a
television screen.

(Alexander Graham Bell Association for the Deaf, 1993d). As more television sets with built-in decoders are purchased and used, an increased number of captioned television programs will be available. Captioning is expanding to local movie theaters as well. Different options are available so those who desire captions can see them while the rest of the audience does not. Reversed text, for example, shows the captions on the rear wall of the theater and the individual looks at a transparent Plexiglas panel to see the captions and forward to see the movie (Hyder, 1995). Clearly, this is allowing deaf people to participate in an important part of American life with hearing people.

Another important piece of equipment, the **text telephone (TTY),** formerly referred to as the telecommunication device for the deaf (TDD), enables those who are deaf to make and receive telephone calls. The first device was created by Robert Weitbrecht, a deaf physicist, and used a *tele*typewriter along with a radio or telephone. TTY prints out the voice message for the person with a hearing loss and can be used to send messages. A lightweight (about one pound), portable version of the TTY is now available. It sells for about the same price as a traditional TTY and comes with a 7–10 hour rechargeable battery.

TTYs are becoming increasingly available to people who need to use them to communicate by telephone. TTY pay phones, for example, are available in most public places. Airports have had TTYs for many years, with the first being installed at these international airports: Minneapolis–St. Paul, Seattle–Tacoma, and Chicago–O'Hare. Moreover, many businesses have added TTYs to their workplaces. For example, the travel industry (travel agencies, major hotel chains, car rental agencies, tour groups) not only has TTY access, it also has special services designed exclusively for deaf patrons. There are many other examples of expanding services for the deaf and hard of hearing. TIAA-CREF, a large retirement plan company, installed a TTY in its main office so that policyholders who have TTYs can communicate with their agents. Merrill Lynch established the Merrill Lynch Deaf/Hard of Hearing Investors Services. The company has equipped a national network of financial advisers with TTYs, voice amplifiers, and toll-free TTY lines and provides access to a twenty-four-hour bulletin board service (Merrill Lynch, 1994).

Most TTYs have one major drawback: A unit is required at both the sending and the receiving end. There are two solutions to this problem. First, the Federal Communications Commission now requires all states to have a **telecommunications relay service (TRS)**, which allows a person using a TTY to communicate with someone using a standard telephone. By using an 800 phone number, the relay service allows deaf individuals to use the phone for everything from calling a doctor to ordering a pizza. When the person who is deaf uses a TTY in a relay system, an operator at a relay center places the call on a voice line and reads the typed message to the non-TTY user. Although a full conversation can be carried on by using a relay system, it is not very private and thus makes phone calls strained and impersonal. However, for making a doctor's appointment, arranging for a car to be fixed, or checking on a homework assignment, the relay system is invaluable. Although the ADA law requires states to have relay systems available, because many deaf and hard of hearing people are not aware of this alternative, they are not used maximally (Sorkin, 1995).

Most deaf and hard of hearing people prefer to use their voice on a phone call, and a new device is now available. The **voice carry over (VCO)** is a TTY that includes the option to use both voice and text. For those who want to use their

text telephone (TTY). A piece of equipment, formerly called the telecommunication device for the deaf (TDD), that allows people to make and receive telephone calls by typing information over the telephone lines.

telecommunications relay service (TRS). A telephone system required by federal law that allows an operator at a relay center to convert a print-telephone message to a voice telephone message.

voice carry over (VCO). A TTY that allows both voice and text use.

voices but need to receive telephone communication through print, these phones allow for both voice and text transmissions. VCOs have many advantages, particularly for hearing people with deaf family members or friends, for businesses that want both options but do not want to invest in two different phones, and for public places so everyone has access to the telephone system. And now even a TTY/Voice Answering machine that takes messages in either format is available.

Computerized Speech-to-Text Translations

Understanding college lectures is difficult for many deaf students. Those who use sign language can use interpreters during class lectures, but simultaneously taking notes and watching an interpreter is almost impossible. A system called C-print solves this problem (Wilson, 1992). By using an inexpensive laptop computer, two commercially available software packages, a standard word processing program, and a computer shorthand system, C-print provides **real-time translations (RTC)** for persons who are deaf. C-print uses a trained operator who listens to the lecture and types special codes that represent words into the computer; the transcription is instantly shown on a special screen that sits on top of an overhead projector. Once the lecture is completed, the student can get a printout. Studies have shown that students have a higher rate of understanding lecture material when using C-print than when using sign language interpreters. Another benefit is that this system is less expensive, because C-print operators, who can be trained college

real-time translations (RTC).
Practically instantaneous translations of speech into print.

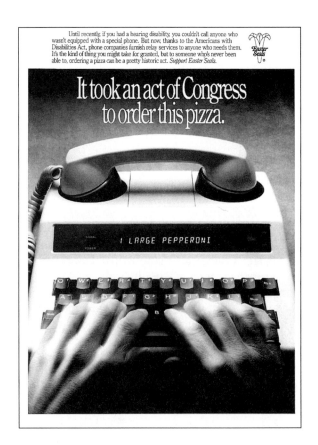

work-study students, cost less than interpreters. In addition, much of the needed equipment and software is readily available at most colleges and universities. Many students who attend traditional colleges and universities and who would have to rely on an interpreter report that RTC does not make them feel different and even improves social possibilities (Kramlinger, 1996).

A system similar to C-print is used in some courtrooms; it also provides real-time translations but employs a court stenographer or court reporter (Sulzberger, 1991). The court reporter uses special computer equipment that instantaneously translates the proceedings onto a display screen. With the addition of a laptop computer, this system can also be used outside the courtroom to take depositions. It is this system that has allowed Richard Ricks to return to his profession (Torry, 1991). Ricks quit his criminal defense practice when he became deaf and could not hear what was being said in the courtroom. Now, with simultaneous transcription, he is back in the court. He says that without this system he would not be able to practice law at all: "I'd be missing too much... I feel great. Now I know I can work again" (Torry, 1991, p. D2).

Alerting Devices

Alerting devices make people who are deaf aware of an event or important sound in their environment by using the senses of sight or touch. A flashing light, loud gong, or vibration can signal a fire alarm, doorbell, alarm clock, or telephone. Some attach to a lamp that flashes on and off for a signal. Others attach to vibrators (in the bed for an alarm clock or on a person's belt as a personal signaler). Some alerting devices include sound-sensitive monitors that let the deaf person know about a baby who is crying or an out-of-the-ordinary sound. Hearing Ear Dogs (or service dogs) also can help alert deaf people to important sounds in their environments. These dogs are trained to act as "ears." They can distinguish between noises and alerts, and can even recognize specific sounds (NICD, 1994).

MAKING CONNECTIONS

- For another example of service dogs, see the Educational Interventions section of Chapter 9.

Concepts and Controversy: Cochlear Implants: To Do or Not To Do?

Tension between hearing people and the deaf existed long before Thomas Gallaudet and Alexander Graham Bell debated before Congress on topics such as whether two deaf people should be allowed to marry or whether sign language was an acceptable form of communication. Across time, hearing people viewed deaf people as less than human because they either did not use oral language or did not use it well. With the emergence of Deaf culture and Deaf pride, the acceptance of these individuals has improved. However, the Deaf are engaged in a new and bitter debate, one they believe assaults their worth and integrity.

The debate now raging concerns whether young deaf children should receive a cochlear implant, technology that allows deaf individuals to perceive sound. The position of many hearing parents of deaf children is that the implant may let their child hear sounds in the environment, develop speech, and participate in mainstream society. Many parents also fear that if their deaf children do not develop speech, they will lose them to the Deaf community. Many in the Deaf community are opposed to implants. They say it is brutal to open up a child's head, wind wires

alerting devices. Devices that use sight, sound, or vibration to make individuals aware of an occurrence or an important sound.

through the inner ear, and force a child through years of speech therapy without knowing what the outcome will be and possibly seeing little improvement in speech intelligibility. They feel that the child is robbed of his or her right to be a member of the Deaf community, which has a rich language and culture of its own. They also point out that no one knows the long-term physical, social, or emotional effects of this irreversible procedure (Barringer, 1993) or whether it will allow children to hear well enough to develop intelligible speech (Tye-Murray, Spencer, & Woodworth, 1995).

Although the medical profession is seeking to cure deafness, some experts in deafness view implants as a misguided effort (Barringer, 1993). For example, Scott Lidell, chairperson of Gallaudet University's Linguistics Department, believes that the typical deaf child will not master the English language with its use, will acquire only a few words, and those very late. He maintains that American Sign Language is the only language these children can acquire on a normal schedule. Others— even some who are deaf themselves—challenge Lidell's claim. They believe that spoken English skills *can* be acquired by children who are deaf and that oral communication is the key to good jobs and integration into mainstream society (Liebman, 1993). Implants do help some individuals, particularly those deafened as adults, hear better. The outcomes for children are less definite, and adults are making decisions for themselves where children are not.

Issues beyond surgery and language acquisition are involved in this debate, however. Many in the Deaf community view the cochlear implant movement as an attack against their culture and worth. Members of the Deaf community believe that implants are a continuation of their history of repression, where they and their culture are denied and minimized (Shapiro, 1993). Many Deaf people believe they do not have a sickness or disability to be pitied and cured, perceptions, they feel, those who hear have of them. As members of the Deaf community, then, implants reinforce the view that deafness is a pathology, something to be cured. Others do not understand why parents would put children through a painful operation that they view as useless and cruel. On the other hand, many hearing people believe that those who are Deaf reject the use of implants because they feel threatened by them and fear that their community would not exist if deafness were eliminated.

Is this debate really about choice? Should cochlear implant surgery be withheld from children until the results of experimental studies are better understood? Is this movement really an attack on the Deaf community? Finally, how important is oral language? Should it be a goal for every deaf child? Until these questions are answered, the cochlear implant debate will continue.

~~~ *SUMMARY* ~~~

Most of us communicate with others through a process of telling and listening. This process is one important way that we learn about the world we live in, subjects at school, and others' perspectives on issues and concerns. The deaf have a more restricted ability to communicate, a difference that should determine the way these students are taught, the content of the curricula, and the related services they require for an appropriate education.

Self-Test Questions

▶ *What variables are used to create different subgroups of students who are deaf or hard of hearing?*

The primary way divides this special education category into three subgroups: amount of loss, age of onset, and type of loss. When classified by the amount of hearing loss, these two groups are used: the deaf and the hard of hearing. The deaf are further divided into two groups relating to age of onset. Those who are prelingually deaf typically lost their hearing at, during, before, or shortly after birth; and those who lost their hearing after they had acquired some language (after the age of 2) are called postlingually deaf. A third way to organize hearing losses is by two general types: conductive and sensorineural. Conductive losses result in a flat profile on an audiogram, respond best to the use of hearing aids, and are caused by damage to the middle or outer ear. Conductive losses are also easier to correct using current medical technology. Sensorineural hearing losses are caused by damage to the inner ear or the auditory nerve and result in an uneven profile on an audiogram.

▶ *What is meant by the concept of Deaf culture?*

To many, particularly the Deaf who use American Sign Language (ASL) and who live in the Deaf community, deafness is not a disability. Rather, it is a historically misunderstood minority group. Deafness has created a language difference, not a disability. The Deaf community and many others support the belief that ASL is a bona-fide language with unique elements of all languages. These individuals are proud of their heritage, history, traditions, and art. They have become successful advocates for themselves and their community's way of life. What they desire is respect, independence, and self-determination, just like most Americans.

▶ *What are the major causes of hearing loss?*

The five major causes of hearing loss are maternal rubella, meningitis, otitis media, heredity, and noise. Other causes are being identified, for example, CMV, but probably over half of the cases in children are genetic. Today, many cases of deafness and hard of hearing in children can be prevented.

▶ *What educational support services do many of these students require?*

With appropriate support systems, many deaf and hard of hearing students can benefit from traditional educational programs at their local neighborhood schools in general education classes where the standard curriculum is presented. This often requires additional services from a variety of specialists: speech/language pathologists, audiologists, educational interpreters, and special education teachers. They may also require some accommodations (seating assignments, handouts, peer assistance) to succeed in general education classes. Also, their general education teachers might need some extra guidance or training from a consulting teacher or an SLP. An expert knowledgeable about hearing can be an important resource to both the teacher and the student.

▶ *How do the major instructional methods for deaf children differ, and how should an individual child's communication style affect the choice of instructional method?*

Most deaf children do not develop oral language without effort. Debates about the best mode of communication to use when educating deaf students continue. Although some can master oral communication, most cannot. Interest is renewed in the oral-only approach, particularly for those children who are receiving cochlear implants, because it stresses developing the students' facility with oral language. Probably as a response to the Deaf community's advocacy of ASL, the bilingual-bicultural approach was developed. This method teaches ASL as the native language and written English as a second language. However, the majority of deaf children's parents are able to hear and do not know ASL. For these children, the natural mastery of a communication system is not the norm. For many, a total communication environment—where manual communication (sign language) supports speech—results in increased learning because all channels available for sending and receiving information are used. For family members who are not deaf themselves, implementing this approach requires learning a new communication system and a very small number have found cued speech to be easier to master. The family and preschool program staff work as a team to provide an educational program that lasts all day, every day, and ensures that some form of language is fully developed.

Challenge Question

▶ *What types of technology are available to assist the deaf, and what advances might the future hold?*

Technology has impacted on the lives of the deaf and hard of hearing. First, assistive listening devices such as hearing aids allow many hard of hearing persons to function independently in environments where oral communication is dominant. The hearing aid is continually being refined to accommodate individuals' specific hearing abilities. Second, telecommunication devices help individuals use both their sight and their hearing to improve communication and television listening. The availability of captioned television has greatly broadened the world of those who are deaf. New breakthroughs in the area of computerized speech-to-text translations will dramatically increase the access of deaf people to mainstream society. These new systems allow for real-time translations of daily situations (college lectures, court room proceedings). Alerting devices help these people become aware of sounds and events in their environments by means other than hearing. Finally, technology is being applied to the teaching of communication skills. Some software programs help individuals improve the understanding of their speech, and others assist with the instruction of manual communication language systems such as ASL. Certainly, the future will bring a new generation of hearing aids that mask out background noise and adjust to an individual's unique hearing pattern. It is for the most clever among us to brainstorm future applications of technology that will improve and facilitate the lives of deaf and hard of hearing individuals.

〜〜 *SUPPLEMENTARY RESOURCES* 〜〜

Scholarly Books

McAnally, P. L., Rose, S., & Quigley, S. P. (1994). *Language learning practices with deaf children.* Austin, TX: Pro-Ed.

Marschark, M. (1993). *Psychological development of deaf children.* NY: Oxford University Press.

Moores, D. F. (1996). *Educating the deaf: Psychology, principles, and practices* (4th ed.). Boston: Houghton Mifflin.

Popular Books

Greenberg, J. (1988). *Of such small differences.* NY: Holt.

Kisor, H. (1990). *What's that pig outdoors? A memoir of deafness.* NY: Hill & Wang.

McCullers, C. (1970). *The heart is a lonely hunter.* NY: Bantam.

Sacks, O. (1989). *Seeing voices.* Berkeley: University of California Press.

Schaller, S. (1991). *A man without words.* NY: Summit Books.

Walker, L. A. (1986). *A loss for words: The story of deafness in a family.* NY: Harper & Row.

Videos

The miracle worker. (1962). United Artists.
The heart is a lonely hunter. (1968). Warner Brothers/
  7 Arts.
Tin man. (1983). Montage Films.

Children of a lesser God. (1986). Paramount Pictures.
See no evil, hear no evil. (1989). Tri-Star Pictures.
Mr. Holland's Opus. (1996). Hollywood Pictures Home
  Video.

Professional, Parent, and Consumer Organizations and Agencies

Alexander Graham Bell Association for the Deaf, Inc.
3417 Volta Place, NW
Washington, DC 20007
Web site: http://www.agbell.org
Phone: (202) 337-5220

National Information Center on Deafness Gallaudet University
800 Florida Ave. NE
Washington, DC 20002
E-mail: nicd@galludet.edu
Web site: http://www.edu/^nicd
Phone: (202) 651-5051

American Speech-Language-Hearing Association (ASHA)
10801 Rockville Pike
Rockville, MD 20852
E-mail: irc@asha.org
Web site: http://www.asha.org

Phone: (800) 638-8255

National Institute on Deafness and other Communication Disorders Information Clearinghouse
1 Communication Ave.
Bethesda, MD 20892
Web site: http://www.nig.gov/nidcd/
Phone: (800) 241-1044

National Association of the Deaf
814 Thayer Ave.
Silver Spring, MD 20910
Phone: (301) 587-1788

Self-Help for Hard of Hearing People (SHHHP), Inc.
7800 Wisconsin Ave.
Bethesda, MD 20814
E-mail: shhh.nancy@genie.com
Phone: (301) 657-2248

Auguste Rodin. *The Thinker.* 1880.

François Auguste René Rodin was born and raised on the Left Bank of Paris. His father was a clerk in the police department. Although the family was not rich, the environment in which Rodin grew up was. His neighborhood was a community for artists, poets, writers, and creative people. He is said to have once remarked that his native Paris gave him "*millions de pensées*" (millions of thoughts) (Hale, 1969, p. 37). Rodin was probably drawn to art because of his poor success at school. His first school experiences were not positive. It is said that after three years he still could not spell, a problem that followed him the rest of his life. At age 10, he was sent off to a country school, but again was unsuccessful and dropped out of school by age 13. It is thought that his frustration and failure at school was because of a severe vision problem, for it is reported that he was so nearsighted that he could not see the blackboard (Hale, 1969). It is probably for these reasons that he chose sculpture as his medium of expression, one that is more tactile than visual. He is considered one of the best sculptors of all time.

Low Vision and Blindness

11

A D V A N C E   O R G A N I Z E R S

▼

OVERVIEW

Vision is a distance sense that provides us with information from outside our bodies. When vision is limited, it affects the individual in significant ways: limiting mobility, access to printed information, and independent living. People with visual impairments also face many stereotypes, social stigma, and bar-riers to full participation in mainstream society. Some believe that blindness is met with more nega-tive attitudes than is any other physical disability. Visual impairments (low vision and blindness) in children is a low-incidence disability, affecting about 0.5 percent of all schoolchildren.

▼

FOCUS QUESTIONS

SELF-TEST QUESTIONS

▶ How is the disability of visual impairments divided into two subgroups?

▶ What are the major causes of visual impair-ments, and what preventive measures protect children from this disability?

▶ What are some ways the learning environment can be modified to accommodate students with visual impairments?

▶ Why must orientation and mobility be long-term curriculum targets for many low vision and most blind students, and what specific skills must be included?

▶ What technological advances can assist peo-ple with visual impairments at school, in the workplace, and in independent living?

CHALLENGE QUESTION

▶ Why has Braille literacy become such an emotionally charged debate, and how do you think it should be resolved?

A *Personal Perspective*: Two Families of Preschoolers with Visual Impairments Talk About Their Children

Amanda and Vincent attend the New Mexico School for the Visually Handicapped Preschool, which is located in Albuquerque. Amanda is a Native American, and she and her family live at Zia Pueblo. They commute eighty miles round trip so that Amanda can attend this special preschool. Vincent is Hispanic. He and his mom live in town. Both children have a severe visual impairment and are classified as legally blind. These parents talk about some experiences and hopes for their children.

Tell me a little bit about yourself.

AMANDA'S DAD: My wife is half Blackfoot from Montana, and she is a quarter Spanish from her mother's side and a quarter Zia. I am seven-eighths Zia blood.

VINCENT'S MOM: I am a single mom. Vincent and I live with my parents here in Albuquerque.

How did you first discover that your child had a visual disability? How did you feel about it?

AMANDA'S DAD: There have been no records of albinos among our people. It was kind of a different feeling, since she was the first albino in the Zia Pueblo as a whole.

VINCENT'S MOM: I first learned about Vincent's visual impairment from his ophthalmologist. I didn't think he would be able to do the things normal kids do. I couldn't see how he could have a normal life.

Please share an incident with us about your child at the preschool.

AMANDA'S MOM: When Amanda first went to school, her teachers were calling her Amanda and she wasn't answering to her name. At first, they thought she had a hearing problem. So we had tests taken and that wasn't the problem. I finally stopped and asked, "What are you calling her?" They said that they were calling her Amanda. "I should have told you, her Indian name is Hèshètè and that's the only thing that she understands."

AMANDA'S DAD: So we sat down and we taught them a little bit about our basic language. They took the time when they did not understand what Amanda was saying or doing to ask us. It was just that she was talking in Indian.

VINCENT'S MOM: When Vincent first started going to school, he wasn't even rolling [over] yet. He was about four months old. He wasn't learning how because he couldn't see how to do it. The preschool teachers taught me how to roll him over. We all work with Vincent on a lot of different things. We worked a lot with textures and touching things, and sounds. He is learning a lot.

What are some of the most important things your child has learned at the preschool?

VINCENT'S MOM: When he first started out he didn't like to be around kids his own age. They were too fast for him. Now, he's gotten to where he is one of the kids, and he hangs around with them. The preschool experience has really helped his self-confidence, because he knows he can keep up.

AMANDA'S DAD: We feel Amanda learned to feel good about herself. She is now very competent and portrays this to her younger sister, who is also albino.

What is next for your child after preschool?

VINCENT'S MOM: Vincent will go to a special class for kids with visual impairments in the public school next year. He will spend time in a regular classroom, as well.

AMANDA'S MOM: We want Amanda to go to school at the Pueblo with all of her friends who live nearby.

What are your thoughts about your child's future?

VINCENT'S MOM: Now I think Vincent will be able to do everything but drive.

AMANDA'S MOM: Amanda will be able to attend our Pueblo schools with help from the New Mexico School for the Visually Handicapped Outreach Services.

1. How have these parents' feelings changed about their child? Why do you think this is the case?

2. What do you think are the benefits to a preschooler with severe visual impairments of a segregated educational setting? What are its disadvantages?

---

*Albinism is a genetic condition that causes abnormal coloration of a person's skin, hair, and eyes because of lack of pigment. These individuals' vision is severely affected because of the eyes' inability to adjust to differences in light and acuity problems associated with the condition.

*A*lthough we act on information gained through our sight, we seldom give much thought to the process of seeing. Sometimes, we stop to reflect on the beauty of a particular sunset, the stars at night, a flower in bloom, or the landscape after a snowstorm. We use our sense of sight all of our waking hours, yet we do not think about vision and how it functions. Most of us use vision in our work. For example, people use sight when they use the Internet, write memos, look up telephone numbers, or direct people to various offices. At the zoo, animal caretakers use their vision to be certain that the animals are not acting differently by changing their typical patterns of behavior and are not injured. We use our vision for recreation when we watch a movie, view television, or read a book. Some of us actually prefer learning by reading or looking at information, rather than listening to a lecture or instructions. These people are known as visual learners. We also use our vision for self-defense; for example, we look in all directions before crossing a street by foot or an intersection when driving a car. Unlike touch and taste, vision and hearing are **distance senses**, senses that provide us with information outside our bodies. These senses developed to alert us to the presence of helpful as well as dangerous elements in the environment.

Clearly, those of us with unimpaired vision profit from this sense. We learn by observing events, we use our vision to move freely in our environment, and we are alert to danger by using our sight. People with visual impairments have limited use of their sight, but with systematic instruction and advances in technology, most can lead fully integrated and independent lives.

This chapter will help you understand visual impairments and the people they affect. For example, you will learn that the great majority of people who have a visual impairment are able to use their sight to function in society. However, their disability affects the ease with which they can cope with daily life. You will also learn about one of the biggest challenges for those who are blind—learning to be independently mobile. You will become aware of the obstacles these people often confront and come to understand that people with visual impairments can assume places alongside others who do not share their disability. Finally, you will learn about the stereotypes and barriers that are uniquely centered on this group of people.

 MAKING CONNECTIONS

For more information about bias and stereotypes people with disabilities face, see these sections:
- Disabilities Defined (Chapter 1)
- Significance (Defined) (Chapters 3–12)
- Transitions (Educational Interventions) (Chapters 3–12)

Visual Impairments Defined

To better understand visual impairments, we must understand how vision normally occurs. For people to see, four elements must be present and operating. The first is light. The second is something that reflects light. The third is the eye processing the reflected image into electric impulses. The fourth is the brain receiving and giving meaning to these impulses. Use the picture of the eye (see Figure 11.1) to trace how the normal visual process works.

Light rays enter the front of the eye through the **cornea**. The cornea is transparent and curved. The **iris** is the colored part of the eye and it expands and contracts in response to the intensity of light it receives. In the center of the iris is the **pupil**, which is a hole. Light rays pass through the pupil to the lens, which is behind the iris. The **lens** brings an object seen into focus by changing its thickness. The process of the lens adjusting to focus things that are close and those that are far away is called **accommodation**. The lens focuses light rays onto the

distance senses. Senses—hearing and vision—that provide us with information external to our bodies, developed to help alert us to danger.

cornea. The transparent, curved part of the front of the eye.

iris. The colored part of the eye.

pupil. Hole in the center of the iris that expands and contracts, admitting light to the eye.

lens. Located behind the iris, brings objects seen into focus.

accommodation. The focusing process of the lens of the eye.

~~~
FIGURE 11.1

How Vision Works

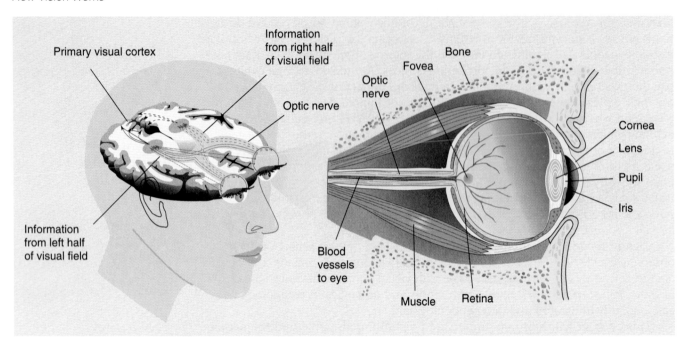

Source: Physiology of Behavior, 5th ed. by N. R. Carlson, 1994, Boston: Allyn and Bacon, Figures 6.4 and 6.12. Adapted by permission.

retina, which is the inside lining of the eye. It is made up of photosensitive cells that react to light rays and send messages along the **optic nerve** to the visual center of the brain.

How well people can use their sight, their **visual efficiency**, is influenced by many factors including the person's acuity and peripheral vision abilities, environmental conditions, and psychological variables. **Visual acuity** describes how well a person can see at various distances. The width of a person's field of vision or the ability to perceive objects outside the direct line of vision is called **peripheral vision**. This aspect of vision helps people move freely through their environment. It helps them see large objects and movement. Severe limitation in peripheral vision is sometimes called **tunnel vision** or restricted **central vision** because of an inability to see a wide area. Some persons with visual impairments have little functional use of sight, but the great majority have substantial use of their vision, particularly with correction (glasses or contact lenses). Although many people do not realize it, the vast majority of people with visual impairments use vision as their primary method of learning, and for many the amount of vision they have left, **residual vision**, can be further developed (Barraga, 1993). The vision of some is static, remaining the same from day to day, while others find their ability to see varying by the day, time of day, or setting (Levin, 1996). For some, higher or lower levels of illumination (amount of light) affect how well they can see, but for others, lighting level makes little difference. For some individuals, distance and

retina. Inside lining of the eye.

optic nerve. The nerve that carries messages from the eye to the visual center of the brain.

visual efficiency. How well a person can use sight.

visual acuity. How well a person can see at various distances.

peripheral vision. The outer area of a person's visual field.

tunnel vision. Severe limitation in peripheral vision.

central vision. The main field of vision in the eye, usually greater than 20 degrees.

residual vision. The amount and degree of vision that one has functional use of despite a visual disability.

The photo on the left shows what a person with a limited visual field, or tunnel vision, sees; the one on the right shows what a person with restricted visual acuity might see.

contrast are important factors affecting how well they can process information presented through the visual channel. Some are color-blind; others are not. For most, optical aids such as glasses have a positive effect.

The eye is a very complicated mechanism. Damage to any part of the eye can result in serious limitations in one's abilities to see and process information through the visual channel. Table 11.1 lists conditions of various parts of the eye by using an organizational system suggested by Tuttle and Ferrell (1995). These conditions can result in blindness or severe visual impairments. Many disorders can be corrected or reduced through medical technology, but not all can be resolved by medical treatment.

Types of Visual Impairments

Many professionals in the field of visual impairments divide persons with visual impairments into two subgroups: low vision and blindness. Individuals with **low vision** use sight to learn, but their visual impairments interfere with daily functioning. **Blindness** means that the person uses touch and hearing to learn and does not have functional use of sight. Parents and professionals now tend to use functional definitions for these two subgroups. Remember, this classification system is based on how well people can use their sight, even if its use is severely limited.

Low Vision. Corn (1989) defines low vision as "a level of vision which, with standard correction, hinders an individual in the planning and/or execution of a task, but which permits enhancement of the functional vision through the use of optical or nonoptical devices, environmental modifications and/or techniques" (p. 28). In other words, children with low vision use their sight for many school activities, including reading. Barraga and Erin (1992), however, caution us not to assume that all children with low vision use print materials, because some use Braille.

low vision. A level of visual impairment where vision is still useful for learning or the execution of a task.

blindness. Not having a functional use of sight.

TABLE 11.1

Types of Visual Impairments

Type	Definition
Conditions of the Eye	
Myopia	Nearsightedness; condition allows focus on objects close but not at a distance.
Hyperopia	Farsightedness; condition allows focus on objects at a distance but not close.
Astigmatism	An eye disorder that produces images on the retina that are not equally in focus.
Conditions of the Eye Muscles	
Strabismus	Improper alignment of the two eyes causes two images being received by the brain, with the possible result of one eye becoming nonfunctional.
Nystagmus	Rapid, involuntary movements of the eye that interfere with bringing objects into focus.
Conditions of the Cornea, Iris, and Lens	
Glaucoma	Fluid in the eye is restricted, causing pressure to build up and damage the retina.
Aniridia	Undeveloped iris, due to lack of pigment (albinism), results in extreme sensitivity to light.
Cataract (opacity of the crystalline lens)	A cloudy film over the lens of the eye.
Conditions of the Retina	
Diabetic retinopathy	Changes in the eye's blood vessels are caused by diabetes.
Macular degeneration	Damage to a small area near the center of the retina results in restricted fine central vision and difficulties in reading and writing.
Retinopathy of prematurity (ROP)	Excess oxygen to infants causes retinal damage; was called retrolental fibroplasia.
Retinal detachment	Detachment of the retina interrupts transmission of visual information to the brain.
Retinitis pigmentosa	Genetic eye disease leads progressively to blindness; night blindness is the first symptom.
Retinoblastoma	Tumor.
Condition of the Optic Nerve	
Atrophy	Reduced function of the optic nerve.

Blindness. Children without functional use of their vision may only perceive shadows or some movement; these youngsters must be educated through tactile and other sensory channels and are considered functionally blind. Blindness can occur at any age, but its impact varies with age. For those with visual impairments, like the deaf and hard of hearing, the age of onset (when the disability occurs) is important. Persons born with a severe impairment are **congenitally blind.** Those who acquire a severe visual impairment sometime after birth (usually after age 2) are called **adventitiously blind.** People who lose their sight after age 2 retain some memory of what they had seen. They remember what some objects look like. The later the disability occurs, the more they remember. Visual memory is an important factor in learning, for it can influence one's development of concepts and other aspects important to learning.

Despite the movement toward functional definitions of visual impairments, the nonfunctional definition, **legally blind**, is still in use. The term *legally blind* does not relate perfectly to functional use of vision. For example, many people who are considered legally blind use print to gain information. However, being classified as legally blind allows the individual to receive special tax benefits and materials from the federal government and private agencies. To be considered legally blind, a person must meet the following criteria: central visual acuity of 20/200 or less in the better eye, with best correction, or the widest diameter of the visual field does not subtend to an angle greater than 20 degrees.

Identification

Important decisions with lifelong implications are often made from those assessments that qualify children with visual impairments for special education services. Professionals and parents use the information to decide whether a child should learn to read print or to read Braille, to specify the level and type of education placements the child will receive, and to determine which assistive services will be included in the child's IEP.

Although parents and professionals are advocating for the use of functional definitions of visual impairments, many states still use measures of acuity to qualify youngsters for special education services. Normal visual acuity is measured by how accurately a person can see an object or image 20 feet away. Therefore normal vision is said to be 20/20. A person whose vision is measured at 20/40 can see at 20

MAKING CONNECTIONS

For a review of IEPs and the services that can be included in special education, read again Chapter 2.

Reprinted by permission: Tribune Media Services

congenitally blind. Those with severe visual impairments present at birth.

adventitiously blind. Those who acquired a severe visual impairment after the age of two.

legally blind. Visual acuity measured as 20/200 or worse in the better eye with correction, or peripheral vision no greater than 20 degrees.

feet what people who do not need visual correction (glasses or contact lenses) can see at 40 feet away. Field of vision is measured in degrees. Those whose visual field is restricted to no more than 20 degrees are classified as legally blind. Although states and school districts vary in the criteria they use to determine eligibility for special services, typically people with visual acuity measuring 20/70 to 20/200 in the better eye with correction are considered to have low vision (Heller, Alberto, Forney, & Schwartzman, 1996). Acuity below 20/200 classifies an individual as legally blind.

When educators use a functional approach, measurement takes on some additional assessment procedures (Blanksby & Langford, 1993). Three factors are considered: visual capacity, visual attention, and visual processing. Visual capacity determines what actually can be seen; it includes acuity, amount of visual field, and how the individual responds to visual information. Visual attention includes four capacities: alertness (ability to maintain sensitivity to environmental stimuli), selection (ability to select information from different sources), degree of attention (ability to maintain attention to a visual stimulus and change to another), and processing capacity (ability to process visual information). Visual processing is assessed to determine which elements expected in normal visual functioning are impaired.

Assessing visual status can be complicated, imprecise, and frequently inaccurate. Information must be gathered from multiple sources. We have identified six: diagnosticians, the children affected, their parents, educators, school nurses, and eye specialists. Diagnosticians are one source of information used to determine visual status. Typically, the diagnostician watches for spontaneous visual behaviors in an environment in which the child is comfortable. Unfortunately, this method has a high probability of underestimating a child's potential functional visual abilities (Batshaw & Perret, 1992), particularly for children whose language is not yet well developed or who do not have good descriptive vocabularies. Because functional assessments of vision include observations of how well children use their other senses, this method can also lead to inaccurate results for youngsters with multiple disabilities, such as limited hearing or motor abilities. Teachers of the visually impaired are excellent resources during the assessment process, for they are likely to be the best trained and well-experienced member of the team. Another source of information is the children themselves, but it may be surprising to learn that they are often very unreliable. Possibly motivated by the desire to please a doctor or a diagnostician, many parents report that their blind children both report and simulate a different level of blindness than they actually possess when in the assessment situation (Erin & Corn, 1994). For example, some children indicate that they can see things they cannot: a car coming, the moon at night, the color of an object. Decisions about visual status must be made from accurate information, but sometimes this task can prove to be quite challenging.

Most states require that all schoolchildren have a visual screening test (Brody, 1993). Children's visual acuity can be tested in the school nurse's office or by a pediatrician using the **Snellen chart**. The Snellen chart, originally developed by a Dutch ophthalmologist in 1862, comes in two versions. One test uses the letter E placed in various positions in different sizes; the other uses alphabet letters in different sizes. For the screening of substantial numbers of people, a more efficient adaptation of the Snellen chart uses the E version projected on a television monitor placed 10 to 20 feet away from the viewer. The viewer matches a key on a computer with the direction or placement of the E on the screen, allowing the computer to analyze the data.

Snellen chart. A chart used to test visual acuity, developed in 1862.

Although not a requirement, each visual screening of a schoolchild should include teachers' observations about the child's classroom behaviors and performance. For example, teachers should indicate whether a particular child complains about scratchy or itchy eyes or headaches, rubs the eyes excessively, or has difficulty discriminating letters or symbols when completing classroom assignments. Such information is helpful especially when the special services committee makes recommendations about placement and the types of special assistance a child should receive.

Two types of eye specialists provide diagnosis and treatment. **Ophthalmologists** are medical doctors who specialize in eye disorders. They can conduct physical examinations of the eye, prescribe corrective lenses and medicines, and perform surgery. **Optometrists** are professionals who measure vision and can prescribe corrective lenses and make functional recommendations. They cannot prescribe drugs or perform surgery. An **optician** fills either the ophthalmologist's or optometrist's prescription for glasses or corrective lenses.

Significance

People experience visual loss due to damage to the eye and the visual processing mechanisms. You have learned through your studies that it is difficult to arrive at a concise definition for most exceptionalities. This is true for visual impairments as well. Those with visual impairments range greatly in their abilities, and some of these individuals have multiple disabilities. You have learned so far that visual efficiency is an important concept; think about it as you continue to learn more about this disability and how it impacts the people affected by it. Interestingly, individuals with the same visual acuity or amount of peripheral vision may differ in their abilities to use their sight. A person's visual efficiency influences how that individual learns (through visual, tactile, or auditory channels) and the modifications to instructional methods that teachers must make. For example, a child's visual efficiency could affect how the classroom needs to be organized, where the child should sit, whether additional equipment (microcomputers, Braillers) is required, or if adapted materials (texts with enlarged print) are necessary.

Unfortunately, blindness often significantly affects individuals in other ways as well. Hudson (1994) believes it is the attitudes that people with visual impairments have to contend with in the community and workplace that cause psychological problems in some of these people. She is joined in her belief that the blind face terrible stereotypes and bias by a team of Dutch researchers (Verplanken, Meijnders, & van de Wege, 1994). In their work, the Dutch team found that sighted people tend to have unfavorable feelings about blind people they had interacted with—unfortunately, more experience and contact did not improve the situation. Verplanken and his colleagues maintain that blindness is met with more negative attitudes than other physical disabilities (Verplanken et al., 1994). Evidently, sighted persons often feel uneasy, afraid, or uncomfortable when interacting with blind people, even if they assess the individual as extremely competent (Hudson, 1994). We must guard against such negative attitudes, which can result in bias in the community, the workplace, and at school. Clearly, bias and negative attitudes can lead to discrimination and missed opportunities for participation in the mainstream of society and should be eliminated. Possibly, sighted people tend to feel uncomfortable with those who are blind because they do not know how to act or whether to offer assistance. Educators can play an important role in helping

MAKING CONNECTIONS

For reminders about special services committees, see A Personal Perspective (Chapter 2).

MAKING CONNECTIONS

For suggestions about adapting the classroom setting for blind and low vision students, see the Making Accommodations box (Inclusion section) in this chapter.

ophthalmologist. Medical doctor who specializes in eye disorders.
optometrist. Professional who measures vision and can prescribe corrective lenses (eyeglasses or contact lenses).
optician. A person who fills either the ophthalmologist's or optometrist's prescriptions for glasses or corrective lenses.

Helping Sighted Students Feel More Comfortable with Blind Peers

1 Speak directly to the individual in a normal tone of voice; do not ask someone else to speak for the person with visual impairments.

2 Let the blind person ask for help; do not force it on the individual.

3 Let the person take your arm and walk a half-step behind (to anticipate curbs and steps) and continue normal conversation when asked to provide mobility assistance.

4 Introduce everyone in the room (including pets) when a blind person enters.

5 Speak when you enter a room to let the blind person know that you are there.

6 Help by being certain that hazards and obstacles are removed from pathways.

7 Do not avoid using the word *see*; it is okay to use phrases like, "See you soon."

8 Do not pity the blind person or talk about the "wonderful compensations" of being blind (like improved senses of hearing and smell).

9 If you have a question about the individual's blindness, ask, but remember that the person has many interests he or she would probably like to discuss.

10 Show the individual each new environment by telling details about the location of rooms and items.

11 Remember blind people have many interests; do not always discuss the individual's blindness.

12 Yield the right of way to blind people using long canes; it is the law in every state.

Source: Adapted from *Courtesy Rules of Blindness*, courtesy of the National Federation of the Blind.

sighted children learn what is appropriate in social interactions with blind peers and, over time, this may improve the situation for all adults. The Tips for Teachers box provides some courtesy rules that may improve people's comfort levels in social interactions and also reduce bias and negative attitudes.

History of the Field

Our knowledge of people with visual impairments in Western civilization dates back to the ancient world. Records from ancient Egypt confirm that people with visual impairments were accepted in society. Homer, the twelfth-century B.C. Greek author who wrote *The Odyssey* and *The Iliad,* was blind. The ancient Greeks held Homer and his work in the highest regard, considering him a source of wisdom and a model of heroic conduct. Despite indications of the acceptance of some blind individuals, there is no record of a systematic attempt to educate and integrate blind people into society until the eighteenth century.

Tradition holds that Homer, a blind Greek poet, lived around the time of the Trojan War (12th century B.C.) in either Chios or Smyrna. He made his living as a court singer and storyteller and is credited with writing the earliest epic poems, The Iliad *and* The Odyssey.

The first school for the blind, the Institution for Blind Youth, was founded in Paris in 1784 by Valentin Haüy. He also conceived a system of raised letters on the printed page. Unfortunately, his developmental efforts ended with the French Revolution in 1789. In the early 1800s, Louis Braille, a Frenchman who was blind, developed a tactile system for reading and writing that used an embossed six-dot cell, which is the Braille system used today.

The first center school for the blind in the United States, the New England Asylum for the Blind (now the Perkins School for the Blind), directed by Samuel Gridley Howe, opened in 1821. Around 1832, the New York Institute for the Blind and the Pennsylvania Institution for the Instruction of the Blind were founded. These nineteenth-century schools were private boarding schools, usually attended by children from wealthy families.

The first day classes began in Scotland in 1872. The Scottish Education Act required children who were blind to be integrated with their sighted classmates and to attend schools in their local communities. Note that our mainstreaming and "inclusion" movements are not new concepts: Their roots are deep in the history of education of children with disabilities. In the United States, the first concentrated attempts to integrate students who were blind into local public schools were in Chicago. In 1900, Frank Hall, the superintendent for the Illinois School for the Blind, convinced people to allow blind students to live at home. Hall developed a plan that divided Chicago into several regions, with one local school in each region to serve blind students. The students attended general classes but also had a special education teacher who taught Braille and encouraged students to participate fully in general education programs. Hall developed a mechanical Braille writer, a small, portable machine for taking notes and completing other written tasks.

 MAKING CONNECTIONS

To review the history of mainstreaming and current trends for integration of students with disabilities, see
• Legislation (Chapter 1),
• Inclusion sections (Educational Interventions) (Chapters 3 through 12).

Natalie Barraga's work on visual efficiency changed the field's research agenda and influenced how low vision and blind children are taught.

MAKING CONNECTIONS

For other discussions of service animals, see
• Transition Through Adulthood (Chapter 9),
• Technology (Chapter 10).

MAKING CONNECTIONS

Read the Technology section of this chapter.

Hoover cane. Long, white cane used in the mobility and orientation system developed in 1944 by Richard Hoover to help people with visual impairments move through the environment independently.

Kurzweil Reader. One of the first computerized systems designed for people with visual impairments that translates print into synthesized speech.

Edward Allen taught the first class for the partially sighted in 1913 in Boston; later that year, Robert Irwin started a class in Cleveland. These programs were modeled after classes in England where schoolwork was exclusively oral. Reading and writing tasks were kept to a minimum, and students attending these classes participated in general education as much as possible. These classes were generally called "sight saving classes." This method was popular for almost fifty years (from about 1915 to 1965), until Natalie Barraga's research on visual efficiency appeared in 1964 (Barraga, 1964; Barraga & Collins, 1979). She proved that people do not have a limited amount of sight that can be used up; rather, vision can become more limited when it is not used.

Many advances that the general population uses and enjoys have provided great benefits for people with visual impairments, such as the telephone, developed by Alexander Graham Bell in 1876, and the phonograph, invented by Thomas Edison in 1877. The first radio broadcast occurred in 1906 in the United States and marked access to both entertainment and information for people with visual impairments. There are many other examples of how the popularity of items with the general population increase access to mainstream society for people with visual impairments (e.g., large-print books, computerized versions of popular novels, audiotapes of texts). However, it is only their general popularity that makes the price reasonable, allows for mass production, and promotes widespread availability.

Although reading and writing present difficult tasks to many individuals who have visual impairments, another major area of difficulty is movement. Between 1918 and 1925, dog guides were trained to help French and German veterans of World War I. Guide dogs (Seeing Eye dogs) were introduced in the United States in 1928, but they have not been a popular method of assisting mobility. Less than 2 percent of people with visual impairments use Seeing Eye dogs (Hill, 1986). Long canes were developed around 1860. Richard Hoover, after whom the **Hoover cane** is named, is credited with developing a mobility and orientation system in 1944. Before this time, there was no systematic method for teaching individuals how to move freely in their environments.

During the 1950s, medical advances that helped save the lives of infants born prematurely ironically caused the disease *retinopathy of prematurity* (ROP), formally known as retrolental fibroplasia, in surviving infants. ROP results in visual impairments that range from mild visual loss to blindness. During the 1960s, the rubella (German measles) epidemic left many children with multiple disabilities, often including visual impairments. The dramatic increase in children with visual impairments strained the capacity of residential schools, which before World War II had served 85 percent of all schoolchildren with visual impairments (Sacks & Rosen, 1994). At the same time, parents began to call for their children to be mainstreamed. The result was increased comprehensive programs for children with visual impairments in local communities. Today, the majority of children with visual impairments live at home and attend local public schools.

Advances in technology have significantly influenced the lives of blind and low vision individuals. Over the past twenty years, improvements in computer capabilities have allowed for readily produced and inexpensive print enlargements and immediate translation of print to Braille. The first print-to-voice translator, the **Kurzweil Reader**, was developed in the 1970s and, though crude and expensive when compared to today's versions of optical scanners, provided immediate access to printed text not available in other formats (Braille, enlarged text, audio). This machine provided the breakthrough technology that allows blind individuals immediate access to all printed information, and only hinted at the remarkable innovations now developed and yet to come.

Prevalence

According to the American Foundation for the Blind, approximately 4.8 million Americans have severe visual impairments, with over 220,000 having no useful vision (American Foundation for the Blind, 1994). However, the vast majority of these people are over the age of 65. The proportion of children with visual impairments is much smaller than the proportion of people with this disability in the general population. This fact is clear when you see the data from the *Eighteenth Annual Report to Congress on the Implementation of the Individuals with Disabilities Act*. About 5 of every 10,000 schoolchildren (less than .05 percent) have visual impairments and receive special services (U.S. Department of Education, 1996). Only 13,099 children between the ages of 6 and 17 are receiving special education because of low vision or blindness. Of this entire group of students, about one-third (5 in every 1,000 students) are legally blind (Tuttle & Ferrell, 1995). Visual impairments are clearly associated with increasing age.

It is difficult to get an accurate or consistent count of students with visual impairments. What factors might explain such differences in the numbers of these students from year to year? A primary reason for differences in such counts is that different states use different definitions and criteria to determine eligibility for special services. Also, more than half of those identified as having severe visual impairments have an additional disability (Tuttle & Ferrell, 1995). Many of these students are counted in the **multiple disabilities** category rather than in the visual impairment category, even if visual impairment is their primary, or most serious, disabling condition. Others have their vision corrected with glasses or through surgery. No longer requiring special services, these students do not remain on the special education rolls. Finally, it is possible that many students with mild and even moderate visual impairments are not identified and do not receive services for which they are eligible.

 MAKING CONNECTIONS

For information about other low-incidence disabilities, see Chapters 8 through 12.

 MAKING CONNECTIONS

For comparable problems with prevalence figures, see that section in Chapter 10.

Causes and Prevention

The prevalence of visual impairments, particularly in children, varies country by country. For example, the incidence of blindness in developing countries is much greater than in more advanced nations, where access to medical treatment is readily available. In developing nations such as India and countries in Africa, the major causes of blindness are infectious diseases, malnutrition, and vitamin A deficiency. Worldwide, fully 80 percent of childhood blindness is caused by poor nutrition or infections; most of these situations can be prevented (American Foundation for the Blind, 1990). However, professionals who try to improve health care in these countries often battle on two fronts—improving health and disproving local myths. Many people in developing countries cling to superstitions about disabilities. "In parts of Latin America, villagers believe that bats' urine fell in the baby's eyes, or that a 'black witch moth' flew in the baby's face" (Werner, 1987, p. 244).

multiple disabilities. Possessing more than one handicapping condition.

Advances in medical technology—such as laser treatment, surgery, and corneal implants—all help to reduce the incidence or lessen the severity of visual impairments among children. Medical technology can cause increases in this disability as well. As we mentioned earlier, many years ago the hospital care of premature infants actually caused blindness or severe visual impairments. Once this relationship was understood, care was taken to prevent this form of visual impairment. Today, because of medical advances, more infants survive birth. Premature babies with very low birthweights, even some who weigh less than two pounds, now survive. Many of these infants have multiple disabilities, including visual impairments. As the survival rate of premature and low birthweight babies increases, so, too, does the incidence of retinopathy of prematurity (ROP). Although new advances in eye surgery can correct some cases of ROP, the retina is reattached successfully only about half the time (Heller, Alberto, Forney, & Schwartzman, 1996). Remember, the advances in medical technology that have reduced the prevalence of visual impairments in children outnumber those that contribute to its increase.

Causes

Visual impairments may be congenital (present at birth) or acquired. Almost half of the children who are blind have the disability because of prenatal factors, mostly hereditary. Researchers are beginning to identify genes that cause some forms of blindness, which is the first step leading to a cure. For example, the gene that causes retinitis pigmentosa has now been located and isolated, with the hope of a cure in the near future. Tumors in the retinal layer or along the optic nerve can also cause blindness and severe visual impairments in schoolchildren and cannot be corrected. Fortunately, two causes of visual impairments have been reduced dramatically over the past ten years. Today, precautions are being taken to prevent many cases of ROP. Rubella, also a significant cause of congenital visual impairments and multiple disabilities in the past, can today be prevented by a vaccine. Unfortunately, not everyone is immunized.

As we have mentioned, many youngsters with visual impairments have multiple disabilities as well, with estimates of about one-half of these individuals having multiple disabilities (Heller et al., 1996). The rate of multiple disabilities is associated with the cause of the disability. For example, premature babies with very low birthweights are at high risk for mental retardation. Rubella babies often have multiple disabilities, but those with visual impairments because of a tumor around the eye do not.

Prevention

Visual screenings can identify children with visual impairments. However, teachers and parents, alert to possible signs of a visual problem, might be able to identify such students even sooner and ultimately reduce the impact of the disability (Brody, 1993). Table 11.2 lists some common characteristics of children with visual impairments. Alert teachers, aware of these characteristics, might contribute to the early identification of a child facing a visual problem. Any child who exhibits one or more of these characteristics should be checked by a school nurse, pediatrician, or ophthalmologist.

MAKING CONNECTIONS

To review information about low-birthweight babies, see
• Causes and Prevention (Chapter 6),
• Prevalence (Chapter 9).
For more about ROP, see
• History section of this chapter,
• Table 11.1.

MAKING CONNECTIONS

To review information about the importance of immunizations, see
• Concepts and Controversy (Chapter 5),
• Causes and Prevention (Chapter 3).

TABLE 11.2

Possible Signs of Visual Impairments

- Eyes water excessively.
- Eyes are red or continually inflamed.
- Eyes are crusty in appearance.
- Eyes look dull, wrinkled, or cloudy.
- Eyes look swollen
- One or both pupils (black center of the eye) look gray or white.
- One or both eyes cross, turn in or out, or move differently from the other.
- Baby of three months or more does not look directly at objects.
- Child bumps into or trips over things.
- Child has difficulty seeing after the sun sets (night blindness).
- Child has difficulty reading small print.
- Child has difficulty identifying details in pictures.
- Child has difficulty going up or down stairs, throwing or catching a ball, buttoning clothes, or tying shoes.
- Child is excessively clumsy.
- Child is unable to discriminate letters.
- Child rubs eyes often.
- Child squints.
- Child complains of dizziness or headaches after a reading assignment.
- Child often tilts head.
- Child uses one eye, possibly shutting or covering the other eye when reading.
- Child dislikes or avoids close work.
- Child holds objects abnormally close to the eyes.

In many cases, visual impairments can now be prevented, but more can be done. For example, by protecting against eye injuries, the incidence of visual impairments can be greatly reduced. For those visual impairments that cannot be avoided, their impact can be lessened through early and consistent treatment. In the next two sections, we call your attention to the importance of public education and safety precautions.

Public Education. As we just mentioned, medical advances have helped reduce the incidence and prevalence of low vision and blindness. Medical treatments can also reduce the severity of the visual impairment, especially when provided as early as possible. In progressive diseases, treatments such as improving the children's diet or supplementing their diets with vitamins may halt damage before it is too serious. For example, adding a vitamin A supplement to a child's diet might prevent dry eye; limiting sugar intake for a child prone for diabetes might prevent the blindness often associated with this disease.

Early identification of a disability is a crucial element in the prevention of visual impairments and is especially important when medical technology cannot prevent or reduce the impact of the disability. If children with visual impairments and their families receive professional help early, they all adjust more quickly to the disability and the child is able to move quickly to the tasks of learning. Unfortunately, not all U.S. children have early access to health care. In fact, poor children are between 1.2 and 1.8 times more likely to have visual impairments (Sherman, 1994).

Some public education measures must seek to break down traditions that, though well meaning, are harmful to children. Unfortunately, many people still try so-called home cures to prevent or cure eye problems. For example, in Mexico, a common home cure is to place a wet chia seed under a person's eyelid to remove dirt or other particles from the eye. However, dirt adheres to the seed because of the seed's sticky surface layer and causes more problems. Other home cures are dangerous and can cause blindness. For example, lemon juice, urine, feces, pieces of shell, and some topical ointments are desperate cures in some cultures, but they are not safe and can injure the eye. With education, however, people can be informed about the dangers of these techniques or cures.

Public education needs to go beyond the school and the playground. In the mid-1980s, Prevent Blindness America launched a public education program to inform professional groups (educators, doctors, nurses) and the general public about eye safety and the importance of early medical treatment. Encouragingly, most states now have referral and information networks, and public information messages on television and radio provide information to the general public on vision and safety precautions.

Safety. Almost one million Americans have lost their vision from an eye injury, about half of which happened at home, and most could have been prevented by wearing the right eye protection (Rabb, 1996). Safety measures can prevent visual impairments caused by accidents. For example, nearly 10 percent of eye injuries in children under age 5 are caused by toys. In children between ages 5 and 14, eye injuries were caused most often by toys, baseball, basketball, adhesives, swimming pool accidents, pens and pencils, bicycles, football, and aerosol containers. Many of these cases could have been avoided with better safety measures such as wearing safety goggles and other protective devices (Prevent Blindness America, 1996).

Low Vision and Blind Children

You may be surprised to learn that only 10 percent of students who are legally blind use Braille as their primary mode of learning (American Printing House for the Blind, 1992). The great majority of students with visual impairments learn to read and write, watch television, and use their vision to function in society. For many of these students, their visual efficiency can be improved with careful guidance and instruction (Barraga, 1993). Certainly, they have less information to act on when compared with individuals who have all of their senses intact. This fact has serious ramifications for interpersonal interactions as well as academic learning. Next time you are interacting with friends, consider how nonverbal cues (facial expressions, a shrug of the shoulders) affect the meaning of a message. Now think about how the literal message (without the nonverbal cues) of the interaction would be understood by someone who could not use sight during the interaction.

Characteristics Affecting Social Skills

Visual information plays an important role in the acquisition of social skills and the ability to interact appropriately with peers. This learning process begins in infancy and continues to develop throughout childhood (Kekelis, 1992). The infant learns to make eye contact, smile, and touch appropriately. The child learns to gain access to play groups, resolve conflicts, attract and direct attention of peers, play, and maintain friendships. Where these skills are learned through typical interactions by sighted children, they need to be directly taught to many blind children (Heller et al., 1996).

Many people with visual impairments are rejected by sighted people (Hudson, 1994), possibly because they might not have been taught what is expected in normal social interactions. For example, many blind youngsters tend to lack play skills, ask too many irrelevant questions, and engage in inappropriate acts of affection (Rettig, 1994). Many of these individuals also exhibit other inappropriate behaviors, such as rocking, moving their hands strangely in space, and eye poking. Possibly because of their inappropriate or immature social behaviors, they tend to interact with and make friends with the least popular peers in their general education classes (MacCuspie, 1992). And, unfortunately, they tend not to interact with other children naturally or spontaneously (Crocker & Orr, 1996). Of course, with careful and direct instruction these situations can be improved or even eliminated.

Perhaps the way blind children are treated and negative experiences with peers during the schoolyears contribute to the following characteristics often attributed to blind people in the research literature: being socially immature, egocentric, self-conscious, isolated, passive, withdrawn, and dependent (Tuttle & Ferrell, 1995). Why else are these behavioral characteristics exhibited by some individuals with visual impairments? Some of these behaviors may be a function of the disability, but some may be caused by the way people treat individuals with visual impairments. For example, people with visual impairments tend to be overprotected; they are not encouraged to take risks, participate in sports, and move around as others do (Ferrell, 1986). Overprotection often begins in early infancy and can result in patterns of behavior that reduce social integration. In addition, many sighted people seem to be uncomfortable with people who have visual impairments (Hudson, 1994). They do not know how to interact with a person who cannot see well and who may look different as well. Overprotection by well-meaning family and friends and the aversion and fear of the general population can cause some individuals with visual impairments to become dependent and withdrawn.

The lack of effective interpersonal social skills can have a lifelong impact. It can influence leisure time activities, success on the job, and overall adjustment. The challenge here is to sighted peers, teachers, and parents and to the individuals themselves. Interpersonal skills can be learned, and the opportunities for using those skills can be increased (MacCuspie, 1992; Sacks & Kekelis, 1992a; Sacks & Reardon, 1992). Sighted peers should be informed about the visual status of their classmates with visual impairments and can be assigned the role of helper for both academic and social situations. They can also be taught to role-model proper behavior. Teachers can encourage students with visual impairments to participate fully in all school activities and to communicate their visual needs to others in a straightforward fashion. Teachers can also help these students understand the explicit and implicit rules of games and social interactions. Meanwhile, parents can organize small play groups at home and provide direct feedback about their youngster's interpersonal interactions. Parents can also foster independence by allowing their child to take some risks.

Academic Performance

Today, a large percentage (about 46 percent) of students with visual impairments spend over 79 percent of their school days in general education classrooms. Two-thirds of low vision and blind students receive their education at their neighborhood school in the general education classroom, possibly with support from a resource or itinerant teacher (U.S. Department of Education, 1996). These students participate in the general education curriculum with their sighted classmates and, if they do not also have multiple disabilities, perform well academically. Many use aids such as glasses or technology that enlarges type to help them enhance their vision for accessing information from printed material. Others learn to use their tactile senses and use Braille as their reading method, and some rely on audio means for gaining information. Regardless of the method they use for reading, all individuals with severe visual limitations must learn to listen well. So, in the following sections, we discuss different methods of reading and writing and the development of listening skills. Clearly, accommodations in classroom settings can help these students function even better; these we discuss in the Educational Interventions section of this chapter.

> MAKING CONNECTIONS
>
> For more about Braille, see in this chapter
> • The Literacy section (Educational Interventions),
> • Concepts and Controversy.

Methods of Reading and Writing. Students with very severe visual impairments may need to learn to read and write using different methods. **Braille** uses a coded system of dots embossed on paper so that individuals can feel a page of text. Surrounded in controversy today, Braille has been used by shrinking proportions of low vision and blind people over recent years (Schoellkopf, 1995; Wittenstein, 1994). In 1963, over 50 percent of persons with severe visual impairments used Braille, while in 1978 less than 20 percent did. By 1992, only 10 percent of students who were blind used Braille (American Printing House for the Blind, 1992).

Many reasons are given to explain why fewer people are using Braille as a reading method today. First, Braille for many can be very cumbersome and slow. Tuttle and Ferrell (1995) report that good Braille readers achieve a rate of only 100 words per minute; others (Ethington, 1956; Nolan, 1967) have found that the average high school student who is blind reads even fewer words per minute—around 86 to 90. Try to read that slowly, you will find it quite difficult and laborious. Becoming even minimally proficient at the Braille method of reading takes extensive training and practice. Braille also uses different codes for different types of reading, such as math and music, making it even more difficult for students with cognitive impairments to master completely.

Braille. A system of reading and writing that uses dot codes that are embossed on paper, developed by Louis Braille in 1929.

Having a Personal Companion lets this high school student take notes, which he will use later, as he writes his social studies paper.

Can you think of some other reasons why Braille is less popular today? Here is a list: teachers who do not know how to use or teach the Braille method, the unavailability of teachers who know how to teach Braille to others, increasing availability of audio-tapes, immediate computerized print-to-voice translations, difficulty of getting Braille versions of books. Braille literacy has become the focus of a great debate. Ironically, advanced technology is both a reason for its resurgence and its unpopularity. The unavailability of Braille versions of texts used in the general education classroom was a great hindrance to this method's widespread use. Now, because of scanning capabilities and special microcomputer software and printers that can translate standard print to Braille instantaneously, Braille editions can be obtained quite quickly through regional materials centers, the American Printing House for the Blind, and Library of Congress. These agencies and the Recordings for the Blind also produce voice versions of printed materials.

What are some other methods blind people use for reading? What other purposes might Braille serve for people with visual impairments? The majority use their vision and read print. According to the American Printing House for the Blind (1992), 27 percent of students who are blind are visual readers, 10 percent are auditory readers (primarily using **personal readers** or recorded materials), and 10 percent use Braille. (Personal readers are people who read aloud to those who are blind.) This study included elementary and secondary students attending local public schools and those attending state center schools, and it found that 22 percent of the students were considered prereaders because they were reading at a readiness level and had not yet determined a preferred reading mode and that 31 percent were nonreaders. Findings like these have caused

personal reader. A person who reads text orally to those who cannot read print.

concern in the field about the low literacy rate among individuals with visual impairments and have sparked debate about the teaching of Braille (Rex, Koenig, Wormsley, & Baker, 1994). "Braille bills" have been and are being introduced and passed in many state legislatures (Schroeder, 1993). And, in part because it found that over 90 percent of working blind people use Braille in their work, the federal government is strongly encouraging a resurgence of Braille instruction (Briand, 1994). None of the state bills or federal guidelines mandate the teaching of Braille; rather they allow it to be part of a student's IEP. Clearly, these actions have brought national attention to the issue of literacy and people who cannot use their sight to read.

Today, some children are taught to read print instead of Braille because experts better understand the concept of visual efficiency: People do not have only so much sight that can be used up; rather, using sight can improve an individual's visual efficiency. Improved practices help people with visual impairments make better use of their residual vision, particularly those with low vision. Also, better optical corrections and technology are now available that allow more of these individuals to use their own vision as they read and write.

Many low vision students who use their vision to read need specially adapted versions of the texts used in their classes. Many such texts have been produced on microcomputer disks and are available from materials centers. An advantage of using computers is the flexibility in output: individually adjusted type size, Braille, or audio. Future technology will add other methods for reading and writing. For example, in the future, speech synthesizers will become less expensive, exceptionally portable, and more commonly available, allowing for instant voice-to-print and print-to-voice translations of documents.

As mentioned previously, the size of print in typical school textbooks is too small for many students with visual impairments. If computers are not available, what other options do these students have? Many states and school districts have materials centers that offer modified materials for students' use, but many books and materials are broadly available through bookstores and mail-order sources. For example, books with enlarged print allow some students to read the same material as their sighted classmates. Also, large-type dictionaries, thesauruses, and atlases are now available. The Book of the Month Club maintains a Large Print Library; *Reader's Digest* produces a large-type version of its magazine every month, as well as a biography and condensed book series; and the *New York Times* publishes a specially edited weekly version of its newspaper in 16 point type and small page size (12 inch x 14 inch). And, of course, materials not originally produced in large type can be enlarged by using common copy machines. Such modifications—essential for most individuals with glaucoma, congenital cataracts, or nystagmus—allow greater participation in American society by blind and low vision people.

For individuals with good central vision but a limited visual field, enlargements may be a hindrance, however. For these students, audiocassette versions of textbooks may be the better choice. Personal readers may also be used. With the new capabilities of computer-generated print-to-voice systems will come greater and easier access to classroom materials for students with severe visual impairments.

Some students must adjust or vary the way they hold texts to read print. For example, many students with nystagmic eye (rapid eye) movements minimize the

MAKING CONNECTIONS

Background about work in the area of visual efficiency is found in the History section of this chapter.

MAKING CONNECTIONS

More information about technology for low vision and blind people is found in the Technology section of this chapter.

distracting movement by pulling their eyes to the right or left corner to read, which lessens the movement of the eye itself. Other students see reading material better if they hold it in a particular position; a reading stand or easel might be helpful to them. Others have difficulties with thick books that do not remain open or flat; for these students, pages of a book can be clipped together. Many find the reading (and other classroom work that places demands on their vision) causes considerable fatigue, particularly if the reading passage is long. Consider this factor when planning the student's school day.

Regardless of the method used, many students with visual impairments have substantial difficulties learning to read (Harley, Truan, & Sanford, 1987). These students require more repetition, more drill, and more practice than other students whether they are learning to read by using print or Braille. Teachers must thus find creative ways to keep these students' attention and prevent boredom and loss of interest. Games, computer-assisted instruction, and peer tutoring are alternatives to the flash cards and mimeographed worksheets teachers generally (over)use.

Listening. All students can benefit from improving their listening skills; however, for students with visual impairments, good listening skills are imperative. Many of these individuals must rely heavily on their hearing. Mack (1984) found that most blind adults commonly use readers and recordings for their reading because of the inconvenience of the Braille method. As the use of audiotaped versions of books and of microcomputers that convert print to voice becomes more common, listening skills gain even more importance.

Listening is part of the communication process and is a crucial skill for students with visual impairments, especially those whose visual loss is severe. To gain information, they listen to teachers, friends, and family; to recorded books and magazines; and to television, radio, and sounds from computers and other electronic devices.

Listening skills can be divided into five categories: attentive, analytic, marginal, appreciative, and selective (Smith, 1972). **Attentive listening** occurs when a person focuses on one form of communication, as in a telephone call. **Analytical listening** requires the individual to think about and analyze what a speaker is saying, possibly even drawing inferences about the content of the other person's message. When we listen to music, poetry, or stories being read, we are using **appreciative listening**; and when we listen to background music when studying or writing, we are using **marginal listening**. In **selective listening**, we eliminate all background noise and listen only to certain sounds or a certain speaker. Many aspects of listening can be improved. So that all students develop good listening skills, teachers should include activities in the school day whose purpose is to develop better listening skills in their students. For example, specific tactics—such as peer coaching—used to remind classmates to listen carefully to a particular part of a lesson can help improve the listening skills of children with attention problems. The relationship between language development and listening skills is strong, and children's listening can be improved through instruction to increase vocabulary, knowledge of multiple meanings, and syntax.

Table 11.3 shows a listening hierarchy teachers can use to develop listening skills in their students. Devised for students with visual impairments, this sequential skill listing is helpful to all students. The questions serve as a guide for the teacher.

attentive listening. Focusing on one form or source of communication.

analytic listening. Listening that includes analysis and possibly interpretation of another person's communication message.

appreciative listening. Listening for the sake of enjoyment, such as to music.

marginal listening. Listening in which part of the auditory content, such as background music, is not the primary focus of attention.

selective listening. Focusing attention on only one sound in the environment, such as the speaker's voice in a lecture.

~~~

TABLE 11.3

Listening Skills Hierarchy

Sound awareness
Does the child change behavior by the presence or absence of sound? (Startle reaction)

Auditory attending
Can the child interpret different sounds to have different meanings? (The sound of a dog barking, doorbell ringing)

Auditory attention span
Can the child attend to sounds for some length of time?

Sound localization
Can the child tell the location or direction of sound?

Auditory discrimination
Can the child recognize the similarities and differences between sounds?

Auditory memory
Can the child store and recall a series of sounds?

Auditory memory span
Can the child associate an event with a sound or remember verbal commands over some period of time?

Auditory sequencing
Can the child remember the order of items named in a sequence?

Auditory projection
Can the child attend to and interpret sounds at a distance?

Auditory figure-ground discrimination
Can the child attend to a particular sound despite competing sounds in the environment?

Auditory blending
Can the child put sounds together to make whole words?

Auditory closure
Can the child complete a word when only a part is presented?

Reauditorization
Can the child remember inflection patterns?

Source: Communication Skills for Visually Impaired Learners (p. 204) by R. K. Harley, M. B. Truan, and L. D. Sanford, 1987. Courtesy of Charles C. Thomas, Publisher, Springfield, IL. Adapted by permission.

Educational Interventions

The vast majority of low vision and blind students live at home and attend their neighborhood elementary and secondary schools. Many receive the same education as classmates who do not share their disability. They may receive extra assistance from resource room teachers and other specialists, particularly in the area of basic skills. Some receive the general education curriculum, with additional instructional support. Students whose functional use of vision is extremely limited require specialized instruction on additional topics such as orientation and mobility and independent living skills.

For those with visual impairments, preschool education is vital. What is a good educational program for a preschooler? What role does this early intervention play in the future of persons with visual impairments? These issues are addressed in the next section. In the Education and the Schoolchild section, you will learn about adapting the instructional setting to better meet the educational needs of low vision and blind students, special curriculum topics (e.g., orientation and mobility) unique to this population of learners, and issues surrounding literacy.

Education and the Preschool Child

Preschool programs for individuals with severe visual impairments help infants and their families from the onset of their visual loss (Barraga & Erin, 1992). Recall that those who are congenitally blind (born blind) and those who became blind at a very early age (adventitiously blind) have little or no memory of how the world looks. These infants are not stimulated like sighted infants and have limited opportunities for learning. They do not see their mother's smile or the toys in their cribs. The right preschool program can give preschoolers with visual impairments the "right start" so that the disadvantages which this disability can cause are minimized.

 MAKING CONNECTIONS

For a review of issues relating to age of onset and types of impairments, see the Defined section of this chapter.

A wide variety of programs are available for preschoolers with visual impairments. In some cities, teachers work with these children and their families at their homes. Sometimes, preschool and day care teachers are assisted by special education teachers who travel from school to school (itinerant specialists). In many cities, special preschool programs are available for these children. Sometimes, these programs are segregated (attended only by preschoolers with visual impairments); other times, they are integrated (they include sighted children). Many special preschool programs are supervised and managed by staff from a state center or residential school. No matter what program is chosen, preschoolers should receive the most intensive early educational experiences possible. To provide the fullest attention to the child, the teacher of a preschooler with visual impairments should coordinate an interdisciplinary team of specialists to work with the child and the family. This team might include an ophthalmologist, occupational therapist, physical therapist, orientation and mobility instructor, and social worker. The makeup of the team depends on the needs of each child and family.

 MAKING CONNECTIONS

The parents who shared their story in the Personal Perspective section and their children participate in a special preschool managed by the state's residential center school.

When not stimulated directly, blind infants often withdraw and do not explore their environments as sighted infants do. Many infants who are blind experience a prolonged period of inactivity during their first year, which inhibits their exploration and discovery of their environment (Tröster & Brambring, 1994). Many develop the inappropriate behaviors we discussed earlier in this chapter, such as rocking or inappropriate hand movements. Babies with visual impairments may acquire some social problems as a result of insufficient interpersonal interactions early in life, so they need assistance as they develop relationships, particularly during the first two years of life. For example, they may need to be taught when to smile and make eye contact appropriately. These are skills that parents can teach their children with the help of early childhood specialists. Infants and toddlers with severe visual impairments do, however, act like sighted babies in other ways. Although there is no difference in the way that these and sighted babies babble, many blind children do have some language delays. However, with some extra guidance from family members, their vocabulary development can be the same as that of sighted babies (Dote-Kwan & Hughes, 1994).

The preschool years provide the foundation for lifelong learning and independence. In that regard, in this section we discuss the development of play skills and initial independence. For many young low vision and blind children and their families, preschool programs are a cornerstone to a good start on the path for strong educational results or outcomes. Selecting the right preschool can be confusing, so we have listed some characteristics or quality indicators of excellent early intervention programs for these youngsters.

MAKING CONNECTIONS

Read again the Educational Interventions section (Preschool) (Chapter 5) for more on young children's play behavior.

Play. Researchers are learning that play is a very important part of human development (Crocker & Orr, 1996; Skellenger & Hill, 1994). Through play, young children learn to socialize, interact with others, and cooperate. Through discovery and exploration, which are encouraged through play activities, young children also learn about their environment, develop motor skills, and often enhance their language skills. Because of their disability, blind children play very differently than their sighted peers (Rettig, 1994), and these play differences may well have lifelong effects. For example, blind children spend 56 percent of their time playing alone; sighted children play alone only 14 percent of the time.

Blind preschoolers explore their surroundings less than their sighted peers (Tröster & Brambring, 1992). Many blind adults also restrict their environments and tend not to explore unfamiliar areas on their own (Clarke, Sainato, & Ward, 1994). Tröster and Brambring (1992; 1994) have identified other play characteristics that follow many blind individuals into adulthood: engaging in high rates of solitary play, not playing spontaneously, seeking play with adults rather than other children, and selecting toys that are concrete, familiar items. It also appears that blind children are unable to play symbolically until much later than their nondisabled peers. This delayed play development might well contribute to later difficulties in social interactions. Sighted children often find it difficult to adjust their play to the ability levels of blind children who prefer noisy play activities that are not abstract or symbolic (Tröster & Brambring, 1994). They may also find that their play styles are in conflict with blind peers'. The quick and sometimes unpredictable movements of sighted children may disorient children with severe visual impairments (Rettig, 1994). Such play differences may well inhibit integrated play activities of sighted and nonsighted peers. Some researchers are convinced that adults have to teach blind preschoolers how to play and be sure those skills are well learned before encouraging play with sighted peers (Skellenger & Hill, 1994). Teachers must be aware of the possible barriers to parallel play between sighted and blind children; they will need to teach these children to learn how to play together, interact appropriately, and work cooperatively.

To eliminate some of the barriers to meaningful interactions, Rettig (1994) believes that play environments designed specifically for children with visual impairments, but with great appeal to sighted children, could encourage interactions between blind and sighted children. For example, playcourts designed along themes that rely on senses other than sight may facilitate play between these two groups. Rettig suggests a number of different themes: rough and tumble hills, tactile towns sized for young children, sensory obstacle courses, gardens. Tactile maps could be developed to guide youngsters through mazes. The options for unique and interesting play areas seem endless.

Learning Independence. Orientation and mobility are major curriculum targets for students with severe visual impairments. Because instruction in this area needs to begin as early as possible, parents and professionals are encouraging the introduction of the long cane to children between the ages of 2 and 6 (Pogrund, Fazzi, & Schreier, 1993). Although some orientation and mobility teachers believe that young children should begin learning how to use a long cane with the one they will use later in life (which would be extra long for their present size), research findings indicate that children are better off learning how to use a mobility cane that is more their size (Clarke, Sainato, & Ward, 1994). Sometimes called the Kiddy Cane or the Connecticut precane, this home-made version of the long cane is tailored to the size of the user, even a preschooler. It is made of rigid, white PVC pipe and is cut at midchest height. It has a red stripe at the bottom and tape across the top for a grip.

Because the home is the most natural setting for infant's and toddler's educational programs, most include home-based instruction with considerable parent involvement. For later independence, one of the most important lessons parents can learn is to allow their babies to explore the environment. Research shows that parents can help their infants become more mobile and independent by teaching them to crawl and walk in a structured program (Joffee, 1988). Some parents of infants with visual impairments, fearful that their baby will fall or be hurt, are overly protective and controlling; attitudes that can foster dependency (Behl, Akers, Boyce, & Taylor, 1996).

Quality Indicators of Preschool Programs. Many infants with visual impairments need more meaningful stimulation than their nondisabled peers, and they need direct intervention to effect an increase in the levels of their involvement with others (Crocker & Orr, 1996). Also, the development of the senses of touch and hearing should begin in the early weeks of life and continue on through childhood. These babies should touch their toys and other objects with purpose. They need to learn to feel for shape, size, and other dimensions. The development of good listening skills also needs to begin early, and one of the first skills children should learn is how to judge where sounds are coming from (**sound localization**). Most typical learners enhance these skills through play; so, too, should preschoolers with visual impairments. Good preschool programs encourage play, a natural recreational activity that can also improve self-confidence and self-esteem (Dominguez & Dominguez, 1991).

Most infants and young children learn through imitation. They see what others are doing and they try to copy it. Imitation is restricted for those with visual impairments (Tröster & Brambring, 1994). Adults therefore need to supplement what the infant touches with a verbal description of the activity or object. Simple statements like "I am washing your hands" help the baby associate the meaning of what is felt and the activity. The child's ability to think in terms of concepts is enhanced when someone communicates and describes in words objects the baby touches but cannot see. Naming concrete objects and describing their physical characteristics (long, soft, hard, heavy, rough) help to develop vocabulary and to improve language development.

 MAKING CONNECTIONS

Orientation and mobility is discussed in the Schoolchildren section of this chapter.

sound localization. Being able to locate the source of sounds.

TABLE 11.4

Quality Indicators for Exemplar Preschool Programs for Students with
Visual Impairments

- Experiences that are fun in a homelike, informal, and secure atmosphere

- Structured experiences in which children can integrate information about themselves and their environment

- Activities that prepare children for formal schooling, assisting them to make a gradual transition from the home to the educational environment

- Opportunities for many different types of interactions with peers

- Instruction in a broad array of areas, including acquisition of language and listening skills; preacademics; gross and fine motor skills; and development of residual vision, mobility, socialization, self-confidence, and independence

- Support and assistance to the entire family

- Instruction in assistive technology through direct instruction using the most advanced equipment currently available

- Experiences to assist the child to benefit from incidental visual experiences, develop problem-solving skills, and use environmental information (gained through sight and other senses) to plan and execute tasks

- Initial development of literacy skills

- Experiences whose aim is the development of a personal identity

Experts in the field of early intervention for youngsters with visual impairments emphasize not only the importance of preschool programs but also the vast array of curriculum targets that should be included (Corn, 1990; Dominguez & Dominguez, 1991; Ingsholt, 1990; Leyenberger, 1990). Table 11.4 lists some of the activities that exemplar preschool programs for these youngsters provide.

Education and the Schoolchild

The educational needs of low vision students differ from those of blind students. Students with low vision might require some extra tutorial assistance to learn the same number of phonetic rules as their classmates or additional time to read their history assignment. Students who are blind might require the introduction of entirely different curriculum topics. For example, they might need to learn independent **life skills** so that they can manage an apartment, pay their bills, shop for food, and cook their meals without assistance from others. The crucial factor is that the educational and developmental goals, and the instruction designed to meet those goals, reflect the specific needs of each individual (Corn, Hatlen, Huebner, Ryan, & Siller, 1995). In the following subsections we discuss some methods of teaching and specific curriculum suggestions for low vision and blind students. Keep in mind that these two groups are not truly distinct; suggestions for low vision students might well apply to many blind students, and those for blind students to some low vision students.

life skills. Those skills used to manage a home, cook, shop, and organize personal living environments.

498 ~~ *CHAPTER 11 Low Vision and Blindness*

Classroom Organization and Instructional Management. Some minor modifications in teaching style can help all students, particularly those with visual impairments, gain more from the learning environment. One such modification is the careful use of oral language. For example, many of us, when speaking, use words that do not refer to other words (referents); we say words like *it*, *this*, *that*, and *there* without naming the topic we are discussing. For example, an adult might say, "Go get it. It's over there," instead of saying, "Please get the red book on my desk." Adults need to realize how unclear the first set of directions are to many children, particularly those with disabilities. Also, adults need to think about how their written language is indirect and can be made more specific by restating terms they write on the blackboard and also explaining their meanings. More careful use of language will benefit all members of the class.

Research has shown that people learn more efficiently when they have been given previews of the lesson about to be taught. Unfortunately, few teachers, particularly at middle and secondary schools, provide students with previews or **advance organizers**. As a formalized teaching strategy, advance organizers were developed by researchers at the University of Kansas Center for Research on Learning to assist students with learning disabilities focus their attention on the upcoming learning task; however, this teaching tactic has proven to be effective with many students with disabilities, especially those with visual impairments. Advance organizers convey information about the lecture that is about to be presented. The purpose is to help students gain some initial understanding of the content and become familiar with the organization of the lecture and understand why they should spend the effort learning the information. The key components included in advance organizers are information about topics and subtopics in the lecture, background information and concepts to be learned, and rationale and expected outcomes for learning (Deshler, Ellis, & Lenz, 1996).

Educators can adjust the instructional environment in other ways that will benefit blind and low vision students. These students need to participate actively in the class, should complete assignments independently, and must turn them in at an assigned time. Many of these students require more time to complete typical assignments given in general education classes. The teacher can set a different due date, but must enforce this deadline and follow through with contingencies if the assignment is not completed on time. Many teachers find that allowing students to use a computer for in-class assignments and homework is beneficial. Because reading and writing may be physically fatiguing to some students, some researchers suggest making some exceptions by abbreviating these students' assignments or giving them more time to complete them (Harley et al., 1987). Regardless of these accommodations, teachers should not lower their expectations for students with visual disabilities. These students should be encouraged to be full class members who share their work and thoughts with others.

Organizing the classroom might take a little more thought when the needs of a blind student are being considered. Let us look at the example of Elizabeth, a third grader who is blind. On the first day of school, Mr. Munroe took the time to show Elizabeth the classroom. He made certain that the furniture and materials were in a consistent pattern and placement, but he warned Elizabeth that the classroom would be reorganized periodically. Reorganizing the room every month or so would help Elizabeth learn to adjust to changes in her environment. Many professionals who work with blind and low vision students recommend that teachers use a consistent daily and weekly schedule so that students will know what is

 MAKING CONNECTIONS

Also see the section on teachers' use of oral language (Educational Interventions) (Chapter 5).

 MAKING CONNECTIONS

- For examples of advance organizers, see those sections at the beginning of every chapter in this text.
- For a review of the learning strategies approach, see the Education and the Schoolchild section in the Educational Interventions section (Chapter 4).

advance organizers. Previews to lectures that acquaint students with the content, its organization, and importance.

Weekly Planning Sheet

Date ___1/17___

	MONDAY	√	TUESDAY	√	WEDNESDAY	√	THURSDAY	√	FRIDAY	√	WEEKEND
Tests							English		Science Algebra		To do: Outline English Paper Re-copy History Notes Read Scarlet Letter
Homework/ Papers Due					Algebra Assignment pp 127–130						
Read	Scarlet Letter History Chapter	√ √	Scarlet Letter	√							
Study					for English Test		for Science Test and Algebra				

expected at various times of the day (math after morning recess) and across the week (spelling tests on Friday). Students need to learn how to manage their study schedule to be sure their work is completed well and on time. The weekly planner shown in the Teaching Tactics box has advantages for many middle and high school students with and without visual impairments.

Other modifications to the classroom can help blind and low vision students. For example, some of these students use bulky equipment and aids (optical aids, magnifiers, tape recorders) that facilitate their learning. Some use brailling equipment, and others use portable microcomputers. These students need larger desks or a small table near an electrical outlet. They might even need cabinet space to store their belongings.

Literacy. Many individuals with severe visual impairments are not proficient readers. In the study conducted by the American Printing House for the Blind (1992), the largest group (31 percent) were nonreaders. When that group is added to the group identified as prereaders (22 percent), it is apparent that the majority of students with visual impairments are neither visual nor tactile (Braille) readers. Literacy is a goal for all Americans and an expectation for all high school graduates. Because literacy presents particular and unique challenges for individuals with visual impairments, we need to look at literacy in different ways. Being able

MAKING CONNECTIONS

Also see in this chapter these sections:
• Methods of Reading and Writing (Low Vision and Blind Students)
• Concepts and Controversy

~~~
TABLE 11.5

Literacy Tasks Requiring Communication with Self and Communication with Others in Four Environments

Audience	Home	School	Community	Work
Communicating with self*	Labeling personal items Maintaining an address and telephone book	Jotting assignments Taking notes in class	Making shopping lists Writing directions to a specific location	Jotting notes to self Making list of "things to do"
Communicating with others†	Writing personal letters to friends Paying bills Reading mail Reading for pleasure Reading newspapers Reading books to others	Reading textbooks and workbooks Reading periodicals Writing term papers Completing assignments Taking tests Completing registration forms	Completing deposit slips at a bank Reading signs Reading menus Signing documents Writing checks at a store Reading labels on items at a store	Reading memos from supervisor Writing reports Reading gauges and dials Filling out forms Reading job manuals Writing work-related correspondence

Source: "A Framework for Understanding the Literacy of Individuals with Visual Impairments" by A. J. Koenig. Reprinted by permission from the *Journal of Visual Impairments & Blindness.* Copyright 1992 by American Foundation for the Blind, 11 Penn Plaza, Suite 300, New York, NY 10001. All rights reserved.

*The individual is both the writer and the intended reader.
†The individual is either the writer or the intended reader, but not both.

to gain access to information presented through print and Braille and to communicate with others through written and oral modes are components of the literacy goal for students with visual impairments. In addition, experts include skills such as technology, computing, checkbook balancing, and independent completion of daily living tasks as literacy goals for this population of learners (Newman & Beverstock, 1990).

Clearly, literacy is a diverse and complex concept. For example, reading skills, whether they be through print or Braille, are needed to succeed in school and to meet academic demands of high school and college. Other sets of skills are required for achievement in the workplace. To help us better understand what comprises literacy in the adult world, Koenig (1992) provides us with some examples of what he calls functional literacy—the ability to accomplish practical real-life tasks required in the home, school, community, and work environments. Table 11.5 shows examples of these skills and gives us some ideas about what should be included in the curriculum presented to blind and low vision students.

Orientation and Mobility. Children with very low visual efficiencies need special training to increase their independence (Clarke et al., 1994). Orientation and mobility training helps those with severe visual impairments to move around independently. **Orientation** can be described as the mental map people have about their surroundings (Hill, 1986). Most of us use landmarks and other cues to

orientation. The mental map people have to move through environments.

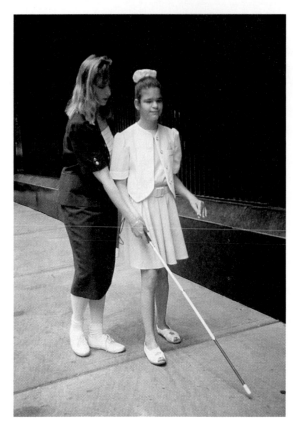

Independent mobility and orientation are two of the greatest challenges that face people with severe visual impairments. Direct instruction in mobility training is necessary.

get from one place to another. Think about how you get from your house to a friend's home or from one class to another on campus. What cues or landmarks do you use? These cues or landmarks make up our mental maps and orientation to our environments. **Mobility** is the ability to travel safely and efficiently from one place to another. Many adults use the **long cane** to help them move around independently. Learning how to be independently mobile by using a long cane is a difficult goal to accomplish. This curriculum target should begin when these children are toddlers and continue as a major instructional area across the schoolyears.

The orientation and mobility curriculum includes more than the use of long canes. For example, using maps is important to everyone who must figure out how to travel from place to place. For blind individuals, **tactile maps** can be very helpful. When students are trained in their use, these maps can assist with independent movement in the community, as street maps do for sighted people. Recent advances in computers and printers now simplify the creation of tactile maps and graphics (Haggen, 1996). In a comparison of different types of tactual maps, easy-to-learn strip maps (3 inch by 5 inch hand-held notebooks) were the most effective and popular with blind users (Luxton, Banai, & Kuperman, 1994). Strip maps may have been the most highly rated because of their portability and small size; but, for whatever reasons, their users explored the subway system of New York City far more when using these maps.

How do people with visual impairments orient themselves to their surroundings and increase their mobility? In doing the background research for their book about guide dog schools, Eames and Eames estimate that 7,250 people in the United States use **guide dogs** (JVIB News Service, 1995). Relatively few adults who are legally blind (less than 4 percent) use guide dogs to help them move about independently (Tuttle & Ferrell, 1995). Substantially more blind and low vision people chose to use long canes. The National Center for Health Statistics reported that in 1990, 109,000 used canes to aid their mobility (JVIB News Service, 1994). The cane makes a sound as it is tapped on the ground while a person is walking. It helps the person know when a hallway ends, when stairs begin and end, and when doors are reached. However, for many obstacles in our world, a cane is not helpful. Silent traffic signals can be very dangerous to persons with visual impairments, and many cities have not yet installed beeper traffic signals. Escalators, elevators, and public transportation can present problems as well.

How do people with visual impairments cope with these problems? In the future, the ADA law should reduce hazards for people with severe visual impairments. This law provides guidelines that will eliminate protruding and overhanging objects that are undetectable with mobility canes. It specifies that passageways must have 80-inch clear headroom or a barrier to warn a blind person and that all stairs in hospitals and public buildings must have uniform riser heights and uniform tread widths (Wiener, 1992). Until such measures are fully implemented, however, people with severe visual impairments need intensive effort and specialized training to cope with these challenges.

Sometimes, like when crossing a busy street or entering an unfamiliar building, blind and low vision people require assistance. But the sighted person must be sensitive to the person's desire to receive help. First, be certain that the individual wants assistance. Ask. If the answer is yes, guide the individual by offering your arm, holding it in a relaxed position. People with a visual impairment usually will gently grasp your arm at or above your elbow and will walk slightly behind or to your side. Never push or pull them as you walk. You will find that this system leaves you free to converse and walk with ease.

Sports and recreation programs and activities can have many benefits to children with severe visual impairments. They not only contribute to better orientation and mobility skills, but also help students become more involved socially. Special events such as the beeping eggs at the White House Easter Egg Hunt make a difference (Associated Press, 1996), but routine activities where consistent participation is possible are best. Many special sports programs are available (for example, skiing, sailing, hiking, baseball, bowling, bicycling, horseback riding), but for everyone it is important to begin the pattern of consistent physical exercise early in life. Many individuals with severe visual impairments excel in sports and can serve as role models and examples for children. For example, Bill Irwin and his guide dog, Orient, spent eight months hiking the entire 2,167-mile Appalachian Trail, which begins in Georgia and ends in Maine (*New York Times*, 1990). After many different excursions, Orient retired in October 1995 (CNN News, 1995). Erik Weihenmayer, the first blind person to hike the sixty-mile-long Inca Trail in Peru (*Sports Illustrated*, 1995), accomplished another first. Erik—along with Jamie Bloomquist, Jeff Evans, Sam Epstein, and two guides—were the first blind people to climb Alaska's Mount

MAKING CONNECTIONS

Service animals are also discussed in these sections:
- Educational Interventions (Chapter 9)
- Transition Through Adulthood in the Educational Interventions section (Chapter 10)

Review again the discussions of mobility canes in these sections of this chapter:
- Preschool
- History

MAKING CONNECTIONS

A photo of the AFB High Sights '95 team is on p. 509.

guide dogs. Animals, also called service animals, trained to assist blind persons to move about independently.

McKinley, the highest peak in North America. Their expedition, called "AFB HighSights '95," was sponsored by the American Foundation for the Blind "to encourage people who are blind or visually impaired to set their sights high and for more and more people across America to see us doing just that" (Augusto, 1993, p.1). This team of climbers, who hold jobs as English and math teacher, computer systems analyst, assistant district attorney, and psychoanalyst, certainly accomplished Weihenmayer's as well as their own personal goals.

Inclusion

Estimates indicate that before the 1940s, 85 percent of students with severe visual impairments attended special residential schools (Sacks & Rosen, 1994). This situation has changed dramatically. Today, about 11 percent attend public residential schools, and about 66 percent attend either general education or resource room programs in their local public schools (U.S. Department of Education, 1996). Many blind and low vision students receive tremendous benefits from attending general education classrooms and living at home. They are taught the same subjects as other children, and generally in the same manner. They grow up where home management (cooking, shopping, cleaning) is part of the daily routine. And, they interact socially with many different people, making them better prepared to take their places in society when schooling is completed. Unfortunately, merely attending a local public school does not guarantee socialization and true integration. These are goals still to be achieved.

Because of the increased understanding of the great benefits of living at home and attending school with neighborhood friends, enrollments at many residential schools are decreasing. In addition to changing philosophical views about educating students with disabilities at their neighborhood schools, many are concerned about high operating costs. When state legislators recently closed Stevie Wonder's alma mater, the Michigan School for the Blind, they cited costs (about $200,000 per year for each student) as their reason for closure (*Albuquerque Journal*, 1995).

The vast majority (85 percent) of children with visual impairments attend public school classes. Except for children with speech or language impairments, this group of youngsters is the most integrated of all students with disabilities. However, to learn all the skills they will need to be successful at school, at home, and later in adulthood, many of these students need intensive education in addition to the instruction they receive in the general classroom. They attend general education classes and receive educational services and supports from specially trained teachers. General education teachers have found that they need to make some adjustments to the learning environment and to their teaching practices to optimize the learning opportunities for their low vision and blind students. The suggestions found in the Making Accommodations box can easily be incorporated into classroom situations and certainly make the general classroom environment more "friendly" to students with substantial visual limitations (Barraga & Morris, 1992; Harley et al., 1987; Sacks & Kekelis, 1992b; Sacks & Reardon, 1992).

In large cities, many teachers of those with visual impairments serve as itinerant teachers, moving from school to school, sometimes spending only part of any school day at one school. Traditionally, their primary role was academic tutor. Like resource room teachers, they helped their students with the assignments from general educa-

1. Place the child's desk close to the teacher's desk, the blackboard, and the classroom door.

2. Reduce distracting glare, arrange the child's desk away from a light source but in a well-lit area.

3. Allow the child to relocate in the classroom for different activities to enhance opportunities to see and hear.

4. Open or close doors fully (a half-open door can be a dangerous obstacle).

5. Eliminate unnecessary noise; do not speak too loudly, for it tends to increase classroom volume level.

6. Eliminate clutter from the room, particularly in aisles and movement paths.

7. Place materials in consistent places, so that students know where particular items are always located.

8. Keep to routine schedules so that students know what to expect on specific days and times.

9. Address students by using their names first to get their attention.

10. Do not leave the classroom without telling the student.

11. Explain the implicit and explicit rules for classroom conduct, games, and social situations.

12. Encourage students with visual impairments to express their visual needs.

13. Repeat orally information written on a board or an overhead projector, and give the student a printed version. (Remember that enlargements on an overhead projector are not helpful to all blind and low vision students.)

14. Prepare enlarged print or Braille handouts, summarizing key points from lectures (an easy task using computers with Braillers and adjustable font and type sizes).

15. Audiotape lectures so that students can use tapes as study aids at home.

16. Select bright and contrasting colors for bulletin boards and other instructional materials for those who benefit from such visual contrasts.

17. Increase visual contrast: Place yellow plastic overlays over purple ditto worksheets (which will help some students see the worksheets more easily), photocopy dittos, use felt tip pens.

18. Seek assistance of a specialist in the area of visual impairments, and have high expectations.

Source: Adapted from *Courtesy Rules of Blindness*, courtesy of the National Federation of the Blind.

tion classes. Today, this role is changing, in part because of data indicating that blind and low vision adults have difficulties coping with daily life and require extensive supports to live independently successfully. Many of these adults experience problems managing their homes and their time. Others have difficulty locating and keeping jobs. Without mastery of these important life skills, which are necessary for independent living, successful academic learning means little. Therefore many teachers of students with visual impairments now spend a substantial portion of their time working on these practical life and career education skills.

Teachers of students with visual impairments who work in rural areas may serve in more of a consulting role. These itinerant teachers work directly with the students but also advise and assist general education teachers who work with low vision and blind students. They also obtain adapted materials and special equipment for students with visual impairments.

For over fifty years, it has been common practice for students with visual impairments to be educated in local public schools in general education classes, but that practice is now being questioned (Sacks, 1992). Many professionals (Corn et al., 1995) advocate for a full array of services for these students, including separate special classes and center or residential schools. Under these arrangements, students with visual impairments would be taught by teachers with very specialized preparation and receive a curriculum designed specifically for them.

Why, after all of these years of inclusion, would there be a call for a change in practice? Many educators are concerned that graduates of general education programs do not possess the skills needed for independence as adults (Curry & Hatlen, 1988; Sacks, Kekelis, & Gaylord-Ross, 1992). To achieve adult independence, youngsters with visual impairments need direct instruction in areas that are not part of the typical curriculum, such as social skills, functional life skills, assistive technology, career education, leisure skills, and orientation and mobility. Some individuals also need instruction in alternative reading methods such as Braille. Sacks (1992) maintains that although these youngsters have spent most, if not all, of their schoolyears with sighted classmates, "this approach left many children socially isolated and academically limited and resulted in a 'more restrictive environment.'" She also believes that "simple social or physical proximity between the groups may be counterproductive" (p. 4). The challenge is for teachers to ensure that, regardless of placement, students with visual impairments receive all the education they require, including social skills development.

Some programs are working to bridge this gap. Residential schools for students with visual impairments can be found in almost every state. In many cases, these schools serve fewer full-time, residential students. The students tend to come from rural areas, where services and the availability of special equipment are limited, and more and more of the students have multiple disabilities. As more students with visual impairments have been included in general education classrooms, the roles of many of the residential schools have changed. In addition to serving residential students, the schools serve as statewide resource and materials centers. Personnel from center schools consult with teachers at the local schools. Many center schools also offer short courses and summer programs for students and teachers. The specialized staff, materials, and equipment enable these schools to provide short courses on mobility and orientation, career education, independent living, and technology instruction not available locally. They also offer **outreach programs** across their state or region. For example, in many cities, preschool programs for children with visual impairments and their families are supervised and operated by these center schools. However, some large cities provide services independent of such center operations.

Transition Through Adulthood

As we discussed earlier, some young adults with visual impairments often have a difficult time adjusting to independence and the world of work. They are less experienced in the job world than are many of their sighted peers. Unfortunately, they also seem to be less prepared for adulthood than we might expect. Many of these

outreach programs. Specialized programs offered in local communities by residential schools or centralized agencies serving students with special needs.

individuals do not possess the level of literacy necessary to be successful in the community or on the job. Many do not possess other skills (for example, social interaction, job, self-advocacy) needed to be competitive in the workplace. When such deficiencies are coupled with the bias and discrimination, the result is underemployment and a group of individuals not achieving to their capabilities. With education specifically directed toward literacy, career education, and job training, this situation can be corrected.

Transition to Work. Traditionally, employment opportunities have not been very good for blind workers. For those of working age (between 21 and 64), only 26 percent were employed. For people with low vision, the situation is still much worse than for sighted people, with only 48 percent employed (JVIB News, 1994). Remember, these are statistics reflecting employment status, not whether the job held is appropriate for the individual. Underemployment or unemployment does not have to be the case for people with visual impairments. Richard Ruffalo certainly proves that point. He was honored with an American Teachers Award and was named the nation's top teacher for 1995 (Piña, 1995). This New Jersey biology teacher, who also coaches the track team's javelin throwers and shot putters, came to Washington, D.C., where Vice President Al Gore gave him his award. Ruffalo's accomplishments should show others that blind people can be outstanding workers if given a chance.

Why are so many blind students at a disadvantage in getting good jobs? Possibly, it is partially because their high school years are filled with educational tasks. During high school, many sighted classmates hold jobs after school or during the summer. These sighted peers learn about finding and keeping jobs and also about salaries, wages, and benefits. Students with severe visual impairments, on the other hand, often spend their summers learning other important skills (such as orientation and mobility) that they need for independence. Unfortunately, not having practical work experience can later put them at a disadvantage in the job market.

Postsecondary education has many benefits for all students but is very important to the increased employability of blind adults. Graduating from college has a significant bearing on that person's career and earning power, but less than half of those with visual impairments who enter college graduate. Their reasons for leaving college are not usually based on the academic demands but rather on the difficulties of living independently. Fortunately, the skills needed for successful college life can be taught. The University of Evansville teaches students who are blind the mobility, orientation, academic, and life skills needed for college life (Martin, 1996). Here, students learn how to master a college campus, do their own laundry, live in a dormitory, and take notes during lectures. For students who have participated in this twenty-two-year-old program, college is a less frightening and more successful experience.

Adults with visual impairments hold jobs at every level. For example, they are scientists, engineers, teachers, office workers, managers of business, and laborers. Unfortunately, despite individual successes and achievements, as a group, people with visual impairments are generally underemployed. What kind of job can a person with visual impairments expect? Even for those people with normal intelligence and high school diplomas, individuals with visual impairments have limited job opportunities that are far below the national average in pay and opportunities for advancement (Kendrick, 1993). Advances in technology, particularly print-to-voice conversions by new equipment, help qualified persons who are blind to have successful careers in a variety of jobs. Unfortunately, many do not

MAKING CONNECTIONS

For discussions of other precollege programs, see these Transitions sections: Chapters 4, 7, 8, and 10.

work in private industry, but instead hold jobs in sheltered workshops that often do work similar to that done in private industry. Besides offering inferior wages and benefits, these workshops have many disadvantages, among them outdated equipment and techniques. Many of the individuals who work in these settings have the skills needed for work in industry but not the opportunity.

 MAKING CONNECTIONS

See the Legislative section of Chapter 1 for a review of the ADA law.

Fortunately, changes are occurring in laws and businesses. Federal antidiscrimination legislation such as the ADA law forbids discrimination against job applicants with disabilities. Hiring workers with disabilities provides a humanitarian benefit to the individual and an economic benefit to the company. Unfortunately, American society has a long way to go before low vision and blind adults gain access to employment opportunities commensurate with their potential. Although some individuals with severe visual impairments now have jobs in private industry, employers' attitudes can still be improved so that more qualified people with visual impairments have an equal opportunity.

Transition to the Community. To better assist their students make the transition from school to adult life, teachers of students with visual impairments need to be familiar with a number of different agencies and facts. Particularly at the high school level, teachers of students with visual impairments should know about the services available to their students after graduation. For example, they need to know how students can become eligible for services from their state's office of vocational rehabilitation.

As we have mentioned, a major problem for people with visual impairments is their lack of acceptance of and the negative attitudes about their disability. These individuals face discrimination in the workplace and in society. As an example, two New York police officers mistakenly thought that a folded white mobility cane in the pocket of a man, David St. John, was a set of nunchakus, an illegal martial arts weapon. The police approached St. John but did not identify themselves, and they asked him to empty the contents of his pockets. St. John thought he was about to be mugged and defended himself, while the police hit him on the legs and arms. The struggle continued until a witness yelled to the police officers that the man was blind (Sulzberger, 1989).

Although students with visual impairments are included in general education at school, many have difficulties as adults because of poor social interaction skills (Sacks et al., 1992). This problem is exacerbated by a society that holds a protective view of adults with severe visual impairments that is even expressed in its language system. For example, we refer to agencies that are "responsible" for or "serve" the blind. People with visual impairments understand that the protective view of them stems from good intentions, but it severely limits their abilities to be contributing members of society. Often, attempts are made to overadapt environments for those with visual impairments. With proper preparation, though, many of these individuals can attend college, live in apartments, and hold jobs just like anyone else. Accordingly, adults with severe visual impairments are calling for their acceptance as individuals who can function well in modern society.

Many adults with visual impairments feel that their access to recreational, leisure, and cultural activities is also limited. Some positive changes are occurring, however. Cultural events are now more accessible as well. At concert programs of the New York Philharmonic, the Chamber Music Society, and the Great Performances at Lincoln Center, music programs are available in different

Jeff Evans, Erik Weihenmayer, and Sam Epstein unfurl the American Foundation for the Blind flag on the summit of Mt. McKinley.

versions: Braille, large-type, and audiotape. Finally, at "Washington: Symbol and City," now a permanent exhibit at the National Building Museum in Washington, D.C., people with severe visual impairments can touch models of the major monuments found in our nation's capital, allowing them to appreciate the beautiful treasures found in that city as sighted people have for years.

Changed attitudes and the ADA law have brought about other opportunities as well. Not only have museums become more accessible, but so too have zoos. The San Diego Zoo, and most others, had had long-standing bans against guide dogs. These bans existed because many of the wild animals were disturbed by the presence of canine animals. Now, at least in part, these bans have been discontinued, although some areas of zoos might remain off-limits to guide dogs (McCutcheon, 1994).

Families

Until the mid-1970s, parent involvement in the educational programs of their children was not commonplace. Education was considered to be the teacher's domain. The role of the family in the educational process has changed today, partly due to the work of some activist professionals and substantially due to parents' involvement in the IEP process as mandated by IDEA. Parents and families should not be viewed as either enemies or friends; they should be thought of as partners in the education of their children.

Helping Children Understand Their Visual Differences

Family members fill very special roles as they help their children grow up. One role is to help their blind and low vision children understand that their vision is different from that of others. Erin and Corn (1994) believe that children with visual impairments must learn that they act on information that is gained differently from seeing people. It is not that their perceptions are faulty but rather are developed through different methods and worked from different sources of information.

As part of understanding their visual differences, these children need to gain knowledge about their visual status, the cause of their impairment, and the probability of its worsening or improving. Many of the children have great confusion about their disabilities, which is apparent by the kind and content of the questions they ask about their blindness. In one very interesting study, parents were asked to list questions their children had asked about their vision. The following indicates topics of frequently asked questions: When would they be able to see? Would they be able to see when they got older? Why God made them blind? Why they could not see some things (like rainbows)? How do their eyes look? Would anything help them see better? Are they special? Why are they different? What is it like to see? Why did they fail the vision test (Erin & Corn, 1994)?

Families Coping with Stress

Sometimes a blind child can overtax a family's resources (both emotional and financial). When this occurs, the family will likely experience stress because family relations are tense or disrupted (Nixon, 1994). The demands on the family are in excess of their available resources. In such situations, many members of the family unit, including the person with the disability, may feel deprived of necessary social support and the family may begin to break apart. Families must learn to cope with stress, and sometimes this requires outside help, which may be difficult for some family members to accept. In some cases, support from school personnel is helpful. In other cases, support groups of families who also have a blind child meet to share experiences and information and to provide each other with assistance. For some, professional help from counselors or therapists is necessary. Educators can serve an important service by guiding parents to the best support system to meet their needs.

As we have discussed throughout the family sections included in this text, disabilities affect not only the individuals but also their entire families. As Nixon (1994) so aptly put it, "coping with impairment is a shared experience" (p. 329). Educators must understand that many of their students have strong extended families, families where their network of social roles, relationships, and shared commitments bind them together. It is important to recognize that working with the student's parents in these situations means honoring and involving the entire extended family unit (see the Focus on Diversity box about the Circle of Life). There is great strength to draw from in such situations. Let's think of Ramon and his family. All of Ramon's relatives share their human and financial resources to meet his needs. Ramon's teacher wants him to transfer some of the skills he has learned at school by playing new, more complex games at home. To be successful, she must teach brothers, sisters, cousins, aunts, uncles, grandfathers, and grandmothers in addition to his parents how to play the game; for Ramon is the shared

Circle of Life

The style and ways of the dominant American culture are often in conflict with other cultures that comprise the United States. Because the dominant culture typically dictates how services are delivered, these services are either inappropriate or ineffective for many Native American children with disabilities and their families. Professionals might be more culturally sensitive by remembering that the circle is a recurring theme of life and health, particularly in Native American cultures. People are born into a circle of family and community that embraces mutual support and oneness (Ponchillia, 1993). When one member is affected by something or an event, the entire community is also affected. So, when one member is involved, everyone should be involved. Rather than focusing on the individual, the focus of services should be with the family and its extended members. For example, when working with students with visual impairments, Ponchillia (1993) recommends that all family members be shown how to use equipment and adaptive techniques, so they can better support the individual with the disability.

responsibility of everybody in the Garcia family. In the culture of the Garcia family, individuals gain strength from the family unit, and it is the family, not just his mother and father, that must be involved in Ramon's educational program. Educators must come to understand that various cultures have different expectations of family units and that some extended family units expect to be involved in the child's education program.

Even with support from a strong family unit, educators must recognize the stress that is often associated with a family member with special needs. Parents and siblings of any child with a disability are at risk for emotional difficulties if their support systems or coping skills are inadequate. An insufficient support system or poor coping skills can affect the child with special needs, too. For example, parents often report a feeling of helplessness. Educators can help these parents find organized family support groups or introduce them to parents who are successfully coping with their child's disability.

A major frustration for parents is finding and gaining access to services for their children. A lack of coordination among the many agencies that work with people with disabilities makes information about what is available fragmented, incomplete, and sometimes inaccurate. Unfortunately, this situation often occurs throughout these individuals' lives, from early intervention through transitional services for adults. And when a child has multiple disabilities (for example, both visual impairment and mental retardation), the lack of coordinated services is more obvious. Fortunately, some of these problems are now being addressed, and parents often help each other to identify quality services that are available. Some state-funded residential schools for students with visual impairments, such as the

 MAKING CONNECTIONS

For other discussions about negotiating special education and social services, see the Family sections in Chapters 5 and 8.

Arizona School for the Blind, offer family support services and even provide educational diagnostic services to better match an individual to the services available in the home community.

The targets for parents to address with their children are many, particularly for children with severe visual impairments. These parents must help their children develop many skills across a range of areas: communication, independent living, mobility, sensory development, fine and gross motor skills, cognition, and social skills. Parents also find themselves in a variety of roles. For example, they should provide the support system and continuity needed in their child's life. They are advocates, teachers, and nurturers. Usually, it is for them to provide the most normalized experiences for their children, for they are the ultimate managers of the child's growth and development.

No resource is more important to a child than his or her parents. While teachers are transitory, parents are the major, consistent factor in children's lives. Parents must provide the consistent, sustained, and systematic support their children require. To do so, parents of children with visual impairments need information and strategies. They need to understand the nature of visual impairments, their child's abilities and disabilities, and their child's learning style. Parents must learn how to set limits and how to allow for the development of independence. It is for them to guide, reinforce, reassure, and build confidence in their child. The demands and stress on parents of children with special needs are great, but with educators as partners, their tasks are manageable.

Technology

For many years, people with visual impairments have used various kinds of technologies to help them learn and function in society. For example, they have used various types of canes, some electronic, to assist in orientation and mobility. Advances in microcomputer technology provide access to printed information. Because of the popularity of the personal computer, books are now available on computer disks. These electronic books, which may soon be as abundant as conventional books, allow the reader, using a laptop computer, to increase the size of print or to switch from print to voice easily. Many even incorporate animation and a wide variety of graphics, such as maps and diagrams (Rogers, 1992). Organizations such as the Visually Impaired and Blind User Group (VIBUG) of the Boston Computer Society are exchanging information to expand computer literacy among persons with visual impairments.

Increasingly, people with visual impairments are gaining access to technology and the assistive devices designed to minimize the effects of their disabilities. For example, sales of products developed exclusively for people with visual impairments reached $57.2 million in 1992 and $65.7 million in 1993 (Stang & Stacey, 1994). Although each of these advances adds to the household budget, the diversity of items is remarkable. For example, talking watches, clocks, calculators, food scales, and machines that tell you the denomination of paper money are now plentiful. Also, Braille and enlarged-type versions of games can be purchased for about the same price as games without special adaptations. For example, a large-print deck of colorful playing cards can be purchased for $2.65, while a Braille set costs $5.65 (The Lighthouse, 1996). Special sets of checkers, chess, scrabble, poker chips, and many other game items are easy to locate.

These exciting technological advances open up a new world for people with severe visual impairments. Clearly, these advances give them greater participation and independence in all aspects of modern society. However, two major barriers inhibit access to the broad array of assistive technology available: cost and information. With the average costs of devices ranging from $1,000 to $20,000 and the vast number of options available, careful selection of the right equipment is important. The rate of high-tech use is positively related to higher occupational status, but most people with severe visual impairments do not use these devices (Uslan, 1992). Cost is probably a crucial factor in this situation, and professionals need to seek new avenues for financial assistance to help people acquire the devices. As we have noted, technology affects many aspects (reading, mobility) of life for persons with visual impairments. These systems use different means of input: visual, auditory, and tactile.

Visual Aids

Closed-circuit television (CCTV) can be used to enlarge the print found in printed texts and books. By using a small television camera with a zoom lens and a sliding reading stand on which the printed materials are placed, one can view printed material greatly enlarged on a television monitor (up to 60 times the original size). Such equipment provides immediate access to all types of printed materials such as magazines, textbooks, and mimeographed or photocopied handouts. A wide range of CCTVs now exist at more reasonable cost, starting at under $500. Of course, the less expensive versions are cumbersome, not particularly mobile, and less convenient than the newer advances that offer many different options: hand-held camera, zoom lens, battery-operated portable systems, and powerful magnification levels. Uslan (1994) describes a new line of CCTVs produced by Acrotech that include some of the latest innovations in technology. One CCTV uses a hand-held camera the size and shape of a large computer mouse that has rollers on the bottom to help track horizontally over a flat surface. This model allows for a range of magnifications and the material scanned can be viewed on video monitors ranging in size from 5 square inches to 25 inches by 45 inches. Other units include reading and writing stands, some of which come with a carrying case and weigh as little as ten pounds. Other units, like the Magni-Cam, produced by Innoventions, now come with liquid crystal displays (LCDs) and battery packs (Shen & Uslan, 1996). Such comprehensive units cost as little as $1,800 but, unfortunately, are still out of reach of many individuals with visual impairments. Imagine future possibilities: headmounted CCTV displays, inexpensive equipment that weighs less than a pound, CCTVs that interface with computers, digital image processing that accommodates for damaged sections of the retina, and near-vision CCTVs that work together with distance-vision orientation and mobility functions (Uslan, Shen, & Shragai, 1996).

Overhead projectors can also enlarge printed materials but are not useful to most individuals with low vision. Microcomputers using special word processing programs can produce large-print displays that allow persons with low vision to adjust the size of print to match their own visual efficiencies. Some programs display print on the microcomputer screen at various sizes, allowing the user to select the type size and style that gives the best readability. Most microcomputers also allow the user to select different sizes of print for hard-copy printout or visual

closed-circuit television (CCTV). A television used for transmissions not accessible to the general public; sometimes, only one camera and television monitor is used.

display on the monitor, and standard copy machines can now also adjust print size. Thus individuals who can only read enlarged print can modify materials to various sizes. Also, teachers who prepare handouts on a microcomputer can prepare different-size print for their students with visual impairments and their nondisabled students while still covering the same material.

Audio Aids

Audio aids allow persons with visual impairments to hear what others can read. **Talking books** have been available through the Library of Congress since 1934, and specially designed record players, tape and compact disk (CD) machines that allow for compressed speech (eliminating natural pauses and accelerating speech) have been developed by the American Printing House for the Blind. A substantial amount of material is available in these forms, but usually it must be ordered from either a regional resource and materials center or a national center. Audiotape versions of many classics and current best-sellers are now available in most bookstores. Although these audiotapes were developed for sale to the general public, they allow greater access to current books for people with visual impairments. A set of audiocassettes available from the U.S. Department of Education provides information about federal student aid programs. First available in 1989, these cassettes give information about eligibility requirements and application procedures for federal grants, loans, and work/study programs, and they list scholarships available only to persons with visual impairments (NASDSE, 1989). Another audio system, Newsline for the Blind (available in New Mexico and other states), allows people who are blind to hear text from their local newspapers over the telephone line each morning.

MAKING CONNECTIONS

The Kurzweil Reader is also discussed in the History section of this chapter.

The Kurzweil Reader changes printed material into synthesized speech, but its early version of synthesized speech had its limitations. It was large, cumbersome, very expensive, unable to recognize all words, and difficult to understand. A newer version, the Xerox/Kurzweil PC, provides a more convenient and quick desktop reading system. This version produces state-of-the-art synthesized speech with a personal computer and either a page scanner or a sensor. When a person moves the sensor along a line of type, information is passed to the computer, which in turn translates the print to speech. The scanner uses a similar system, but a page of print is placed on a template. The computer then scans the material with the same result: Print is turned into voice. The listener can select the rate of speech (how fast it is delivered), the pitch, and gender of the voice/sound the computer generates. This system has many advantages for individuals who cannot read print. Students can use the same books and materials as their sighted classmates; they are not dependent on the availability of materials at a regional materials center. Users of this system also do not have to order special materials or wait for their delivery. Even those who are able to read print benefit from this system. Those who need to use enlarged type do not have to wait for special versions to be prepared. Of course, there is concern that those who can read print will prefer this audio system and will not develop proficient reading skills. For those who can read print, educators should still emphasize proficiency with reading. For those who are unable to read print, there is no guarantee that they will be able to access this new technology. Cost may be a significant barrier for many people. Although considerably less expensive now, the cost of a desktop reading system is still high (between $7,000 and $9,000), particularly when one considers the relatively low salaries people with visual impairment earn. If,

talking books. Books available in auditory format.

however, these systems follow the pattern of other computers, the cost should decrease as the demand for the product increases.

An exciting recent development, **audiodescription**, allows people with severe visual impairments to better participate in American life and entertainment. Their ability to enjoy plays, movies, television, and home videos is also limited. However, with audiodescription, they hear a narration of the visual cues and non-verbal information presented on the screen or stage. This system, initially developed for television by Margaret Pfanstiehl, uses the added sound track available in stereo televisions to describe aspects (costumes, scenes, sets, body language) important to a fuller understanding of the story. A similar system has been devised for theaters; it uses an earphone and a tiny FM receiver. The explanations occur in the pauses or otherwise silent parts of the film or play. Audiodescriptions are available for movie videos and some public television shows (DVS Home Video Catalog, 1996). Chet Avery shares his excitement over this development:

> Audiodescription enables blind and visually impaired persons to become more fully integrated into the mainstream of family and social life. Indeed, it removes the alienation that often arises between blind and visually impaired persons and the television set or movie screen as well as from family and friends who, despite the best goodwill, feel describing all the nonverbal elements is a chore. (American Foundation for the Blind, 1991, p. 17)

Tactile Aids

As you know, some persons who are blind use Braille as their preferred reading method. The Perkins Brailler is a compact and portable machine that uses keys that, when pressed down, emboss special paper with the Braille code. It is inexpensive but not as efficient as newer electronic versions that use microprocessors to store and retrieve information. Also, microcomputer systems, even those designed for sighted users, can support various types of Braille and can even be networked so that many people can use the Braille adaptation simultaneously. As with audiocassettes and talking books, a wealth of materials are available in Braille. Remember that enlarged-print, audiocassettes, and Braille versions of printed materials are not always available for every text or supplemental material used in the general education classroom. This was and still is a severe limitation for those who cannot read print.

Access to Braille is becoming less of a challenge, though. For example, the Xerox/Kurzweil desktop reading system, discussed earlier, can also scan printed materials and produce a Braille version of the text. A Braille version of a telephone credit card is available; it stores the user's access number so that he or she can charge the toll and call on any phone. Most major appliance companies now provide Braille options for their equipment. For example, GE and Hotpoint provide free Braille panels for their ovens, refrigerators, and laundry equipment. Whirlpool also offers Braille instructional manuals or audiocassettes to accompany its equipment. Finally, personal computers with special printers transform print to Braille. When a specially designed Braille printer is attached to a microcomputer, standard text can be translated into Braille, allowing a teacher who does not know how to use Braille to produce Braille copies of handouts, tests, maps, charts, and other class materials. And, some new printers, such as the ones made by American Thermoform, can produce Braille and print on the same page. Some of these printers cost less than $3,000.

audiodescription. A technique in which trained narrators describe visual and nonverbal information during the pauses in the audio or scripted dialogue of plays, films, and television shows by using FM transmissions or the extra sound track available on stereo televisions.

Concepts and Controversy: Is Literacy Necessary in the Twenty-First Century?

MAKING CONNECTIONS

For other discussions of Braille literacy, see these sections in this chapter:
• Methods of Reading and Writing (Low Vision and Blind Children)
• Literacy (Educational Interventions)

Increasing America's rate of literacy has become a national goal. The federal government has articulated the importance of literacy for the nation in its *Goals 2000* document (U.S. Department of Education, 1994) and in the President's 1997 State of the Union address. The declining literacy rate of individuals with severe visual impairments has become the focus of a national, emotionally charged debate. According to the American Printing House for the Blind (1992), 27 percent of students who are blind are visual readers and 10 percent use Braille. It is estimated that 10 percent are auditory readers (primarily using personal readers or recorded materials) and that the remainder are nonliterate. Some estimate that in the last forty years the percentage of blind people who can read and write Braille has dropped from 50 to 9 percent (Schoellkopf, 1995). Judith Heumann, the U.S. Department of Education's assistant secretary for Special Education and Rehabilitative Services, said that data "show that over 90 percent of working blind people use Braille in the performance of their jobs," which led her to conclude that Braille literacy is important for blind students (Briand, 1994, p. 6).

Many factors have contributed to the decline in the use of Braille by people who are blind or who have low vision. First, less that half (46 percent) of teachers of students with visual impairments feel competent in their ability to teach in Braille, despite their own proficiency using this reading skill (76 percent), positive attitudes about Braille as a means of reading, and belief that Braille should be the primary literacy medium of blind people (Wittenstein, 1994). Second, the availability of teachers of the visually impaired is limited. In some parts of this country, itinerant teachers have caseloads consisting of over fifty students (Corn et al., 1995). Third, there seems to be a growing reliance on audio versions for gaining information from printed materials (audio cassettes, talking books, print-to-voice technology). Fourth, there is an educational philosophy that students with visual impairments should use their residual vision as much as possible, including reading print. Fifth, there exists a growing number of blind students with multiple impairments who are less able to master either Braille or print-based reading skills.

Consider the changes in technology and in American society. Is it necessary to be able to read and write using print? And, will it be in the next century? Directions for appliances come on video tape. Most people use the telephone instead of writing letters. The technology that converts print to voice and voice to print is now available and will soon be affordable, portable, and commonplace. All Americans will have access to this technology. So, will print become outmoded? Can years of instructional time be justified for those who cannot master the skill easily and quickly? Will reading become as obsolete as teaching Greek and Latin? As you think about literacy for those with visual impairments, broaden your thinking to the entire population.

Why is this national conversation about literacy and the use of Braille by blind people so emotional? Of course, one factor is the great concern about the declining literacy rate among people with visual impairments. Will widespread inability to read print among this group bring them more discrimination and bias? Many of the strongest supporters of Braille literacy are blind adults (Augusto, 1993; Schroeder, 1993) who consider Braille as a symbol that could unite blind people, as sign language has bonded the deaf community. Is that reason enough to support the Braille literacy movement?

For most of us, the primary way we learn is through vision. Often, when in the process of learning how to perform a new skill, we are shown how to do the task. We observe the actions of others and imitate their behaviors. We gain information by watching television or reading a newspaper, book, or magazine. People with visual impairments have a restricted ability to use their sight, and that can affect how they function as independent adults. For schoolchildren, visual impairments is one of the smallest special education categories. The incidence of visual impairments increases with age: the older a person, the higher the likelihood of that person having some visual impairment. Although these students have been successfully included in general education for many years, they do not find integration the norm when they are adults. Many have not found competitive employment but, rather, work in sheltered workshops. They are not included in the mainstream of American society. In fact, stereotypes and old traditions impede their participation in normal activities as adults. Most clearly, this area will require the concerted efforts of adults with this disability, their families, and their advocates. With changed attitudes, this group will participate more fully in society and take their places alongside sighted people.

FOCUS QUESTIONS

Self-Test Questions

▶ *How is the disability of visual impairments divided into two subgroups?*

Individuals with visual impairments comprise two general groups: those who are blind and those who have low vision. These distinctions relate to the severity of the disability or the amount of functional use of sight an individual has. Another way to divide the category of visual impairments is by age of onset, when the disability occurred. Those who are congenitally blind have been blind since birth or infancy, while those who are adventitiously blind became profoundly visually impaired sometime after the age of 2. This latter group comprises persons who usually remember what things in their environment look like, a mental image that can influence how well they learn about concepts during their schoolyears.

▶ *What are the major causes of visual impairments, and what preventive measures protect children from this disability?*

Many different conditions or situations can cause blindness. Worldwide, the vast majority of cases are caused by poor nutrition or infections and could have been prevented. In the United States, the most common causes are factors related to increasing age. For American children, heredity and accidents are the most frequently cited causes for those who are blind and have a single disability. However, more than half of children with visual impairments have another disability as well, often placing them in the multiple disabilities category.

▶ *What are some ways the learning environment can be modified to accommodate students with visual impairments?*

The learning environment can be modified and adjusted in many ways to optimize the integration and learning opportunities for low vision and blind students. Some commonsense teaching strategies (using advance organizers, orally summarizing printed information, providing handouts of lectures) often prove to be the most useful. Students should be allowed to position themselves in the best place for them to gain as much as possible from each instructional activity. Sometimes, this will be close to the chalkboard, other times away from the glare of an unshaded window. The students must assess their visual efficiencies for each situation. All dangerous obstacles and hazards need to be eliminated, and a consistent organization of both the physical and instructional environments are of great benefit. Teachers must encourage students to participate, let them know what is expected and the consequences when they break the rules (even the subtle ones), have high expectations, and consult with an expert when they need assistance.

> *Why must orientation and mobility be long-term curriculum targets for many low vision and most blind students, and what specific skills must be included?*

One of the greatest difficulties for blind adults is living independently. Those who are successful are able to move independently to maintain a household, take care of themselves, use whatever transportation necessary to get to and from work, and be independently mobile in the workplace. The development of these orientation and mobility skills takes years of instruction and practice. This is true whether the individual uses a long cane or a guide dog. Although the ADA law will eventually help blind and low vision people by removing the physical hazards in the environment, many challenges will remain: escalators, elevators, public transportation, orientation to new places, use of maps. Participation in sports and leisure activities is important to everyone, and those with severe visual impairments should participate as well. Although the opportunities through special sports programs are increasing, actual instruction in sports and recreation activities needs to become a consistent instructional topic for these individuals.

> *What technological advances can assist people with visual impairments at school, in the workplace, and in independent living?*

Advances and developments in technology have and will continue to change the lives of all Americans, particularly those with disabilities. With the availability and relatively low price of personal computers, persons with severe visual impairments will use technology-based machines to assist them when they need to read and write. Whether their preferred mode is enlarged print, Braille, or listening, computers can provide immediate access to all printed documents. Other technologies are beneficial to blind and low vision people. They can be organized into three groups: visual aids, audio aids, and tactile aids. These devices improve independent living opportunities (enlarged print displays, talking watches and clocks, Braille labels for household appliances) and enhance participation in recreational and leisure time activities (large-print newspapers, audiodescriptions, tactile maps to enjoy museums and national parks).

Challenge Question

> *Why has Braille literacy become such an emotionally charged debate, and how do you think it should be resolved?*

The great majority of persons with visual impairments use sight to learn and gain information. Although most read print, some require that the print be enlarged. A small number read and write using Braille, a system of raised dot codes that requires considerable training and practice to become proficient in its use. For students with substantial cognitive disabilities and visual impairments, it may not be a skill that can be mastered. At the center of an emotionally charged debate is whether Braille literacy should be a goal for these students. Until the passage of many "Braille Bills" across the country, instruction in Braille was not available to all students who attended their local public school because of the unavailability of teachers proficient in Braille instruction. Those states that have passed Braille bills now have an option for inclusion on the child's IEP. As with most services in special education, this debate will probably be resolved by encouraging that decisions about Braille instruction be made on an individual basis.

~~~ *SUPPLEMENTARY RESOURCES* ~~~

Scholarly Books

Barraga, N. C., & Erin, J. N. (1992). *Visual handicaps and learning* (3rd ed.). Austin, TX: Pro-Ed.

Heller, K. W., Alberto, P. A., Forney, P. E., & Schwartzman, M. N. (1996). *Understanding physical, sensory, & health impairments.* Pacific Grove, CA: Brooks/Cole.

Popular Books

Hine, R. V. (1993). *Second Sight*. Berkeley: University of California Press.

Keller, H. (1988). *The story of my life*. New York: Sig Classics.

Mehta, V. (1989). *The stolen light*. New York: Norton.

Milsap, R., & Carter, T. (1990). *Almost like a song*. New York: McGraw-Hill.

Videos

The miracle worker. (1962). United Artists.
Places in the heart. (1984). Tri-Star Pictures.
Mask. (1985). Universal Films.

Sneakers. (1991). Universal Pictures.
Scent of a woman. (1992). Universal/MCA.

Professional, Parent, and Consumer Organizations and Agencies

American Foundation for the Blind
15 West Sixteenth Street
New York, NY 10011
E-mail afbinfo@afb.org
Phone: (800) 232-5463
       (212) 502-7657

Division of the Blind and Visually Impaired
Rehabilitation Services Administration
U.S. Department of Education
330 C Street, SW
Washington, DC 20202
E-mail: chet_avery@ed.gov
Phone: (202) 401-3000

American Printing House for the Blind
P.O. Box 6085
1839 Frankfort Ave.
Louisville, KY 40206
Web site: http://www.aph.org
Phone: (800) 223-1839

National Federation of the Blind
1800 Johnson Street
Baltimore, MD 21230
E-mail: nfb@access.digex.net
Phone: (410) 659-9314

Division for the Visually Handicapped
Council for Exceptional Children
1920 Association Drive
Reston, VA 22091
Web site: http://www.cec.sped.org
Phone: (800) 224-6830

Prevent Blindness America
500 E. Remington Rd.
Schaumburg, IL 60173
Web site: http://www.prevent-blindness.org
E-mail: 74777.100@compuserve.com
Phone: (847) 843-2020

Stephen Wiltshire. Chinatown. No date.

Stephen Wiltshire is an artist with autism. He was mute as a child, and at age 5 he began to communicate by drawing on scraps of paper. He now talks with reporters and others who want to interview him about his work. Wiltshire lives in England, but has made a number of trips to America. These trips stimulated the "American Dream" series of art. The cover art for this book of the Grand Canyon was inspired by his visit to Arizona. This scene of San Francisco is more typical of his work—black line drawings. Wiltshire uses his visual memory to remember scenes he wants to sketch later, which he does very prolifically.

Very Low-Incidence Disabilities: Autism, Deaf–Blindness, Traumatic Brain Injury

12

OVERVIEW

Three special education categories can be referred to as very low incidence areas: autism, deaf–blindness, and traumatic brain injury. Children with autism present a complex array of excessive behaviors, an inability to develop relationships, complex speech and language problems, and insistence on sameness. Children with deaf–blindness have very special learning needs because of their dual dis-

abilities. The vast majority of members from both groups also have mental retardation. Children with traumatic brain injury (TBI) possess a range of cognitive and behavior problems, which for some become lifelong and for others only temporary. Many children with these disabilities have very severe problems and require comprehensive, well-coordinated, specialized services.

FOCUS QUESTIONS

SELF-TEST QUESTIONS

▶ What are the major characteristics of children with autism?
▶ How would you describe the impact of deaf–blindness on those affected?
▶ What additional disabilities do children with autism and children with deaf–blindness often possess?

▶ How can many cases of TBI be prevented?
▶ How are functional assessments and the development of functionally equivalent behaviors used together?

CHALLENGE QUESTION

▶ Should autism, deaf–blindness, and traumatic brain injury each be considered a separate special education category? Why? Why not?

A *Personal Perspective*: An American Mom in Paris Negotiates a Different Educational System for Her Autistic Son

Leslie Palanker, an American who went to Paris on a sojourn from college, met the man who is now her husband and made a life for herself in France. She has two sons, Joey, a precocious 8-year-old who was bilingual by the age of 3, and Luke, who is 5 and autistic. Leslie shares their story, one that is still unfolding. Their experiences can help us understand how confusing it can be for parents who are trying to sort through education and social service systems to arrange for the best services for their children.

Luke's story is not unusual for children with autism. As a baby, he was too fussy, too agitated, not at all like our first boy, Joey. The woman who ran the play group that Joey was going to for preschool suggested that I have Luke's hearing tested. That led to visits to the ear, nose, and throat doctor and a subsequent operation. Despite efforts from these medical professionals, Luke did not improve. So, began visit after visit to various child psychiatrists, most of whom (at least here in France) seemed shrouded in archaic attitudes and theories with their roots in Freudian psychology. We still had no answers to our questions, and Luke was not getting better.

Our luck changed on a trip home to America. My father was able to arrange for the diagnostic team from the local public school to see Luke. One of the team members was fluent in French, so the bilingual environment that we have maintained for our children at home was part of the testing situation. On the trip home to France, we were equipped with a label and a vocabulary about autism that allowed us to begin our search for the best educational program for Luke in earnest.

Back in France we found a speech pathologist/psychologist from one of the major children's hospitals who was able to help us. At age 3, Luke began seeing a psychologist two times a week. Also, once a week he went to a prespeech rhythmic class at the hospital, and we found a private bilingual school that accepted Luke on the condition that he was accompanied by what we call "a helper." The most important thing is that we all learned how to spend more time together in a happier fashion. We continued this program for two years, and Luke progressed considerably. Even though he was not expressing himself verbally, he enjoyed himself with his family and was generally more manageable.

This year we decided to do something different. France's mandatory schooling age is 6, and until that age if the publicly supported schools are full and do not have any openings, they do not have to provide for every child requesting placement. We could not find a public program for Luke. At age 5, having Luke at home with no other children was unthinkable. Partly because we could not find many suitable alternatives, we enrolled Luke in a private school for children with learning difficulties. Within the first month, we knew that this was not the right program for our son. They could not adapt to meet Luke's needs. We began a search for another placement, but every place was full. Obviously, the need for preschool programs for children like Luke surpasses availability. Meanwhile, we are left with seemingly no options.

The search continues. School after school, professional after professional has been called. All of this has revealed that there are at least two distinct camps, philosophies, about educating children with autism. It seems to me that on the one hand are psychiatrists who analyze and observe. On the other seems to be those who favor an approach similar to the inclusion practices in America. These professionals seek to provide as many "typical" role models for children with disabilities as possible. The programs they provide integrate children like Luke with normal peers. I am afraid of putting Luke in segregated programs. In France, there are many "day hospitals or institutions" where children with autism can go to school, but I don't think that is what our family wants for Luke. One thing this search has taught me is to ask a lot of questions and listen very carefully to be sure we understand.

So, we are now waiting for an opening at a school that can meet Luke's needs. In the meantime I have found a speech therapist who sees children individually. We will see how this works out. Luke still sees a psychologist, who has helped him a lot. This American in Paris will continue to pick her way through the many private and public schools, the theories, the procedures, and the methods until I find what seems best for my son.

1. Could Leslie's experience be repeated here in the United States?

2. What do think is in store for Leslie, Luke, and their family?

*T*his chapter includes information about three very different disabilities: autism, deaf–blindness, and traumatic brain injury. Each is a *separate special education category* recognized in IDEA. One characteristic shared by these three disabilities is their low incidence: They are not very common. It is likely that most general education teachers will not teach many youngsters with these conditions during their careers. Just like other disabilities, these conditions can range in severity from mild to severe. However, most typically, children with these disabilities require substantial and intensive special education services and support. The problems their disabilities present are typically complex and extremely serious.

You will notice that the organization of this chapter is somewhat different from the chapters that focus on only one special education area. Separate sections for each disability include Defined, Prevalence, Causes and Prevention, and Children with this Disability. Then you will find combined sections for Educational Interventions, Families, and Technology.

◣ MAKING CONNECTIONS

In Chapter 6, review the sections about support in these sections:
• Emerging Classification Systems (Types of Mental Retardation)
• Support (Children with Mental Retardation)
• Family

Autism

Although **autism** has probably always been part of the human condition, its discrete identification is recent. Leo Kanner is credited with first coining the term and describing the condition in 1943 (Koegel, Koegel, Frea, & Smith, 1995). His goal was to separate what he thought was an exceptionally rare condition from the more global classification of childhood psychosis. Autism, as a separate condition, has gained considerable attention across the years. In 1965, Bernard Rimland, a psychologist

Truly including a child with autism can be a challenge for even the most engaging teacher.

autism. A severe disorder of thinking, communication, interpersonal relationships, and behavior.

who has devoted his career to the study of autism and is also a parent of a child with this disability, joined with other parents to form the National Society for Autistic Children (now called Autism Society of America). This major advocacy group, assisted by the data collected by the Autism Research Institute which was started in 1967, was able in the 1990 reauthorization of IDEA to gain independent classification status for autism. It is now considered a separate special education category. Previously, it was a subgroup of other disabilities. Some considered it part of mental retardation, others believed that it should be included in the physical impairment category, and others felt strongly that it should be considered a subgroup of emotional disturbance and behavior disorders (Kauffman, 1997). There is considerable merit to Mesibov's (1994) observation, "Autism is a poorly understood low incidence disability" (p. 88). Let's see whether we can come to an understanding of autism, the nature of this disability, and how it affects these individuals and their families.

Autism Defined

When Kanner originally identified autism, he believed that the condition had two primary symptoms: extreme isolation present from the first years of life and excessive insistence on preserving "sameness" (Rimland, 1994). Although many parents and professionals have sought to broaden the definition of autism to include children who experience onset of the symptoms often associated with autism later in life, many believe that the original, more rigid, criterion should be kept. Let's look at two different definitions of autism. Think about who would be included when using each definition and what different special needs teachers must address when different definitions are applied.

According to IDEA, autism means:

> A developmental disability significantly affecting verbal and nonverbal communication and social interaction, generally evident before age 3, that adversely affects a child's performance. Other characteristics often associated with autism are engagement in repetitive activities and stereotyped movements, resistance to environmental change or change in daily routines, and unusual responses to sensory experiences. The term does not apply if a child's educational performance is adversely affected primarily because the child has a serious emotional disturbance. (U.S. Department of Education, 1992, p. 44,841)

The Autism Society of America defines autism in this way:

> The essential features are typically manifested prior to 30 months of age, including disturbances of (a) developmental rates and/or sequences; (b) responses to sensory stimuli; (c) speech, language, and cognitive capacities; and (d) capacities to relate to people, events, and objects. Disturbances in developmental rates may include delays, arrests, or regressions in motor, cognitive, or social behavior. Disturbances in response to sensory stimuli may include overreactivity or underreactivity to visual, auditory, tactile, or olfactory stimuli. (Sturmey & Sevin, 1994, p. 16)

Autism is a very serious disability. Great strides are being made in the development of effective teaching strategies that positively change these individuals' patterns of isolation, inability to initiate or sustain meaningful social interchanges, and lack of functional language development. However, more research is needed to better understand this disability and to develop best practices and effective treatment procedures. The outcome for most of these individuals is not good and their ability to function as independent adults is extremely limited. However, as more is learned about the causes of this disability, ways to prevent its occurrence and to reduce its impact will surely follow.

Types of Autism

Because not all individuals with autism manifest exactly the same or similar characteristics with the same intensity, researchers have been searching for ways to subgroup autism (Sturmey & Sevin, 1994). A number of different dimensions have been explored for subgrouping. For example, some have proposed that different subgroups be created according to level of intellectual functioning, the time of the condition's onset, or the number and severity of the symptoms. Others have found that different clusters can be created by their distinctly different patterns of brain activity (Dawson, Klinger, Panagiotides, Lewy, & Castelloe, 1995). Sevin and his colleagues (Sevin, Matson, Coe, Fee, & Sevin, 1991) propose a system of four groups that seems to have considerable internal consistency. The *atypical group* has the fewest autistic characteristics and the highest mean levels of intelligence. The *mildly autistic group* has social problems and also a strong need for things and events to be routine, the same. Members of this group also have mild mental retardation and some functional language. The *moderately autistic group* includes individuals with these characteristics: limited social responding, severe patterns of stereotypic behaviors (such as rocking, hand flapping), limited functional language, and mental retardation requiring considerable supports. Individuals included in the *severely autistic group* are socially aloof, have no functional communication skills, and function at significant levels of mental retardation.

Probably because of their almost bizarre inconsistencies in ability (being unable to initiate or maintain a conversation yet remembering trivia), people tend to focus considerable attention on **autistic savants**. Remember that this subgroup of individuals with autism is very small, possibly comprising only 5 percent of those with autism (Begley & Springen, 1996). Needless to say, their abilities and talents are unusual. Some, like the character Raymond in the film *Rain Man*, can instantly count the number of wooden matches that have fallen on the floor, remember the dates and day of the week of important events, or recall the numbers of all of the winning lottery tickets for the past year. Some have outstanding musical or artistic abilities. Such *splinter skills* can be fascinating to the observer, but they are rarely functional for the individual.

Identification

One of the first assessment devices used to identify children with autism was a checklist. Developed by Rimland, it is based on Kanner's original definition of the condition (Rimland, 1964). Since that time, many different identification procedures have been developed. Some use checklists, for example, the *Autism Behavior Checklist (ABC)*, that are easy to use, even by untrained people (Krug, Arick, & Almond, 1980). Most of these systems have been criticized, however, because they use information gathered from people familiar with the target child rather than using direct observations made by unbiased evaluators (Sturmey & Sevin, 1994). Other instruments use rating scales. For example, the *Childhood Autism Rating Scale (CARS)* uses data gathered from behavioral observations in the home setting and is completed by trained observers.

MAKING CONNECTIONS

See the Children with Autism section of this chapter.

autistic savant. An individual who displays many behaviors associated with autism, yet also possesses discrete abilities and unusual talents.

 MAKING CONNECTIONS

For more on functional assessment and the ABC model of behavioral analysis, see the Prevention section of Chapter 8.

Remember, in most cases of autism the symptoms are so definitive and unique that the diagnosis is obvious to most professionals who specialize in this area. Today, many advocate the use of behavioral or functional assessments (Harris, Belchic, Blum, & Celiberti, 1994). Under this system (sometimes called an ABC analysis), each individual is considered unique, a person

> whose biological capacities, learning history, and present environment combine to create a set of strengths, behavioral deficits, and special needs...and grapples with questions such as "When does this maladaptive behavior occur?" "What environmental events may bear upon the expression of that symptom?" and "How can contextual events be manipulated to enable this client to function more effectively?" (p. 127)

Such functional assessments are beneficial in that they identify individuals with autism and provide guidance during design of the treatment program. When functional assessments are conducted in the child's natural (home and school) environments, the actual frequency and intensity of the behaviors of concern become apparent (Mullen & Frea, 1995). It is also possible to determine under what conditions the behaviors are more likely to occur. This helps teachers understand how to reshape the environment to reduce the likelihood of the inappropriate behaviors occurring and to assist the child in developing more **functionally equivalent behaviors** instead (Koegel, Koegel, Frea, & Smith, 1995).

 MAKING CONNECTIONS

Additional information about developing functionally equivalent behaviors is found in these places in this chapter:
• Teaching Tactics box
• Educational Interventions

functionally equivalent behaviors. Identifying behaviors that can replace inappropriate behaviors because they serve similar purposes.

Teaching students functionally equivalent behaviors, like raising a hand and waiting to be called on, can replace inappropriate behaviors with appropriate ones.

Significance

Individuals with autism process information and understand the world differently from those who do not have this disability (Mesibov, 1994). Most require comprehensive services and extensive supports for their entire lives. Effective services and supports require high levels of coordination and consistency. Unfortunately, these are difficult goals to achieve through the often fragmented services provided by social service agencies, health care providers, and the educational system.

Even high-functioning individuals with autism face considerable challenges as adults. For example, Gary Peterson works for the Psychology Department at the University of Washington (UW) (King, 1996). He does library searches, office work, and even guest lectures to classes about autism. He lives independently, rides public transportation to work, and cooks his own meals. Gary is exceptionally high functioning for someone with autism, probably in the top 10 to 15 percent. Even so, his disability makes him markedly different from other people. According to Geraldine Dawson, UW psychology professor, Gary is "very autistic." He becomes upset when clothing does not match. He tells people, very bluntly, things about their personal appearance. He also has savant tendencies. Within seconds, Gary is able to tell someone the day of the week any future birthday will fall. He can remember the exact dates (and day of the week) of specific events, like the last time the electricity went out at UW.

Although Gary Peterson is able to function in the community with limited supports, most adults with autism do not fare as well. Their adaptive behaviors are impaired. It is now known that deficiencies in adaptive behavior are apparent at very early ages (Vig & Jedrysek, 1995). Even at the time of preschool, children with autism show signs of difficulties across many adaptive areas, not just the area of communication and socialization. Significant problems exist in such skill areas as daily living, abstract thinking, problem solving, and motor skills. And, it appears that such problems become more serious as these individuals grow older. The reason may be that many of these individuals are less receptive to training (Partington, Sundberg, Newhouse, & Spengler, 1994) and do not naturally or spontaneously develop the ability to imitate others (Krantz, McClannahan, & Poulson, 1994). The job of learning is a major feat for many of these individuals.

Prevalence

How many children are included in any special education category is directly related to the definition used, and for autism this is a significant issue to think about (Rimland, 1994). Some definitions of autism, like Kanner's, are very restrictive. Using this definition results in as few as 0.7 or as many as 2.3 individuals per 10,000 being identified (Locke, Banken, & Mahone, 1994). Less restrictive definitions would qualify more children, perhaps as many as 7 to 14 per 10,000. Qualifying more children, however, affects other factors beside the number served under this special education label (Koegel, Koegel, Frea, & Smith, 1995). It increases the variability in behaviors and symptoms observed in the population, and it results in the inclusion of more children with higher intelligence in this category.

So, how many students are served under this special education category? According to the *Eighteenth Annual Report to Congress on the Implementation of*

MAKING CONNECTIONS

For related information, see Negotiating the Mental Health Care System (Family Section) in Chapter 8.

MAKING CONNECTIONS

Adaptive behavior is fully explained in Chapter 6 in these sections:
• Mental Retardation Defined
• Children with Mental Retardation

MAKING CONNECTIONS

To review the definitions of autism, see the earlier section Autism Defined.

IDEA (U.S. Department of Education, 1996), a total of 22,780 children (ages 6 to 21) across the nation were classified as having autism. This represents about .04 percent of schoolchildren. It is clear that even though the IDEA definition is much less stringent than Kanner's original conceptualization of the condition, autism is a very low disability area.

Causes and Prevention

Causes, reasons for autism, have been sought since the condition was originally identified. Autism was first thought to be an emotional disorder caused by something the child's mother did wrong (Rimland, 1994). This incorrect theory added to mothers' burden. Feelings of guilt and shame were the result of theories of early psychologists like Bruno Bettelheim who laid clear blame for children's disabilities on mothers' attitudes and poor parenting skills. Eventually, researchers were able to show that autism is a neurological rather than an emotional disorder. Such research findings have changed the beliefs of professionals and the public. Mothers are no longer wrongly blamed for causing autism in their children.

Although definite answers are still unavailable, most experts now agree: Autism is probably organic in nature (Sturmey & Sevin, 1994) and most likely caused by brain damage (Begley & Springen, 1996). Many theories point to damage in the brain stem (Koegel, Koegel, Frea, & Smith, 1995); however, some contend that autism is due to a single gene disorder, similar to what causes PKU (Locke, Banken, & Mahone, 1994). This theory explains why some cases of autism (or autistic-like behaviors) seem to be associated with Fragile X syndrome. Other theories suggest that a virus that affected the mother during pregnancy may be the culprit (Begley & Springen, 1996).

 MAKING CONNECTIONS

For more information about PKU and Fragile X syndrome, see the Causes and Prevention section of Chapter 6.

As it is for all disabilities, it is so important that researchers focus on identifying the cause(s) of autism. The hope is that once the etiology is understood, a preventive technique should soon follow. For now, some factors have been observed to improve the condition, but the reasons for improvement are not known. For example, Vitamin B6 and magnesium have helped reduce the symptoms of autism in many children, and for those it has not helped it has caused no harm (Rimland, 1994). Why it is effective with some and not others is a puzzle. At the present time, no consistently effective treatment—other than well-designed educational programs based on behavioral interventions—is available (Scheuermann, 1996). Certainly, much effort needs to be placed toward proving or disproving the many theories that surround autism. Once that happens, reliable techniques can be developed and implemented to prevent the condition and reduce its effects for those who have it.

Children with Autism

A unique profile of stereotypic behaviors comprise the symptoms, or characteristics, of autism. Each characteristic alone does not signal autism, but in combination they define a very serious disability. It is a disability that at the present time means challenging outcomes for the individuals with the condition and their families. (See Mark Rimland's story written by his "pioneering dad.") Table 12.1 presents an overview of those characteristics—organized into four major groups—that

TABLE 12.1

Signs or Characteristics of Autism

Impairment in Reciprocal Social Interactions
- Normal attachments to parents, family members, or caregivers do not develop.
- Friendships with peers fail to develop.
- Cooperative or peer play is rarely observed.
- Emotions such as affection and empathy are rarely displayed.
- Nonverbal signals (smiling, gestures, physical contact) of social intent tend not to be used.
- Eye contact is not initiated or maintained.
- Imaginative play is an activity seldom observed.
- The lack of social-communicative gestures and utterances is apparent during the first few months of life.
- Preferred interaction style could be characterized as *extreme isolation*.

Poor Communication Abilities
- Functional language is not acquired fully or mastered.
- Content of language is usually unrelated to immediate environmental events.
- Utterances are stereotypic and repetitive.
- Conversations are not maintained.
- Spontaneous conversations are rarely initiated.
- Speech can be meaningless, repetitive, and echolalic.
- Many fail to use the words *I* and *yes*, and problems with pronouns in general are apparent.
- Both expressive and receptive language is extremely literal.

Insistence on Sameness
- Marked distress is typically experienced over trivial or minor changes in the environment.
- Aspects of daily routine can become ritualized.
- Obsessive behavior is frequently displayed.
- The requirement to complete self-imposed, required actions is intense.
- Stereotypic behaviors (rocking, hand flapping) are repeated in cycles difficult to stop.

Unusual Behavior Patterns
- Hypersensitive and/or inconsistent behaviors are the response to visual, tactile, or auditory stimulation.
- Aggression to others is common, particularly when compliance is requested.
- Self-injurious or outwardly aggressive behavior (hitting, biting, kicking, head banging) is common and frequent.
- Extreme social fears are manifested toward strangers, crowds, unusual situations, and new environments.
- Loud noises (barking dogs, street noises) can result in startle or fearful reactions.
- Noncompliant behavior to requests from others results in disruption to the individual and others (tantrums).
- Self-stimulation (twirling objects, rocking) consumes a considerable amount of time and energy.

～～～ A Pioneering Dad's Story ～～～

Dr. Bernard Rimland—psychologist, researcher, founder of the Autism Research Institute, and parent of a child with autism—tells us about his son and through that story we can learn what it was like for parents when the field was just beginning.

My wife, Gloria, and I were delighted when Mark, our first baby, arrived, after a picture-perfect pregnancy, on March 28, 1956. A beautiful healthy bright-eyed baby boy. End of dream—beginning of nightmare: Mark almost never stopped screaming. He screamed so violently he could hardly be nursed.

Infant Mark did not want to be held. He needed to be rocked to go to sleep, but he violently resisted being held. We found that by placing him in his baby carriage and rocking it back and forth we could get him to sleep for a few hours a night. I also discovered that by taping a yardstick to the floor and running the wheels of the baby carriage over the yardstick, we could impart a slight bouncing motion that helped relax him and let him sleep. (Now, with the benefit of hindsight and several decades of research on autism, we can understand that Mark craved vestibular stimulation but could not tolerate tactile stimulation. It is at least possible that the screaming was due to hyperacute hearing.)

As Mark grew older, he manifested all the symptoms we now know to be characteristics of autism, including severe ritualistic behavior, rocking, and head banging, insistence on the preservation of sameness, eating oddities of various kinds, "autistic" staring into space, bizarre fears, failure to develop relationships with his parents, grandparents, or other humans, and fascination with mechanical objects, especially vacuum cleaners.

Our pediatrician, a venerable and respected physician with forty years of experience, had never seen or heard of a screaming, ritualistic, alienated child such as Mark.

Mark started to say words at 8 months of age. His first words were "spoon," "bear," "all done," and "come on, let's play ball," all spoken with perfect articulation. The words were uttered in somewhat appropriate contexts, but Mark did not seem to be aware of what he was saying—like a living tape recorder.

One day when Mark was about 2 years old, walking aimlessly around the house repeating nursery rhymes and radio commercials in a hollow, parrot-like monotonic voice, Gloria (Mark's mother) remembered reading something in one of her college textbooks about a child with similar behaviors. We went to the garage, located the box of old college texts, and there found a point-by-point description of our little boy, accompanied by the strange-looking words "infantile autism."

I was now 5 years beyond my Ph.D. in psychology and was seeing the word *autism* for the first time. Today the term is familiar to almost every high school student because of films such as *Rain Man* and other media coverage.

Gloria's textbook listed several references to the literature. I jotted those down and went to the university library to see what more I could learn about this strange and puzzling disorder. I did not know it then, but I was hooked. Hooked on autism. I have stayed hooked on autism for almost three and a half decades now.

Source: From "The modern history of autism: A personal perspective" by Bernard Rimland, 1994, in *Autism in Children and Adults: Etiology, Assessment, and Intervention*, pp. 1–2. Reprinted with permission.

many practitioners, researchers, and family members have identified (Mesibov, 1994; Rimland, 1994; Sturmey & Sevin, 1994; Koegel, Koegel, Frea, & Smith, 1995). Study that table as you read how some of the outcomes relate to these characteristics.

Data about characteristics of autism that have a lifelong impact are quite significant. Let's look at some data gathered by a number of different researchers (Sturmey & Sevin, 1994). Of children with autism,

- 80 percent have a concurrent diagnosis of mental retardation,
- 50 percent probably never will develop functional speech or language,
- 40 percent engage in high levels of **self-injurious behaviors (SIB)**,
- four out of five are males, and
- 33 percent develop seizures.

The disability can be characterized by both behavior excesses and deficits. Excesses can include ritualistic, bizarre, and stereotypic behaviors. For example, some of these individuals express unfounded fears of changes in the environment, strangers, strange sounds, and pets and other animals. The frequency of self-stimulatory behavior is often high and repetitive in which the individual engages in such behaviors as loud repetitive verbalizations, rocking, hand flapping, gazing at lights. Their rate of SIB (hair pulling, hitting, scratching) is exceptionally high, even when compared to others with severe disabilities. For example, SIB among students with mental retardation is estimated to be between 7 and 22 percent; whereas it is 40 percent for students with autism. Behavior deficits commonly found in individuals with autism include difficulties establishing relationships with others, inappropriate toy play, muteness or echolalia, and inappropriate or lack of affect. If language develops, it is usually nonfunctional. The signs of autism appear during the first few months of life. Family members often note that eye gaze, smiles, desires to be held, recognition of parents, and the ability to be consoled are missing in many of these children.

Deaf–Blindness

The world of children with **deaf–blindness** can be exceptionally restricted. For those whose hearing *and* vision fall into the ranges of severe or profound losses, their immediate world may well end at their fingertips (Miles, 1995). Some of these students have enough residual vision to allow them to read enlarged print, see sign language, move about in their environment, and recognize friends and family. Some have sufficient hearing to understand some speech sounds or hear loud noises. Some can develop speech themselves, and others have such limited vision and hearing that they profit little from either sense. The majority of these individuals have other disabilities in addition to visual and hearing losses. Most individuals with deaf–blindness need support from others to make their worlds safe and accessible.

Deaf–Blindness Defined

A separate funding base for students with deaf–blindness was initiated in 1969. This was the time of a major national crisis, a period when the rubella epidemic caused dramatic increases in the number of babies with disabilities, particularly those who were blind, deaf, and deaf–blind. Definitions of deaf–blindness

self-injurious behavior (SIB). Self-inflicted injuries (head banging, eye poking).

deaf–blindness. A dual disability whereby the individual has both vision and hearing problems.

Helen Keller and her teacher, Anne Sullivan, became a pair who proved that deaf and blind people can achieve beyond many people's expectations.

vary by state. The result is inconsistent identification results and service outcomes, which are compounded by the fact that most of these youngsters have disabilities in addition to their visual and hearing problems. For these reasons, many of these youngsters are served in a category referred to as multihandicapped (or multiple disabilities). The category of deaf–blindness is defined in IDEA as

> such severe communication and other developmental and learning needs that the persons cannot be appropriately educated in special education programs solely for children and youth with hearing impairments or severe disabilities, without supplementary assistance to address their education needs due to these dual, concurrent disabilities. (IDEA, 1990 p. 1119)

The IDEA definition, some professionals believe, does not assist in accurate or correct identification, and ultimately appropriate services, of all children with this disability (Baldwin, 1996). Many state coordinators therefore advocate for a more functional definition. They are seeking a definition that focuses on the conditions needed for optimal learning and considers the unique conditions caused by the interplay of two sensory impairments. This functional definition is proposed by Victor Baldwin:

> If the deficit in hearing *and* vision is sufficient to *require* special adaptations in instruction in *both* the auditory and visual modes to produce maximum learning, then the person qualifies to be identified as deaf–blind and should be included in the annual census. (Baldwin, 1995, p. 2)

Identification

Most professionals suggest that inclusion in the deaf–blind category requires that "a person needs, at a minimum, to have a visual acuity of 20/70 in the better eye with correction *and* an auditory deficit of 30 db in the better ear" (Baldwin, 1995, p. 5).

MAKING CONNECTIONS

Review the Defined sections in
• Chapter 10,
• Chapter 11.

Significance

The most famous person with deaf–blindness was most likely Helen Keller. Keller was a woman of many accomplishments, but her achievements, including graduating from Radcliffe with honors in 1904, would not have been possible without the efforts of her teacher, Anne Sullivan (Holcomb & Wood, 1989). Sullivan's "family tree" is interesting and noteworthy. Samuel Gridley Howe was the founder of the Perkins School for the Blind. Located in Boston, it was the first school for blind students in the United States. One of Howe's pupils was Laura Dewey Bridgman. Bridgman, herself a person with deaf–blindness, talked to other people by tapping letters and using a manual alphabet. She used Braille for reading. Bridgman became a teacher, and one of her students was a partially blind girl named Anne Sullivan. When Anne Sullivan grew up, she learned of a 6-year-old girl with deaf–blindness living in Alabama. Sullivan visited young Helen Keller and brought her a gift, a doll given to her by Laura Bridgman. Anne Sullivan became Helen Keller's teacher and lifelong companion. Of her disabilities, Keller said, "Blindness separates a person from things, but deafness separates him from people" (Miles, 1995, p. 4). Clearly, the case of Helen Keller is most unique and remarkable. Although it is unrealistic to expect the outcomes for all individuals with deaf–blindness to be like hers, her story does remind us all of the importance of high expectations, hard work, intensive instruction, and meaningful support.

MAKING CONNECTIONS

• For more on methods of reading and writing for students with visual impairments, see the Low Vision and Blind Children section in Chapter 11.
• For more about the development of oral language in deaf children, review the section on speech ability in Deaf or Hard of Hearing Children in Chapter 10.

Just as it would be a mistake to assume that all people with deaf–blindness can become "Helen Kellers," it is a mistake to make an alternative assumption about people in this group. Kim Powers is a good example (Rosenberg, 1995). Powers hosts a new Saturday television show for kids, "Kim's World." She is a unique and daring host who has played with tarantulas and tigers, bungee jumped, and ridden horses and elephants. Being a person with deaf–blindness has not stopped her from skiing and scuba diving on TV. The cable network, Kaleidoscope, that airs her show focuses mostly on programs for people with disabilities and hopes to go nationwide soon. Let's turn our attention to three more common results of this disability, problems that the individuals affected, their family members, and their teachers must address: isolation, communication, and mobility.

Feelings of isolation are a particular problem for many individuals with deaf–blindness and an area that educators must address. The world of these individuals is restricted. It is educators' role to expand their "world-view" and connect them with other people and their environments (Haring & Romer, 1995;

Kim Powers, who is deaf and blind, stars in Kaleidoscope's Kim's World. Kaleidoscope is a 24-hour cable network that also produces a web site of interesting and useful information (www.ktv-i.com).

MAKING CONNECTIONS

In Chapter 6, review these sections about supports:
• Emerging Classification Systems (Types of Mental Retardation)
• Support (Children with Mental Retardation)
• Family

 MAKING CONNECTIONS

The concept of "age of onset" is discussed in both Chapters 10 and 11 in the Defined sections.

 MAKING CONNECTIONS

In Chapter 10,
• review information about sign language; see the Deaf Culture section (Children Who Are Deaf or Hard of Hearing),
• to find more about different communication systems, including Total Communication, see the Instructional Methods for Deaf Students section (Educational Interventions).

 MAKING CONNECTIONS

See the section in Chapter 11 on Orientation and Mobility (Educational Interventions).

 MAKING CONNECTIONS

• Review the Deaf–Blindness Defined section of this chapter.
• For the definition of ataxia, read again the section about cerebral palsy (Chapter 9).

incidental learning. Gaining knowledge and skills without being directly taught.

Heubner, Prickett, Welch, & Joffee, 1995). Remember, many individuals with deaf–blindness have enough vision to move around, recognize familiar faces, read enlarged print, and even read sign language at close distances. Some have sufficient hearing to understand some sounds, recognize familiar voices, and maybe even develop speech. Many of these students also have mental retardation. So the compounding effects of all of these disabilities result in the vast majority of these individuals requiring extensive supports throughout their lives.

For those of us without disabilities, much of our learning is almost effortless. Through what is called **incidental learning**, we gain knowledge about our environment, we learn about the subtle rules and social conventions about interacting with others, and we come to understand how to access our communities. Efficient incidental learning uses intact vision and hearing, for it is through these channels that others communicate and convey important information. Depending on the degree of visual or hearing loss and the age of onset of the disability, the transfer of this knowledge is impaired (Prickett & Welch, 1995). For many of these youngsters, total communication becomes their means of interchange and allows for the integrated use of oral and manual communication. And, for many of these individuals profit from manual communication actually becoming tactile, where the signs are conveyed through touch. What can teachers do to help lessen the impact of both visual and hearing problems on the communication abilities of their students? Prickett (1995, p. 62) provides some suggestions in this regard:

- Interact frequently and consistently
- Use multisensory information
- Use tactile and close-range signing as appropriate
- Focus on individual interaction
- Encourage direct communication among classmates.

Movement is important to all of us. We move to exercise, to recreate, to get from one location to another for so many purposes, and to communicate our emotions. The ability to move freely in our environments is a natural human behavior, but for those who have significant visual losses, movement is often restricted and can even be dangerous. The components of purposeful movement need to become instructional targets for students with deaf–blindness. To help us understand the complexity of what is so natural for so many, Groce & Isaacson (1995) identified and defined these components (see Table 12.2).

What should be clear for this discussion is that the significance of deaf–blindness, and its associated problems, is great. The impact on the individuals affected is substantial. The work and effort to overcome these challenges is considerable and involves teams of dedicated people that include the individuals themselves, their families, educators, and experts from many disciplines.

Prevalence

According to the State and Multi-State Service Centers for Children with Deaf–Blindness, in 1995 some 10,415 deaf–blind students—ages birth to 21—were served under IDEA (Baldwin, 1996). At least 85 percent of children with deaf–blindness have additional disabilities as well (*JVIB News Service*, 1995). Because students can be reported by the states to the federal government by only one disability area, many deaf–blind students are reported in other categories, so prevalence reports often vary significantly from one source to another.

TABLE 12.2

Components of Purposeful Movement

Be Aware of Surroundings

The world is comprised of people, places, and things that must be understood independently and in relationship to self.

Initiate and Sustain Movement

Reaching a desired location requires that movement begin and be sustained until the destination is reached.

Recognize Destinations

Movement has an object—the destination—that must be recognized and dealt with appropriately.

Protect Self from Danger

Obstacles and other immediate dangers must be handled safely.

Make Decisions

Choosing when and how to move requires the individual to decide whether there is sufficient reason to move, whether it is the right time to move, whether there is preference for this act of moving, and which mode of transportation to use.

Source: From "Purposeful Movement" by M. M. Groce and A. B. Isaacson, 1995, in K. M. Heubner, J. G. Prickett, R. R. Welch, and E. Joffee (Eds.), *Hand in hand: Essentials of communication and orientation and mobility for your students who are deaf blind* (pp. 94–95). New York: AFB Press. Adapted by permission.

Causes and Prevention

The most frequent, specified cause of deaf–blindness is prematurity (Baldwin, 1996). However, it is important to note that in the majority of cases the cause of these multiple disabilities is unknown. Besides prematurity, some causes or factors associated with deaf–blindness are understood.

Usher syndrome is a hereditary cause of congenital deafness, progressive blindness, along with mental retardation. In addition to these three disabilities, many individuals with Usher syndrome also have walking and motor problems associated with ataxia. Neuropsychological problems are also observed in about 25 percent of these cases (Accardo, Whitman, Laszewski, Haake, & Morrow, 1996). This recessive X-linked, genetic syndrome accounts for about 5 percent of all children with severe hearing losses, about 2 percent of children with deaf–blindness, and about 50 percent of adults with deaf–blindness. This rare syndrome occurs in about 3 out of every 100,000 people. There are several types of deaf–blindness, and with one of these the onset of visual impairments does not begin until adolescence (Prickett & Welch, 1995). These individuals often face additional emotional challenges because they spent most of their schoolyears alongside deaf peers, included in Deaf culture. As their vision becomes more and more restricted, they find that they can no longer fully participate in the Deaf community, which leads to frustration and disappointment.

 MAKING CONNECTIONS

• For more information about prematurity and its relationship to disabilities, see the section on Low Birthweight (Causes) in Chapter 6.
• For more information about the causes and types of visual impairments and deafness, see those sections in Chapters 10 and 11.

 MAKING CONNECTIONS

For more information about Deaf culture, review Deaf or Hard of Hearing Children in Chapter 10.

Usher syndrome. A genetic syndrome that includes a nonprogressive sensorineural hearing loss, retinitis pigmentosa and progressively restricted field of vision, loss of the sense of smell, and impaired balance and motor skills.

Deaf–blindness is associated with other conditions beside Usher syndrome. For example, about 2 percent of those with deaf–blindness have Down syndrome, about 4 percent have hydrocephaly, and another 4 percent were affected by rubella. Prematurity, the most frequently reported cause, accounts for only 9 percent of the cases of deaf–blindness, and this listed cause itself has many different causes. Thus proportionally few causes are understood, so we do not have reliable preventive measures.

Children with Deaf–Blindness

As we mentioned earlier, the vast majority (some 85 percent) of students who are deaf–blind have additional disabilities beyond their visual and hearing problems (*JVIB News Service*, 1995). The most common additional disability is mental retar-

---

MAKING ACCOMMODATIONS

Here are some helpful guidelines to follow when "working and playing" with individuals with deaf–blindness.

Courtesy

- Be human.
- Let the person know you are nearby with a gentle touch on the hand that is nearest to you.
- If you want to communicate, touch the person's hands gently and then slide your hands underneath the other person's.
- Every time you meet the person, identify yourself (maybe with a special sign).
- Respect the person. Give him time to respond. Let that person think for himself.
- Let the person know when you are going to leave the room.
- Leave the environment as you found it (furniture should be in its standard places, doors either fully open or closed).
- Offer assistance only when it looks appropriate or necessary.

Guidance

- Pay attention when helping someone walk safely, and remember you are estimating space for two people, not just yourself.

- Take your time, because it is easier to retain balance and adjust for hazards in the path when the pace is slow and steady.
- Be consistent when guiding another person by keeping steps and paces about the same in distance and speed.
- When you are not sure whether a few steps or a ramp is the best path, ask.

Communication

- Know the individual's primary mode of communication and how subtle messages are conveyed (confusion, understanding, request for a restatement).
- Communicate clearly. Use direct and descriptive language with clear referents.
- Explain why the situation is why it is (why everyone has to move, why you came back without the popcorn).
- When serving as an interpreter, the rules of privacy and respect are the same as for interpreters for the deaf.

---

dation, followed by a speech or language impairment, a physical disability, and a health problem (Baldwin, 1995). Some of these children have more than one additional disability. Their multiple disabilities clearly make meeting their instructional needs challenging and require specially prepared teachers and related service providers. However, it is important to look beyond those disabilities and naturally make accommodations for these individuals' differences. Smith (1992) developed the organizational scheme and suggested some of the guidelines found in the Making Accommodations box. After reading those guidelines, it should be apparent that "working and playing" with individuals with deaf–blindness may well be easier than we think. Notice that these commonsense suggestions could be easily applied to many students, particularly others with low-incidence disabilities.

One question that you should be asking relates to the seriousness of these youngsters' visual and hearing disabilities. You should also be wondering about how these degrees of loss combine. For example, do most of these children have a mild vision loss but a profound hearing loss? Do they have little or no functional use of either sense? First, let's look at the levels of loss for hearing and vision separately. Then, we'll look at their combinations. According to Baldwin (1996), most often these youngsters have a severe hearing loss. So, as a whole, the entire population is more deaf than blind. What is the most common combination of hearing loss and visual loss (e.g., mild loss for vision and severe loss for hearing)? The most frequent combination is being legally blind along with a severe hearing loss (Baldwin, 1995). Figure 12.1 displays these overall data.

~~~

FIGURE 12.1

The Frequency of Various Combinations of Hearing and Visual Losses in Children with Deaf–Blindness

		Hearing Loss			
		Mild	Moderate	Severe	Profound
Vision Loss	Partially sighted	575	545	470	323
	Legally blind	432	709	685	490
	Light perception only	172	280	305	129
	Totally blind	178	213	212	219

Note: Not included are those children:
(a) not tested (or)
(b) Tested but not conclusive

Source: From "Summary of Hearing vs. Vision Loss" by V. Baldwin, 1997. Monmouth, OR: Teaching Research, Western Oregon State College.

Traumatic Brain Injury

Modern medicine has propelled many families into becoming lifelong sources of care and concern for children who experience acquired brain injury resulting in severe disabilities—an unprecedented circumstance in American family life. Prior to the 1960s, most children whose brains were seriously hurt died soon after the trauma. Changes in emergency treatment, imaging technology, and surgical and pharmaceutical treatments have begun to routinely save the lives of approximately 30,000 of these children each year. (Singer, Glang, & Williams, 1996, p. xix)

About one million children annually experience a head injury, and about 165,000 of them require hospitalization (Heller, Alberto, Forney, & Schwartzman, 1996). Some youngsters, after their injuries, require special education. Children with **traumatic brain injury (TBI)** have been served in special education since IDEA was originally passed in 1975. In fact, many children with TBI were served long before then. It is quite possible that some were recognized during the 1940s. Strauss and Lehtinen published a groundbreaking book, *Psychopathology and Education of the Brain-Injured Child*, in 1947. There, they recommended highly structured educational approaches for children whom they described having many of the characteristics observed in today's students with TBI.

TBI was not, however, considered a separate disability area until the 1990 reauthorization of IDEA (PL 101-476), the special education law. Until that time, these students were counted in the categories that most closely matched their primary learning needs and were educated with peers without disabilities and those with similar learning characteristics. For example, many students with TBI were (and most continue to be) educated alongside those with learning disabilities because of the similarity in their learning and behavioral characteristics. Like their classmates with learning disabilities, these students often exhibit memory deficits, attention problems, language impairments, and reduced academic performance. Many benefit from instructional procedures proven effective with children with learning disabilities: direct instruction, structured school days, and organized classes where expectations are clearly specified. Others, because of their head injuries, experience seizures and receive many of the same accommodations as children with epilepsy. Although specific programs for students with TBI are emerging across the nation (Weld County TBI Task Force outside of Greeley, Colorado; Rehabilitation Center in Austin, Texas; Wisconsin Department of Public Instruction), most are served within existing programs for students with other disabilities.

TBI Defined

traumatic brain injury. The result of a head injury; the individual experiences reduced cognitive functioning, limited attention, and impulsivity.

In 1990, Congress added TBI to the list of special education categories. IDEA defines this disability as

an acquired injury to the brain caused by an external physical force, resulting in total or partial functional disability or psychosocial impairment, or both, that adversely affects a child's educational performance. The term applies to open or closed head injuries resulting in impairments in one or more areas, such as cognition; language; memory; attention; reasoning; abstract thinking; judgment; problem solving; sensory, perceptual and motor abilities; psychosocial behavior; physical functions; information processing; and speech. The term does not apply to brain injuries that are congenital or degenerative, or brain injuries induced by birth trauma. (U.S. Department of Education, 1992, p. 44,842)

TBI occurs when a traumatic event "causes a loss of consciousness, memory loss for immediately preceding or subsequent events, confusion, disorientation, or a dazed feeling" (Hux & Hacksley, 1996, p. 158). TBI has several synonyms: acquired brain injury, head injury, closed head injury. It does not include injuries resulting from skull fractures. Table 12.3 provides some explanations of what TBI is and what it is not.

Types of TBI

As with other disabilities, TBI ranges in severity from mild to severe, with most cases falling into the mild range. The vast majority are mild and do not raise alarm with most doctors (Hux & Hacksley, 1996). Mild episodes of brain injury often result in these symptoms: dizziness, headache, selective attention problems, irritability, anxiety, blurred vision, insomnia, fatigue, motor difficulties, language problems, behavior and emotional problems, cognitive problems, and memory problems (Clark, 1996; Heller, Alberto, Forney, & Schwartzman, 1996).

TABLE 12.3

What Is and What Is Not TBI

TBI	*Not TBI*
Concussion is another term for TBI.	An internal cause of brain damage— such as a stroke, brain tumor, or infection of the brain—is not TBI.
A TBI can occur without a direct blow to the head—as in shaken baby syndrome and other forms of child abuse.	A medically documented event potentially causing brain damage but not accompanied by a documentable change in educational performance does not justify TBI verification.
A person does *not* have to lose consciousness to sustain a TBI.	
Brain damage resulting from TBI is often *not* visible through medical tests such as EEGs or brain imaging techniques such as computerized tomography scans or magnetic resonance imaging.	
Repeated mild TBIs can have a cumulative effect.	

Source: From "Mild traumatic brain injury: Facilitating school success" by K. Hux and C. Hacksley, 1996, *Intervention in School and Clinic, 31*, p. 160. Reprinted by permission.

These problems can last for a very short time or for years. In many cases, the effects eventually disappear, but some cases of TBI result in lifelong problems. Youngsters with moderate to severe injuries often experience dramatic changes in their cognitive, language, motor, sensory, and behavioral performances. Some of these children are typical learners one day but after their injury have significant disabilities. In these cases, it is also common for the individual to experience depression or withdrawal.

Identification

Many children with TBI are not identified immediately after their injuries. This happens because many of these youngsters show no visible signs (cuts, bruises) of brain injury (NICHY, 1994). The impact of what has been sometimes called the "silent epidemic" may go misunderstood for months. How can this be? Think about Ryan who was not wearing a helmet, despite his mother's warnings, and fell while skateboarding. Because he did not want to tell his mother that he was not wearing his helmet, he also did not tell her about the accident. Instead he told his mom that he was tired and went off to his room to take a nap.

Even when accidents are serious, injury to the brain may go unnoticed at first. Too often, families bring their children home from the hospital not knowing that long after broken bones are mended that it is the head injury that could result in long-term disabilities (Singer, 1996). Most families are unaware of the signs associated with TBI, and were not informed by medical staff at the hospital that their children might have long-term cognitive effects from their injuries. Sometimes it is educators who must confirm families' worst (and often unspoken) fears: The accident several weeks ago caused more than a broken leg; it also caused brain injury.

In many cases, families do not inform school personnel of the possibility of mild TBI. This might happen if the accident occurred during the summer. It might be that family members did not make the connection between an accident, physical injuries, and changes in behavior (Hux & Hacksley, 1996). The result can be serious. Educators may spend unnecessary time trying to determine why a child, who never had academic or behavior problems before, is having great difficulty at school. Educators may not know that they should be making specific accommodations for the child's academic or social performance.

Since the federal government created its definition of TBI, states have worked toward implementing it. Most have developed eligibility criteria (Katsiyannis & Conderman, 1994). Almost all states require a neurological or medical examination and documentation of the adverse effects of the injury on the student's educational performance. The result is that health specialists and physicians are serving on these children's IEP committees and multidisciplinary teams. Using nonschool district personnel, particularly from the health field, can cause difficulties with scheduling meetings, having the designated team members readily available, understanding or being familiar with educational terms, and budgeting for increased costs. The result could well be that under these circumstances only students with severe disabilities are identified as having TBI. Regardless, multidisciplinary teams are vital to the successful design and implementation of appropriate educational plans for students with disabilities. Table 12.4 reminds us of the key features of such teams and their work.

~~~

TABLE 12.4

Responsibilities of Multidisciplinary Teams

1. *Create working relationships with the student's entire support team*

   Partnerships must be developed between the school and the family, between the school and the medical providers, and among school personnel to coordinate services and share information.

2. *Develop systems for collaboration and communication, at the beginning of every schoolyear (or as the child is being identified for special education services)*

   At a meeting with all parties present, be sure to create understandings for as many "what-if" situations as possible, conduct a needs assessment (if necessary), develop an evaluation plan, create formal and informal channels for communication, and set dates for contacts and meetings.

3. *Establish a school-based team that will coordinate services*

   Particularly for students who receive services from related services personnel who are not from the school district, key contact persons must be identified to coordinate services, approaches, and information.

4. *Achieve mutual understandings of long-term goals for the child*

   Specific goals for transition, adult independence, and employment—held by each stakeholder—should be shared among and understood by all members of the child's support team.

5. *Implement ongoing evaluation procedures*

   The student's progress must be monitored directly, consistently, and frequently with those results shared with all members of the child's support team.

6. *Adjust the student's program as needed*

   The student's performance should determine modifications in the educational program, which must reflect any changes in the psychological needs of the child, as well as educational and behavioral needs.

Significance

The impact of TBI is related to the severity of the injury. In many minor cases, recovery occurs within a few months (Heller, Alberto, Forney, & Schwartzman, 1996). In devastating situations, recovery and relearning can be a slow and frustrating process. Motor skills usually return first. For those with already well developed speech and language skills, basic communication abilities tend to recover quickly. More complex language use and comprehension of subtle verbal and nonverbal cues remain difficult for some students. High-level cognitive functions (problem-solving, memory, high-level, and complex-thinking skills) often return later. The pattern seems to be rapid progress during the first few months after the injury, followed by substantial improvement throughout the first year. Then, gradual improvement is often noted across even a five-year period (Heller, Alberto, Forney, & Schwartzman, 1996).

Educators can play important roles in the recovery of students with TBI. In particular, they can provide considerable assistance during the often difficult period when the student is just returning to school and still in the process of adjusting to unusual fatigue, reduced energy, and loss of ability (Doelling & Bryde, 1995).

Prevalence

More than 100,000 children and youth between the ages of birth and 21 are hospitalized each year for injuries to the head. Estimates vary about the long-term effects of these injuries. Some believe that 1 in 500 of these children develop persistent learning and behavior problems (Katsiyannis & Conderman, 1994), and others think that over one-third of those injuries result in lifelong disabilities (Singer, 1996).

Causes and Prevention

The most common causes of TBI are falls, domestic accidents, motor vehicle accidents, pedestrian and bicycle accidents, assaults, and sports accidents (Hux & Hacksley, 1996). These injuries typically occur among older children. Unfortunately, the sad fact is that for children under the age of 2, the most common cause of TBI is child abuse (Heller, et al., 1996).

Those schoolchildren most at risk for TBI are teenage males (Singer, 1996). The majority of cases occur in youngsters 15 and older (West, Gibson, & Unger, 1996). Why is this so? They are the group who engage in high-risk behaviors such as driving too fast, mixing alcohol or drugs and driving, skateboarding without pro-

Wearing the proper protective gear can prevent head injuries.

tective equipment, and participating in contact sports. Preventing many of these accidents merely involves some commonsense measures. For example, wearing helmets when bicycling or skateboarding, not driving a car or motorcycle when using intoxicating substances, or avoiding high-risk behaviors can prevent tragic accidents.

The effects of TBI can be reduced and long-term negative outcomes prevented in many cases by the actions of family members and professionals. The influence of the family on the long-term outcomes of their children with TBI should never be minimized, for the results can be great. In one study, significant improvements in academic and behavior performance a year after the injury could be attributed directly to the family's involvement (Singer, 1996).

It is obvious that appropriate medical treatment and rehabilitation are critical to preventing the devastating outcomes seen in untreated individuals. Education is also a powerful tool, and students are helped by their special education and general education teachers. Teachers can do many things to enhance these students' ability to succeed. Tyler and Mira (1993) recommend the following steps:

- Retrain and teach cognitive skills.
- Consider whether the student is thinking and processing appropriately.
- Check on any prerequisite cognitive skills.
- Provide frequent feedback.
- Refocus student's attention if necessary.
- Repeat and review.
- Provide examples and models.
- Give simple and frequent instructions, both verbal and written.
- Provide enough time to respond.
- Use computers, especially for drill and practice. (p. 25)

Children with TBI

Children with TBI and their families face great emotional turmoil during the time shortly after the injury. They must adjust to changes in ability, performance, and behavior (Hux & Hacksley, 1996). Even those with mild cases of TBI must cope with sudden changes in performance and many of the common symptoms shown in Table 12.5. What came easily one day is filled with frustration and confusion the next. Tasks that were previously easy to perform now present repeated failure. Many youngsters with TBI tend to have uneven abilities, a fact that is confusing to the individuals and to their teachers. These students also often experience reduced stamina, seizures, headaches, hearing losses, and vision problems (Tyler & Myles, 1991). They get tired easily, so some receive home instruction, often for a year, before returning to school part time. Many of these youngsters have difficulty adjusting to and accepting their newly acquired disability. Because of the frustrations of having difficulty doing tasks that used to be easy, many display behavior problems and reduced self-esteem.

With some simple adjustments to and accommodations in the classroom routine, though, students with brain injuries can be reintegrated into school settings with relative ease (Mira, Tucker, & Tyler, 1992; Tyler & Myles, 1991). If students spend only half a day at school, the teacher can schedule instruction on important academic tasks during the morning, when they are alert and present. Homework assignments can be abbreviated to accommodate their reduced stamina. If some

TABLE 12.5

Characteristics of TBI

Medical/Neurological	Physical	Cognitive	Behavioral/Emotional
Blurred vision	Decreased motor coordination	Decreased attention	Denial of deficits
Concussion	Sensory deficits affecting vision, hearing, taste, or smell	Decreased organizational skills	Depression
Dizziness		Decreased problem solving	Disinhibition
Headache		Slowed information processing	Distractibility
Seizure activity		Difficulty with abstract reasoning	Flat affect
Skull fracture		Memory deficits	Impulsivity
Sleep disorder		Perceptual deficits	Inappropriate laughing or crying
		Poor judgment	Irritability
		Rigidity of thought	Limited initiation
		Word-finding difficulty	Social isolation

Source: From "Mild traumatic brain injury: Facilitating school success" by K. Hux and C. Hacksley, 1996, *Intervention in School and Clinic, 31,* p. 161. Reprinted by permission.

students find that their balance, coordination, and ability to carry materials are more limited than before the accident, the teacher can provide another set of textbooks for home use to make life much easier for them and their families. Because many of these students get confused easily, teachers should clearly specify and adhere to classroom rules and expectations. It is also helpful to use instructional tactics that incorporate a considerable amount of drill and practice to help students remember what is being taught.

Very Low-Incidence Disabilities

We have just provided some specific information about three very low-incidence disabilities. For each, we talked about definitions, prevalence, causes and preventive techniques, and characteristics. Now let's turn our attention to more general information about three issues: educational interventions, families, and technology. Recognize that the following information will not apply to every individual and that it may pertain to one of these three groups of learners more than the others. Still, we think it is applicable to many children with these disabilities. For example, the supports needed by most individuals with autism, deaf–blindness, and moderate to severe cases of TBI are often both intensive and pervasive. The special needs of these individuals are quite challenging for all who work with them.

Participating in recess activities with classmates without diabilities makes a school day complete.

Educational Interventions

Students with very low incidence disabilities present complex profiles to their families and to their teachers. Despite being assigned to a category, each student should be considered a unique member of a diverse group of learners, all possessing different learning styles and characteristics. As such, instructional programs need to be designed on an individual basis to meet each student's needs. Despite their diversity, these children often share many common goals and desired outcomes. For example, a common goal among children with multiple and severe disabilities is improving communication skills. Another is the development of proficient social skills. These students also experience persistent academic problems, probably because of their poor abilities to generalize their learning of one skill to another. Skills often need to be taught in small increments through consistent, systematic, and direct instructional techniques (Strain, Danko, & Kohler, 1995). Many discussions about teaching these skills to preschoolers and schoolchildren with disabilities are found in earlier chapters of this text, so limited discussion about one new intervention strategy is found here.

But first, educators should never lose sight of the prevailing principles of special education (Matson, 1994; Koegel & Koegel, 1995; Szekeres & Meserve, 1994). These principles should be the foundation for all instruction provided to every child with a disability:

 MAKING CONNECTIONS
Review the Educational Interventions sections in Chapters 3 though 11.

- ▦ Student assessments are functionally related to instruction.
- ▦ Educational decisions are made on an individual basis.
- ▦ Instruction is applied directly to the target behavior.

MAKING CONNECTIONS

In Chapter 2, review the sections about
• collaboration,
• multidisciplinary teams.

MAKING CONNECTIONS

In more about functional assessments, see
• Identification section (Autism Defined) in this chapter,
• Prevention section of Chapter 8.

MAKING CONNECTIONS

For more discussion about free appropriate education and the least restrictive environment, see Chapters 1 and 2.

MAKING CONNECTIONS

See the sections about IDEA in Chapter 1.

◾ Collaboration among members of multidisciplinary teams promotes appropriate education.

◾ Accommodations are made for the unique learning styles of each student.

◾ Frequent student evaluation (curriculum based instruction) guides the development and modifications of instructional programs.

Functional assessment procedures help parents and educators better understand the relationship between environmental events and target behaviors (Harris, Belchic, Blum, & Celiberti, 1994; Mullen & Frea, 1995). These techniques often reveal those events that cause the inappropriate or undesirable behavior to occur and the reasons why the behaviors continue to occur. In many cases, educators find that some unproductive behaviors occur for purposes of either escape, attention, or communication. For example, a tantrum—for children who do not know how to ask for help—may be a means of escaping school work that is too difficult or frustrating. When such is the case, educators have found that teaching a student to engage in functionally equivalent behaviors (e.g., "Is this right?" "I need help") often replaces the disruptive behavior (Koegel, Koegel, Frea, & Smith, 1995). These behaviors serve to teach the student very useful skills. (See the Teaching Tactics box for an example of teaching functionally equivalent behaviors.)

Inclusion

By now, we assume that you are nearing the end of the semester and have almost completed this text. It should be clear: At the heart of great debate and consternation lie issues about where students with disabilities should receive their education. Related issues focus on what that education should comprise and what the first and second priority outcomes for these students should be. In other words, What comprises an appropriate education and what is meant by least restrictive environment? Some parents and professionals believe adamantly that "students with disabilities should be full-time members of age-appropriate, typical classrooms in their home schools (whatever school they would attend if they did not have disabilities) and receive all supports necessary to participate in both the academic and social communities of their peers" (Goetz, 1995, p. 3). The courts, however, do not always agree (*Early Childhood Report*, 1996). In one recent ruling, a 13-year-old student with severe and multiple disabilities, despite his parents' wishes, was denied full-time general education placement. Special education class with integration in activities across the school day was determined to be the LRE. So, the debate about LRE continues. But, what are its origins, and why is the issue so inflammatory?

Historically, students with severe disabilities were excluded from U.S. public education. For most of these individuals, it took a federal law (PL 94-142, passed in 1975) and many court decisions to guarantee them a place in the educational system. As programs were initiated and services evolved, special classes were developed (some at segregated schools). With all good intentions, these programs were thought to be highly specialized. Students were brought together where they could form a group sufficiently large enough to allow highly trained specialists (PTs, OTs, SLPs, nurses, assistive technology specialists) to work with expensive and special equipment (therapeutic swimming pools, technology). In part because students with severe disabilities were not making hoped-for progress in the devel-

Developing Functionally Equivalent Behaviors

Jack, a 5-year-old child with autism, engaged in high rates of self-stimulation. He flapped his hands, he rocked back and forth, he repeated words and phrases that had no communicative meaning, and he pounded his hands on his desk. He did all things excessively. Ms. Curren, Jack's special education kindergarten teacher, and her assistant, Mrs. Alanya, conducted a functional assessment of these behaviors. In the classroom and on a home visit, they collected data and information about these inappropriate behaviors, to determine the functional relationships between environmental events and the disruptive behaviors. They interviewed family members and other caregivers (babysitters). They discussed the situation among themselves. They directly observed Jack using the ABC model of data collection. In this stage, they described the behaviors in detail, the events that preceded (antecedent to) the self-stimulatory behaviors, and those consequences that followed the behaviors. When they summarized all of the information while searching for functional relationships, they determined that a significant amount of Jack's disruptive behavior was an attempt to seek attention.

This information, along with knowledge of research findings indicating that developing functionally equivalent behaviors would cause a reduction in the frequency of the related inappropriate behaviors, led them to design an intervention program. They taught Jack to say, "Is this right?" when he wanted Ms. Curren's or Mrs. Alanya's attention. When Jack needed assistance with his work, they taught him to say, "I need help." Jack's family members also rewarded Jack when he did not engage in self-stimulation but instead used these two phrases appropriately. Without directly targeting the stereotypic behaviors and instead teaching and reinforcing functionally equivalent behaviors, Jack's parents and teachers saw dramatic improvement in his performance.

 MAKING CONNECTIONS

- Review the sections on Inclusion (Educational Interventions) in Chapters 3 though 11.
- In Chapters 1 and 2, review the sections about LRE.

opment of social skills, were not integrated into mainstream society, and were not generalizing skills learned at school to other settings, The Association for Persons with Severe Disabilities (TASH) has vigorously advocated for all students with disabilities to be educated exclusively in the general education classroom. This model has been referred to as *full inclusion*.

It appears that the hopes and promises some parents and professionals have for this educational model are not being achieved. Consensus still exists among this group: Full inclusion is the best service delivery model for these students (Haring & Romer, 1995). However, some—even those instrumental in creating the full inclusion model—are suggesting modifications (Romer & Haring, 1995). What are the concerns? Inclusion does not guarantee performance outcomes. In fact, no educational placement can make such guarantees. For students with disabilities, if a skill is not directly taught, it is usually not learned. Experts in deaf–blindness make this point well:

> Merely being present with peers without disabilities in general education settings is not sufficient to bring about those outcomes… We have seen too many students with deaf–blindness included with their peers for many hours a day, only to find

that no meaningful relationships were developed with those peers, that no psychological sense of community was felt. We believe this is because, like behavioral technology, we have confused a process, or a behavior, with an outcome. (Romer & Haring, 1995, p. 426)

These experts are not abandoning the concept of integration but are questioning whether placement alone can achieve outcome goals. They also raise an interesting point for those with very low incidence disabilities: Full inclusion could be interpreted as sending a message that the only relationships valued are those with people without disabilities. Being included at the neighborhood school may well mean that no other student with that disability attends school there. Support needs should be met from a variety of communities: families, peers without disabilities, and peers with similar disabilities (Romer & Haring, 1995). People need to be allowed to gain a sense of community with those who have similar interests, concerns, and needs. They need, for example, to band together to advocate for each other when the necessity arises, or share problems and solutions with each other. These connections can be made outside of school, as well as at school. Certainly, issues about placement need continual consideration. This discussion raises an important question: What comprises segregation? Is it being excluded for some part of the school day from students without disabilities? Or, is segregation not being able to participate with others with similar concerns, interests, and abilities?

So despite all of the rhetoric about full inclusion, where do students with severe and multiple disabilities attend school? Let's look at placement patterns. About 9 percent of children with autism receive the majority of their educational programs in general education class settings (U.S. Department of Education, 1995). About the same percentage spend somewhere between 21 and 60 percent of their school day attending a resource room, and 50 percent attend separate special education classes, 28 percent attend special schools, and 3 percent are placed in residential facilities. The majority of students with deaf–blindness receive their education in special education classes (Baldwin, 1995). Some 38 percent attend special classes, while 24 percent attend either public or private special schools. Probably reflecting the complexity of their disabilities, only 6 percent attend general education classes and 4 percent attend resource rooms as their primary educational placements. The pattern for students with TBI is somewhat similar to the other two groups (U.S. Department of Education, 1995). The majority of students attend either a special class (28 percent) or special school (28 percent). Many fewer students (some 16 percent) participate the majority of the school day in a general education classroom, and almost 20 percent attend resource rooms. Almost 3 percent of these students receive hospital or homebound services, and 4 percent attend school at residential facilities. It is important to understand that the full inclusion movement has made some difference in where these students are educated, but still very few attend general education programs most of the day.

Transition

One important goal of transition programs is for individuals with severe disabilities to achieve social integration in workplace, residential, and recreational settings. This along with two other goals—holding a job and living independently—provide the core of many education programs during the transition years. Clearly, being employed, possessing functional life skills, and meeting the requirements of daily life (managing a budget, maintaining a household, cooking, shopping) are important to what is considered successful adulthood. However, social integration is thought of by some as associated with quality of life (Chadsey-Rusch & Heal, 1995). Table 12.6 lists some important instructional targets that should improve social outcomes of young people.

For more information about functional or life skills, see the Functional Curriculum section (Education and the Schoolchild) in Chapter 6.

Families

Particularly since the 1992 AAMR definition of mental retardation, professionals in the field of special education have been reconceptualizing programs and services for people with disabilities (Luckasson, Coulter, Polloway, Reiss, Schalock, Snell, Spitalnik, & Stark, 1992). The worth of these programs is measured in terms of outcomes (or results) for these individuals when they are adults, with their merit being judged by adults' independence. The focus is on the type and amount of support the individual needs to remain in the community, living, working, and playing alongside and with people without disabilities (Bradley, Ashbough, & Blaney, 1993). The family is one of the most obvious sources of natural support for all individuals with disabilities, particularly those with low-incidence disabilities. Support requires commitment. As you read Bernard Rimland's story, note how his child impacted on his whole life and the commitment to his child with a disability results in support.

For more information about the 1992 AAMR definition of mental retardation, see the Defined section of Chapter 6.

Singer (1996) provides us with some key concepts about creating family supports:

- Service agency personnel should consider the family as the primary unit of concern.

- The family should be assisted in remaining involved in the community and avoiding isolation and withdrawal from friends and activities.

- Support services should be arranged specifically for each family's needs, rather than expecting a family to avail itself of services that happen to be available.

- Many families need a case manager, one person to coordinate all services and supports for the family and the individual.

- Supports must be available across the individual's lifespan and change as needs change.

- Families should be empowered, so they can provide supports and meet challenges without always depending on social service agencies or others.

- People with low-incidence disabilities should be an integral part of the community.

- Services that encourage family support must adapt to cultural diversity.

Let's take a look at what these concepts really mean. Simply put, the family's concerns, needs, capacity, and potential for providing support must be moved to the forefront. No longer can the individual with low-incidence or severe disabilities be isolated or viewed as an individual who exists without natural supports available. In practice, it means that parents, brothers and sisters, and extended family members should be included in the individual's school, rehabilitation, and

TABLE 12.6

Transition Outcomes

Individuals know how to
- ask for help, offer assistance, ask questions.
- answer questions, respond to criticism.
- interact with others socially at work.
- initiate conversations appropriately.
- advocate for themselves.
- interpret and discriminate social cues.

Personal acceptance is demonstrated by co-workers
- voluntarily eating lunch with the individual.
- seeing the individual after work.
- taking breaks with the individual.
- indicating that the individual is a friend.
- encouraging the individual to attend company social events.

Co-workers or the employer
- initiates social interactions with the individual.
- responds to social interactions initiated by the individual.
- advocates for the individual.
- teaches the individual new social skills.

Individuals participate socially by interacting with co-workers
- about work upon arrival, at breaks, during lunch, several times throughout the day, and after work.
- on nonwork topics upon arrival, at breaks, during lunch, and after work.
- at company-sponsored events.
- social occasions that occur outside of work.

Individuals experience social support as demonstrated by increased
- happiness at work.
- self-esteem.
- friendship network.
- support network.

Individuals are accepted in the workplace as indicated by co-workers
- indicating they like the person.
- advocating or supporting the person.
- considering the person to be an acquaintance.
- considering the person to be a team player.
- displaying positive, general interactions.
- training the person to perform work tasks better.

Source: From "Building consensus from transition experts on social integration outcomes and interventions" by J. Chadsey-Rusch and L. W. Heal, 1995, *Exceptional Children, 62,* pp. 170–174. Adapted with permission.

Being Culturally Sensitive When Developing Family Supports

Family involvement for individuals requiring intensive and pervasive supports to participate in the community varies across cultures. Professionals must be sensitive to each family's needs and understand how culture influences family involvement and its potential for providing supports the individual might need (Singer, 1996). For example, attitudes about disabilities are culturally influenced: The disability may be considered a sign of divine displeasure or punishment. Such attitudes may affect how willing an immediate family member may be in acknowledging the disability. People from cultures in which it is improper to question authority figures may find it impossible to be fully participating members of IEP teams. Those who come from cultures in which problem behavior is considered shameful might have difficulties attending community events with their family member with disabilities. It is important not to make assumptions as well, for traditional values may not be held by everyone from a particular cultural group.

social service programs. They should be invited for involvement. When arranging planning sessions, their schedules and desires should be considered. However, it is crucial that their needs be understood. Some may not wish to be involved in the life of the individual with the disability. Professionals from mainstream culture must be sensitive and adapt to others' cultural beliefs and expectations. The Focus on Diversity box further expands on cultural diversity and developing family support.

Services and programs for the individuals with low-incidence disabilities should be an integral part of the community. The premise is that sustained family involvement in the lives of those with disabilities increases the probability of success and independence in the community. For example, instead of living in an institution miles from their home communities, these individuals live in settings (homes, apartments, neighborhoods) like everyone else. In many cases, this cannot occur without considerable support from a variety of sources. To prevent the terrible treatment experienced by many individuals with disabilities living in institutions far removed from public scrutiny, family support and community support need to be aware of the signs of abuse. To some, not only is the **family system** the best source of support, but its members have some clear roles to fill (DePompei & Williams, 1994). If they chose to accept that role, they should be considered full members of the child's multidisciplinary team. They also can be information providers, active participants in assessment and treatment, and advocates. Individuals from the family system can extend treatment programs to all aspects of the individual's life and assist with generalization. This network of people express the hopes and dreams for the achievement of goals for the targeted family member.

 MAKING CONNECTIONS

For more about family support, see the Family section of Chapter 6.

family system. Potential sources of support for people with disabilities, including sons and daughters, spouses, parents, siblings, in-laws, aunts and uncles, grandparents, extended family members, and step-family members.

Technology

⌂ MAKING CONNECTIONS

For the wide array of technological advances that can assist people with disabilities learn, communicate, see, hear, interact with others, and function better in daily life, see the Technology sections throughout this text.

A major, positive change in the lives of people with disabilities and their families is the development of technology that can address and compensate for their disabilities. Many of these technological advances (alternative and augmentative communication devices, assistive technology, computer-assisted and -enhanced instruction) are very beneficial to individuals with low-incidence disabilities. In this chapter, we decided to focus on yet another contribution that technology can make to the lives of individuals with disabilities and those who work with them.

A major challenge faced by school administrators who work in rural and remote areas is a lack of sufficient numbers of children who share low-incidence disabilities to support the costs of experts from a variety of different disciplines to work with these children and their families. For example, there may be only one deaf–blind child in an entire school district that is hundreds of miles from a large metropolitan area and comprehensive medical services. There may be only two children with autism in adjacent school districts that together cover a thousand square miles. Simply put, it is quite likely that there is insufficient expertise at these school sites to provide an appropriate education for these children, regardless of age and unique learning needs. Compounding the problem are the difficulties of communicating with many people: parents who live many miles from school, members of the multidisciplinary team who come from different parts of the state, itinerant teachers and related service providers, and the student's school-based teachers.

Today, some of these problems can be solved through technology by using the practices, hardware, and software developed for another purpose: **distance education**. This technology was created to deliver instruction to remote areas, typically a substantial distance from a university campus. Although a very important activity for the benefit of students with disabilities and their families, the applications of this technology extend far beyond the enhancement of teachers' skills and knowledge. For example, distance education could create "statewide classrooms" where special educators who live even hundreds of miles away can collaborate, team teach, and work together to meet the needs of students with very special learning needs. Consulting teachers and related service providers can work with classroom teachers hundreds of miles away. Through live and interactive television, behavior can be evaluated by a multidisciplinary team as it is occurring in the classroom. Team members can also help the teacher develop and implement an educational program as it is being tested with the child.

Distance education technology can be applied to work with families. Many families have televisions and videotape players in their homes or can arrange to borrow the equipment from the school or a neighbor. This "video connection" can enhance the interaction between the family and the school, even when work and distance make it difficult for family members to make frequent school visits. Teachers can use videotapes to introduce members of the multidisciplinary team to the family, even though their visits to school could not be coordinated to occur at the same time or even on the same day when the parents could be present. Distance education technology can help bridge the gap with families who do not speak sufficient English to understand technical terms and descriptions of how to best work with their child with limited vision and hearing. Lessons might be taped in the family's home language and sent home with the child. Using this strategy, parents can help with generalization by implementing school programs at home that they now understand because they were explained in their primary language (even when none of the teachers at their child's school are proficient in that

distance education. Uses telecommunications technologies to deliver instruction by experts to areas where particular expertise is needed.

Video Technology and Communication with Family

The teacher or itinerant specialist might videotape

▸ a tour of the school and classrooms the child uses.

▸ an introduction of all of the teachers and related services.

▸ messages to the family.

▸ examples of the child's educational programs at school.

▸ demonstrations of activities for follow-up at home.

▸ initial performance and "progress" performances.

▸ activities as a video "report card."

▸ the child engaged in "excellent levels" of performance as examples or models of results that can be achieved.

▸ home language and English comparisons for families who might not be English proficient.

The parents or family might videotape

▸ introductions of family members, including the extended family and other caregivers (important neighbors, babysitters, close friends).

▸ introductions of important members of the child's community.

▸ the child performing chores and family functions.

▸ behaviors the family would like help in improving.

▸ the child participating in significant community events.

▸ messages to the teachers.

language). By using a camcorder, the family can also record behaviors they find problematic at home and seek help from the professionals at school. The Tips for Teachers box has ideas for other possible uses of video technology.

Let's look at some other examples of distance education technology that can be expanded to meet the needs of children with low-incidence disabilities and their families. One project in Montana, VIDEOSHARE, uses this technology to document children's accomplishments in special education classrooms with social service agency personnel and the children's families (Alliance 2000, 1993a). In Wyoming, parents can receive training about IEP meetings and how to advocate better for their children's service needs through workshops offered by a parent information center. For parents who cannot attend one of the fourteen regional centers, classes are offered through videos and teleconferencing (Alliance 2000, 1993b). In Kentucky, the newest advances in assistive technology are shared with rural educators through distance education strategies (Alliance 2000, 1993c). The applications of distance education for the benefit of children with low-incidence disabilities who live in rural and remote areas are still being developed. They have and will continue to improve the educational opportunities for these children. Perhaps the greatest overall benefit is

 MAKING CONNECTIONS

For a review, see the Assistive Technology section in Chapter 9.

that it has allowed children whose families make this choice to live at home and attend schools along with their brothers and sisters, instead of having to live at a state-funded residential institution because no educator in proximity to them has the skills to develop their abilities.

Concepts and Controversy: Are Separate Special Education Categories Necessary?

Almost concurrent with the national move to reduce or eliminate special education categories (particularly from classroom programs), the federal government added two disability categories to special education and the potential of yet another category in the future. In many school districts across the nation, classes specifically for students with one type of disability taught by teachers with specialized preparation in that area have disappeared. They have been replaced by cross-categorical programs where students with mild disabilities are taught together, possibly in a resource room setting. Those with moderate disabilities might be grouped for specific job training activities, and students with similar severe disabilities might receive community based instruction on functional or life skills. In districts adopting full inclusion plans, students receive pull-in services based on their individual needs, not on their disability label.

In the 1990 reauthorization of IDEA (PL 101-457), autism and TBI were given separate disability classifications, and attention deficit disorder (ADD) was put under study for possible future designation as a separate disability category for special education services. Children with autism and children with TBI have been guaranteed educational services since IDEA was first passed in 1975. It is doubtful that any child with either of these conditions has been excluded from school or denied special education services (Thompson & Freeman, 1995). In these cases, the change in the law probably did not bring any previously unserved children to special education. (If ADD were added as a special category, this is probably not the case and many children not previously eligible would receive special education services.) It did move these two groups to independent status. Previously, students with autism had been included with different groups. For a while, they were considered part of the behavior disorders or emotional disturbance category. At other times, they were included with students with physical impairments and special health care needs. Individual students with TBI have been classified as having learning disabilities, emotional disturbance, or mental retardation.

In separating these students, some hoped that new special programs would be developed. For example, for students with TBI some made the case that "the designation of TBI as a separate category of disability signals that schools should provide children and youth with access to and funding for neuropsychological, speech and language, educational, and other evaluations necessary to provide the information needed for the development of an appropriate individualized education program" (NICHY, 1994 p. 1). Has this occurred for either group of youngsters? Has the separate classification led to the development of new programs specifically for these students? Has it led to new personnel preparation programs that produce teachers specifically trained to staff these classes? Are these separate categories justified? Should they be eliminated or should more discrete categories be identified?

MAKING CONNECTIONS

For a review of ADD, see these sections in Chapter 4:
• History
• Children with Learning Disabilities

Although the size of the disability group is probably not very important to the individuals or the families affected, these three special education categories are each comprised of very few students. Together, autism, deaf–blindness, and traumatic brain injury account for about .06 percent of schoolchildren. Although relatively small in numbers, these disabilities are often severe, affecting overall performance significantly. Many of these individuals also have additional problems in one or more of these areas: cognition, language, speech, and motor skills. Many have mental retardation. Individuals with low-incidence disabilities have complex learning needs that require the collaborative input from many experts from comprehensive multidisciplinary teams.

FOCUS QUESTIONS

Self-Test Questions

▶ *What are the major characteristics of children with autism?*

In 1943, when Leo Kanner first coined the term *autism* and described the condition, he specified two primary characteristics: extreme isolation and excessive insistence on *sameness*. He also required that these two symptoms be present during infancy. Kanner's is probably the strictest definition of autism and therefore permits the fewest number of individuals to be included. Less restrictive definitions also include excessive behaviors, the need for sameness, and social withdrawal. They also describe these behaviors as typifying the condition: stereotyped movements, repetitive activities, unusual responses to auditory and visual stimuli, poor educational performance, inability to initiate or maintain social interactions, and poor language development. Other behaviors are often observed among members of this population. For example, many (about 40 percent) engage in self-injurious behaviors, such as head banging, eye poking, and biting. The vast majority (some 80 percent) of these individuals also have mental retardation, and over half do not develop functional speech or language. About a third of the group develop seizures, and four out of five are males. Some individuals exhibit bizarre inconsistencies in their abilities, but only 5 percent are considered savants and possess unique musical, artistic, or memory (such as remembering trivia) abilities.

▶ *How would you describe the impact of deaf–blindness on those affected?*

People with deaf–blindness live in very restricted environments. Their dual disability impacts their communication and mobility abilities. As a group, their hearing problems tend to be more severe than their visual impairments, but their losses in both areas require special adaptations and instruction in *both* modes for maximal learning to occur. The most typical combination is for the individual to be classified as legally blind and also have a severe hearing loss. Some develop speech and can learn to read print, and others cannot. In almost all cases, these individuals need support from others to make their environments safe and accessible. Because of their limited vision and hearing, many experience significant feelings of isolation. In addition, a great number of these individuals have additional disabilities, such as mental retardation, speech or language impairments, physical disabilities, and health problems.

▶ *What additional disabilities do children with autism and children with deaf–blindness often possess?*

The majority of children with autism and children with deaf–blindness could also qualify as belonging to the special education category of multiple disabilities. It is very common for individuals from both groups to also have mental retardation. About 80 percent of those in the autism category have mental retardation, and this is the most common additional disability for those with deaf–blindness. Speech and language development is a problem area for many of these individuals as well. Those with cognitive impairments often do not fully develop language skills, and those who are deaf usually do not develop speech (and may use sign language instead). Their severe disabilities impact their lives in significant and complex ways.

▶ *How can many cases of TBI be prevented?*

The most common causes of traumatic brain injury (TBI) are domestic accidents, motorcycle accidents, car accidents, pedestrian and bicycle accidents, assaults, sports injuries, and child abuse. Except for child abuse, most TBI cases occur among teenage males who engage in high-risk behaviors. Wearing protective gear such as seat belts and helmets can prevent many of these injuries. Avoiding substances such as drugs and alcohol when operating a vehicle can also prevent the accidents that cause many cases of TBI among teenagers. Preventing the dangerous cycle of domestic violence is a complex and major problem in our nation today, but children must be protected and the home environments in which they are raised must be made safe.

▶ *How are functional assessments and the development of functionally equivalent behaviors used together?*

Many special educators across many different disability areas use functional assessments (sometimes referred to as an ABC analysis). This behavioral technique helps to more clearly understand an individual's inappropriate behavior patterns. It helps to define the behavior better. For example, for a specific individual self-injurious behavior includes head banging and biting but does not include any other harmful behavior. By analyzing under what conditions the behavior occurs, educators can come to understand what causes and what events maintain the behavior of concern. For example, head banging occurs most often when the individual is asked to perform a difficult and frustrating task and seems to

be maintained because considerable attention is given to the person when that behavior is happening. In this situation, educators will teach the individual how to engage in a functionally equivalent behavior with the aim of replacing the inappropriate behavior with a more useful one. In this case, the teacher might encourage the student to raise his hand and say, "I need help," when presented with difficult learning situations. The pairing of functional assessments with teaching functionally equivalent behaviors can lead to the reduction in undesirable behaviors and the increase of helpful and productive skills.

Challenge Question

▶ *Should autism, deaf–blindness, and traumatic brain injury each be considered a separate special education category? Why? Why not?*

Over the years—while creating and while amending IDEA—Congress has debated the issue of creating more discrete special education categories. Disability categories are used to identify children who should qualify for services under this federal law. In many instances, they also assist with the design of appropriate individualized educational programs for each student with a disability. However, in the cases of autism, deaf–blindness, and traumatic brain injury (TBI), students were not being denied special educational services and were being provided with an appropriate education under already existing disability categories. Many parents and professionals who advocated for separate classifications for these disabilities believed that more appropriate educational opportunities would be the result: the development of new classes or services specifically for each group of children, special teacher preparation programs, and additional funding for new experts to be part of multidisciplinary teams. In some cases, they also felt that individuals with these disabilities and their families might experience less stigma by no longer being associated with another special education label.

Scholarly Books

Haring, N. G., & Romer, L. T. (Eds.). (1995). *Welcoming students who are deaf–blind into typical classrooms: Facilitating school participation, learning, and friendships.* Baltimore: Paul H. Brookes.

Heubner, K. M., Prickett, J. G., Welch, R. R., & Joffee, E. (Eds.). (1995). *Hand in hand: Essentials of communication and orientation and mobility for your students who are deaf blind.* New York: AFB Press.

Koegel, R. L., & Koegel, L. K. (Eds.). (1995). *Teaching children with autism: Strategies for initiating positive interactions and improving learning opportunities.* Baltimore: Paul H. Brookes.

Matson, J. L. (Ed.). (1994). *Autism in children and adults: Etiology, assessment and intervention.* Pacific Grove, CA: Brooks/Cole.

Mira, M. P., Tucker, B. F., & Tyler, J. S. (1992). *Traumatic brain injury in children and adolescents: A sourcebook for teachers and other school personnel.* Austin, TX: Pro-Ed.

Singer, G. H. S., Glang, A., & Williams, J. M. (Eds.). (1996). *Children with acquired brain injury: Educating and supporting families.* Baltimore: Paul H. Brookes.

Popular Books

Keller, H. (1988). *The story of my life.* New York: Sig Classics.

Williams, D. (1992). *Nobody nowhere: The extraordinary autobiography of an autistic.* New York: Times Books/Random House.

Popular Videos

James Brady Story. (1991). HBO.
The Miracle Worker. (1962). United Artists.

Rain Man. (1989). United Artists.
Regarding Henry. (1991). Paramount.

Professional, Parent, and Consumer Organizations and Agencies

Autism Hotline
Autism Services Center
P.O. Box 507
Huntington, WV 25710-0507
Phone: (304) 525-8014
Web site:
http://www.cetfsu.edu/tree/nichcy/autism/org.html

Autism Society of America
7910 Woodmont Ave., Suite 650
Bethesda, MD 20814
Phone: (301) 657-0881 and (800) 3-AUTISM
Web site: http://www.autism.society.org

National Information Clearinghouse on Children Who Are Deaf–Blind (DB-LINK)
345 N. Monmouth Ave.
Monmouth, OR 97361
Voice: (800) 438-9376
TTY: (800) 854-7013
Web site: http//www.tr.wosc.osshe.edu/db.link

American Association of Deaf–Blind
814 Thayer Ave., Room 300
Silver Spring, MD 20910
(301) 588-6545 TTY only

Helen Keller National Center for Deaf–Blind Youths and Adults
111 Middle Neck Road
Sands Point, NY 11050
Voice: (516) 944-8900
TTY: (516) 944-8637

Brain Injury Association, Inc.
1775 Massachusetts Ave., NW
Suite 100
Washington, DC 20036-1904
Phone: (202) 296-6443

GLOSSARY

ABC model. A behavioral way to analyze and select interventions by looking at whether they occur antecedent to (before), concurrent with (during), or consequent to (after) the target behavior.

ability grouping. Placing students with comparable achievement and skill levels in the same classes or courses.

absence seizures. Seizures with a short lapse in consciousness (also called petit mal seizures).

acceleration. Moving students through a curriculum or years of schooling in a shorter period of time than usual.

accessibility. Barrier-free environments allowing maximal participation by individuals with disabilities.

accommodation. The focusing process of the lens of the eye.

acquired immunodeficiency syndrome (AIDS). A usually fatal medical syndrome caused by infection from the human immunodeficiency virus.

acuity. Sharpness of response to visual, auditory, or tactile stimuli.

adaptive behavior. Performance of everyday life skills expected of adults.

adaptive skill areas. Targets of instruction that focus on the ability of an individual to function in a typical environment and on successful adult outcomes (independent living, employment, and community participation).

advance organizers. Previews to lectures that acquaint students with the content, its organization, and importance.

advanced placement courses. High school courses that carry college credit.

adventitiously blind. Those who acquired a severe visual impairment after age 2.

aggression. Hostile and attacking behavior, which can include verbal communication, directed toward self, others, or the physical environment.

air conduction audiometry method. A method to test hearing that uses a pure-tone sound generated by an audiometer.

alerting devices. Devices that use sight, sound, or vibration to make individuals aware of an occurrence or an important sound.

alternative and augmentative communication. Assistive technology devices that specifically help individuals communicate, including those that actually produce speech.

American Sign Language (ASL). The sign language or manual communication system preferred by many adults who are deaf in this country.

Americans with Disabilities Act (ADA). Federal disability antidiscrimination legislation passed in 1990.

analytic listening. Listening that includes analysis and possibly interpretation of another person's communication message.

anchored instruction. The use of videotaped real-life situations to make learning more relevant and meaningful.

anorexia. Intense fear of gaining weight, disturbed body image, chronic absence or refusal of appetite for food, causing severe weight loss (25 percent of body weight).

anoxia. Inadequate supply of oxygen to the body, usually at birth.

anvil (incus). One of the three tiny bones (ossicles) in the middle ear.

anxiety disorders. Conditions causing painful uneasiness, emotional tension, or emotional confusion.

aphasia. Loss or impairment of language ability due to brain injury.

appreciative listening. Listening for the sake of enjoyment, such as to music.

array of services. A constellation of services, personnel, and educational placements.

articulation problems. Abnormal production of speech sounds.

asphyxia. Deprivation of oxygen, often through near drowning or smoke inhalation.

assistive devices. Any equipment or technology that facilitates people's work, communication, mobility, or any aspect of daily life.

assistive listening devices (ALDs). Equipment such as hearing aids that helps deaf and hard of hearing individuals use their residual hearing.

assistive technology. Devices that help students with disabilities in their daily lives; they include hearing aids, wheelchairs, computers that offer augmentative communication, and a wide array of equipment that helps compensate for an individual's disabilities.

association. In thinking, the ability to see relationships among different concepts or knowledge bases.

asthma. A common, chronic condition resulting in difficulty in breathing.

at risk. Children whose condition or situation makes it probable for them to develop disabilities.

ataxia. A type of cerebral palsy characterized by movement disrupted by impaired balance and depth perception.

athetoid. A type of cerebral palsy characterized by purposeless and uncontrolled involuntary movements.

attention deficit disorder (ADD). A condition that describes students who display hyperactive behaviors, have difficulty attending to the task at hand, and tend to be impulsive.

attention deficits. A characteristic often associated with learning disabilities in which students do not pay attention to the task or the correct features of a task to learn how to perform it well.

attentive listening. Focusing on one form or source of communication.

attributes. Common characteristics or features of a group.

attributions. The explanations individuals give themselves for their successes or failures.

audio loop. A device that directs sound from the source directly to the listener's ear through a specially designed hearing aid.

audiodescription. A technique in which trained narrators describe visual and nonverbal information during the pauses in the audio or scripted dialogue of plays, films, and television shows by using FM transmissions or the extra sound track available on stereo televisions.

audiogram. The grid or graph used to display a person's hearing abilities.

audiologist. Professional trained to diagnose hearing losses and auditory problems.

audiometer. An electrical instrument for measuring the threshold of hearing tests using an audiometer; charts individuals' thresholds of hearing at various frequencies against sound intensities in decibels.

auditory nerve. Nerve that carries messages received through the ear to the brain; known in neurology as the eighth cranial nerve.

augumentative communication systems. Alternative methods of communicating, such as communication boards, communication books, sign language, and computerized voices.

aura. A signal of an impending seizure, sometimes called the preictal stage.

authentic assessments. Performance measures that use work generated by the student or observational data on social behaviors for assessment and evaluation purposes.

autism. A severe disorder of thinking, communication, interpersonal relationships, and behavior.

autistic savant. An individual who displays many behaviors associated with autism, yet also possesses discrete abilities and unusual talents.

barrier games. Drill and practice activities that require the application of verbal skills to solve problems, using a game format.

basic interpersonal communicative skills (BICS). Face-to-face conversational language.

behavior disorders. A condition of disruptive or inappropriate behaviors that interferes with a student's learning, relationships with others, or personal satisfaction to such a degree that intervention is required.

behind the ear (BTE). A hearing aid that cups behind the ear with a cord that runs into the person's ear canal.

Best Buddies. A program that pairs college students with people with mental retardation to build relationships, friendships, and opportunities for support.

best practices. Instructional techniques or methods proven through research to be effective.

bilingual maintenance approach. Teaching students partly in English using ESL strategies and partly in their home language so that they maintain proficiency.

bilingual transitional approach. Teaching students primarily in English and partly in their home language until they learn enough English to learn academic subjects.

bilingual-bicultural approach. The application of ESL and bilingual techniques to deaf education where ASL is the native language and reading and writing in English are taught as a second language.

bionic artificial limbs. Artificial arms and legs that replace full functioning of nonfunctional limbs.

blindness. Not having a functional use of sight.

bone conduction audiometry method. A test for conductive hearing loss in which a vibrator is placed on a person's forehead so that sound bypasses the outer and middle ear and goes directly to the inner ear; tests for conductive hearing losses.

Braille. A system of reading and writing that uses dot codes that are embossed on paper, developed by Louis Braille in 1929.

brainstorming. An instructional technique in which students quickly generate as many ideas as they can.

bulimia. Chronically causing oneself to vomit, limiting weight gain.

captions. Subtitles that print the words spoken in film or video; can be either closed or open.

cascade of services. A linear and sequential model used to describe educational environments from the most to the least restrictive.

categorical. A system of classification using specific categories such as learning disabilities or mental retardation.

categorize. Classify or group concepts or items; a thinking skill.

center schools. Separate schools (some residential), typically dedicated to serving students with a particular disability.

central nervous system dysfunction. Some brain or neurological damage that impedes individuals' motor and/or learning abilities.

central vision. The main field of vision in the eye, usually greater than 20 degrees.

cerebral palsy. A disorder of movement and posture caused by damage to the developing brain.

chaining. A strategy to teach the steps of skills that have been task analyzed either first step first (forward chaining) or last step first (backward chaining).

chronic illness. Being sick for long periods of time.

chunking. Grouping information into smaller pieces so that it can be more easily remembered.

classification. A structured system that identifies and organizes characteristics to establish order.

classifying. The ability to categorize items or concepts by their common characteristics.

cleft palate. An opening in the roof of the mouth, causing too much air to pass through the nasal cavity when the individual is speaking.

closed captions. Captions that can be seen on the television screen only with the use of a decoder.

closed-circuit television (CCTV). A television used for transmissions not accessible to the general public; sometimes, only one camera and television monitor is used.

cluster programs. A plan whereby gifted students spend a part of their day in the general classroom on enriched or accelerated activities.

cochlea. Part of the inner ear that contains fluid and hairlike nerve cells that transmit information to the brain.

cochlear implant. Electronic microprocessor that replaces the cochlea and allows some people who are deaf to process sounds.

cognitive behavior modification. Instructional strategies that teach internal control methods (such as self-talk) in structured ways to help students learn how to learn.

cognitive/academic linguistic proficiency (CALP). The abstract language abilities required for academic work.

collaboration. Professionals working cooperatively to provide educational services.

communication. The transfer of knowledge, ideas, opinions, and feelings.

communication board. A flat device on which words, pictures, or other symbols are used to expand the verbal interactions of people with limited vocal abilities.

communication signals. A variety of messages that announce some immediate event, person, action, or emotion.

communication symbols. Voice, letters of the alphabet, or gestures used to relay communication messages.

communicative competence. Proficiency in the use of language allowing people to participate in all aspects of communication in social and learning situations.

community based instruction (CBI). A strategy of teaching functional skills in the environments in which they occur; for example, shopping skills should be taught in the local market rather than a classroom "store."

complex partial seizures. Periods of automatic behavior resulting from discharge in a localized area of the brain (sometimes called psychomotor or focal seizures).

computer-assisted instruction (CAI). Self-contained instructional software programs that students use to supplement or replace traditional teacher-directed instructional methods.

computer-enhanced instruction. Software programs that students use to supplement traditional instruction, used primarily for drill and practice.

computerized language translators. Microcomputers that provide translations of written text from one language to another.

conduct disorders. Behavior patterns that are externalizing and include "acting out" and hyperactivity, but this condition alone does not qualify as a disability according to IDEA.

conductive hearing loss. Hearing loss caused by damage or obstruction to the outer or middle ear that prevents transfer of sound to the inner ear.

confidential school records. Private files of a student.

congenitally blind. Those with severe visual impairments present at birth.

content. An aspect of language that governs the intent and meaning of the message delivered in a communication; includes semantics.

continuum of services. A graduated range of educational services, each level of service leading directly to the next one.

contractures. Joint stiffening, often because of muscle shortening, to the point that the joint can no longer move through its normal range.

cooperative learning. Groups of more than two students collaborating as they learn the same material.

cornea. The transparent, curved part of the front of the eye.

creativity. A form of intelligence characterized by advanced divergent thought, the production of many original ideas, and the ability to develop flexible and detailed responses and ideas.

cross-cultural dissonance. When the home and school cultures are in conflict.

cued speech. Hand signals for difficult-to-see speech sounds that accompany oral speech to assist in lip reading.

cultural pluralism. All cultural groups are valued components of the society, and the language and traditions of each group are maintained.

curriculum based assessment (CBA). A method of evaluating children's performance by collecting data on their daily progress.

curriculum compacting. Reducing instructional time spent on typical academic subjects so that enrichment activities can be included in the curriculum.

Deaf culture. The structures of social relationships, language (ASL), dance, theater, and other cultural activities that bind the Deaf community.

Deaf pride. A term used to signify the accomplishments and achievements of members of the Deaf community.

deaf-blindness. A dual disability whereby the individual has both vision and hearing problems.

deafness. Inability to usefully perceive sounds in the environment with or without the use of a hearing aid; inability to use hearing as the primary way to gain information.

decibel (dB). Unit of measure for intensity of sound.

decoder. A device that allows closed captions to appear on a television screen.

deduction. Coming to a logical conclusion from facts or general principles that are known to be true.

deinstitutionalization. Decreasing the number of individuals with mental retardation living in large congregate facilities.

depression. A state of despair and dejected mood.

desktop publishing. Using a microcomputer and special software to prepare written and graphic material in publication format and quality.

diagnostician. A professional trained to test and analyze a student's areas of strength and weakness to determine whether an individual is eligible for special services and to help in setting educational goals and planning for instruction.

dialect. Words and pronunciation from a particular area, different from the form of the language used by the normative group.

differentiated curriculum. The flexible application of curriculum targets that ensures content mastery, in-depth and independent learning, and exploration of issues and themes and allows for acceleration when needed.

dignity of risk. The principle that taking ordinary risks and chances is part of growing up and is essentially human.

direct instruction. Specifically focusing instruction on the desired, targeted behavior.

discalculia. Severely impaired ability to calculate or perform mathematical functions; presumed to be caused by central nervous system dysfunction.

discrepancy formulas. Formulas developed by state educational agencies or local districts to determine the difference between a child's actual achievement and expected achievement based on the student's IQ scores.

discrepancy scores. The scores used in some states to determine eligibility for services designed for students with learning disabilities.

disgraphia. Severely impaired ability to write; presumed to be caused by central nervous system dysfunction.

distance education. The use of telecommunications technologies to deliver instruction by experts to areas where particular expertise is needed.

distance senses. Senses—hearing and vision—that provide us with information external to our bodies, developed to help alert us to danger.

Down syndrome. A chromosomal disorder that causes identifiable physical characteristics and usually causes delays in physical and intellectual development.

due process hearing. A noncourt proceeding before an impartial hearing officer that can be used if parents and school personnel disagree on a special education issue.

dysfluencies. Aspects of speech that interrupt the pattern of speech; typical of normal speech development in young children.

dyslexia. Severely impaired ability to read; presumed to be caused by a central nervous system dysfunction.

eardrum (tympanic membrane). Part of the ear on which sound waves and their vibrations fall and cause the ossicles to move; separates the outer and middle ear.

ecological assessment. A procedure that includes observational data collected in the student's natural environments for the purpose of identifying the antecedent events that cause a problem behavior or consequent events that maintain or increase the target behavior.

Education for All Handicapped Children Act (EHA). A federal law, PL 94-142, passed in 1975 with many provisions for assuring free appropriate public education for all students with disabilities; later renamed the Individuals with Disabilities Education Act (IDEA).

educational interpreters. Related service providers who translate or convert spoken messages to the deaf person's preferred mode of manual communication.

educational placement. The location or type of classroom program (e.g., resource room) arranged for a child's education; the setting in which a student receives educational services.

e-mail. A computerized mail system allowing people using personal computers, the phone system, and a host mainframe computer to communicate.

eminence. Superiority in ability.

emotional disturbance. A term that is often used interchangeably with behavior disorder.

English as a second language (ESL). Instructing children in English in their classrooms or in special classes until English proficiency is achieved.

enrichment. Adding topics or skills to the traditional curriculum or presenting a particular topic in more depth.

enrichment triad/revolving door model. A model for gifted education where 15 to 20 percent rather than 3 percent of a school's students periodically participate in advanced activities planned to develop thinking skills, problem solving, and creativity.

epicanthic fold. A flap of skin over the innermost corners of the eye.

epilepsy. A tendency to recurrent seizures.

evaluation. Assessment or judgment of special characteristics such as intelligence, physical abilities, sensory abilities, learning preferences, and achievement.

excess cost. Expenses for the education of a child with disabilities that exceed the average expenses of education for a child without disabilities.

extended family. Includes immediate family members—mother, father, and siblings and other relatives—aunts, uncles, grandparents.

externalizing behaviors. Behaviors, especially aggressive behaviors, that seem to be directed toward others.

family system. Potential sources of support for people with disabilities, including sons and daughters, spouses, parents, siblings, in-laws, aunts and uncles, grandparents, extended family members, and step-family members.

fetal alcohol syndrome (FAS). Congenital mental impairments, behavior problems, and perhaps some physical disabilities, caused by the mother's drinking alcohol during pregnancy.

finger spelling. A form of manual communication that assigns to each letter of the alphabet a sign.

fluency problems. Hesitations or repetitions of sounds or words that interrupt a person's flow of speech.

FM transmission device. Equipment used in many classes for students with severe hearing loss that allows direct oral transmissions from the teacher to each individual student.

follow-up study. To provide later evaluation, diagnosis, or treatment of a condition.

form. The rule system of language; it is comprised of phonology, morphology, and syntax.

fragile X syndrome. An inherited genetic disorder associated with disabilities and is particularly linked to mental retardation.

free appropriate public education (FAPE). One of the provisions of IDEA that ensures that children with disabilities receive necessary education and services without cost to the child and family.

frequency of sound. The number of vibrations per second of molecules through some medium like air, water, or wires.

full inclusion. An interpretation that states that the least restrictive environment for all children with disabilities is the general education classroom.

functional academics. Using life skills as the means to teach academic tasks.

functional assessments. Similar to ecological assessment except that behaviors are manipulated (where they are not in the other system) to determine those events that cause and maintain target behaviors.

functionally equivalent behaviors. Identifying behaviors that can replace inappropriate behaviors because they serve similar purposes.

Future Problem Solving Program. A national competition and instructional program to teach creative problem solving, in which students attempt to find positive solutions to real issues such as the nuclear arms race and water conservation.

gait training. Analysis and instruction of walking.

Gallaudet University. The United States's federally funded liberal arts university serving deaf undergraduate and graduate students.

general education. A typical classroom and curriculum designed to serve students without disabilities.

generalization. The transfer of learning from particular instances to other environments, people, times, and events.

generic supports. Nondisability-specific public benefits to which all eligible people have access.

gifted. A term describing individuals with high levels of intelligence, outstanding abilities, and capacity for high performance.

group homes. Apartments or homes in which a small number of individuals with mental retardation live together as part of their community with the assistance of service providers.

guide dogs. Animals trained to assist blind persons to move about independently, also called service animals.

hair cells. The structures in the inner ear that produce the electrochemical signals that pass through the auditory nerve to the brain, where these signals, which originated as sound waves, are perceived as tones.

hammer (malleus). One of the three tiny bones (ossicles) in the middle ear.

hard of hearing. Having sufficient residual hearing to be able, with a hearing aid, to comprehend others' speech and oral communication.

hearing aid. A device that intensifies sound to help hard of hearing people process information presented orally.

hearing threshold. The point at which a person can perceive the softest sound at each frequency level.

hertz (Hz). Unit of measure for sound frequency.

heterogeneity. Variation among members in a group.

high achievers. Students who expect success and view it as an incentive to work harder.

high-tech devices. Complex technical devices such as computers.

HIV infection. Human immunodeficiency virus; a microorganism that infects the immune system, impairing the body's ability to fight infections.

home or hospital teacher. A special teacher who teaches in the child's home or hospital when the child must be absent from school due to health problems.

honors sections. Advanced classes for any student who shows high achievement in specific subject areas.

Hoover cane. Long, white cane used in the mobility and orientation system developed in 1944 by Richard Hoover to help people with visual impairments move through the environment independently.

hyperactivity. Impaired ability to sit or concentrate for long periods of time.

Hypermedia. Computer programs that incorporate text, graphics, sound, photographic images, and video clips.

Hypertext. A computer program that can be used to modify textbook materials through rewording, defining vocabulary, and providing further explanations.

identification. The process of seeking out and designating children with disabilities who require special education and related services.

impulsive. Impaired ability to control one's own behavior.

in the canal (ITC). A hearing aid that is worn inside the person's ear canal.

in the ear (ITE). A hearing aid that fits inside the person's outer ear.

inactive learners. Students who do not become involved in learning situations, do not approach the learning task purposefully, do not ask questions, do not seek help, or do not initiate learning.

incidence. The number of new cases that occur within a certain time period.

incidental learning. Gaining knowledge and skills without being directly taught.

independent study. A common approach to the education of the gifted that allows a student to pursue and study a topic in depth on an individual basis.

Individualized Education Program (IEP). A management tool used to identify and organize individualized educational and related services for preschoolers and schoolchildren.

Individualized Family Service Plan (IFSP). A written plan that identifies and organizes services and resources for infants and toddlers with special needs who are under age 3 and their families

Individualized Transition Plan (ITP). A statement of the transition services required for coordination and delivery of services as the student moves to adulthood.

Individuals with Disabilities Education Act (IDEA). New name given in 1990 to the Education for All Handicapped Children Act (EHA).

infectious diseases. Contagious diseases.

inferences. Incomplete decisions or opinions, based on assumptions or reasoning.

information-processing theory. Suggests that learning disabilities are caused by an inability to organize thinking and approach learning tasks systematically.

infused. The incorporation of enrichment activities into the general education curriculum.

integration. Being included and having full access to mainstream society.

intellectual functioning. The actual performance of tasks believed to represent intelligence, such as observing, problem solving, and communicating.

interdisciplinary instruction. An approach to the education of the gifted that involves studying a topic and its issues in the context of several different disciplines.

internalizing behaviors. Behavior that is withdrawn, into the individual.

internship. Programs that place gifted students, usually high school seniors, in job settings related to their career goals in order to challenge them and apply knowledge in real-life skills.

the Intervention Ladder. A hierarchy of disciplinary tactics organized from the least intrusive and least complex to the most intrusive and most complicated.

iris. The colored part of the eye.

itinerant teachers. Teachers who teach students or consult with others in more than one setting.

job coach. An individual who works alongside people with disabilities, helping them to learn all parts of a job.

job developer. An individual who seeks out, shapes, and designs employment opportunities in the community for people with disabilities.

judicial hearing. A hearing before a judge in court.

juvenile arthritis. Chronic and painful muscular condition seen in children.

Kurzweil Reader. One of the first computerized systems designed for people with visual impairments that translates print into synthesized speech.

labeling. Assigning a special education category to an individual.

language. The formalized method of communication by which ideas are transmitted to others.

language delay. Development of language skills that is slower than in the majority of peers; may signal language that will require assistance of a specialist to use language proficiently.

language impairment. Difficulty or inability to master the various systems of rules in language, which then interferes with communication.

language-different. Children who are not native English speakers and those who speak nonstandard English and do not have an impairment even though their language is not typical.

lateral dominance. A preference for using either the right or the left side of the body for one's motoric responses; some believe that mixed dominance or lateral confusion is associated with poor reading performance.

learned helplessness. A phenomenon in which individuals gradually, usually as a result of repeated failure or control by others, become less willing to attempt tasks.

learning disabilities (LD). A disability in which the individual possesses average intelligence but is substantially delayed in academic achievement.

learning strategies. Instructional methods to help students read, comprehend, and study better by helping them organize and collect information strategically.

least restrictive environment (LRE). One of the principles outlined in IDEA that must be balanced when considering the best educational placement for an individual student with disabilities.

legally blind. Visual acuity measured as 20/200 or worse in the better eye with correction, or peripheral vision no greater than 20 degrees.

legislation. Laws passed by a legislature or the Congress and signed by a governor or the President.

lens. Located behind the iris, brings objects seen into focus.

life skills. Those skills used to manage a home, cook, shop, and organize personal living environments.

limb deficiencies. Resulting from missing or non-functioning arms or legs.

limited English proficient (LEP). Limited ability to read, write, or speak English.

litigation. A lawsuit or legal proceeding.

long cane. White canes used to assist blind people be independently mobile, developed by Hoover during World War II.

loudness. An aspect of voice, referring to the intensity of the sound produced while speaking.

low achievers. Students who expect failure and see little use in expending effort to learn.

low vision. A level of visual impairment where vision is still useful for learning or the execution of a task.

low-incidence disability. A disability that occurs infrequently; the prevalence and incidence are very low.

low-tech devices. Simple technical devices such as home-made cushions or a classroom railing.

magnet schools. Center schools that serve children who do not live in the immediate neighborhood; some magnet schools are designed to serve children whose parents work in a nearby area; other magnet schools emphasize a particular theme (such as theater arts, math, and science).

mainstreaming. Including students with special needs in general education classrooms for some or all of their school day.

manual communication. Using the hands, not the voice, as the means of communication, as in sign language or finger spelling.

marginal listening. Listening in which part of the auditory content, such as background music, is not the primary focus of attention.

medically fragile. Used to describe children with special health care needs.

melting pot. The concept of an homogenized United States where cultural traditions and home languages are abandoned for the new American culture.

meninges. Membranes that cover the spinal cord and brain.

meningitis. A disease that affects the central nervous system and often causes hearing loss.

mental age (MA). An age estimate of an individual's mental ability, derived from an artificial comparison of the individual's IQ score and chronological age.

mental retardation. A disability characterized by cognitive impairment, limited adapted behavior, need for support, and initial occurrence before age 18.

mentorship. A program in which a gifted student is paired with an adult in order to learn to apply knowledge in real-life situations.

metacognition. Understanding one's own learning process.

Mimosa Cottage Project. One of the earliest demonstration and research sites, located at a state-funded institution in Kansas, where institutionalized individuals were shown to be able to learn a variety of tasks.

mnemonics. A learning strategy that promotes the remembering of names by associating the first letters of items in a list with a word, sentence, or picture.

mobility. The ability to travel safely and efficiently from one place to another.

morphology. Rules that govern the structure and form of words and comprise the basic meaning of words.

motivation. Internal incentives that are influenced by previous success or failure.

multiple disabilities. Possessing more than one handicapping condition.

multiple intelligences. A multidimensional approach to intelligence, providing an alternative view for the concept of IQ, allowing those exceptional in any one of seven areas to be identified as being gifted.

muscular/skeletal conditions. Conditions affecting muscles or bones and resulting in limited functioning.

myoelectric limbs. Artificial limbs, powered by batteries and controlled by electric signals transmitted by the individual's brain (sometimes called bionic).

natural supports. Supports that occur as a natural result of typical family and community living.

neonatal intensive care (NIC). A specialized hospital unit for infants who are in need of intensive medical attention.

neural tube disorders. Another name for spinal cord disorders, which always involve the spinal column and usually the spinal cord.

neuromotor impairment. Condition involving the nerves, muscles, and motor functioning.

noncategorical approach. In special education, not classifying or differentiating among disabilities in providing services.

nondiscriminatory testing. Assessment that properly takes into account a child's cultural and linguistic diversity.

nonpaid supports. Ordinary assistance given by friends and neighbors.

normal curve. A theoretical construct of the normal distribution of human traits such as intelligence.

normalization. Making available ordinary patterns of life and conditions of everyday living.

obturator. A device that creates a closure between the oral and nasal cavities when the soft palate is missing or damaged.

occupational therapist (OT). A professional who directs activities that help improve muscular control and develop self-help skills.

open captions. Captions that appear on the television screen for all viewers to see.

ophthalmologist. Medical doctor who specializes in eye disorders.

optic nerve. The nerve that carries messages from the eye to the visual center of the brain.

optician. A person who fills either the ophthalmologist's or optometrist's prescriptions for glasses or corrective lenses.

optometrist. Professional who measures vision and can prescribe corrective lenses (eyeglasses or contact lenses).

oral-only approach. One method of instruction advocated for students who are deaf, where they learn to communicate (both receiving and sending information) orally, not using sign language.

orientation. The mental map people have to move through environments.

orthopedic impairments. Conditions related to a physical deformity or disability of the skeletal system and associated motor function.

ossicles. Three tiny bones in the middle ear that transmit sound waves from the eardrum through the middle ear to the cochlea.

other health impairments. Chronic or acute health problems resulting in limited strength, vitality, or alertness.

otitis media. Middle ear infection that can result in hearing loss, communication impairments, or learning disabilities if it becomes a chronic condition.

outcomes. The results of decisions and actions.

outreach programs. Specialized programs offered in local communities by residential schools or centralized agencies serving students with special needs.

paradigm shifts. A change in conceptual framework that is a basic understanding or explanation for a field of study.

perinatal. At the time of birth.

peripheral vision. The outer area of a person's visual field.

personal reader. A person who reads text orally to those who cannot read print.

phonology. The rules within a language used to govern the combination of speech sounds to form words and sentences.

physical therapist (PT). A professional who treats physical disabilities through many nonmedical means.

pitch. An aspect of voice; its perceived high or low sound quality.

portfolio assessment. An alternative form of individualized assessment that includes many samples of the student's work across all curriculum targets and reports of teachers and parents about that individual's social skills.

postlingually deaf. Having lost the ability to hear after developing language.

postnatal. After birth.

postsecondary. Education that comes after high school (e.g., community college, technical/vocational school, college, university, continuing education).

pragmatics. A key element of communication; the relationship among language, perception, and cognition.

prelingually deaf. Having lost the ability to hear before developing language.

prenatal. Before birth.

prevalence. The total number of cases at a given time.

primary epilepsy. Predictable seizure disorders that appear at a young age and seem to be hereditary.

problem solving. Finding answers or solutions to situations.

process/product debate. Argument that either perceptual training or direct instruction was more effective for instruction.

Public Law (PL) 94-142. Education for All Handicapped Children Act (now IDEA).

pull-in programming. Rather than having students with disabilities leave general education classes for special education or for related services, delivering those services to them in the general education classroom.

pull-out programs. The most common educational placement for gifted students, who spend part of the school day in a special class.

pupil. Hole in the center of the iris that expands and contracts, admitting light to the eye.

Purdue Secondary Model for Gifted and Talented Youth. A high school curriculum for gifted students that combines enrichment and acceleration.

pure sounds. Sound waves of specific frequencies used to test an individual's hearing ability.

real-time translations (RTC). Practically instantaneous translations of speech into print.

reauthorization. The act of amending and renewing a law.

rehabilitation engineering. Application of mechanical and engineering principles to improve human physical functioning.

related services. A part of special education that includes services from professionals from a wide range of disciplines typically outside of education, all designed to meet the learning needs of individual children with disabilities.

residual vision. The amount and degree of vision that one has functional use of despite a visual disability.

resonating system. Oral and nasal cavities where speech sounds are formed.

respiratory system. The system of organs whose primary function is to take in oxygen and expel gases.

retina. Inside lining of the eye.

reversals. Letters, words, or numbers written or read backward.

robotics. Use of high-tech devices to perform motor skills.

schizophrenia. A rare disorder in children that includes bizarre delusions and dissociation with reality.

school nurses. Professionals who participate in delivering FAPE to students with disabilities, though not listed by IDEA as an actual related service.

school psychologist. Psychologist trained to test and evaluate individual students' abilities.

secondary (lesional) epilepsy. Seizure disorders that appear at any age and seem to occur in response to particular damage.

seizure. A spontaneous abnormal discharge of the electrical impulses of the brain, sometimes referred to as a convulsive disorder.

selective attention. Ability to attend to the crucial features of a task.

selective listening. Focusing attention on only one sound in the environment, such as the speaker's voice in a lecture.

self-advocacy movement. A social and political movement started by and for people with mental retardation to speak for themselves on important issues such as housing, employment, legal rights, and personal relationships.

self-determination. A set of behaviors that include making decisions, choosing preferences, and practicing self-advocacy.

self-injurious behavior (SIB). Self-inflicted injuries (head banging, eye poking).

self-management technique. A set of instructional procedures whereby the individual uses self-instruction, self-monitoring, or self-reinforcement to change behavior.

semantics. The system within a language that governs content, intent, and meanings of spoken and written language.

sensorineural hearing loss. Hearing loss caused by damage to the inner ear or the auditory nerve.

sequencing. Mentally categorizing and putting items, facts, or ideas in order according to various dimensions.

serious emotional disturbance. The term used in IDEA to classify students with behavior disorders and emotional disturbance.

service delivery options. Different special education services and placements sometimes described as a continuum and other times as an array.

service manager. The case manager who oversees the implementation and evaluation of an Individualized Family Service Plan.

setting demands. The behavioral requirements, both obvious and subtle, of an environment.

shunt. A tube used in a medical procedure that draws excess fluid from the brain and head area and disposes it in a safe area in the body, such as the stomach.

sickle cell anemia. A hereditary blood disorder that inhibits blood flow.

sign language. An organized established system of manual gestures used for communication.

simple partial seizures. Not always apparent; often affect behavior and feelings.

Snellen chart. A chart used to test visual acuity, developed in 1862.

social maladjustment. Referring to a group of children who do not act within society's norms but are excluded from the definition of children with serious emotional disturbance.

socioeconomic status. The status an individual or family unit holds in society, usually determined by job, level of education, and the amount of money available to spend.

sound localization. Being able to locate the source of sounds.

spastic. A type of cerebral palsy characterized by uncontrolled tightening or pulling of muscles.

special education. Individualized education for children and youth with special needs.

special services committee. The multidisciplinary team of professionals that determines whether a student qualifies for special education and, if so, develops the individualized plan.

specialized supports. Disability-specific benefits.

speech. The vocal production of language.

speech impairment. Abnormal speech that is unintelligible, is unpleasant, or interferes with communication.

speech mechanisms. Includes the various parts of the body—tongue, lips, teeth, mandible, and palate—required for oral speech.

speech synthesizers. Equipment that creates voice.

speech/language pathologist (SLP). A professional who diagnoses and treats problems in the area of speech and language development.

spina bifida. A developmental defect whereby the spinal column fails to close properly.

spinal cord. The cord of nervous tissue that extends through the bony spinal column to the brain.

spinal cord disorders. Always involve the spinal column, usually both the nerves and muscles.

Sputnik. The name of the Russian spaceship that was launched in 1957 and caused a renewed interest in the education of the gifted in this country.

standard deviation (SD). A statistical measure that expresses the variability and the distribution from the mean of a set of scores.

standard scores. Converted test scores that equalize scores from different tests to allow comparison.

Stay-Put Provision. The legal mandate prohibiting students with disabilities from being expelled because of behavior associated with their disabilities.

stirrup (stapes). One of the three tiny bones (ossicles) in the middle ear.

STORCH infections. Includes many different congenital viruses.

stuttering. The lack of fluency in an individual's speech pattern, often characterized by hesitations or repetitions of sounds or words.

submersion. Placing a child with native English speakers in all-English classrooms with no special language assistance. Also known as the "sink or swim" method.

supported employment. Used in job training, whereby students are placed in paying jobs for which they receive significant assistance and support, and the employer is helped with the compensation.

syntax. Rules that govern word endings and order of words in phrases and sentences.

tactile maps. Maps that utilize touch to orient people to specific locales.

talent development. The process of translating ability into achievement.

talking books. Books available in auditory format.

task analysis. Breaking down problems and tasks into smaller, sequenced components.

technology-dependent children. Children who probably could not survive without high-tech devices such as ventilators.

telecoil. Also called induction coils, an added option on many hearing aids that allows access to telephones, audio loops, and other assistive listening devices.

telecommunications. Various electronic devices that allow students and teachers to access and send materials and information using a computer network system.

telecommunications relay service (TRS). A telephone system required by federal law that allows an operator at a relay center to convert a print-telephone message to a voice telephone message.

text telephone (TTY). A piece of equipment, formerly called the telecommunication device for the deaf (TDD), that allows people to make and receive telephone calls by typing information over the telephone lines.

theoretical construct. A model based on theory, not practice or experience.

time of onset. When the disability occurred.

tonic-clonic seizures. Seizures characterized by a stiff (tonic) phase in which the muscles become rigid, followed by a jerking (clonic) phase in which the arms and legs snap (formerly referred to as grand mal seizures).

total communication approach. A system of instruction for deaf students that employs any and all methods of communication (oral speech, manual communication, ASL, gestures) that is easy, efficient, and preferred by the student for communication.

total immersion. The student is taught entirely in English; all the other students are also non-native

English speakers, and the teacher can speak the students' home language.

Tourette's syndrome. A low-incidence disability that is characterized by multiple and uncontrollable motor and/or verbal tics.

toxin. A poisonous substance that can cause immediate or long-term harm to the body.

trauma. An injury.

traumatic brain injury. The result of a head injury; the individual experiences reduced cognitive functioning, limited attention, and impulsivity.

tunnel vision. Severe limitation in peripheral vision.

twice-exceptional students. Students who have a disability and who are gifted.

use. An aspect of language; applying language appropriately; includes pragmatics.

Usher syndrome. A genetic syndrome that includes a nonprogressive sensorineural hearing loss, retinitis pigmentosa and progressively restricted field of vision, loss of the sense of smell, and impaired balance and motor skills.

ventilators. Machines to assist with breathing.

vibrating system. The orderly function of the larynx and vocal folds to vibrate and produce sounds and pitch.

videodisc instruction. An alternative to CAI; instructional discs contain narrated segments of visual images.

visual acuity. How well a person can see at various distances.

visual efficiency. How well a person can use sight.

vocal symbols. Oral means of relaying messages, such as speech sounds.

vocal system. Parts of the respiratory system used to create voice.

voice carryover (VCO). A TTY that allows both voice and text use.

voice problem. An abnormal spoken language production, characterized by unusual pitch, loudness, or quality of sounds.

word banks. Computer-generated lists of words.

World Wide Web. Using the Internet, the Web allows the accessing of information through a personal computer.

wrap-around services. A service delivery model whereby all of the child's needs are met through the coordination of the education system, mental health agencies, social services, and community agencies.

written symbols. Graphic means, such as the written alphabet, used to relay messages.

REFERENCES

CHAPTER 1: THE CONTEXT OF SPECIAL EDUCATION

Art

Denvir, B. (1991). *Toulouse-Lautrec*. London: Thames and Hudson.

Perruchot, H. (1962). *Toulouse-Lautrec*. NY: Collier Books.

Personal Perspective

Cheng, L. R. (1996). *The Starfish Story*. Personal communication.

Disabilities Defined

Americans with Disabilities Act of 1990, Pub. L. No. 101–336. 104 Stat. 327.

Atkins, M., & Pelham, W. (1992). School-based assessment of attention-deficit hyperactivity disorder. *Journal of Learning Disabilities, 24,* 197–204, 255.

Cromwell, R. L., Blashfield, R. K., & Strauss, J. S. (1975). Criteria for classification systems. In N. Hobbs (Ed.), *Issues in the classification of children* (Vol. 1, pp. 4–25). San Francisco: Jossey-Bass.

Green, J. (1996). The concepts of disability and handicaps in Native communities. Personal communication.

Groce, N. E. (1985). *Everyone here spoke sign language: Hereditary deafness on Martha's Vineyard*. Cambridge, MA: Harvard University Press.

Harrison, D. (Ed.). (November 29, 1995). Proposed new category rekindles IDEA debate. *Special Education Report, 21,* 5.

Learning Disabilities Association of America. (September/October, 1995). The importance of the category of specific learning disability. *LDA Newsbrief, 30,* 1, 9.

Mercer, J. (1973). *Labeling the mentally retarded*. Berkeley: University of California Press.

Reschly, D. (1988). Minority representation and special education reform. *Exceptional Children, 54,* 316–223.

Turner, C. S. V., & Louis, K. S. (1996). Society's response to differences: A sociological perspective. *Remedial and Special Education, 17,* 134–141.

U.S. Department of Education. (1995a). *Individuals with Disabilities Education Act Amendments of 1995*. Washington, DC: Office of Special Education and Rehabilitative Services.

Special Education Defined

National Association of State Directors of Special Education (NASDSE). (1994). State education agency strategies for recruiting culturally and linguistically diverse special education professionals. *Liaison Bulletin, 22,* 1.

U.S. Department of Education. (1992). Assistance to states for the education of children with disabilities program and preschool grants for children with disabilities; final rule. *Federal Register, 34,* CRF Parts 300 and 301.

U.S. Department of Education. (1996). *Eighteenth annual report to Congress on the implementation of the Individuals with Disabilities Education Act*. Washington, DC: U.S. Government Printing Office.

History of Special Education

Aiello, B. (1976). Especially for special educators: A sense of our own history. *Exceptional Children, 42,* 244–252.

Ballard, J., Ramirez, B. A., & Weintraub, F. J. (1982). *Special education in America: Its legal and governmental foundations*. Reston, VA: Council for Exceptional Children.

Barr, M. W. (1913). *Mental defectives: Their history, treatment and training*. Philadelphia: Blakiston.

Barsh, R. H. (1965). *A movigenic curriculum* (Bulletin No. 25). Madison, WI: Department of Public Instruction, Bureau for the Handicapped.

Biklen, D. (1985). *Achieving the complete school: Strategies for effective mainstreaming*. New York: Teachers College Press.

Eberle, L. (August, 1922). The maimed, the halt and the race. *Hospital Social Service, VI,* 59–63. Reprinted in R. H. Bremner

(Ed.), *Children and youth in America, a documentary history: Vol. II, 1866–1932* (pp. 1026–1028). Cambridge, MA: Harvard University Press.

Frostig, M., & Horne, D. (1964). *The Frostig program for the development of visual perception.* Chicago: Follett.

Itard, J. M. G. (1806). *The wild boy of Aveyron* (G. Humphrey & M. Humphrey, Trans.). (1962). Englewood Cliffs, NJ: Prentice-Hall.

Kanner, L. (1964). *A history of the care and study of the mentally retarded.* Springfield, IL: Thomas.

Kauffman, J. M. (1997). *Characteristics of behavior disorders of children and youth* (6th ed.). Columbus, OH: Merrill.

Kephart, N. (1960). *The slow learner in the classroom.* Columbus, OH: Merrill.

Longmore, P. K. (September/October 1995). The second phase: From disability rights to disability culture. *Disability Rag & Resource, 16,* 4–22.

Montessori, M. (1912). *The Montessori method* (A. George, Trans.). New York: Stokes.

Nazzaro, J. N. (1977). *Exceptional timetables: Historic events affecting the handicapped and gifted.* Reston, VA: The Council for Exceptional Children.

Nirje, B. (1969). The normalization principle and its human management implications. In R. B. Kugel and W. Wolfensberger (Eds.), *Changing patterns in residential services for the mentally retarded* (pp. 179–195). Washington, DC: President's Committee on Mental Retardation.

Nirje, B. (1976). The normalization principle. In R. B. Kugel and A. Shearer (Eds.), *Changing patterns in residential services for the mentally retarded* (rev. ed., pp. 231–240). Washington, DC: President's Committee on Mental Retardation.

Nirje, B. (1985). The basis and logic of the normalization principle. *Australia and New Zealand Journal of Developmental Disabilities, 11,* 65–68.

Roos, P. (1970). Trends and issues in special education for the mentally retarded. *Education and Training of the Mentally Retarded, 5,* 51–61.

Sarason, S. B., & Doris, J. (1979). *Educational handicap, public policy, and social history.* New York: Free Press.

Scheerenberger, R. C. (1983). *A history of mental retardation.* Baltimore: Brookes.

Seguin, E. (1846). *The moral treatment, hygiene, and education of idiots and other backward children.* Paris: Balliere.

State ex. rel. Beattie v. Board of Education, 169 Wis. 231, 172 N. W. 153, 154 (1919).

The summer school for teachers. (February 1907). *Training School Bulletin, 36,* 17.

Treanor, R. B. (1993). *We overcame: The story of civil rights for disabled people.* Falls Church, VA: Regal Direct Publishing.

Wolfensberger, W. (Ed.). (1972). *The principle of normalization in human services.* Toronto: National Institute on Mental Retardation.

Wolfensberger, W. (1995). Of "normalization," lifestyles, the Special Olympics, deinstitutionalization, mainstreaming, integration, cabbages and kings. *Mental Retardation, 33,* 128–131.

Legislation

Americans with Disabilities Act of 1990, Pub. L. No. 101–336, 104 Stat. 327.

American Society of Interior Designers. (1994). *A guidebook to Washington, DC for people with disabilities.* Washington, DC: Author.

Bateman, B. (1996). *Better IEPs: How to develop legally correct and educationally useful programs.* Longmong, CO: Sopris West.

Briand, X. (Ed.). (May 17, 1995a). Suspension, special education data reveal mixed picture. *Special Education Report, 21,* 1, 3–4.

Conderman, G., & Katsiyannis, A. (1995). Section 504 Accommodation Plans. *Intervention in School and Clinic, 31,* 42–45.

Council for Exceptional Children. (1993). CEC policy on inclusive schools and community settings: A position statement. *Supplement to Teaching Exceptional Children, 25.*

Council for Exceptional Children. (June 1994). Violence in our school community. *CEC Today, 1,* 102.

Dupont (1993). *Equal to the task: II.* Wilmington, DE: Author

Education of Individuals with Disabilities Act. U. S. C. 1988 Title 20, Sections 1400 et seq.

Garnett, K. (Spring/Summer 1996). What is wrong with the Senate bill? *The DLD Times, 13,* 7–8.

Klein, J. (October 28, 1996). Up close and personal. *Newsweek,* p. 31.

Levoy, J. (March 20, 1995). Despite law jobs are scarce for the disabled. *Los Angeles Times,* pp. A1, A3, A21.

LaRue, S. (Ed.). (February 2, 1996). Judicial decisions. *The Special Educator, 11,* 13–14.

Maroldo, R. A. (October 13, 1995). Time waits for no man: An attorneys' fee petitions. *The Special Educator, 11,* 1–2.

Mills, K. (August 27, 1995). Disabilities act yet to achieve tricky legal balance. *Albuquerque Journal, Dimensions,* pp. B1, B4.

Montes, E. (1995). Texas suit confronts barriers to polling sites for disabled. *Albuquerque Journal,* p. C2.

National Association of State Directors of Special Education (NASDSE). (July 1996). Federal financial support for special education: What's the right formula? *Liaison Bulletin, 26,* 1–5.

Parrish, T. B. (1996). Special education finance: Past, present and future. Palo Alto: Center for Special Education Finance.

Perske, R. (1972). The dignity of risk. In W. Wolfensberger (Ed.), *The principle of normalization in human services* (pp. 194–205). Toronto: National Institute of Mental Retardation.

Pfieffer, D. (1996). "We won't go back": The ADA on the grass roots. *Disability & Society, 11*, 271–284.

Rehabilitation Act of 1973 Section 504, 19 U.S.C. section 794.

Reid, R. & Katsiyannis, A. (1995). Attention-deficit/hyperactivity disorder and Section 504. *Remedial and Special Education, 16*, 44–52.

Roberts, R., & Mather, N. (1995). Legal protections for individuals with learning disabilities: The IDEA, Section 504, and the ADA.

U.S. Department of Education. (1995a). *Individuals with Disabilities Education Act Amendments of 1995*. Washington, DC: Office of Special Education and Rehabilitative Services.

U.S. Department of Education. (1996). *The seventeenth annual report to Congress on the implementation of the Individuals with Disabilities Education Act*. Washington, DC: U.S. Government Printing Office.

Vukelich, D. (November 1995). Serving disabled clients pays. *The Albuquerque Tribune*, p. C6.

Werne, S. (November 12, 1995). Accessible by design. *Albuquerque Journal, Trends*, pp. I1, I7.

West, J. (1994). *Federal Implementation of the Americans with Disabilities Act, 1991–1994*. New York: Milbank Memorial Fund.

West, J. (November 1996). *IDEA, Where do we go from here?* National Teacher Education Division Annual Conference, Keynote Speech, Washington, DC.

Whitmire, R. (June 17, 1996). Special ed: Is the price too high? *USA Today*, p. 6D.

Litigation

Brown v. Board of Education, 347 U.S. 483 (1954).

Burlington School Committee v. Department of Education of the Commonwealth of Massachusetts, 471 U.S. 359 (1985).

Carter v. Florence County School District Four, 950 F.2d 156, 71 Ed. Law Rep. 633 (1991).

Doe v. Withers, 20 IDELR 422 (1993).

Honig v. Doe, 484 U.S. 305, 108 S. Ct. 592 (1988).

Irving Independent School District v. Tatro, 468 U.S. 883 (1984).

Mills v. Board of Education of the District of Columbia, 348 F. Supp. 866 (1972).

Pennsylvania Association for Retarded Children v. Commonwealth of Pennsylvania, 343 F. Supp. 279 (E. D. Pa., 1972).

Rowley v. Hendrick Hudson School District, 458 U.S. 176 (1982).

Smith v. Robinson, 468 U.S. 992 (1984).

Timothy W. v. Rochester, New Hampshire, School District, 1987–88 EHLR DEC. 559:480 (D. N. H. 1988).

Timothy W. v. Rochester, New Hampshire, School District, 875 F. 2d 954 (1st Cir. 1989), *cert. denied* 110 S. Ct. 519 (1989).

Zobrest v. Catalina Foothills School District, 963 F. 2d 190.

Prevalence of Children with Special Needs

Briand, X. (November 1, 1995b). Disabled student numbers rising at record pace. *Special Education Report, 21*, 1, 3.

U.S. Department of Education. (1996). *The eighteenth annual report to Congress on the implementation of the Individuals with Disabilities Education Act*. Washington, DC: U.S. Government Printing Office.

Outcomes or Results

Accreditation Council on Services for People with Disabilities. (1993). *Outcome based performance measures*. Landover, MD: Author.

Blackorby, J., & Wagner, M. (1996). Longitudinal postschool outcomes of youth with disabilities: Findings from the national longitudinal transition study. *Exceptional Children, 62*, 399–413.

Hehir, T. (September 1966). *The achievements of people with disabilities because of IDEA*. Paper presented at the meeting of Project SUCCESS for annual project directors, Washington, DC.

Hughes, C., Hwang, B., Kim, J-H, Eisenman, L. T., & Killian, D. J. (1995). Quality of life in applied research: A review and analysis of empirical measures. *American Journal on Mental Retardation, 99*, 623–641.

O'Brien, J., & Lyle-O'Brien, C. (1992). Perspectives on social support. In J. Nisbet (Ed.), *Natural supports in school, at work, and in the community for people with severe disabilities*. Baltimore: Brookes.

U.S. Department of Education. (1995b). *Sixteenth annual report to Congress on the implementation of the Individuals with Disabilities Education Act*. Washington, DC: U.S. Government Printing Office.

Concepts and Controversy

Briand, X. (Ed.). (May 17, 1995a). Suspension, special education data reveal mixed picture. *Special Education Report, 21*, 1, 3–4.

Garnett, K. (Spring/Summer 1996). What is wrong with the Senate bill? *The DLD Times, 13*, 7–8.

U.S. Department of Education. (1995a). *Individuals with Disabilities Education Act Amendments of 1995*. Washington, DC: Office of Special Education and Rehabilitative Services.

CHAPTER 2: IFSP, IEP, ITP: PLANNING AND DELIVERING SERVICES

Art

Bolton, L. (1989). *Manet: The history and times of great masters.* Secaucus, NJ: Chartwell Books.

Schneider, P., & the Editors of Time-Life Books (1968). *The world of Manet: 1832–1883.* NY: Time-Life Books.

Special Education Services

Deno, E. (1970). Special education as developmental capital. *Exceptional Children, 37,* 229–237.

Lovitt, T. C. (1995). Curriculum options and services for youth with disabilities. *Journal of Behavioral Education, 5,* 211–213.

Padeliadu, S., & Zigmond, N. (1996). Perspectives of students with learning disabilities about special education placement. *Learning Disabilities Research and Practice, 11,* 15–23.

Rivera, D. P., & Smith, D. D. (1997). *Teaching students with learning and behavior problems* (3rd ed.). Boston: Allyn and Bacon.

U.S. Department of Education. (1996). *Eighteenth annual report to Congress on the implementation of the Education for Handicapped Act.* Washington, DC: U.S. Government Printing Office.

Welch, M., Richards, G., Okada, R., Richards, J., & Prescott, S. (1995). A consultation and paraprofessional pull-in system of service delivery. *Remedial and Special Education, 16,* 16–28.

Individualized Special Education Programs

Algozzine, B., Ysseldyke, J. E., & Christenson, S. (1983). An analysis of the incidence of special class placement: The masses are burgeoning. *Journal of Special Education, 17,* 141–147.

Bateman, B. (1996). *Better IEPs: How to develop legally correct and educationally useful programs.* Longmont, CO: Sopris West.

Blalock, G. (1996). Community transition teams as the foundation for transition services for youth with learning disabilities. *Journal of Learning Disabilities, 29,* 148–159.

Bloom, L, & Bacon, E. (1995). Using portfolios for individual learning and assessment. *Teacher Education and Special Education, 18,* 1–9.

Carpenter, C. D., Ray, M. S., & Bloom, L. A. (1995). Portfolio assessment: Opportunities and challenges. *Intervention in School and Clinic, 31,* 34–41.

Clark, G. M. (1996). Transition planning assessment for secondary-level students with learning disabilities. *Journal of Learning Disabilities, 29,* 79–92.

Curran, C. M., & Harris, M. B. (1996). Uses and purposes of portfolio assessment for general and special educators. Albuquerque: University of New Mexico.

Edelen-Smith, P. (1995). Eight elements to guide goal determination for IEPs. *Intervention in School and Clinic, 30,* 297–301.

Edgar, E., & Polloway, E. A. (1994). Education for adolescents with disabilities: Curriculum and placement issues. *Journal of Special Education, 27,* 438–452.

Figueroa, R. A., & Garcia, E. (1994). Issues in testing students from culturally and linguistically diverse backgrounds. *Multicultural Education, 2,* 10–19.

Fowler, S. A., Schwartz, I., & Atwater, J. (1991). Perspectives on the transition from preschool to kindergarten for children with disabilities and their families. *Exceptional Children, 58,* 136–145.

Fuchs, L. S., & Deno, S. L. (1994). Must instructionally useful performance assessment be based in the curriculum? *Exceptional Children, 61,* 15–24.

Hallahan, D. P., & Kauffman, J. M. (1995). *The Illusion of Inclusion.* Austin, TX: Pro-Ed.

Haring, K. A., Lovett, D. L., & Saren, D. (1991). Parent perspectives of their adult offspring with disabilities. *Teaching Exceptional Children, 23,* 6–10.

Johnson, B. H., McGonigel, M. J., & Kaufmann, R. K. (1989). *Guidelines and recommended practices for the individualized family service plan.* Washington, DC: National Early Childhood Technical Assistance System and Association for the Care of Children's Health.

Keogh, B. K. (1988). Perspectives on the regular education initiative. *Learning Disabilities Focus, 4,* 3–5.

Kroth, R. (1990). *A report of the referral and identification rate of students in the Albuquerque public schools.* Unpublished manuscript, University of New Mexico, Albuquerque.

Levine, P., & Edgar, E. (1994). An analysis by gender of long-term postschool outcomes for youth with and without disabilities. *Exceptional Children, 61,* 282–300.

Lovitt, T. C., Cushing, S. S., & Stump, C. (1994). High school students rate their IEPs: Low opinions and lack of ownership. *Intervention in School and Clinic, 30,* 34–37.

Luckasson, R., Coulter, D. L., Polloway, E. A., Reis, S., Schalock, R. L., Snell, M. E., Spitalnik, D. M., & Stark, J. A. (1992). *Mental retardation: Definition, classification, and systems of supports.* Washington, DC: American Association on Mental Retardation.

Maker, C. J. (1994). Authentic assessment of problem solving and giftedness in secondary school students. *The Journal of Secondary Gifted Education, 6,* 19–29.

Menlove, M. (1996). A checklist for identifying funding sources for assistive technology. *Teaching Exceptional Children, 28,* 20–24.

Midgett, T. E. (1995). Assessment of African American exceptional learners: New strategies and perspectives. In B. A. Ford, F. E. Obiakor, & J. M. Patton (Eds.), *Effective education of African American exceptional learners: New perspectives.* Austin, TX: Pro-Ed.

Notari-Syverson, A. R., & Shuster, S. L. (1995). Putting real-life skills into IEP/IFSPs for infants and young children. *Teaching Exceptional Children, 27*, 29–32.

Parette, Jr., H. P., Murdick, N. L., & Gartin, B. C. (1996). Mini-grant to the rescue. *Teaching Exceptional Children, 28*, 20–23.

Patton, J. R., & Blalock, G. (1996). *Transition and students with learning disabilities: Facilitating the movement from school to adult life.* Austin, TX: Pro-Ed.

Pautier, N. F. (April 6, 1995). Area high schools flunk in attempt to teach learning disabled. *University Week*, p. 5.

Pike, K., & Salend, S. J. (1995). Authentic assessment strategies. *Teaching Exceptional Children, 28*, 15–20.

Smith, D. D. (1988). No more noises to the glass: A response. *Exceptional Children, 54*, 476.

Strickland, B. B., & Trunbull, A. P. (1993). *Developing and implementing individualized education programs* (3rd ed.). Englewood Cliffs, NJ: Macmillan.

Turnbull, H. R., III, Turnbull, A., Shank, M., & Leal, D. (1995). *Exceptional Lives: Special education in today's schools.* Columbus, OH: Merrill, an imprint of Prentice-Hall.

U.S. Department of Education. (1996). *Eighteenth annual report to Congress on the implementation of the Education for Handicapped Act.* Washington, DC: U.S. Government Printing Office.

Van Reusen, A. K., Bos, C. S., Schumaker, J. B., & Deshler, D. D. (1994). *The Self-Advocacy Strategy for Education & Transition Planning.* Lawrence, KS: Edge Enterprises, Inc.

Ysseldyke, J. E., Thurlow, M. L., & Erickson, R. N. (1994). *Possible sources of data for early childhood (age 3) indicators.* Minneapolis: University of Minnesota.

Concepts and Controversy

Briand, X. (July 27, 1994). AFT inclusion survey documents teachers' ambivalence. *Special Education Report, 20*, 3–4.

Briand, X. (November 29, 1995). Disabled students' parents eye neighborhood schools. *Special Education Report, 21*, 7.

Commission on the Education of the Deaf. (1988). *Toward equality: Education of the deaf.* Washington, DC: U.S. Government Printing Office.

Hallahan, D. P., & Kauffman, J. M. (1995). *The illusion of inclusion.* Austin, TX: Pro-Ed.

Huestis, T. (December 15, 1993). AFT calls for pause in full inclusion push. *Special Education Report, 19*, 1, 3.

Hyman, I. A. (May 26, 1993). The dumbing of special education. *Education Week*, p. 25.

LaRue, S. (January 19, 1996). Courts take another view of inclusion. *The Special Educator, 11*, 1, 7.

National Association for State Boards of Education (NASBE). (1992). *Winners all: A call for inclusive schools.* Alexandria, VA: Author.

Roach, V., Ascroft, J., Stamp, A., & Kysilko, D. (1995). *Winning ways: Creating inclusive schools, classrooms and communities.* Alexandria, VA: National Association of State Boards of Education (NASBE).

Sailor, W. (1991). Special education in the restructured school. *Remedial and Special Education, 12*, 8–22.

Silber, L. B. (1991). The regular education initiative: A déjà vu remembered with sadness and concern. *Journal of Learning Disabilities, 24*, 389–390.

Snell, M. E. (1988). Gartner and Lipsky's beyond special education: Toward a quality system for all students: Messages to TASH. *Journal of the Association for Persons with Severe Handicaps, 13*, 137–140.

Stainback, S., & Stainback, W. (1989). No more teachers of students with severe handicaps. *TASH Newsletter, 15*, 9–10.

Stainback, S., Stainback, W., East, K., & Sapon-Shevin, M. (1994). A commentary on inclusion and the development of a positive self-identity by people with disabilities. *Exceptional Children, 60*, 486–490.

U.S. Department of Education. (1996). *Eighteenth annual report to Congress on the implementation of the Education for Handicapped Act.* Washington, DC: U.S. Government Printing Office.

Vaughn, S., & Schumm, J. S. (1995). Responsible inclusion for students with learning disabilities. *Journal of Learning Disabilities, 28*, 264–290.

Will, M. (1986). *Educating students with learning problems: A shared responsibility: A report to the secretary.* Washington, DC: U.S. Department of Education, Office of Special Education and Rehabilitative Services.

CHAPTER 3: MULTICULTURAL AND BILINGUAL SPECIAL EDUCATION

Art

Smith, J. K., & Plimpton, G. (1993). *Chronicles of courage: Very special artists.* NY: Random House.

Introduction

Smith-Davis, J., & Billingsley, B. S. (1993). The supply/demand puzzle. *Teacher Education and Special Education, 16*, 205–220.

Multicultural and Bilingual Special Education Defined

Baca, L. M., & Cervantes, H. T. (Eds.). (1989). *The bilingual special education interface* (2nd ed.). Columbus, OH: Merrill.

Banks, J. A. (1994a). *An introduction to multicultural education.* Boston: Allyn and Bacon.

Banks, J. A., & Banks, C. A. M. (1993). *Multicultural education: Issues and perspectives* (2nd ed.). Boston: Allyn and Bacon.

Callahan, C. M., & McIntire, J. A. (1994). *Identifying outstanding talent in American Indian and Alaska Native students.* Washington, DC: U.S. Department of Education, Office of Educational Research and Improvement.

Cheng, L. L. (Ed.). (1995). *Integrating language and learning for inclusion: An Asian-Pacific focus.* San Diego: Singular Publishing Group.

Cheng, L. L., Nakasato, J., & Wallace, G. J. (1995). The Pacific islander population and the challenges they face. In L. L. Cheng (Ed.), *Integrating language and learning for inclusion: An Asian-Pacific focus* (pp. 63–105). San Diego: Singular Publishing Group.

Cuccaro, K. (April 3, 1996). Teacher observations key in bilingual assessment. *Special Education Report, 22,* pp. 1, 3.

Diana v. State Board of Education, No. C–70–37 Rfp (N. D. Calif. 1970).

Erickson, F. (1993). Transformation and school success: The politics and culture of educational achievement. In E. Jacob & C. Jordon (Eds.), *Minority educations: Anthropological perspective* (pp. 27–51). Norwood, NJ: Ablen Publishing.

Figueroa, R. A., & Garcia E. (1994). Issues in testing students from culturally and linguistically diverse backgrounds. *Multicultural Education, 2,* 10–18.

Gardner, H. (1983). *Frames of mind: The theory of multiple intelligences.* New York: Basic Books.

Gottlieb, J., Alter, M., Gottlieb, B. W., & Wishner, J. (1994). Special education in urban America: It's not justified for many. *Journal of Special Education, 27,* 453–465.

Krause, M. (1992). Testimony to the Select Senate Committee on Indian Affairs on S. 2044, *Native American Languages Act of 1991,* to assist Native Americans in assuring the survival and continuing vitality of their languages, pp. 16–18.

Larry P. v. Riles, Civil Action No. C–70–37 (N. D. Calif. 1971).

Maker, C. J. (1994). *Identification of gifted minority students: A national problem and an emerging paradigm.* Manuscript submitted for publication.

Maker, C. J., Nielson, A. B., & Rogers, J. A. (1994). Giftedness, diversity and problem solving. *Teaching Exceptional Children, 27,* 4–18.

Ogbu, J. U. (1992). Understanding cultural diversity and learning. *Educational Researcher, 21* 5–14.

Palmer, D. J., Olivarez, Jr., A., Willson, V. L. & Fordyce, T. (1989). Ethnicity and language dominance—influence on the prediction of achievement based on intelligence test scores in nonreferred and referred samples. *Learning Disability Quarterly, 12,* 261–274.

Patton, J. M. (1992). Assessment and identification of African-American learners with gifts and talents. *Exceptional Children, 59,* 150–159.

Patton, J. M., & Baytops, J. L. (1995). Identifying and transforming the potential of young gifted African Americans: A clarion call for action. In B. A. Ford, F. E. Obiakor, and J. M. Patton (Eds.), *Effective education of African American exceptional learners: New perspectives* (pp. 27–68). Austin: Pro-Ed.

Ruiz, N. (1995a). The social construction of ability and disability: I. Profile types of Latino children identified as language learning disabled. *Journal of Learning Disabilities, 28,* 476–490.

Ruiz, N. (1995b). The social construction of ability and disability: II. Optimal and at-risk lessons in a bilingual special education classroom. *Journal of Learning Disabilities, 28,* 491–502.

Salas, B. (1994) Assessment of individuals with disabilities with linguistic, cultural and ethnic diversity. *LD Forum, 19,* 48–50.

Siccone, F. (1995). *Celebrating diversity: Building self-esteem in today's multicultural classrooms.* Boston: Allyn and Bacon.

20 U.S.C. Section 1412 [5][c].

U.S. Department of Education (1993). *Fifteenth annual report to Congress on the implementation of the Individuals with Disabilities Education Act.* Washington, DC: U.S. Government Printing Office.

U.S. Department of Education (1994). *Sixteenth annual report to Congress on the implementation of the Individuals with Disabilities Education Act.* Washington, DC: U.S. Government Printing Office.

U.S. Office of Education, Office of Bilingual Education (1980). Manual for application for grants under bilingual education, 1974. In A. H. Leivbowitz, *The bilingual education act: A legislative analysis.* Rosslyn, VA: National Clearinghouse for Bilingual Education.

History of the Field

Baca, L. M., & Cervantes, H. T. (Eds.). (1984). *The bilingual special education interface.* St. Louis: Times Mirror/Mosby.

Banks, J. A. (1994a). *An introduction to multicultural education.* Boston: Allyn and Bacon.

Bransford, L., Baca, L., & Lane, K. (Eds.). (1974). Special issue: Cultural diversity. *Exceptional Children, 40* (8).

Diana v. State Board of Education, No. C–70–37 Rfp (N. D. Calif. 1970).

Dunn, L. M. (1968). Special education for the mildly retarded: Is much of it justifiable? *Exceptional Children, 35,* 5–22.

Gollnick, D. M., & Chinn, P. C. (1983). *Multicultural education in a pluralistic society* (1st ed.). New York: Macmillan.

Gonzales, E. (1989). Issues in the assessment of minorities. In H. L. Swanson and B. Watson (Eds.), *Educational and psychological assessment of exceptional children: Theories, strategies, and applications* (pp. 383–402). Columbus, OH: Merrill.

Larry P. v. Riles, Civil Action No. C–70–37 (N. D. Calif. 1971).

Lau v. Nichols, 414 U.S. 563 (1974).

Mercer, J. (1973). *Labeling the mentally retarded.* Berkeley: University of California Press.

Mercer, J. R., & Lewis, J. F. (1978). *System of multicultural pluralistic assessment: Student assessment manual.* New York: Psychological Corporation.

Phyler v. Doe, 102 S. Ct. 2382 (1982).

President's Committee on Mental Retardation. (1970). *The six hour retarded child.* Washington, DC: U.S. Government Printing Office.

Prevalence

Artiles, A. J., & Trent, S. C. (1994). Overrepresentation of minority students in special education: A continuing debate. *The Journal of Special Education, 27,* 410–437.

Booth, W. (1993, December 30). Florida plans to sue U.S. over illegal immigrants. *The Washington Post,* pp. A1, A12.

Bureau of the Census. (1991). *Final 1990 census population counts.* Washington, DC: U.S. Department of Commerce.

Center for Research on Elementary and Middle Schools. (1990). *The changing nature of the disadvantaged population: Current dimensions and future trends.* Baltimore: Johns Hopkins University.

Cheng, L. L., & Chang, J. (1995). Asian/Pacific islander students in need of effective services. In L. L. Cheng (Ed.), *Integrating language and learning for inclusion: An Asian-Pacific focus* (pp. 3–59). San Diego: Singular Publishing Group.

Children's Defense Fund. (1995). *The state of America's children: Yearbook.* Washington, DC: Author.

Children's Defense Fund (August 1995). Vaccines for children program: Children's health boosted nationally. *CDF Reports, 16,* 1–2, 4.

Deno, E. (1970). Special education as developmental capital. *Exceptional Children, 37,* 229–237.

Diana v. State Board of Education, No. C–70–37 Rfp (N. D. Calif. 1970).

Dunn, L. M. (1968). Special education for the mildly retarded: Is much of it justifiable? *Exceptional Children, 23,* 5–21.

Figueroa, R. A., & Garcia E. (1994). Issues in testing students from culturally and linguistically diverse backgrounds. *Multicultural Education, 2,* 10–18.

Gottlieb, J., Alter, M., Gottlieb, B. W., & Wishner, J. (1994). Special education in urban America: It's not justified for many. *Journal of Special Education, 27,* 453–465.

Harry, B. (1992a). *Cultural diversity, families, and the special education system: Communication and empowerment.* New York: Teachers College Press.

Harry, B. (1994). *The disproportionate representation of minority students in special education: Theories and recommendations.* Alexandria, VA: National Association of State Directors of Special Education.

Individuals with Disabilities Education Act (IDEA), Pub. L. No. 101–476, 104 Stat.

Larry P. v. Riles, Civil Action No. C–70–37 (N. D. Calif. 1971).

Lau v. Nichols, 414 U.S. 563 (1974).

Office of Civil Rights. (1992). *1990 elementary and secondary school civil rights survey.* DC: Author.

Peenan, J. (September 1995). Danger signs of overrepresentation of minorities in special education, *CEC Today, 2,* 7.

Reschly, D. J. (1991). The effects of placement litigation on psychological and education classification. *Diagnostique, 17,* 6–20.

Reschly, D. J., Kicklighter, R. H., & McKee, P. (1988). Recent placement litigation, Part III: Analysis of difference in Larry P., Marshall, and S–1 and implications for future practices. *School Psychology Review, 17,* 9–50.

Smith-Davis, J., & Billingsley, B. S. (1993). The supply/demand puzzle. *Teacher Education and Special Education, 16,* 205–220.

U.S. Department of Education (1993). *Fifteenth annual report to Congress on the implementation of the Individuals with Disabilities Education Act.* Washington, DC: U.S. Government Printing Office.

Zawaiza, T. W. (1995). Stand and deliver: Multiculturalism and special education reform in the early twenty-first century. In S. Walker, K. A. Turner, M. Haile-Michael, A. Vincent, and M. D. Miles (Eds.), *Disability and diversity: New leadership for a new era.* Washington, DC: President's Committee on Employment of People with Disabilities.

Causes and Prevention

The Black Community Crusade for Children, Children's Defense Fund. (1995). *A black community crusade and covenant for protecting children.* Washington, DC: Children's Defense Fund.

Cheng, L. L. (Ed.). (1995). *Integrating language and learning for inclusion: An Asian–Pacific focus.* San Diego: Singular Publishing Group.

Children's Defense Fund. (1995). *The state of America's children: Yearbook.* Washington, DC: Author.

Children's Defense Fund. (August 1995). Vaccines for children program: Children's health boosted nationally. *CDF Reports, 16,* 1–2, 4.

Hanson, M. J., Lynch, E. W., & Wayman, K. I. (1990). Honoring the cultural diversity of families when gathering data. *Topics in Early Childhood Special Education, 10,* 112–131.

Kozol, J. (1991). *Savage inequalities: Children in America's schools.* New York: Crown.

Kozol, J. (1995). *Amazing grace: The lives of children and the conscience of a nation.* New York: Crown.

Larry P. v. Riles, Civil Action No. C–70–37 (N. D. Calif. 1971).

Reed, S., & Sautter, R. C. (1990, June). Children of poverty: Kappan special report. *Phi Delta Kappan, 71,* K1–K12.

Exceptional Culturally and Linguistically Diverse Children

The Black Community Crusade for Children and Children's Defense Fund (1995). *A black community crusade and covenant for protecting children.* Washington, DC: Children's Defense Fund.

Banks, J. A. (1994a). *An introduction to multicultural education.* Boston: Allyn and Bacon.

Cheng, L. L. (Ed.). (1995). *Integrating language and learning for inclusion: An Asian–Pacific focus.* San Diego: Singular Publishing Group.

Cheng, L. L., & Chang, J. (1995). Asian/Pacific islander students in need of effective services. In L. L. Cheng (Ed.), *Integrating language and learning for inclusion: An Asian-Pacific focus* (pp. 3–59). San Diego: Singular Publishing Group.

Children's Defense Fund. (1995). *The state of America's children: Yearbook.* Washington, DC: Author.

Cummins, J. (1984). *Bilingualism and special education: Issues in assessment and pedagogy.* San Diego: College-Hill.

Henning-Stout, M. (1996). ¿Que Podemos Hacer?: Roles for school psychologists with Mexican and Latino migrant children and families. *School Psychology Review, 25,* 152–164.

Improving America's Schools Act of 1994, Pub. L. 103–382, 108 Stat. 3518.

Kozol, J. (1988). *Rachel and her children: Homeless families in America.* New York: Crown.

Krause, M. (1992). Testimony to the Select Senate Committee on Indian Affairs on S. 2044, *Native American Languages Act of 1991,* to assist Native Americans in assuring the survival and continuing vitality of their languages, pp. 16–18.

Langdon, H. W., with Cheng, L. -R. L. (1992). *Hispanic children and adults with communication disorders: Assessment and intervention.* Gaithersburg, MD: Aspen.

Obiakor, F. E. (1994). *The eight-step multicultural approach: Learning and teaching with a smile.* Dubuque, IA: Kendall/Hunt.

Pyle, A. (June 11, 1996). Teaching the silent students. *Los Angeles Times,* pp. A1, A18.

Rogers-Dulan, J., & Blacher, J. (1995). African American families, religion, and disability: A conceptual framework. *Mental Retardation, 33,* 226–238.

Sileo, T. W., Sileo, A. P., & Prather, M. A. (1996). Parent and professional partnerships in special education: Multicultural considerations. *Intervention in School and Clinic, 31,* 145–153.

Smith-Davis, J. & Smith, D. D. (1993). *Demographic, social, and economic trends affecting children and youth in the United States.* Albuquerque: Alliance 2000 Project.

U.S. Department of Education (1992). *Fourteenth annual report to Congress on the implementation of the Individuals with Disabilities Education Act.* Washington, DC: U.S. Government Printing Office.

Waggoner, D. (1993). 1990 Census shows dramatic change in the foreign-born population in the U.S. *NABE News, 16,* 1, 18–19.

Educational Interventions

Arreaga-Mayer, C., Carta, J. J., & Tapia, Y. (1994). Ecobehavioral assessment: A new methodology for evaluating instruction for exceptional culturally and linguistically diverse students. In S. Garcia (Ed.), *Addressing cultural and linguistic diversity in special education.* Reston, VA: The Council for Exceptional Children.

Baca, L. M., & Cervantes, H. T. (Eds.). (1989). *The bilingual special education interface* (2nd ed.). Columbus, OH: Merrill.

Banks, J. A. (1994b). *Multiethnic education: Theory and practice* (3rd ed.). Boston: Allyn and Bacon.

Bilingual Education Act of 1968, PL 90–247.

Cheng, L. R. (1996). Beyond bilingualism: A quest for communication competence. *Topics in Language Disorders, 16,* 9–21.

Children's Defense Fund (1995). *The state of America's children: Yearbook.* Washington, DC: Author.

Cloud, N. (1993). Language, culture and disability: Implications for instruction and teacher preparation. *Teacher Education and Special Education, 16,* 60–72.

Collier, V. P. (1995). Acquiring a second language for school. *Directions in Language & Education.* Washington, DC National Clearinghouse for Bilingual Education.

Corson, D. (1993). *Language, minority education and gender: Linking social justice and power.* Toronto: Ontario Institute for Studies in Education.

Crawford, L. W. (1993). *Language and literacy learning in multicultural classrooms.* Boston: Allyn and Bacon.

Cummins, J. (1984). *Bilingualism and special education: Issues in assessment and pedagogy.* San Diego: College-Hill.

Cummins, J. (1989). A theoretical framework for bilingual special education. *Exceptional Children, 56,* 111–119.

Currie, J., & Thomas, D. (1995). *Does Head Start make a difference?* Santa Monica: Rand.

Ford, B. A., Obiakor, F. E., & Patton, J. M. (Eds.). *Effective education of African American exceptional learners: New perspectives.* Austin: Pro-Ed.

Garcia, S., & Yates, J. (1994). Diversity: Teaching special population. *CEC Today, 1,* 1, 10.

Gersten, R., Brengilman, S., & Jiménez, R. (1994). Effective instruction for culturally and linguistically diverse students: A reconceptualization. *Focus on Exceptional Children, 27,* 12–16.

Gollnick, D. M., & Chinn, P. C. (1994). *Multicultural education in a pluralistic society* (4th ed.). New York: Macmillan.

Henry, T. (September 22, 1994). Doubts over bilingual schooling. *USA Today,* p. 8D.

Hoff, D. (Ed.) (June 15, 1995). New York city special ed suit targets preschoolers. *Special Education Reports, 21,* 2–3.

King, E. W, Chipman, M., & Cruz-Janzen, M. (1994). *Educating young children in a diverse society.* Boston: Allyn and Bacon.

Langdon, H. W., with Cheng, L. L. (1992). *Hispanic children and adults with communication disorders: Assessment and intervention.* Gaithersburg, MD: Aspen.

Lynch, E. W., & Hanson, M. J. (1992). *Developing cross-cultural competence: A guide for working with young children and their families.* Baltimore: Brookes.

Miner, H. (1956). Body ritual among the Nacirema. *American Anthropologist, 58,* 503–507.

National Center for Educational Statistics (1994). *Dropout rates in the United States: 1993.* Washington, DC: U.S. Government Printing Office.

New York Times (July 6, 1990). Cavazos asks bilingualism among teachers. p. A7.

Obiakor, F. E. (1994). *The eight-step multicultural approach: Learning and teaching with a smile.* Dubuque, IA: Kendall/Hunt.

Obiakor, F. E., Patton, J. M., & Ford, B. A. (Eds.). (1992). Special issue: Issues in the education of African-American youth in special education settings. *Exceptional Children, 59,* 97–176.

Ortiz, A. A., Yates, J. R., & Garcia, S. B. (1990). Competencies associated with serving exceptional language minority students. *Bilingual Special Education Perspective, 9,* 1, 3–5.

Panel on Educational Opportunity and Postsecondary Desegregation (1995). *Redeeming the American promise.* Atlanta: Southern Education Foundation.

Pyle, A. (January 14, 1996). Long-term study touts bilingual education. *Albuquerque Journal,* p. A7.

Ramasamy, R. (1996). Post-high school employment: A follow-up of Apache Native American youth. *Journal of Learning Disabilities, 29,* 174–179.

Siccone, F. (1995). *Celebrating diversity: Building self-esteem in today's multicultural classrooms.* Boston: Allyn and Bacon.

U.S. Department of Education (1993). *Fifteenth annual report to Congress on the implementation of the Individuals with Disabilities Education Act.* Washington, DC: U.S. Government Printing Office.

Very Special Arts (1995). Spirit weavers create rich heritage. *The Creative Spirit, Very Special Arts News & Information,* Summer, p. 3.

Webb-Johnson, G., Obiaker, F. E., & Algozzine, R. (1995). Self-concept development: An effective tool for behavior management. In F. E. Obiakor & R. Algozzine (Eds.), *Managing problem behaviors: Perspectives for generic and special educators* (pp. 161–177). Dubuque, IA: Kendall/Hunt.

Families

Bell, M. L., & Smith, B. R. (1996). Grandparents as primary caregivers: Lessons in love. *Teaching Exceptional Children, 28,* 18–19.

Harry, B. (1992b). Restructuring the participation of African-American parents in special education. *Exceptional Children, 59,* 123–131.

Harry, B., Allen, N., & McLaughlin, M. (1996). "Old fashioned, good teachers:" African American parents' views of effective early instruction. *Learning Disabilities Research and Practices, 11,* 193–201.

Prater, L. P., & Tanner, M. P. (1995). Collaboration with families: An imperative for managing problem behaviors. In F. E. Obiakor & R. Algozzine (Eds.), *Managing problem behaviors: Perspectives for general and special educators* (pp. 178–206). Dubuque, IA: Kendall/Hunt.

Rogers-Dulan, J., & Blacher, J. (1995). African American families, religion, and disability: A conceptual framework. *Mental Retardation, 33*, 226–238.

Voltz, D. (1994). Developing collaborative parent–teacher relationships with culturally diverse parents. *Intervention in School and Clinic, 29*, 288–291.

Wilson, C. L., & Hughes, M. (1994). Parents: Involving linguistically diverse parents. *LD Forum, 19*, 25–27.

Technology
Earl, G. (1984). *The Spanish Hangman*. Computer program. San Antonio, TX: Author.

Concepts and Controversy
Biskupic, J. (March 26, 1996). High court takes on "English only" law. *Albuquerque Journal*, pp. A1, A5.

Piatt, B. (1990). *¿Only English? Law & language policy in the United States*. Albuquerque: University of New Mexico.

Tatalovich, R. (1995). *Nativism Reborn? The official English language movement and the American states*. Lexington: The University of Kentucky Press.

CHAPTER 4: LEARNING DISABILITIES

Art
Moss, P. B. (1989). *P. Buckley Moss: The people's artist: An autobiography*. Waynesboro, VA: Shenandoah Heritage.

Learning Disabilities Defined
Abrahamsen, E. P., & Sprouse, P. T. (1995). Fable comprehension by children with learning disabilities. *Journal of Learning Disabilities, 28*, 302–308.

Algozzine, B., & Ysseldyke, J. E. (1986). The future of the LD field: Screening and diagnosis. *Journal of Learning Disabilities, 19*, 394–398.

Esposito, J. (Spring 1995). Finding the correct "label" was my turning point. *New Mexico LDA Newsletter*, New Mexico Learning Disabilities Association.

Frankenberger, W., & Fronzaglio, K. (1991). A review of states' criteria and procedures for identifying children with learning disabilities. *Journal of Learning Disabilities, 24*, 495–500.

Gollnick, D. M., & Chinn, P. C. (1994). *Multicultural education in a pluralistic society* (4th ed.) New York: Macmillan

Haager, D., & Vaughn, S. (1995). Parent, teacher, peer, and self-reports of the social competence of students with learning disabilities. *Journal of Learning Disabilities, 28*, 205–231.

Kavale, K. A., & Forness, S. R. (1996). Social skill deficits and learning disabilities: A meta-analysis. *Journal of Learning Disabilities, 29*, 226–237.

Kavale, K. A., & Reese, J. H. (1992). The character of learning disabilities: An Iowa profile. *Learning Disability Quarterly, 15*, 74–94.

Lyon, G. R., Gray, D. B., Kavanagh, J. F., & Krasnegor, N. A. (1993). *Better understanding of learning disabilities: New views from research and their implications for education and public policies*. Baltimore: Paul H. Brookes.

McLeskey, J. (1992). Students with learning disabilities at primary, intermediate, and secondary grade levels. *Learning Disability Quarterly, 15*, 13–19.

McLeskey, J., Lancaster, M., & Grizzle, K. L. (1995). Learning disabilities and grade retention: A review of issues with recommendations for practice. *Learning Disabilities Research and Practice, 10*, 120–128.

McLeskey, J., & Waldron, N. L. (1991). The identification and characteristics of students with learning disabilities in Indiana. *Learning Disabilities Research, 1990*, 72–78.

Mercer, C. D., King-Sears, P., & Mercer, A. R. (1990). Learning disabilities definitions and criteria used by state education departments. *Learning Disability Quarterly, 13*, 141–152.

National Joint Committee on Learning Disabilities. (1988). Letter to NJCLD member organizations.

New Mexico Learning Disabilities Association. (Spring 1994). Grade retention may not help students catch up. *LDA Newsletter*, pp. 1–3.

Reynolds, C. R. (1992). Two key concepts in the diagnosis of learning disabilities and the habilitation of learning. *Learning Disability Quarterly, 15*, 2–12.

Robinson, S. M., & Deshler, D. D. (1995). Learning disabled. In E. L. Meyen and T. M. Skritc (Eds.), *Special education and student disability: An introduction* (4th ed.). Denver: Love Publishing.

Rourke, B. P. (1994). Neurological assessment of children with learning disabilities: Measurement issues. In G. R. Lyon (Ed.), *Frames of reference for the assessment of learning disabilities: New views on measurement issues*. Baltimore: Paul H. Brookes.

Ruiz, N. (1995). The social construction of ability and disability: I. Profile types of Latino children identified as language learning disabled. *Journal of Learning Disabilities, 28*, 476–490.

Schumaker, J. B., Deshler, D. D., Alley, G. R., & Warner, M. M. (1983). Toward the development of an intervention model for learning disabled adolescents: The University of Kansas Institute. *Exceptional Education Quarterly, 4*, 45–74.

Shafrir, U., & Siegel, L. S. (1994). Subtypes of learning disabilities in adolescents and adults. *Journal of Learning Disabilities, 27*, 123–134.

Shaw, S. F., Cullen, J. P., McGuire, J. M., and Brinckerhoff, L. C. (1995). Operationalizing a definition of learning disabilities. *Journal of Learning Disabilities, 28,* 586–597.

Stanovich, K. E. (1991). Conceptual and empirical problems with discrepancy definitions of reading disability. *Learning Disability Quarterly, 14,* 269–280.

Swanson, H. L. (Ed.). (1991). Special issue on definitions. *Learning Disability Quarterly, 14,* 242–254.

Swanson, H. L., & Christie, L. (1994). Implicit notions about learning disabilities: Some directions for definitions. *Learning Disabilities Research and Practice, 9,* 244–254.

U.S. Department of Education. (1992). Assistance to states for the education of children with disabilities program and preschool grants for children with disabilities; final rule. *Federal Register, 34,* CRF Parts 300 and 301.

U.S. Department of Education. (1993). *Fifteenth annual report to Congress on the implementation of IDEA.* Washington, DC: U.S. Government Printing Office.

Wallach, G. P., & Butler, K. G. (1995). Language learning disabilities: Moving in from the edge. *Topics in Language Disorders, 16,* 1–26.

Ysseldyke, J., Algozzine, B., & Epps, S. (1983). A logical and empirical analysis of current practice in classifying students as handicapped. *Exceptional Children, 50,* 160–165.

History of the Field

Hammill, D., & Larsen, S. (1974). The effectiveness of psycholinguistic abilities. *Exceptional Children, 41,* 5–14.

Kirk, S. A., McCarthy, J. J., & Kirk, W. D. (1968). *Illinois Test of Psycholinguistic Abilities (ITPA).* Urbana: University of Illinois Press.

Wiederholt, J. L. (1974). Historical perspectives on the education of the learning disabled. In L. Mann and D. Sabatino (Eds.), *The second review of special education* (pp. 103–152). Philadelphia: Journal of Special Education Press.

Prevalence

U.S. Department of Education. (1996). *Eighteenth annual report to Congress on the implementation of the Education for Handicapped Act.* Washington, DC: U.S. Government Printing Office.

Causes and Prevention

Bender, W. N. (1992). *Learning disabilities: Characteristics, identification, and teaching strategies.* Boston: Allyn and Bacon.

Bos, C. S., & Vaughn, S. (1994). *Strategies for teaching students with learning and behavior problems.* Boston: Allyn and Bacon.

Currie, J., & Thomas, D. (1995). *Does Head Start make a difference?* Santa Monica: Rand.

Decker, S. N., & Defries, J. C. (1980). Cognitive abilities in families of reading disabled children. *Journal of Learning Disabilities, 13,* 517–522.

Decker, S. N., & Defries, J. C. (1981). Cognitive ability profiles in families of reading disabled children. *Developmental Medicine and Child Neurology, 23,* 217–227.

Deshler, D. D., & Schumaker, J. B. (1986). Learning strategies: An instructional alternative for low-achieving adolescents. *Exceptional Children, 52,* 583–590.

Englemann, S. E. (1977). Sequencing cognitive and academic tasks. In R. D. Kneedler & S. G. Tarver (Eds.), *Changing perspectives in special education* (pp. 46–61). Columbus, OH: Merrill.

Gibbs, D. P., & Cooper, E. B. (1989). Prevalence of communication disorders in students with learning disabilities. *Journal of Learning Disabilities, 22,* 60–63.

Hallahan, D. P., & Bryan, T. H. (1981). Learning disabilities. In J. M. Kauffman and D. P. Hallahan (Eds.), *Handbook of special education.* Englewood Cliffs, NJ: Prentice-Hall.

Hallahan, D. P, Kauffman, J. M., & Lloyd, J. W. (1996). *Introduction to learning disabilities.* Boston: Allyn and Bacon.

Lerner, J. (1993). *Learning disabilities: Theories, diagnosis, and teaching strategies* (6th ed.). Boston: Houghton Mifflin.

Lovitt, T. C. (1977). *In spite of my resistance … I've learned from children.* Columbus, OH: Merrill.

New Mexico Learning Disabilities Association. (Fall 1994). Dyslexia gene region identified. *New Mexico LDA Newsletter,* p. 1.

Oliver, J. M., Cole, N. H., & Hollingsworth, H. (1991). Learning disabilities as functions of familial learning problems and developmental problems. *Exceptional Children, 57,* 427–440.

Reichman, J., & Healey, W. C. (1983). Learning disabilities and conductive loss involving otitis media. *Journal of Learning Disabilities, 16,* 272–278.

Wallach, G. P., & Butler, K. G. (1995). Language learning disabilities: Moving in from the edge. *Topics in Language Disorders, 16,* 1–26.

Children with Learning Disabilities

Abrahamsen, E. P., & Sprouse, P. T. (1995). Fable comprehension by children with learning disabilities. *Journal of Learning Disabilities, 28,* 302–308.

American Psychiatric Association (1994). *Diagnostic and statistical manual of mental disorders* (4th ed.) (DSM IV). Washington, DC: American Psychiatric Association.

Armstrong, T. (1995). *The myth of the ADD child.* New York: Dutton.

Bryan, T. (1994). The social competence of students with learning disabilities over time: A response to Vaughn and Hogan. *Journal of Learning Disabilities, 27*, 304–308.

Dohrn, E., & Bryan, T. (1994). Attribution instruction. *Teaching Exceptional Children, 26*, 61–63.

Ellis, E. S. (1986). The role of motivation and pedagogy on the generalization of cognitive strategy training. *Journal of Learning Disabilities, 19*, 66–70.

Fox, C. L. (1989). Peer acceptance of learning disabled children in the regular classroom. *Exceptional Children, 56*, 50–59.

Fulk. B. M. (1996). The effects of combined strategy and attribution training on LD adolescents' spelling performance. *Exceptionality, 6*, 13–17.

Geisthardt, C., & Munsch, J. (1996). Coping with school stress: A comparison of adolescents with and without learning disabilities. *Journal of Learning Disabilities, 29*, 287–296.

Haager, D., & Vaughn, S. (1995). Parent, teacher, peer, and self-reports of the social competence of students with learning disabilities. *Journal of Learning Disabilities, 28*, 205–231.

Kavale, K. A., & Forness, S. R. (1996). Social skill deficits and learning disabilities: A meta-analysis. *Journal of Learning Disabilities, 29*, 226–237.

Lenz, B. K., Alley, G. R., & Schumaker, J. B. (1987). Activating the inactive learner: Advance organizers in the secondary content classroom. *Learning Disability Quarterly, 10*, 53–67.

Lerner, J. (1993). *Learning disabilities: Theories, diagnosis, and teaching strategies* (6th ed.). Boston: Houghton Mifflin.

Lerner, J. W., Lowenthal, B., & Lerner, S. R. (1995). *Attention deficit disorder.* Pacific Grove, CA: Brooks/Cole.

Mercer, C. D. (1997). *Students with learning disabilities* (5th ed.). Columbus, OH: Merrill, an imprint of Prentice-Hall.

Nabuzoka, D., & Smith, P. K. (1995). Identification of expressions of emotions by children with and without learning disabilities. *Learning Disabilities Research and Practice, 10*, 91–101.

Pearl, R. (1982). LD children's attributions for success and failure: A replication with a labeled LD sample. *Learning Disability Quarterly, 5*, 173–176.

Riccio, C. A., Gonzalez, J. J., & Hynd, G. W. (1994). Attention-Deficit Hyperactivity Disorder (ADHD) and learning disabilities. *Learning Disabilities Quarterly, 17*, 311–322.

Rivera, D., & Smith, D. D. (1988). Using a demonstration strategy to teach midschool students with learning disabilities how to compute long division. *Journal of Learning Disabilities, 21*, 77–81.

Rivera, D. P., & Smith, D. D. (1997). *Teaching students with learning and behavior problems.* Boston: Allyn and Bacon.

Roberts, C., & Zubrick, S. (1993). Factors influencing the social status of children with mild academic disabilities in regular classrooms. *Exceptional Children, 59*, 192–202.

Sabornie, E. J. (1994). Social-affective characteristics in early adolescents identified as learning disabled and nondisabled. *Learning Disability Quarterly, 17*, 268–279.

Shaywitz, S. E., & Shaywitz, B. A. (Eds.). (1992). *Attention deficit disorder comes of age: Toward the twenty-first century.* Austin: Pro-Ed.

Shelton, T. L., & Barkley, R. A. (1994). Critical issues in the assessment of attention deficit disorders in children. *Topics in Language Disorders, 14*, 26–41.

Swanson, H. L. (1987). Information processing theory and learning disabilities: An overview. *Journal of Learning Disabilities, 20*, 3–7.

Swanson, H. L. (1990). Intelligence and learning disabilities: An introduction. In H. L. Swanson and B. Keogh (Eds.), *Learning disabilities: Theoretical and research issues* (pp. 23–39). Hillsdale, NJ: Erlbaum.

Switzky, H. N., & Schultz, G. F. (1988). Intrinsic motivation and learning performance: Implications for individual educational programming for learners with mild handicaps. *Remedial and Special Education, 9*, 7–14.

Torgesen, J. K., & Licht, B. G. (1983). The learning disabled child as an inactive learner: Retrospect and prospects. In J. D. McKinney and F. Feagan (Eds.), *Current topics in learning disabilities* (vol. 1, pp. 3–31). Norwood, NJ: Ablex.

Tur-Kaspa, H., & Bryan, T. (1995). Teachers' ratings of the social competence and school adjustment of students with LD in elementary and junior high school. *Journal of Learning Disabilities, 28*, 44–52, 64.

Wallace, G., & McLoughlin, J. A. (1988). *Learning disabilities: Concepts and characteristics* (3rd ed.). Columbus, OH: Merrill.

Yasutake, D., & Bryan, T. (1995). The influence of affect on the achievement and behavior of students with learning disabilities. *Journal of Learning Disabilities, 28*, 329–334.

Educational Interventions

American Academy of Pediatrics. (1992). *Infant health and development program for low birth weight, premature infants: Program elements, family participation, and child intelligence.* Elk Grove Village, IL: Author.

Aune, B., & Friehe, M. (1996). Transition to postsecondary education: Institutional and individual issues. *Topics in Language Disorders, 16*, 1–22.

Baldwin, J. (1996). *Who took the GED?* Washington, DC: American Council on Education.

Banerji, M., & Dailey, R. A. (1995). A study of the effects of an inclusion model on students with specific learning disabilities. *Journal of Learning Disabilities, 28*, 511–522.

Bassett, D. S., & Smith, T. E. C. (1996). Transition in an era of reform. *Journal of Learning Disabilities, 29,* 161–166.

Berkow, I. (October 15, 1995). *A small-college football starter tries to stand out in two worlds.* The New York Times, p. S3.

Blalock, G. (1997). Transition. In D. P. Rivera and D. D. Smith, *Teaching students with learning and behavior problems* (3rd ed., pp. 414–449). Boston: Allyn and Bacon.

Bryan, T. (1995). Strategies for improving homework completion and the home–school connection. Paper presented at the Council for Learning Disabilities Conference, October 1995.

Bryan, T., Nelson, C., & Mathur, S. (1995). Doing homework: Perspectives of primary students in mainstream, resource, and self-contained special education classrooms. *Learning Disabilities Research & Practice, 10,* 85–90.

Bryan, T., & Sullivan, K. (1994a). *Planning for success: A teacher's self-study guide to homework.* Phoenix: Planning for Success

Bryan, T., & Sullivan, K. (1994b). *Planning for success: A parent's self-study guide to homework.* Phoenix: Planning for Success

Carr, M. N. (1993). A mother's thoughts on inclusion. *Journal of Learning Disabilities, 26,* 590–592.

CEC Today. (October 1995). Research shows phonological awareness key to reading success. Reston, VA: Council for Exceptional Children.

Colvin, R. L. (April 30, 1996). Word of honor. *Los Angeles Times,* pp. E1, E5.

Cooper, H., & Nye, B. (1994). Homework for students with learning disabilities: The implications of research for policy and practice. *Journal of Learning Disabilities, 27,* 465–536.

Council for Learning Disabilities Board of Trustees. (1993). Council for Learning Disabilities position statement, April 1993. *Learning Disability Quarterly, 16,* 126.

Cronin, M. E. (1996). Life skills curricula for students with learning disabilities: A review of the literature. *Journal of Learning Disabilities, 29,* 53–68.

Daly, E. J. III, & Martens, B. K. (1994). *Journal of Applied Behavior Analysis, 27,* 459–469.

Deshler, D. D., Ellis, E. S., & Lenz, B. K. (1996). *Teaching adolescents with learning disabilities: Strategies and methods* (2nd ed.). Denver: Love Publishing.

Deshler, D. D., & Schumaker, J. B. (1986). Learning strategies: An instructional alternative for low-achieving adolescents. *Exceptional Children, 52,* 583–590.

Dunn, C. (1996). A status report on transition planning for individuals with learning disabilities. *Journal of Learning Disabilities, 29,* 17–30.

Geisthardt, C., & Munsch, J. (1996). Coping with school stress: A comparison of adolescents with and without learning disabilities. *Journal of Learning Disabilities, 29,* 287–296.

Greenbaum, B., Graham, S., & Scales, W. (1995). Adults with learning disabilities: Educational and social experiences during college. *Exceptional Children, 61,* 460–471.

Greenbaum, B., Graham, S., & Scales, W. (1996). Adults with learning disabilities: Occupational and social status after college. *Journal of Learning Disabilities, 29,* 167–173.

Greene, G. (1994). The magic of mnemonics. *LD Forum, 19,* 34–37.

Gutterman, B. R. (1995). The validity of categorical learning disabilities services: The consumer's view. *Exceptional Children, 62,* 111–124.

Haring, K. A., Lovett, D. L., & Smith, D. D. (1990). Recent special education graduates of learning disabilities programs. *Journal of Learning Disabilities, 23,* 108–113.

HEATH. (1996). *Summer pre-college programs for students with learning disabilities.* Washington, DC: American Council on Education.

Henderson, C. (1995). *College freshman with disabilities: A triennial statistical profile.* Washington, DC: American Council on Education, HEATH.

Higbee-Mandelbaum, L. (1992/1993). Homework: Getting it done. *New Mexico LDA Newsletter,* pp. 1–2.

Hoehn, T. P., & Baumeister, A. A. (1994). A critique of the application of sensory integration therapy to children with learning disabilities. *Journal of Learning Disabilities, 27,* 338–350.

Hurford, D. P., Johnston, M., Nepote, P., Hampton, S., Moore, S., Neal, J., Mueller, G., McGeorge, K., Huff, L., Awad, A., Tatyro, C., Juliano, C., & Huffman, D. (1994). Early identification and remediation of phonological-processing deficits in first-grade children at risk for reading disabilities. *Journal of Learning Disabilities, 27,* 647–659.

Hurford, D. P., Schauf, J. D., Bunce, L., Blaich, T., & Moore, T. (1994). Early identification of children at risk for reading disabilities. *Journal of Learning Disabilities, 27,* 371–382.

Johnson, D. J., & Blalock, J. W. (1987). *Adults with learning disabilities: Clinical studies.* Orlando, FL: Grune & Stratton.

Kahn, K. R. (Ed.). (August 2, 1996). LRE/Inclusion: Inclusion which made student feel "different" was inappropriate. *The Special Educator,* pp. 14–15.

Katims, D. S. (1994). Emergence of literacy in preschool children with disabilities. *Learning Disabilities Quarterly, 17,* 58–69.

Kos, R. (1991). Persistence of reading disabilities: The voices of four middle school students. *American Educational Research Journal, 28,* 875–895.

Kravets, M., & Wax, I. F. (1995). *The K & W guide to colleges for the learning disabled: A resource book for students, parents, and professionals* (3rd ed.). New York: Harper Collins.

Learning Disabilities Association of America. (September/October 1994). Adults with learning disabilities: Preliminary analysis of survey data. *LDA Newsletter, 29*, 3–4.

Lovitt, T. C. (1995). *Tactics for teaching* (2nd ed.). Columbus, OH: Merrill, an imprint of Prentice Hall.

Majsterek, D. J., & Ellenwood, A. E. (1995). Phonological awareness and beginning reading: Evaluation of a school-based screening procedure. *Journal of Learning Disabilities, 28*, 449–456.

Mangrum II, C. T., & Strichart, S. S. (Eds.). (1994). *Peterson's colleges with programs for learning disabled students* (4th ed.). Princeton, NJ: Peterson's Guides.

Mather, N. (1992). Whole language reading instruction for students with learning disabilities: Caught in the cross fire. *Learning Disabilities Research & Practice, 7*, 87–95.

McIntosh, R., Vaughn, S., Schumm, J. S., Haager, D., & Lee, O. (1993). Observations of students with learning disabilities in general education classrooms. *Exceptional Children, 60*, 249–261.

Moats, L. C., & Lyon, R. G. (1993). Learning disabilities in the United States: Advocacy, science, and the future of the field. *Journal of Learning Disabilities, 26*, 282–294.

National Joint Committee on Learning Disabilities. (1993). Providing appropriate education for students with learning disabilities in regular education classrooms. *Journal of Learning Disabilities, 26*, 330–332.

Neubert, D. A., Tilson, G. P., & Ianacone, R. N. (1989). Postsecondary transition needs and employment patterns of individuals with mild disabilities. *Exceptional Children, 55*, 494–500.

O'Connor, R. E., & Jenkins, J. R. (1996a). Cooperative learning as an inclusion strategy: A closer look. *Exceptionality, 6*, 29–51.

O'Connor, R. E., & Jenkins, J. R. (1996b). Choosing individuals as the focus to study cooperative learning. *Exceptionality, 6*, 65–68.

O'Connor, R. E., Jenkins, J. R., Leicester, N., & Slocum, T. A. (1993). Teaching phonological awareness to young children with learning disabilities. *Exceptional Children, 59*, 532–546.

O'Connor, S. C., & Spreen, O. (1988). The relationship between parents' socioeconomic status and education level, and adult occupational and educational achievement of children with learning disabilities. *Journal of Learning Disabilities, 21*, 148–153.

O'Melia, M. C., & Rosenberg, M. S. (1994). Effects of cooperative homework teams on the acquisition of mathematics skills by secondary students with mild disabilities. *Exceptional Children, 60*, 538–548.

Padeliadu, S., & Zigmond, N. (1996). Perspectives of students with learning disabilities about special education placement. *Learning Disabilities Research & Practice, 11*, 15–23.

Patton, J. R., & Blalock, G. (Eds.). (1996a). *Transition and students with learning disabilities: Facilitating the movement from school to adult life.* Austin: Pro-Ed.

Patton, J. R., & Blalock, G. (1996b). Transition and students with learning disabilities: Creating sound futures. *Journal of Learning Disabilities, 29*, 7–16.

Pressley, M., & Rankin, J. (1994). More about whole language methods of reading instruction for students at risk for early reading failure. *Learning Disabilities Research & Practice, 9*, 157–168.

Roberts, R., & Mather, N. (1995). The return of students with learning disabilities to regular classrooms: A sellout. *Learning Disabilities Research and Practice, 10*, 46–58.

Scanlon, D., Deshler, D. D. & Schumaker, J. B. (1996). Can a strategy be taught and learned in secondary inclusive classrooms? *Learning Disabilities Research & Practice, 11*, 41–57.

Schalock, R. L., Holl, C., Elliott, B., & Ross, I. (1992). A longitudinal follow-up of graduates from a rural special education program. *Learning Disability Quarterly, 15*, 29–38.

Scruggs, T. E., & Mastropieri, M. A. (1992). Classroom applications of mnemonic instruction: Acquisition, maintenance, and generalization. *Exceptional Children, 59*, 219–229.

Seidel, J. F., & Vaughn, S. (1991). Social alienation and the learning disabled school dropout. *Learning Disabilities Research and Practice, 6*, 152–157.

Sharkey, N. (Ed.) (May 22, 1996). California leads revival of teaching phonics. *The New York Times*, Education, p. B8.

Siegel, S., & Gaylord-Ross, R. (1991). Factors associated with employment success among youths with learning disabilities. *Journal of Learning Disabilities, 24*, 40–47.

Sitlington, P. L., & Frank, A. R. (1993). Dropouts with learning disabilities: What happens to them as young adults. *Learning Disabilities Research and Practice, 8*, 244–252.

Skinner, C. H., Adamson, K. L., Woodward, J. R., Jackson Jr., R. R., Atchison, L. A., & Mims, J. W. (1993). A comparison of fast-rate, slow-rate, and silent previewing interventions on reading performance. *Journal of Learning Disabilities, 26*, 674–681.

Smith, B. J., & Schakel, J. A. (1986). Noncategorical identification of preschool handicapped children: Policy issues and options. *Journal of the Division for Early Childhood, 11*, 78–86.

Smith, J. O. (1992). Falling through the cracks: Rehabilitation services for adults with learning disabilities. *Exceptional Children, 58*, 451–460.

Smith, T. E. C., & Dowdy, C. A. (1993). Accessing vocational rehabilitation services for individuals with learning disabilities. *LD Forum, 18,* 29–30.

Talbott, E., Lloyd, J. W., & Tankersley, M. (1994). Effects of reading comprehension interventions for students with learning disabilities. *Learning Disabilities Quarterly, 17,* 223–232.

Torgesen, J. K., Wagner, R. K., & Rashotte, C. A. (1994). Longitudinal studies of phonological processing and reading. *Journal of Learning Disabilities, 27,* 276–286.

U.S. Department of Education. (1995). *Sixteenth annual report to Congress on the implementation of IDEA.* Washington, DC: U.S. Government Printing Office.

Vaughn, S, & Schumm, J. S. (1995). Responsible inclusion for students with learning disabilities. *Journal of Learning Disabilities, 28,* 164–270, 290.

Westberry, S. J. (1994). A review of learning strategies for adults with learning disabilities preparing for the GED exam. *Journal of Learning Disabilities, 27,* 202–209.

White, W. J. (1992). The postschool adjustment of persons with learning disabilities: Current status and future projections. *Journal of Learning Disabilities, 25,* 448–456.

Winnery, K. W., & Fuchs, L. S. (1993). Effects of goal and test-taking strategies on the computation performance of students with learning disabilities. *Learning Disabilities Research & Practice, 8,* 204–214.

Zigmond, N., & Baker, J. M. (1994). Is the mainstream a more appropriate educational setting for Randy? A case study of one student with learning disabilities. *Learning Disabilities Research and Practice, 9,* 108–117.

Zumwalt School District v. Missouri State Board of Education, 24 IDELR 222 (E.D. Mo. 1996).

Families

Dyson, L. L. (1996). The experiences of families of children with learning disabilities: Parental stress, family functioning, and sibling self-concept. *Journal of Learning Disabilities, 29,* 280–286.

Gartland, D. (1993). Teacher-parent partnerships: Effective conferencing strategies. *LD Forum, 18,* 17–20.

Hudson, P., & Miller, S. P. (1993). Home and school partnerships: Parent as teacher. *LD Forum, 18,* 31–33.

Jayanthi, M., Swayer, V., Nelson, J. S., Bursuck, W. D., & Epstein, M. H. (1995). Recommendations for homework-communication problems. *Remedial and Special Education, 16,* 212–225.

Kroth, R. (1978). Parents: Powerful and necessary allies. *Teaching Exceptional Children, 10,* 88–91.

Kroth, R. L. and Edge, D. (1997). *Strategies for communicating with parents and families of exceptional children* (3rd ed.) Denver: Love.

O'Shea, D. J. (1993). Professionals and families in team alliances. *LD Forum, 18,* 22–26.

O'Shea, D. J., O'Shea, L. J., & Hammitte, D. J. (1994). Expanding roles for teachers of students with learning disabilities: Working with family members. *LD Forum, 19,* 28–30.

Simpson, R. L. (1996). *Working with parents and families of exceptional children and youth: Techniques for successful conferencing and collaboration* (3rd ed.). Austin: Pro-Ed.

Technology

Babbitt, B. C., & Miller, S. P. (1996). Using Hypermedia to improve the mathematics problem solving skills of students with learning disabilities. *Journal of Learning Disabilities, 29,* 391–401.

Carnine, D. (1989). Teaching complex content to learning disabled students: The role of technology. *Exceptional Children, 55,* 524–533.

Carroll, N. (June 5, 1996). Many school computers are outdated. *USA Today,* pp. D1, D6.

Cochran-Smith, M. (1991). Word processing and writing in elementary classrooms: A critical review of related literature. *Review of Educational Research, 61,* 107–155.

Higgins, K., & Boone, R. (1990). Hypertext computer study guides and the social studies achievement of students with learning disabilities, remedial students, and regular education students. *Journal of Learning Disabilities, 23,* 529–540.

Higgins, K., Boone, R., & Lovitt, T. C. (1996). Hypertext support for remedial students and students with learning disabilities. *Journal of Learning Disabilities, 29,* 402–412.

Hunt-Berg, M., Rankin, J. L., & Benkelman, D. R.. (1994). Ponder the possibilities: Computer-supported writing for struggling writers. *Learning Disabilities Research & Practice, 9,* 169–178.

Koscinski, S. T., & Gast, D. L. (1993). Computer-assisted instruction with constant time delay to teach multiplication facts to students with learning disabilities. *Learning Disabilities Research & Practice, 8,* 157–168.

Lewis, R. B. (1993). *Special education technology: Classroom applications.* Pacific Grove, CA: Brooks/Cole.

Lovitt, T. C., & Horton, S. V. (1994). Strategies for adapting science textbooks for youth with learning disabilities. *Remedial and Special Education, 13,* 105–116.

MacArthur, C. A. (1996). Using technology to enhance the writing process of students with learning disabilities. *Journal of Learning Disabilities, 29,* 344–355.

MacArthur, C. A., Graham, S., Haynes, J. B., & DeLaPaz, S. (1996). Spelling checkers and students with learning disabilities: Performance comparisons and impact on spelling. *The Journal of Special Education, 30,* 35–57.

MacArthur, C. A., & Schwartz, S. S. (1991). An integrated approach to writing instruction: The computers and writing instruction. *LD Forum, 16,* 35–41.

Wilson, R., Majsterek, D., & Simmons, D. (1996). The effects of computer-assisted versus teacher-directed instruction on the multiplication performance of elementary students with learning disabilities. *Journal of Learning Disabilities, 29,* 382–290l

Woodward, J., & Gersten, R. (1992). Innovative technology for secondary studentrs with learning disabilities. *Exceptional Children, 58,* 407–421.

Concepts and Controversy: Is ADD a Disability?
Armstrong, T. (1995). *The myth of the ADD child.* New York: Dutton.

Reid, R., Maag, J. W., & Vasa, S. F. (1993). Attention deficit hyperactivity disorder as a disability category: A critique. *Exceptional Children, 60,* 198–214.

Riccio, C. A., Gonzalez, J. J., & Hynd, G. W. (1994). Attention deficit hyperactivity disorder (ADHD) and learning disabilities. *Learning Disabilities Quarterly, 17,* 311–322.

Shaywitz, S. E., & Shaywitz, B. A. (Eds.). (1992). *Attention deficit disorder comes of age: Toward the twenty-first century.* Austin: Pro-Ed.

Weiderholt, J. L. (1991). Editor's comments. *Journal of Learning Disabilities, 24,* 68.

CHAPTER 5: SPEECH OR LANGUAGE IMPAIRMENTS

Art
Hinde, T. (1991). *Lewis Carroll: Looking-Glass Letters.* NY: Rizzoli.

General
Warren, S. F. (1993). The transdisciplinary view of communication. Personal communication.

Speech and Language Impairments Defined
Blank, M., Rose, S. A., & Berlin, L. J. (1978). *The language of learning: The preschool years.* New York: Grune & Stratton.

Boone, D. R., & Plante, E. (1993). *Human communication and its disorders* (2nd ed.). Englewood Cliffs, NJ: Prentice-Hall.

Johnston, J. R., Miller, J. F., Curtiss, S., & Tallal, P. (1993). Conversations with children who are language impaired: Asking questions. *Journal of Speech and Hearing Research, 36,* 973–978.

Marvin, C. (1989). Language and learning. In D. D. Smith, *Teaching students with learning and behavior problems* (pp. 147–181). Englewood Cliffs, NJ: Prentice-Hall.

Onslow, M., Andrews, C., & Lincoln, M. (1994). A control/experimental trial of an operant treatment for early stuttering. *Journal of Speech and Hearing Research, 37,* 1244–1259.

Owens, R. E., Jr. (1994). Development of communication, language, and speech. In G. H. Shames, E. H. Wiig, and W. A. Secord (Eds.), *Human communication disorders: An introduction* (4th ed., pp. 36–81). NY: Merrill, an imprint of Macmillan.

Ratner, N. B. (1995). Language complexity and stuttering in children. *Topics in Language Disorders, 15,* 32–47.

Rice, M. L. (1995). Speech and language impairments. In E. L. Meyen and T. M. Skrtic (Eds.), *Special education and student disability: An introduction* (4th ed., pp. 339–376). Denver: Love.

Ruiz, N. T. (1995). The social construction of ability and disability: I. Profile types of Latino children identified as language learning disabled. *Journal of Learning Disabilities, 28,* 476–490.

Sander, E. K. (1972). When are speech sounds learned? *Journal of Speech and Hearing Disorders, 37,* 62.

Shames, G. H., & Ramig, P. R. (1994). Stuttering and other disorders of fluency. In G. H. Shames, E. H. Wiig, and W. A. Secord (Eds.), *Human communication disorders: An introduction* (4th ed, pp. 336–386). NY: Merrill, an imprint of Macmillan.

Van Riper, C., & Erickson, R. L. (1996). *Speech correction: An introduction to speech pathology and audiology* (9th ed.). Boston: Allyn and Bacon.

Walker, H. M., Schwarz, I. E., Nippold, M. A., Irving, L. K., & Noell, J. W. (1994). Social skills in school-age children and youth: Issues and best practices in assessment and intervention. *Topics in Language Disorders, 14,* 70–82.

Weiss, A. L. (1995). Conversational demands and their effects on fluency and stuttering. *Topics in Language Disorders, 15,* 18–31.

Wingate, M. E. (1962). Personality needs of stutterers. *Logos, 5,* 35–37.

History of the Field
Moore, G. P., & Kester, D. (1953). Historical notes on speech correction in the preassociation era. *Journal of Speech and Hearing Disorders, 18,* 48–53.

Van Riper, C. (1981). An early history of ASHA. *ASHA, 23,* 855–858.

Van Riper, C., & Erickson, R. L. (1996). *Speech correction: An introduction to speech pathology and audiology* (9th ed.). Boston: Allyn and Bacon.

Prevalence
Boone, D. R., & Plante, E. (1993). *Human communication and its disorders* (2nd ed.). Englewood Cliffs, NJ: Prentice-Hall.

Dublinski, S. (1981). Block grant proposal introduced: What does it mean? *Language, Speech, and Hearing Services in the Schools, 12,* 192–199.

Rice, M. L. (1995). Speech and language impairments. In E. L. Meyen and T. M. Skrtic (Eds.), *Special education and student disability: An introduction* (4th ed., pp. 339–376). Denver: Love.

Tallal, P. Miller, S. L., Bedi, G., Byma, G., Wang, X., Nagarajan, S. S., Schreenei, C., Jenkins, W. M. & Merzenich, M. M. (1996). Language comprehension in language learning impaired children improved with acoustically modified speech. *Science, 27,* 81–84.

U.S. Department of Education. (1996). *Eighteenth annual report to Congress on the implementation of the Individuals with Disabilities Education Act.* Washington, DC: U.S. Government Printing Office.

Wallach, G. P., & Butler, K. G. (1995). Language learning disabilities: Moving in from the edge. *Topics in Language Disorders, 16,* 1–26.

Causes and Prevention

Battle, D. (1996). Language learning and use by African American children. *Topics in Language Disorders, 16,* 22–37.

Finn, P., & Ingham, R. J. (1994). Stutterers' self-rating of how natural speech sounds and feels. *Journal of Speech and Hearing Research, 37,* 326–340.

Lahey, M., & Edwards, J. (1995). Specific language impairment: Preliminary investigation of factors associated with family history and with patterns of language performance. *Journal of Speech and Hearing Research, 38,* 634–657.

Langdon, H. W., & Cheng, L-R, L. (1992). *Hispanic children and adults with communication disorders.* Gaithersburg, MD: Aspen.

Leonard, L. (1994). Language disorders in preschool children. In G. H. Shames, E. H. Wiig, and W. A. Secord (Eds.), *Human communication disorders: An introduction* (4th ed, pp. 174–211). NY: Merrill, an imprint of Macmillan.

Marge, M. (1984). The prevention of communication disorders. *ASHA, 26,* 29–37.

Maughn II, T. H. (August 11, 1995). Study finds folic acid cuts risk of cleft palate. *Los Angeles Times,* p. A20.

McWilliams, B. J., & Witzel, M. A. (1994). Cleft palate. In G. H. Shames, E. H. Wiig, and W. A. Secord (Eds.), *Human communication disorders: An introduction* (4th ed, pp. 438–479). NY: Merrill, an imprint of Macmillan.

Ratner, N. B. (1995). Language complexity and stuttering in children. *Topics in Language Disorders, 15,* 32–47.

Ruiz, N. T. (1995). The social construction of ability and disability: I. Profile types of Latino children identified as language learning disabled. *Journal of Learning Disabilities, 28,* 476–490.

Silverman, F. H. (1996). *Stuttering and other fluency disorders* (2nd ed.). Boston: Allyn and Bacon.

Stark, R. E., Bernstein, L. E., & Demorest, M. E. (1993). Vocal communication in the first 18 months of life. *Journal of Speech and Hearing Research, 36,* 548–558.

Taylor, O. L., & Payne, K. T. (1994). Differences and disorders of language. In G. H. Shames, E. H. Wiig, and W. A. Secord (Eds.), *Human communication disorders: An introduction* (4th ed; pp. 136–175). NY: Merrill, an imprint of Macmillan.

Terrell, B. Y. (1993). Multicultural perspectives: Are the issues and questions different? *ASHA, 35,* 51–52, 62.

Van Riper, C., & Erickson, R. L. (1996). *Speech correction: An introduction to speech pathology and audiology* (9th ed.). Boston: Allyn and Bacon.

Weiss, A. L. (1995). Conversational demands and their effects on fluency and stuttering. *Topics in Language Disorders, 15,* 18–31.

Children with Speech or Language Impairments

Catts, H. W. (1993). The relationship between speech-language impairments and reading disabilities. *Journal of Speech and Hearing Research, 36,* 948–958.

Catts, H. W, Hu, C-F., Larrivee, L., & Swank, L. (1994). Early identification of reading disabilities in children with speech-language impairments. In R. V. Watkins and M. L. Rice (Eds.), *Specific language impairments in children: Volume 4* (pp. 145–160). Baltimore: Paul H. Brookes.

Fey, M. E., Windsor, J., & Warren, S. F. (Eds). (1995). *Language intervention: Preschool through the elementary years.* Baltimore: Paul H. Brookes.

Lloyd, P. (1994). Referential communication: Assessment and intervention. *Topics in Language Disorders, 14,* 55–59.

Nippold, M. A. (1994). Persuasive talk in social contexts: Development, assessment and intervention. *Topics in Language Disorders, 14,* 1–12.

Shames, G. H., & Ramig, P. R. (1994). Stuttering and other disorders of fluency. In G. H. Shames, E. H. Wiig, and W. A. Secord (Eds.), *Human communication disorders: An introduction* (4th ed, pp. 336–386). NY: Merrill, an imprint of Macmillan.

Stevens, L. J., & Bliss, L. S. (1995). Conflict resolution abilities of children with specific language impairment and children with normal language. *Journal of Speech and Hearing Research, 38,* 599–611.

U.S. Department of Education. (1995). *Fifteenth annual report to Congress on the implementation of the Education of the Handicapped Act.* Washington, DC: U.S. Government Printing Office.

Van Riper, C., & Erickson, R. L. (1996). *Speech correction: An introduction to speech pathology and audiology* (9th ed.). Boston: Allyn and Bacon.

Walker, H. M., Schwarz, I. E., Nippold, M. A., Irvin, L. K., & Noell, J. W. (1994). Social skills in school-age children and youth: Issues and best practices in assessment and intervention. *Topics in Language Disorders, 14,* 70–82.

Wallach, G. P., & Butler, K. G. (1995). Language learning disabilities: Moving in from the edge. *Topics in Language Disorders, 16,* 1–26.

Wiig, E. H., & Secord, W. A. (1994). Language disabilities in school-age children and youth. In G. H. Shames, E. H. Wiig, and W. A. Secord (Eds.), *Human communication disorders: An introduction* (4th ed, pp. 212–248). NY: Merrill, an imprint of Macmillan.

Educational Interventions

Aune, B., & Friehe, M. (1996). Transition to postsecondary education: Institutional and individual issues. *Topics in Language Disorders, 16,* 1–22.

Blank, M., & Marquis, A. M. (1987). *Directing discourse.* Tucson: Communication Skill Builders.

Boone, D. R., & Plante, E. (1993). *Human communication and its disorders* (2nd ed.). Englewood Cliffs, NJ: Prentice-Hall.

Cannon, G. S., Idol, L., & West, J. F. (1992). Educating students with mild handicaps in general classrooms: Essential teaching practices for general and special educators. *Journal of Learning Disabilities, 25,* 300–317.

Catts, H. W, Hu, C-F, Larrivee, L., & Swank, L. (1994). Early identification of reading disabilities in children with speech-language impairments. In R. V. Watkins and M. L. Rice (Eds.), *Specific language impairments in children* (pp. 145–160). Baltimore: Paul H. Brookes.

Clarke, J. (1996). Language development in children prenatally drug exposed: Consideration for assessment and intervention. *The Source, 6,* 12–14.

Conner, R. N., & Welsh, R. (1993). Teams and teamwork: Educational settings. *ASHA, 35,* 35–36.

Crais, E. R., & Lorch, N. (1994). Oral narratives in school-age children. *Topics in Language Disorders, 14,* 13–28.

Cuda, R. A., & Nelson, N. (1976). *Analysis of teacher speaking rate, syntactic complexity and hesitation phenomena as a function of grade level.* Paper presented at the annual meeting of the American Speech-Language-Hearing Association, Houston. As reported in G. Wallach and K. Butler (Eds.), (1984), *Language learning disabilities in school-age children.* Baltimore: Williams & Wilkins.

Dinkmeyer, D., & Dinkmeyer, D. (1982). *DUSO-revised: Developing understanding of self and others.* Circle Pines, MN: American Guidance Service.

Dunn, L. M., Dunn, L. M., Smith, J. O., Smith, D. D., & Horton, K. (1983). *Peabody picture collection.* Circle Pines, MN: American Guidance Service.

Dunn, L. M., Smith, J. O., Dunn, L. M., Horton, K., & Smith, D. D. (1981). *Peabody language development kits (rev. ed.), levels P & 1.* Circle Pines, MN: American Guidance Service.

Education of the Handicapped (February 26, 1992). Early intervention greatly reduces learning problems, study says. Author, p. 7.

Ellett, L. (1993). Instructional practices in mainstreamed secondary classrooms. *Journal of Learning Disabilities, 26,* 57–64.

Fuchs, D., & Fuchs, L. S. (1994/1995). Sometimes separate is better. *Educational Leadership, 52,* 22–26.

Geluke, N., & Lovitt, T. C. (1992). *Conversations with general education teachers about their work with mainstreamed students.* Unpublished paper, High School Curriculum Project, University of Washington, Seattle.

Gruenewald, L., & Pollack, S. (1984). *Language interaction in teaching and learning.* Austin, TX: Pro-Ed.

Hart, B., & Risley, T. (1995). *Meaningful differences in the everyday lives of American Children.* Baltimore: Paul H. Brookes.

Hoskins, B. (1987). *Conversations: Language intervention for adolescents.* Allen, TX: DLM—Teaching Resources.

Katims, D. S. (1994). Emergence of literacy in preschool children with disabilities. *Learning Disabilities Quarterly, 17,* 58–69.

LaBlance, G. R., Steckol, K. F., & Smith, V. L. (1994). Stuttering: The role of the classroom teacher. *Teaching Exceptional Children, 27,* 10–12.

Marvin, C. (1989). Language and learning. In D. D. Smith, *Teaching students with learning and behavior problems* (pp. 147–181). Englewood Cliffs, NJ: Prentice-Hall.

Ostrosky, M. M., & Kaiser, A. P. (1991). Preschool classroom environments that promote communication. *Teaching Exceptional Children, 23,* 6–10.

Plourde, L. (1985). *Classroom listening and speaking (CLAS).* Tucson: Communication Skill Builders.

Rogow, S. (1991). Teachers at play: Observed strategies to promote social play between children with special needs and their non-handicapped peers. *B. C. Journal of Special Education, 15,* 201–209.

Rouse, M. (Spring 1993). *Searching for inclusive schools in the snow.* University of Cambridge Institute of Education Newsletter, p. 1.

Schumm, J. S., & Vaughn, S. (1991). Making adaptations for mainstreamed students: General classroom teachers' perspectives. *Remedial and Special Education, 12,* 18–27.

Schumm, J. S., & Vaughn, S. (1992). Reflections on planning for mainstreamed special education students: Perceptions of general classroom teachers. *Exceptionality, 3,* 121–126.

Simon, C. (1981). *Communicative competence: A functional-pragmatic approach to language therapy.* Tucson: Communication Skill Builders.

Sirotnick, K., & Lovitt, T. C. (1992). *Interviews with high school principals: Preliminary impressions.* Unpublished paper, High School Curriculum Project, University of Washington, Seattle.

Snider, K. (April 27, 1992). Department of labor report outlines skills, personal abilities needed for the workplace. *American Association of Colleges for Teacher Education Briefs, 13,* 1.

U.S. Department of Education. (1994). *Fourteenth annual report to Congress on the implementation of the Individuals with Disabilities Education Act.* Washington, DC: U.S. Government Printing Office.

Wagner, M. M., D'Amico, R., Marder, C., Newman, L., & Blackorby, J. (1992). *What happens next? Trends in postschool outcomes of youth with disabilities. The second comprehensive report from the National Longitudinal Transition Study of Special Education Students.* Menlo Park, CA: SRI International.

Warren, S. F., Yoder, P. J., Gazden, G. E., Kim, K., & Jones, H. A. (1993). Facilitating prelinguistic communication skills in young children with developmental delay. *Journal of Speech and Hearing Research, 36,* 83–97.

Watkins, R. V., & Rice, M. L. (Eds.). (1994). *Specific language impairments in children.* Baltimore: Paul H. Brookes.

Westby, C. E. (1995). Culture and literacy: Frameworks for understanding. *Topics in Language Disorders, 16,* 50–66.

Wiig, E. (1982). *Let's talk: Developing prosocial communication skills.* Columbus, OH: Merrill.

Families

Children's Defense Fund. (1996). *The state of America's children: Yearbook 1996.* Washington, DC: Author.

Cleminshaw, H., DePompei, R., Crais, E. R., Blosser, J., Gillette, Y., & Hooper, C. R, (1996). Working with families. *ASHA, 38,* 34–45.

Crais, E. R., & Lorch, N. (1994). Oral narratives in school-age children. *Topics in Language Disorders, 14,* 13–28.

Fishman, I. (1987). *Electronic communication aids: Selection and use.* Boston: Little, Brown.

Leonard, L. (1994). Language disorders in preschool children. In G. H. Shames, E. H. Wiig, and W. A. Secord (Eds.), *Human communication disorders: An introduction* (4th ed., pp. 174–211). NY: Merrill, an imprint of Macmillan.

Nippold, M. A., & Rudzinski, M. (1995). Parents' speech and children's stuttering: A critique of the literature. *Journal of Speech and Hearing Research, 38,* 978–989.

Parette, H. P., & Angelo, D. H. (1996). Augmentative and alternative communication impact on families: Trends and future directions. The *Journal of Special Education, 30,* 77–99.

Stark, R. E., Bernstein, L. E., & Demorest, M. E. (1993). Vocal communication in the first 18 months of life. *Journal of Speech and Hearing Research, 36,* 548–558.

Technology

Beukelman, D. R., & Mirenda, P. (1992). *Augmentative and alternative communication: Management of severe communication disorders in children and adults.* Baltimore: Brookes.

Maugh II, T. H. (January 5, 1996). New therapy aids pupils with speech problems. The *Los Angeles Times,* pp. A1, A25.

Merzenich, M. M., Jenkins, W. M., Johnston, P., Schreiner, C., Miller, S. L., Tallal, P. (January 5, 1996). Temporal processing deficits of language-learning impaired children ameliorated by training. *Science, 271,* 77–80.

Parette, H. P., & Angelo, D. H. (1996). Augmentative and alternative communication impact on families: Trends and future directions. The *Journal of Special Education, 30,* 77–99.

Peavler, B. (Spring 1996). New studies may yield treatment for language-based learning disabilities. *New Mexico Learning Disabilities Association Newsletter,* pp. 1–2, 8.

Tallal, P. Miller, S. L., Bedi, G., Byma, G., Wang, X., Nagarajan, S. S., Schreenei, C., Jenkins, W. M. & Merzenich, M. M. (1996). Language comprehension in language learning impaired children improved with acoustically modified speech. *Science, 27,* 81–84.

Concepts and Controversy

Anderson, C. (1972). *Society pays: The high costs of minimal brain damage in America.* New York: Walker.

ASHA Committee on Prevention of Speech-Language and Hearing Problems. (1984). Prevention: A challenge for the profession. *ASHA, 26,* 35–37.

Associated Press. (January 9, 1991). Panel urges measles-vaccination fund boost. *Albuquerque Journal,* p. D10.

Bradley, A. (May 16, 1990). Lack of funds halts measles-vaccination program. *Education Week,* p. 5.

Children's Defense Fund (1996). *The state of America's children: Yearbook 1996.* Washington, DC: Author.

Hilts, P. J. (May 9, 1990). Fight measles stalls on money: U.S. runs out of funds for emergency vaccinations to fight the epidemic. *New York Times,* p. A13.

CHAPTER 6: MENTAL RETARDATION

Mental Retardation Defined

Bryant, B. R., Taylor, R. L., & Rivera, D. P. (1996). *Assessment of adaptive areas (AAA): Examiner's manual.* Austin, TX: Pro-Ed.

Edgerton, R. (1967). *The cloak of competence.* Berkeley: University of California.

Grossman, H. J. (Ed.). (1983). *Classification in mental retardation.* Washington, DC: American Association on Mental Retardation.

Hernandez Jr., E. (July 26, 1995). Learning about disabilities. *Los Angeles Times,* p. B2.

Jutkiewicz, R. (April 2, 1994). Special children. *Albuquerque Tribune* (Lifestyles), pp. C1–C2.

Luckasson, R., Coulter, D. L., Polloway, E. A., Reis, S., Schalock, R. L., Snell, M. E., Spitalnik, D. M., & Stark, J. A. (1992). *Mental retardation: Definition, classification, and systems of supports.* Washington, DC: American Association on Mental Retardation.

Szivos, S. E., & Griffiths, E. (1990). Group processes involved in coming to terms with a mentally retarded identity. *Mental Retardation, 28,* 333–341.

Thomson, G. O. B., Ward, K. M., & Wishart, J. G. (1995). The transition to adulthood for children with Down's syndrome. *Disability and Society, 10,* 325–339.

History of the Field

Ayllon, T., & Azrin, N. H. (1964). Reinforcement and instructions with mental patients. *Journal of Experimental Analysis of Behavior, 7,* 327–331.

Ayllon, R., & Azrin, N. H. (1968). Reinforcer sampling: A technique for increasing the behavior of mental patients. *Journal of Applied Behavior Analysis, 1,* 13–20.

Brinbrauer, J. S., Wolf, M. M., Kidder, J. D., & Tague, C. E. (1965). Classroom behavior of retarded pupils with token reinforcement. *Journal of Experimental Child Psychology, 2,* 219–235.

Bryant, B. R., Taylor, R. L., & Rivera, D. P. (1996). *Assessment of adaptive areas (AAA): Examiner's manual.* Austin, TX: Pro-Ed.

Gelf, S. (1995). The beast in man: Degenerationism and mental retardation, 1900–1920. *Mental Retardation, 33,* 1–9.

Howe, S. G. (1866). On the proper role of state institutions for the disabled. Speech given at ceremonies on laying the cornerstone of the New York State Institution for the Blind at Batavia, Genesee County, New York. Batavia, NY: Henry Todd.

Itard, J. M. G. (1806). *Wild boy of Aveyron.* (G. Humphrey and M. Humphrey, Trans.). (1962). Englewood Cliffs, NJ: Prentice-Hall. Originally published Paris: Gouyon (1801).

Lent, J. R., & McLean, B. M. (1976). The trainable retarded: The technology of teaching. In N. G. Haring and R. L., Schiefelbush (Eds.), *Teaching special children* (pp. 197–223). New York: McGraw-Hill.

Longhurst, N. A. (1994). *The self-advocacy movement by people with developmental disabilities: A demographic study and directory of self-advocacy groups in the United States.* Washington, DC: The American Association on Mental Retardation.

Nirje, B. (1969). The normalization principle and its human management implications. In R. Kugel and W. Wolfensberger (Eds.), *Changing patterns in residential services for the mentally retarded* (pp. 179–195). Washington, DC: President's Committee on Mental Retardation.

Nirje, B. (1976). The normalization principle. In R. Kugel and A. Schearer (Eds.), *Changing patterns in residential services for the mentally retarded* (pp. 231–240). Washington, DC: President's Committee on Mental Retardation.

Perske, R. (1972). The dignity of risk. In W. Wolfensberger (Ed.), *The principle of normalization in human services* (pp. 194–200). Toronto: National Institute on Mental Retardation.

Winzer, M. A. (1993). The history of special education: From isolation to integration. Washington, DC: Gallaudet University Press.

Wolfensberger, W. (1972). *The principle of normalization in human services.* Toronto: National Institute on Mental Retardation.

Prevalence

MacMillan, D. L., Siperstein, G. N., & Gresham, F. M. (1996). A challenge to the viability of mild mental retardation as a diagnostic category. *Exceptional Children, 62,* 356–371.

U.S. Department of Education. (1996). *Eighteenth annual report to Congress on the implementation of the Individuals with Disabilities Education Act.* Washington, DC: U.S. Government Printing Office.

Causes and Prevention

Bates, B. (January/February, 1996). Extremely low birth weight child trails peers. *LDA Newsbrief, 31,* p. 8.

Coulter, D. L. (1996). Prevention as a form of support: Implications for the new definition. *Mental Retardation, 34,* 108–116.

Dorris, M. (1989). *The broken cord: A family's ongoing struggle with fetal alcohol syndrome.* New York: Harper & Row.

Griego, T. (October 13, 1994). Conference deals with ravages of fetal alcohol syndrome. *Albuquerque Tribune,* p. A6.

Hagerman, R. J., & Silverman, A. C. (Eds.). (1991). *Fragile X syndrome: Diagnosis, treatment and research.* Baltimore: John Hopkins University Press.

Haney, D. Q. (September 22, 1994). Disabilities plague the tiniest preemies: Medical miracle has a dark side. *Albuquerque Journal,* p. A4.

Jutkiewicz, R. (April 2, 1994). Special children. *Albuquerque Tribune* (Lifestyles), pp. C1–C2.

Lowenthal, B. (1996). Educational Implications of child abuse. *Intervention in School and Clinic, 32,* 21–25.

Luckasson, R., Coulter, D. L., Polloway, E. A., Reis, S., Schalock, R. L., Snell, M. E., Spitalnik, D. M., & Stark, J. A. (1992). *Mental retardation: Definition, classification, and systems of supports.* Washington, DC: American Association on Mental Retardation.

Mandell, C. J., & Stewart, J. (1994). Fetal crack cocaine exposure: Dispelling the myths. *LD Forum, 19,* 16–14.

March of Dimes. (1993). Substance abuse. *StatBook.* White Plains, NY: March of Dimes Birth Defects Foundation.

New York Times News Service. (June 28, 1995). Dr. Robert Guthrie saved thousands from mental retardation. *Albuquerque Tribune,* p. C12.

President's Committee on Mental Retardation. (n. d.). *A guide for state planning: For the prevention of mental retardation and related disabilities.* Washington, DC: Author.

Santos, K. (1992). Fragile X syndrome: An educator's role in identification, prevention, and intervention. *Remedial and Special Education, 13,* 32–39.

Schopmeyer, B. B., & Lowe, F. H. (Eds.). (1992). *The fragile X child.* San Diego, CA: Singular Publishing Group.

Sherman, A. (1994). *Wasting America's failure: The Children's Defense fund report on the costs of child poverty.* Boston: Beacon Press.

Stevenson, R. E., Massey, P. S., Schroer, R. J., McDermott, S., & Richter, B. (1996). Preventable fraction of mental retardation: Analysis based on individuals with severe mental retardation. *Mental Retardation, 34,* 182–188.

Tanner, L. (April 10, 1996). Studies: Obese women's babies run higher defect risk. *Albuquerque Journal,* p. A9.

Thomson, G. O. B., Ward, K. M., & Wishart, J. G. (1995). The transition to adulthood for children with Down's syndrome. *Disability and Society, 10,* 325–339.

Torres, V. (January 25, 1995). $150,000 awarded in case of lead poisoning. *Los Angeles Times,* pp. B7, B9.

Youth Record. (August 15, 1995). Child abuse leads to lower IQ and body responsiveness. *Author, 15,* p. 1.

Children with Mental Retardation

Best Buddies. (n. d.). *Best buddies colleges.* Miami, FL: Best Buddies Headquarters.

Bradley, V. J., Ashbough, J. W., & Blaney, B. (Eds.). (1993). *Creating individual supports for people with developmental disabilities: A mandate for change at many levels.* Baltimore: Brookes.

Drew, C. J., Logan, D. R., & Hardman, M. L. (1992). *Mental retardation: A life cycle approach.* New York: Merrill, an imprint of MacMillan.

McDonnell, J., Mathot-Buckner, C., & Ferguson, B. (1996). *Transition programs for students with moderate/severe disabilities.* Pacific Grove, CA: Brooks/Cole.

Parette, H. P., & Angelo, D. H. (1996). Augmentative and alternative communication impact on families: Trends and future directions. *The Journal of Special Education, 30,* 77–98.

Yoder, P. J., Kaiser, A. P., & Alpert, C. (1993). Following the child's lead when teaching nouns to preschoolers with mental retardation. *Journal of Speech and Hearing Research, 36,* 158–167.

Educational Interventions

Associated Press. (November 10, 1995). Down syndrome tailback turns game around for team: Teen's spirit takes football to higher level. *The Honolulu Advisor,* p. A2.

Belfiore, P. J., & Toro-Zambrana, W. (1994). *Recognizing choices in community settings by people with significant disabilities.* Washington, DC: American Association on Mental Retardation.

Blair, C., Ramey, C. R., & Hardin, J. M. (1995). Early intervention for low birthweight, premature infants: Participation and intellectual development. *American Journal on Mental Retardation, 99,* 542–554.

Cook County Cooperative Extension Service. (1990). *Meeting the urban challenge: Annual report.* Urbana-Champaign: University of Illinois.

Drew, C. J., Logan, D. R., & Hardman, M. L. (1992). *Mental retardation: A life cycle approach.* New York: Merrill, an imprint of MacMillan.

Guralnick, M. J., Connor, R. T., & Hammond, M. (1995). Parent perspectives of peer relationships and friendships in integrated and specialized programs. *American Journal on Mental Retardation, 99,* 457–476.

Hickson, L., Blackman, L. S., & Reis, E. M. (1995). *Mental retardation: Foundations of educational programming.* Boston: Allyn and Bacon.

Jitendra, A., & Nolet, V. (1995). Teaching how to use a check register: Procedures for instruction and selection. *Intervention in School and Clinic, 31,* 28–33.

Krauss, M. W., Seltzer, M. M., Gordon, R. M., & Friedman, D. H. (1996). Binding ties: The roles of adult siblings of persons with mental retardation. *Mental Retardation, 34,* 83–93.

Longhurst, N. A. (1994). *The self-advocacy movement by people with developmental disabilities: A demographic study and directory of self-advocacy groups in the United States.* Washington, DC: The American Association on Mental Retardation.

McNair, J., & Rusch, F. R. (1991). Parent involvement in transition programs. *Mental Retardation, 29,* 93–101.

Ramey, C. T., Bryant, D. M., Wasik, B. H., Sparling, J. J., Fendt, K. H., & LaVange, L. M. (March 1992). Infant health and development program for low birth weight, premature infants: Program elements, family participation, and child intelligence. *Pediatrics, 3*, 454–465.

SRI. (1991). *The early youth experiences of youth with disabilities: Trends in employment rates and job characteristics.* Menlo Park, CA: Author.

SRI. (1992). *Being female—A secondary disability? Gender differences in the transition experiences of young people with disabilities.* Menlo Park, CA: Author.

Sullivan, C. (October 25, 1992). Tots' plot. *Chicago Tribune, TempoLake,* p. E1.

Thomson, G. O. B., Ward, K. M., & Wishart, J. G. (1995). The transition to adulthood for children with Down's syndrome. *Disability and Society, 10*, 325–339.

Thorin, E., Yovanoff, P., & Irvin, L. (1996). Dilemmas faced by families during their young adults' transitions to adulthood: A brief report. *Mental Retardation, 34*, 117–120.

Tobin, J. (March 6, 1996). Many handicapped kids function well in classroom. *The Acorn,* pp. 1–8.

Urban Update. (Winter 1992). *"4-H for All" means new opportunities for all.* Author, 4, 1–2.

U.S. Department of Education. (1995). *Seventeenth annual report to Congress on the implementation of the Individuals with Disabilities Education Act.* Washington, DC: U.S. Government Printing Office.

Wehmeyer, M. L., Kelchner, K., & Richards, S. (1996). Essential characteristics of self-determined behavior of individuals with mental retardation. *American Journal on Mental Retardation, 100*, 632–642.

Wehmeyer, M. L., & Metzler, C. A. (1995). How self-determined are people with mental retardation? The national consumer survey. *Mental Retardation, 33*, 111–119.

Families

Beach Center on Families and Disability. (1995a). Dads and disability. *Families and Disability Newsletter, 6*, p. 1.

Beach Center on Families and Disability. (1995b). Dads feel left out. *Families and Disability Newsletter, 6*, p. 4.

Beach Center on Families and Disability. (1995c). How to involve fathers more with their children with special needs. *Families and Disability Newsletter, 6*, pp. 5–6.

Birenbaum, A., & Cohen, H. J. (1993). On the importance of helping families: Policy implications from a national study. *Mental Retardation, 31*, 67–74.

Bradley, V. J., Knoll, J., & Agosta, J. M. (1992). *Emerging issues in family support.* Washington, DC: American Association on Mental Retardation.

Krauss, M. W., Seltzer, M. M., Gordon, R. M., & Friedman, D. H. (1996). Binding ties: The roles of adult siblings of persons with mental retardation. *Mental Retardation, 34*, 83–93.

Sandler, A. G., Warren, S. H., & Raver, S. A. (1995). Grandparents as a source of support for parents of children with disabilities: A brief report. *Mental Retardation, 33*, 248–250.

Thorin, E., Yovanoff, P., & Irvin L. (1966). Dilemmas faced by families during their young adults' transitions to adulthood: A brief report. *Mental Retardation, 34*, 117–120.

Willoughby, J. C., & Glidden, L. M. (1995). Fathers helping out: Shared child care and marital satisfaction of parents of children with disabilities. *American Journal on Mental Retardation, 99*, 399–406.

Technology

Hickson, L., Blackman, L. S., & Reis, E. M. (1995). *Mental retardation: Foundations of educational programming.* Boston: Allyn and Bacon.

Horton, S. V., Lovitt, T. C., & White, O. R. (1992). Teaching mathematics to adolescents classified as educable mentally handicapped: Using calculators to remove the computational onus. *Remedial and Special Education, 13*, 36–60.

Kolata, G. (July 6, 1993). Miniature scope gives the earliest pictures of a developing embryo. *New York Times,* p. B6.

Parette, H. P., & Angelo, D. H. (1996). Augmentative and alternative communication impact on families: Trends and future directions. The *Journal of Special Education, 30*, 77–98.

Pollack, A. (February 9, 1993). Computers taking wish as their command. *New York Times,* p. A1.

Concepts and Controversy

Herrnstein, R., & Murray, C. (1994). *The bell curve: Intelligence and class structure in American life.* New York: The Free Press.

Rock, R. J. (1996). Eugenics and euthanasia: A cause for concern for disabled people, particularly disabled women. *Disability and Society, 11*, 121–127.

Rodriguez-Trias, H. (1982). Sterilization abuse. In R. Hubbard, M. S. Henitin, and B. Fried (Eds.), *Biological woman: The convenient myth.* Cambridge, MA: Schenkman.

Smith, J. D. (October 1994). Mental retardation and eugenics: The persistent argument. *The Front Line, 1*, pp. 6–11. Pacific Grove, CA: Brooks/Cole.

Smith, J. D. (1995). For whom the bell curves: Old texts, mental retardation, and the persistent argument. *Mental Retardation, 33*, 199–202.

CHAPTER 7: GIFTEDNESS AND TALENT DEVELOPMENT

Art

Coughlan, R., & the Editors of Time-Life Books. (1966). *The world of Michelangelo: 1475–1564*. NY: Time, Inc.

Reynal and Company. (1966). *The complete work of Michelangelo*. NY: William Morrow and Company.

General

Morelock, M. J., & Feldman, D. H. (1997). High IQ children, extreme precocity, and savant syndrome. In N. Colangelo and G. A. Davis (Eds.), *Handbook of gifted education* (2nd ed., pp. 439–459). Boston: Allyn and Bacon.

Simonton, D. K. (1997). When giftedness becomes genius: How does talent achieve eminence? In N. Colangelo and G. A. Davis (Eds.), *Handbook of gifted education* (2nd ed., pp. 335–349). Boston: Allyn and Bacon.

Giftedness and Talent Defined

Borland, J. H. (1996). Gifted education and the threat of irrelevance. *Journal for the Education of the Gifted, 19,* 129–147.

Coleman, L. (Ed.) (1996). Special Issue: Critical appraisals of gifted education. *Journal for the Education of the Gifted, 19,* 127–250.

Coleman, M. R., & Gallagher, J. J. (1994). *Report on states' policies related to the identification of gifted students*. Chapel Hill: Gifted Education Policy Studies Program.

Cornell, D. G., Delcourt, M. A. B., Goldberg, M. D., & Bland, L. C. (1995). Achievement and self-concept of minority students in elementary school gifted programs. *Journal for the Education of the Gifted, 18,* 189–209.

Feldhusen, J. F. (1992). *TIDE: Talent identification and development in education*. Sarasota, FL: Center for Creative Learning.

Feldhusen, J. F. (Ed.). (1995). Talent development: The new direction in gifted education. *Roeper Review, 18,* 92.

Gagné, F. (1996). From giftedness to talent: A developmental model and its impact on the language of the field. *Roeper Review, 18,* 92, 103–111.

Gallagher, J. J. (1985). *Teaching the gifted child* (3rd ed.). Boston: Allyn and Bacon.

Gallagher, J. J. (1996). A critique of critiques of gifted education. *Journal for the Education of the Gifted, 19,* 234–249.

Garcia, E. (1994). *Understanding and meeting the challenges of student cultural diversity*. Boston: Houghton Mifflin.

Gardner, H. (1983). *Frames of mind: The theory of multiple intelligences*. New York: Basic Books.

Hunsaker, S. L. (1995). The gifted metaphor from the perspective of traditional civilizations. *Journal for the Education of the Gifted, 18,* 255–268.

Kitano, M. K., & Espinosa, R. (1995). Language diversity and giftedness: Working with gifted English language learners. *Journal for the Education of the Gifted, 18,* 234–254.

Margolin, L. (1996). A pedagogy of privilege. *Journal for the Education of the Gifted, 19,* 164–180.

Marland, S. (1972). *Education of the gifted and talented* (Report to the Congress of the United States by the U.S. Commissioner of Education). Washington, DC: U.S. Government Printing Office.

Morgan, A. D. (Fall 1994). *Opportunities to learn through multiple intelligences. School Renewal Update*. Santa Fe: Effective Schools Unit, New Mexico State Department of Education.

Pendarvis, E., & Howley, A. (1996). Playing fair: The possibilities of gifted education. *Journal for the Education of the Gifted, 19,* 215–233.

Ramos-Ford, V., & Gardner, H. (1991). Giftedness from a multiple intelligence perspective. In N. Colangelo and G. A. Davis (Eds.), *Handbook of gifted education* (pp. 55–64). Boston: Allyn and Bacon.

Renzulli, J. (1978). What makes giftedness? Reexamining a definition. *Phi Delta Kappan, 60,* 180–184, 261.

Renzulli, J. S., & Reis, S. M. (1997). The schoolwide enrichment model: New directions for developing high-end learning. In N. Colangelo and G. A. Davis (Eds.), *Handbook of gifted education* (2nd ed., pp. 136–154). Boston: Allyn and Bacon.

Sapon-Shevin, M. (1996). Beyond gifted education: Building a shared agenda for school reform. *Journal for the Education of the Gifted, 19,* 192–214.

Terman, L. (1925). *Genetic studies of genius* (Vol. 1). Stanford, CA: Stanford University Press.

Thornkike, R. L., Hagen, E. P., & Sattler, J. M. (1996). *Stanford-Binet Intelligence Scale* (4th ed.). Itasca, Illinois: Riverside.

Treffinger, D. J., & Feldhusen, J. F. (1996). Talent recognition and development: Successor to gifted education. *Journal for the Education of the Gifted, 19,* 181–193.

VanTassel-Baska, J. (1995). The development of talent through curriculum. *Roeper Review, 18,* 98–102.

Wechsler, D. (1991). *Wechsler Intelligence Scale for Children III (WISC-III)*. San Antonio, Texas: Psychological Corporation.

History of the Field

Callahan, C. M. (1996). A critical self-study of gifted education: Healthy practice, necessary evil, or sedition? *Journal for the Education of the Gifted, 19,* 148–163.

Clark, B. (1992). *Growing up gifted*. New York: Merrill-Macmillan.

Davis, G. A. & Rimm, S. B. (1994). *Education of gifted and talented* (3rd ed.). Boston: Allyn and Bacon.

Gallagher, J. J. (1988). National agenda for educating gifted students: Statement of priorities. *Exceptional Children, 55,* 107–114.

Galton, F. (1869). *Hereditary genius: An inquiry into its laws and consequences.* London: Macmillan.

Gardner, J. W. (1984). *Excellence: Can we be equal and excellent too?* (rev. ed.). New York: Norton.

Hunsaker, S. L. (1995). The gifted metaphor from the perspective of traditional civilizations. *Journal for the Education of the Gifted, 18,* 255–268.

Maker, C. J. (1986). Education of the gifted: Significant trends. In R. J. Morris and B. Blatt (Eds.), *Special education: Research and trends* (pp. 190–221). New York: Pergamon.

Sapon-Shevin, M. (1996). Beyond gifted education: Building a shared agenda for school reform. *Journal for the Education of the Gifted, 19,* 192–214.

Silverman, L. K. (1988). Gifted and talented. In E. G. Meyen and T. M. Skrtic (Eds.), *Exceptional children and youth: An introduction* (3rd ed., pp. 263–292). Denver: Love.

Silverman, L. K. (1992). Leta Stetter Hollingworth: Champion of the psychology of women and gifted children. *Journal of Educational Psychology, 84,* 20–27.

Terman, L. (1925). *Genetic studies of genius* (Vol. 1). Stanford, CA: Stanford University Press.

Prevalence
Cartwright, G. P., Cartwright, C. A., & Ward, M. A. (1995). *Educating special learners* (4th ed.). Belmont, CA: Wadsworth.

Davis, G. A., & Rimm, S. B. (1994). *Education of the gifted and talented* (3rd ed.). Boston: Allyn and Bacon.

Harry, B. (1994). *The disproportionate representation of minority students in special education: Theories and recommendations.* Alexandria, VA: National Association of State Directors of Special Education.

Marland, S. (1972). *Education of the gifted and talented* (Report to the Congress of the United States by the U.S. Commissioner of Education). Washington, DC: U.S. Government Printing Office.

Mitchell, B. (1982). An update on the state of gifted/talented education in the U.S. *Phi Delta Kappan, 64,* 357–358.

National Center for Education Statistics. (1994). *Digest of Education Statistics.* Washington, DC: U.S. Government Printing Office.

Renzulli, J. S., & Reis, S. M. (1997). The schoolwide enrichment model: New directions for developing high-end learning. In N. Colangelo and G. A. Davis (Eds.), *Handbook of gifted education* (2nd ed., pp. 136–154). Boston: Allyn and Bacon.

Schmidt, R. (May 20, 1993). Seeking to identify the gifted among LEP students. *Education Weekly,* pp. 1, 12.

U.S. Department of Education. (1993). *Fifteenth annual report to Congress on the implementation of the Individuals with Disabilities Education Act.* Washington, DC: U.S. Government Printing Office.

Causes
Delisle, J. R. (1984). *Gifted children speak out.* New York: Walker.

Hunsaker, S. L. (1995). The gifted metaphor from the perspective of traditional civilizations. *Journal for the Education of the Gifted, 18,* 255–268.

Krippner, S. (1967). The ten commandments that block creativity. *Gifted Child Quarterly, 11,* 144–151.

Renzulli, J. (1978). What makes giftedness? Reexamining a definition. *Phi Delta Kappan, 60,* 180–184, 261.

Simonton, D. K. (1997). When giftedness becomes genius: How does talent achieve eminence? In N. Colangelo and G. A. Davis (Eds.), *Handbook of gifted education* (2nd ed., pp. 335–349). Boston: Allyn and Bacon.

Terman, L. (1925). *Genetic studies of genius* (Vol. 1). Stanford, CA: Stanford University Press.

Gifted Children
AAUW. (1992). *The AAUW report: How schools shortchange girls: Executive summary.* Washington, DC: American Association of University Women Educational Foundation.

Bireley, M. (1995). *Crossover children: A sourcebook for helping children who are gifted and learning disabled* (2nd ed.). Reston, VA: The Council for Exceptional Children.

Borland, J. H. (1996). Gifted education and the threat of irrelevance. *Journal for the Education of the Gifted, 19,* 129–147.

Callahan, C. M., & McIntire, J. A. (1994). *Identifying outstanding talent in American Indian and Alaska Native students.* Washington, DC: U.S. Department of Education, Office of Educational Research and Improvement.

Clark, B. (1992). *Growing up gifted.* New York: Merrill-Macmillan.

Davis, G. A. (1996). *Review of giftedness and talent development for Smith and Luckasson.* Personal Communication.

Davis, G. A., & Rimm, S. B. (1994). *Education of the gifted and talented* (3rd ed.). Boston: Allyn and Bacon.

Dickens, M. N., & Cornell, D. G. (1993). Parent influences on the mathematics self-concept of high ability and adolescent girls. *Journal for the Education of the Gifted, 17,* 53–73.

Dunning, J. (May 27, 1991). Seeking out ballet talent in public schools. *New York Times,* p. B1.

Eccles, J. (1985). Why doesn't Jane run? Sex differences in educational and occupational patterns. In F. Horowitz and M. O'Brien (Eds.), *The gifted and talented: Developmental perspectives* (pp. 251–295). Washington, DC: American Psychological Association.

Ford, D. Y. (1995). *Counseling Gifted African American Students: Promoting Achievement, Identity, and Social and Emotional Well-being.* Storrs, CT: National Research Center on the Gifted and Talented at the University of Connecticut.

Ford, D. Y., & Harris, J. J. (1994). Reform and gifted black students: Promising practices in Kentucky. *Journal of Gifted Education, 17,* 216–240.

Ford, B. A., Obiakor, F. E., & Patton J. M. (Eds.). (1995). *Effective education of African American exceptional learners: New perspectives.* Austin, TX: Pro-Ed.

Freeman, J. (1994). Some emotional aspects of being gifted. *Journal for the Education of the Gifted, 17,* 180–197.

Gallagher, J. J. (1988). National agenda for educating gifted students: Statement of priorities. *Exceptional Children, 55,* 107–114.

Gallagher, J. J., & Gallagher, S. A. (1994). *Teaching the gifted child* (4th ed.). Boston: Allyn and Bacon.

Hollingworth, L. S. (1942). *Children above 180 IQ, Stanford-Binet: Origin and development.* Yonkers, NY: World Book.

Hunsaker, S. L. (1994). Adjustments to traditional procedures for identifying underserved students: Successes and failures. *Exceptional Children, 61,* 72–76.

Jenkins-Friedman, R., & Nielsen, M. E. (1990). Gifted and talented students. In E. L. Meyen (Ed.), *Exceptional children in today's schools* (2nd ed., pp. 451–493). Denver: Love.

Lamb, J., & Daniels, R. (1993). Gifted girls in a rural community: Math attitudes and career options. *Exceptional Children, 59,* 513–517.

Laycock, F. (1979) *Gifted children.* Glenview, IL: Scott, Foresman.

Maker, C. J. (1977). *Providing programs for the gifted handicapped.* Reston, VA: Council for Exceptional Children.

Maker, C. J. (1986). Education of the gifted: Significant trends. In R. J. Morris and B. Blatt (Eds.), *Special education: Research and trends* (pp. 190–221). New York: Pergamon.

Maker, C. J., Nielson, A. B., & Rogers, J. A. (1994). Giftedness, diversity and problem solving. *Teaching Exceptional Children, 27,* 4–19.

Maker, C. J., & Schiever, S. W. (1989). Defining the Hispanic population. In C. J. Maker and S. W. Schiever (Eds.), *Critical issues in gifted education: Defensible programs for cultural and ethnic minorities* (Vol. 2, pp. 1–4). Austin, TX: Pro-Ed.

Morgan, T. (May 30, 1991). A sugar plum dream in a homeless shelter. *New York Times,* p. B1.

Nielsen, M. E., Higgins, L. D., & Hammond, A. E. (1993). The twice-exceptional child project: Identifying and serving gifted/handicapped learners. In C. M. Callahan, D. A. Tomlinson, and P. M. Pizzat (Eds.), *Contexts for promise: Noteworthy practices and innovations in the identification of gifted students* (pp. 145–168). Charlottesville, VA: National Research Center on the Gifted and Talented.

Nielsen, M. E., Higgins, L. D., Hammond. A. E., & Williams, R. A. (1993). Gifted children with disabilities: The twice-exceptional child project. *Gifted Child Today, 16,* 9–12.

Patton, J. M., & Baytops, J. L. (1995). Identifying and transforming the potential of young, gifted African Americans: A clarion call for action. In B. A. Ford, F. E. Obiakor, and J. M. Patton (Eds.), *Effective education of African American exceptional learners: New perspectives* (pp. 27–58). Austin, TX: Pro-Ed.

Piechowski, M. (1997). Emotional giftedness: The measure of intrapersonal intelligence. In N. Colangelo and G. A. Davis (Eds.), *Handbook of gifted education* (2nd ed., pp. 366–381). Boston: Allyn and Bacon.

Rand, D., & Gibb, L. H. (1989). A model program for gifted girls in science. *Journal for the Education of the Gifted, 12,* 142–155.

Roberts, S. M., & Lovett, S. B. (1994). Examining the "F" in Gifted: Academically gifted adolescents' physiological and affective responses to scholastic failure. *Journal for the Education of the Gifted, 17,* 241–259.

Silverman, L. K. (1995). Gifted and talented. In E. L. Meyen and T. M. Skrtic (Eds.), *Exceptional children and youth: An introduction* (4th ed., pp. 377–414). Denver: Love.

Terman, L. (1925). *Genetic studies of genius* (Vol. 1). Stanford, CA: Stanford University Press.

Van Tassel-Baska, J. (1995). The development of talent through curriculum. *Roeper Review, 18,* 98–102.

Wilkerson, I. (February 21, 1990). Class for gifted requires more than brains. *New York Times,* pp. A1, B10.

Yong, F. L., & McIntyre, J. D. (1992). A comparative study of the learning style preferences of students with learning disabilities and students who are gifted. *Journal of Learning Disabilities, 25,* 124–132.

Educational Interventions

Archambault, Jr., F. X., Westberg, K. L., Brown, S. W., Hallmark, B. W., Zhang, W., & Emmons, C. L. (1993). Classroom practices used with gifted third and fourth grade students. *Journal for the Education of the Gifted, 16,* 103–119.

Banks, J. A. (1994). *An introduction to multicultural education.* Boston: Allyn and Bacon.

Bloom, B. S., & Sosniak, L. A. (1981). Talent development vs. schooling. *Educational Leadership, 39,* 86–94.

Clark, B. (1992). *Growing up gifted*. New York: Merrill-Macmillan.

Cornell, D. G., Delcourt, M. A. B., Goldberg, M. D., & Bland, L. C. (1995). Achievement and self-concept of minority students in elementary school gifted programs. *Journal for the Education of the Gifted, 18*, 189–209.

Cox, J., Daniel, N., & Boston, B. (1985). *Educating able learners: Programs and promising practices*. Austin: University of Texas Press.

Davis, G. A., & Rimm, S. B. (1994). *Education of the gifted and talented* (2nd ed.). Englewood Cliffs, NJ: Prentice-Hall.

Feldhusen, J., & Robinson, A. (1986). The Purdue secondary model for gifted and talented youth. In J. S. Renzulli (Ed.), *Systems and models for developing programs for the gifted and talented* (pp. 153–178). Mansfield Center, CT: Creative Learning Press.

Gallagher, J. J. (1996). A critique of critiques of gifted education. *Journal for the Education of the Gifted, 19*, 234–249.

Gallagher, J. J., & Gallagher, S. A. (1994). *Teaching the gifted child* (4th ed.). Boston: Allyn and Bacon.

Gallagher, J. J., Weiss, P., Oglesby, K., & Thomas, T. (1983). *The status of gifted/talented education: United States survey of needs, practices, and policies*. Ventura, CA: Ventura County Superintendent of Schools Office.

Goertzel, V., & Goertzel, M. G. (1962). *Cradles of eminence*. Boston: Little, Brown.

Gray, B. B. (December 26, 1991). Enrollment up in program for high achievers. *Los Angeles Times*, Valley View, p. E7.

Hirsch, S. P. (1979). *Young, gifted, and handicapped: Mainstreaming high-potential handicapped students into the Executive High School Internship Program*. Washington, DC: U.S. Office of Education.

Hobson v. Hansen, 269 F. Supp. 401 (D. D. C. 1967), affirmed subnom. Smuck v. Hobson, 408 F. 2d 175 (DC Cir 1969).

Hughes, H. H., & Converse, H. D. (1962). Characteristics of the gifted: A case for a sequel to Terman's study. *Exceptional Children, 29*, 179–183.

Karnes, M. B., Shwedel, A. M., & Linnemeyer, S. A. (1982). The young gifted/talented child: Programs at the University of Illinois. *Elementary School Journal, 82*, 196–213.

Kolloff, P. B. (1997). Special residential high schools. In N. Colangelo and G. A. Davis (Eds.), *Handbook of gifted education* (2nd ed., pp. 198–206). Boston: Allyn and Bacon.

Kulik, J. A., & Kulik, C. -L. C. (1997). Ability grouping. In N. Colangelo and G. A. Davis (Eds.), *Handbook of gifted education* (2nd ed., pp. 230–242). Boston: Allyn and Bacon.

Lewis, M., & Louis, B. (1991). Young gifted children. In N. Colangelo and G. A. Davis (Eds.), *Handbook of gifted education* (pp. 365–381). Boston: Allyn and Bacon.

Maker, C. J. (Ed.). (1993). *Critical issues in gifted education*. Austin, TX: Pro-Ed.

McBride-Chang, C., Manis, F. R., & Wagner, R. K. (1996). Correlates of phonological awareness: Implications for gifted education. *Roeper Review, 19*, 27–30.

McDaniel, T. R. (1993). Education of the gifted and the excellence-equity debate: Lessons from history. In C. J. Maker (Ed.), *Critical issues in gifted education: Programs for the gifted in regular classrooms* (pp. 6–18). Austin, TX: Pro-Ed.

McDowell, L. (1989). *Prepackaged program experimentation assignment*. Unpublished manuscript, University of New Mexico, Albuquerque.

Oden, M. H. (1968). The fulfillment of promise: 40-year follow-up of the Terman gifted group. *Genetic Psychology Monographs, 77*, 3–93.

Pendarvis, E., & Howley, A. (1996). Playing fair: The possibilities of gifted education. *Journal for the Education of the Gifted, 19*, 215–233.

Reis, S. M., & Purcell, J. H. (1993). An analysis of content elimination and strategies used by elementary classroom teachers in the curriculum compacting process. *Journal for the Education of the Gifted, 16*, 147–170.

Renzulli, J. S. (1994/1995). Teachers as talent scouts. *Educational Leadership, 52*, 75–81.

Renzulli, J. S., & Reis, S. M. (1997). The schoolwide enrichment model: New directions for developing high-end learning. In N. Colangelo and G. A. Davis (Eds.), *Handbook of gifted education* (2nd ed., pp. 136–154). Boston: Allyn and Bacon.

Sapon-Shevin, M. (1996). Beyond gifted education: Building a shared agenda for school reform. *Journal for the Education of the Gifted, 19*, 192–214.

Scheidemann, N. V. (1931). *The psychology of exceptional children*. New York: Houghton Mifflin.

Schiever, S. W., & Maker, C. J. (1991). Enrichment and acceleration: An overview and new directions. In N. Colangelo and G. A. Davis (Eds.), *Handbook of gifted education* (pp. 99–110). Boston: Allyn and Bacon.

Schneider, B. H., & Daniels, T. (1992). Peer acceptance and social play of gifted kindergarten children. *Exceptionality, 3*, 17–29.

Sisk, D. (1987). *Creative teaching of the gifted*. New York: McGraw-Hill.

Slavin, R. E. (1990). Ability grouping, cooperative learning and the gifted. *Journal for the Education of the Gifted, 14*, 3–8.

Sommerfeld, M. (April 29, 1992). B. U. to open accelerated high school for gifted students. *Education Week*, p. 5.

Southern, W. T., & Jones, E. D. (1991). *The academic acceleration of gifted children*. New York: Teachers College Press.

Subotnik, R. F., & Arnold, K. D. (1994). *Beyond Terman: Contemporary longitudinal studies of giftedness and talent.* Norwood, NJ: Ablex.

Terman, L. (1925). *Genetic studies of genius* (Vol. 1). Stanford, CA: Stanford University Press.

Terman, L. M., & Oden, M. H. (1959). *The gifted group at midlife.* Stanford, CA: Stanford University Press.

Torrance, E. P. (1972). Career patterns and peak creative achievements of creative high school students twelve years later. The *Gifted Child Quarterly, 16,* 75–88.

Torrance, E. P., & Torrance, J. P. (1978). Future problem solving: National interscholastic competition and curriculum project. *Journal of Creative Behavior, 12,* 87–89.

Treffinger, D. J. (1986). Fostering effective, independent learning through individualized programming. In J. S. Renzulli (Ed.), *Systems and models for developing programs for the gifted and talented* (pp. 429–460). Mansfield Center, CT: Creative Learning Press.

Van Tassel-Baska, J. (1992). *Planning effective curriculum for gifted learners.* Denver: Love.

VanTassel-Baska, J. (1995). The development of talent through curriculum. *Roeper Review, 18,* 98–102.

Walsh, M. (June 19, 1991). College-credit law for high-school students assailed. *Education Week,* p. 21.

Wernick, S. (July 8, 1992). *Interest renewed in grade skipping as inexpensive way to aid the gifted.* New York Times (Education), p. B7.

Yong, F. L., & McIntyre, J. D. (1992). A comparative study of the learning style preferences of students with learning disabilities and students who are gifted. *Journal of Learning Disabilities, 25,* 124–132.

Yewchuk, C. R. (1995). The "mad genius" controversy: Implications for gifted education. *Journal for the Education of the Gifted, 19,* 3–29.

Families

Albert, R. S. (1991). People, processes, and developmental paths to eminence: A developmental-interactional model. In R. M. Milgram (Ed.), *Genius and eminence* (pp. 19–35). NY: Pergamon.

Davis, G. A., & Rimm, S. B. (1994). *Education of the gifted and talented* (2nd ed.). Englewood Cliffs, NJ: Prentice-Hall.

Dickens, M. N., & Cornell, D. G. (1993). Parent influences on the mathematics self-concept of high ability and adolescent girls. *Journal for the Education of the Gifted, 17,* 53–73.

Subotnik, R., Kassan, L., Summers, E., & Wasser, A. (1993). *Genius revisited: High IQ children grow up.* Norwood, NJ: Ablex Publishing.

Yewchuk, C. R. (1995). The "mad genius" controversy: Implications for gifted education. *Journal for the Education of the Gifted, 19,* 3–29.

Technology

McBride, R. O., & Lewis, G. (1993). Sharing the resources: Electronic outreach programs. *Journal for the Education of the Gifted, 16,* 372–386.

Morgan, T. D. (1993). Technology: An essential tool for gifted and talented education. *Journal for the Education of the Gifted, 16,* 358–371.

Concepts and Controversy

Banks, J. A. (1994). *An introduction to multicultural education.* Boston: Allyn and Bacon.

Callahan, C. M., & McIntire, J. A. (1994). *Identifying outstanding talent in American Indian and Alaska Native students.* Washington, DC: U.S. Department of Education, Office of Educational Research and Improvement.

Coleman, M. R., & Gallagher, J. J. (1994). *Report on states' policies related to the identification of gifted students.* Chapel Hill: Gifted Education Policy Studies Program.

Harry, B. (1994). *The disproportionate representation of minority students in special education: Theories and recommendations.* Alexandria, VA: National Association of State Directors of Special Education.

Maker, C. J., Nielson, A. B., & Rogers, J. A. (1994). Giftedness, diversity and problem solving. *Teaching Exceptional Children, 27,* 4–19.

U.S. Department of Education. (1993). *Fifteenth annual report to Congress on the implementation of the Individuals with Disabilities Education Act.* Washington, DC: U.S. Government Printing Office.

CHAPTER 8: BEHAVIORAL DISORDERS AND EMOTIONAL DISTURBANCE

Art

Bischoff, U. (1988). *Edvard Munch: 1863–1944.* Köln, Germany: Benedikt Taschen Verlag GmbH & Co.

Grolier. (1993). *The new Grolier multimedia encyclopedia.* Danbury, CT: Grolier Electronic Publishing.

Messer, T. M. (1985). *Munch.* New York: Harry N. Abrams.

Behavior Disorders and Emotional Disturbance Defined

Ahearn, E. (Ed.). (February 1995). Summary of the 16th annual report to Congress on special education. *Liaison Bulletin,* pp. 1–3. Alexandria: NASDSE.

American Psychiatric Association. (1994). *Diagnostic and statistical manual of mental disorders (DSM-IV)*

(4th ed.), edited by C. Reinburg. Washington, DC: Author.

Bower, E. M. (1960). *Early identification of emotionally disturbed children in school* (rev. ed.). Springfield, IL: Thomas.

Bower, E. M. (1982). Defining emotional disturbance: Public policy and research. *Psychology in the Schools, 19,* 55–60.

Forness, S. R., & Knitzer, J. (1992). A new proposed definition and terminology to replace "serious emotional disturbance" in IDEA. *School Psychology Review, 21,* 12–20.

George, N. L., George, M. P., Gersten, R., & Grosenick, J. K. (1995). To leave or to stay? An exploratory study of teachers of students with emotional and behavioral disorders. *Remedial and Special Education, 16,* 227–236.

Hallahan, D. P., & Kauffman, J. M. (1997). *Exceptional children: Introduction to special education* (7th ed.). Boston: Allyn and Bacon.

Kauffman, J. M. (1997). *Characteristics of behavioral disorders of children and youth* (6th ed.). Columbus, OH: Merrill.

Koyanagi, C., & Gaines, S. (1993). *All systems failure.* Alexandria, VA: National Mental Health Association.

Landrum, T. J., Singh, N. N., Nemil, M. S., Ellis, C. R., & Best, A. M. (1995). Characteristics of children and adolescents with serious emotional disturbance in systems of care. Part II: Community-based services. *Journal of Emotional and Behavioral Disorders, 3,* 141–149.

Newcomer, P. L. (1993). *Understanding and teaching emotionally disturbed children and adolescents* (2nd ed.). Austin, TX: Pro-Ed.

Oswald, D. P., & Coutinho, M. J. (1996a). Identification and placement of students with serious emotional disturbance. Part I: Correlates of state child-count data. *Journal of Emotional and Behavioral Disorders, 3,* 224–229.

U.S. Department of Education. (1992). Assistance to states for the education of children with disabilities program and preschool grants for children with disabilities, final rule. *Federal Register, 34* CRF Parts 300 and 301.

U.S. Department of Education. (1994). *Sixteenth annual report to Congress on the implementation of the Individuals with Disabilities Education Act.* Washington, DC: U.S. Government Printing Office.

Walker, H. M., & Severson, H. H., Nicholson, F., Kehle, T., Jenson, W. R., & Clark, E. (1994). Replication of the systematic screening of behavior disorders (SSBD) procedure for the identification of at-risk children. *Journal of Emotional and Behavioral Disorders, 2,* 66–77.

History
Bower, E. M., & Lambert, N. M. (1962). *A process for in-school screening of children with emotional handicaps.* Princeton, NJ: Educational Testing Service.

Brigham, A. (1847). The moral treatment of insanity. *American Journal of Insanity, 4,* 1–15.

Deutsch, A. (1949). *The mentally ill in America: A history of their care and treatment from colonial times* (2nd ed.). New York: Columbia University Press.

Haring, N. J., & Phillips, E. L. (1962). *Educating emotionally disturbed children.* New York: McGraw-Hill.

Healy, W., & Bronner, A. F. (1926). *Delinquents and criminals: Their making and unmaking.* New York: Macmillan.

Hobbs, N. (1966). Helping disturbed children: Psychological and ecological strategies. *American Psychologist, 21,* 1105–1115.

Koyanagi, C., & Gaines, S. (1993). *All systems failure.* Alexandria, VA: National Mental Health Association.

Safford, P. L., & Safford, E. J. (1996). *A history of childhood and disability.* New York: Teachers College Press.

Prevalence
Kauffman, J. M. (1997). *Characteristics of behavioral disorders of children and youth* (5th ed.). Columbus, OH: Merrill.

Oswald, D. P., & Coutinho, M. J. (1996a). Identification and placement of students with serious emotional disturbance. Part I: Correlates of state child-count data. *Journal of Emotional and Behavioral Disorders, 3,* 224–229.

Peterson, R. L., & Ishii-Jordon, S. (Eds.). (1994). *Multicultural issues in the education of students with behavioral disorders.* Cambridge, MA: Brookline.

U.S. Department of Education. (1994). *Sixteenth annual report to Congress on the implementation of the Individuals with Disabilities Education Act.* Washington, DC: U.S. Government Printing Office.

Causes and Prevention
Ahearn, E. (Ed.) (February 1995). Summary of the 16th annual report to Congress on special education. *Liaison Bulletin,* pp. 1–3. Alexandria: NASDSE.

American Psychiatric Association. (1994). *Diagnostic and statistical manual of mental disorders (DSM-IV)* (4th ed.), edited by C. Reinburg. Washington, DC: Author.

Children's Defense Fund. (1995). *The state of America's children: Yearbook 1995,* edited by B. Finlay. Washington, DC: Author.

Hallahan, D. P., & Kauffman, J. M. (1997). *Exceptional children: Introduction to special education* (7th ed.). Boston: Allyn and Bacon.

Rivera, D. P., & Smith, D. D. (1997). *Teaching students with learning and behavior problems.* Boston: Allyn and Bacon.

Smith, D. D., and Rivera, D. P. (1993). *Effective discipline.* Austin: Pro-Ed.

Tobin, T., Sugai, G., & Colvin, G. (1996). Patterns in middle school discipline records. *Journal of Emotional and Behavioral Disorders, 4,* 82–94.

Werner, E. E., & Smith, R. S. (1992). *Overcoming the odds: High risk children from birth to adulthood.* Ithaca, NY: Cornell University Press.

Children with Behavior Disorders and Emotional Disturbance

Day, D. M., & Hunt, A. C. (1996). A multivariate assessment of a risk model for juvenile delinquency with an "under 12 offender" sample. *Journal of Emotional and Behavioral Disorders, 4,* 66–72.

Hackett, David (Ed.) (December 31, 1995a). New national pool finds majority of young children fear they might die young; Youth exposed to serious health and safety threats. *Youth Record, 7,* 1–2.

Hackett, David (Ed.). (September 15, 1995b) Gangs and victimization at school, *Youth Record, 7,* 1–2.

Kauffman, J. M. (1997). *Characteristics of behavioral disorders of children and youth* (6th ed.). Columbus, OH: Merrill.

Locke, W. R., & Fuchs, L. S. (1995). Effects of peer-mediated reading instruction on the on-task behavior and social interaction of children with behavior disorders. *Journal of Emotional and Behavioral Disorders, 3,* 92–99.

Montgomery, L. (April 11, 1996). Age of youths on crime path sounds alarm. *Albuquerque Journal,* pp. A1–A2.

Safran, S. P. (1995). Peers' perceptions of emotional and behavioral disorders: What are students thinking? *Journal of Emotional and Behavioral Disorders, 3,* 66–75.

Walker, H. M., Schwarz, I. E., Nippold, M. A., Irvin, L. K. & Noell, J. W. (1994). Social skills in school-age children and youth: Issues and best practices in assessment and intervention. *Topics in Language Disorders, 14,* 70–82.

Walker, H. M. & Sylvester, R. (1994). Where is school along the path to prison? *The Frontline, 1,* 3–6.

Educational Interventions

Cheney, D., & Barringer, C. (1995). Teacher competence, student diversity, and staff training for the inclusion of middle school students with emotional and behavioral disorders. *Journal of Emotional and Behavioral Disorders, 3,* 174–182.

Chesapeake Institute. (1994). *National agenda for achieving better results for children and youth with serious emotional disturbance.* Washington, DC: U.S. Department of Education Office of Special Education Programs.

Coutinho, M. J., & Oswald, D. (1996b). Identification and placement of students with serious emotional disturbance. Part II: Nation and state trends in the implementation of LRE. *Journal of Emotional and Behavioral Disorders, 4,* 40–52.

Evans, E. D., & Richardson, R. C. (1995). Corporal punishment: What teachers should know. *Teaching Exceptional Children, 27,* 33–36.

Feil, E. G., Walker, H. M., & Severson, H. H. (1995). The early screening project for young children with behavior problems. *Journal of Emotional and Behavioral Disorders, 3,* 194–202.

Frank, A. R., Sitlington, P. L., & Carson, R. R. (1995). Young adults with behavioral disorders: A comparison with peers with mild disabilities. *Journal of Emotional and Behavioral Disorders, 3,* 156–164.

Hallenbeck, B. A., & Kauffman, J. M. (1995). How does observational learning affect the behavior of students with emotional or behavioral disorders? A review of research. The *Journal of Special Education, 29,* 45–71.

Martin, J. E,, & Marshall, L. H. (1995). Choicemaker: A comprehensive self-determination transition program. *Intervention in School and Clinic, 30,* 147–156.

Nelson, C. M., Rutherford, R. B., & Wolford, B. I. (1987). *Special education in the criminal justice system.* Columbus, OH: Merrill.

Nelson, J. R., Johnson, A., & Marchand-Martella, N. (1996). Effects of direct instruction, cooperative learning, and independent learning practices on the classroom behavior of students with behavioral disorders: A comparative analysis. *Journal of Emotional and Behavioral Disorders, 4,* 53–62.

Repp, A. C., and Deitz, D. E. (1978). On the selective use of punishment—Suggested guidelines for administrators. *Mental Retardation, 16,* 250–254.

Smith, D. D., & Rivera, D. P. (1993). *Effective discipline* (2nd ed.). Austin: Pro-Ed.

Serna, L. A., & Lau-Smith, J. (1995). Learning with purpose: Self-determination skills for students who are at risk for school and community failure. *Intervention in School and Clinic, 30,* 142–146.

Voyles, Linda (Ed.). (June 1994) CEC guides Congress on school discipline. *CEC Today, 1,* 1–3, 22.

Walker, H. M., Colvin, G., & Ramsey, E. (1995). *Antisocial behavior in school: Strategies and best practices.* Pacific Grove, CA: Brooks/Cole.

Wall, M. E., & Dattilo, J. (1995). Creating option-rich learning environments: Facilitating self-determination. The *Journal of Special Education, 29,* 276–294.

Families

Ahearn, E. (Ed.). (February 1995). Summary of the 16th annual report to Congress on special education. *Liaison Bulletin,* pp. 1–3. Alexandria: NASDSE.

Children's Defense Fund. (1995). *The state of America's children: Yearbook 1995,* edited by B. Finlay. Washington, DC: Author.

Children's Defense Fund. (1996). *The state of America's children: Yearbook 1996,* edited by B. Finlay. Washington, DC.

Koroloff, N. M., Elliott, D. J., Koren, P. E., & Friesen, B. J. (1996). Linking low-income families to children's mental health services: An outcome study. *Journal of Emotional and Behavioral Disorders, 4,* 2–11.

Sherman, A. (1994). *Wasting America's future: The Children's Defense Fund report on the costs of child poverty.* Boston: Beacon Press.

Smucker, K. S., Kauffman, J. M., & Ball, D. W. (1996). School-related problems of special education foster-care students with emotional or behavioral disorders: A comparison to other groups. *Journal of Emotional and Behavioral Disorders, 4,* 30–39.

Technology
Rivera, D. P., & Smith, D. D. (1997). *Teaching students with learning and behavior problems* (3rd ed.). Boston: Allyn and Bacon.

Concepts and Controversy
Armstrong, T. (1995). *The myth of the ADD child.* New York: Dutton.

Carpenter, R. L., & Sells, C. J. (1974). Measuring effects of psychoactive medication in a child with a learning disability. *Journal of Learning Disabilities, 7,* 545–550.

Hancock, L. N. (March 18, 1996). Mother's little helper. *Newsweek,* pp. 51–56.

Hoff, David (Ed.). (February 10, 1993). Research: Drugs don't help ADD students learn. *Special Education Report, 19,* pp. 1–2.

Landrum, T. J., Singh, N. N., Nemil, M. S., Ellis, C. R., & Best, A. M. (1995). Characteristics of children and adolescents with serious emotional disturbance in systems of care. Part II: Community-based services. *Journal of Emotional and Behavioral Disorders, 3,* 141–149.

Sulzbacher, S. I. (1972). Behavior analysis of drug effects in the classroom. In G. Semb (Ed.), *Behavior analysis and education—1972* (pp. 37–52). Lawrence: The University of Kansas Support and Development Center for Follow Through.

CHAPTER 9: PHYSICAL IMPAIRMENTS AND SPECIAL HEALTH CARE NEEDS

Art
Horgan, P. (1994). *The artifice of blue light: Henriette Wyeth.* Santa Fe: Museum of New Mexico.

Physical Impairments and Special Health Care Needs Defined
Altman, L. K. (May 4, 1993). Rise in asthma deaths is tied to ignorance of many physicians. *New York Times,* p. B8.

Barry, J. (December 13, 1994). Disabled model makes comeback—a step at a time. *Albuquerque Journal,* p. B4.

Best, S. J., Bigge, J. L., & Sirvis, B. P. (1994). Physical and health impairments. In N. G. Haring, L. McCormick, and T. G. Haring, *Exceptional children and youth* (6th ed., pp. 300–341). New York: Macmillan College Publishing.

Briand, X. (Ed.). (December 13, 1995). OCR letters tackles access, bias for disabled students. *Special Education Report, 21,* 1–2.

Epilepsy Foundation of America. (1994a). *Epilepsy: Questions and Answers.* Landover, MD: Author.

Epilepsy Foundation of America. (1994b). *Seizure recognition and first aid.* Landover, MD: Author.

Farrell, M. A. (December 13, 1994). Disabled comics tell audience: It's OK to laugh. *Albuquerque Journal,* p. B5.

Hallahan, D. P., & Kauffman, J. M. (1994). *Exceptional children: Introduction to special education* (6th ed.). Boston: Allyn and Bacon.

Heller, K. W., Alberto, P. A., Forney, P. E., & Schwartzman, M. N. (1996). *Understanding physical, sensory, & health impairments.* Pacific Grove: Brooks/Cole.

Neergaard, L. (July 11, 1995). Safer polio vaccines raise fears of new epidemics. *Albuquerque Journal,* pp. A1, A5.

Ponchillia, S. V. (1993). The effect of cultural beliefs on the treatment of native peoples with diabetes and visual impairment. *Journal of Visual Impairment and Blindness, 87,* 333–335.

Samuels, R. (April 2, 1995). South beach access: Miami offers disabled visitors a variety of activities. *Albuquerque Journal* (Travel), p. C1.

Sirvis, B. P., & Caldwell, T. H. (1995). Physical disabilities and chronic health impairments. In E. L. Meyen and T. M. Skrtic (Eds.), *Special education and student disability: An introduction* (4th ed., pp. 533–564). Denver: Love.

Taylor, J. M., & Taylor, W. S. (1989). *Communicable disease and young children in group settings.* Boston: College-Hill.

United Cerebral Palsy Associations. (1993). *Cerebral palsy—Facts and figures.* Washington, DC: Author.

Urbano, M. T. (1992). *Preschool children with special health care needs.* San Diego: Singular Press.

U.S. Department of Education (1992). Assistance to states for the education of children with disabilities program and preschool grants for children with disabilities; final rule. *Federal Register,* 34 CRF Parts 300 and 301.

Woods, E. (May 14, 1994). Spirit of the game. *Albuquerque Tribune* (Lifetimes), p. C1.

History
Dolch, E. W. (1948). *Helping handicapped children in school.* Champaign, IL: Garrard Press.

Eberle, L. (August 1922). The maimed, the halt and the race. Hospital Social Service, 6, 59–63. Reprinted in R. H. Bremner (Ed.), *Children and youth in America, A documentary history: Vol. II, 1866–1932* (pp. 1026–1928). Cambridge, MA: Harvard University Press.

Frayer, D. W., Horton, W. A., Macchiarelli, R., & Mussi, M. (November 5, 1987). Dwarfism in an adolescent from the Italian late Upper Palaeolithic. *Nature, 330,* 60–61.

Heller, K. W., Alberto, P. A., Forney, P. E., & Schwartzman, M. N. (1996). *Understanding physical, sensory, & health impairments.* Pacific Grove: Brooks/Cole.

Kriegel, L. (1969). Uncle Tom and Tiny Tim: Some reflections on the cripple as Negro. *American Scholar, 38*(3), 412–430.

La Vor, M. L. (1976). Federal legislation for exceptional persons: A history. In F. J. Weintraub, A. Abeson, J. Ballard, and M. L. La Vor (Eds.), *Public policy and the education of exceptional children* (pp. 96–111). Reston, VA: Council for Exceptional Children.

Maddox, S. (Ed.). (1987). *Spinal network: The total resource for the wheelchair community.* Boulder, CO: Author.

Scheerenberger, R. C. (1983). *A history of mental retardation.* Baltimore: Brookes.

Shaw, B. (May/June 1995). Ed Roberts: 1939–1995. *Disability Rag,* p. 25.

Stone, K. G. (March 19, 1995). Disability rights pioneer inspired his community. *Albuquerque Journal,* p. C6.

Winzer, M. A. (1993). *The history of special education: From isolation to integration.* Washington, DC: Gallaudet University.

Prevalence

Epilepsy Education Department of Neurology University of Minnesota. (1993). *Epilepsy: Medical aspects.* Landover, MD: Author.

Heller, K. W., Alberto, P. A., Forney, P. E., & Schwartzman, M. N. (1996). *Understanding physical, sensory, & health impairments.* Pacific Grove: Brooks/Cole.

Kuban, K. C. K. & Leviton, A. (1994). Cerebral palsy. *New England Journal of Medicine, 330,* 188–195.

Lesar, S., Gerber, M. M., & Semmel, M. I. (1995). The HIV infection in children: Family stress, social support, and adaptation, *Exceptional Children, 62,* 224–236.

March of Dimes. (1992). *Spina bifida: Public health education information sheet.* White Plains, NY: Author.

Rowley-Kelly, F. L., & Reigel, D. H. (1993). *Teaching the student with spina bifida.* Baltimore: Paul H. Brookes.

United Cerebral Palsy Associations. (1993). *Cerebral palsy—Facts and figures.* Washington, DC: Author.

U.S. Department of Education. (1996). *Eighteenth annual report to Congress on the implementation of the Individuals with Disabilities Education Act.* Washington, DC: U.S. Government Printing Office.

Causes and Prevention

Albuquerque Journal. (January 16, 1995a). Guidelines for childhood vaccinations (Health), p. B1.

Albuquerque Journal. (July 15, 1995b). Measles exposure spread to three counties, p. A2.

Associated Press (January 9, 1991). Panel urges measles-vaccination fund boost. *Albuquerque Journal,* p. D10.

Charney, E. B. (1992). Neural tube defects: Spina bifida and myelomeningocele. In M. L. Batshaw and Y. M. Perret, (Eds.), *Children with disabilities: A medical primer* (pp. 471–488). Baltimore: Paul H. Brookes.

Epilepsy Foundation of America. (1992). *Children and epilepsy: The teacher's role.* Landover, MD: Author.

Epilepsy Foundation of America. (1994a). *Epilepsy: Questions and answers.* Landover, MD: Author.

Epilepsy Foundation of America. (1994b). *Seizure recognition and first aid.* Landover, MD: Author.

Epilepsy Foundation of America. (1995). *Epilepsy: Part of your life.* Landover, MD: Author.

Finlay, B. (May 1995). Service clubs promote immunizations. Children's Defense Fund, *CDF Reports, 16,* 13.

Heller, K. W., Alberto, P. A., Forney, P. E., & Schwartzman, M. N. (1996). *Understanding physical, sensory, & health impairments.* Pacific Grove: Brooks/Cole.

Kelker, K., Hecimovic, A., & LeRoy, D. H. (1994). Designing a classroom and school environment for students with AIDS: A checklist for teachers. *Teaching Exceptional Children, 26,* 52–53.

Lerro, M. (1994). Teaching adolescents about AIDS. *Teaching Exceptional Children, 26,* 49–51.

Neergaard, L. (July 11, 1995). Safer polio vaccines raise fears of new epidemics. *Albuquerque Journal,* pp. A1, A5.

Rapport, M. J. K. (1996). Legal guidelines for the delivery of special health care services in schools. *Exceptional Children, 62,* 537–549.

Children with Physical Impairments and Special Health Care Needs

Crump, I. (Ed.). (1987). *Nutrition and feeding of the handicapped child.* Boston: College-Hill/Little, Brown.

Prendergast, D. E. (1995). Preparing for children who are medically fragile in educational programs. *Teaching Exceptional Children, 27,* 37–41.

Sirvis, B. P., & Caldwell, T. H. (1995). Physical disabilities and chronic health impairments. In E. L. Meyen and T. M. Skrtic (Eds.), *Special education and student disability: An introduction* (4th ed., pp. 533–564). Denver: Love.

Educational Interventions

Associated Press. (June 23, 1995). 13-year-old has no hands, good glove. *Albuquerque Journal*, p. C1.

Campbell, P. H. (1987a). Physical management and handling procedures with students with movement dysfunction. In M. E. Snell (Ed.), *Systematic instruction of persons with severe handicaps* (3rd ed., pp. 174–187). Columbus, OH: Merrill.

Campbell, P. H. (1987b). Programming for students with dysfunction in posture and movement. In M. E. Snell (Ed.), *Systematic instruction of persons with severe handicaps* (3rd ed., pp. 188–211). Columbus, OH: Merrill.

Ferrer, S. H. (1996). Monkeys give helping hand to paralyzed. *Albuquerque Journal* (Health), p. A8.

Hannaway, P. (1992). *Asthma self-help book: How to live a normal life inspite of the condition*. Rocklin, CA: Prima.

Koltick, J. C. (December 25/January 1, 1995/1996). Christopher Reeve. *People*, pp. 52–53.

Krementz, J. (1989). *How it feels to fight for your life*. Boston: Joy Street/Little, Brown.

Orelove, F. P., & Sobsey, D. (1987). *Educating children with multiple disabilities: A transdisciplinary approach*. Baltimore: Brookes.

Sandler, A. (1989) Learning by design: The AIA elementary and secondary education program. *Art Education, 42*, 13–16.

Schultz, T. (December 29, 1994). DC guard doesn't "think twice" about having an underdeveloped arm. *USA Today*, p. C8.

Smith, L. (June 1996). We draw strength from each other. *Good Housekeeping Magazine*, pp. 86–89, 172.

Taylor, A. (1990). The place of design education in art education. *Design for Arts in Education, 43*, 22–28.

Taylor, A., & Warden, M. G. (1994). Learning environments for the twenty-first century. *Curriculum in Context, 22*, 12–14.

Urbano, M. T. (1992). *Preschool children with special health care needs*. San Diego: Singular Press.

U.S. Department of Education. (1996). *Eighteenth annual report to Congress on the implementation of the Individuals with Disabilities Education Act*. Washington, DC: U.S. Government Printing Office.

Woods, E. (May 14, 1994). Spirit of the game. *Albuquerque Tribune* (Lifetimes), p. C1.

Families

Davis, H. (1983). *Counseling parents of children with chronic illness or disability*. Baltimore: Brookes.

Martin, S. S., Brady, M. P., & Kotarba, J. A. (1992). Families with chronically ill young children: The unsinkable family. *Remedial and Special Education, 13*, 6–15.

Smith, P. M. (1993). You are not alone: For parents when they learn that their child has a disability. *NICHCY News Digest, 3*, 1–15.

Technology

Maddox, S. (Ed.). (1987). *Spinal network: The total resource for the wheelchair community*. Boulder, CO: Author.

Ramstad, E. (April 2, 1995). High tech helps engineer work despite his disease. *Albuquerque Journal*, p. E15.

Weiss, K. E., & Dykes, M. K. (1995). Legal issues in special education: Assistive technology and support services. *Physical Disabilities: Education and Related Services 11*, 1, 29–36.

Concepts and Controversy

U.S. Department of Education. (1995). *Seventeenth annual report to Congress on the implementation of the Individuals with Disabilities Education Act*. Washington, DC: U.S. Government Printing Office.

CHAPTER 10: DEAFNESS AND HARD OF HEARING

Deafness and Hard of Hearing–Art

Hignett, S. (1983). *Brett from Bloomsbury to New Mexico: A biography*. New York: Franklin Watts.

Deafness and Hard of Hearing Defined

Carlson, N. R. (1994). *Physiology of Behavior* (5th ed.). Boston: Allyn and Bacon.

Leary, W. E. (March 10, 1993). U.S. Panel backs testing all babies to uncover hearing losses early. *New York Times*, p. B7.

Lowenbraun, S. (1995). Hearing impairment. In E. L. Meyen and T. M. Skrtic (Eds.), *Exceptional children and youth: An introduction* (4th ed., pp. 453–486). Denver: Love.

Lowenbraun, S., & Thompson, M. D. (1994). Hearing impairments. In N. G. Haring, L. McCormick, and T. G. Haring (Eds.), *Exceptional children and youth* (6th ed., pp. 378–413). NY: Merrill, an Imprint of Macmillan College Publishing.

Moores, D. F. (1996). *Educating the deaf: Psychology, principles, and practices* (4th ed.). Boston: Houghton Mifflin.

Northern, J. L., & Downs, M. P. (1984). *Hearing in children* (3rd ed.). Los Angeles: Williams & Wilkins.

Schildroth, A., & Hotto, S. (1994). Annual survey of hearing impaired children and youth, 1992–1993. *American Annals of the Deaf, 139*, 239–243.

Wright, G. L. (February 6, 1994). Deaf man free after 68 years in mental ward: N. C. hospital mistook handicap for mental illness. *Albuquerque Journal*, p. A6.

History of the Field

Adams, M. E. (November 1929). 1865–1935: A few memories of Alexander Graham Bell. *American Annals of the Deaf, 74,* 467–479.

Alby, J. F. (Spring 1962). The educational philosophy of Thomas Hopkins Gallaudet. *Buff and Blue,* pp. 17–23.

Gannon, J. R. (1989). *The week the world heard Gallaudet.* Washington, DC: Gallaudet University Press.

Soloman, A. (August 28, 1994). Defiantly deaf. *New York Times Magazine,* pp. 38–45, 64–68.

Winefield, R. (1987). *Never shall the twain meet: The communications debate.* Washington, DC: Gallaudet University Press.

Prevalence

Schildroth, A. N., & Hotto, S. A. (1996). Changes in student and program characteristics, 1984–1985 and 1994–1995. *American Annals of the Deaf, 141,* 68–71.

Soloman, A. (August 28, 1994). Defiantly deaf. *New York Times Magazine,* pp. 38–45, 64–68.

U.S. Department of Education. (1996). *Eighteenth annual report to Congress on the implementation of the Individuals with Disabilities Education Act.* Washington, DC: U.S. Government Printing Office.

Causes and Prevention

Alexander Graham Bell Association for the Deaf. (November 1992). Rhode Island passes breakthrough newborn hearing screening bill. *Newsounds, 17,* 1.

Alexander Graham Bell Association for the Deaf. (April 1993a). NIH panel recommends hearing screening for all newborns. *Newsounds, 18,* 1.

Alexander Graham Bell Association for the Deaf. (June/July 1993b). Successful auditory brainstem implant surgeries performed. *Newsounds, 18,* 1.

Browne, M. W. (May 14, 1992). Noise experts agree: America has become the land of battered eardrums. *New York Times* (National), p. A14.

Fryauf-Bertschy, H., & Gantz, B. J. (1994). Cochlear implants for children: Candidacy and performance results to date. *Shhh Journal, 16,* 20–12, 23

Goldberg, B. (1993). Universal hearing screening of newborns: An idea whose time has come. *ASHA, 35,* 63–64.

Heller, K. W., Alberto, P. A., Forney, P. E., & Schwartzman, M. N. (1996). *Understanding physical, sensory, and health impairments.* Pacific Grove, CA: Brooks/Cole.

Holthouser, M. (October 14, 1994). Can you hear me? *Newsweek,* p. 8.

Hotchkiss, D. (1989). *Demographics of hearing impairment: Questions and answers* (2nd ed.). Washington, DC: Center for Assessment and Demographic Studies, Gallaudet University.

Lane, H. (1995). Construction of deafness. *Disability & Society, 10,* 171–187.

Lowenbraun, S., & Thompson, M. D. (1994). Hearing impairments. In N. G. Haring, L. McCormick, & T. G. Haring (Eds.), *Exceptional children and youth* (6th ed., pp. 378–413). NY: Merrill, an Imprint of Macmillan College Publishing.

Marcotty, J. (May 3, 1996). Sound of silence. *The Salina Journal,* (Health), pp. C1–C2.

Moores, D. F. (1996). *Educating the deaf: Psychology, principles, and practices* (4th ed.). Boston: Houghton Mifflin.

Rosenthal, E. (December 6, 1990). Jarring aerobics linked to inner-ear damage. *New York Times* (National), p. A14.

Schildroth, A. (1993). Causes of hearing impairments from the 1993 Annual Survey of Hearing Impaired Children and Youth. Personal communication.

Schildroth, A. N., & Hotto, S. A. (1996). Changes in student and program characteristics, 1984–1985 and 1994–1995. *American Annals of the Deaf, 141,* 68–71.

Soloman, A. (August 28, 1994). Defiantly deaf. *New York Times* Magazine. pp. 38–45, 64–68.

Tye-Murray, N., Spencer, L., & Woodworth G. G. (1995). Acquisition of speech by children who have prolonged cochlear implant experience. *Journal of Speech and Hearing Research, 38,* 327–337.

Ubell, E. (January 15, 1995). New devices can help you hear. *Parade Magazine,* pp. 14–15.

Children Who Are Deaf or Hard of Hearing

Allen, T. E. (Winter/Spring 1986). A demographic view of deaf students and mainstreaming in the United States. *Research at Gallaudet,* p. 6.

Dolnick, E. (September 1993). Deafness as culture. *Atlantic Monthly.*

Fletcher, R. (1994). On Deaf culture and cultures. *Border Walking, 2,* 2.

Gallaudet Research Institute. (1994). *Working Papers 89–3.* Washington, DC: Gallaudet University.

Goehl, H., & Kaufman, D. K. (1984). Do the effects of adventitious deafness include disordered speech? *Journal of Speech and Hearing Disorders, 49,* 58–64.

Goldberg, B. (1995). Families facing choices: Options for parents of children who are deaf or hard of hearing. *ASHA, 37,* 38–45.

Good, T. L., & Brophy, J. E. (1986). School effects. In M. C. Wittrock (Ed.), *Handbook of research on teaching* (3rd ed.). New York: Macmillan.

Lane, H. (1995). Construction of deafness. *Disability & Society, 10,* 171–187.

Moores, D. F. (1996). *Educating the deaf: Psychology, principles, and practices* (4th ed.). Boston: Houghton Mifflin.

Rieth, H. J., Polsgrove, L., & Semmel, M. I. (1979). Relationship between instructional time and academic achievement: Implications for research and practice. *Education Unlimited, 1,* 53–56.

Soloman, A. (August 28, 1994). Defiantly deaf. *New York Times Magazine,* pp. 38–45, 64–68.

Wolk, S., & Schildroth, A. N. (1986). Deaf children and speech intelligibility: A national study. In A. N. Schildroth and M. A. Karchmer (Eds.), *Deaf children in America* (pp. 139–159). Austin, TX: Pro-Ed.

Educational Interventions

Allen, R. E., Rawlings, B. W., & Schildroth, A. N. (1989). *Deaf students and the school-to-work transition.* Baltimore: Brookes.

Associated Press. (August 27, 1994). Driver charged after deaf man cut in dispute. *Albuquerque Journal,* p. A2.

Ayres, B. D., Jr. (December 18, 1990). College carries standard in revolution for the deaf. *New York Times* (National), p. A14.

Cardenas, J. (April 5, 1996). Magnet: Deaf and hearing students together. *The Los Angeles Times Valley,* pp. B1, B6–B7.

Cohen, O. P. (1994). Introduction. In R. C. Johnson and O. P. Cole (Eds.), *Implications and complications for Deaf students of the full inclusion movement* (pp. 1–6). Washington, DC: Gallaudet Research Institute, Gallaudet University.

Counterpoint. (Summer 1992). Deaf students invited to eye their futures, p. 17.

Dolnick, E. (September 1993). Deafness as culture. *Atlantic Monthly.*

Flexer, C., Wray, D., Millin, J., & Leavitt, R. (1993). Mainstreamed college students with hearing loss: Comparison of receptive vocabulary to peers with normal hearing. *The Volta Review, 95,* 125–133.

Forbath, P. (October 29, 1990). Disabled workers struggling to find acceptance. *Albuquerque Journal* (Business Outlook), p. 7.

Harvey, S. (1993). Executive corner: Full inclusion movement may restrict choices. *The Endeavor, 2,* 1, 12.

Hawkins, L. (1993). Opinion: full inclusion or isolation? *The Endeavor, 2,* 7.

Jacobs, L. M. (1989). *A deaf adult speaks out* (3rd ed.). Washington, DC: Gallaudet College Press.

Johnson, R. C., & Cohen, O. P. (1994). *Implications and complications for Deaf students of the full inclusion movement.* Washington, DC: Gallaudet Research Institute, Gallaudet University.

Lane, H. (1995). Construction of deafness. *Disability & Society, 10,* 171–187.

Lee, D., & Antia, S. (1992). A sociological approach to the social integration of hearing-impaired and normally hearing students. *The Volta Review, 95,* 425–434.

Lowenbraun, S. (1992). *Secondary education interviews: Hearing impaired.* Unpublished report, High School Curriculum Project, University of Washington, Seattle.

Lowenbraun, S. (1995). Hearing impairment. In E. L. Meyen and T. M. Skrtic (Eds.), *Exceptional children and youth: An introduction* (4th ed., pp. 453–486). Denver: Love.

McIntire, M. (1994). *The acquisition of American Sign Language by Deaf children.* Burtonsville, MD: Linstok Press.

Mahshie, S. N. (1995). *Educating Deaf children bilingually.* Washington, DC: Gallaudet University.

Manning A., & Briggs, R. W. (September 19, 1994). Miss America, proud sign for the deaf world. *USA Today* (Life), p. D1.

Marschark, M. (1993). *Psychological development of deaf children.* NY: University of Oxford Press.

Matlin, M. (July 15, 1995). The real "handicap" of deafness is attitude. *The Los Angeles Times* (Ann Landers), p. E7.

Maurer, R. (1995). Signs for the times. *Quantum, 12,* 6–8.

Moores, D. F. (1996). *Educating the deaf: Psychology, principles, and practices* (4th ed.). Boston: Houghton Mifflin.

Paul, P. V., & Quigley, S. P. (1994). American Sign Language—English bilingual education. In P. L. McAnally, S. Rose, and S. P. Quigley (Eds.), *Language learning practices with deaf children* (2nd ed., pp. 219–254). Austin, TX: Pro-Ed.

Quintanilla, R. (October 31, 1994). Miss deaf America serves as advocate. *Albuquerque Journal* (Health), p. D2.

Rasing, E. J., & Duker, P. C. (1992). Effects of a multifaceted training procedure on the acquisition and generalization of social behaviors in language-disabled deaf children. *Journal of Applied Behavior Analysis, 25,* 723–734.

Rawlings, B. W., Karchmer, M. A., & DeCaro, J. J. (1987). Postsecondary programs for deaf students at the peak of the rubella bulge. *American Annals for the Deaf, 132,* 36–42.

Rawlings, B. W., Karchmer, M. A., DeCaro, J. J., & Allen, T. E. (1995). *College & career programs for deaf students* (9th ed.). Washington, DC and Rochester, NY: Gallaudet University and National Technical Institute for the Deaf.

Rawlings, B. W., & King, S. J. (1986). Postsecondary educational opportunities for deaf students. In A. N. Schildroth and M. A. Karchmer (Eds.), *Deaf children in America* (pp. 231–257). Austin, TX: Pro-Ed.

Rawlings, B., King, S., Skilton, J., & Rose, D. (1993). *Gallaudet University Alumni Survey, 1993.* Washington, DC:

Gallaudet Research Institute and Office of Institutional Research, Gallaudet University.

Rose, P., & Kiger, G. (1995). Intergroup relations: Political action and identity in the deaf community. *Disability & Society, 10,* 521–528

Salend, S. J., & Longo, M. (1994). The roles of the educational interpreter in mainstreaming. *Teaching Exceptional Children, 26,* 22–28.

Schildroth, A. N., & Hotto, S. A. (1994). Deaf students and full inclusion: Who wants to be excluded? In R. C. Johnson and O. P. Cole (Eds.)., *Implications and complications for Deaf students of the full inclusion movement,* (pp. 31–40). Washington, DC: Gallaudet Research Institute, Gallaudet University.

Schildroth, A. N., & Karchmer, M. A. (Eds.). (1994). *Deaf children in America.* Austin, TX: Pro-Ed.

Schroedel, J. G., & Watson, D. (Summer 1991). Postsecondary education for students who are deaf: A summary of a national study. *OSERS News in Print, 4,* 7–13.

Shaw, B. (September/October 1991). Deaf women refused interpreters in California. *Disability Rag,* p. 32.

Stiger, S. (June 25, 1996). Two-way dictionary. *Albuquerque Journal,* pp. B1–B2.

Sulzberger, A. O. (November 6, 1990). Deaf chief for a school in New Jersey. *New York Times,* p. A-14.

U.S. Department of Education. (1996). *Eighteenth annual report to Congress on the implementation of the Individuals with Disabilities Education Act.* Washington, DC: U.S. Government Printing Office.

Williams, J. S. (1994). Bilingual experience of a deaf child. In M. McIntire, *The acquisition of American Sign Language by Deaf children* (pp. 11–16). Burtonsville, MD: Linstok Press.

Wojciechowksi, G. (September 7, 1991). This rookie hears sound of silence and cheers. *Albuquerque Journal,* pp. C1, C5.

Woodward, J., Allen, T., & Schildroth, A. (1985). Teachers and deaf students: An ethnography of classroom communication. In S. DeLancey and R. Tomling (Eds.), *Proceedings of the first annual meeting of the Pacific Linguistics Conference* (pp. 479–493). Eugene: University of Oregon.

Families

Angier, N. (March 22, 1991). Deaf babies use their hands to babble, researcher finds. *New York Times,* pp. A1, A11.

Blade, R. (October 31, 1994). Sign language is beautiful, close-knit Deaf community says. *Albuquerque Tribune,* p. A5.

Gallaudet Research Institute. (Fall 1991). Language development at home and school: From gesture to language in hearing and deaf children. *Research at Gallaudet,* pp. 1, 2–3.

McIntire, M. (1994). *The acquisition of American Sign Language by Deaf children.* Burtonsville, MD: Linstok Press.

Moores, D. F. (1996). *Educating the deaf: Psychology, principles, and practices* (4th ed.). Boston: Houghton Mifflin.

Proctor, L. A. (n. d.). *Growing together: Information for parents of hearing impaired children.* Washington, DC: National Information Center on Deafness.

Research at Gallaudet. (Spring 1995). Infancy program studies family interactions. Washington, DC: Graduate School and Research at Gallaudet University.

Somers, M. N. (1984). The parent-infant program at Kendall Demonstration School. In D. Ling (Ed.), *Early intervention for hearing-impaired children: Total communication options* (pp. 183–229). San Diego: College-Hill.

Technology

Alexander Graham Bell Association for the Deaf. (January/February 1993c). Making tracks for better hearing and speech. *Newsounds, 18,* 1.

Alexander Graham Bell Association for the Deaf. (August 1993d). July 1, 1993 marks history in advancement of TV captioning. *Newsounds, 18,* 1.

Anderson, L. (May 19, 1995). Ryun inspires deaf children with quiet, clear message. *Seattle Post-Intelligencer,* pp. A1, E1, E6.

Bakke, M. H. (1995). Hearing aids and the consumer: An overview of current hearing aid wisdom. *SHHH Journal, 16,* 13–17.

Compton, C. L., & Kaplan, H. (1988). Up close and personal: Assistive devices increase access to speech and sound. *Gallaudet Today, 18,* 18–23.

Cutler, W. B., & Boone, M. A. (1996). Hearing help: Using assistive listening systems in public areas. *SHHH Journal, 17,* 7–9.

Hyder, J. (April 17, 1995). *Letter to caption test participants.* Washington, DC: National Air and Space Museum.

Kraminger, J. (1996). Making noise in a silent world: A profile of the deaf college experience. *Volta Voices, 3,* 20–21.

LaSasso, C. J., & King, C. M. (1992). Television Decoder Circuitry Act of 1990: Will it really benefit people who are deaf? *Newsounds, 17,* 5.

Merrill Lynch. (1994). Merrill Lynch Deaf/Hard of Hearing Investor Services. Code #11054–0594.

National Information Center on Deafness. (1994). *Hearing ear dogs for people who are deaf and hard of hearing.* Washington, DC: Gallaudet University.

Olson, J. M. (1994). In pursuit of communication access: FM use endangered by FCC ruling. *SHHH Journal, 15,* 17–18.

Preves, D. (1994). A look at the telecoil—its development and potential. *SHHH Journal, 15*, 7–10.

Robinson, S. (1993). Hearing aid breaks the silence. *Quantum: A Journal of Research and Scholarship at the University of New Mexico, 9*, 4–6.

Ross, M. (1994). Update: Telecoils, audio loops and hearing aids. *SHHH Journal, 15*, 24–25.

Sorkin, D. L. (1995). Understanding our needs: The SHHH member survey looks at telecommunications relay services. *SHHH Journal, 16*, 24–25.

Stang, P., & Stacey, J. (October 14, 1994). Pushing handicaps aside. *USA Today*, p. B1.

Sulzberger, A. O. (October 16, 1990). Closed-caption law: Victory for the deaf. *New York Times*, p. A11.

Sulzberger, A. O. (August 23, 1991). Technology lending a hand to the deaf in court. *New York Times*, p. B8.

Torry, S. (January 31, 1991). In D. C. court, a career reborn: Technology helps lawyer overcome hearing loss. *Washington Post*, pp. D1–D2.

Wilson, D. L. (July 15, 1992). Dramatic breakthroughs for deaf students: New technologies offer greater participation. *The Chronicle of Higher Education*, pp. A16–A17

Concepts and Controversy

Barringer, F. (May 16, 1993). Pride in a soundless world: Deaf oppose a hearing aid. *New York Times*, pp. A1, A14.

Liebman, J. (May 27, 1993). The deaf learn English and pursue careers (Letter to the editor). *New York Times*, p. A14.

Shapiro, J. P. (May 27, 1993). The deaf learn English and pursue careers (Letter to the editor). *New York Times*, p. A14.

Tye-Murray, N., Spencer, L., & Woodworth G. G. (1995). Acquisition of speech by children who have prolonged cochlear implant experience. *Journal of Speech and Hearing Research, 38*, 327–337.

CHAPTER 11: BLINDNESS AND LOW VISION

Art

Hale, W. H., and the editors of Time-Life. (1969). *The world of Rodin: 1840–1917*. New York: Time-Life Books.

Visual Impairments Defined

Barraga, N. (1993). Reflections of the past. In J. N. Erin, A. L. Corn, and V. E. Bishop (eds.). *Low vision: Reflections of the past and issues for the future*. New York: AFB Press.

Barraga, N. C., & Erin, J. N. (1992). *Visual handicaps and learning* (3rd ed.). Austin, TX: Pro-Ed.

Batshaw, M. L., & Perret, Y. M. (1992). *Children with disabilities: A medical primer*. Baltimore: Paul H. Brookes.

Blanksby, D. C., & Langford, P. E. (1993). VAP-CAP: A procedure to assess the visual functioning of young visually impaired children. *Journal of Visual Impairment & Blindness, 86*, 46–49.

Brody, J. W. (November 3, 1993). Vision problems in children often go undetected. *New York Times* (Health), p. B8.

Corn, A. L. (1989). Instruction in the use of vision for children and adults with low vision: A proposed program model. *RE:view, 21*, 26–38.

Erin, J. N. & Corn, A. L. (1994). A survey of children's first understanding of being visually impaired. *Journal of Visual Impairment & Blindness, 88*, 132–139.

Heller, K. W., Alberto, P. A., Forney, P. E., & Schwartzman, M. N. (1996). *Understanding physical, sensory, & health impairments*. Pacific Grove: Brooks/Cole.

Hudson, D. (1994). Causes of emotional and psychological reactions to adventitious blindness. *Journal of Visual Impairment & Blindness, 88*, 498–503.

Levin, A. V. (1996). Common visual problems in classrooms. In R. H. A. Haslam and P. J. Valletutti (Eds.), *Medical problems in the classroom: The teacher's role in diagnosis and management* (pps. 161–180). Austin, TX: Pro-ed.

Tuttle, D. W., & Ferrell, K. A. (1995). Visually impaired. In E. L. Meyen and T. M. Skrtic (Eds.), *Exceptional children and youth: An introduction* (4th ed., pp. 487–532). Denver: Love.

Verplanken, B., Meijnders, A., & van de Wege, A. (1994). Emotion and cognition: Attitudes toward persons who are visually impaired. *Journal of Visual Impairment & Blindness, 88*, 504–511.

History of the Field

Barraga, N. C. (1964). *Increased visual behavior in low vision children*. New York: American Foundation for the Blind.

Barraga, N. C., & Collins, M. E. (1979). Development of efficiency in visual functioning. *Journal of Visual Impairment & Blindness, 73*, 121–126.

Hill, E. W. (1986). Orientation and mobility. In G. R. Scholl (Ed.), *Foundations of education for blind and visually handicapped children and youth: Theory and practice* (pp. 315–340). New York: American Foundation for the Blind.

Sacks, S. Z., & Rosen, S. (1994). Visual impairment. In N. G. Haring, L. McCormick, and T. G. Haring (Eds.), *Exceptional children and youth* (6th ed., pp. 403–446). Columbus, OH: Merrill.

Prevalence

American Foundation for the Blind. (1994). *Prevalence estimates of blindness and visual impairment in the United States: Early 1990s*. New York: Programs and Policy Research.

Tuttle, D. W., & Ferrell, K. A. (1995). Visually impaired. In E. L. Meyen and T. M. Skrtic (Eds.), *Exceptional children and youth: An introduction* (4th ed.) (pp. 487–532). Denver: Love.

U.S. Department of Education. (1996). *Eighteenth annual report to Congress on the implementation of the Individuals with Disabilities Act.* Washington, DC: U.S. Government Printing Office.

Causes and Prevention

American Foundation for the Blind. (1990). *More alike than different: Blind and visually impaired children around the world.* New York: Author.

Brody, J. W. (November 3, 1993). Vision problems in children often go undetected. The *New York Times* (Health), p. B8.

Heller, K. W., Alberto, P. A., Forney, P. E., & Schwartzman, M. N. (1996). *Understanding physical, sensory, & health impairments.* Pacific Grove: Brooks/Cole.

Prevent Blindness America. (1996). *Children's eye injuries fact sheet.* Schaumburg, IL.

Rabb, M. F. (Ed.) (1996). Richard Karn speaks out on eye safety at home. *Prevent Blindness News,* Winter, p. 1.

Sherman, A. (1994). *Wasting America's future: The Children's Defense Fund on the cost of child poverty.* Boston: Beacon Press.

Werner, D. (1987). *Disabled village children.* Palo Alto: Hesperian Foundation.

Low Vision and Blind Children

American Printing House for the Blind. (1992). *Annual report.* Louisville, KY: Author.

Barraga, N. (1993). Reflections of the past. In J. N. Erin, A. L. Corn, and V. E. Bishop (Eds.). *Low vision: Reflections of the past and issues for the future.* New York: AFB Press.

Briand, X. (July 13, 1994). ED top set new guidelines promoting braille instruction. *Special Education Report,* p. 6.

Crocker, A. D., & Orr, R. R. (1996). Social behaviors of children with visual impairments enrolled in preschool programs. *Exceptional Children, 62,* 451–462.

Ethington, D. (1956). The readability of braille as a function of three spacing variables. Unpublished master's thesis, University of Kentucky, Lexington, KY. As cited in Harley, Truan, & Stanford (1987).

Ferrell, K. A. (1986). Infancy and early childhood. In G. R. Scholl (Ed.), *Foundations of education for blind and visually handicapped children and youth: Theory and practice* (pp. 119–136). New York: American Foundation for the Blind.

Harley, R. K., Truan, M. B., & Sanford, L. D. (1987). *Communication skills for visually impaired learners.* Springfield, IL: Thomas.

Heller, K. W., Alberto, P. A., Forney, P. E., & Schwartzman, M. N. (1996). *Understanding physical, sensory, & health impairments.* Pacific Grove: Brooks/Cole.

Hudson, D. (1994). Causes of emotional and psychological reactions to adventitious blindness. *Journal of Visual Impairment & Blindness, 88,* 498–503.

Kekelis, L. S. (1992). Peer interactions in childhood: The impact of visual impairment. In S. Z. Sacks, L. S. Kekelis, and R. J. Gaylord-Ross (Eds.), *The development of social skills by blind and visually impaired students* (pp. 13–35). New York: American Foundation for the Blind.

MacCuspie, P. A. (1992). The social acceptance and interaction of visually impaired children in integrated settings. In S. Z. Sacks, L. S. Kekelis, and R. J. Gaylord-Ross (Eds.), *The development of social skills by blind and visually impaired students* (pp. 83–102). New York: American Foundation for the Blind.

Mack, C. (1984). How useful is braille? Reports of blind adults. *Journal of Visual Impairment & Blindness, 78,* 311–313.

Nolan, C. Y. (1967). A 1966 reappraisal of the relationship between visual acuity and mode of reading for blind children. *The New Outlook, 61,* 255–261.

Rettig, M. (1994). The play of young children with visual impairments: Characteristics and interventions. *Journal of Visual Impairment & Blindness, 88,* 410–420.

Rex, E. J., Koenig, A. J., Wormsley, D. P., & Baker, R. L. (1994). *Foundations of braille literacy.* New York: AFB Press.

Sacks, S. Z., & Kekelis, L. S. (1992a). The effects of visual impairment on children's social interactions in regular education programs. In S. Z. Sacks, L. S. Kekelis, and R. J. Gaylord-Ross (Eds.), *The development of social skills by blind and visually impaired students* (pp. 59–82). New York: American Foundation for the Blind.

Sacks, S. Z., & Reardon, M. P. (1992). Maximizing social integration for visually impaired students: Applications and practice. In S. Z. Sacks, L. S. Kekelis, and R. J. Gaylord-Ross (Eds.), *The development of social skills by blind and visually impaired students* (pp. 151–170). New York: American Foundation for the Blind.

Schoellkopf, A. (March 25, 1995). Declining braille skills alarm advocates. *Albuquerque Journal* (Metropolitan), p. B1.

Schroeder, F. K. (1993). *Braille usage: Perspectives of legally blind adults and policy implications for school administrators.* Unpublished doctoral dissertation, Albuquerque: University of New Mexico.

Smith, J. A. (1972). *Adventures in communication.* Boston: Allyn and Bacon.

Tuttle, D. W., & Ferrell, K. A. (1995). Visually impaired. In E. L. Meyen and T. M. Skrtic (Eds.), *Exceptional children and youth: An introduction* (4th ed., pp. 487–532). Denver: Love.

Wittenstein, S. H. (1994). Braille literacy: Preservice training and teacher's attitudes. *Journal of Visual Impairments & Blindness, 88,* 516–524

U.S. Department of Education. (1996). *Eighteenth annual report to Congress on the implementation of the Individuals with Disabilities Act.* Washington, DC: U.S. Government Printing Office.

Educational Interventions

Augusto, C. R. (1993). Reading, writing, and literacy. *AFB News, 28,* pp. 1, 8.

Albuquerque Journal. (September 7, 1995). Alma mater closing doors. p. A5.

American Printing House for the Blind. (1992). *Annual report.* Louisville, KY: Author.

Associated Press. (April 9, 1996). Clintons forgo bunny suit, set Easter egg roll hopping. *The Los Angeles Times,* p. A11.

Haggen, R. (June 7, 1996). Letter. City of Commerce, CA: American Thermoform Co.

Barraga, N. C., & Erin, J. N. (1992). *Visual handicaps & learning* (3rd. ed.). Austin: Pro-Ed.

Barraga, N. C., & Morris, J. E. (1992). *Program to develop efficiency in visual function: Source book on low vision.* Louisville, KY: American Printing House for the Blind.

Behl, D. D., Akers, G. C., Boyce, M. J., & Taylor, M. J. (1996). Do mothers interact differently with children who are visually impaired. *Journal of Visual Impairment and Blindness, 90,* 501–511.

Clarke, K. L., Sainato, D. M., & Ward, M. E. (1994). Travel performance of preschoolers: The effects of mobility training with a long cane versus a precane. *Journal of Visual Impairment & Blindness, 88,* 19–30.

CNN Headline News. (October and November 1995). *Orient the guide dog retires.*

Corn, A. L. (1990). Curriculum and goals: Two components in a program for the use of low vision. In S. A. Aitken, M. Buultjens, and S. J. Spungin (Eds.), *Realities and opportunities: Early intervention with visually handicapped infants and children* (pp. 92–95). New York: American Foundation for the Blind.

Corn, A. L., Hatlen, P., Huebner, K. M., Ryan, F., & Siller, M. A. (1995). *The national agenda for the education of children and youths with visual impairments, including those with multiple disabilities.* New York: AFB Press, American Foundation for the Blind.

Crocker, A. D., & Orr, R. R. (1996). Social behaviors of children with visual impairments enrolled in preschool programs. *Exceptional Children, 62,* 451–462.

Curry, S. A., & Hatlen, P. H. (1988). Meeting the unique educational needs of visually impaired pupils through appropri-

ate placement. *Journal of Visual Impairment & Blindness, 82,* 417–422.

Deshler, D. D., Ellis, E. S., & Lenz, B. K. (1996). *Teaching adolescents with learning disabilities: Strategies and methods* (2nd ed.). Denver: Love.

Dominguez, B., & Dominguez, J. (1991). *Building blocks: Foundations for learning for young blind and visually impaired children: An English-Spanish book.* New York: American Foundation for the Blind.

Dote-Kwan, J., & Hughes, M. (1994). The home environments of young blind children. *Journal of Visual Impairment & Blindness, 88,* 31–42.

Harley, R. K., Truan, M. B., & Sanford, L. D. (1987). *Communication skills for visually impaired learners.* Springfield, IL: Thomas.

Hill, E. W. (1986). Orientation and mobility. In G. R. Scholl (Ed.), *Foundations of education for blind and visually handicapped children and youth: Theory and practice* (pp. 315–340). New York: American Foundation for the Blind.

Ingsholt, A. (1990). How does a blind infant develop an identity? In S. A. Aitken, M. Buultjens, and S. J. Spungin (Eds.), *Realities and opportunities: Early intervention with visually handicapped infants and children* (pp. 160–170). New York: American Foundation for the Blind.

Joffee, E. (1988). A home-based orientation and mobility program for infants and toddlers. *Journal of Visual Impairments & Blindness, 82,* 282–285.

JVIB News Service. (March-April 1995). Demographics update: Alternate estimate of the number of guide dog users. *Journal of Visual Impairment & Blindness, 89,* 4.

JVIB News Service. (January-February 1994). Demographics update: Use of "white" ("long") canes. *Journal of Visual Impairment & Blindness, 88,* 4.

Kendrick, D. (1993). *Jobs to be proud of: Profiles off workers who are visually impaired.* New York: American Foundation for the Blind.

Koenig, A. J. (1992). A framework for understanding the literacy of individuals with visual impairments. *Journal of Visual Impairment & Blindness, 85,* 277–284.

Leyenberger, E. (1990). Reaching for literacy. In S. A. Aitken, M. Buultjens, and S. J. Spungin (Eds.), *Realities and opportunities: Early intervention with visually handicapped infants and children* (pp. 102–107). New York: American Foundation for the Blind.

Luxton, K., Banai, M., & Kuperman, R. (1994). The usefulness of tactual maps of the New York City subway system. *Journal of Visual Impairment & Blindness, 88,* 75–84.

McCutcheon, C. (May 5, 1994). First guide dog goes to the zoo. *Albuquerque Journal* (Metropolitan), p. C1.

Martin, K. (1996). *Summer college program for students with disabilities on the campus of the University of Evansville.* Evansville, IN: Evansville Association for the Blind.

Newman, A. P., & Beverstock, C. (1990). *Adult literacy: Contexts and challenges.* Newark, DE: International Reading Association.

New York Times. (November 22, 1990). Blind hiker finishes an 8-month journey, p. A14.

Piña, P. (November 6, 1995). Blindness doesn't dim ability of man named nation's top teacher. *USA Today,* p. D6.

Pogrund, R. L., Fazzi, D. L., & Schreier, E. M. (1993). Development of a preschool "Kiddy Cane." *Journal of Visual Impairment & Blindness, 86,* 52–54.

Rettig, M. (1994). The play of young children with visual impairments: Characteristics and interventions. *Journal of Visual Impairment & Blindness, 88,* 410–420.

Sacks, S. Z. (1992). The social development of visually impaired children: A theoretical perspective. In S. Z. Sacks, L. S. Kekelis, and R. J. Gaylord-Ross (Eds.), *The development of social skills by blind and visually impaired students* (pp. 3–12). New York: American Foundation for the Blind.

Sacks, S. Z., & Kekelis, L. S. (1992b). Guidelines for mainstreaming blind and visually impaired children. In S. Z. Sacks, L. S. Kekelis, and R. J. Gaylord-Ross (Eds.), *The development of social skills by blind and visually impaired students* (pp. 133–149). New York: American Foundation for the Blind.

Sacks, S. Z., Kekelis, L. S., & Gaylord-Ross, R. J. (1992). *The development of social skills by blind and visually impaired students.* New York: American Foundation for the Blind.

Sacks, S. Z., & Reardon, M. P. (1992). Maximizing social integration for visually impaired students: Applications and practice. In S. Z. Sacks, L. S. Kekelis, and R. J. Gaylord-Ross (Eds.), *The development of social skills by blind and visually impaired students* (pp. 151–170). New York: American Foundation for the Blind.

Sacks, S. Z., & Rosen, S. (1994). Visual impairment. In N. G. Haring, L. McCormick, and T. G. Haring (Eds.), *Exceptional children and youth* (6th ed., pp. 403–446). Columbus, OH: Merrill.

Skellenger, A. C., & Hill, E. W. (1994). Effects of a shared teacher-child play intervention on the play skills of three young children who are blind. *Journal of Visual Impairment & Blindness, 88,* 433–445.

Sports Illustrated. (August 7, 1995). Faces in the crowd: Erik Weihenmayer. p. 10.

Sulzberger, A. O. (May 17, 1989). Police officers beat blind man. *New York Times,* p. A7.

Tröster, H., & Brambring, M. (1992). Early social-emotional development in blind infants. *Child: Care, Health and Development, 18,* 421–432.

Tröster, H. & Brambring, M. (1994). The play behavior and play materials of blind and sighted infants and preschoolers. *Journal of Visual Impairment & Blindness, 88,* 421–432.

Tuttle, D. W., & Ferrell., K. A. (1995). Visually impaired. In E. L. Meyen and T. M. Skrtic (Eds.), *Exceptional children and youth: An introduction* (4th ed., pp. 487–531). Denver: Love.

U.S. Department of Education. (1996). *Eighteenth annual report to Congress on the implementation of the Individuals with Disabilities Act.* Washington, DC: U.S. Government Printing Office.

Wiener, W. R. (1992). Orientation and mobility. In American Foundation for the Blind (Ed.), *Accommodation and accessibility: Implementing the ADA on a local level* (pp. 14–17). New York: Author.

Families

Erin, J. N. & Corn, A. L. (1994). A survey of children's first understanding of being visually impaired. *Journal of Visual Impairment & Blindness, 88,* 132–139.

Nixon, H. (1994). Looking sociologically at family coping with visual impairments. *Journal of Visual Impairment & Blindness, 88,* 329–337.

Ponchillia, S. V. (1993). The effect of cultural beliefs on the treatment of native peoples with diabetes and visual impairment. *Journal of Visual Impairment & Blindness, 87,* 333–335.

Technology

American Foundation for the Blind. (1991). *A picture is worth a thousand words for the blind and visually impaired persons too!: An introduction to audiodescription.* New York: Author.

DVS Home Video Catalog. (1996). *Catalogue.* St. Paul: WGBH Educational Foundation.

The Lighthouse. (1996). Products to help people with impaired vision: 1996 consumer catalog. New York: The Lighthouse Store.

NASDSE. (May 4, 1989). Visually impaired can receive student aid information on cassette. *SpecialNet,* Electronic Mail.

Rogers, M. (June 20, 1992). The literary circuitry. *Newsweek,* pp. 66–67.

Shen, R., & Uslan, M. M. (1996). A review of two low-cost closed-circuit television systems: The big picture and the magni-cam. *JVIB News Service, 90,* 6–10.

Stang, P. & Stacey, J. (October 14, 1994). Pushing handicaps aside. *USA Today,* p. D1.

Uslan, M. M. (1992). Barriers to acquiring assistive technology: Cost and lack of information. *Journal of Visual Impairment & Blindness, 85,* 402–407.

Uslan, M. M. (1994). A review of acrontech's "executive" series of closed-circuit television systems. *Journal of Visual Impairment & Blindness, 88,* 14–20.

Uslan, M. M., Shen, R., & Shragai, Y. (1996). The evolution of video magnification technology. *Journal of Visual Impairments and Blindness, 90*, 465–478.

Concepts and Controversy

American Printing House for the Blind. (1992). *Annual report.* Louisville, KY: Author.

Augusto, C. R. (1993). Reading, writing, and literacy. *AFB News, 28*, pp. 1, 8.

Briand, X. (July 13, 1994). ED top set new guidelines promoting braille instruction. *Special Education Report,* p. 6.

Corn, A. L., Hatlen, P., Huebner, K. M., Ryan, F., & Siller, M. A. (1995). *The national agenda for the education of children and youths with visual impairments, including those with multiple disabilities.* New York: AFB Press, American Foundation for the Blind.

Schoellkopf, A. (March 25, 1995). Declining braille skills alarm advocates. *Albuquerque Journal* (Metropolitan), p. B1.

Schroeder, F. K. (1993). *Braille usage: Perspectives of legally blind adults and policy implications for school administrators.* Unpublished doctoral dissertation, Albuquerque: University of New Mexico.

U.S. Department of Education. (1994). *The Goals 2000: Educate America Act—Launching a new era in education.* Washington, DC: U.S. Government Printing Office.

Wittenstein, S. H. (1994). Braille literacy: Preservice training and teacher's attitudes. *Journal of Visual Impairments & Blindness, 88*, 516–524.

CHAPTER 12: VERY LOW-INCIDENCE DISABILITIES

Autism

Kauffman, J. M. (1997). *Characteristics of behavioral disorders of children and youth* (5th ed.). Columbus, OH: Merrill.

Koegel, R. L., Koegel, L. K., Frea, W. D., & Smith, A. E. (1995). Emerging interventions for children with autism: Longitudinal and lifestyle implications. In R. L. Koegel and L. K. Koegel (Eds.), *Teaching children with autism: Strategies for initiating positive interactions and improving learning opportunities* (pp. 1–16). Baltimore: Paul H. Brookes.

Mesibov, G. B. (1994). A comprehensive program for serving people with autism and their families: The TEACCH model. In J. L. Matson (Ed.), *Autism in children and adults: Etiology, assessment, and intervention* (pp. 85–98). Pacific Grove, CA: Brooks/Cole.

Autism Defined

Begley, S., & Springen, K. (May 13, 1996). Life in a parallel world: A bold new approach to the mystery of autism. *Newsweek,* p. 70.

Dawson, G., Klinger, L. G., Panagiotides, H., Lewy, A., & Castelloe, P. (1995). Subgroups of autistic children based on social behavior display distinct patterns of brain activity. *Journal of Abnormal Child Psychology, 23*, 569–583.

Harris, S. L., Belchic, J., Blum, L., & Celiberti, D. (1994). Behavioral assessment of autistic disorder. In J. L. Matson (Ed.), *Autism in children and adults: Etiology, assessment, and intervention* (pp. 127–146). Pacific Grove, CA: Brooks/Cole.

King, W. (March 18, 1996). A different focus: Autistic worker lives with unique perspectives. *Albuquerque Journal* (Health), pp. C1–C2.

Koegel, R. L., Koegel, L. K., Frea, W. D., & Smith, A. E. (1995). Emerging interventions for children with autism: Longitudinal and lifestyle implications. In R. L. Koegel and L. K. Koegel (Eds.), *Teaching children with autism: Strategies for initiating positive interactions and improving learning opportunities* (pp. 1–16). Baltimore: Paul H. Brookes.

Krantz, P. J., McClannahan, L. E., & Poulson, C. L. (1994). Generalized imitation and response—class formation in children with autism. *Journal of Applied Behavior Analysis, 27*, 685–697.

Krug, D. A., Arick, J., & Almond, P. (1980). Behavior checklist for identifying severely handicapped individuals with high levels of autistic behavior. *Journal of Child Psychology and Psychiatry, 21*, 221–229.

Mesibov, G. B. (1994). A comprehensive program for serving people with autism and their families: The TEACCH model. In J. L. Matson (Ed.), *Autism in children and adults: Etiology, assessment, and intervention* (pp. 85–98). Pacific Grove, CA: Brooks/Cole.

Mullen, K. B., & Frea, W. D. (1995). A parent-professional collaboration model for functional analysis. In R. L. Koegel and L. K. Koegel (Eds.), *Teaching children with autism: Strategies for initiating positive interactions and improving learning opportunities* (pp. 175–188). Baltimore: Paul H. Brookes.

The 1990 Amendments to the Individuals with Disabilities Education Act (IDEA), Pub. L. No. 101–476, 34 C. F. R. section 300. 7 [b] [1] [1992].

Partington, J. W., Sundberg, M. L., Newhouse, L., & Spengler, S. M. (1994). Overcoming an autistic child's failure to acquire a tact repertoire. *Journal of Applied Behavior Analysis, 27*, 733–734.

Rimland, B. (1964). *Infantile autism: The syndrome and its implications for neural theory of behavior.* Englewood Cliffs, NJ: Prentice-Hall.

Rimland, B. (1994). The modern history of autism: A personal perspective. In J. L. Matson (Ed.), *Autism in children and adults: Etiology, assessment, and intervention* (pp. 1–12). Pacific Grove, CA: Brooks/Cole.

Schopler, E., Reichler, R. J., & Renner, B. R. (1988). *The Childhood Autism Rating Scale (CARS)*. Los Angeles: Western Psychological Services.

Sevin, J. A., Matson, J. L., Coe, D., Fee, V., & Sevin, B. M. (1991). Evaluation and comparison of three commonly used autism scales. *Journal of Autism and Developmental Disorders, 21*, 417–432.

Sturmey, P., & Sevin, J. A. (1994). Defining and assessing autism. In J. L. Matson (Ed.), *Autism in children and adults: Etiology, assessment, and intervention* (pp. 13–36). Pacific Grove, CA: Brooks/Cole.

Vig, S., & Jedrysek, E. (1995). Adaptive behavior of young urban children with developmental disabilities. *Mental Retardation, 33*, 90–98.

Prevalence

Koegel, R. L., Koegel, L. K., Frea, W. D., & Smith, A. E. (1995). Emerging interventions for children with autism: Longitudinal and lifestyle implications. In R. L. Koegel and L. K. Koegel (Eds.), *Teaching children with autism: Strategies for initiating positive interactions and improving learning opportunities* (pp. 1–16). Baltimore: Paul H. Brookes.

Locke, B. J., Banken, J. A., & Mahone, C. H. (1994). The graying of autism: Etiology and prevalence at fifty. In J. L. Matson (Ed.), *Autism in children and adults: Etiology, assessment, and intervention* (pp. 37–58). Pacific Grove, CA: Brooks/Cole.

Rimland, B. (1994). The modern history of autism: A personal perspective. In J. L. Matson (Ed.), *Autism in children and adults: Etiology, assessment, and intervention* (pp. 1–12). Pacific Grove, CA: Brooks/Cole.

U.S. Department of Education. (1996). *Eighteenth annual report to Congress on the implementation of the Individuals with Disabilities Education Act*. Washington, DC: U.S. Government Printing Office.

Causes and Prevention

Begley, S., & Springen, K. (May 13, 1996). Life in a parallel world: A bold new approach to the mystery of autism. *Newsweek*, p. 70.

Koegel, R. L., Koegel, L. K., Frea, W. D., & Smith, A. E. (1995). Emerging interventions for children with autism: Longitudinal and lifestyle implications. In R. L. Koegel and L. K. Koegel (Eds.), *Teaching children with autism: Strategies for initiating positive interactions and improving learning opportunities* (pp. 1–16). Baltimore: Paul H. Brookes.

Locke, B. J., Banken, J. A., & Mahone, C. H. (1994). The graying of autism: Etiology and prevalence at fifty. In J. L. Matson (Ed.), *Autism in children and adults: Etiology, assessment, and intervention* (pp. 37–58). Pacific Grove, CA: Brooks/Cole.

Rimland, B. (1994). The modern history of autism: A personal perspective. In J. L. Matson (Ed.), *Autism in children and adults: Etiology, assessment, and intervention* (pp. 1–12). Pacific Grove, CA: Brooks/Cole.

Scheuermann, B. (1996). Chapter review. Boston: Allyn and Bacon.

Sturmey, P., & Sevin, J. A. (1994). Defining and assessing autism. In J. L. Matson (Ed.), *Autism in children and adults: Etiology, assessment, and intervention* (pp. 13–36). Pacific Grove, CA: Brooks/Cole.

Children with Autism

Koegel, R. L., Koegel, L. K., Frea, W. D., & Smith, A. E. (1995). Emerging interventions for children with autism: Longitudinal and lifestyle implications. In R. L. Koegel and L. K. Koegel (Eds.), *Teaching children with autism: Strategies for initiating positive interactions and improving learning opportunities* (pp. 1–16). Baltimore: Paul H. Brookes.

Mesibov, G. B. (1994). A comprehensive program for serving people with autism and their families: The TEACCH model. In J. L. Matson (Ed.), *Autism in children and adults: Etiology, assessment, and intervention* (pp. 85–98). Pacific Grove, CA: Brooks/Cole.

Rimland, B. (1994). The modern history of autism: A personal perspective. In J. L. Matson (Ed.), *Autism in children and adults: Etiology, assessment, and intervention* (pp. 1–12). Pacific Grove, CA: Brooks/Cole.

Sturmey, P., & Sevin, J. A. (1994). Defining and assessing autism. In J. L. Matson (Ed.), *Autism in children and adults: Etiology, assessment, and intervention* (pp. 13–36). Pacific Grove, CA: Brooks/Cole.

Deaf-Blindness

Miles, B. (December 1995). *Overview on deaf-blindness*. Monmouth, OR: DB-LINK, The National Information Clearinghouse on Children Who Are Deaf-Blind.

Deaf-Blindness Defined

Baldwin, V. (1995). *Annual Deaf-Blind Census*. Monmouth, OR: Teaching Research, Western Oregon State College.

Baldwin, V. (1996). *Population/Demographics*. Monmouth, OR: Teaching Research, Western Oregon State College.

Groce, M. M., & Isaacson, A. B. (1995). Purposeful movement. In K. M. Heubner, J. G. Prickett, R. R. Welch, and E. Joffee (Eds.), *Hand in hand: Essentials of communication and orientation and mobility for your students who are deaf blind* (pp. 91–110). New York: AFB Press.

Haring, N. G., & Romer, L. T. (Eds.). (1995). *Welcoming students who are deaf-blind into typical classrooms: Facilitating school participation, learning, and friendships*. Baltimore: Paul H. Brookes.

Heubner, K. M., Prickett, J. G., Welch, R. R., & Joffee, E. (Eds.). (1995). *Hand in hand: Essentials of communication and* orientation and mobility for your students who are deaf blind. New York: AFB Press.

Holcomb, M., & Wood, S. (1989). *Deaf woman: A parade through the decades*. Berkeley, CA: DawnSignPress.

Individuals with Disabilities Act (IDEA), Pub. L. No. 101–476, 101 Stat 1119.

Miles, B. (December 1995). *Overview on deaf-blindness*. Monmouth, OR: DB-LINK, The National Information Clearinghouse on Children Who Are Deaf-Blind.

Prickett, J. G. (1995). Deaf-blindness and communication. In K. M. Heubner, J. G. Prickett, R. R. Welch, and E. Joffee (Eds.), *Hand in hand: Essentials of communication and orientation and mobility for your students who are deaf blind* (pp. 61–90). New York: AFB Press.

Prickett, J. G., & Welch, T. R. (1995). Deaf-blindness: Implications for learning. In K. M. Heubner, J. G. Prickett, R. R. Welch, and E. Joffee (Eds.), *Hand in hand: Essentials of communication and orientation and mobility for your students who are deaf blind* (pp. 25–60). New York: AFB Press.

Rosenberg, H. (February 27, 1995). "Kim's World" open to disabled and beyond. *Los Angeles Times* (Calendar), pp. F1, F10.

Prevalence
Baldwin, V. (1996). *Population/Demographics*. Monmouth, OR: Teaching Research, Western Oregon State College.

JVIB News Service. (May-June 1995). Demographics update: The number of deaf-blind children in the U.S., *89*, 13–14.

Causes and Prevention
Accardo, P. J., Whitman, B. U., Laszewski, C., Haake, C. A., & Morrow, J. D. (1996). *Dictionary of developmental disabilities terminology*. Baltimore: Paul H. Brookes.

Baldwin, V. (1996). *Population/Demographics*. Monmouth, OR: Teaching Research, Western Oregon State College.

Prickett, J. G., & Welch, T. R. (1995). Deaf-blindness: Implications for learning. In K. M. Heubner, J. G. Prickett, R. R. Welch, and E. Joffee (Eds.), *Hand in hand: Essentials of communication and orientation and mobility for your students who are deaf blind* (pp. 25–60). New York: AFB Press.

Children with Deaf-Blindness
Baldwin, V. (1995). *Annual deaf-blind census*. Monmouth, OR: Teaching Research, Western Oregon State College.

Baldwin, V. (1996). *Population/Demographics*. Monmouth, OR: Teaching Research, Western Oregon State College.

JVIB News Service. (May–June 1995). Demographics update: The number of deaf-blind children in the U.S., *89*, 13–14.

Smith, R. B. (1992). *Guidelines for working and playing with deaf-blind people*. Monmouth, OR: DB-LINK (the National Information Clearinghouse on Children Who Are Deaf-Blind).

Traumatic Brain Injury
Heller, K. W., Alberto. P. A., Forney, P. E., & Schwartzman, M. N. (1996). *Understanding physical, sensory, and health impairments*. Pacific Grove, CA: Brooks/Cole.

Singer, G. H. S., Glang, A., & Williams, J. M. (Eds.). (1996). *Children with acquired brain injury: Educating and supporting families*. Baltimore: Paul H. Brookes.

Strauss, A., & Lehtinen, L. (1947). *Psychopathology and education of the brain-injured child*. New York: Grune & Stratton.

TBI Defined
Clark, E. (1996). Children and adolescents with traumatic brain injury: Reintegraton challenges in educational settings. *Journal of Learning Disabilities, 29*, 549–560.

Doelling, J. E., & Bryde, S. (1995). School reentry and educational planning for the individual with traumatic brain injury. *Intervention in School and Clinic 31*, 101–107.

Heller, K. W., Alberto, P. A., Forney, P. E., & Schwartzman, M. N. (1996). *Understanding physical, sensory, and health impairments*. Pacific Grove, CA: Brooks/Cole.

Hux, K., & Hacksley, C. (1996). Mild traumatic brain injury: Facilitating school success. *Intervention in School and Clinic, 31*, 158–165.

Katsiyannis, A., & Conderman, G. (1994). Serving individuals with traumatic brain injury: A national survey. *Remedial and Special Education, 13*, 319–325.

NICHCY, (1994). *General information about traumatic brain injury: Fact Sheet #18*. Washington, DC: National Information Center for Children and Youth with Disabilities.

Singer, G. H. S. (1996). Constructing supports: Helping families of children with acquired brain injury. In G. H. S. Singer, A. Glang, and J. M. Williams (Eds.), *Children with acquired brain injury: Educating and supporting families* (pp. 1–22). Baltimore: Paul H. Brookes.

U.S. Department of Education (1992). Assistance to states for the education of children with disabilities program and preschool grants for children with disabilities; final rule. *Federal Register, 34*, CRF Parts 300 and 301.

Prevalence
Katsiyannis, A., & Conderman, G. (1994). Serving individuals with traumatic brain injury: A national survey. *Remedial and Special Education, 13*, 319–325.

Singer, G. H. S. (1996). Constructing supports: Helping families of children with acquired brain injury. In G. H. S. Singer, A. Glang, and J. M. Williams (Eds.), *Children with acquired* brain injury: *Educating and supporting families* (pp. 1–22). Baltimore: Paul H. Brookes.

Causes and Prevention

Heller, K. W., Alberto, P. A., Forney, P. E., & Schwartzman, M. N. (1996). *Understanding physical, sensory, and health impairments.* Pacific Grove, CA: Brooks/Cole.

Hux, K., & Hacksley, C. (1996). Mild traumatic brain injury: Facilitating school success. *Intervention in School and Clinic, 31,* 158–165.

Singer, G. H. S. (1996). Constructing supports: Helping families of children with acquired brain injury. In G. H. S. Singer, A. Glang, and J. M. Williams (Eds.), *Children with acquired brain injury: Educating and supporting families* (pp. 1–22). Baltimore: Paul H. Brookes.

Tyler, J., & Mira, M. (1993). Educational modifications for students with head injuries. *Teaching Exceptional Children, 25,* 24–27.

West, M. D., Gibson, K., & Unger, D. (1996). The role of the family in school-to-work transition. In G. H. S. Singer, A. Glang, and J. M. Williams (Eds.), *Children with acquired brain injury: Educating and supporting families* (pp. 197–220). Baltimore: Paul H. Brookes.

Children with TBI

Hux, K., & Hacksley, C. (1996). Mild traumatic brain injury: Facilitating school success. *Intervention in School and Clinic, 31,* 158–165.

Mira, M. P., Tucker, B. F., & Tyler, J. S. (1992). *Traumatic brain injury in children and adolescents: A sourcebook for teachers and other school personnel.* Austin, TX: Pro-Ed.

Tyler, J. S., & Myles, B. S. (1991). Serving students with traumatic brain injury: A new challenge for teachers of students with learning disabilities. *LD Forum, 16,* 69–74.

Very Low-Incidence Disabilities
Educational Interventions

Baldwin, V. (1995). *Annual deaf-blind census.* Monmouth, OR: Teaching Research.

Chadsey-Rusch, J., & Heal, L. W. (1995). Building consensus from transition experts on social integration outcomes and interventions. *Exceptional Children, 62,* 165–187.

Early Childhood Report. (July 1996). Special education LRE for 12-year-old student with multiple disabilities, p. 8. Horsham, PA: LRP Publications.

Goetz, L. (1995). Inclusion of students who are deaf-blind: What does the future hold? In Haring, N. G., and Romer, L. T. (Eds.), *Welcoming students who are deaf-blind into typical classrooms: Facilitating school participation, learning, and friendships* (pp. 3–16). Baltimore: Paul H. Brookes.

Haring, N. G., & Romer, L. T. (Eds.). (1995). *Welcoming students who are deaf-blind into typical classrooms: Facilitating school participation, learning, and friendships.* Baltimore: Paul H. Brookes.

Harris, S. L., Belchic, J., Blum, L., & Celiberti, D. (1994). Behavioral assessment of autistic disorder. In J. L. Matson (Ed.), *Autism in children and adults: Etiology, assessment, and intervention* (pp. 127–146). Pacific Grove, CA: Brooks/Cole.

Koegel, R. L., & Koegel, L. K. (Eds.). (1995). *Teaching children with autism: Strategies for initiating positive interactions and improving learning opportunities.* Baltimore: Paul H. Brookes.

Koegel, R. L., Koegel, L. K., Frea, W. D., & Smith, A. E. (1995). Emerging interventions for children with autism: Longitudinal and lifestyle implications. In R. L. Koegel and L. K. Koegel (Eds.), *Teaching children with autism: Strategies for initiating positive interactions and improving learning opportunities* (pp. 1–16). Baltimore: Paul H. Brookes.

Matson, J. L. (Ed.). *Autism in children and adults: Etiology, assessment, and intervention.* Pacific Grove, CA: Brooks/Cole.

Mullen, K. B., & Frea, W. D. (1995). A parent-professional collaboration model for functional analysis. In R. L. Koegel and L. K. Koegel (Eds.), *Teaching children with autism: Strategies for initiating positive interactions and improving learning opportunities* (pp. 175–188). Baltimore: Paul H. Brookes.

Romer, L. R,, & Haring, N. G. (1995). Including educational outcomes for students with deaf-blindness: Rethinking current practices. In Haring, N. G., and Romer, L. T. (Eds.), *Welcoming students who are deaf-blind into typical classrooms: Facilitating school participation, learning, and friendships* (pp. 421–430). Baltimore: Paul H. Brookes.

Strain, P. S., Danko, C. D., & Kohler, F. (1995). Activity engagement and social interaction development in young children with autism: An examination of "free" intervention effects. *Journal of Emotional and Behavioral Disorders, 3,* 108–123.

Szekeres, S. F., & Meserve, N. F. (1994). Collaborative intervention in schools after traumatic brain injury. *Topics in Language Disorders, 15,* 21–36.

U.S. Department of Education. (1995). *Seventeenth annual report to Congress on the implementation of the Individuals with Disabilities Education Act.* Washington, DC: U.S. Government Printing Office.

Families

Bradley, V. J., Ashbough, J. W., & Blaney, B. (Eds.). (1993). *Creating individual supports for people with developmental disabilities: A mandate for change at many levels.* Baltimore: Brookes.

DePompei, R., & Williams, J. (1994). Working with families after TBI: A family-centered approach. *Topics in Language Disorders, 15,* 68–81.

Luckasson, R., Coulter, D. L., Polloway, E. A., Reis, S., Schalock, R. L., Snell, M. E., Spitalnik, D. M., & Stark, J. A. (1992). *Mental retardation: Definition, classification, and systems of supports.* Washington, DC: American Association on Mental Retardation.

Singer, G. H. S. (1996). Constructing supports: Helping families of children with acquired brain injury. In G. H. S. Singer, A. Glang, and J. M. Williams (Eds.), *Children with acquired brain injury: Educating and supporting families* (pp. 1–22). Baltimore: Paul H. Brookes.

Technology

Alliance 2000. (1993a). VIDEOSHARE Outreach project. *Video based innovations.* Albuquerque: Alliance 2000 Project, University of New Mexico.

Alliance 2000. (1993b). Assistive technology: Interactive multimedia for training preservice and inservice special education and related services personnel. *Video based innovations.* Albuquerque: Alliance 2000 Project, University of New Mexico.

Alliance 2000. (1993c). The Wyoming parent information center. *Distance education: A program review.* Albuquerque: Alliance 2000 Project, University of New Mexico.

Concepts and Controversy

NICHCY (1994). *General information about traumatic brain injury:* Fact Sheet #18. Washington, DC: National Information Center for Children and Youth with Disabilities.

Thompson, R. P., & Freeman, C. W. (1995). A history of federal support for students with deaf-blindness. In N. G. Haring and L. T. Romer (Eds.), *Welcoming students who are deaf-blind into typical classrooms: Facilitating school participation, learning, and friendships* (pp. 17–36). Baltimore: Paul H. Brookes.

NAME INDEX

SUBJECT INDEX

Council for Learning Disabilities (CLD), 177
  inclusion and, 157
Counselors, 15
Court stenographers, 466
C-print, 466
Crane High School (Chicago), 296
Creativity, 290, 304. See also Giftedness
  definition of
  Renzulli's definition of, 278
  techniques for teaching, 304
  transition and, 316
Crisis teaching, 154
Critical thinking skills, teaching, 303, 306, 310
"Cross-cultural dissonance," 115, 202
Crossover children, 298
Cued speech approach, 449, 458
Cultural awareness, 114, 119, 131, 219–220, 294–297, 382, 551
Cultural diversity and perceptions about disabilities, 7, 38, 88–89, 95, 106
Culturally and linguistically diverse students. See Multicultural and bilingual education; Multicultural and bilingual individuals
Cultural pluralism, 89
Curriculum, differentiated, for gifted students, 304
Curriculum-based assessment (CBA), 62–63
  behavioral disorders/emotional disturbance and, 349–352
  learning disabilities and, 151, 153, 155
Curriculum compacting, 305, 308
Cystic fibrosis, 249, 380, 403
Cytomegalovirus (CMV) infection, 249, 380–381, 387, 390, 434–435. See also STORCH infections

Dark Crystal, 369
David, 272
Deaf-blindness, 531–537
  causes, 535, 536
  children with, 536–537
  definitions of, 531–532
  IDEA and, 532, 554
  identification of, 533
  inclusion and, 547–548
  families of, 549, 551
  placement patterns, 548
  prevalence, 10, 521, 534
  prevention of, 535–536
  purposeful movement and, 535
  transition and, 548, 550
  separate categories and, 554
  significance of, 533–534, 555–556
  vision and hearing patterns of, 537
Deaf community, 419, 460, 535
  advocacy and, 431,452, 457
  ASL and, 447, 469
  cochlear implants and, 438–439, 467–468
  minority group as, 441
Deaf culture, 430, 440–442, 469, 535. See also Deaf Pride

Deaf of deaf, 441, 447
Deaf Mosaic, 457
Deafness and hard of hearing, 8–9, 418–470
  causes of, 443–446, 469
  children with, 440–446
  cochlear transplants and, 437–439, 446, 467–468
  communication approaches and, 448, 458–459
  debates about communication methods, 429–430, 467–468
  definitions of, 421–429
  determining LRE for, 453
  employment outcomes, 453–455
  families of children with, 458–460
  history of, 429–431
  identification of, 424–426, 439
  inclusion and, 451–453
  instructional methods for, 448–450
  Martha's Vineyard, 8–9
  mental retardation and, 428
  as a minority group, 441
  preschool education and, 446–447
  prevalence of, 10, 431–432
  prevention of, 436–440
  school-age education and, 447–453
  significance of, 426–428
  speech ability, 444–446
  technology and, 460–467, 470
  transition through adulthood and, 453–457
  types of, 423–424, 468
Deaf President Now Movement, 430–431, 441
Deaf Pride, 430, 467
Deaf Theater, 441–442, 457
Decibels (dB), 424–426, 436
Decision-making skills, mental retardation and, 259–260
Declaration of Independence, 338
Decoders, for television captions, 464–465
Deductive thinking, 310
Deinstitutionalization, of individuals with mental retardation, 240
Delinquency, 331–332, 346–348
Denver Broncos, 457
Depression, 333, 342, 344
Descriptive Video Services of Boston,
Desktop publishing, gifted students and, 318–319
Developing Understanding of Self and Others (DUSO), 213
Deviance model, 8
Dexedrine, for behavior control, 148, 173, 362
Diabetes, 380
Diabetic retinopathy, 478
Diagnosis. See Identification
Diagnostic and Statistical Manual of Mental Disorders (4th ed.) (DSM IV), 148–149, 330–332
Diagnosticians, 11, 15
Dialects, 98–99, 187–188, 201
Diana v. State Board of Education, 90, 93

Differentiated curriculum, 304
Dignity of risk, 28
Directing Discourse, 213
Direct instruction. See also Curriculum based assessment; Effective discipline
  for behavioral control, 148, 364
  language instruction and, 206
  learning disabilities and, 133
  mental retardation and, 240, 251
  physical impairments and, 405
  process/product debate and, 134
  reading and, 133, 152–153
  traumatic brain injury and, 538
  twice exceptional students and, 299
  very low-incidence disabilities and, 545
  visual impairments and, 506
Disabilities,
  cultural concepts, 7, 38
  defined, 6–13
  as handicaps, 7–8
  language of, 11–13
Discalculia, 128
Discipline, 29. See also Effective Discipline, Intervention Ladder
Discrepancy formulas, 129–130, 135
Discrepancy scores, 128
Discrimination. See also Attitudes; Multicultural and Bilingual Special Education
  ability grouping as, 280, 285–286
  against blind individuals, 481, 507–508
  against deaf individuals, 456–457
  against people with disabilities, 7–8, 31, 231, 263, 386
  in testing 54–57, 85–88, 119, 238, 294, 320–321
Disgraphia, 128
Disney World, 409
Distance education and learning, 319–320, 552–554
Distance senses, 419, 473, 475. See also Hearing; Deafness and hard of hearing; Vision; Visual impairments
Distortions in articulation, 192
Divergent thinking, 310
Division of the Blind and Visually Impaired Rehabilitative Services, 519
Division for Children with Communication Disorders (CEC), 227
Division for Culturally and Linguistically Diverse Exceptional Learners (DDEL) of CEC, 121
Division for Learning Disabilities (DLD) (CEC), 177
Division on Mental Retardation (CEC), 271
Division on the Physically Handicapped (CEC), 417
Division for the Visually Handicapped (CEC), 519

Schizophrenia, 149, 330, 333
School children
    behavioral disorders/emotional
        disturbance in, 349–357
    deafness/hard of hearing and, 447–453
    gifted, 302–315, 322
    with learning disabilities, 151–166
    with mental retardation, 256–261
    multicultural/bilingual, 105–112
    physical impairments/special health
        care needs, 403–410
    speech or language impairments and,
        211–217
School failure
    learning disabilities and, 148, 150
    motivation and, 140–143
School nurses, 49, 57, 260, 398–399, 486,
    546
School psychologist, 55 *See also*
    Psychologist
School records, confidentiality of, 57
Scoliosis, 373
Scottish Education Act, 483
The Screamer, 324
Seattle Community College, 455
Secondary (lesional) epilepsy, 390
Section 504 of the Rehabilitation Act of
    1973, 30–32, 386, 396
Seeing eye dogs. *See* Service animals
Segregation. *See* Inclusion
Seizure disorders, 326, 372–375, 415. *See
    also* Epilepsy
    in IEP conferences, 70–71
    causes of, 389–390
    classroom management for 394–395
    recognition of, 375
    treatment guidelines, 395
    types of, 374–375
Selective attention, 138
Selective listening, 493
Self-advocacy, 70–71, 241, 262–263
Self-determination, 262, 355
    and individuals with behavior
        disorders/emotional disturbance,
        355–357
    and individuals with learning
        disabilities, 165
    and individuals with mental
        retardation, 262–263
Self-direction, 357
Self-esteem, 293
    in blind students, 497
    in diverse students, 111, 114
    in students with behavior
        disorders/emotional disturbance,
        333
    in students with learning disabilities,
        131, 145, 157, 166
    students with TBI, 543
Self-evaluation, 357
Self-fulfilling prophecy, 150
Self-Help for Hard of Hearing People
    (SHHHP), Inc., 471
Self-injurious behavior (SIB), 531
Self-management techniques, 135, 148
Semantics, 189

Semicular canals (ear), 422–423
Sensorineural hearing losses, 425–426,
    461, 469
Sequencing, (problem solving skill),
    144–145
Sensory integration, 151
Serious emotional disturbance. *See*
    Behavior disorders and emotional
    disturbance
Service animals
    dogs, 409, 467
    monkeys, 409
    seeing eye dogs, 484
Service centers for children with deaf-
    blindness, state and multistate, 534
Service delivery options, 43. *See also*
    Educational placements.
Service managers, 66
Setting demands, 214–215, 353
Sexually transmitted diseases. *See* AIDS
    (acquired immunodeficiency
    syndrome)
Shake-a-Leg (organization), 383–384
Shunts, 248, 250, 266, 269, 394
Sickle-cell anemia, 249, 379–380, 387,
    403
Sickling crisis, 379 *See also* Sickle-cell
    anemia
"Sight saving classes," 484
Sign language, 182, 429, 446, 459. *See
    also* American Sign Language
    (ASL); Manual communication
"Silent epidemic" (of TBI), 540
Simple partial seizure, 374–375, 396
Sistine Chapel, 272
Skeletal disorders, 373. *See also*
    Muscular/Skeletal conditions.
Smith v. Robinson, 34
Snellen chart, 480
Social-cognitive approach, 350
Social competence, 145–146, 175,
    205–206. *See also* Social skills.
Social interactions. *See* Peer relationships
Socially maladjusted children, 329, 332
Social skills
    autism and, 529
    behavioral disorders/emotional
        disturbance and, 344–346, 357
    learning disabilities and, 145–147
    low vision/blindness and, 489–490
Social status and learning disabilities,
    146–147
Social workers, 15
*Society Pays: The High Costs of Minimal
    Brain Damage in America*
    (Anderson), 224
Socioeconomic status learning disabilities
    and, 163
Software evaluation. *See* Computers
Soldiers' Rehabilitation Act, 386
Sonography (during pregnancy). *See*
    Ultrasound
Sound(s), frequency of. *See* Decibels (dB);
    Hertz (Hz)
Sound localization, 497
Spastic cerebral palsy, 376

Special Challenger Division (sports), 384,
    408
Special education, *See also* Array of
    services, Categorical systems;
    Multicultural and Bilingual
    special education
    costs of, 26, 30, 57–58, 136, 173
    definition of, 13–14, 37
    history of, 14–22
    prevalence of children needing, 33–34
    prevailing principles of, 545–546
    services, 13–14, 43–47, 57–59
Special education placement rates, 45.
    See also Educational placements.
Special education and related service
    professionals, 14–15, 49–50
Special education schools. *See* Center
    schools.
Special health care needs. *See* Physical
    impairments/special health care
    needs.
Specialized supports, 253
Special services committee, 53, 59, 61,
    75. *See also* Multidisciplinary
    teams
Specific learning disabilities. *See* Learning
    disabilities
Speech
    definition of, 183
    hearing losses and, 444–446
Speech banana, 425–426
Speech impairments, 178–227
    articulation problems, 184–188
    causes of, 198–199
    children with, 204–207
    deaf-blindness and, 537
    defined, 181–195, 225
    diverse children and, 87
    families of children with, 218–220
    fluency problems, 185
    history of, 195–196
    identification of, 190–193
    inclusion and, 214–217
    parent perspective, 180
    preschool education and, 207–211
    prevalence of, 10, 196–198, 225
    prevention of, 202–204, 224
    school-age education and, 211–214
    significance of, 194–195
    signs and characteristics of, 204
    technology and, 221–224, 226
    transition through adulthood and,
        217–218
    types of 184–188
    voice problems, 185–186
Speech/language pathologists (SLPs),
    178–227
    articulation problems and, 186
    assessment and, 56, 191, 193–194,
        199, 208
    collaboration and, 211–212, 214, 220,
        226
    computers and,
    hearing loss and, 420, 446, 448, 451
    language delays and, 200
    mental retardation and, 251, 260

Chapter	Teaching Tactics	Inclusion
1. Context of Special Education		CEC's position
2. IFSP, IEP, ITP: Planning and Delivering Services	Strategies for promoting student involvement in the IEP conference	LRE considerations, array of services, professionals
3. Multicultural and Bilingual Special Education	The Nacerima–an exercise in cultural perceptions	Responsiveness to cultural and language needs
4. Learning Disabilities	Homework self-study quiz for teachers	Array of special services, accommodations, and curricular options available
5. Speech or Language Impairments	The shopping spree	Necessary student and teacher behaviors
6. Mental Retardation	Task analysis and chaining	Community programs viewed as inclusive settings
7. Giftedness and Talent Development	Critical-thinking skills	Cluster programs, pullout programs, magnet schools
8. Behavior Disorders and Emotional Disturbance	The Intervention Ladder	Placement of rates of students w/BD in general education
9. Physical Impairments and Special Health Care Needs	Designing a learning environment	Inclusion in the learning environment and recreation
10. Deafness and Hard of Hearing	The Puzzle Technique	Array of services, placement, FAPE & LRE for distinct needs
11. Low Vision and Blindness	Weekly planning sheet	Outreach programs, itinerant support teachers
12 Very Low-Incidence Disabilities: Autism, Deaf-Blindness, and Traumatic Brain Injury	Developing functionally equivalent behaviors	Full inclusion, support needs